INSTITUTIONAL SELF-REGULATION (COMPLIANCE)

To Kurt
The master of
self-Regulation

Tamer

Institutional Self-Regulation (Compliance)

Tamar Frankel

Published by:

 Vandeplas Publishing, LLC – August 2018

801 International Parkway, 5th Floor
Lake Mary, FL. 32746
USA

www.vandeplaspublishing.com

ISBN 978-1-60042-299-7

INSTITUTIONAL SELF-REGULATION (COMPLIANCE)

TAMAR FRANKEL

Professor of Law Emerita
Boston University School of Law

ACKNOWLEDGEMENTS

Many thanks to Lee Augsburger, who opened the door to the area that this book addresses. Many thanks to Nathaniel Lindzen, Esq. who read and extensively commented on the text. Thanks to Charles Senatore for his insights and ideas. I am deeply indebted to Hila Conforti, LL.M. (BU Law School), Israel, for sharing her insights, ideas and experience, and to Eva Maryskova for her editing and suggestions. Special thanks to Mr. Nathan Malcolm, Esq. for his thoughtful and helpful comments. I am grateful to the students at Boston University Law School, who studied from a draft of this book, and offered their valuable comments. William Hecker has contributed to the research for this book, as he has been doing for all of my books.

Institutional Self-Regulation

This book discusses self-regulation by institutions that engage in financial activities. However, the fundamental building blocks of self regulation apply to institutions that engage in any business. In our context, the term "institutions" is used regardless of the legal form in which a group of actors is legally organized.to engage in any business. As institutions have grown larger; they engage in complex transactions, expand their activities around the globe, and impact interactions locally, as well as internationally. Their failures and successes can impact economic and financial as well as health and other systems of this country and those of other countries as well. The size, interaction, and impact of these institutions can render government regulators and examiners less effective. It has been suggested that these institutions are currently not only too big to fail, but also too big to regulate.[1] Yet the issue of corporate behavior is not new. In 1975, Christopher D. Stone wrote a book entitled *Where the Law Ends, The Social Control of Corporate Behavior*[2] in which he criticized corporate wrongdoing and noted the attendant corporate culture. This book is shocking in its modernity.

Waiting for the courts to punish wayward financial institutions is waiting too long to achieve too little. Once the harm is done, its effects can be devastating. Thus, in addition to demands for external regulation, oversight, and prosecution, a strong movement has risen to demand self-enforcement of the law within corporations to prevent such violations from occurring.

Indeed, an increasing number of laws require institutions to establish and effectively operate programs to ensure their compliance with the law.[3] The programs are also named Codes. A number of differences distinguish self regulation from regulation by law. This book focuses on elf-regulation. This book is organized as follows:

Chapter one: The institutional power structure and institutional rules aimed at maintain institutional legal behavior,

---

1 Ryan Tracy & Victoria McGrane, *Fed to Banks: Shape Up or Risk Breakup*, Wall St. J. Oct. 21, 2014, at C1, LEXIS, News Library, Wsj File.

2 Christopher D. Stone, Where the Law Ends ch. 20 (1975).

3 *See, e.g.*, 31 U.S.C. § 5318 (2012) (requiring the creation and maintenance of an anti-money laundering program under the Bank Secrecy Act).

Chapter Two, Law and self-regulation inlclude preventive rules (i) monitoring activities and (ii) investigating possible activities.

Chapter Three, Culture: the role of internal institutional rules

Chapter Four, Rewarding for reporting violations and especially correcting and preventing future possible violations.

Chapter Five, The Profession of Law and the Profession of Compliance.[4]

Chapter Six. An aalysis of failed institutional self-regulation and resurrection of a failed institution.

The legal system has traditionally used outside policing of possible violations. However, outside policing is costly, and may have negative effects, such as inducing an atmosphere of suspicion and mistrust among the actors within the institutions. Although some of these attendant results might be inevitable, we examine effective alternatives to external policing to minimize legal and financial risks by the institutions and their participants.

One type of self-regulation is reflected in the name most corporate compliance programs carry. These programs are called "compliance" programs, which usually means: "*obey* the rules." Yet, the programs are often designated as "ethics programs." Under an ethics program, one is guided to follow one's own internal rules of honesty. Similarly, institutions may have a less formal and more flexible overarching system of self-governance that fills the gaps between their formal codes of ethics and compliance systems. We call this overarching internal system "culture." Culture includes rules of behavior, which are accepted and enforced by and within the institution.

Usually, both ethics and culture constitute habitual rules of behavior. Ethics speaks to the habits of *individuals*, and culture speaks to the habits of *groups. This book deals with the latter.* Yet, good ethical habits, including the habit of reviewing our habits periodically, can be powerful components of a compliance culture. We will learn how culture and habits, as well as their response to change, can be instilled as parts of a self-regulation program.

Another form of enforcement that exists beyond the walls of a particular institution is the standard of fair competition in the marketplace. In our context, fairness is not necessarily a legal standard. It means acting legitimately, in accordance with industry standards of conduct or rules. Such rules may induce self-regulation, provided that the rules are impartial, unbiased, and acceptable by most, if not all, actors. These rules represent the culture of the particular industry to which the institution belongs. Illegal or "almost illegal" competition that ventures close to the

---

4   Monica Langley & Dan Fitzpatrick, *Embattled J.P. Morgan Bulks Up Oversight*, Wall St. J., Sept. 12, 2013, at A1.

prohibited line may be unfair. Such a behavior, especially if profitable, may make it harder for those who exercise greater self-restraint to avoid following and reaching closer to the prohibited line. We deal with these forms of enforcement mechanisms throughout this book.

One aspect of any compliance system is the evaluation of trends rather than the enforcement of specific "do or do not" actions. The focus is not on the ultimate judgment, nor on a dictionary definition. There is a measure of vagueness in trends. But we can focus on the beginning and on the direction of the problematic activities or approaches. One of the main lessons of this book is to recognize this vagueness, to measure it as much as possible, and to react to it appropriately, for example, by chilling it, or nipping it in the bud.

The ideas of Lord Moulton, a British judge and mathematician, might offer a guide. He noted "the three great domains of Human Action." "First comes the domain of Positive Law, where our actions are prescribed by laws binding upon us which must be obeyed." Next comes the domain of Free Choice, which includes all those actions as to which we claim and enjoy complete freedom."[5]

"But between these two there is a third large and important domain in which the rules are neither Positive Law nor Absolute Freedom. In that domain there is no law which inexorably determines our course of action, and yet we feel that we are not free to choose as we would." This is called "the domain of Obedience to the Unenforceable."[6]

Lord Moulton noted: "The real greatness of a nation . . . is measured by the extent of this land of Obedience to the Unenforceable. It measures the extent to which the nation trusts its citizens . . . ."[7] "I have no wish that Positive Law should annex this intermediate country. On the other hand, I dread it. Instead of the iron rule of law being thrown over it I would rather see it well policed by the inhabitants. I am too well acquainted with the inadequacy of the formal language of statutes to prefer them to the living action of public and private sense of Duty."[8]

Thus, to some extent, this book deals with the following problem: How can institutions pursue profitable self-interest, and yet be trustworthy and concerned with the welfare of the nation and its citizens. Following this balance, we may achieve, as Lord Moulton noted, less of the "iron rule of law." The vast area that this Judge describes is not void of rules and their enforcement. But these rules and their enforcement differ,. We may call this area of rules system the "culture" of the nation or society or the institutions.

Culture rather than legal rules of compliance is one of the main aspects that we explore in this book. Our current model of compliance reflects our approach to law enforcement. We recognize that compliance includes prevention of activities that are legal, if they lead to illegal actions. Institutions should monitor employees for possible, not only actual wrongdoing;

---

5   Right Honorable Lord Moulton, *Law and Manners*, ATLANTIC MONTHLY, July 1924, at 1.

6   *Id.*

7   *Id.* at 2.

8   *Id.* at 4.

supervise them; investigate them; might punish them, and prepare for examinations by government regulators. All actors in the corporation, from top management to low-level employees, are subject to coercive rules and—in the case of the violation of the rules—to punishment. As we study our current evolving system, we might consider other forms of compliance programs. For example: a program in which middle managers combine management with self-enforced law, and in which they are rewarded for identifying and correcting mistakes and wrongful actions. This system evolves at each level of the organization, instead of from the top down. We will study the potential advantages and disadvantages of various organizational structures to achieve institutional self-regulation.

This book draws examples from financial institutions, such as brokerage, insurance, mutual funds, investment advisers, and banking. But the attitudes and systems can apply to institutions that are involved in any activity that is subject to law.

We pay attention first to activities, the actors, and the law involved.

I trust you will enjoy studying institutional self-regulation by legal analysis, and by considering culture, ethics, rewards of self-regulation, monitoring, investigating, collaborating, and, of course, learning from mistakes. Welcome to "The Law of Institutional Self-Regulation."

Tamar Frankel, 2017

TABLE OF CONTENTS

The Rise of the Institutional Compliance Movement

INTRODUCTION

This chapter introduces self-regulation by financial institutions, such as banks and mutual funds, and their history and contributions to society.

Section I offers a short description of the nature and the role of money and the financial system in society, discussing the history, nature, and use of money and listing the main financial institutions. Section II focuses on the reasons for the regulation of financial institutions. It notes the fundamental distinction between law and self-regulation, and discusses the reasons for the rising need for self-regulation by financial institutions. Section III lists the distinction between legal rules and institutional rules, and their issuers and enforcers. Section IV introduces the legal liabilities of institutions, the allocation of responsibilities for corporate activities, and the corporate Constitutional rights. Section V **lists** institutional internal power structures: the legal, business, compliance, and personal power groups. Section VI describes those who bear the consequences for institutional violations of the law. Section VII offers a short discussion of the role of culture, which we will examine as we focus on different subjects, and the lawyer's role in most institutions. Section VIII closes this Chapter with a Rule issued by the Securities and Exchange Commission, directing institutions to impose and enforce internal codes of behavior.

I. THE NATURE AND THE ROLE OF MONEY AND THE FINANCIAL INSTITUTIONS IN SOCIETY

A. The Nature and Use of Money.

We start by discussing Bitcoins, the evolution of money, and the role of the law. The purpose of this introduction is to raise questions regarding the movement towards electronic money and its impact. The answer is yet unclear, but the questions are worth considering now.[9]

1. For centuries, money was used for a number of purposes. It was used as currency, as ornament, and as sacrifices to the Gods. Centuries ago, humans began to exchange foods and other assets. That was a wise evolution that enriched both parties, each of whom had too much of one thing but not enough of another. Exchange may have been hard to measure with precision. Therefore, humans developed ways to more accurately measure different products not only by amounts and weights, but also by their value and public demand. To compare the values of different assets, humans found another type of an asset that was fairly abundant and whose value and form were relatively stable. Such assets included "amber, beads, cowries, drums, eggs, feathers, gongs, hoes, ivory, jade, kettles, leather, mats, nails, oxen, pigs, quartz, rice, salt," tobacco in the south of the United States, gold in England, and sheep in ancient Israel (note that the word "kessef" in Hebrew means money, silver, and a garbled word for sheep, which in Hebrew is "keves"). Later, humans used more transportable assets, such as gold coins and paper, backed by the real assets. In fact, until 1971, the US dollar was backed by gold stored at Fort Knox. Later, the value of money was determined not by assets but by government obligations. By law, the government was vested with exclusive power to issue money.

2. The role of government in regulating money and the money supply has been controversial. Money could be viewed not only as a "thing" but also as "social technology." The effect of money on the well-being of the population is demonstrated by the suffering of Germany's peoples at the end of the First World War, when the Allies imposed money reparations on Germany and devastated the nation's financial system. [10]

Thus, arguably, money should be controlled by the government in order to maintain financial and economic stability. In the United States money may not be copied or mutilated by certain ways of trading. In addition, by law, banks must report to the government suspected legal violations. These suspicions may be triggered by the amounts, frequency of transfers, and sources

---

9   This introduction is adapted from Tamar Frankel, *Bitcoins: The Evolution of Money and the Enforcement of the Law*, VERDICT, Dec. 21, 2017, *available at* https://verdict.justia.com/2017/12/21/bitcoins-evolution-money-enforcement-law (last visited Jan. 18, 2018). Some authorities omitted.

10   JACK WEATHERFORD, THE HISTORY OF MONEY 200-01 (1997).

of payments[11] or by the destination of payments. The transfer abroad of excessive amounts of money must be reported as well. Because most countries use and regulate their own types of money, the International Monetary Fund was established to maintain a measure of predictability in the exchange of different countries' money. [12]

3. The search for ways to avoid government supervision over gaining, holding, and transferring money has grown throughout the years. The reasons for the search include avoiding taxes, hiding illegal sources of the money,[13] or the desire to support countries that United States law prohibits supporting.[14] These incentives may have driven the creation of electronic money. After all, electronic money is harder to detect because it need not pass through a regulated banking system; it may be used so long as it is acceptable to the recipients.

Thus, electronic money offers freedom from complying with legal constraining rules, but it can undermine the collection of taxes and the government's supervision and controls over the financial system. This type of money is different from money issued by other countries because the exchange of foreign and domestic currency is governed by law, while the exchange of electronic money is not.[15]

What we see is the emergence of an electronic "asset" (information) that is used to measure the value of dissimilar assets, that is: another kind of money. This electronic "asset" may be named coins or Bitcoin or any other name for electronic money.

4. There are three features that distinguish [bit]coins from other forms of money: (1) bitcoins can be expressed in an electronic form; (2) they are, and can be, traded in the markets, so their value can change, sometimes significantly, through forces of demand and supply; and (3) they are not regulated by the government as money. Therefore, at least currently, they can be used

---

11 31 U.S.C. § 5313 (2012) (requiring financial institutions to report certain coins and currency transactions as required by regulations); 31 C.F.R. §1010.311 (2017) (filing obligations for reports of transactions in currency); 31 U.S.C. § 5318A (2012) (requiring special measures for jurisdictions, financial institutions, international transactions, or types of accounts of primary money laundering concern) 31 U.S.C. § 5326 (2012) (requiring additional records and reports for certain transactions).

12 Int'l Monetary Fund, *About the IMF, available at* http://www.imf.org/en/About (last visited Dec. 15, 2017) (noting that "IMF's primary purpose is to ensure the stability of the international monetary system—the system of exchange rates and international payments that enables countries (and their citizens) to transact with each other).

13 H. R. Rep. No. 91-975, at 12-13 (1970), *quoted in* California Bankers Ass'n v. Shultz, 416 U.S. 21, 28 (1974) (avoiding taxes); *id.* (noting that foreign bank accounts and institutions "have served as the cleansing agent for 'hot' or illegally obtained monies").

14 *See, e.g.,* 31 U.S.C. § 5315(a)(3) (2012) (noting importance of collecting information on capital flows under Trading With the Enemy Act and Bretton Woods Agreement Act); Ofc. Foreign Assets Control, OFAC Regulations for the Financial Community (Jan. 24, 2012), *available at* https://www.treasury.gov/resource-center/sanctions/Documents/facbk.pdf (last visited Dec. 15, 2017) (discussing responsibilities of financial institutions regarding countries that are targets of U.S. economic sanctions).

15 *See* 31 U.S.C. § 5315 (2012) (requiring financial institutions to report foreign currency transactions conducted by U.S. person or foreign person controlled by U.S. person); 7 U.S.C. § 2(c)(2) (2012) (providing that Commodity Exchange Act and Commodity Futures Trading Commission jurisdiction apply to certain foreign currency transactions).

to hide the transfer of wealth outside government regulation. To be sure, governments could develop electronic supervision to substitute for bank supervision. But most governments have not done so, at least not yet, although some governments have acted to control electronic money, as noted later.

The Securities and Exchange Commission cautioned one company that offered electronic money that it might be offering securities. The consequences of this classification would be to legally require these electronic signals to be described and disclosed not only to users but to the government as well.

If these offers might be securities, what should be described? (1) the issuer, (2) the underwriter, (3) perhaps the pricing and market price, and (4) the trading cost. The next stage in this development might be pooling different electronic coins into baskets and trading each type of coin in the basket. The cost of trading and the market value of these money-securities may have to be disclosed, but users may find it difficult to determine the value at any particular time when this money will be used. Perhaps the function of the banks would change. Who would need banks in that environment? However, it is not surprising that a number of banks have accepted Bitcoins or similar electronic money.

Thus, the ultimate issue posed by electronic currency is government control rather than disclosure to future investors. The ultimate question is: Can the market control the price of our money? If we need a stable money-value, the answer is: No, at least in the present environment in the United States.

5. A related issue may be: "who should manage the economy?" Is it the government, or is it the market makers and broker-dealers? Will the price of bread, among other things, be linked to the market price of electronic money as well? If the government will not control the value of the money, then those who issue electronic money might influence, if not control, the economy: Money, as well as taxes, might fly to other parts of the world with electronic wings.

Bloomberg's columnist Matt Levine noted:

> Look, on the one hand: Sure, yes, when everyone can buy bitcoins over the phone from their banks, the price *will* go a lot higher. On the other hand, soon you'll be able to buy bitcoins, the disruptive alternative currency that was meant to rebuild the financial system on the basis of computer-science principles, by *picking up the phone and calling your bank!* Because that›s what people want! It does seem simultaneously bullish for bitcoin—more buyers!—and yet somehow deeply bearish: People will be buying bitcoin while rejecting its premise.[16]

---

16   Matt Levine, *SEC Halts a Silly Initial Coin Offering*, BLOOMBERG VIEW, Dec. 5, 2017, *available at* https://www.bloomberg.com/view/articles/2017-12-05/sec-halts-a-silly-initial-coin-offering (last visited Jan. 19, 2018).

Some of the current securities markets have spawned a casino environment. Small investors may indirectly invest in hedge funds, less regulated mutual funds. Now the tendency to take risks is growing. The largest such fund is about $6 billion, spawned by a former Goldman Sachs executive. Concentrated investments may carry more gain and more risk. Where will the electronic evolution of money lead?

6. Different degrees of concern relating to electronic money have been expressed in various countries.

a. A number of countries viewed electronic money as money that competes or otherwise affects the monetary system. These countries include:
- China, whose central bank has taken full control over this electronic currency, seemingly treating it as currency;
- Morocco and India, which do not allow the introduction of electronic money;
- Russia, which denounced the types of electronic money as "Pyramid Schemes";
- Australia, which viewed it as speculative mania.

b. A number of countries expressed concern. These countries include:
- New Zealand describes bitcoins as too unstable to be classified as money;
- France views the developments with "great caution";
- The Netherlands described bitcoins as "most daring" type of money;
- The United Kingdom views electronic money as a potential revolution;
- Germany has expressed concern about bitcoins' effect on money, although perhaps not to that extent (as in the UK);
- The United States is concerned about privacy rights;
- European Central Bank expressed concerns about instability of markets rather than currency effects.

c. A number of countries have taken a "wait and see" attitude:
- Japan is in a "Study Mode";
- Canada accepts electronic money as assets;
- Scandinavia is exploring options;
- Turkey views the developments as important;
- The Bank for International Settlements is paying full attention to developments;
- One country supports the innovations:
- Brazil.

B. The role of the financial system and its contribution to society

We may take the financial system for granted. After all, it has been with us and served us for a long time. Yet the system reminds us of its importance when it fails, and when we believe that its intermediaries have betrayed us. We depend on it more than we usually realize. Therefore, let us remind ourselves of its importance when it is functioning properly, rather than when it begins to fail or when it fails.

Why is the financial system so important? It is important because it can create money or alternatives to other forms of money. Money is the means we use to evaluate and compare the value of various assets. It facilitates our trading in land, goods, ideas, services, and other valuable and exchangeable things. Money could take many forms. In ancient Israel, for example, where most tribes were shepherds, the unit of exchange was sheep and goats. In America's south, the unit of exchange was tobacco leaf. Both morphed into coin and paper. In the middle of 2017, Bitcoins have emerged as money. They are worth whatever everyone agrees they are worth, that is, whatever can be acquired by offering them.

It is not surprising that in Great Britain goldsmiths created money and evolved their businesses into banks. Their services included the safekeeping of gold, which the goldsmith gave a receipt for. Not surprisingly, the receipts began to be used and accepted as the gold itself, and were given instead of gold to buy or sell properties. So long as the goldsmiths were respectable and reliable these receipts became convenient money.

With time, the goldsmiths began to issue receipts without gold backup. Nonetheless, they paid for the receipts in gold, when the gold was demanded. After all, not all gold owners demanded their gold the same day or month. Thus, the amount of gold that served as a backup of the entire amount of the goldsmiths' receipts was lower than the amount of the receipts the goldsmiths issued. It was lower, but sufficient to accommodate those customers that demanded their gold.

When a goldsmith did not have sufficient coverage, the goldsmith experienced a "run." That is when its reputation was questioned and more than the usual amount of gold was demanded by receipt holders. And if any goldsmith did not have sufficient gold to meet the demand, it went bankrupt, and sometimes lost its freedom as well, ending in jail. The "run" on one goldsmith could result in a run on other goldsmiths, as mistrust spread. When money was invested in businesses, the investments, the shares issued by the businesses organized as corporations took the form of money, that is, paper. The paper represented the issuing entities' obligations or participation in a pool of paper representing claims; as with gold receipts, the paper could be more easily traded than the actual property or pool it represented. Broker-dealers enabled the owners to convert their financial instruments into money, which the owners could convert into actual assets, such as homes and food.

Today's financial intermediaries are as numerous and as complex as the "paper" they deal with. For example, pools of paper (securities) that issue securities, mutual funds, issue securities to the public and invest in securities. Thus, financial institutions are a mechanism for transferring and trading in money and financial paper usually tradable paper. Although they are named an "industry" they are in fact a service, through which money and money alternatives are traded and transferred.

Discussion topic

Why are banks regulated? Is their structure different from the structure of the British goldsmiths? If so, what is the difference?

What are Bitcoins? How different are they from dollars? Can their use be abused? If so, who are the potential abusers and their victims?

What problems and benefits can Bitcoins pose to the financial system and to the individuals that use them?

Should Bitcoins be regulated? If so, who should be the regulator?

C. The main financial institutions that we note are the following:

*Banks, including Bank Holding Companies: These holding companies may offer many, if not all, of the available financial services, and financial guarantees.

*Investment companies: Institutions that issue and invest in securities, thus offering diversified portfolios of securities to shareholders.

*Investment advisory services: Advisers provide both individuals and institutions advice concerning the management of their financial assets.

*Broker-dealers: Broker-dealers provide the service of trading in financial assets and sometimes include advice to clients as well.

*Insurance companies: Insurance companies provide insurance, brokerage, and variable annuities and variable insurance, which are hybrids of insurance and mutual funds services.

*Private financial advisers and intermediaries that are more highly controlled by their owners.

A. The problems that financial institutions pose and the reasons for their regulation by law

1. Today's society is increasingly dependent on the financial system. Can we imagine living without money, or without a bank, or without a credit card? Can we imagine investments without securities, or advisers, or mutual funds? However, dependence poses dangers to society and to its members. First, financial institutions command great power over the economy and the well-being of society. These institutions hold or affect the price of the assets backing the means of exchange—money or its equivalent. Money is easily hidden, transferred, and misappropriated. Second, money can be used for good or for evil. It can be used to avoid legal restrictions, avoid paying taxes, and illegally buy arms or support illegal activities and dangerous organizations.

Banks that transfer money and offer similar services are required by law to notify the authorities of suspicious transfers. Yet a notification may reduce banks' profitable business and pose an enforcement problem when banks are faced with conflicting interests. People may overcome their fear and guilt by various justifications for acting in violation of the law, such as, high costs and unreasonable or unfair laws, and, of course, by asserting that "everyone does it."

2. In addition, financial institutions are either entrusted with, or hold, other people's money, or advise people who are less knowledgeable about financial matters including their own. Therefore, by definition, financial servicers have greater controls over other people's money and more expertise in the matters of financial management. Regardless of what the legal relationships between people who entrust their money to financial servicers (entrustors) and the financial servicers are, financial servicers must be trusted. Therefore, by definition they are fiduciaries. In law, the two aspects of the clients' vulnerability impose two types of duties on fiduciaries. One duty is the duty of care. This duty requires fiduciaries to exercise expertise and attention in serving their clients. The other is the duty to avoid conflicts of interests with those of the clients, unless the fiduciaries receive their clients' consent.[17]

Fiduciary duties in the area of finance are difficult to supervise and control because the fiduciaries deal with money or equivalents of money. As noted, money is easily transferred and hard to identify, especially when the connections and transfer have become easier and contacts of information less controllable. In sum, the rules governing financial institutions are neither uniformly clear nor specific; and are based on the necessary and justified trust in fiduciaries being balanced against the justified rights of fiduciaries to compensation and perhaps other interests.

---

17   *See* TAMAR FRANKEL, FIDUCIARY LAW (2011) (Oxford University Press).

Thus, the rules of law and the ambitions and purposes of financial institutions' leaders and personnel are not always compatible, let alone identical. Even if the institutions are required to comply with enforcing the laws, the relationship between the law and the self-regulatory rules are not always compatible.

Therefore, the balance of power between government lawmakers and institutional rule makers can be unstable. Even though both the legal system and the required compliance system are designed to support the same objectives, they may not reach the goals to the same degree. The incentive of the British goldsmiths to issue more receipts than the gold they held is similar to the incentive of the banks to use depositors' money for income-producing purposes, such as loans and trading in securities. If they make risky loans, they might charge higher fees, but at the same time they may not only fail to meet the depositors' demands, but also to create the panic that leads to a run on the bank, which may spread to other banks if their depositors also lose trust in their banks.

Law aims at the long-term success, development, and stability of the financial system. In contrast, many business and financial institutions might aim at a more short-term financial success of their own institution. In addition, institutions may be engaged in tougher outside competition and may harbor more internal competition that propels actions that might eventually conflict with the law.

To be sure, law has heavier clout over a violating institution and its actors, compared to the power of the institutions to hide gray areas of wrongdoing. Yet, law has less enforcement and close supervisory power over internal actions and actors within institutions. These differences are hard to measure. However, they shape the requirements and support that law may provide to institutional self-regulation.

The conflicting drives of the law and its enforcers, on the one hand, and the actors in the financial system are often a "moving target." A new technological innovation may raise conflicts between law enforcers and innovative institutions, as well as among members within the institutions. In both cases the law and internal compliance systems interact in many areas. In both cases the interaction involves: (i) the power structure of financial institutions that are subject to compliance with the substance of the rules; (ii) the identity of those who make the rules; (iii) the identity of the enforcers of the rules; (iv) the form and methods by which the rules are enforced; and (v) the financial and other reasons that may divert the interests of the parties.

B. Why is today's law less effective in regulating financial institutions? What gave rise to the need for financial institutions self-regulation?

Two main reasons for the recent weakening of financial institution regulation is that financial institutions have grown in size and complexity, and their activities have expanded around the globe. The ability of outside regulators to monitor, investigate, and generally supervise the activities within these large institutions has become weaker and less effective.

1. The evolving solution to the regulatory problem is increasingly to relegate the duties to prevent legal violations and enforce the law to the institutions themselves. The law requires institutions to self-regulate and ensure that they do not violate the law. This is the system of institutional self-regulation that we explore and study.

Thus, today, the law that regulates financial institutions includes two kinds of legal rules: (i) the rules of law that institutions should follow, and (ii) the rules of law commanding, and guiding, some of the detailed ways in which the institutions should ensure their self-enforcement of the law. This duality of the law should be kept in mind. When a legal problem arises, the lawyer should identify the rules imposed on the client institution, as well as well as the rules that require the institution to create an enforcement system of those legal rules.

2. There is a fundamental difference between law and the law imposing self-regulation on institutions. Self-regulation requires not only compliance with the prohibitions and dictates of the laws, but also the imposition of a system of preventing or avoiding actions that might mature into violations. Thus, we will study the mechanisms that follow permissible activities but that signal possible activities or absence of activities that might, but not necessarily will, result in violations of the law. That is, we will study the concept, evaluation, and the detection of legal risk.

Among the institutional mechanisms designed to implement the law and prevent violations are monitoring, as well as monitoring the law, discussed in Chapter 10; investigation, discussed in Chapter 11; and the issue of whistleblowers, which is discussed in Chapter 12.

C. In sum, institutional self-regulation draws on three systems.

(i) Legal rules imposed on the institutions; (ii) legal rules imposing on institutions the duty to internally enforcing legal rules and the ways this duty should be performed; and (iii) self-imposed rules, imposed by the institutions on their leaders and employees and on related entities and their employees, as well as the enforcement of the these rules by, and within, institutions.

These self-imposed rules can be embodied in the culture of the institution. In fact, the contents of culture can include a constitution: principles of behavior, as well as itemized rules of behavior, similar to law. We should note that combined law and institutional or group culture are not unique to financial institutions. Law and internal self-regulation— culture—are linked. Both relate to the substance and activities they regulate.

For example, family law imposes on parents certain requirements in the way they treat their children. However, each family is regulated by an internal structure and culture, which may differ from those of other families. The rule-maker within a family may be the father, the mother, and sometimes the three-year-old tyrant. The rules regarding food, sleeping time, and manners, etc. may differ as well. Yet they must comply with the overarching law. Spanking a child is likely to be permissible under the law. But beating a weaker child or spouse is not.

A similar combination of applicable law and internal regulations and culture applies to institutions. As noted, institutional rules, power, personal relationships, and behavior constitute the institutional culture. While in some institutions the CEO's word is the law, in other institutions a group of money producers calls the shots (and can bring the institution down by illegal activities), and, as we shall see, in yet another institution, the acceptable behavior is the rule, regardless of who imposes it.

It is therefore worth repeating that, as we study institutional self-regulation, we inquire into: (i) the applicable rules of law; (ii) the legal rules requiring and directing institutional self-regulation; and (iii) the rules and enforcement system by which institutions establish self-regulation. These rules include the culture of the institution.

Both government and governance and their rule-enforcement are usually hierarchal. In government (law) the Constitution trumps federal law, which in turn trumps state law, and so on. The decisions of higher courts overrule the decisions of the lower courts. The decisions of the board of directors in the corporation may trump the decisions of the lower corporate echelon, but, as we shall see, not always. In fact, the current move of the power core is to the middle.

As noted, government and governance differ in the timing of enforcement and methods of preventing violations. Most new government rules and enforcement of past violations come after violations have been proven. The preventive effect of law consists of threats of punishment. In contrast, governance is far more focused on preventive rules and their enforcement. Its rules highlight signs of possible violations, and are aimed at preventing violations before they have occurred. Ideally, governance is effective before a violation has occurred.

In addition, as noted, the punishment methods of each system differ. Violations of government laws can involve fines and prison sentences, and sometimes disqualification and prohibition of professional practice, while violation of institutional governance rules may involve termination of employment, reduced compensation and bonuses, or demotion. Presumably, both systems aim at deterring actors from violating the laws.

Thus, a fundamental distinction between law and self-regulation is that self-regulation requires not only compliance with the prohibitions and dictates of the laws, but also prevention of violations before actions mature into violations. Thus, we will study the mechanisms that follow permissible activities but look for signals of possible activities or absence of activities that might, yet not necessarily will, result in violations of the law. That is, we will study the concept and the detection of risk, of possible or probable violations.

D. Neither the legal nor the self-regulatory systems or their interaction are uniformly clear and specific.

After all, institutions differ in size, history, personality of their leadership, and other employees, as well as in their methods of deterring violations of the law. Not only is the relationship between the law and the self-regulatory rules unstable, but the powers and the substance of the dual rules are unstable as well. However, both systems are aimed at accommodating the same purposes, that is, preventing violation of the law.

III. LEGAL RULES AND INSTITUTIONAL CULTURAL RULES: THEIR ISSUERS AND ENFORCERS

A. Applicability of legal rules.

Laws apply to all persons who inhabit, or are citizens of, a relevant political unit, such as a state or a municipality. The laws of the United States are created by the Constitution, laws passed by Congress, the States, the regulating agencies, the subordinate authorities, the local councils, and the courts. The laws deal with the conduct of individuals and organizations in society, and apply to all, or most, of their members. The enforcers of the laws are the courts, enforcement agencies, such as the police, and regulatory agencies, such as the Securities and Exchange Commission. Violators of the law may be punished by monetary sanction or restrictions on certain activities, as well as by imprisonment.

1. Non-legal, institutional (cultural) rules are imposed by institutions on their employees and related parties. For example, a firm may prohibit its brokers from meeting often with brokers of another firm in order to avoid possible reciprocal relationships in trading, which might adversely affect both the client's interests and the interests of the firm. Violations of institutional rules may result in termination of the employment or business relationship, reduced salaries, demotion, transfer to less desirable places within the institution's operations, and social embarrassment

2. Usually, both legal and institutional cultural systems are hierarchal. In law and in governance, the hierarchy of authority is most often top down. However, as we shall see later in this book, there are structures that involve the middle management of an entity and encourage "group think" as well as enforcement and avoidance of violation. This is institutional culture, which we will view in detail, that creates internal rules and their enforcement. Mostly it is

institutional culture that affects and sometimes shapes the patterns of habitual behavior within the institutions.

Thus, institutional enforcement of the laws differs significantly from the legal enforcement of the same laws. For example, the institution cannot imprison the violating employee, as the law can, but institutions can terminate their relationship. Both can impose financial punishment in different ways and by different decision makers. The law can impose fines, while institutions can charge the employee by reducing their salaries or bonuses.

3. We focus on self-regulation (named governance or compliance) and on the rules designed to enforce the law within institutions, that is, rules of institutional cultural. Rules of institutional cultural are "self-made" rules, issued by those who control the institutional actors' functions and services. We focus on these self-regulatory rules, aimed at preventing violations of the law. Although many self-regulatory rules are discretionary, we note that some laws mandate their imposition and enforcement by and within the institutions.

4. Most importantly, we must remember that our environment is not the courtroom. It is the business store, the securities trading floor, and the markets in the United States and abroad. In fact, much, if not most, of a lawyer's practice in other areas as well involves issues of self regulation to prevent violations of the law (compliance). Generally, business clients try hard to avoid prosecution and the courtroom. They may take a deep breath (sometimes in frustration) and opt for self-limitation to avoid even the gray areas of the law. In this book, we aim to serve clients that prefer self-limitation. Yet, even where there is preference for self-limitation over the courtroom, conflicting desires and barriers arise continuously; they must be recognized and dealt with.

B. Who interprets the laws and the non-legal, culture rules?

The meaning of a law—the legal rules—can be decisively interpreted by the courts or by legislation. Lawyers interpret legal rules and might eventually lead to a resolution of a conflict in various available ways. Different people and organizations can interpret institutional rules. For example, directors, executives, and supervisors may interpret the institutional rules designed to enforce the law as well as cultural rules, just as referees formally interpret the rules of a football game.

The non-legal culture rules, such as the rules of a game of marbles, may be informally interpreted by a group of players, or even by a group of spectators. Thus, the interpretation and enforcement of non-legal rules can be culture-based: "we do not do it here!" Most importantly, as we shall see, in an institution, the corporate legal counsel (CLO) can interpret non-legal rules than the chief compliance officer (CCO).

1. What are the consequences of breaking the legal and institutional rules? Law may impose monetary sanction, injunctions, and imprisonment. The punishment of institutional-based rules violations is usually monetary and sometimes includes exclusion from the community. We may obey institutional rules because we know that violating these rules may bring unpleasant consequences, including demotion, loss of employment, painful social embarrassment, or exclusion from the group.

2. Why and how do problems arise in enforcing the laws and the institutional, cultural self-regulating (governance) rules? In fact, each legal and self-regulating rule raises three main problems. One problem involves disagreement about the legitimacy of the law-issuers—the government and institutional governance—questioning their authority or power to issue and enforce their rules: What does the Securities and Exchange Commission or these examiners really know about the business, the difficulties, and the pressures!?

A second problem can arise from disagreements about the meaning of the rules. After all, most rules are amenable to more than one interpretation. For example, if a broker made a mistake and a client lost money, how much money should the brokerage firm pay the customer? The mistake may have caused the client a $5,000 loss or a $200,000 loss. The client may accept $5,000 with thanks, and the event will be forgotten, unless the client discovers the discrepancy and problems arise. If the larger amount is noted, it may draw the government examiners' attention to the event, and they may alert the client. How should the lawyer advise institutional management to act?

A third problem that can arise from violating legal and the institutional compliance internal rules is: Is merely stating a prohibition or a requirement sufficient to prevent disobedience with the rule? What actions should be prohibited, even though they have not reached a full-blown violation, but are moving in the direction of a violation? Are such actions to be observed, monitored, and investigated? What about a cashier who borrows $100 from the till for the weekend, and promises himself to return the money on Monday? What if the cashier does return this amount? What if such borrowing becomes a habit? What if other cashiers do the same? Do these activities raise any problems? If so, how should the internal rules react to the activities?

3. Usually, enforcement of law differs from enforcement of institutional rules. The main objective of institutional rules is to further a successful business or other objectives; the main objective of government is to further public prosperity, trust in the financial system, and peace. These objectives are not always compatible. The laws may limit the activities that might maximize business benefits, although the laws may take institutional business objectives into consideration. After all, numerous restrictive legal rules can limit risky institutional activities that may become profitable. The drive to take a risk is especially strong if the profits and losses are

not equally divided among the actors and investors. Therefore, the search for accommodating law and internal, cultural, non-legal rules is continuous.

Yet, how can we resolve a possible conflict between the commands and objectives of the rules on the one hand, and the drives and desires of those, who are subject to the rules on the other hand? Individuals and groups may seek to "bend the rules" just a bit, and yet, this "bending" may lead to enormously socially harmful violations. In addition, government regulators and corporate compliance officers may have ambitions and objectives that are not entirely in harmony with laws and institutional rules. Both may restrict or relax their interpretations with similar negative consequences. Thus, neither legal rules, nor self-regulation (governance) rules, make everyone happy all the time.

The 2008-9 meltdown of the financial system has led to numerous analyses and conflicting opinions. Some blamed the laws and government law-enforcement system for inadequate controls of the financial disaster. Some blamed the financial institutions for disobeying the laws. Some blamed corporate governance of financial institutions for failing to prevent illegal actions from occurring in the first place. And some blamed the investors' greed that arguably drove institutional personnel to violations. Other causes of the problems have been proposed as well.[18] The purpose of our study is to examine ways to prevent a repetition of the 2008 meltdown. At the same time we hope to support successful and trustworthy service to clients and to the country. We are searching for a balance that over time will bring prosperity to all participants and to society as a whole and satisfy most actors, even if not fully.

Discussion topic

The following are a number of the most difficult issues that we will deal with: how should conflicting interests, desires, and drives, such as competition in the marketplace, be dealt with?
How should the strong ambition to win and gain *more* be resolved and constrained in a non-destructive way? How can "unhealthy and risky" tendencies be avoided?
How can self-limitation be rewarded?
How can one succeed in the marketplace if "everyone violates the law" because the law is not being effectively enforced?
How can an institution that manages other people's money determine the level of risk that its activities should or may undertake?
How should the drive for profits and success be balance against the constraints of the law? Is this question legitimate?

---

18 *See* Tamar Frankel, Trust and Honesty: America's Business Culture at a Crossroad pt. 1 (2006).

A. The Nature of a Corporation.

We begin our inquiry by examining the relationship of the corporation with its employees and controlling shareholders. This inquiry covers "family" corporations, such as parent, subsidiary and sister corporations. A Parent or Holding Company is a corporation that holds the shares of another corporation, named Subsidiary. A "Sister Corporation" is a Subsidiary's relationship with another Subsidiary of a Holding Company.

The law recognizes a corporation to be a person. The corporation consists of an organized group of interacting persons, who collaborate for a specified purpose or purposes. Being a legal entity, rather than a human actor, "it" can function only through its agents. These agents can be humans or other legal entities, acting through humans. In the final analysis, a corporation is composed of groups of people, and acts under people's directions. This "humanizes" the corporate entity.[19]

As a legal "person" a corporation is entitled to a number of constitutional protections such as "due process" and "equal protection" under the law. Unless otherwise provided by statute or in the constitution, a corporation is entitled to the same protections and rights as a natural person is.[20] In addition, a corporation has the power to act as a natural person. "It" can trade, hire, and engage in the same activities as individuals do. "It" could also violate the law, as individuals might.

B. Corporations raise capital from investors and lenders (whether individuals or corporations or other entities) and issue them shares (stock) or obligations (bonds).

Even though they elect the corporate directors, the corporations' shareholders' (equity investors') liability for the corporation's violations, obligations, and activities is limited. These shareholders require limited liability because they have no direct control over the corporation's actions. Therefore, they should not bear the responsibility for these actions. Nonetheless, the investors' freedom from liability for the corporation's actions is not foolproof. A court may "pierce the corporate veil" to reach the shareholders, and impose on them liability, if they

---

19   *See, e.g.,* River Woods Chappaqua Corp. v. Marine Midland Bank, N.A., 30 F.3d 339, 344 (2d Cir. 1994) ("Because a corporation can only function through its employees and agents, any act of the corporation can be viewed as an act of such an enterprise, and the enterprise is in reality no more than the defendant itself.")

20   The Privileges and Immunities Clause of the Constitution does not apply to corporations. Therefore, restrictions on a foreign corporation's activities are not unconstitutional if the restrictions represent a reasonable exercise of the state's police power. U. S. Const. art. IV, § 2, cl. 1; Paul v. Virginia, 75 U.S. 168, 8 Wall 168 (1869); Am. Nat'l Life Ins. Co. v. Dir. of Revenue, 269 S.W.3d 19 (Mo. 2008).

controlled the corporation and caused it to act the way it did.[21] In addition, passive investors may, through capital losses, bear the bitter fruits of fraud and misappropriation by a corporation's controlling persons.

C. Two fundamental differences between corporations and individuals are relevant to our topic:

First, corporations do not die; at least, they do not die a "natural death." Second, corporations cannot act except through others, whether individuals or other corporations. Therefore, corporations *as such* cannot prohibit or allow the activities that are performed on their behalf. Only individuals can prohibit or allow activities on behalf of the corporation. These distinctions are relevant to our subject. Not only is the corporation liable for the actions of its agents, the agents might also use the corporation as a shield against the liabilities caused by their own actions. The following examples demonstrate these issues.

D. The Corporation as a Legal Person.

May a corporation's employee refuse to produce certain documents by relying on the Fifth Amendment? In *Three Grand Jury Subpoenas*[22] the Second Circuit answered this question by distinguishing between a current employee and a past employee. Current employees are the corporation's agents. Therefore, they must produce required documents. The order to produce the documents is directed to the corporation; the employees hold the documents not in their personal capacity, but as the corporation's agents. Therefore, they, personally, are not entitled to claim a Fifth Amendment protection. In contrast, *past* employees hold such documents personally, rather than on behalf of the corporation. Therefore, they are entitled to claim a Fifth Amendment protection in refusing to produce these documents.[23]

The distinction between the corporation and those who represent it in any capacity is recognized in other contexts. Yet, the dissenting judge in this case argued that the majority opinion "creates 'an obvious haven for those who seek to frustrate the legitimate demands for the production of relevant corporate records made by a grand jury.'"[24] An investigated person, who is well-informed in the law, "will have a clear incentive to leave the organization, take with him— with or without the assistance of the organization—any documents that he knows may contain

---

21　*See, e.g.,* Richmond McPherson & Raja Nader, *Corporate Justice: An Empirical Study of Piercing Rates and Factors Courts Consider When Piercing the Corporate Veil,* 45 Wake Forest L. Rev. 931 (2010).

22　United States v. Doe (*In re* Three Grand Jury Subpoenas Dukes Talcum dated January 29,1999), 191 F.3d 173, 183-84 (2d Cir. 1999).

23　*Id.*

24　*Id.* at 187.

evidence of wrongdoing, and then resist production of these documents by asserting a claim of privilege against compelled self-incrimination."[25] The decision might provide incentives for "this sort of obstructionist behavior."[26]

Discussion topics

You represent a corporation, whose employee-brokers have misappropriated the clients' money:

Are there any reasons why the clients, who suffered the harm, or the regulators, having viewed the documents, would judge the corporation as one of the guilty parties?

Representing the corporation, what facts would you seek to uncover in order to protect the corporation from liability? What fairness arguments would you make in defense of the corporation?

Representing the plaintiffs, what facts would you seek to establish in order to render the corporation liable for the misappropriation? What fairness arguments would you make in support of the plaintiffs' claims?

E. Under What Conditions, and to What Extent, Should Wrongdoing by Corporate Employees or Agents be Attributed to the Corporation?

Here are two cases to consider. The Second Circuit held: "It is settled law that a corporation may be held criminally responsible for [criminal] violations committed by its employees or agents acting within the scope of their authority."[27] Another Second Circuit court decision noted: "[T]he Supreme Court has long ago determined that the corporation may be held criminally liable for the acts of an agent within the scope of his employment."[28] "Whether an agent is acting within the scope of his employment can then be measured by whether he or she is acting with authority and with intent to benefit the employer."[29] "An agent need not have conferred an

---

25 *Id.*

26 *Id.*

27 United States v. Twentieth Century Fox Film Corp., 882 F.2d 656, 660 (2d Cir. 1989), *quoted in* United States v. Ionia Mgmt. S.A., 526 F. Supp. 2d 319, 323 (D. Conn. 2007).

28 United States v. George F. Fish, Inc., 154 F.2d 798, 801 (2d Cir. 1946), citing New York Cent. & H.R.R. Co. v. United States, 212 U.S. 481, 29 S. Ct. 304, 53 L. Ed. 613 (1909), *quoted in* United States v. Ionia Mgmt. S.A., 526 F. Supp. 2d 319, 323 (D. Conn. 2007).

29 United States v. Kippers, Inc., 652 F.2d 290, 298 (2d Cir. 1981), *quoted in* United States v. Ionia Mgmt. S.A., 526 F. Supp. 2d 319, 323 (D. Conn. 2007).

actual benefit, however; it is sufficient that there was an intent, at least in part, to benefit the employer."[30]

> The suggestion that the employee's wrongful act did not advance the interests of the employer, and therefore should not be imputed to it, entirely overlooks the basic concept of respondeat superior. Presumably, no tortious act by an agent redounds to the benefit of the principal where the latter is held responsible for the resulting damages. Yet if this reasoning were followed no principal would ever be liable.[31]

Clarifying the link between lack of authority and employees' illegal acts, the court continued, "[I]f the fact that [the defendants here] were not authorized to make illegal sales would exculpate the employer, it would be practically impossible to impose any penalties."[32] Therefore a court may hold corporations liable for its agents that engaged in illegal conduct while operating within the scope of their authority.

In *United States of America v. Ionia Management S.A.,*[33] the Court followed the Second Circuit rationale, holding that "a corporation may be held criminally responsible for [criminal] violations committed by its employees or agents acting within the scope of their authority."[34] The corporation argued that it had "a strict policy against" the violation and that its employees "were each trained and promised to abide by this policy."[35] Therefore, "any illegal activities undertaken by these crewmembers were not within the scope of their employment or for the actual benefit of [the corporation]."[36] However, "criminal liability may be imposed on the corporation only when the agent is acting within the scope of his or her employment."[37]

What defines the scope of an agent's employment?

The acts of a corporate agent or corporation's employee are within the scope of his authority if those acts are done on the corporation's behalf or for its benefit in the performance of the

---

30   J.C.B. Super Markets, Inc. v. United States, 530 F.2d 1119, 1122 (2d Cir. 1976), *quoted in* United States v. Ionia Mgmt. S.A., 526 F. Supp. 2d 319, 323 (D. Conn. 2007).

31   *Id.* Under the doctrine of respondeat superior, generally "[a]n employer is subject to liability for torts committed by employees while acting within the scope of their employment." Restatement (Third) of Agency § 2.04 (2006) (LEXIS version).

32   United States of America v. Ionia Mgmt. S.A., 526 F. Supp. 2d 319, 323 (D. Conn. 2007), *quoting* J.C.B. Super Markets, Inc. v. United States, 530 F.2d 1119, 1122 (2d Cir.1976).

33   United States of America v. Ionia Mgmt. S.A., 526 F. Supp. 2d 319, 323 (D. Conn. 2007), *quoting* J.C.B. Super Markets, Inc. v. United States, 530 F.2d 1119, 1122 (2d Cir.1976).

34   United States of America v. Ionia Mgmt. S.A., 526 F. Supp. 2d 319, 323 (D. Conn. 2007), *citing* United States v. Twentieth Century Fox Film Corp., 882 F.2d 656, 660 (2d Cir.1989).

35   *Id.* at 322.

36   *Id.*

37   *Id.* at 324, *citing* United States v. Ricotta, 689 F.2d 238, 241-42 (1st Cir. 1982).

agent's general duties. . . . In order to be acting within the scope of his authority, the employee must be found to be acting on behalf of the corporation with the purpose of benefiting the corporation or serving some corporate purpose.[38]

As to the relationship between an employer's official policies, informal instructions, illegal conduct, and the imputation of vicarious liability, the judge's instruction to the jury was:

> If you find that the agent was acting within the scope of his employment, the fact that the agent's act was illegal, contrary to his employer's instructions, or against the corporation's policies will not relieve the corporation of responsibility for it. However, you may consider the fact that the agent disobeyed instructions or violated company policy in determining whether the agent intended to benefit the corporation, or was acting within this authority.[39]

Violations of the law by entities with which the corporation does business, or on whom it relies for services, could result in severe harm to the corporation's reputation. For example, in August 2014 F-Squared Investments Inc., an investment advisory firm, admitted that it had received a "Wells notice"[40] from the SEC, indicating that the SEC may bring an enforcement action against the company for improperly advertising its returns. Another advisory firm, Virtus Investment Partners Inc., jointly managed a line of mutual funds with F-Squared.[41] The activities of F-Squared Investments Inc. affected the reputation of Virtus. Within a week, the stock price of Virtus declined by 17%.[42] In addition, two brokerage firms prohibited the purchase of shares in the jointly managed Virtus funds. The SEC later investigated Virtus and other firms that used F-Square's performance data, and instituted a proceeding against Virtus.[43]

------

38   *Id.* at 324, *citing* United States v. Bausch, 596 F.2d 871, 877 (9th Cir. 1979).

39   *Id., citing* 1 Leonard B. Sand Et Al., Modern Federal Jury Instructions - Criminal ¶ 2.01, Instr. 27 (2007).

40   A Wells notice is a communication from the staff of the Securities and Exchange Commission to a person involved in an investigation that: (1) informs the person the staff has made a preliminary determination to recommend that the Commission file an action or institute a proceeding against them; (2) identifies the securities law violations that the staff has preliminarily determined to include in the recommendation; and (3) provides notice that the person may make a submission to the Division and the Commission concerning the proposed recommendation.

    Div. of Enforcement, Sec. & Exch. Comm'n, Enforcement Manual 20 (Oct. 28, 2016), *available at* https://www.sec.gov/divisions/enforce/enforcementmanual.pdf (last visited Jan. 5, 2017). *See also* Joshua A. Naphtalis , Note, *"Wells Submissions" to the SEC as Offers of Settlement Under Federal Rule of Evidence 408 and Their Protection from Third-Party Discovery,* 102 Colum. L. Rev. 1912, 1931 (2002).

41   Chris Dietrich & Carrie Driebusch, *Firms Ban New Cash in Some Virtus Funds,* Wall St. J., Sept. 18, 2014, at C3, LEXIS, News Library, Wsj File. The SEC subsequently charged F-Squared and its former CEO with making false and misleading statements, and the firm settled and admitted wrongdoing. U.S. Sec. & Exch. Comm'n, *SEC Charges Investment Manager F-Squared and Former CEO with Making False Performance Claims* (Dec. 22, 2014), *available at* http://www.sec.gov/news/pressrelease/2014-289.html (last visited Feb. 2, 2016).

42   Chris Dieterich, *Virtus Gets Dinged in F-Squared Flap,* Wall St. J., Sept. 6, 2014, at B5, LEXIS, News Library, Wsj File.

43   U.S. Sec. & Exch. Comm'n, (Nov. 16, 2015), *available at* http://www.sec.gov/news/pressrelease/2015-258.html (last visited Feb. 2, 2016).

Discussion Topics

In light of the cases cited above, what steps should a corporation take to avoid criminal liability for its employees' and agents' actions? Please choose among the following actions:

*Establish appropriate policies and internal instructions.

*Limit the freedom of the employees to act and itemize the actions that they may take on behalf of the corporation.

*Require that employees report their daily activities to their supervisors.

*Vest the authority to determine what an appropriate action is in the direct managers of the acting employees, and reward them for avoiding inappropriate actions.

F. The Liability of a Corporation for the Actions or Inactions of an Acquired Fully-Owned Subsidiary

"Florida follows the traditional corporate law rule that if a corporation acquires 100 percent of another corporation's stock or assets, it 'does *not* as a matter of law, assume the liabilities of the prior business' [of the acquired corporation or its assets]."[44] It does, however, assume the future activities of the full subsidiary.

As to past liabilities, however, "[o]n the other hand, where there is a 'corporate merger,' and one entity ceases to exist, the general rule is that 'the surviving corporation becomes liable for the debts, contracts and torts' of the former corporation."[45] Other exceptions to the rule that the successor corporation does not assume liabilities include where: '(1) the successor corporation expressly or impliedly assumes obligations of the predecessor; (2) the transaction is a *de facto* merger; (3) the successor is a mere continuation of the predecessor; or (4) the transaction is a fraudulent effort to avoid liabilities of the predecessor.'"[46] "A de facto merger occurs when one corporation is absorbed by another, i.e., there is a continuity of the selling corporation evidenced

---

44 Infante v. Bank of Am. Corp., 680 F. Supp. 2d 1298, 1305 (S.D. Fla. 2009), *quoting* Corporate Express Office Products, 847 So. 2d 406, 412 (Fla. 2003) (emphasis added).

45 *Id.* at 1305, quoting Corporate Express Office Products, 847 So. 2d 406, 413 (Fla. 2003), *citing* Barnes v. Liebig, 146 Fla. 219, 1 So. 2d 247, 253 (1941) and Fla. Stat. § 607.1106 (2002).

46 *Id., first quoting* Corporate Express Office Products, 847 So. 2d 406, 412 (Fla. 2003), and then *quoting* Bernard v. Kee Mfg. Co., 409 So. 2d 1047, 1049 (Fla. 1982)) (emphasis added) (footnote omitted). *See also* In re Indy Mac Mortgage-Backed Sec. Litig., 718 F. Supp. 2d 495, 508 (S.D.N.Y. 2010) (noting exceptions to rule), *citing* Cargo Partner AG v. Albatrans, Inc., 352 F.3d 41, 46 n.4 (2d Cir. 2003) ("recognizing de facto merger doctrine as one avenue for imposing successor liability under New York law"); *In re* NYSE Specialists Sec. Litig., 405 F. Supp. 2d 281, 316 (S.D.N.Y. 2005) ("listing exceptions, under New York law, to the general non-liability rule, including an agreement to assume liability, continuity of ownership and corporate structure, and a fraudulent transaction arranged to evade debts"); American Buying Ins. Servs., Inc. v. Kornreich & Sons, Inc., 944 F. Supp. 240, 249 (S.D.N.Y. 1996) ("describing circumstances under which successor liability will lie under Racketeering Influenced and Corrupt Organizations Act").

by such things as the same management, personnel, assets, location and stockholders."[47] The reason is that all the shareholders have approved the merger. They have no reason to complain.

However, a merger does not exonerate a corporation from any criminal liability; this difference represents the distinction between liabilities for obligations v. liabilities for wrongful activities.[48] It also highlights the difference between those who consented to the activities and those who were bound by the activities without their consent. For the same reason, this view applies to the case of de facto mergers.

G. To What Extent is a Corporation Responsible for a "Sister" Corporation's Violations?

The plot thickens when corporations or other legal entities are related, but, unlike individuals, their relationships depend on factors other than birth or marriage. Rather, their responsibilities for each other depend on their corporate purposes and their control relationships.[49] The main question is: at what point does a sister corporation become sufficiently involved, in terms of operations and control, to become responsible for the acts or omissions that lead to compliance breaches at a related entity? The following case demonstrates the issue in such situations and the guidelines to resolve them.

Grand Aerie Fraternal Order of Eagles v. Haygood.[50] Grand Aerie, a highly reputable charitable organization, had chapters throughout the United States, including one named Broncho Aerie 2914 (Broncho) located in Texas. After leaving a bar at Broncho's, a drunken Broncho's Chapter member, who was a former Chapter president, had a head-on collision with the Plaintiff's car, killing the Plaintiff's fiancée and seriously injuring the Plaintiff. The Plaintiff sued the drunken driver, as well as Broncho and Grand Aerie.

The lower court held Grand Aerie liable, and Grand Aerie appealed. It argued, among other things, "that the evidence is legally insufficient to establish that its control over Broncho was atypical of a normal parent-subsidiary relationship."[51] Evidence showed that Broncho governed its own alcohol practices. However, its bylaws were subject to approval by Grand Aerie. In addition, "Grand Aerie undertook to aid Broncho in problematic aspects of its activities, and . . . had the means of discovering and remedying dangerous alcohol policies.[52] [Arguably] Grand

---

47 Infante v. Bank of Am. Corp., 680 F. Supp. 2d 1298, at 1305 n.8 (S.D. Fla. 2009), *quoting* Chaul v. Abu-Ghazaleh, 994 So. 2d 465 (Fla. 3d DCA 2008).

48 Franklin A. Gevurtz, Corporation Law § 7.2.1.b, at 686 (2d ed. 2010).

49 Boy Scouts, Girl Scouts, and other civic organizations present similar issues with respect to their organizational "relatives."

50 Grand Aerie Fraternal Order of Eagles v. Haygood, 402 S.W.3d 766 (Tex. App. 2013).

51 *Id.* at 772.

52 *Id.* at 777.

Aerie's failure to notice and remedy Broncho's 'dangerous practices' constituted negligence in its supervision, oversight, and/or dominion [by Grand Aerie]."[53]

The Court of Appeals reversed. It held that "[r]egardless of whether Grand Aerie in fact exercised control, there must be a substantial connection between Grand Aerie's control and the subject matter of the claim[,]" that is, connection "to alcohol service."[54] Even though "Grand Aerie reserved the right to approve bylaws," its "constitution states that both the house rules and bylaws of a local [A]erie are the exclusive governing authority of members and guests in social rooms."[55] The Court noted that Broncho's policies required its bartenders to pass a Texas-approved alcohol seller training program. "Although the compliance officer, general auditor, and program department assisted, audited, and counseled the local [A]eries, without evidence that these activities related to alcohol service or Broncho's relationship with its employees, any alleged control is insufficient to establish jurisdiction over the nonresident corporation."[56]

> [The] courts will not because of stock ownership or interlocking directorship disregard the separate legal identities of corporations, unless such relationship is used to defeat public convenience, justify wrongs, such as violation of the anti-trust laws, protect fraud, or defend crime.
> ... The parent's degree of control must be more than is typical with common ownership and directorship.... To disregard the corporate fiction, there must be evidence that 'the two entities cease to be separate.' [57]

Therefore, Grand Aerie did not exercise "the type of control over Broncho that is required to impute the local chapter's contacts to Grand Aerie for jurisdictional purposes."[58]

As noted in *Grand Aerie,* there is the issue of abuse of the corporate form to shield assets. Courts may "pierce the corporate veil" or disregard the corporate form to reach assets of the shareholders of a corporation "to prevent fraud or to achieve equity."[59] Under the "general rules of agency," an agent may be liable under respondeat superior if it uses control of a corporation to further its own business rather than that of the corporation.[60]

In *Walkovszky v. Carlton,* a plaintiff was injured by a taxicab owned by one of ten corporations owned by the individual defendant. Each of the corporations owns one of the two cabs but

---

53   *Id.*

54   *Id.*

55   *Id.*

56   *Id.*

57   *Id.* at 779, *quoting and citing* BMC Software Belgium, N.V. v. Marchand, 83 S.W.3d 789, 798-99 (Tex. 2002) (citation omitted).

58   *Id.*

59   Walkovszky v. Carlton, 223 N.E.2d 6, 7 (N.Y. App. 1966).

60   Id. at 7-8.

the corporations "allegedly[] are operated as a single entity with regard to financing, supplies, repairs, employees, and garaging."[61]

The Court cited a previous case where a cab was operated by one of four corporations ("operating companies") affiliated with the defendant company. The defendant company and operating companies were essentially owned by the same parties; the defendant company's name was used on the taxis; and the defendant company "serviced, inspected, repaired, and dispatched them." Therefore, the Court pierced the corporate veil and found the defendant company liable, finding that "[t]he operating companies were simply instrumentalities for carrying on the business of the defendant without imposing upon it financial and other liabilities incident to the actual ownership and operation of the cabs."[62]

However, in *Walkovszky*, the Court declined to find the individual defendant liable. The Court found that the plaintiff failed to allege facts sufficient to show that the individual corporations were undercapitalized or that the individual defendant was otherwise doing business through the corporations in his individual capacity.[63] One judge dissented, stating that the corporations were intentionally undercapitalized to avoid liability and income was drained out of them for this purpose.[64]

Discussion topics:

In *Grand Aerie,* how did the higher Court weigh the elements of the relationship between the two entities? Please list the Court's rules representing the relationships that you derive from the reading of this case.

Do you agree with the higher Court's decision?

What would be the consequences for Grand Aerie and similar organizations, if the Plaintiff had been allowed to collect his judgment from Grand Aerie?

Finally: should a court consider these issues? If not, who should?

V. THE INSTITUTIONAL POWER STRUCTURES: LEGAL, BUSINESS, COMPLIANCE, AND PERSONAL POWER GROUPS

Institutions can be viewed as societies, populated by people who interact, working towards a common goal, in various degrees of passion and ability. The corporation's goal is balanced

---

61 *Id.* at 7.

62 *Id.* at 8, *citing* Mangan v. Terminal Transp. System, 247 App. Div. 853, *mot. for lv. to app. den.,* 272 N. Y. 676 (1936).

63 *Id.* at 10; *see also, e.g.,* Worthy v. N.Y. City Hous. Auth., 21 A.D.3d 284, 287 (N.Y. App. Div. 2005).

64 223 N.E.2d at 10-11 (Keating, J., dissenting).

against the people's individual objectives on the one hand and the society's objectives on the other hand. Corporate institutional structure tells us about the corporation's general social and business goals. It also points to the power position of individuals within the corporate organization.

A full picture of an institutional power structure includes not only the legal structure but also the business structure, the compliance-self-regulatory-structure and a special power group. Here is a short description of each. The first is the formal legal structure. It usually is a corporation, although it may include a limited partnership, a trust, and other organizational legal forms. This structure includes the power hierarchy as outlined by the law. A second structure is the business structure. The third is the compliance structure. The fourth is a power group, based on the personality of its members. We deal with each of these structures to highlight the power focus of each group and its role in ensuring corporate compliance with the law.

A. The Legal Structure.

In law, a corporation is generally deemed to be a person, legally responsible for the actions of its employees and related corporations, provided those actions are performed on the corporation's behalf, or under the command of its personnel. Like an individual, the corporation's operations or failure to act may bestow benefits or cause injury, internally and externally. It should be noted that our discussion of "the corporation" may include any other legal-social entities that are recognized by law as a "person," such as limited partnerships, and trusts. Each of these organizational forms is subject to "piercing their veil" and uncovering the people behind their veils. However, generally, each of these organizations is deemed to be a person.

Corporation law establishes a leadership group and its members' associated duties to be performed with care and loyalty. In addition, the structure lays out the position of those who contribute to the corporate enterprise, but have a relatively limited power to direct it, such as shareholders. With minor exceptions, corporations have a board of directors, a Chief Executive Officer (CEO) and executive officers, each of whom is responsible for a particular aspect of the corporation's business operations. In addition there are laws that require financial institutions to impose added roles on any legal structure or to regulate their form. For example, section 10 of the Investment Company Act of 1940 requires the board of an investment company to have at least 40% independent members, and the definition of an independent director is defined in great detail. Exemptions by the Securities and Exchange Commission usually require the percentage of independent board members to be 51%.[65]

As in most corporations, financial institutions have a President, Vice President, board members, legal adviser, Chief Executive Officer, who operates and manages the institution, and lower-rank executives in charge of parts of the institutional operations, an internal Chief Financial

---

65 *See* Investment Company Act of 1940 section 10(a), 15 U.S.C. § 80a-10(a) (2012).

Officer, a Law Officer, and a Compliance Officer. Institutions may seek support from outside independent experts in areas such as technical analysis, and a network of compliance officers.

This traditional corporate power structure mirrors the legal structure of "top down" power, with the CEO and board at the top and "down you go" through the hierarchies. There is a recent development of a different power structure in organizations that aims not at internal competition, but at internal support and cooperation. We will deal at length with this development both because it is pointing to the future, and because it may be more effective than the legal structure or the compliance structure imposed by the law and rules.

However, as will be emphasized time and again, other structures may be more complex. For example, investment companies (mutual funds) are organized as corporations that hold investors' money. These corporations have the usual corporate structure, including a board of directors. However, all of the operational functions of the mutual funds are executed by an investment adviser, under a contract between the adviser and the fund's directors, subject to regulation.[66] The adviser's corporate form can become extremely complex, if it is designed as a holding company of holding companies, and if, in addition, it involves contractual and other forms of outside support and is publicly held.

Although we focus on the actors within the corporate entity, their interest and that of the entity should be balanced against the interests of other members in society and against the interests of society as a whole. The search for this balance brings the issues of self-regulation to the fore. For example, while the sale of addictive products, e.g., cigarettes, is profitable, these products may be physically injurious to users and to the society that supports them when they are unable to earn a living.[67] With time, corporations have grown to affect the health and wealth of an increasingly large number of members of society. These include investors, consumers, employees, and other institutions. Corporate risks and losses have been increasingly shifting from the corporations to their agents, investors, and sometimes to the country's citizens. This shift has prompted a movement to require heightened supervision of corporate activities, on the one hand, and the rise of "the good citizen corporation," on the other.[68]

Most financial institutions are established under a corporation law. Most laws are state laws, but there are also federal laws that authorize or require the creation of a corporation for particular businesses, such as banking. "Associations for carrying on the business of banking under this Title may be formed by any number of natural persons, not less in any case than five. They shall enter into articles of association, which shall specify in general terms the object for which

---

66 See Investment Company Act of 1940 section 15, 15 U.S.C. § 80a- 15 (2012)

67 *See* Cipollone v. Liggett Grp., Inc., 644 F. Supp. 283, 285 (D.N.J. 1986) (quoting cigarette manufacturer's contention that Congress determined that social utility of cigarettes (including benefits to cigarette industry and economy) outweighs costs associated with their use).

68 For a discussion of how the law has influenced corporate responsibility, *see* Lyman Johnson, *Law and Legal Theory in the History of Corporate Responsibility: Corporate Personhood*, 35 Seattle U. L. Rev. 1135 (2012). "Good citizen" corporations are those whose operational decisions factor-in the interests of society.

the association is formed, and may contain any other provisions, not inconsistent with law, which the association may see fit to adopt for the regulation of its business and the conduct of its affairs. These articles shall be signed by the persons uniting to form the association, and a copy of them shall be forwarded to the Comptroller of the Currency, to be filed and preserved in his office."[69]

As noted, a corporation is generally deemed to be a person, legally responsible for the actions of its employees and related corporations, provided those actions are performed on the corporation's behalf or under the command of its personnel. Like an individual, the corporation's operations or failure to act may bestow benefits or cause injury, internally and externally. It should be remembered that our discussion of "the corporation" may include any other legal-social entities that are recognized by law as a "person," such as limited partnerships, and trusts.[70]

With minor exceptions corporations have a board of directors, a chief executive officer ("CEO") and executive officers, each of which is responsible for a particular aspect of the corporation's business. Thus, the legal and business structures, and sometimes the self-regulation compliance structures, are linked at the top of the corporate management pyramid. Yet, many corporations differ in their hierarchal management structure. As noted below, self-regulation compliance may be, but not always must be, part of the higher echelon in a corporate management structure.

The Board of Directors supervises the management of a corporation's business enterprise. Board members include the Chief Executive Officer ("CEO"), who heads the corporate business enterprise, and other high-ranking executive officers, who manage the various parts of the business. Usually, "outside directors," who are not executives, join the board as "independent directors." They are typically retired corporate executives, and social, academic, or government leaders. In some corporations board members may include the founders and their family members.

The board of directors is legally the highest authority that directs corporate activities. Arguably, the board is responsible for protecting the shareholders' interests, although there are conflicting views on that score.[71] The Board meets and works with the business managers. It receives relevant information from the managers and determines the directives management should implement. Boards are often divided into subcommittees that focus on particular aspects of the corporate operations, such as audit and management's compensation.[72]

---

69 12 U.S.C. § 21 (2015).

70 Each of these organizational forms is subject to "piercing their veil" and uncovering the people behind their veils. However, generally, these organizations are deemed to be a person.

71 *See, e.g.*, Anne Tucker Nees, *Who's the Boss – Unmasking Oversight Liability Within the Corporate Power Puzzle*, 35 DEL. J. CORP. L. 199, 211-215 (2010).

72 *See, e.g.*, 8 DEL. CODE ANN., § 141(c)(1)-(3) (allowing boards to designate committees and subcommittees).

The internal power of boards can differ, reflecting different power and functional structures. For example, the board of directors may choose the CEO as the board's Chairperson. Among other things, the Chairperson determines the agendas of the board meetings. This power may be more important than it seems. If a topic is not on the agenda for discussion, no board decision is likely to be reached. Therefore, this issue, among others, can be subject to debate. As noted in an article in the *Wall Street Journal,* the appointment of Bank of America's CEO as board Chairperson "was disputed by some large shareholders while it was supported by other large shareholders." But the Chief Executive Officer retained his chairmanship.[73] In sum, the chairmanship of the Board may bestow on the holder a special power.

B. The Business Structure

The business structure within a corporation varies, depending on the nature of the corporate business. Most positions in this structure are not required by law but are rather designed at the discretion of corporate management according to the needs of the corporation's business. This structure may be redesigned with changes of the corporate business and leadership. For example, if the corporation expands its business, it may hire and appoint experts to manage that particular business.

C. The Self-Regulatory Compliance Structure

The compliance structure is designed to place compliance officers (CCOs) in various corporate functional locations that are sensitive to possible violations of legal requirements. After all, business operations and legal constraints do not always interact harmoniously. CCOs may be placed regardless of their location in the organizational hierarchy, regardless of whether they perform other business or managerial functions in addition to enforcing self-regulatory compliance. No one structure's responsibility and power fits all people, or works well in every corporation. As we shall see, business managers may occupy a position of compliance in certain structures, but not in others.

However, it seems that one crucial attribute of any self-regulatory (compliance) position of a Chief Compliance Officer is independence and direct contact with the board of directors. These two elements are considered necessary to ensure that the corporation manages its business within the dictates of the law, both in the short- and the long-term. There are corporate managers that view self-regulation as "risk management," designed to limit the risk of corporate liability, similar to an insurance function. Other managers may view the corporation's good

---

[73] Christina Rexrode, *BofA Under Fire for Leader's Dual Role,* WALL ST. J., Nov. 24, 2014, at C3, LEXIS, News Library, Wsj File; Christina Rexrode, *Bank of America's Brian Moynihan Survives Chairman-CEO Vote,* WALL ST. J., (last updated Sept. 22, 2015).

behavior as a beneficial and profitable approach, especially if it is accompanied by appropriate publicity. And some managers take a balanced approach in an attempt to weigh the different purposes and claims on powerful corporations.

CCOs may include not only internal officers but also external personnel. Kenneth L. Bryant suggested that a comprehensive self-regulatory compliance risk management framework should, at a minimum, include four internal control functions: (1) internal audit; (2) legal;[74] (3) risk management;[75] and (4) compliance.[76] In addition, we note the difference between the involvement of directors who do not manage the business operations, that is, "external directors" and directors who are also managers of the corporate enterprise, that is, the "senior management."[77] The internal control functions are on the same level as senior management; the board has ultimate responsibility for the framework.[78]

Traditionally the Chief Compliance Officer (CCO) operated within the office of the Chief Legal Officer (CLO). There are signs that in the future the CCO's position may be an independent position, in cooperation with the CLO. The Office of the Comptroller (OCC), that regulates the banks, has adopted a different model. The OCC may require banks to hire independent consultants and then to provide the OCC with the particulars of these consultants, as part of the Independent Foreclosure Review (IFR). "More recently, in a substantial number of cases, the OCC has ordered banks of all sizes to retain independent consultants to address deficiencies in compliance with the BSA and anti-money laundering laws and regulations."[79] However, as we shall see, at least in one case, the independent consultant seems to have done more than what was permissible to help banks in their quest for profits, and has paid a price for this action. Hopefully, this was a unique case rather than a general pattern of behavior.[80] In sum, there are always exceptions.

---

74   *See, e.g.,* DEL. CODE ANN.(state corporate law).

75   *See, e.g.,* Chapters 7, 10-11 (discussing conduct risk, monitoring, and investigations).

76   KENNETH L. BRYANT, DESIGNING A COMPREHENSIVE COMPLIANCE RISK MANAGEMENT FRAMEWORK (2004). (n.p.). *See, e.g.,* Chapters 17-18 (discussing the CCO); Chapter 5 (discussing compliance programs required by law).

77   KENNETH L. BRYANT, DESIGNING A COMPREHENSIVE COMPLIANCE RISK MANAGEMENT FRAMEWORK (2004). (n.p.).

78   *Id. See also* Norman Marks, *How to Assess the Effectiveness of Internal Audit,* INTERNAL AUDITOR, Jan. 30, 2013, *available at* https://iaonline.theiia.org/how-to-assess-the-effectiveness-of-internal-audit (last visited Apr. 4, 2017); Richard Chambers, *When It Comes to Fraud, Internal Auditors Need to Get There Early,* INTERNAL AUDITOR, June 25, 2013, *available at* https://iaonline.theiia.org/when-it-comes-to-fraud-internal-auditors-need-to-get-there-early (last visited Apr. 4, 2017); BASEL COMMITTEE ON BANKING SUPERVISION, THE INTERNAL AUDIT FUNCTION IN BANKS (June 2012), available at http://www.bis.org/publ/bcbs223.pdf (last visited Apr. 4, 2017).

79   *Outsourcing Accountability? Examining the Role of Independent Consultants: Hearing before the Subcomm. on Financial Institutions and Consumer Protection of the S. Comm. on Banking, Housing, and Urban Affairs,* 113th Cong. (2013), CONG. DOCUMENTS & PUBLICATIONS, LEXIS, News Lib, Arcnws File (testimony of Daniel Stipano, Deputy Chief Counsel, Office of the Comptroller of the Currency)

80   N.Y. State Dep't of Fin. Servs., *NYDFS Announces PricewaterhouseCoopers Regulatory Advisory Services Will Face 24-Month Consulting Suspension; Pay $25 Million; Implement Reforms After Misconduct During Work at Bank of Tokyo Mitsubishi* (Aug. 18, 2014), *available at* http://www.dfs.ny.gov/about/press/pr1408181.htm (last visited Apr. 4, 2017); Settlement Agreement, N.Y. State Dep't of Fin. Servs., In re *PricewaterhouseCoopers LLP* (Aug. 14, 2014), *available at* http://www.

D. The "Inner Circle"

A fourth unit within the power structure in a corporation is a power group of individuals or, as it is sometimes called, an "inner circle." We should distinguish between the formal structure, business structure, self-regulatory compliance structure and the "inner circle." An inner circle's power need not be known to all, and its members might not be subject to the constraints that apply to formal powerholders. The power of this "inner circle" is linked to particular persons, rather than to a particular formal position. In fact, personality and personal relationship have an impact on the group's membership and degree of influence. Not all directors or chief operating officers exercise the same power, even when they occupy the same position in the formal structure. This power-allocation may or may not be reflected in the formal, business, or self-regulatory compliance structures. Most importantly, a formal authority in a corporation may be trumped by, or combined with, an inner circle power group.

In a marvelously well-documented and thoughtful article, Professor James Fanto discussed the formation and power of "inner circles" within institutions.[81] In a corporation, the "circle" can be formed by the CEO, supported by a group of loyal followers, who enforce the CEO's views and commands. Group members think alike (group-think) and strengthen each other's views. The ideas of others, whether contradictory or questioning, will not easily penetrate the institution's group-think, because the group is cohesive and its members are comfortable with this cohesion.

When the leader of the group is powerful, group members attain some of the leaders' power and at the same time reinforce it. With this power come benefits in various forms, such as higher pay and bonuses, and the ability to hire favorites and to exercise nepotism. If the group is not particularly concerned with following legal self-limitations, the possibility of wrongful activities by the corporation becomes more likely as well.

"Inner circles" have been strong both in very successful corporations and in failed institutions like Enron Corporation.[82] Enron Corporation took significant risks that brought about its collapse, even though the risks could be easily identified, if one looked at the right places. Yet, accounts and their numbers alone do not always reveal the tricks used by corporations such as Enron Corporation.

Following Enron, the Sarbanes-Oxley Act of 2002 tightened corporate regulation and imposed a higher level of internal controls and documentation.[83] Yet, there is little consensus

---

dfs.ny.gov/about/ea/ea140818.pdf (last visited Apr. 4, 2017); Danielle Douglas, *Pricewaterhouse to Pay $25 Million Fine,* Wash. Post, Aug. 19, 2014, at A09, LEXIS, News Library, Curnws File

81   James Fanto, *Whistleblowing and the Public Director: Countering Corporate Inner Circles,* 83 Or. L. Rev. 435 (2004).

82   *Id.* at 444-49.

83   Sarbanes-Oxley Act of 2002, Pub. L. No. 107-204, 116 Stat. 745 (codified as amended in scattered sections of 15 and 18 U.S.C.).

on its effectiveness. Arguably, the statutory controls create "the risk of re-enforcing compliance mentalities." Arguably, the statute is a "sledgehammer." It is too far-reaching, rendering too many companies highly risk-adverse and backwards-looking. Peter Bartram, however, points to Switzerland, and to the way regulation can be more proportionate, in recognition of the need for strong internal controls and managing a successful business as well.[84] Whether the Swiss model is effective, however, is open to arguments. Thus, there is a continuous search for the balance between the law, business, and personal drives. Besides, "the truth, the whole truth, and nothing but the truth" is hard to design and identify. Some companies may not show the amount of products returned by buyers. Some companies may not demonstrate cost clearly. Yet their operators may be convinced that their behavior is justified.

In your reading, please focus on identifying the informal power group, for instance, by examining group functionality, size, and interwoven relationships. The power group is extremely important because, for better or worse, it might constitute the actual leadership of an institution. Furthermore, formal power distribution may be influenced by additional factors, such as the corporation's history and the personality, expertise, and roles of particular individuals within the corporation. Rarely does a corporation or any organization avoid the duality of formal and real power structure. That is because the formal structure appears in the documents and the law, while the real power structure depends on the particular actors, their abilities, inclinations, and their relationships with other actors within, and sometimes outside, the corporation.

A formal authority in a corporation may be overcome by, or may combine with, an "inner circle" within the organization. The difference between the two is significant. Formal structures can be changed by filing the appropriate papers. Power structures change depending on individuals and their personal relationships. People may be removed from a position; they may retire. Their experience may have become outdated expertise, or their personal situations have changed and these affected their performance. The corporation may change as well. It may require different kinds of experienced individuals, and new developing expertise.

VI. WHO BEARS THE CONSEQUENCES FOR INSTITUTIONAL VIOLATIONS OF THE LAW?

While corporate structures demonstrate functional and power relationships, they do not, however, demonstrate the allocation of responsibility for violations of the law. An incorrect forecast, for example, is made within the business structure, and its punishment could be applied to the top or low echelon personnel. In the case of Walgreens, the young CFO (Chief Financial Officer) had to leave immediately, after an "event," together with the older CEO, who would ultimately

---

84   Peter Bartram, Enron: *10 Years On*, FINANCIALDIRECTOR, Jan. 2012, at 42, 42, (Dec. 8, 2011), *available at* https://www.financialdirector.co.uk/financial-director/feature/2133327/enron (last visited Apr. 4, 2017).

retire at the end of the year. They were paid severance fees, although by industry standards, not that much. The employees, who actually produced the false forecast, were not mentioned, and it is unclear whether they have been reprimanded.[85] This story demonstrates a faulty internal information system, and the failure of top management to effectively perform its oversight role. The incident suggests a situation in which ambition overcame caution and precise reporting, and where senior management bore the cost of error. This event could be predictive of the manner in which such blunders will be dealt with in the future.

Arguably, corporations that engage in wrongful activities could remain free of responsibility by blaming their wayward agents for committing the wrongs. This approach would protect the investors in such corporations, especially if the investors had no impact on the corporation's decisions and actions. Yet, as William S. Laufer noted, if the investors in a corporation have a measure of influence on corporate decisions, relieving a corporation from any responsibility for wrongful actions may undermine the objectives and spirit of the law.[86] Besides, it is unclear whether investors in fraudulent corporations should reap benefits from fraud.

To be sure, if a corporation is punished, the constituents of the corporation that contributed to the wrongful acts might be punished as well. They may have to compensate the victims who suffered losses. Besides, when a corporation is punished by having to pay a large fine, the affected parties might be both the management, if they lose face and their jobs, the employees, if they lose their jobs and ability to get new jobs, and the investors, if they lose the value of their investments. In addition, outside related entities and persons may bear the burden of the corporation's activities. The relationship may contaminate them as well.

Discussion Topics:

Assume that you are preparing for an interview for a position in a law firm. You are going to meet with a number of firm members. Please list the facts you would like to know about the firm and the persons with whom you are going to interview. Where would you look for and verify these facts?

Assume that you are required to prepare a case against an investment adviser on behalf of the advisers' investors. The claim is based on faulty disclosures of the firm to its investors in violation of the Advisers Act of 1940. Your task is to identify the persons who might be sued,

---

85 Michael Siconolfi, *$1 Billion Blunder Trips Up Walgreen*, WALL ST. J., Aug. 20, 2014, at A1, LEXIS, News Library, Wsj File, *online version*, Michael Siconolfi, *Walgreen Shakeup Followed Bad Projection*, WALL ST. J., Aug. 20, 2014, *available at* https://www.wsj.com/articles/walgreen-shakeup-followed-bad-projection-1408494546 (last visited June 15, 2017) (registration required); Ed Silverman, *Walgreen Sued by Former CFO for Defamation Over Forecasting Error*, WALL ST. J. (Oct. 17, 2014, 11:07 AM), *available at* https://blogs.wsj.com/pharmalot/2014/10/17/walgreen-sued-by-former-cfo-for-defamation-over-forecasting-error/ (last visited June 15, 2017).

86 *See generally* William S. Laufer, *Corporate Liability, Risk Shifting, and the Paradox of Compliance*, 52 VAND. L. REV. 1343 (1999).

including the firm. Please list the positions of persons that you might consider responsible for the violation of the Investment Advisers Act of 1940.

VII. THE ROLE OF CULTURE AND THE LAWYER'S ROLE IN THE INSTITUTION

A. A Crucial Aspect of Institutional Self-Regulation is the Institutional Culture

We do not live alone and cannot live alone. Most of us belong to many groups, such as a family, school, sports group, workplace, professional association, the town or settlement where we live, and the state and country whose citizens we are. The different rules that govern and are enforced in different groups may overlap; and some rules, such as the legal rules, trump other or all rules of other groups. Thus, in our families we comply with the law as well as with family rules, which the law does not impose. We may raise our children strictly or permissibly, but we must send them to school or home schooling, in accordance with the law.

As noted, today, law imposes two types of rules on institutions. One type consists of rules of behavior, backed by punishment (the law of the land) and the other type is rules that require the institutions to ensure legal behavior by self-regulation (rules of self-regulation). For example, the law of the land prohibits brokers from misappropriating their customers' money. An additional law currently requires brokers to establish an internal system that would preclude and prevent brokers from misappropriating the customers' money.

Even though the objective of the law and the rules of self-regulation coincide, the substance of the law differs from the substance of the rules of self-regulation. The rules of the law address certain prohibitions or requirements of behavior. These rules are accompanied by punishment for violations. For example, the law prohibits misappropriation of property and the law's violation is accompanied by punishment from fines to a prison sentence. In addition, the law of the land may impose a duty to self-regulate to avoid such violations.

The rules of self-regulation may be backed by a threat of punishment as well. But in addition, these rules aim at preventing such violations from occurring. For example, prevention includes examining applicant employees before hiring them, and monitoring institutional activities to uncover signals of a "road to violations." The signals themselves are not prohibited. But if they might lead to prohibited activities, the institutions are required to identify the existence of such signals and prevent the maturing of these signals into actual violations.

The laws that impose on institutions a duty of self-regulation are not detailed. That is because institutions differ in their size, history, and the nature of their business. After all, a small brokerage and a huge bank that offers brokerage services may require different types of self-regulatory system and resources.

B. Institutional Enforcement

What is the impact of institutional rules on behavior? Institutional rules of behavior are not necessarily specifically enforced by the law. These rules include many prohibitions or requirements designed to prevent ultimate violation. The prohibited or required actions themselves may be permissible by law. But if they lead to possible violations they may be prohibited by the institutional rules or may require reporting of the particular actions. Institutional rules focus on "slippery slopes" and on risks of future wrongful actions.

Who enforces the institutional rules? Within institutions the rules are enforced by the bearers of power, from the board to executive officers and compliance officers. Compliance officers use monitoring and investigating to uncover and prevent wrongful activities, as well as threats of different types of punishments. Punishment may include money fines or reduced salaries or bonuses, changing the workplace to a less desirable one, demotion, and termination of employment and relationship. Refusal to provide a recommendation upon termination of employment and relationship may create enormous hardship in finding other employment.

Who interprets the rules of behavior? Within most institutions the interpreters are the Chief Legal Officer (CLO), and the Chief Compliance Officer (COO). Their relationship[s] has not yet been generally defined and is evolving. We will deal with their different functions, positions, and approaches.

Last but far from being least, the concept and system of culture are introduced in our studies. That is because culture is crucial to effective self-regulatory compliance by institutions. You might find the words "ethics" and "trust" and similar expressions denoting "good behavior." Yet, ethics focuses on the personal behavior of particular people. Culture is a group ethics. Culture is a system that parallels law. It is a group system that imposes and enforces rules on its members. Sometimes it is established by the top executives, but it can also be established by a group that holds power within the institution. We will examine at least one such case, which led to the failure of the entire brokerage firm.

To be sure, not every court pays full attention to the culture within an institution, but this issue is of crucial importance in our study. Increasingly culture plays a role in establishing group behavior that avoids or leads to violations of the law. We will deal with culture at length as well.

Discussion Topic

A very large bank has an active and growing brokerage division. To continue its growth the brokers are promised bonuses if they "open new brokerage accounts." One of the brokers, who is creative and hungry for more money, has an idea. He has a brokerage account for Mr. Dumb, who is an old and trusting gentleman. When the broker executes a new transaction for Mr. Dumb, the broker does not use Mr. Dumb's existing account but opens another, new account for his client. Account opening has two benefits. One is acquiring a new client. The other is imposing on the client the cost of opening a new account, and perhaps an added cost of rewarding the broker for opening the account.

With time, Mr. Dumb has five such accounts. Needless to say, the other brokers believe that opening new accounts for existing customers is great, and follow the model. Whether the supervisor of the brokers knows that the new accounts do not represent new clients but existing clients is unclear. What seems clear is that the supervisor is delighted with the growth of new accounts and is rewarded for the growth of accounts by bonuses. Regardless of what he or she thinks about it, the practice is justified at the time. Literally, "new accounts" are "new" accounts. Nowhere in the internal rule did it say "New clients." "In this bank, we follow specific rules just as we do in the law! Whatever is not prohibited is permitted. Right? Right!"

After a number of years, however, the system is discovered, and the overcharge to clients amounts to billions. The bank must repay the money to the clients (and what about interest?) and pay a hefty fine as well. Numerous brokers are discharged. The bank's reputation is marred.[87]

Discussion Topic:

In light of the legal and institutional designs you just read and your general knowledge:
- Was there any violation of the law in this case?
- If not, why not? If yes, what went wrong and why did it go wrong?
- Was the internal rule violated?
- Should the laws and rules be differently written?
- Who should have been responsible for this disaster, and why?
- Please run an Internet search for "Whatever is not prohibited is permitted" and assess the extent to which this approach is accepted.

What is your reaction to the following test: Stand in front of the mirror. Look at yourself. And then ask: Would I like to be treated this way?

---

87   This is precisely what happened to Wells Fargo, resulting in $185M in fines, the firing of more than 5,300 employees, a scathing Senate hearing, and the eventual ousting of formerly revered C.E.O. John Stumpf . . . after employees were found to have created more than two million unauthorized bank and credit card accounts between 2011 and 2016. Consumer Fin. Protection Bureau, *Consumer Financial Protection Bureau Fines Wells Fargo $100 Million for Widespread Illegal Practice of Secretly Opening Unauthorized Accounts* (Sept. 8, 2016), *available at* https://www.consumerfinance.gov/about-us/newsroom/consumer-financial-protection-bureau-fines-wells-fargo-100-million-widespread-illegal-practice-secretly-opening-unauthorized-accounts/ (last visited Mar. 23, 2017); *Testimony of John Stumpf, Chairman and Chief Executive Officer of Wells Fargo & Co., Before the U.S. Senate Committee on Banking, Housing and Urban Affairs* (2016), *available at* http://www.banking.senate.gov/public/_cache/files/18312ce0-5590-4677-b1ab-981b03d1cbbb/3B18AA6E3A 96E50C446E2F601B854CF1.092016-stumpf-testimony.pdf (last visited Mar. 21, 2017); *Wells Fargo CEO John Stumpf Steps Down*, WALL ST. J. ONLINE, Oct. 13, 2016, LEXIS, News Library, Wsj File.

As noted we have two types of laws. The rules of law directing required behavior and the rules of law directing institutions to impose and enforce codes of behavior. Here is an example of the latter type of rules, which requires advisers to impose a particular code of behavior. Please note that the requirement is more general because it takes into consideration the probable differences among advisory institutions.

U.S. Sec. & Exch. Comm'n, *The Evolving Compliance Environment: Examination Focus Areas*, Apr. 2009 (2009 CCOutreach Regional Seminars)[88]

* * *

I. UNDERSTANDING AN ADVISER'S COMPLIANCE PROGRAM

A. Identifying Compliance Risks and Conflicts of Interest

Investment advisers are exposed to numerous risks and conflicts of interest that can result in harm to investors and may cause a firm to deviate from regulatory requirements. Many risks and conflicts of interest are common among firms. Examples of such risks and problems include portfolio managers making decisions that are contrary to a client's investment objectives, traders placing orders for clients' accounts to generate soft dollar credits rather than seeking best execution, and misrepresenting investment performance of a fund to enhance its position in the competitive marketplace. However, advisers may also have risks and conflicts of interest that are unique as a result of the firm's organizational arrangements, affiliations, business partners, diversity of client base, products and services offered to clients, geographical locations, and personnel.

To implement a compliance program reasonably designed to prevent violations of the Advisers Act and rules thereunder, each adviser should identify the risks and conflicts of interest that are relevant to its business. The identification process should be repeatable and firm wide. Such a process may include any or a combination of the following:

Top-down: a simple approach to risk assessment in which management identifies the conflicts of interest and other risks the firm confronts.

Layered: committees are used to identify the conflicts of interest and other risks present within each area of expertise (e.g., portfolio management committee, brokerage committee,

---

88 U.S. Sec. & Exch. Comm'n, *The Evolving Compliance Environment: Examination Focus Areas*, Apr. 2009 (2009 CCOutreach Regional Seminars), *available at* https://www.sec.gov/info/iaiccco/iaiccco-focusareas.pdf (last visited June 15, 2017).

pricing committee, IT oversight committee, internal controls committee, and corporate governance committee). Such committee input is compiled and summarized into a firm-wide program.

Bottom-up: each employee or group of employees provides input regarding the potential conflicts of interest and other risks that the firm confronts in the employees respective areas of expertise.

Dedicated risk staff: a group of individuals are responsible for managing the risk assessment process and ensuring risks are properly assessed, inventoried, and managed.

Regardless of the process used by an adviser to identify its risks, the end result of the firm's risk assessment process should be an inventory of potential risks that reflects the current environment of the firm. Such an inventory of risks should not be static. In addition to gathering and analyzing information about an adviser's risk assessment process, examiners review the firm's inventory of risks and determine whether it is current and sufficiently comprehensive.

B. Mapping Potential Compliance Risks to Policies and Procedures

An effective compliance program could include a standardized process for creating written policies and procedures to address each risk in its inventory. Similar to the process for identifying risks, the process for creating and maintaining corresponding policies and procedures should be an evergreen process and also may be structured as a top-down, layered, bottom-up, or dedicated risk staff process.

The written policies and procedures established by an adviser should create the necessary separation of duties vital to the creation of an effective control environment and should address responsibilities for the administration and oversight of each risk area. Typically, such policies and procedures dictate that testing and reconciliations are built into routine operations, require that periodic exceptions and completion reports be prepared, and address the process for escalating information and reporting to higher levels of management.

As part of their assessment of the compliance program, examiners typically evaluate an adviser's process for creating effective policies and procedures to manage and control the risks present at the firm.

C. Implementing Policies and Procedures

The goal of implementing an effective compliance program is to facilitate the adviser fulfilling its fiduciary duty and its disclosure obligations to clients and to guide the firm toward operating in a manner that is consistent with the Advisers Act. Thus, compliance with the policies and procedures should be an integral part of daily operations. In addition, routine testing of information and operations should be done against established guidelines and limitations to identify exceptions that need to be followed up. Implementation of policies and procedures also covers the follow-up work required to investigate exceptions and outlier results, and information and remedial actions taken to correct non-compliant practices.

Examiners typically evaluate the implementation process used by an adviser, including oversight activities by the CCO, to assist in determining if the compliance program is effective.

D. Monitoring the Effectiveness of the Policies and Procedures

One goal of compliance programs is to prevent compliance problems from occurring. However, some compliance breaches still may occur. As a result, examiners expect to find exception reports, compliance checklists, and management reports that note problems and issues. Conversely, if a review of compliance records and/or a discussion with an adviser's compliance staff reveals that the firm has not found any compliance problems during its reviews, an examiner may be skeptical of these results and conduct additional testing to confirm such an outcome. To evaluate the timeliness with which compliance problems are found and corrected, examiners request information from the adviser regarding: when problems were found; when the problems occurred; when and how each such problem was resolved; and whether factors that allowed the problem to happen were identified, corrected, or improved.

Monitoring the effectiveness of a compliance program includes conducting transactional testing, analyzing exception reports, and conducting forensic tests. Forensic tests are designed to identify patterns of data that represent anomalies with respect to expected outcomes and may identify weaknesses in a firm's compliance program that are not readily evident. Such anomalies may be indicators of possible fraudulent conduct. Forensic tests corroborate the results of daily transaction tests and the related exception and management reports.

Each adviser is required by the Compliance Rule to conduct at least an annual review of its compliance program. However, ideally, the process of reviewing and evaluating compliance risks and policies and procedures should be a continuous part of any compliance program. For example, problems identified in exception reports or as a result of forensic testing may require analysis of the firm's operations in select areas, evaluation of the control procedures in those areas, and corrective action. The rule does not require the CCO of an adviser to prepare a report that summarizes the results of the annual review. However, it is a good business practice to prepare a report to document the work that was performed, the findings from the review, and the recommendations for improvements. This information is frequently requested and reviewed by examiners to determine the effectiveness of an adviser's own reviews.

Discussed in more detail below are some areas examiners review, deficiencies they uncovered, and controls they have observed which may be effective for each of these areas of special emphasis. When determining areas to review, the staff assesses the conflicts of interest and risks that are present at a particular firm and the extent to which the firm's compliance program mitigates and manages those conflicts and risks. The existence of a conflict or risk does not suggest that a deficiency will be present. Advisers should note that the risks identified and specific procedures discussed do not represent an exhaustive list and are not required by the federal securities laws.

Examiners assess whether an adviser has engaged in any activity that conflicts with the interests of the adviser's clients, validate that the firm has employed reasonable care to mitigate and manage such risks and to avoid misleading clients, and evaluate whether the adviser has provided full and fair disclosure of all material facts to clients and prospective clients. In today's evolving economic and regulatory environment, examiners are placing special emphasis on the following operational areas: portfolio management, outsourcing services, safeguarding client funds and securities, performance claims, and valuation.

A. Portfolio Management

The term "portfolio management" covers a broad array of advisory activities. It includes the allocation of investment opportunities among clients, the consistency of portfolios with clients' investment objectives, disclosures to clients, and consistency of operations with applicable regulatory requirements and the firm's code of ethics. Because of their importance, these areas are typically reviewed during all examinations.

Risks in the area of portfolio management are greatly dependent on an adviser's operations, services, affiliations, and the specificity of guidelines and restrictions clients place on the firm regarding their individualized services. Also relevant is how the firm handles its receipt of non-public information, and how the firm maintains the confidentiality of information regarding its clients.

1. Understanding the Firm's Business and Operations

a. When examiners review the activities of an adviser, they analyze the firm's business operations, business relationships, affiliations, and disclosures to confirm that the adviser has procedures in place to ensure that: it only engages in investment decisions that are consistent with client mandates and objectives; it reviews accounts to confirm consistency; and it provides full and complete disclosure to clients regarding portfolio management services. In addition, the staff confirms that there is a framework for testing whether investment decisions have been allocated equitably among eligible clients.

b. If the adviser has discretionary authority, the power to engage in conflicting transactions rises. Situations in which the adviser has conflicts of interest, for example: (i) Adviser benefits from a broker-dealer that is interested in selling or buying certain securities. (ii) Adviser manages different types of accounts in a parallel manner (i.e., registered investment company, private investment company, and/or separately managed accounts – all with the same investment objective); (iii) Adviser manages accounts with competing investment strategies.

c. On February 7, 2017, the Office of Compliance Inspections and Examinations of the Securities and Exchange Commission (OCIE) published a Risk Alert listing of the five compliance topics most frequently identified in deficiency letters that were sent to SECregistered investment advisers ("Advisers") during the past two years. Within each of these topics, a few examples of typical deficiencies were discussed to highlight the risks and issues that examiners commonly identified.[89]

The five compliance topics addressed in this Risk Alert are deficiencies or weaknesses involving: Rule 206(4)-7 (the Compliance Rule) under the Investment Advisers Act of 1940 (the Advisers Act); (ii) required regulatory filings; ((iii) Rule 206(4)-2 under the Advisers Act (the Custody Rule); (iv) Rule 204A-1 under the Advisers Act (the Code of Ethics Rule); and (v) Rule 204-2 under the Advisers Act (the Books and Records Rule). The Staff emphasized that: "*Advisers should review their compliance programs and practices in light of the topics noted in this Risk Alert.*"

Although the list of deficiencies and weaknesses was based upon examinations of SEC-registered investment advisers, these findings should be considered as regulatory guidance by "exempt reporting advisers," as well, that is, particularly relating to those whose business is anticipated to grow beyond the scope of the exemption they are relying on.

For example, the failure to adopt and maintain a Code of Ethics, which is an obligation applicable to all investment advisers, whether or not registered; the failure to adopt compliance manuals that are reasonably tailored to the Adviser's business practices; the failure of Advisers to follow their compliance manual policies and procedures; and the failure of Advisers to maintain accurate books and records with regard to their investment adviser business, including typical accounting and other business records.

In other situations, an adviser manages accounts with differing compensation structures, such as performance-based compensation versus asset-based management fees.

---

89 Office of Compliance Inspections and Examinations Issues Risk Alert on the Five Most Frequent Compliance Topics Identified in Examinations of Investment Advisers

Conflicts arise when: (i) The adviser makes proprietary investments in the same securities that are recommended to clients. (ii) The adviser invests client assets in affiliated entities; (iii) The adviser votes client proxies.

2. Identifying Deficient Practices and Control Weaknesses

Deficient practices might exist in situations where firms did not: adopt or maintain policies and procedures relating to the firms' investment decision-making; maintain required books and records to corroborate investment decisions (e.g., trade tickets and confirmations); and/or disclose all conflicts of interest to clients that may affect the impartiality of the advisers' investment decisions (e.g., a material relationship, compensation arrangement, or other conflict of interest). The severity of the issues identified during an examination with respect to an adviser's portfolio management review may vary.

Below are examples of questions examiners may ask to determine if an adviser has deficient practices and control weaknesses:

*Does the adviser have processes, including supervisory procedures, to ensure that the investment advice provided to each client is consistent with: (a) the client's circumstances, expectations, restrictions, direction, and risk tolerance; (b) the information provided to each client in brochures, marketing materials, contracts, and otherwise; and (c) the regulatory regime?

*How does the adviser ensure that its compliance policies and procedures are adequate with respect to the investment advice the adviser provides?

*Does the adviser have an effective means for evaluating investment decisions after implementation to determine if outcomes were consistent with clients' expectations and restrictions? If outcomes deviated from expectations, were appropriate remedial actions taken?

*Does the adviser maintain current and complete information regarding each client's financial and family circumstances, investment objectives and restrictions, and risk tolerance?

*Does the adviser maintain an effective due diligence process through which all relevant features and risks associated with proposed investment products, styles, and processes are vetted and approved before being implemented?

*Are the adviser's investment recommendations consistent with the disclosures made to clients? Do its investment recommendations carry a greater or lesser risk than disclosed to clients?

*If the adviser uses an approved list of investments, how does it ensure that actual client investments are consistent with this list?

*Does the adviser recommend derivative instruments, such as swaps and inverse floaters? Is its client accounting system able to fully accommodate the sometimes unusual terms and conditions relating to these instruments?

*Does the adviser have effective processes to identify, contain, and prevent the unauthorized and/or inappropriate use of non-public information that comes into its possession?

*If the adviser's employees come into possession of non-public information, is this information effectively identified, documented, and contained so that it is used appropriately?

*If the adviser's employees come into possession of non-public information about an issuer as a result of a client's position in that issuer (e.g., a participation in a bank loan), is this information controlled effectively so that it is not used to unlawfully trade in other instruments of the issuer (e.g., shorting the issuer's equity if the issuer's financial condition deteriorates)?

*If the adviser provides investment advice to clients regarding companies with which the adviser has business relationships, does the adviser have processes to prevent providing conflicted investment advice to clients and to ensure that clients receive full and fair disclosures regarding these conflicts?

*Does the adviser engage in "window dressing" (i.e., are decisions to effect trades in client or proprietary accounts undertaken in an attempt to manipulate the closing price of a security or to be able to present to clients a list of portfolio positions that is consistent with their investment objectives but which is substantially different than the positions held in between reporting periods)?

*How does the adviser deal with conflicts in advice it gives to clients (e.g., advising one client to sell a thinly traded security, while at the same time recommending that another client purchase the same security)?

*Is portfolio turnover (frequency and amount of trading in clients' accounts) consistent with clients' investment objectives, or is it the result of decisions by employees to generate commission credits that the adviser can use for its own purposes?

*How does the adviser prevent cherry-picking of favorable trades on behalf of favored clients or proprietary accounts? Are changes in order allocations consistent with its fiduciary relationship with clients, code of ethics, and disclosures?

*How does the adviser prevent scalping of investment advice provided to clients (i.e., the illegal practice of recommending that clients purchase a security and secretly selling the same security in a personal or proprietary account contrary to the recommendation)?

*Does the adviser have any side letters or agreements with any participant in a pooled vehicle the adviser advises or manages? Are the terms and conditions of these agreements consistent with the adviser's disclosures to clients and pooled vehicle participants?

*Does the adviser vote proxies consistent with its proxy voting policies and procedures, disclosures to clients, and status as a fiduciary?

*Is documentation or other output generated to substantiate that the adviser obtained all information related to providing investment advice in a timely, accurate, and complete manner?

3. Controls Observed

An adviser should have controls to ensure that the policies and procedures in place with respect to its portfolio management functions are adequate to detect fraudulent conduct and decrease the ability for personnel to perpetuate and conceal fraudulent activity. Below are examples of such controls examiners have observed.

*Adviser has segregation of duties (when practicable) among personnel performing certain functions, especially portfolio management, marketing, and valuation of clients' positions.

*Adviser performs forensic testing to identify accounts or portfolio managers that have outlier performance and determines the cause for these unusual results.

*Portfolio managers periodically review offering documents, client contracts, disclosure information, and/or marketing materials to ensure that the strategy or investments utilized are accurately described and that accounts are managed consistently.

*Adviser periodically reminds clients of their need to update the firm of any changes in their contact information, objectives, or financial situation and documents all changes received (whether they are received verbally or in writing).

*Adviser carefully considers appropriate procedures to address those situations in which the firm might benefit from client relationships or transactions (e.g., if the firm keeps the proceeds from the correction of trade errors that were profitable, are the firm's procedures adequate to address the conflicts?).

*Adviser establishes front-end compliance parameters to ensure that client mandates, such as restrictions and diversification standards, are followed.

*Adviser provides disclosure (rather than merely offering to provide disclosure) and discusses highlights and changes during periodic client communications.

*Clients are informed of violations of restrictions and the corrective action taken, even if promptly found and corrected.

*Adviser regularly reviews the Commission's website for changes to required practices and recent enforcement actions and reconciles these developments with the firm's policies and procedures to determine if updates are warranted.

B. Outsourcing Services

An adviser may choose to engage service providers to perform a number of important services for advisory clients, including management or contractual responsibilities. Service providers often serve as administrator, pricing agent, proxy voting agent, and/or fund accountant. These service providers may: provide financial reporting, tax, and regulatory services; create and maintain required books and records; value portfolio securities and accounts; prepare regulatory filings; calculate client account expenses; vote client proxies; and monitor arrangements with other service providers. However, when a service provider is utilized, the adviser still retains its fiduciary responsibilities for the delegated services. As a result, advisers should review each service provider's overall compliance program for compliance with the federal securities laws and should ensure that service providers are complying with the firm's specific policies and procedures.

1. Understanding the Firm's Business and Operations

a. Examiners review an adviser's disclosures, contracts with clients, and contracts with service providers to determine whether the services and reporting obligations are consistent with disclosures and that all obligations are adequately addressed and overseen by the adviser. Examiners assess whether the adviser is familiar with the service provider's staff responsible for performing the contracted services and assess whether the advisory staff assigned to review the documentation and information received from the service providers are adequately overseeing the service provider's activities.

For example, if the service provider utilizes internal audit to review its services and operations, does advisory staff overseeing service providers inquire as to the topics covered by these reviews and seek to learn whether there were any material deficiencies? The staff will review whether the adviser's staff responsible for service provider oversight ensures that the services are implemented as agreed upon and monitors compliance with the contracted terms and conditions. The staff will also focus on identifying any undisclosed arrangements between the adviser and the service providers, such as fee rebates or tie-ins.

b. Conflicts of interest or risk areas may include:

* Adviser relies heavily on service providers.

* Adviser changes service providers.

* Service provider modifies its reporting processes or procedures.

* Adviser and service provider (or its principals) are "related persons."

c. Identifying Deficient Practices and Control Weaknesses.

Deficient practices might exist in situations where firms did not: adopt or maintain policies and procedures relating to the firms' use of service providers; adequately oversee the activities of services providers; and/or disclose any affiliations and related conflicts of interest related to the use of a service provider.

(i) Below are examples of questions examiners may ask to determine if an adviser has deficient practices and control weaknesses:

* Does the adviser obtain a confidentiality agreement from third-party service providers that may be given access to confidential client information? Have service providers inadvertently disclosed such information?

* Does the adviser represent that the service provider is "independent" when, in fact, the firms are under common control or otherwise have a close connection that should be disclosed?

*. Does the adviser periodically verify that the fees deducted from client accounts are consistent with contractual terms? Have clients overpaid fees?

* Do clients pay excessive and duplicative fees for administration and/or accounting services?

* Does the adviser take steps to validate the accuracy of pricing provided by third parties?

*Are there any arrangements whereby clients make payments to various third-party service providers and, in turn, the service providers make payments directly to the advisers ("quid pro quo" arrangements)?

* If the adviser recommends other managers to clients, does the adviser have policies and procedures regarding researching and monitoring separate account managers and mutual funds?

* Does the adviser use client funds to pay third-party consultant fees that should be paid by the adviser?

* Does the adviser deem a contractor with access to client investment recommendations to be an access person?

3. Controls Observed

Advisers should perform adequate initial and on-going due diligence of each service provider to confirm that the contracted services and the implementation processes are appropriate for the firm and its clients. Such due diligence is important when reviewing the services provided by [outsiders]. . . .

Discussion topic

As you review the rule directing institutions to impose and enforce codes of behavior, how different is this rule from a rule directing behavior. Please start by outlining the topics on which the rules touches. If you were to write the code at an adviser institution, what would you add? What would be too broad? What would be too narrow and specific?:

IX. WHAT IS THE LAWYER'S ROLE IN THE AREA OF INSTITUTIONAL SELF-REGULATION?

Lawyers take many roles with respect to their clients depending on the clients' desires and the lawyers' tendencies. Some lawyers are advisers with respect to the law. Others venture to advise with respect to the business, especially if they have witnessed the experience of other clients and can evaluate the clients' nature, tendencies, and purposes.

The lawyer need not know the business of the client in depth and detail. However, a lawyer should understand the basic functions of the client institution and what drives its activities. In addition to understanding the financial system and the activities of the particular financial intermediaries our study will pursue a basic understanding of institutional business management, organizational management, and personal group and individual human behavior. To be sure, understanding human behavior is part of studying any area of the law. In subject, these understandings will be highlighted in the context of the financial activities by the institution. They are crucial to any lawyer who advises the institutional enterprise.

How should a lawyer review and research the law in this area? First, the lawyer will research the law to determine the particular prohibitions or required behavior and the punishments for their violations. Second, the lawyer will examine the laws requiring institutional self-regulation, and internal policing to prevent violations from occurring. Third, the lawyer will examine the institutions' internal rules, aimed at preventing violations, and fourth, the lawyer will examine the implementation of these internal preventive rules to ensure reasonable prevention of violations. However, the last two steps are not only, or even mainly, the lawyer's function; they are the function of the Compliance Officer as well. Yet as we shall see, the law and compliance functions are not entirely separate. They may be moving in the future towards a cooperative format.

Chapter 2

THE ROLE AND LIABILITY OF CORPORATE DIRECTORS AND THE SELF-REGULATORY SYSTEM

INTRODUCTION: CORPORATE DIRECTORS

The following are summaries of three court cases and a decision by an administrative judge of the Securities and Exchange Commission. The three court decisions demonstrate the judges' views of the corporate director's role in designing and enforcing compliance programs. However, the facts of these cases and the business aspects of the corporations involved may highlight other aspects and lead to our subject of inquiry, that is, institutional self-regulation.

I. THE *CAREMARK* CASE: A CORPORATE BOARD'S LIABILITY FOR SELF-REGULATION IN A SALES BUSINESS STRUCTURE

The main revenues of Caremark Corporation "derived from third party payments, insurers, and Medicare and Medicaid reimbursement programs."[90] This source of payments was "subject to the terms of the Anti-Referral Payments Law (ARPL), which prohibits health care providers from paying any form of remuneration to induce the referral of Medicare or Medicaid patients." "From its inception, Caremark entered into . . . agreements with hospitals, physicians, and health care providers for advice and services, as well as distribution agreements with drug manufacturers." Caremark's practice was to contract physicians for services, through such means as consultation agreements and research grants, to the extent that such contracts were not prohibited by the ARPL. However, these contracts "raised the possibility of unlawful 'kickbacks.'"

"As early as 1989, Caremark's predecessor issued an internal employee 'Guide to Contractual Relationships' (Guide)" regarding "contracts with physicians and hospitals." The Guide was subject to annual review and update by lawyers. Each updated version of the Guide "stated [the] policy that no payments would be made in exchange for or to induce patient referrals." The prohibited reciprocity, however, was not always easy to discern because court interpretations on

---

90   Excerpted from *In re Caremark Int'l Inc. Derivative Litigation*, 698 A.2d 959, 961-962 (Del. Ch. 1996). Edited.

this prohibition were scarce. Caremark "repeatedly publicly stated that there was uncertainty" about ARPL's legal interpretation.

In 1991, the United States Department of Health and Human Services (HHS) issued "safe harbor" regulations listing the "conditions under which financial relationships between health care service providers and patient referral sources . . . would not violate the ARPL." Caremark argued that the regulations had given "limited guidance" to Caremark's predecessor, but that contemporaneously the corporation "amended many of its standard forms of agreement with health care providers and revised the Guide . . . to comply with the new regulations."

However, "[i]n August 1991, the HHS Office of the Inspector General (OIG) initiated an investigation of Caremark's predecessor" and served it with a "subpoena requiring the production of . . . contracts between Caremark's predecessor and physicians." "Under [those agreements], Caremark's predecessor appears to have paid physicians fees for monitoring patients under [its] care, including Medicare and Medicaid." "In March 1992, the Department of Justice (DOJ) joined the OIG investigation." Other government agencies started investigations as well.

"During [that] period, Caremark had approximately 7,000 employees and 90 branch operations." Its management structure was decentralized. "By May 1991, however, Caremark . . . had begun . . . attempts to centralize its management structure in order to increase supervision over its branch operations." The corporation announced that, as of October 1, 1991, it would cease paying management fees to physicians for services rendered to Medicare and Medicaid patients. However, "pursuant to advice," Caremark management noted that it "did not believe that such payments were illegal under [current] laws and regulations."

Further, in an effort to have the company and its forms comply with the ARPL policies, Caremark's Board "published a fourth revised version of its Guide." The revisions were "apparently designed to ensure that its agreements either complied with the ARPL and regulations or excluded Medicare and Medicaid patients altogether." In September 1992, the corporation "instituted a policy requiring its regional officers . . . to approve each contractual relationship" between Caremark and physicians.

"[I]nside and outside counsel . . . advised Caremark's directors" that the existing corporate contracts complied with the law. But Caremark "recognized that [there was] some uncertainty respecting the correct interpretation of the law." "In its 1992 annual report, Caremark disclosed the ongoing government investigations, [and] acknowledged that if penalties were imposed on the company they could have a material adverse effect on Caremark's business." The company "stated that no assurance could be given that its interpretation of the ARPL would prevail if challenged."

During the government investigations, "Caremark had an internal audit plan . . . to assure compliance with [its] business and ethics policies." "Caremark employed Price Waterhouse as its outside auditor. On February 8, 1993, the Ethics Committee of Caremark's Board received and reviewed [a] report by Price Waterhouse which concluded that there were no material weaknesses in Caremark's control structure." Yet, "on April 20, 1993, [Caremark's] Audit & Ethics Committee adopted a new internal audit charter requiring a comprehensive review of compliance policies and the compilation of an employee ethics handbook concerning such policies." Price Waterhouse worked together with the Internal Audit Department on this project.

"[Caremark's board] appears to have been informed about this project and other efforts to assure compliance with the law. For example, . . . management reported to the Board that [the] sales force [received] ongoing education regarding the ARPL and the . . . use of Caremark's form contracts[,] . . . approved by in-house counsel."

In 1993, the new ethics manual "expressly prohibit[ed] payments for referrals and require[ed] employees to report all illegal conduct to a toll-free confidential ethics hotline." Employees were given revised versions of the manual. "During 1993, Caremark took . . . additional steps which appear to have been aimed at increasing management supervision, . . . including new policies requiring local branch managers to secure home office approval for all disbursements under agreements with health care providers and to certify compliance with the ethics program." "[T]he [CFO] was appointed to serve as Caremark's [CCO] [and] [i]n 1994, a fifth revised Guide was published."

Nevertheless, "[o]n August 4, 1994, a federal grand jury in Minnesota issued a 47-page indictment charging Caremark . . . with violating the ARPL." The indictment included two Caremark officers (but not the firm's CEO), "an individual who had been a sales employee of Genentech, Inc., and . . . a [private] physician practicing in Minneapolis." The parties were charged with violating ARPL from 1986 to 1993. This physician was paid over $ 1.1 million to "induce him to distribute Protropin, a human growth hormone drug marketed by Caremark. . . . Some payments were 'in the guise of research grants' and others were made pursuant to 'consulting agreements.'"[91] According to the indictment the physician "performed virtually none of the consulting functions described in his 1991 agreement with Caremark, but [he was not] required to return the money . . . or precluded from receiving future funding from Caremark."

Management informed Caremark's Board "that the investigation had resulted in an indictment." In response, "Caremark denied any wrongdoing" and "reiterated" that its contracts complied with law. However, "[o]n September 21, 1994, a federal grand jury in Columbus, Ohio issued another indictment alleging that an Ohio physician had defrauded the Medicare program." The physician had "request[ed] and receiv[ed] $134,600 [from Caremark] in exchange for referrals of patients whose medical costs were in part reimbursed by Medicare." These actions constituted a violation of ARPL.

On October 28, 1994 new allegations of "over billing" and "referral payments" were brought in Atlanta, involving "referral practices in Michigan" and "fraudulent billing of insurers." After this indictment "Caremark publicly announced that as of January 1, 1995, it would terminate all remaining . . . relationships with physicians in [some lines of its] business." Caremark "extended

---

91   *Id.* at 964 (citing the federal indictment against Caremark, ¶20) (citations omitted).

its restrictive policies to all of its contractual relationships with physicians, rather than just those involving Medicare and Medicaid patients, and terminated its research grant program which had always involved some recipients who referred patients to Caremark."

Caremark settled with the government. It pleaded guilty "to a single count of mail fraud," and agreed to pay a "criminal fine" and "substantial civil damages."[92] In December 1995, in the wake of the plea agreements, Caremark learned of impending suits against it by several private insurers for damages they incurred as a result of the "improper business practices." In response, Caremark's Board negotiated, and on March 18, 1996 approved, a $98.5 million settlement agreement with the insurers. The following outline summarizes part of the settlement:

(1) Caremark undertook, for itself, employees and agents, to avoid paying any form of compensation to any third party in exchange for referring Medicare or Medicaid covered patients (or those covered under similar state administered programs) to a Caremark facility. The same obligations applied to referrals for any other services provided by Caremark, or for "the prescription of drugs marketed or distributed by Caremark."

(2) Caremark agreed to avoid paying, or splitting its fees with, "physicians, joint ventures, [or] any business combination in which Caremark maintain[ed] a direct financial interest."

(3) Caremark's full Board agreed to discuss semi-annually "all relevant material changes in government health care regulations and their effect on [their] relationships with health care providers."

(4) Caremark's officers agreed to "remove all [of Caremark's] personnel from health care facilities or hospitals."

(5) Caremark agreed that each of its patients would "receive written disclosure of any financial relationship between Caremark and the health care professional or provider who made the referral."

(6) Caremark's Board agreed to establish a Compliance and Ethics Committee consisting of four directors (two of which would be independent). This committee would "meet at least four times a

---

92 The government agreed to negotiate a permission for Caremark to "continue participating in Medicare and Medicaid programs" and the board approved an overall settlement. None of the management was charged. "[A]s part of the sentencing in the Ohio action on June 19, 1995, the United States stipulated that *no senior executive of Caremark participated in, condoned, or was willfully ignorant of wrongdoing in connection with the home infusion business practices.*" "The federal settlement included certain provisions in a 'Corporate Integrity Agreement' designed to 'enhance future compliance.'" *Id.* at 965.

year to [assure implementation of] these policies and monitor business segment compliance with the ARPL." This same committee would brief the Board on their findings semiannually.

(7) Finally, the corporate officers leading each of Caremark's business segments were required to "serve as compliance officers" for their units and to "report semi-annually to the Compliance and Ethics Committee." These compliance officers were also required, "with the assistance of outside counsel," to "review existing contracts and [receive advance] approval of any new contract forms."

Caremark investors sued the corporation's directors for violating their duties to the corporation and, indirectly, to its investors. What follows is a summary of the Court's legal principles regarding the directors' duties to establish and monitor corporate operations to comply with the law.

The court held that the directors' liability for a breach of the duty to exercise appropriate care may arise from a *"board decision* that results in a loss because that decision was ill advised or 'negligent.'"[93] In this case the directors are nonetheless protected by the "business judgment rule." This is a rule under which the courts defer to the directors' business judgment. After all, the directors are the ones who should manage the business, not the court. However, the courts will defer to the directors' decision so long as the directors' judgment is not tainted or affected by conflicts of interest.

Second, the directors' breach may "arise from an *unconsidered failure of the board to act* in circumstances in which due attention would, arguably, have prevented the loss." If one of the above contexts is present, the court will then determine the appropriate level of care (and any breach thereof). This level of care will not be determined "by reference to *the content of the board decision* that leads to a corporate loss."[94]

In crafting the standard, judges must only consider the good faith or rationality of the process employed. There is no "moral basis" to "attack a *good faith* business decision of a director as 'unreasonable' or 'irrational'" because, while the board should authorize the most important corporate actions, most decisions are, in fact, made by officers and employees.[95] Therefore a board has only the "responsibility to assure that appropriate information and reporting systems are established by management."[96]

---

93   *Id. at 967.*

94   *Id.*

95   *Id. at 968.* The court cites the *Salomon* case discussed later. *Id. at 968-69.* "[A] court must determine whether or not the particularized factual allegations of a derivative stockholder complaint create a reasonable doubt that, as of the time the complaint is filed, the board of directors could have properly exercised its independent and disinterested business judgment in responding to a demand." Rales v. Blasband, 634 A.2d 927, 934 (Del. 1993).

96   698 A.2d *at 969-70.*

The court concluded "a director's obligation includes a duty to attempt in good faith to assure that [the] corporate information and reporting system . . . [exists and is adequate]." Failure to fulfill this may, "under some circumstances," "render a director liable for losses caused by non-compliance with applicable legal standards."[97] In Caremark's case, the court found that "[t]he board was informed that the company's reimbursement for patient care was frequently from government funded sources and that such services were subject to the ARPL."[98]

The board was not aware that Caremark had in fact violated ARPL. The board merely understood that the company had entered into a variety of contracts with physicians, researchers, and health care providers, and that some of these parties also had prescribed treatments that Caremark participated in providing.

"[T]he board appears to have been informed by experts" that these arrangements, "while contestable, were lawful." The court concluded that there was "no evidence that reliance on such reports was not reasonable." And while the board had a good faith duty to be informed, this duty was not the same as possessing "detailed information about all aspects of the operation of the enterprise. Such a requirement would simply be inconsistent with the scale and scope of efficient organization size in this technological age." Consequently, the directors had met their obligations.[99]

Discussion topics

*How did Caremark earn profit? Where did the bribery money come from? Why were the bribes to hospitals and physicians by Caremark's salespeople beneficial to the corporation? Who ultimately paid for the medicines and other products and paid the higher prices?

*What law did Caremark violate? What wrongs was the law designed to prevent?

*Why was the payment for the medicines, or payments in connection with the purchase of the medicines, called a "bribe"? Why did the law get involved in these payments in the first place? What was wrong with paying the hospitals and doctors for buying and using the corporation's products?

*What were the pressures and conflicted interests that led to the legal problems?

*What, if anything, was unclear about the law?

---

97   *Id.* at 970.

98   *Id.* at 971.

99   *Id.*

*How did the Court analyze the directors' liability in relation to compliance?

*Who in Caremark was involved in creating or exacerbating these problems?

*Was Caremark management aware of these potential problems?

*What steps, if any, did the management take to deal with the problems? What position did the directors of Caremark occupy under the corporation's Compliance Guidelines?

*Did the contracts used by the salespersons relate to these issues?

*What steps did the board take to strengthen compliance with the law? What prompted the board to make changes to the compliance system?

*Did Caremark's lawyers do their job well? What approach did they take?

*What is the difference between high-level personnel and substantial-authority personnel?

*The Caremark Corporation employed more than 7,000 salespersons and had a decentralized structure. Given this business reality, Caremark's board of directors had to establish principles and general rules of behavior for the entire institution; but it could not follow each actor to determine compliance with its directives. How could the board have induced the salespeople to avoid offering kickbacks to hospitals and physicians?

*Whose money was used to pay the prohibited bribes? Who authorized the salespeople making the bribes? Where was the funding for the bribes recorded? Who recorded them?

*Who in the corporation lost as a result of the legal violations? Who gained?

*What was the incentive system in Caremark for the salespeople, their supervisors, and the board? What about the incentives of the lawyers? How did the incentive system affect the investors?

*How did the Court analyze the directors' liability in relation to compliance? Did the Court invoke the issue of the corporation's culture or immoral behavior? Should it have invoked these issues?

*Finally: How did the investors gain and how did they lose from their investment in this corporation?

In light of our inquiry, if we examine and focus on (i) the corporation's business structure; (ii) who paid an inflated price or amount for the medicines; and (iii) who benefited from the increased amounts of medicines prescribed and used, do you agree with the court's analysis and conclusion,?

II. THE *STONE V. RITTER* CASE: DIRECTORS' LIABILITY FOR SELF-REGULATION IN A BANKING BUSINESS STRUCTURE

In *Stone v. Ritter* [100] the investors sued the directors of a bank, AmSouth, for violation of its duty to file a legally required Suspicious Activities Report (SAR). A bank is required to file a written report with the Financial Crimes Enforcement Network (FinCEN), a bureau of the U.S. Department of the Treasury, whenever a banking transaction involves at least $5,000 "and the bank knows, suspects, or has reason to suspect" that, among other possibilities, the "transaction involves funds derived from illegal activities or is intended or conducted in order to hide or disguise funds or assets derived from illegal activities . . ."[101]

The nominal defendant, AmSouth, was a Delaware corporation. The plaintiffs "owned AmSouth common stock 'at all relevant times.'" "During the relevant period, AmSouth's wholly-owned subsidiary, AmSouth Bank, operated about 600 commercial banking branches in six states throughout the southeastern United States and employed more than 11,600 people."[102]

The source of the original government investigations was "an unlawful 'Ponzi' scheme" in AmSouth's wholly owned subsidiary. This bank subsidiary opened "custodial trust accounts for 'investors' in a 'business venture.'" The venture was allegedly "construction of medical clinics overseas." In fact, however, the venture was a Ponzi scheme. The payment to earlier investors was made out of funds provided by later investors. AmSouth employees in Tennessee "agreed to provide custodial accounts for the investors and to distribute monthly interest payments to each custodial account upon receipt of a check . . . and [further instructions from the fraudsters.]"[103] The movement of the "new money" to the "old money" should have raised concern. Rather than a mere oversight, the banks could have been induced by a desire to keep a good bank client and avoid learning the truth of the scheme.

---

100 Excerpted from *Stone v. Ritter,* 911 A.2d 362 (Del. 2006). Edited

101 *Id.* at 365, *citing* 31 U.S.C. § 5318 (2006) et seq.

102 *Id.*

103 *Id.*

The scheme "was discovered in March 2002, when the investors did not receive their monthly interest payments" (because there were no more new investors). Consequently, investors in Tennessee and Mississippi sued the fraudsters and AmSouth. The fraudsters and AmSouth were separately subject to a Mississippi federal grand jury investigation related to the same conduct. Ultimately, two fraudsters "pled guilty" and "were indicted on federal money-laundering charges."[104]

In 2004, AmSouth and AmSouth Bank paid $40 million in fines to resolve the government charges that the bank's employees failed to file SARs as required by the BSA and Anti-Money-Laundering rules (AML). After the United States Attorney's Office advised AmSouth that it was the subject of a criminal investigation the bank entered into a Deferred Prosecution Agreement. It was noted in the agreement that although "at least one" bank employee suspected the fraudulent scheme, the bank "failed to file SARs in a timely manner."[105] However, no blame was ascribed to the board.[106]

"On October 12, 2004, the [banking authorities] . . . issued a Cease and Desist Order against AmSouth, requiring it, for the first time, to improve its BSA/AML program [and to hire] an independent consultant 'to conduct a comprehensive review of the Bank's AML Compliance program and make recommendations, as appropriate, for new policies and procedures to be implemented by the Bank.'"[107]

Then "[the banking authorities] . . . assessed a $10 million civil penalty against AmSouth for operating an inadequate anti-money-laundering program and for failing to file SARs," and "a written Assessment of Civil Money Penalty." "[These authorities] found that 'AmSouth violated the suspicious activity reporting requirements of the Bank Secrecy Act,' and that '[s]ince April 24, 2002, AmSouth has been in violation of the anti-money-laundering program requirements of the Bank Secrecy Act.'" FinCEN's report also concluded that "'AmSouth's [AML compliance] program lacked adequate board and management oversight,' and that 'reporting to management for the purposes of monitoring and oversight of compliance activities was materially deficient.' AmSouth neither admitted nor denied FinCEN's determinations."[108]

"No fines or penalties were imposed on AmSouth's directors, and no other regulatory action was taken against them."[109] The Court stated that pursuant to Delaware General Corporation

---

104 *Id.* at 365-66.

105 The court posed the question of whether the directors were liable for the bank's legal failures, stating that "Caremark articulates the necessary conditions predicate for director oversight liability: (a) the directors utterly failed to implement any reporting or information system or controls; *or* (b) having implemented such a system or controls, consciously failed to monitor or oversee its operations thus disabling themselves from being informed of risks or problems requiring their attention." *Id.* at 371.

106 *Id.* at 366.

107 *Id.*

108 *Id.*

109 *Id.* at 365.

Law, Delaware corporations are managed under the direction of the corporate board of directors.[110] The fifteen board member defendants included both officers employed by the corporation (as well as the Chairman) and independent directors, who had never worked for AmSouth.[111]

The court held that "the directors' potential personal liability depends upon whether or not their conduct can be exculpated by the section 102(b)(7) provision contained in the AmSouth certificate of incorporation. Such a provision can exculpate directors from monetary liability for a breach of the duty of care,[112] but not for [failure to act in good faith][113] or a breach of the duty of loyalty.[114] The standard for assessing a director's potential personal liability for failing to act in good faith in discharging his or her oversight responsibilities has evolved . . . ."[115] While the plaintiffs alleged just that, "[t]he Court of Chancery found that the plaintiffs did not plead the existence of 'red flags,' that is, 'facts showing that the board ever was aware that AmSouth's internal controls were inadequate, that these inadequacies would result in illegal activity, and that the board chose to do nothing about problems it allegedly knew existed.'"[116]

In dismissing the shareholders' derivative complaint, the Court of Chancery concluded:

> This case is not about a board's failure to carefully consider a material corporate decision that was presented to the board. This is a case where information was not reaching the board because of ineffective internal controls. . . . With the benefit of hindsight, it is beyond question that AmSouth's internal controls with respect to the Bank Secrecy Act and anti-money laundering regulations compliance were inadequate. . . . [T]he lack of internal controls resulted in a huge fine, $50 million . . . [but losses are] not alone enough . . . to conclude that [the directors cannot terminate the action, which is a business decision, within their jurisdiction.][117]

The court found that a reasonable reporting system existed since 1998.

---

110 *Id.* at 366, *citing* DEL. CODE ANN. tit. 8, § 141(a) (2006).

111 *Id.* at 367 n.12.

112 The *Caremark* Court said that "the core element of any corporate law duty of care inquiry" is "whether there was good faith effort to be informed and exercise judgment." In re *Caremark Int'l Inc. Derivative Litigation*, 698 A.2d 959, 961-962 (Del. Ch. 1996).

113 "[A] failure to act in good faith requires conduct that is qualitatively different from, and more culpable than, the conduct giving rise to a violation of the fiduciary duty of care (i.e., gross negligence)." *Id.* at 369, *citing* In re *Walt Disney Co. Deriv. Litig.*, 906 A.2d 27 (Del. 2006). Examples include "where the fiduciary intentionally acts with a purpose other than that of advancing the best interests of the corporation, where the fiduciary acts with the intent to violate applicable positive law, or where the fiduciary intentionally fails to act in the face of a known duty to act, demonstrating a conscious disregard for his duties." *Id.*, *citng* 906 A.2d at 67.

114 "Essentially, the duty of loyalty mandates that the best interest of the corporation and its shareholders takes precedence over any interest possessed by a director, officer or controlling shareholder and not shared by the stockholders generally." *Cede & Co. v. Technicolor*, 634 A.2d 345, 361 (Del. 1993).

115 911 A.2d at 367. Footnotes added.

116 *Id.* at 370.

117 *Id.* at 370-71.

. . . AmSouth has had [an officer] "responsible for all BSA/AML-related matters including employee training, general communications, CTR reporting and SAR reporting," and "presenting AML policy and program changes to the Board of Directors, the managers at the various lines of business, and participants in the annual training of security and audit personnel[;]"

. . . AmSouth has had for years a BSA/AML Compliance Department, headed by the BSA Officer and comprised of nineteen professionals, including a BSA/AML Compliance Manager and a Compliance Reporting Manager;

. . . AmSouth's Corporate Security Department has been at all relevant times responsible for the detection and reporting of suspicious activity as it relates to fraudulent activity . . . ;

. . . Since 2001, the "Suspicious Activity Oversight Committee" and its predecessor, the "AML Committee," have actively overseen AmSouth's BSA/AML compliance program. The Suspicious Activity Oversight Committee's mission has for years been to "oversee the policy, procedure, and process issues affecting the Corporate Security and BSA/AML Compliance Programs, to ensure that an effective program exists at AmSouth to deter, detect, and report money laundering, suspicious activity and other fraudulent activity."

The KPMG Report reflects that the directors not only discharged their oversight responsibility to establish an information and reporting system, but also proved that the system was designed to permit the directors to periodically monitor AmSouth's compliance with BSA and AML regulations. For example, as KPMG noted in 2004, AmSouth's designated BSA Officer "has made annual high-level presentations to the Board of Directors in each of the last five years." Further, the Board's Audit and Community Responsibility Committee (the "Audit Committee") oversaw AmSouth's BSA/AML compliance program on a quarterly basis.

The KPMG Report shows that AmSouth's Board at various times enacted written policies and procedures designed to ensure compliance with the BSA and AML regulations. For example, the Board adopted an amended bank-wide "BSA/AML Policy" on July 17, 2003–four months before AmSouth became aware that it was the target of a government investigation. That policy was produced to plaintiffs in response to their demand to inspect AmSouth's books and records pursuant to section 22038 and is included in plaintiffs' appendix. Among other things, the July 17, 2003, BSA/AML Policy directs all AmSouth employees to immediately report suspicious transactions or activity to the BSA/AML Compliance Department or Corporate Security.[118]

Thus, the plaintiff did not demonstrate "a sustained or systematic failure of the board to exercise oversight—such as an utter failure to attempt to assure a reasonable information and reporting system exists—[which] will establish the lack of good faith that is a necessary condition to liability."[119]

The court noted that the KPMG Report refutes:

_____

118   *Id.* at 371-72.

119   *Id.* at 372-73, *citing In re* Caremark Int'l Inc. Deriv. Litig., 698 A.2d 959, 971 (Del.Ch. 1996).

the assertion that the directors "never took the necessary steps . . . to ensure that a reasonable BSA compliance and reporting system existed." KPMG's findings reflect that the Board received and approved relevant policies and procedures, delegated to certain employees and departments the responsibility for filing SARs and monitoring compliance, and exercised oversight by relying on periodic reports from them. Although there ultimately may have been failures by employees to report deficiencies to the Board, there is no basis for an oversight claim seeking to hold the directors personally liable for such failures by the employees.

. . . .

The lacuna in the plaintiffs' argument is a failure to recognize that the directors' good faith exercise of oversight responsibility may not invariably prevent employees from violating criminal laws, or from causing the corporation to incur significant financial liability, or both . . . In the absence of red flags, good faith in the context of oversight must be measured by the directors' actions "to assure a reasonable information and reporting system exists" and not by second-guessing after the occurrence of employee conduct that results in an unintended adverse outcome. Accordingly, we hold that the Court of Chancery properly applied and dismissed the plaintiffs' derivative complaint for failure to excuse demand by alleging particularized facts that created reason to doubt whether the directors had acted in good faith in exercising their oversight responsibilities.[120]

The Court affirmed the judgment of the Court of Chancery.[121]

Discussion Topic

*What is a Ponzi scheme?

*Why should any bank be liable for failing to notify the authorities about the possible Ponzi scheme?

*How does the use of "custody accounts" help Ponzi schemers? How did these accounts serve the fraudsters?

*What caused the bank employee to suspect a Ponzi scheme?

*It seems that at least one employee suspected the existence of a Ponzi scheme. Why didn't more employees suspect that?

---

120 *Id.* at 372-73, *citing In re Caremark* Int'l Inc. Deriv. Litig., 698 A.2d 959, 967-68, 971 (Del.Ch. 1996).

121 *Id.* at 373.'

*Why did the employee who suspected the Ponzi scheme fail to notify or convince his superiors of this suspicion?

*What activities, approaches, or experts helped exonerate the board in the *Stone v. Ritter* case?

Please compare the *Caremark* and the *Stone v. Ritter* cases: In which case was it harder to uncover the wrongdoing? Which violation was more serious from a societal perspective? Which violation was more serious from a governmental perspective?

———————

III. *IN THE MATTER OF J. KENNETH ALDERMAN, CPA, ETAL.* SEC CASE. THE DIRECTORS' LIABILITY FOR A SPECIFIC STATUTORY DIRECTORS' DUTY

The valuation of mutual fund shares is crucial for investors, especially investors in the "open-end" fund. The shareholders of such a fund do not trade their shares in the markets but rather gain "liquidity" by having the right to redeem their shares from the fund. In such a case the fund sells a sufficient number of shares it holds in order to pay the redeeming shareholder the value of his or her shares. In most cases the fund shareholders do not know what securities the fund holds, and therefore cannot quickly determine the net asset value of the shares that the investor seeks to redeem.

How should fund shareholders ascertain that the redemption price was the true price, representing the pro rata share of the fund's portfolio? What if the insiders and managers did not give the redeeming shareholders the true information concerning the value of the fund's portfolio? What if the insiders, who knew the value, redeemed and bought fund shares based on their insider information about the fund holdings?

To resolve this issue, the fund's board of directors was assigned a significant role in determining the accurate value of the fund shares. The following case describes possible problems posed by the valuation of such open-end fund's shares and directors' responsibilities regarding the valuation process. The case is also interesting because it relates to mortgage-backed securities, a type of securities that was linked to the market crash of 2008.

"Sub-prime" mortgages have an ambiguous name. "Prime" generally denoted the low interest that banks charged "prime" or high-quality borrowers. Those who borrowed sub-prime mortgages were not high-quality borrowers, yet they did carry a rate that was low relative to their inherent credit risk. These sub-prime mortgages were frequently structured as "adjustable rate" instruments in which there was a "reset" period, for example, of two years, after which the interest rate the borrowers were required to pay increased substantially. The step-like interest rate profile made the loans highly attractive to risky borrowers at the start of the mortgage period and highly unattractive after the reset date was reached unless the value of the real estate subject to the mortgage had risen significantly. For many lower-quality borrowers, the possible rate increases were often poorly communicated by lenders or brokers, and when the rate increases occurred, the shock contributed greatly to high default rates beginning around 2007. These defaults in turn played a significant role in the financial crash of the late 2000s.

The following case deals with "collateralized debt obligations (CDOs), collateralized mortgage obligations (CMOs), collateralized loan obligations (CLOs), home-equity loan-backed securities, various types of asset-backed securities, and certificate-backed obligations."[122] For our purpose, suffice to say that the borrowers under these types of securities were usually very risky borrowers. The securities were wrapped in various legal structures, but the source of payment under these securities was unstable and unassured.

To convert loans of various amounts and payments into standardized securities, the loans were transferred to a separate legal entity: the special purpose vehicle (SPV). Usually, the entity establishes what was known as the "waterfall" structure. It issues four classes of securities named "tranches." A "tranche" is a class of securities that entitles its holders to payment before or after another class or tranches.

The securities of a more senior level tranche are paid before the securities of a subordinate tranche; securities of a subordinate tranche are entitled to receive payment only after the securities of more senior tranches have been paid. Because they thus are less risky, more senior tranches entitle investors to less return. The securities of the highest tranche receive income from the underlying loans first, but receive the lowest return. The last, or fourth, tranche is the most risky security because it entitles investors to payment only if all three other tranches have been paid. However, to offset the risk of default, fourth tranche investors are entitled to the highest return, provided the debtor did not default.

However, often, mortgagors defaulted. As a result, the more subordinate tranches often did not receive any payments. In those cases, these securities produced smaller than expected gains, if not large outright losses, for their investors. The following case describes the duties of the directors in evaluating the securities held by their funds.

In the Matter of J. Kenneth Alderman, CPA, et al.[123] On December 10, 2012, the SEC instituted administrative and cease-and-desist proceedings under the Investment Company Act of 1940 against eight directors of an investment company (Directors). All the Directors served on the boards of five registered investment companies (Funds). "Between at least January 2007 and August 2007, significant portions of the Funds' portfolios contained below-investment grade debt securities, some of which were backed by subprime mortgages, for which market quotations were not readily available."

---

122 Excerpted from *In re* J. Kenneth Alderman, CPA, Investment Company Act Release No. 30,300 (Dec. 10, 2013). Edited.

123 Excerpted from *In re* J. Kenneth Alderman, CPA, Investment Company Act Release No. 30,300 (Dec. 10, 2013). Edited.

Under the Investment Company Act of 1940[124], the fair value of those securities should be determined in good faith by the fund's directors. The directors should "determine the method of arriving at the fair value of each such security. To the extent considered necessary, the board may appoint persons to assist it in determining these values, and to make the actual calculations pursuant to the board's direction. Consistent with this responsibility, the board should also continuously review the appropriateness of the method used in valuing each issue of security in the company's portfolio."[125]

In *Alderman*, the Directors neither established a fair valuation methodology nor continuously reviewed any such valuation methodology. The Directors delegated their responsibility to determine fair value to the Valuation Committee of the investment adviser to the Funds. However, the Directors did not "provid[e] any meaningful substantive guidance on how those determinations should be made."[126] In addition, the Directors did not inform themselves on "how fair values were actually being determined."[127] "They received . . . limited information on the factors considered in making fair value determinations and almost no information explaining why particular fair values were assigned to portfolio securities."[128] These failures were particularly significant because fair valued securities made up in most cases at least 60% of the Funds' net asset values (NAVs) during the relevant period.

In addition to the Directors, Morgan Asset Management, Inc. (Morgan Asset), an investment adviser headquartered in Alabama, served as adviser to the Funds and Morgan Keegan & Company, Inc. (Morgan Keegan), a broker-dealer and an investment adviser in Memphis, Tennessee, "provided accounting services to the Funds through its Fund Accounting group (Fund Accounting)."[129] "The Funds consisted of five registered investment companies." "Each Fund had a board of directors." Two directors were "interested directors," that is, they had a potential conflict of interest with the funds' interests, and six independent directors did not have these conflicts. "All of the independent directors sat on each Fund's Audit Committee."[130]

"As of March 31, 2007, the Funds held securities with a combined net asset value of approximately $3.85 billion." "The Funds owned many of the same securities and . . . invested the majority of their total assets in complex securities *known as structured products that included collateralized debt obligations, collateralized mortgage obligations, collateralized loan obligations,*

---

124 *Id.*

125 Accounting Series Release No. 118 (ASR 118) (Dec. 23, 1970)

126 Excerpted from *In re* J. Kenneth Alderman, CPA, Investment Company Act Release No. 30,300 (Dec. 10, 2013). Edited.

127 *Id.*

128 *Id.*

129 Excerpted from *In re* J. Kenneth Alderman, CPA, Investment Company Act Release No. 30,557 (June 13, 2013). Edited.

130 *Id.*

home-equity loan-backed securities, various types of asset-backed securities, and certificate-backed obligations."[131]

The Funds' assets were heavily invested in "below-investment grade debt securities, which carried inherent risks." These risks included "more frequent and pronounced changes in the perceived creditworthiness of issuers, greater price volatility, reduced liquidity, and the presence of fewer dealers in the [secondary] market for such securities."[132]

Another, particularly relevant, characteristic of the Funds' holdings was their significant concentrations in mortgage-backed securities. "*A significant number of the structured products held by the Funds were subordinated tranches of various securitizations,*[133] *for which market quotations were not readily available* during the [r]elevant [p]eriod." "As a result, a large percentage of the Funds' portfolios had to be fair valued as determined in good faith by the Funds' boards, in accordance with the requirements of Section 2(a)(41)(B) of the Investment Company Act of 1940."[134]

Funds have a number of manuals that direct the funds' activities. "In the Funds' Policy and Procedure Manual (the 'Manual'), the Directors delegated to Morgan Asset 'the responsibility for carrying out certain functions relating to the valuation of portfolio securities . . . in connection with calculating the NAV per share of the Funds.'"[135] "The Manual also stated that 'portfolio securities for which market quotations are readily available are valued at current market value [while] . . . [a]ll other portfolio securities will be valued at 'fair value' as determined in good faith by [Morgan Asset] in accordance with the Funds' Valuation Procedures.'"[136]

The Valuation Procedures in the Manual stated: "When price quotations for certain securities are not readily available from the sources noted above [i.e., sources of market prices] or if the available quotations are not believed to be reflective of market value, those securities shall be valued at 'fair value' as determined in good faith by [Morgan Asset's] Valuation Committee." "The Valuation Procedures then listed various general and specific factors, which the Valuation Committee was supposed to consider when making fair value determinations."[137]

---

131 *Id.*

132 *Id.*

133 Securitization begins with transfer of loans to an entity (SPV). That entity has usually four classes (tranches). The first receives payments first, has lower risk of non-payment and consequently is paid a lower interest rate. The second comes next and receives higher interest rate. The last, fourth one receives the last amount, bears the highest risk of non-payment and is entitled to a higher return.

134 *In re* J. Kenneth Alderman, CPA, Investment Company Act Release No. 30,300 (Dec. 10, 2013), *citing* 15 U.S.C. § 80a-2(a)(41)(B) (2012).

135 Excerpted from *In re* J. Kenneth Alderman, CPA, Investment Company Act Release No. 30,557 (June 13, 2013). Edited.

136 *Id.*

137 *Id.*

"Other than listing these factors, which were copied nearly verbatim from ASR 118,[138] the Valuation Procedures provided no meaningful methodology or other specific direction on *how* to make fair value determinations for specific portfolio assets or classes of assets." "Additionally, the Valuation Procedures did not specify what valuation methodology should be employed for each type of security or, in the absence of a specified methodology, how to evaluate whether a particular methodology was appropriate or inappropriate." "Also, the Valuation Procedures did not include any mechanism for identifying and reviewing fair-valued securities whose prices remained unchanged for weeks, months and even entire quarters." "The Directors did not provide any other guidance—either written or oral— on how to determine fair value beyond what was stated in the Valuation Procedures."[139]

"The Valuation Committee, which consisted of Fund officers and Fund Accounting employees, and which did not include any Directors, was responsible according to the Funds' procedures, for overseeing the fair valuation process." "In practice, the task of assigning fair values on a daily basis was performed by Fund Accounting, a unit which consisted of Morgan Keegan employees."[140]

"In determining fair value, Fund Accounting did not use any reasonable analytical method to arrive at fair value." "For example, neither Fund Accounting nor the Valuation Committee used a pricing model or made any *meaningful effort* to analyze future cash flows, or the present values thereof, that a particular bond in the portfolio would likely generate."[141]

"Under the actual fair valuation process, Fund Accounting typically set a security's initial fair value as its purchase price (its cost) and, thereafter, . . . [i]n addition, the Portfolio Manager repeatedly contacted Fund Accounting, by email or other means, and provided price adjustments for particular securities." "Without any explanation of the basis for such prices, Fund Accounting routinely accepted the prices provided by the Portfolio Manager." "Neither the Directors nor Morgan Keegan or Morgan Asset ever provided guidelines by which Fund Accounting or the Valuation Committee should evaluate the reasonableness of such adjustments."[142]

"Shortly after each month's end, Fund Accounting selected and sought price confirmations for a random sample of the Funds' securities that were required to be fair valued, except for March and June when, in connection with annual audits, confirmations were sought by the Funds' independent auditors for 100% of the fair-valued securities." "The price confirmations

---

138 The 1940 Act requires the SEC to establish and enforce financial reporting policies. Pursuant to this authority the SEC issued Accounting Series Release 118 in 1970. This interpretive release prescribes the SEC's standards and policies for mutual fund valuation of assets in which secondary market quotations are not readily available. *See* Dr. Janet Kiholm Smith et. al., *The SEC's "Fair Value" Standard for Mutual Fund Investment in Restricted Shares and Other Illiquid Securities,* 6 FORDHAM J. CORP. & FIN. L. 421, 422 (2001).

139 Excerpted from *In re* J. Kenneth Alderman, CPA, Investment Company Act Release No. 30,300 (Dec. 10, 2013). Edited.

140 Excerpted from *In re* J. Kenneth Alderman, CPA, Investment Company Act Release No. 30,557 (June 13, 2013). Edited.

141 Excerpted from *In re* J. Kenneth Alderman, CPA, Investment Company Act Release No. 30,300 (Dec. 10, 2013). Edited.

142 *Id.*

were essentially opinions . . . rather than bids or firm quotes.'" In addition, the price confirmations generally related to month-end prices, but were obtained several weeks after the respective month-ends." "Accordingly, they could not have sufficed as the primary valuation method." That is because a certain type of a Fund's obligation had to price the securities it held daily; and another type of a fund had to publicize its Net Asset Values daily.[143]

"The Valuation Procedures contained a section entitled 'Price Override Procedures,' which provided that the Adviser could 'override prices provided by a pricing service or broker-dealer only when it had a reasonable basis to believe that the price . . . does not accurately reflect the fair value of the portfolio security.'" "The section further provided that 'the basis for overriding the price shall be documented and provided to the Valuation Committee for its review.'" "Because the Valuation Committee and Fund Accounting interpreted this provision as applying only to broker-dealer quotes (i.e., actual offers to buy or sell [rather than "price confirmations"]), the Valuation Committee was not advised, and could not advise the Directors, as to the basis upon which Fund Accounting chose to ignore the price confirmations."[144]

"In the event a price confirmation indicated a more than 5% variance from the previously assigned fair value, Fund Accounting effectively allowed the Portfolio Manager to determine the fair value." "The Portfolio Manager arbitrarily set values without a reasonable basis and did so in a way that postponed the degree of decline in the NAVs [net asset value] of the Funds which should have occurred during the Relevant Period." "Fund Accounting also engaged in smoothing prices," i.e., daily reductions in the fund value provided by the Portfolio Manager, "to gradually reduce, over days or weeks, a bond to its current proper valuation."[145]

"As a result of the foregoing practices, during the Relevant Period, the NAVs of the Funds were inaccurate at least from March 31, 2007 through August 9, 2007." "Consequently, the prices at which the open-end series sold, redeemed, and repurchased their shares were also inaccurate." "[T]he Directors did not determine what methodology was actually used by Fund Accounting and the Valuation Committee to fair value particular securities or types of securities. The information and reports provided to Directors at their board meetings did not provide sufficient information for the Directors to understand what methodology was being used by Fund Accounting to fair value particular securities."[146]

"Outside counsel advised the Directors in connection with the adoption of the written Valuation Procedures." "Further, . . . independent auditors audited the financial statements for the closed-end funds [that did not redeem their shares but had a market in the shares] for the fiscal year ended March 31, 2007 and the open-end fund's financial statements for the fiscal year

---

143 *Id.*

144 *Id.*

145 *Id.*

146 Excerpted from *In re* J. Kenneth Alderman, CPA, Investment Company Act Release No. 30,557 (June 13, 2013). Edited.

ended June 30, 2007." "During each of these audits, the auditor provided unqualified opinions and advised the Directors that the Valuation Procedures were appropriate and reasonable."[147]

"These audits did not provide the Directors with sufficient information about the valuation methodologies actually employed by Fund Accounting and the Valuation Committee to satisfy the Directors' obligations." "The auditors were not retained to opine on the Funds' internal controls and, in fact, advised the Directors that the auditors' 'consideration will not be sufficient to enable us to provide assurances on the effectiveness of internal control over financial reporting.'" "As a result, the auditors did not advise the Directors in any meaningful detail as to what pricing methodologies were actually being employed."[148]

"In 1970, the [Securities and Exchange Commission (SEC)] issued guidance on various questions relating to the accounting by registered investment companies for investment securities, including the valuation of such securities." "The Commission emphasized that it is the responsibility of a fund's board of directors to determine fair values and cautioned that, while a board may enlist the assistance of individuals who are not board members, it remains the board's duty to establish the fair value methodology to be used and to continuously review the appropriateness of the methods used in valuing each issue of security and the valuation findings resulting from such methods."[149]

"Specifically, the Commission stated:"

[I]t is incumbent upon the Board of Directors to satisfy themselves that all appropriate factors relevant to the value of securities for which market quotations are not readily available have been considered and to determine the method of arriving at the fair value of each such security. To the extent considered necessary, the board may appoint persons to assist them in the determination of such value, and to make the actual calculations pursuant to the board's direction. The board must also, consistent with this responsibility, continuously review the appropriateness of the method used in valuing each issue of security in the company's portfolio. The directors must recognize their responsibilities in this matter and whenever technical assistance is requested

---

147 *Id.*

148 Funds are required to adopt and implement policies and procedures reasonably designed to prevent violations of the securities laws, including policies and procedures concerning a fund's determination of the fair value of portfolio securities. . . . It is a responsibility of a fund's board to ensure that the fund fulfills these obligations, particularly with respect to policies and procedures concerning the determination of fair value. The Directors' explicit statutory responsibilities with regard to the determining of the fair value of securities for which market quotations were not readily available are set forth in the definition of "value" in Section 2(a)(41)(B) of the Investment Company Act, which states in pertinent part: "'Value', with respect to assets of registered investment companies means . . . (i) with respect to securities for which market quotations are readily available, the market value of such securities; and (ii) with respect to other securities and assets, *fair value as determined in good faith by the board of directors.*" 15 U.S.C. § 80a-2(a)(41)(B) (2012).

149 Excerpted from *In re* J. Kenneth Alderman, CPA, Investment Company Act Release No. 30,557 (June 13, 2013). Edited.

from individuals who are not directors, the findings of such individuals must be carefully reviewed by the directors in order to satisfy themselves that the resulting valuations are fair.[150]

"In connection with determining fair values, the Directors [1] did not calculate the valuations themselves, and [2] neither established clear and specific valuation methodologies nor [3] followed up their general guidance to review and approve the actual methodologies used and the resulting valuations."[151]

"Instead, they [1] approved policies generally describing the factors to be considered but [2] failed to determine what was actually being done to implement those policies." "As a result, Fund Accounting implemented deficient procedures, effectively allowing the Portfolio Manager to determine valuations without a reasonable basis." "In this regard, the Directors failed to exercise their responsibilities with regard to the adoption and implementation by the Funds of procedures reasonably designed to prevent violations of the federal securities laws." "These failures were particularly significant given that fair-valued securities made up a substantial percentage of the portfolios of each of the Funds . . ."[152]

In view of the foregoing, the Commission deems it appropriate and in the public interest to impose the sanctions agreed to in Respondents' Offer. Accordingly, pursuant to Section 9(f) of the Investment Company Act, it is hereby ORDERED that: Respondents Alderman, Morgan, Blair, Johnson, McFadden, Pittman, Stone and Willis shall cease and desist from committing or causing any violations and any future violations of, Rule 38a-1 promulgated under the Investment Company Act.[153]

Discussion Topics:

Why should the directors be involved in the details of valuing a fund's securities?
Why were these particular asset-backed securities picked for the directors' valuation?
Who was harmed by the inaccurate valuations? Who benefited?

---

150 Accounting Series Release No. 118 (Dec. 23, 1970), *quoted in In re* J. Kenneth Alderman, CPA, Investment Company Act Release No. 30,557 (June 13, 2013). *See also* 15 U.S.C. §80a-2(a)(41)(B) (2012) (generally defining "value" under Investment Company Act as "fair value as determined in good faith by the board of directors" except for securities for which market quotations are readily available); 17 C.F.R. § 270.2a-4 (2015) (defining for open-end funds the "Current Net Asset Value" for use in computing periodically the current price of redeemable securities).

151 Excerpted from *In re* J. Kenneth Alderman, CPA, Investment Company Act Release No. 30,557 (June 13, 2013). Edited.

152 *Id.* This behavior constituted a violation of Rule 22c-1 and Rule 30a-3(a) and 38a-1 under the Investment Company Act, 17 C.F.R. §§ 270.22c-1, 30a-3(a), 38a-1 (2015), and violations of other securities acts. Excerpted from *In re* J. Kenneth Alderman, CPA, Investment Company Act Release No. 30,300 (Dec. 10, 2013). Edited.

153 *In re* J. Kenneth Alderman, CPA, Investment Company Act Release No. 30,557 (June 13, 2013).

Another example is the case against Jon Corzine, the head of MF Global, which collapsed in 2011 at the cost of $1 billion. Corzine was sued by the Commodity Futures Trading Commission. The claim was based not on corruption but on management's lack of supervision. The defendant was a former manager at Goldman Sachs, and a New Jersey senator and governor. He agreed to a lifetime prohibition from leading a futures broker or registering with the Commodity Futures Trading Commission. He may trade with his own money, but not with anyone else's money, and he may also trade in other markets. [154] The following is the text of the press release announcing the decision.

Washington - The U.S. Commodity Futures Trading Commission (CFTC) has obtained a federal court Consent Order against Defendant Jon S. Corzine (Corzine Order), former CEO of MF Global Inc. (MF Global), requiring him to pay a $5 million civil monetary penalty for his role in MF Global's unlawful use of customer funds totaling nearly one billion dollars and for his failure to diligently supervise the handling of customer funds. Per the Corzine Order, Corzine cannot seek or accept, directly or indirectly, reimbursement or indemnification from any insurance policy with regard to the penalty amount. The Corzine Order also requires Corzine to undertake that he will never act as a principal, agent, officer, director, or employee of a Futures Commission Merchant (FCM) and that he will never register with the CFTC in any capacity. As to Defendant Edith O'Brien, the former Assistant Treasurer of MF Global, the Court entered an Order (O'Brien Order) requiring her to pay a $500,000 civil monetary penalty for aiding and abetting MF Global's violations and prevents her from associating with an FCM or registering with the CFTC in any capacity for a period of eighteen (18) months.

Previously, the CFTC obtained Orders against MF Global and its parent company MF Global Holdings Ltd. (Holdings), which Orders required restitution in amounts sufficient to pay all customer claims.

The Orders against Corzine and O'Brien were entered on January 5, 2017, by Judge Victor Marrero of the U.S. District Court for the Southern District of New York.

Aitan Goelman, the CFTC's Enforcement Director, stated: "This resolution demonstrates the importance that the Commission attaches to customer protection, which has long been a hallmark of our mission."

The Orders arise out of the CFTC's amended Complaint, filed on December 6, 2013. The Corzine Order finds that Corzine was the CEO of MF Global from September 1, 2010 through the commencement of its liquidation proceedings on October 31, 2011 as well as the CEO and

---

154 Ben Protess, *Corzine and Regulators Settle in MF Global Case*, N.Y. TIMES, Jan. 6, 2017, at B3, *available at* http://www.nytimes.com/2017/01/05/business/dealbook/mf-global-jon-corzine-penalty-settlement.html?_r=0 (last visited Jan. 6, 2017).

Chairman of the Board of Directors of its parent company Holdings. The O'Brien Order finds that Edith O'Brien supervised MF Global's Treasury Department, which handled the cash management of MF Global, and was responsible for directing, approving, and/or causing certain wire transfers and other payments into and out of MF Global's customer accounts. Both Orders find that, during the last week of October 2011, in violation of U.S. commodity laws, MF Global unlawfully used nearly one billion dollars of customer segregated funds to support its own proprietary operations and the operations of its affiliates and to pay broker-dealer securities customers and pay FCM customers for withdrawals of secured customer funds.

The Orders find that MF Global violated the Commodity Exchange Act (CEA) and CFTC Regulations by failing to treat, deal with, and account for its FCM customers' segregated funds as belonging to such customers; failing to account separately for, properly segregate, and treat its FCM customers' segregated funds as belonging to such customers; commingling its FCM customers' segregated funds with the funds of any other person; using its FCM customers' segregated funds to fund the operations of MF Global and its affiliates, thereby using or permitting the use of the funds of one futures customer for the benefit of a person other than such futures customer; and withdrawing from its FCM customer segregated funds beyond MF Global's actual interest therein.

When the transfers occurred, Corzine controlled MF Global, which was experiencing a worsening liquidity crisis. Because of this control and by his conduct, Corzine is liable for MF Global's violations as its controlling person. Furthermore, from at least August 2011 through October 31, 2011, Corzine failed to supervise diligently the activities of the officers, employees, and agents of MF Global in their handling of customer funds. By this conduct, Corzine violated CFTC Regulation 166.3, 17 C.F.R. § 166.3.

The O'Brien Order finds that O'Brien, knowing that certain funds would be transferred from customer segregated accounts to MF Global's proprietary accounts, on Thursday, October 27, 2011 and Friday, October 28, 2011, directed, approved, and/or caused seven transfers of funds from customer segregated accounts to MF Global's proprietary accounts totaling hundreds of millions of dollars—more than MF Global had in excess segregated funds as last reported to O'Brien—that caused and/or contributed to a deficiency in the customer segregated accounts. By this conduct, O'Brien aided and abetted MF Global's segregation violations.

The CFTC previously settled charges against MF Global and its parent Holdings for their violations of the CEA and CFTC Regulations (see CFTC Press Releases 6776-13 [November 18, 2013] and 7095-14 [December 24, 2014]). On November 8, 2013, the CFTC obtained a federal Consent Order against MF Global for misuse of customer funds and related supervisory failures in violation of the CEA and CFTC Regulations (see CFTC Press Release 6776-13, November 18, 2013). MF Global was required to pay $1.212 billion in restitution to its customers, as well as a $100 million civil monetary penalty. On December 23, 2014, the CFTC obtained a federal court Consent Order against Holdings also requiring it to pay $1.212 billion in restitution, joint and several with MF Global, and imposed a $100 million penalty (see CFTC Order and Press Release 7095-14, December 24, 2014).

Pursuant to these Orders against MF Global and Holdings, restitution has been paid to satisfy all customer claims (see CFTC Press Prelease 6904-14, April 3, 2014).[155]

Directors either choose and appoint or manage the corporation's management. The following story does not seem to fit this or any other chapter in this book, and yet, it does. It introduces a topic we will deal with throughout the course, that is, the role of management. The purpose of this story, here, is to keep the role of management as well as its limits in mind throughout our discussion of corporate self-regulation, even if it not directly relevant to finance or to our particular subject.

Company Canoe Race

Role of the various actors: Who failed and contributed to the failure? How should have the race been managed?

A Japanese company and an American company decided to have a canoe race on the Missouri River. Each company's team practiced long and hard to reach peak performance before the race. On the day of the race, the Japanese company's team won by a mile.

The American company's team was crushed; they felt discouraged and depressed. The company's management prepared a mission statement and made it their goal to uncover the reason for the defeat. A team of senior management personnel was formed. They would investigate and recommend appropriate action.

They found that the Japanese company's team had eight people rowing and one person steering, whereas their team (the American company) had one person rowing and eight people steering. So the American company hired a consulting firm for an enormous amount of money to advise them. The consulting company concluded that too many people were steering the boat and not enough people were rowing.

To prevent another humiliating loss to the Japanese team the following year, the American rowing team was reorganized. The new management structure included four steering managers, three area-steering superintendents, and one assistant area-steering superintendent liaison. The group then implemented a new performance system intended to give the one person rowing the boat greater incentives to work harder. The system was called the Rowing Team Quality-First

----

155 U.S. Commodity Futures Trading Comm'n, *Federal Court in New York Orders Jon S. Corzine to Pay $5 Million Penalty for His Role in MF Global's Unlawful Use of Nearly $1 Billion of Customer Funds and Prohibits Corzine from Registering with the CFTC in Any Capacity or Associating with an FCM*, Press Release No. pr7508-17 (Jan. 5, 2017), *available at* http://www.cftc.gov/PressRoom/PressReleases/pr7508-17#PrRoWMBL (last visited Jan. 6, 2017).

Program, designed to give the rower empowerment and job enrichment. The program was kicked off with meetings, dinners, and free pens and T-shirts for the rower.

The next year, the Japanese team won the boat race by two miles. The American company's management fired the rower for poor performance, halted funds for the development of a new canoe, sold the paddles, and canceled capital investment for new equipment. They gave awards for high performance to the steering managers and distributed the money saved as bonuses to the senior executives.[156]

Discussion topics

*What is the moral of this story?
*Why is it funny to some and sad to others?
*How does it relate to self-regulation?

---

[156] *The Company Canoe Race, in* DUANE SCHULTZ & SYDNEY ELLEN SCHULTZ, PSYCHOLOGY AND WORK TODAY 168 (10th ed. 2016) ("An Internet legend of unknown source, provided by Marty Salo").

COMPLIANCE, GOVERNANCE AND SELF-REGULATION

INTRODUCTION

In our discussions, we use, in addition to "law" the terms "compliance," "governance," and "self-regulation" either together or alternatively. These concepts share some elements, yet are distinguishable. Chapter 3 discusses these concepts. Section I defines the meaning of compliance, governance, and self-regulation. Section II outlines the focus of our study. Section III explains the need for self-regulation in addition to law, and why government regulation alone is not enough. Section IV summarizes part of the history of corporate self-governance through the story of Boeing Corporation.

I. WHAT IS THE MEANING OF COMPLIANCE, GOVERNANCE, AND SELF-REGULATION?

A. What Does "Compliance" Mean?

The literal meaning of the word "compliance" is "following or agreeing with another's wish, request, or demand." Underlying compliance is the willingness of those who comply to follow a prescribed course of behavior or treatment, and a disposition, tendency, or choice to yield to the will of others.[157] Therefore, a prisoner's obedience is not compliance; the prisoner obeys rules or commands for lack of other options. This distinction is important because underlying the design of compliance is an assumption that the persons who manage and operate the corporation's business intend and desire to comply with the law. Nonetheless, compliance contains a germ of coercion, a threat of punishment. The corporation and the actors on its behalf must obey the law, or face dire consequences if they are caught in violation of the law. Therefore, compliance may be viewed as "mild" coercion, that is, coercion by law, which is presumed to be

---

157 AMERICAN HERITAGE® DICTIONARY OF THE ENGLISH LANGUAGE 377-78 (5TH ED. 2011) ("The act of complying with a wish, request, or demand; acquiescence.").

just. This definition of compliance applies to each and every one of us in everyday life. Yet, in our study, the reach of this text is not that broad. It applies only to compliance by institutions, as well as individuals and groups related to, and within, institutions.

Compliance may also include the readiness to correct prior wrongful acts and self-impose limitations in the future. One example is the case of *United States CFTC v. Oystacher.*[158] Pursuant to section 6(c) of the Commodity Exchange Act,[159] the U.S. Commodity Futures Trading Commission (the CFTC) sought to enjoin the defendants, a trader and a trading company, from committing further violations of the Commodities Exchange Act and to bar the trader from trading certain commodity futures.

Following a hearing, the court determined that the totality of the circumstances did not warrant a preliminary injunction. Ultimately, the defendants' self-implemented corrective measures, supplemented with the court's additional requirements and the limited time until the date of the trial, rendered future violations unlikely. The defendants' self-implemented tools significantly restricted both trading size and trading speed, thereby restricting the trader's ability to manipulate the market by "spoofing," i.e., "bidding or offering with the intent to cancel the bid or offer before execution," a violation of section 6c of the Act.[160] Consequently, the court denied the motion of the government for a preliminary injunction.

B. What Does "Governance" Mean?

"Governance" reflects the function—the activity—of governing, including the imposition of rules of behavior, punishment for violating the rules, and inducements to obey the rules. The function of governance can be performed by the government as well as by different groups that impose rules on their members. Thus, governance does not necessarily tell us the identity of the governing body, but rather describes the way any governing function imposes and enforces rules. It focuses on the way governing entities govern. Universities and law schools within the universities have governance structures. They consist of the board of trustees, the president, the deans, as well as the financial structure and, just as importantly, the way courses are designed and approved as well as the teachers' hiring process.

C. What Does Group "Self-Regulation" Mean?

The term "regulator" signals the kind of person or entity that must be obeyed. Self-regulation denotes both the power of group members and the relative freedom of their entity from the

---

158 *CFTC v. Oystacher,* No. 15-CV-9196, 2016 U.S. Dist. LEXIS 89934 (N.D. Ill. July 12, 2016).

159 7 U.S.C. § 13a-1 (2012).

160 7 U.S.C. § 6c(a)(5)(C) (2012).

outsiders' regulation. In democratic countries, one can say that their citizens self-regulate. Financial entities are externally regulated by the government, as well as internally self-regulated.

To be sure, governing bodies differ in their governance and enforcement power. Government is empowered to punish by fines and imprisonment. The holder of governance power, such as the employer, may hire and fire employees, raise and reduce their salary and benefits, and accord them high or low prestige. In a self-governing group, the governed have more power to determine the rules and form of their enforcement. Both government and a self-governing body can interfere in people's private lives and freedoms, and both can affect the management and well being of the country's citizens. Both involve compliance.

The distinctions between the systems of government, of governance, and of self-regulation are not clear-cut. To be sure, government can punish by fines and imprisonment, but governance, and especially self-regulation, can punish by fines as well. It can also punish by withholding or limiting the means of earning a living, and by exclusion. Likewise, self-governance can reward, with money and job promotion. Government can impose taxes and regulate street traffic, but self-regulation can control individuals' work and leisure time, the way they dress and address each other, and the way they spend the better part of their waking hours. Both government and self-regulation have political influence at home and abroad. Both have an impact on the economy and the financial system, directly and indirectly. Every area of life carries the fingerprints of both.

In our context the two systems interact quite closely. Governance (self-regulation) is expected and required to enforce the government's rules. This leads us to inquire: How does governance by self-regulation work? How does it balance real powers within the institution? And how does it interact with government and international governing organizations?

Self-regulation is a system by which free group members self-limit their freedom. The limit is not imposed by others: neither by government nor by another system of governance. Each and every member of the group is his or her own regulator. In fact, this self-regulation is close to ethical behavior. Each member of the group is not only a part of the group, whose members behave in a certain way; each member is also a member of the group or the government that imposes the rules of behavior. The governed is also the governing. Some of the more recognized self-governing institutions are the Financial Industry Regulatory Authority (FINRA)[161] and the American Bar Association (ABA).[162]

---

[161] *FINRA, available at* http://www.finra.org/ (last visited Apr. 5, 2017).

[162] *American Bar Association, available at* http://www.americanbar.org/aba.html (last visited Apr. 5, 2017).

Our study examines the search for effective self-regulatory systems within institutions. We explore the ways in which a group of people would determine: "Here we do not do this! Or here we do this! And we would not change our behavior, even if we might benefit from the change, and even if our changing behavior is not easily discovered!"

We seek to learn about systems and cultures in which people feel proud of not violating the rules. In part such pride may prevail because the rules are not imposed on the people but rather because the people may participate in making the rules. The rules become their rules. In addition, the members of such groups are likely to trust each other and support each other's efforts. Group achievement becomes personal achievement. Trust among the actors becomes a crucial element to reach this form of cooperation.

Trust is efficient. It reduces the cost of verifying other parties' statements and guaranteeing parties' promises. Therefore, it is not surprising that self-regulatory systems often accompany highly efficient trade and financial relationships, as efficient traders developed governance and self-regulatory systems. Arguably, governance and self-regulation drive efficiency, and therefore trust. Needless to say, not everyone agrees with these assumptions. After all, it is easier to defraud trusting persons rather than suspicious persons.

How do members of a self-regulatory system relate to each other? It seems that members of these systems, such as traders and large extended families, cooperate and yet compete with each other. While competing, they support each other, to the extent that they sense a danger to their group system. They unite when a government attempts to limit their autonomy. For example, they often fight together against rising taxation or stricter regulation.[163] They often band together to maintain a fair course of industry dealing, necessary to protect their reputations and that of their services as a whole (ensuring true weight and measures standards, for example).[164]

The membership in a self-regulating group can become more united and cohesive. The U.S. Chamber of Commerce, for example, performs the function of lobbying and bringing court claims on behalf of its members.[165] There is a movement to merge in the private sector, for

---

163 *See, e.g.,* Inv. Co. Inst., *U.S. House of Representatives Committee on Ways and Means, Tax Reform Working Group on Financial Services, Comments of the Investment Company Institute on the Discussion Draft Regarding Taxation of Financial Products* (Apr. 5, 2013), *available at* https://www.ici.org/pdf/27183.pdf (last visited Feb. 4, 2016); INV. CO. INST., RE: OPEN-END FUND LIQUIDITY RISK MANAGEMENT PROGRAMS; SWING PRICING; RE-OPENING OF COMMENT PERIOD FOR INVESTMENT COMPANY REPORTING MODERNIZATION RELEASE (Jan. 13, 2016), *available at* https://www.ici.org/pdf/16_ici_sec_lrm_dera_comment.pdf (last visited Feb. 4, 2016).

164 *See, e.g., NCWM to Celebrate Its 100th Annual Meeting,* PRWEB NEWSWIRE, June 2, 2015, LEXIS, NEWS LIBRARY, CURNWS FILE (noting that "[i]Industry and regulatory officials will ... discuss and vote on amendments to the national weights and measures standards that affect the daily lives of Americans and the livelihood of businesses that depend on a level playing field to conduct business").

165 *See, e.g., U.S. Chamber of Commerce, The Policymaking Process, available at* https://www.uschamber.com/about-us/about-us-chamber/policymaking-process (last visited Feb. 4, 2016) (noting that U.S. Chamber of Commerce "testifies before Congress or regulatory agencies, disseminates reports or statements to the media, [and] sends comments or letters to Capitol Hill and to policymakers[]"); Business Roundtable v. SEC, 647 F.3d 1144 (D.C. Cir. 2011) (opposing rule requiring

example, among the banks and mutual funds in the U.S. The volume of merger deals worldwide surged 41% in 2004 from the year earlier to $1.95 trillion, the highest level since 2000.[166] That was the case in those days. The trend may have been different later on. It seems that in mid-2016, with tighter regulation, which leads to lower profits, banks have begun to shed some pieces of their "financial mall."[167]How is this merger trend relevant to self-regulation? It signals the movement of competitors that come together not only by agreement but also by merger, especially when reduced competition may be violating the antitrust law.

Another example of the increasing unity and cohesion in private sector governance and self-regulating groups is the U.S. business community's preparation of a program to choose and support judges who are sympathetic to business, in order to combat "frivolous litigation."[168] The movement involves pressing legislators to approve sympathetic judges by signaling to the legislators the voters' sentiments as well as the ephemeral nature of the legislator's own tenure. Plans include expressing popular support for these sympathetic judges through television and other media advertising.[169] The implication of the programs is far-reaching. Unlike lobbying, which has been justified as the education of the legislators, these programs are a more direct political action.. Regardless of whether such a program will be launched and whether it will be successful, it demonstrates the rise of the business community to challenge, and to get openly involved, not only in legislative matters but also in the choice of the judiciary.

Labor organizations are expected to launch a counter-campaign[170] to change the system of choosing judges. Long term, the triumphant campaign may depend on which campaign has the most effective organizational machine and the most money. The method of choosing judges is debatable, but what is not debatable is that both movements exemplify the application of governance power over government power.

In sum, relative to traditional government power, governance power has been rising. Of the two, sometimes competing systems, government structure is better known and more open. Governance and self-governing structure is, by contrast, less known and perhaps unknowable.

How is private power controlled? Self-regulation is controlled by the members of the various institutions. As Professor Lucian Bebchuk noted, there has been a movement to strengthen the

---

public companies to provide shareholders with information about shareholder-nominated candidates for board of directors; noting that Chamber of Commerce "has corporate members that issue publicly traded securities[]").

166 Dennis K. Berman, *Simmering M&A Sector Reaches a Boil*, WALL ST. J., Jan. 3, 2005, at R10, LEXIS, News Library, Wsj File.

167 *See, e.g.*, Lindsay Gellman & Justin Baer, *Goldman Workers Are More than a Number*, WALL ST. J., May 27, 2016, at A1, LEXIS, News Library, Wsj File ("New regulations have crimped profits, forcing banks to retreat from certain businesses and cut staff")..

168 Jeanne Cummings, *Business Gears Up to Support White House Judicial Nominees*, Wall St. J., Jan. 7, 2005, at A4, LEXIS, News Library, Wsj File.

169 *Id.*

170 *Id.*

power of shareholders in public corporations.[171] Professor Lisa M. Fairfax noted that there arose a movement to limit the compensation of corporate management.[172] And there are examples of self-governance where the employees set the rules and impose compliance with the law. Thus, what we are witnessing is an ongoing process.

III. WHY ARE CORPORATIONS REQUIRED TO IMPOSE INTERNAL COMPLIANCE? WHY ARE LAWS AND REGULATIONS NOT ENOUGH?

These questions are not unreasonable. We hear complaints about the rising costs of the enormous number of rules that corporations must know and follow. Here are six possible answers to this complaint.

First, to be sure, violations expose the corporations to risks of sanctions that could undermine reputation and result in serious monetary fines and losses.[173] This is especially true when the corporations are large and deal with complex processes that pose danger to the public. However, many business and financial relationships involve a high level of trust. Loss of trust may mean total financial disaster for a business enterprise. Short-term benefits and "slippery slopes" of minor actions can lead to serious crimes, resulting in frauds on a grand scale.

The individuals involved are harmed as well. For example, a university administrator purported to have completed an undergraduate degree and a graduate degree. She had done neither. However, she was an able and ambitious person, and advanced to become Dean in 1997. She did not have the courage to correct her resume and paid the price of the discovery.[174] A 2005 business ethics survey showed that although formal ethics programs (written standards of conduct, ethics training, etc.) had increased over the last five years, the expected positive outcomes had not increased.[175]

---

171 *E.g.*, Lucian A. Bebchuk, *The Myth that Isolating Boards Serves Long-Term Value*, 113 COLUM. L. REV. 1637, 1654 (2013) (noting attempts to provide shareholders with power to place director candidates on ballot); Facilitating Shareholder Director Nominations, 33-9136; 34-62764; IC-29384 (Aug. 25, 2010), 75 Fed. Reg. 56,668 (Sept. 16, 2010) (codified in scattered sections of 17 C.F.R.); *id.* at 56,669-70 (noting other SEC proposals to enhance shareholders' rights).

172 *E.g.*, Lisa M. Fairfax, *Sue on Pay: Say on Pay's Impact on Directors' Fiduciary Duties*, 55 ARIZ. L. REV. 1, 18-21 (2013) (listing proposals for reforms relating to executive compensation); Dodd-Frank Wall Street Reform and Consumer Protection Act, Pub. L. 111-203, sec. 951, § 14, 124 Stat. 1376, 1899-1900 (2010) (codified as amended at 15 U.S.C. § 78n-1 (2012)) (requiring shareholder approval of certain executive compensation golden parachute payments)

173 BASEL COMMITTEE ON BANKING SUPERVISION, COMPLIANCE AND THE COMPLIANCE FUNCTION IN BANKS 7 (Apr. 2005), *available at* http://www.bis.org/publ/bcbs113.pdf (last visited Feb. 6, 2016).

174 Keith J. Winstein & Daniel Golden, *MIT Admission Dean Lied on Resume in 1979, Quits*, WALL ST. J., Apr. 27, 2007, at B1, LEXIS, News Library, Wsj File.

175 Simon Webley & Andrea Werner, *Corporate Codes of Ethics: Necessary but Not Sufficient*, 17 BUS. ETHICS: A EUROPEAN REV. 405, 408 (2008), *available at* https://www.researchgate.net/publication/227834830_Corporate_codes_of_ethics_Necessary_but_not_sufficient (last visited Oct. 10, 2016), *citing* ETHICS RESOURCE CTR., THE NATIONAL BUSINESS ETHICS SURVEY, HOW EMPLOYEES VIEW ETHICS IN THEIR ORGANIZATION, 1994-2005 (2005).

The punishment for some violations can be horrendous and hard to imagine. For example, MBA students were taken to a minimum-security facility to meet with inmates convicted of business crimes. The students realized that prison officials controlled the inmates' lives, determining, for example, when they would eat and sleep. The inmates consistently said that their wrongful activities were not a single act but a "slippery slope" that began when they wanted to accomplish a goal or help the company.[176]

Thus, corporations and their stakeholders should protect themselves from violations of the law by their own "populations," including employees, management, close independent contractors, and affiliates. The required compliance is not necessarily a punishing; it may provide protection from liability and its dire results. Yet, short term, when rules create barriers to immediate, or shorter-term, prospects of higher profits, complying with restrictive rules can be resented and viewed as constraining market freedom. If activities are not clearly illegal—and many are not—these constraints may initially seem patently unreasonable.

Second, corporate legal violations can cause serious harm to their own investors and employees, as well as to the country's citizens and its economic and financial well being. Unemployment may rise; the gap between the wealthy and the poor may widen; a corporate or even national culture of costly dishonest behavior may develop. In many cases the harm can spread to other countries as well as to the international economic and financial system.

Third, as corporations grow larger and more complex and operate internationally, monitoring by regulators becomes increasingly difficult and sometimes impossible. Internal corporate compliance programs, if operated effectively, may be better at limiting malfeasance than government regulation.

Fourth, rules and detailed regulations are very costly to enforce, both by corporations and by the regulators. A culture of voluntary compliance is likely to reduce these horrendous costs.

Fifth, the demand for specific rules leads to a search around specific prohibitions, and to the claim: "Where is it written?!!" But circumventing a specific rule may lead to another specific written rule, and so on. When more general principles lead to a culture—a social habit of behavior that interprets the prohibition in light of the general problems that the rule was designed to resolve—then fewer rules would be needed. Thus, one of the main enforcement mechanisms of compliance is culture: the accepted general rules that are followed by the group, rather than the specific rules that lead to the search for exceptions.

Sixth, compliance involves international relationships.[177] A growing number of multilateral agreements are negotiated by members of the international community. Mistrust can undermine such beneficial interactions.

---

176 Jenny B. Davis, *Corporate-Crime Fighter: Ex-Prosecutor Teams with Prisoners to Teach Ethics to Executives*, A.B.A.J., Feb. 2003, at26, LEXIS, News Library, Arcnws File.

177 Teall Crossen, *Multilateral Environmental Agreements and the Compliance Continuum*, 16 Geo. Int'l Envtl. L. Rev. 473, 474 (2004).

Teall Crossen has proposed a number of solutions to ensure corporate compliance with obligations and to strengthen parties' trust in each other: first, the notion that a treaty relates not only to its obligations but also to the underlying problem,[178] second, the notion that compliance is driven not only by sanctions but also by reputational injury,[179] and third, the notion that international law is based on legitimacy—the recognition that different ways of doing things are the right thing to do.[180]

Fourth, on a higher level, many, but not all, corporations should share the basic principles of the same culture.[181]

Fifth, as the number of the corporate shareholders grows, so do oversight problems. The larger the number of shareholders, the more difficult it becomes for them to organize and monitor the corporation. With the monitoring weakness of investors and outsiders, the managers' discretion and freedom of action expands, and their accountability shrinks. Managers may then seek, and sometimes receive, justifications for claiming ownership rights: after all, it is they who produce corporate profits, rather than the shareholders. Shareholders are then viewed as parasites.

Yet, unless culture and ethics constrain the managers' claims and justification for entitlement—in effect, agency costs and/or conflicts of interest—prosecutors' activities will increase. Prosecutors seek indictments and convictions, resort to civil and administrative actions against such corporations, and drive for criminal indictments and other means of punishments against their leadership. With this trend, which may be in sight, corporations and their leaders increasingly view corporate compliance and ethics as risk management, similar to insurance. The risk that is being managed is the risk of prosecutorial punishment and loss of reputation._____

Discussion Topics

*If compliance is so good for corporations, why do so many corporations experience fraudulent activities, detailed compliance programs notwithstanding?

*What should corporate leaders do if their competitors do not follow the law, and consequently are more profitable in the short term? How can a corporation follow the law and yet avoid losses? What if the investors and customers prefer short-term profits or more competitive pricing to law-abiding corporate behavior? Is there anyone who might suffer then?

---

178 *Id.* at 478-79.

179 *Id.* at 481-83.

180 *Id.* at 483-85.

181 ROBERT F. ROACH, COMPLIANCE AT LARGER INSTITUTIONS 1 (Nov. 11-13, 2009), *available at* http://www. higheredcompliance.org/compliance/resources/larger-institutions.pdf (last visited Feb. 8, 2016), *citing* REPORT OF THE AD HOC ADVISORY GROUP ON THE ORGANIZATIONAL SENTENCING GUIDELINES (Oct. 2003); *see also* Lynn Sharp Paine, *Managing for Organizational Integrity*, HARV. BUS. REV., Mar.-Apr. 1994, at 106, 111.

*What if competitors are not clearly breaking the law but are merely interpreting it differently, due to the law's inherent ambiguity? How, if at all, does this situation change your answers?

*Please consider and opine on the following statement:

A view of the required corporate compliance is expressed in market terms, as follows: According to William S. Laufer, if corporations purchase only the compliance necessary to avoid their own liability, there is a moral hazard problem. There is no incentive to purchase a higher level of compliance, so crimes will still occur but be imputed to individuals.[182] In addition, according to Philip A. Wellner, if corporations receive a sentence reduction for having compliance programs, they may use resources inefficiently, developing compliance programs that are ineffective or expensive.[183]

IV. THE STORY OF THE BOEING CORPORATION: AN EXAMPLE OF THE EVOLUTION OF CORPORATE SELF-GOVERNANCE

The seeds of modern compliance programs were planted in the 1980s. In 1985 there were concerns about fraud and misconduct involving defense contractors.[184] At one point there were 131 pending investigations against 45 major contractors.[185]

President Reagan appointed a commission (the "Packard Commission") to study and report on defense management issues.[186] The commission issued an Interim Report in February 1986[187] and a final report in June 1986.[188] The interim report suggested that defense contractors adopt and enforce codes of ethics and internal controls to monitor them.[189]

---

182 William S. Laufer, *Corporate Liability, Risk Shifting, and the Paradox of Compliance*, 52 Vand. L. Rev. 1343, (1999).

183 Philip A. Wellner, Note, *Effective Compliance Programs and Corporate Criminal Prosecutions*, 27 Cardozo L. Rev. 497, 498-99 (2005).

184 President's Blue Ribbon Commission on Defense Management, A Quest for Excellence: Final Report to the President 75-77 (1986), *available at* http://www.ndia.org/Advocacy/AcquisitionReformInitiative/Documents/Packard-Commission-Report.pdf (last visited Jan. 22, 2016).

185 *Id.* at 75 n.2.

186 *Id.* at xi, xviii.

187 President's Blue Ribbon Commission on Defense Management, An Interim Report to the President (1989), *available at* http://oai.dtic.mil/oai/oai?verb=getRecord&metadataPrefix=html&identifier=ADA165901 (last visited Jan. 22, 2016).

188 President's Blue Ribbon Commission on Defense Management, A Quest for Excellence: Final Report to the President (1986), *available at* http://www.ndia.org/Advocacy/AcquisitionReformInitiative/Documents/Packard-Commission-Report.pdf (last visited Jan. 22, 2016).

189 President's Blue Ribbon Commission on Defense Management, An Interim Report to the President 21 (1989), *available at* http://oai.dtic.mil/oai/oai?verb=getRecord&metadataPrefix=html&identifier=ADA165901 (last visited Jan. 22, 2016) ("defense contractors must promulgate and vigilantly enforce codes of ethics that address the unique problems

As a result of the Interim Report, senior officials at 18 defense contractors agreed on principles that became the Defense Industry Initiative on Business Ethics and Conduct (DII). By July 1986, 32 contractors had signed on, and as of January 2016 the DII was comprised of 77 companies.[190]

DII contractors agree to the following principles:

(1) We shall act honestly in all business dealings with the U.S. government, protect taxpayer resources, and provide high-quality products and services for the men and women of the U.S. Armed Forces.

(2) We shall promote the highest ethical values as expressed in our written codes of business conduct, nurture an ethical culture through communications, training, and other means, and comply with and honor all governing laws and regulations.

(3) We shall establish and sustain effective business ethics and compliance programs that reflect our commitment to self-governance, and shall encourage employees to report suspected misconduct, forbid retaliation for such reporting, and ensure the existence of a process for mandatory and voluntary disclosures of violations of relevant laws and regulations.

(4) We shall share best practices with respect to business ethics and compliance, and participate in the annual DII Best Practices Forum.

(5) We shall be accountable to the public, through regular sharing and reporting of signatory activities in public fora, including www.dii.org. These reports will describe members' efforts to build and sustain a strong culture of business ethics and compliance.[191]

At about the same time, following concerns about sentencing in a number of corporate scandals,[192] Congress passed the Sentencing Reform Act of 1984, establishing the United States Sentencing Commission to promulgate sentencing guidelines in criminal cases.[193]

---

and procedures incident to defense procurement" and "develop and implement internal controls to monitor these codes of ethics and sensitive aspects of contract compliance").

190 Defense Industry Initiative on Business Ethics and Conduct, *About Us, available at http://www.dii.org/about-us* (last visited Feb. 25, 2016).

191 Defense Industry Initiative on Business Ethics and Conduct, *DII Principles, available at* http://www.dii.org/dii-principles (last visited Feb. 25, 2016).

192 *See* S. Rep. No. 98-225, at 77 (1984), reprinted in 1984 U.S.C.C.A.N. 3182, 3260, *quoted in* John D. Esterhay, *Apples and Oranges: Securities Market Losses Should Be Treated Differently for Major White-Collar Criminal Sentencing Under the Federal Guidelines,* 76 Mo. L. Rev. 1113, 1122 (2011) ("Some major offenders, particularly white collar offenders … frequently do not receive sentences that reflect the seriousness of their offenses.").

193 Act of Oct. 12, 1984, Pub. L. No. 98-473, §§ 211-238, 98 Stat. 1837, 1987-2040.

In 1991, the Commission specifically addressed compliance programs when it adopted guidelines for the sentencing of organizations. These guidelines included amendments to provide a reduction in culpability if an organization had "an effective program to prevent and detect violations of law" and set out seven minimum steps for a compliance program.[194] At about the same time, in 1992, the Committee of Sponsoring Organizations of the Treadway Commission (COSO), a joint initiative of private sector accounting organizations, issued a report, *Internal Control—Integrated Framework,* providing a definition and standard for internal control. It defined internal control as "a process, effected by an entity's board of directors, management, and other personnel, designed to provide reasonable assurance regarding the achievement of objectives in the following categories: (1) effectiveness and efficiency of operations, (2) reliability of financial reporting, and (3) compliance with applicable laws and regulations."[195]

However, the Enron and WorldCom accounting scandals of the early 2000s "exposed serious weaknesses in industry self-regulatory reporting requirements,"[196] and Congress responded by passing the Sarbanes-Oxley Act of 2002. The Act addressed the issue of codes of ethics for public companies. The Act directed the SEC to require a public company to disclose whether it had adopted a code of ethics for senior financial officers.[197] A code of ethics is defined as:

> such standards as are reasonably necessary to promote (1) honest and ethical conduct, including the ethical handling of actual or apparent conflicts of interest between personal and professional relationships; (2) full, fair, accurate, timely, and understandable disclosure in the periodic reports required to be filed by the issuer; and (3) compliance with applicable governmental rules and regulations.[198]

---

194 AMENDMENTS TO THE SENTENCING GUIDELINES FOR UNITED STATES COURTS, 56 Fed. Reg. 22,762 (May 16, 1991). The requirements were incorporated into a new guideline in 2003. SENTENCING GUIDELINES FOR UNITED STATES COURTS, 68 Fed. Reg. 75,340 (Dec. 30, 2003). For the current Sentencing Guidelines applicable to corporations, *see* U.S. SENTENCING GUIDELINES MANUAL ch. 8 (Nov. 1, 2015), *available at* http://www.ussc.gov/sites/default/files/pdf/guidelines-manual/2015/GLMFull.pdf (last visited Mar. 7, 2016). For the Guidelines' requirements for an effective compliance and ethics program, see U.S. SENTENCING GUIDELINES MANUAL §8B2.1 (Nov. 1, 2015), *available at* http://www.ussc.gov/sites/default/files/pdf/guidelines-manual/2015/GLMFull.pdf (last visited Mar. 7, 2016).

195 COMMITTEE OF SPONSORING ORGANIZATIONS, INTERNAL CONTROL — INTEGRATED FRAMEWORK (2013) (executive summary), *available at https://www.coso.org/Documents/990025P-Executive-Summary-final-may20.pdf* (last visited Dec. 28, 2016).

196 Free Enter. Fund v. Public Co. Accounting Oversight Bd., 537 F.3d 667, 669 (D.C. Cir. 2008, *citing* S. REP. No. 107-205, at 2 (2002); H.R. REP. NO. 107-414, at 18-19 (2002); *aff'd in part, rev'd in part, remanded,* 561 U.S. 477 (2010).

197 Sarbanes-Oxley Act of 2002, Pub. L. No. 107-204, § 406(a), 116 Stat. 745, 789. The requirement generally applies to a company that issues securities to the public, *i.e.,* an issuer whose securities are registered under the Securities Act of 1933, an issuer that is required to file reports under the Securities Exchange Act of 1934, or an issuer that files a registration statement under the Securities Act of 1933. *Id.* at § (a)(7), 116 Stat. at 747.

198 *Id.* at § 406(c), 116 Stat. at 789-90.

In addition, the Act resulted in strengthening the requirements for an effective compliance and ethics program. The Act directed the Sentencing Commission to ensure that the organizational sentencing guidelines "are sufficient to deter and punish organizational criminal misconduct."[199]

Accordingly, the Commission required that, for an effective compliance and ethics program, an organization "promote an organizational culture that encourages ethical conduct and a commitment to compliance with the law."[200] The Commission also required an organization, in implementing a program, to "periodically assess the risk of criminal conduct" and "take appropriate steps to design, implement, or modify [the other requirements] to reduce the risk of criminal conduct identified through this process."[201]

Reading Focus

As you read the *Boeing* case below, ask yourself what problems the government identified and uncovered. What steps did it take to resolve the problems? Were the solutions effective?

The following event demonstrates corruption and its deleterious effect on the corporation and government alike. This is not the only case of corporate misdeeds. It is an example of a corruptive effect that harmed not only Boeing shareholder value, but also the U.S. Defense Department. This event resulted in the imposition of compliance programs by the Justice Department.

The Boeing Corporation story[202] demonstrates the dual effect of a scandal on self-regulation and on compliance law. Before the scandal, Boeing had been producing planes for the U.S. Defense Department for many years. This business provided more than half of its annual revenues. In 2003, the corporation became involved in a scandal that severely reduced its business with the Defense Department, shook its management, and tarnished its reputation. In the wake of the affair, the Air Force excluded the firm from a rocket launch project, and put Boeing's $23 billion bid to build 100 aerial refueling tankers on hold.[203] In addition, the government cancelled

---

199 *Id.* at § 805(a)(5), 116 Stat. at 802.

200 SENTENCING GUIDELINES FOR UNITED STATES COURTS, 69 Fed. Reg. 28,994, 29,020 (May 19, 2004).

201 *Id.*

202 J. Lynn Lunsford & Anne Marie Squeo, *Boeing Dismisses Two Executives for Violating Ethical Standards*, WALL ST. J., Nov. 25, 2003, at A1, LEXIS, News Library, Wsj File; J. Lynn Lunsford & Andy Pasztor, *Higher Plane: New Boss Struggles to Lift Boeing Above Military Scandals --- Harry Stonecipher Stresses Ethics, Cost-Cutting,; McCain's Continuing Probe --- 'Don't Lie, Cheat and Steal,'* WALL ST. J., July 14, 2004, at A1, LEXIS, News Library, Wsj File; Andy Pasztor & Anne Marie Squeo, *Boeing Could Avoid Prosecution, Pay up to $500 Million to U.S.*, WALL ST. J., Sept. 9, 2005, at A1, LEXIS, News Library, Wsj File.

203 J. Lynn Lunsford & Andy Pasztor, *Higher Plane: New Boss Struggles to Lift Boeing Above Military Scandals --- Harry Stonecipher Stresses Ethics, Cost-Cutting,; McCain's Continuing Probe --- 'Don't Lie, Cheat and Steal,'* WALL ST. J., July 14, 2004, at A1, LEXIS, News Library, Wsj File.

a contract with Boeing for seven military satellite-launch rockets and indefinitely banned the company from bidding on future satellite launching contracts.[204] Despite a change in its management, the company lost—and did not regain—$1 billion in federal contracts.[205]

How did this happen? Boeing's Chief Financial Officer "dangled a job offer" before a high-level Air Force official, who was responsible for Boeing's contracts.[206] The Boeing officer negotiated hiring this official while she was negotiating contracts with Boeing on behalf of the government.[207] The law prohibits a company or its executives from making an offer or promise of employment to a federal procurement officer. There was "compelling evidence" that the CFO and procurement officer attempted to conceal their alleged misconduct from the lawyers hired by Boeing to investigate the issue. But the information surfaced, and when it did, Boeing dismissed both its CFO and the former procurement officer.[208] However, it was too late.

What happened next? At the end of that year Boeing's Chairman/CEO resigned and was replaced. The new CEO sent Boeing's employees the message that integrity and ethics matter, and ordered the firm's 157,000 employees to sign a Code of Conduct that emphasized ethics. The new CEO overhauled the company's ethics programs, and told the employees: "We don't want you to lie, cheat, and steal." He set up a new ethics office charged with functions including "ethics hotlines," "revamped its hiring practices, establishing new rules about who can approach job candidates," and established a new policy to "review activities of new employees on certain sensitive programs for potential conflicts of interest for three years after hiring."[209]

In reaction to the scandals, the Boeing Chairman/CEO stated that there was no evidence that the company benefited from the conduct. He hoped that the company's "decisive actions" in firing the CFO and former procurement officer would show the government that "we are serious about what we have been saying" regarding ethics. Yet, these changes and announcements did

---

204 Melissa Allison, *Boeing Out to Return to Good Graces; Response on Tap to Air Force Ban on Launch Bids*, CHI. TRIB., Aug. 21, 2003, Business, at 1, LEXIS, News Library, Arcnws File.

205 J. Lynn Lunsford & Andy Pasztor, *Higher Plane: New Boss Struggles to Lift Boeing Above Military Scandals --- Harry Stonecipher Stresses Ethics, Cost-Cutting,; McCain's Continuing Probe --- 'Don't Lie, Cheat and Steal,'* WALL ST. J., July 14, 2004, at A1, LEXIS, News Library, Wsj File.

206 *Id.*

207 J. Lynn Lunsford & Anne Marie Squeo, *Boeing Dismisses Two Executives for Violating Ethical Standards*, WALL ST. J., Nov. 25, 2003, at A1, LEXIS, News Library, WSJ File. The government official's daughter, who works for Boeing, contacted the CFO by e-mail to say that the official was considering post-government employment. *Id.*

208 *Id.* Before he was elevated to the position of the CFO, this person had "risen through the ranks" at Boeing and was considered a top candidate to succeed the then-Chairman/CEO. As the scandal evolved, Boeing's board voted unanimously to dismiss the CFO for unethical behavior and for violating company policy by communicating with an Air Force official to discuss potential employment while she was negotiating contracts with Boeing on behalf of the government. *Id.*

209 J. Lynn Lunsford & Andy Pasztor, *Higher Plane: New Boss Struggles to Lift Boeing Above Military Scandals --- Harry Stonecipher Stresses Ethics, Cost-Cutting,; McCain's Continuing Probe --- 'Don't Lie, Cheat and Steal,'* WALL ST. J., July 14, 2004, at A1, LEXIS, News Library, Wsj File.

not stop the ongoing government investigations of the company, or did mitigate congressional criticism of the Pentagon "for being too cozy with the defense industry."[210]

In September 2005, it was reported that Boeing and the Justice Department were negotiating an overall settlement of the Air Force scandal and another settlement concerning the company's improper acquisition of confidential Lockheed Martin documents dealing with rocket programs. The company would be required to pay up to $500 million, but would avoid prosecution. At that time, this penalty would have been the most severe ever imposed on a U.S. defense contractor.[211]

Discussion Topic

What, in your opinion, drove the legal requirement for internal compliance? Is the *Boeing* case a good example of this congressional and government movement?

We end our discussion with two cases that demonstrate the principles and rules discussed above:

Associated Bank, N.A., Green Bay, Wisconsin

The Comptroller of the Currency of the United States of America (Comptroller), through his examiners and other staff of the Office of the Comptroller of the Currency (OCC), has conducted an examination of Associated Bank, N.A., Green Bay, Wisconsin (Bank), specifically to determine the adequacy of the Bank's Bank Secrecy Act and Anti-Money Laundering (BSA/AML) compliance program. The OCC identified BSA/AML deficiencies in the Bank's internal controls, independent testing, day-to-day monitoring and coordination, and training. These BSA/AML deficiencies occurred primarily during the period 2010–2012 and were addressed by a Consent Order issued by the OCC on February 23, 2012 (Consent Order), which in part required the Bank to undertake remedial actions with respect to its BSA/AML program. The OCC terminated the Consent Order on March 11, 2014. The Bank . . . has executed a Stipulation and Consent to the Issuance of a Consent Order for a Civil Money Penalty (Stipulation) that is accepted by the Comptroller. . .

(1) The Comptroller finds, and the Bank neither admits nor denies that, primarily during the period of 2010-2012:

------

210 J. Lynn Lunsford & Anne Marie Squeo, *Boeing Dismisses Two Executives for Violating Ethical Standards,* WALL ST. J., Nov. 25, 2003, at A1, LEXIS, News Library .

211 Andy Pasztor & Anne Marie Squeo, *Boeing Could Avoid Prosecution, Pay up to $500 Million to U.S.,* WALL ST. J., Sept. 9, 2005, at A1, LEXIS, News Library, Wsj File.

(a) the Bank failed to (i) conduct adequate risk assessments, (ii) conduct sufficient customer due diligence, (iii) properly identify high-risk customers, and (iv) implement an adequate suspicious activity monitoring system;

(b) the Bank's independent testing of the Bank's BSA/AML compliance program was inadequate;

(c) the Bank's BSA officer and staff lacked the necessary resources and expertise, including knowledge of regulatory requirements;

(d) the Bank's BSA training efforts for staff were inadequate; and

(e) after conducting a lookback, the Bank filed 670 new Suspicious Activity Reports (SARs).

(2) In light of the findings of paragraph (1) of this Article, the OCC determined that the Bank violated the following BSA laws and regulations:

(a) 12 C.F.R. § 21.21, including specifically that the Bank (i) lacked a system of internal controls to ensure ongoing compliance with the BSA, (ii) failed to provide for independent testing for compliance with the BSA, (iii) lacked a qualified BSA officer, and (iv) failed to provide adequate training to Bank personnel on the requirements of the BSA; and

(b) 12 C.F.R. § 21.11, by failing to file SARs in a timely manner.[212]

. . . .

New Millenium Cash Exchange, Inc.

The Financial Crimes Enforcement Network has determined that grounds exist to assess a civil money penalty against New Millennium Cash Exchange, Inc. (NMCE or MSB) and its President and Owner, Flor Angella Lopez (Ms. Lopez), pursuant to the Bank Secrecy Act and regulations issued pursuant to that Act.

. . .

The Financial Crimes Enforcement Network conducted an investigation and determined that, since at least February 2008, NMCE and Ms. Lopez willfully violated the Bank Secrecy Act's program, reporting, and recordkeeping requirements.

These violations included:

(A) Failure to register as a money service business, including submission of filings with inaccurate information regarding the services rendered by the MSB;

(B) Violations of the requirement to establish and implement an effective written anti-money laundering program; including

---

212 Excerpted from OCC, *In re* Associated Bank, N.A., (June 26, 2014), *available at* http://www.occ.gov/static/enforcement-actions/ea2014-094.pdf (last visited Oct. 20, 2016).

(1) Lack of adequate AML programs for its check cashing and money order activities as well as its currency exchange transactions;

(2) Inadequate policies, procedures, and internal controls (a) to verify the identities of persons conducting transactions; (b) to monitor for suspicious activities; (c) to identify currency transactions exceeding $10,000; and (d) to ensure that NMCE filed the required currency transaction reports (CTRs);

(3) Inadequate internal controls for creating and retaining adequate Bank Secrecy Act records related to currency exchange;

(4) Failure to conduct a Bank Secrecy Act/AML risk assessment of the MSB and failure to include "red flags" in the MSB's procedures for each type of business;

(5) Failure to recognize the potential conflicts of interest in establishing a relationship with a consultant that: (a) created NMCE's written AML program, (b) performed the only independent testing of the AML program, and (c) provided the only source of Bank Secrecy Act training for the MSB; such training used a generic module that was provided by the consultant that also created its written AML program; the training was not comprehensive and was not tailored to the MSB's specific business lines and associated risk.

(C) Violations of the reporting and recordkeeping requirements; including (1) filing 51 CTRs significantly late and (2) failure to file at least 149 CTRs for exchanges of currency with other financial institutions.[213]

Discussion topics

*What precisely did the institution fail to do in order to meet the requirement of self-regulation?

---

213 Excerpted from *In re* New Milenium Cash Exchange, Inc. (Apr. 23, 2014), *available at* https://www.fincen.gov/sites/default/files/shared/NMCE%20Assessment.pdf (last visited Oct. 20, 2016).

Chapter 4

INTRODUCING THE REGULATORS OF THE FINANCIAL SYSTEM

I. THE SECURITIES AND EXCHANGE COMMISSION[214]

The Securities and Exchange Commission (SEC) was established after the 1929 market crash. Since then it has been supervising securities markets, the broker-dealers' self-regulatory organization (FINRA, formerly NASD), municipal securities markets, investment advisers, and mutual funds. In addition, the SEC supervises, together with the Commodity Futures Trading Commission (CFTC), which is described below, some of the organizations and activities subject to regulation by both organizations, such as the issuance of and trading in derivatives. The SEC has statutory jurisdiction over some hybrid entities and securities. For example, it has jurisdiction over mutual funds and other forms of pooled securities, and entities established to pool mortgage obligations or other securities and issue and distribute their securities to the markets. Usually, entities that invest in securities and issue securities would be regulated, unless they are exempt.[215]

A. SEC Powers to exempt from legal requirements

1. Statutory exemptions[216]

The Securities and Exchange Commission is authorized under specific sections of statutes to exempt applicants from the provisions of certain acts, conditionally or unconditionally. The Investment Company Act of 1940 provides exemptive powers with or without conditions in various sections of the Act, and under various conditions.[217]

---

214 U.S. Sec. & Exch. Comm'n, *The Investor's Advocate: How the SEC Protects Investors, Maintains Market Integrity, and Facilitates Capital Formation* (last modified June 10, 2013), *available at* http://www.sec.gov/about/whatwedo.shtml (last visited July 17, 2015).

215 Investment Company Act of 1940, 15 U.S.C. § 80a et seq. (2012).

216 *See* Tamar Frankel & Ann Taylor Schwing, The Regulation of Money Managers: Mutual Funds and Advisers ch. 2 (2d ed. 2001 & Supp. 2015).

217 *See, e.g.,* Investment Company Act of 1940 section 17, 15 U.S.C. § 80a-17(b) (2012).

2. "No-action" letters[218]

The Commission's staff may issue "no-action letters" stating that the staff will not recommend action against the applicant to the Commission. This would happen when a lawyer determines that the client's plans might come too close to prohibited activities. The lawyer then asks to meet with the Commission's staff and seek a no-action letter. In the request, the lawyer will describe the specific proposed actions and the justification for their permissibility. The questions should be specific because the staff would have an easier time answering. The staff might refuse to become a legal adviser, but when issues cannot be easily answered, the staff has traditionally responded to queries. These queries are presented in writing and receive a written response.[219] The response offers an informal view and position on the proposed activities. The no-action letter states that the staff will not recommend an enforcement action if the proposed activities take place. Hence the name: "no-action letters."[220]

The no-action letters are published, and even though they do not constitute a final authority, they do signal the staff's approach and opinion, which the Commission listens to. In addition the Commission has stated that it would not overrule no-action letters except prospectively. In addition, the courts have in most cases respected the staff's no-action letters. After all, the staff has expertise in particular situations. For the petitioner, the "no-action letters" process has an advantage over a request for an exemption in that it is less public, which is important to most applicants. The process might also be shorter than an exemption process and less costly.

For the SEC and its staff, the process also offers benefits. The requests for the staff's opinion offer information about market actors' possible or desired transactions, and signal possible legal and policy problems. In addition, responses to the letters might substitute for and reduce the SEC's enforcement actions and regulated litigation. Further, the letters open the door to negotiations to restructure and legitimize the proposals. Finally, no-action letters publicize the staff's interpretation and benefit the public facilitating application of the law.

A no-action letter does not constitute a precedent. However, the letter provides comfort, at least against prosecution by the regulator—a partial safe harbor—and some guidance to practitioners, because the letters are fairly consistent. Letters and exemptions are eventually signed by the director of the Division. No-action letters have been criticized as "rulemaking in disguise."[221] A letter is usually expressed as an agreement or disagreement with the applicant's views, yet may grant the "no-action" request even if it disagrees with the applicant's legal arguments, or may emphasize the lack of a clear rule on the issue. Even though it is not a precedent, lawyers

---

218 For a full treatment of the topic *see 1* Tamar Frankel & Ann Taylor Schwing, The Regulation of Money Managers: Mutual Funds and Advisers § 2.12 (2d ed. 2001 & Supp. 2015).

219 *Id.*

220 *Id.*

221 *Id.* at 2-77.

use no-action letters as guidance because the staff cannot be inconsistent in similar situations without raising questions. It should be noted, however, that when a no-action letter is erased from publication, it might signal a change in the Commission's views on the legal matter.[222] Otherwise, however, no-action letters are not overruled by the Commission and can be relied upon as a guide.

B. SEC Guidance.

The staff of the SEC has been issuing "Guidance Updates" of its views, including its views of compliance issues. The "updates" provide guidance and should be read carefully. For example, the staff issued an update on "the conflict of interest that arises when the personnel of a fund's investment adviser are presented with gifts, favors, or other forms of consideration (gifts or entertainment) from persons doing business, or hoping to do business, with the fund."[223] The codes of ethics of investment advisers and registered investment companies generally address this issue.[224] The update elaborates on how investment companies should address the issue in their compliance policies.[225]

In addition, SEC Commissioners and staff give speeches, which may address compliance issues. For example, one staff member noted in a speech that the staff "understand[s] the importance of . . . compliance and custody rule violations." The staff member noted that compliance was a staff priority for private funds and separately managed and/or retail accounts, noting a recent case involving "a compliance theme—recidivism," and also noted the staff's recent initiative which "targets firms that have been previously warned by SEC examiners about compliance deficiencies but failed to effectively act upon those warnings, or firms that have wide-ranging

---

222 *See also* Thomas P. Lemke, *The SEC No-Action Letter Process*, 42 Bus. Law. 1019, 1021 (1987); Donna M. Nagy, *Judicial Reliance on Regulatory Interpretations in SEC No-Action Letters: Current Problems and a Proposed Framework*, 83 Cornell L. Rev. 921 (1998). Note, *The SEC and "No-Action" Decisions Under Proxy Rule 14a-8: The Case for Direct Judicial Review*, 84 Harv. L. Rev. 835 (1971).

223 SEC Guidance Update, *Acceptance of Gifts or Entertainment by Fund Advisory Personnel - Section 17(e)(1) of the Investment Company Act*, No. 2015-01 (Feb. 2015), *available at* http://www.sec.gov/ investment/im-guidance-2015-01.pdf (last visited June 4, 2017).

224 *Id.* at 1; 17 C.F.R. § 275.204A-1 (2017) (requiring codes of ethics for investment advisers); 17 C.F.R. § 270.38a-1 (2017) (requiring codes of ethics for registered investment companies); 17 CFR § 275.206(4)-7(2017) (prohibiting registered investment advisers from advising clients unless they adopt compliance policies and procedures); Chapter 5 (compliance codes required by law).

225 SEC Guidance Update, *Acceptance of Gifts or Entertainment by Fund Advisory Personnel - Section 17(e)(1) of the Investment Company Act,* No. 2015-01 at 2 (Feb. 2015), *available at* http://www.sec.gov/ investment/im-guidance-2015-01.pdf (last visited June 4, 2017) ("The particular policies and procedures concerning the receipt of gifts or entertainment that might be appropriate would depend on the nature of the adviser's business, among other considerations. Some funds and advisers might find a blanket prohibition on the receipt of gifts or entertainment by fund advisory personnel to be appropriate. Other funds and advisers might find other measures to be more appropriate, such as some type of a pre-clearance mechanism for acceptances of gifts or entertainment to assess whether they would be for the purchase or sale of any property to or for the fund and therefore prohibited . . .).".

compliance failures." The staff also noted the importance of "the adviser keeping the chief compliance officer . . . informed about conflicts of interest."[226]

The following is part of a speech by the SEC Director of Compliance, Mr. Bowden.[227]

My recent experience with the Commission has confirmed the complexity and adaptability of the market ... a complexity and rate of change that can be fascinating, exhilarating, challenging, or frustrating ... but that can also cause us to forget our fundamentals and to lose the forest for the trees. We can get lost in the many regulatory agencies, laws, rules, and regulations. Am I dealing with the SEC, the Fed, the OCC, the CFTC, the FCA, or others? How can I take advantage of SEC Rule 506(c) without losing my exemption under CFTC Rule 4.13(a)(3)? . . . Even though the complex and changing rulebooks, regulations, algorithms, and fiber-optic cables (going to lasers now) shaping the market today are interesting and important, they're not what I want to address today. I want to go old school. I want to go back to basics. I want to talk about *people*. More specifically, I want to talk about people handling other peoples' money. For, at its most simple, isn't that what the financial services industry is all about? ... *people* handling other peoples' money?

Good People Trying to Do the Right Thing. . . by their clients, colleagues, owners, and ... even, regulators.. . .. It's not an easy task. Indeed, it's a very difficult task given some of the complexities and innovations we've touched on already. Yet, when OCIE staff engages with business leaders, lawyers, and compliance officers and identifies deficiencies or weaknesses in controls ... whether we're addressing issues generally across the entire market or those specific to a firm ... most make a good-faith attempt to remediate on their own.

We in OCIE [Office of Compliance Inspections and Examinations] therefore spend a lot of our time and resources trying to help the good people get it right. We are transparent. . . we've published our examination priorities to let you know the areas we'll be examining so you have the opportunity to self-evaluate and remediate. We have also been publishing Risk Alerts to flag areas where we have found noncompliance across firms, again giving you the opportunity to look into these issues preemptively in your organizations. We are hosting increasing numbers of outreach and "in-reach" events, where we share with you what we are seeing and what the law requires. . . the goal is not to play "gotcha!" We in OCIE are much more interested in seeing the many good people in the industry self-correct and succeed.

We can dispense with the first vice quickly. . . the methods used by some people to separate their brethren from their money are relatively unchanged. They lie, cheat, and steal. . . You may have seen that the Enforcement Division recently charged a Los Angeles-based attorney as the

---

226 Conflicts, Conflicts Everywhere, Julie Riewe, Co-Chief, Asset Management Unit, Division of Enforcement, IA Watch 17th Annual IA Compliance Conference: The Full 360 View, Washington, D.C. (Feb. 26, 2015), *available at* https://www.sec.gov/news/speech/conflicts-everywhere-full-360-view.html (last visited June 4, 2017).

227 People Handling Other Peoples' Money, Andrew J. Bowden, Director, Office of Compliance Inspections and Examinations, Investment Adviser Association Compliance Conference, Arlington, Va. (Mar. 6, 2014), *available at* https://www.sec.gov/news/speech/2014-spch030614ab (last modified Mar 24, 2014) (last visited June 4, 2017) (footnotes omitted).

alleged architect of a fraudulent scheme that raised money through a boiler room operation. It is alleged that high-pressure salespeople persuaded more than 60 investors nationwide to invest a total of $1.8 million in a movie first titled *Marcel* and later changed to *The Smuggler*. Investors were allegedly falsely told that actors ranging from Donald Sutherland to Jean-Claude Van Damme would appear in the movie when in fact they were never even approached. Instead of using investor funds for movie production expenses as promised, the defendants are charged with spending most of the money on themselves. The SEC press release states that the investor funds that remain aren't enough to produce a public service announcement let alone a full-length motion picture capable of securing the theatrical release promised to investors.

While I believe that liars, cheaters, and thieves are a very small minority of the industry, the SEC spends a significant amount of time and resources trying to detect their bad behavior and to prevent them from harming investors. You must also. From the moment you hire your second employee, or your 20th, or your 2,000th, the odds increase that you have employed someone who will resort to bad acts to separate other people from their money.

My first boss in the industry ran our legal and compliance department, which oversaw well over one thousand employees. In a memorable, but earthy, metaphor, he used to declare, "We have it good. We get to work with smart people in an interesting business. We help our clients achieve their financial goals. Our employees make a good living and provide for their families. This is a great company. We (*and here he was talking about the leadership of the firm, not just the compliance team*) are like lifeguards at the community pool, watching the swimmers' heads bob in the water. Most are having fun, following the rules of the pool, but you just know that someone may be out there, peeing in the pool, ruining it for everyone. Our job is to find that person."

Reckless People. OCIE also sees people who behave recklessly. They forget that they are fiduciaries and caretakers of their clients' money. For example, you may have seen that the Division of Enforcement recently brought a settled case[1] against a firm that adopted practices that gave the firm's 60 employees total control of clients' funds without implementing any appropriate safeguards. The firm enabled its employees to access and to transfer client funds through the use of (1) pre-signed letters of authorization; (2) cutting and pasting client signatures on LOAs; (3) and retaining logins and passwords to access their clients' outside accounts.

. . . But, importantly, the record is devoid of any facts indicating that the firm had adopted reasonable controls to ensure that disbursements of client funds by pre-signed LOAs, or cut-and-pasted signatures, or remote log-in were actually authorized by the client. It was an accident waiting to happen.

It could have been a problem employee with a drug, alcohol, or gambling problem who was tempted to misappropriate client funds ... or it could have been a client who tried to stick it to the firm and falsely claim that a withdrawal or series of withdrawals were unauthorized and there would be no record of the authorization. Someday, somehow, the absence of controls was going to bite the firm. As it turned out, the inadequacy of the firm's controls was exposed when a hacker gained control of a client's email account and, posing as the client, emailed instructions for the firm to wire almost $300,000 to a foreign bank account designated by the hacker. The firm acted upon the hijacked e-mail without question or further inquiry, and the client's money was gone.

Identifying people behaving recklessly within your firms can be difficult. Financial services is fiercely competitive. You are trying to keep up. Resources are finite. And, depending on the size of your firm, people can sometimes roam out of your sight and over the hill before you realize they are no longer with the herd.

I therefore implore you to stay current on what's happening in your business and to continually probe and test to evaluate whether you have people within your organization who are rushing headlong into, or up to their necks in, activities in the absence of the kinds of controls that a fiduciary should have in place. It could be new products ... or new lines of business ... or rapid growth ... or acquisitions ... or contractions and retrenchment ... or bending over backwards to serve your clients. It is critical to identify and remediate any instances within your organization where people are handling other peoples' money in the absence of reasonable controls.

When OCIE staff and I look out into the industry today, one of the areas where we are beginning to conduct exams to assess the existence and effectiveness of controls is in the alternative mutual fund space. Increasingly, advisers to mutual funds are establishing and marketing funds that are labeled "alternative" and hold non-traditional investments or engage in complex trading strategies.... There is certainly nothing wrong with alternative investments or alternative investment strategies, per se. Many investors have benefitted from their inclusion in portfolios.

But ... and it's a big but ... the use of hard to value and/or illiquid securities in an open end mutual fund, which requires daily valuation and offers daily liquidity, is fraught with risk. This is particularly true for advisers that may have experience with alternatives in private funds but are new to implementing them within the strictures of the Investment Company Act ... and for advisers that may have experience with the Investment Company Act but are new to alternatives. In short, daily valuation and daily liquidity require a tremendous amount of control and discipline.... If any of you have launched, or are considering launching, a mutual fund that uses alternative investments or strategies, I implore you to evaluate the reasonableness and effectiveness of your controls.

Conflicts of Interest... [are] the vice that is most difficult for the people within an organization to detect because they are often impaired by it. OCIE staff and I see instances where otherwise honest, hard-working people are blind to the fact that they are putting their interests ahead of their clients. We can come into such situations independently and unaffected by the same pressures and incentives as the adviser and see immediately that client money is being handled primarily for the benefit of the adviser, not the client... but the adviser will cling insistently to the notion that its heart and actions are pure.

There's an apocryphal story about Abraham Lincoln and conflicts of interest during the Lincoln-Douglas debates... [They] engaged in a series of debates in 1858 on the issue of slavery. They alternated who went first. The leader was scheduled to speak for 60 minutes, and then the other would take the stage. One time, Douglas led off and expounded at length on "the great good of slavery." When it was Lincoln's turn to speak, Lincoln sauntered to the stage and simply held two gold coins in front of his eyes. He said, "You know, it's sometimes difficult for a man to see clearly with these in front of his eyes."...If gold was sufficient to blind peoples' vision to the horrors and injustice of human bondage, then it will certainly suffice to cloud peoples' vision when it comes to what investment to buy ... or where to buy it ... or how much to pay ... or who, among several clients, gets a piece.

Conflicts are also interesting and insidious, because we see them at an individual, firm, and industry level. One person, a close group of people, or seemingly everyone in the entire system, can incrementally, over time, through the accretion of justifications, customs, and excuses, convince themselves that they are entitled to money and opportunities that fairly belong to their clients.

Take a conflict at an individual level. In 2012, the Commission charged the founder, majority owner, and CIO of a Los Angeles-based adviser (that at its peak managed more than $10 BB) with allegedly unfairly allocating options trades... over a period of more than two years, the principal allocated almost 2,500 option trades more than an hour after their execution, enabling him to routinely cherry pick winning trades and allocate them to favored accounts (including his own). Even though the firm's policy manual required employees "to adhere to the highest standards with respect to any potential conflicts of interest with client accounts," here was not just a potential conflict, but an actual conflict ("Who gets these profitable trades?") that is alleged to have been consistently resolved in favor of the principal over a 27-month period at the expense of his clients.

OCIE also sees conflicts that appear to ensnare an entire firm's way of doing business. In 2012, the Commission settled charges against a Portland, Oregon-based firm that was receiving compensation for placing its clients in certain mutual funds. The firm, which managed nearly $2 BB (not insignificant), offered turn-key asset management services and back-office custodial support to about 60 advisers. The firm also created and offered proprietary asset allocation models to its advisor clients. The models used a variety of mutual funds, . . . From time to time, the adviser would change weightings, as well as the funds used, in the models. If the participating advisors acquiesced, then the changes were made across all of the advisor's client accounts.. . Incentives and conflicts and the human mind are powerful things. Indeed, individual and firm-level conflicts can sometimes snowball into "groupthink," or industry-wide conflicts.

I could go on ... but suffice it to say the move into fee-based wrap accounts is a widespread practice. A lot of people have jumped into the pool. We fear that the rationalization that "everyone is doing it" may be adversely affecting peoples' thinking about how some of these arrangements are in the best interest of their clients. If you didn't see it, the Commission published recently a good investor bulletin on the adverse impact of fees on investor returns over time. The stakes for investors (and advisers), and the risk that the gold coins are clouding their vision, is high.

Conclusion. . . . I hope you'll have the opportunity to examine the market and your business through the window of the many laws, rules, and regulations with which you must comply ... and the window of the technological changes sweeping through the industry and your firms that you must navigate. But I also hope you will get back to basics and spend some time thinking about the people who work in the industry and in your firms. Most of them are good people, trying to do the right thing by their clients, colleagues, and owners.

But you will occasionally cross paths with someone who is simply trying to separate other people from their money through falsehoods or misappropriation ... or who is handling other people's money recklessly and in the absence of a true fiduciary's reasonable controls ... or whose incentives and thought process has left him (or them ... and sometimes a whole bunch of them) conflicted and behaving in ways that put their selfish interests ahead of those they agreed to serve.

When attempting to identify and address these people, particularly people who are conflicted, please, on behalf of your clients, colleagues, and owners, think and act independently, rigorously, and objectively ... constantly asking, "How is this product, or account, or course of conduct, in the best interest of our clients, who have given us their money, and whose interests we have agreed to put ahead of our own?" And if and when you can't get a square answer to that question, that you can easily understand and explain to others, you've done it! You've identified who's peeing in the pool. Thank you, and have a great conference!

Similarly, on February 7, 2017, the Office of Compliance Inspections and Examinations (OCIE) of the Securities and Exchange Commission published a Risk Alert listing of the five compliance topics most frequently identified in deficiency letters that were sent to SEC registered investment advisers ("Advisers") during the past two years. Within each of these topics, a few examples of typical deficiencies were discussed to highlight the risks and issues that examiners commonly identified.[228]

The five compliance topics addressed in this Risk Alert are deficiencies or weaknesses involving: Rule 206(4)-7 (the Compliance Rule) under the Investment Advisers Act of 1940 (the Advisers Act); (ii) required regulatory filings; (iii) Rule 206(4)-2 under the Advisers Act (the Custody Rule); (iv) Rule 204A-1 under the Advisers Act (the Code of Ethics Rule); and (v) Rule 204-2 under the Advisers Act (the Books and Records Rule). The Staff emphasized that advisers

---

228 Office of Compliance Inspections and Examinations , U.S. Sec & Exch. Comm'n, The Five Most Frequent Compliance Topics Identified in Examinations of Investment Advisers, Feb. 7, 2017, available at https://www.sec.gov/ocie/Article/risk-alert-5-most-frequent-ia-compliance-topics.pdf (last visited May 9, 2017).

"should review their compliance programs and practices in light of the topics noted in this Risk Alert."

Although the list of deficiencies and weaknesses was based on examinations of SECregistered investment advisers, these findings should be considered as regulatory guidance by "exempt reporting advisers" as well. In particular, these findings should be considered by those whose business is anticipated to grow beyond the scope of the exemption on which they are relying; for example, the failure to adopt and maintain a Code of Ethics (an obligation applicable to all investment advisers, whether or not registered), the failure to adopt compliance manuals that are reasonably tailored to the Adviser's business practices, the failure of Advisers to follow their compliance manual policies and procedures, and the failure of Advisers to maintain accurate books and records with regard to their investment adviser business, including typical accounting and other business records. . . .

C. SEC Examinations

The SEC is authorized to conduct examinations of broker-dealers, investment companies, and investment advisers.[229] The SEC conducts examinations through its Office of Compliance Inspections and Examinations (OCIE) and its regional offices. "Staff examinations are designed to: (1) improve compliance; (2) prevent fraud; (3) monitor risk; and (4) inform regulatory policy."[230] OCIE generally sets out some of its examination priorities for each year.[231]

In the context of investment advisers:

> OCIE generally conducts three types of examinations: (1) examinations of higher-risk investment advisers; (2) cause examinations resulting from tips, complaints and referrals; and (3) special purpose reviews such as risk-targeted examination sweeps and risk assessment reviews. Risk-targeted examination sweeps are generally limited in scope and focus on specific areas of concern within the financial services industry and cover a broad sample of regulated entities regarding those areas. Risk assessment reviews are limited scope examinations of an investment adviser's general business activities and a targeted set of the adviser's books and records that help OCIE better assess the risk profile of an investment adviser.[232]

---

229 15 U.S.C. § 78q(b) (2012) (broker-dealers); 15 U.S.C. § 80a-30(b) (2012) (investment companies); 15 U.S.C. § 80b-4(b)(6) (2012) (investment advisers); Chapter 11 (investigations, examinations).

230 U.S. Sec. & Exch. Comm'n, Study on Enhancing Investment Adviser Examinations 5 (Jan. 2011), *available at* https://www.sec.gov/news/studies/2011/914studyfinal.pdf (last visited June 5, 2017).

231 Sec. & Exch. Comm'n, Ofc. of Compliance, Inspections & Examinations, Examination Priorities for 2017, *available at* https://www.sec.gov/about/offices/ocie/national-examination-program-priorities-2017.pdf (last visited June 5, 2017).

232 *Id.* (footnote omitted).

An investment adviser examination begins with an initial request for information. The OCIE staff has set out an overview of the core set of information requested at this stage.[233]

Most SEC staff reactions result in non-public deficiency letters describing the deficiency and asking for a response. If there are serious problems, the staff will refer the matter for enforcement.

In determining whether to make an enforcement referral, the staff considers factors including:

Does it appear that fraud has occurred?
Were investors harmed?

If the conduct does not include fraud, is it serious (i.e., ongoing, repetitive, systemic or severe)?

Did the firm apprise us of the conduct and take meaningful corrective action?

Is the conduct of a type/degree that is most appropriate for the SEC to handle, rather than another regulator?
Is the activity in a particular area that the SEC wants to emphasize (i.e. emerging types of wrongdoing)?

Did the actor profit from the conduct?
Did the actor appear to act intentionally?

Is the conduct recidivist in nature?
Were the firm's supervisory procedures inadequate?[234]

D. The Investment Company Institute

The Investment Company Institute (ICI) is the association for the U.S. investment companies. Its members include SEC-registered investment companies, including mutual funds (i.e., open-end investment companies, closed-end investment companies, and exchange-traded funds); a

---

233 U.S. Sec. & Exch. Comm'n, Ofc. Of Compliance Inspections & Examinations, *Investment Adviser Examinations: Core Initial Request for Information,* Nov. 2008, *available at* https://www.sec.gov/info/cco/requestlistcore1108.htm (last visited June 5, 2017).

234 Speech by SEC Staff: Frequently-Asked Questions About SEC Examinations (Lori Richards, Director, Ofc. Of Compliance Inspections & Examinations, SIFMA Compliance and Legal Division January General Luncheon Meeting, New York, N.Y., Jan. 17, 2008), *available at* https://www.sec.gov/news/speech/2008/spch011708lar.htm (last visited June 5, 2017).

member investment company's investment adviser, principal underwriter, and directors are considered members.[235]

The ICI is not actually a self-regulatory organization and is not supervised as such by the SEC.[236] Nonetheless, it has "long represented the sector in negotiating its own regulation."[237]

II. THE FINANCIAL INDUSTRY REGULATORY AUTHORITY (FINRA)[238]

FINRA is a self-regulatory organization (SRO). It is similar to many such organizations, for example, the American Bar Association. Members of these organizations have an interest in regulating the behavior of their members for a number of reasons. First, they wish to be able to depend on the other members when they deal with each other. Second, they wish to create and maintain a good reputation for their professions and their services. They know that one or a few "rotten apples" can spoil the entire crop. Finally, some of these organizations, such as FINRA, are vested with regulatory powers over their membership, which increases and assures the value of such a membership.

FINRA is a self-regulatory organization of broker-dealers. Broker-dealers deal with each other, so they have a vested interest in ensuring fair competition among themselves, as well as in protecting their interests from non-broker competitors. After the 1929 crash, Congress recognized the authority of broker-dealers' to self-regulate. However, Congress subjected the National Association of Securities Dealers (NASD), now named FINRA, which includes the New York Stock Exchange, to supervision by the Securities and Exchange Commission. Beginning in the 1960s, broker-dealers became the focus of regulatory actions regarding the failure to supervise their sales personnel. In the 1960s and 1970s, the requirement for broker-dealers to provide clients with "suitable" advice and the requirement of "know-your-customer"[239] became increasingly prominent and powerful. In addition, the SEC began requiring that brokerage companies establish committees consisting of independent directors. After 2008 and especially in 2010–16,

---

235 Inv. Co. Inst., *Criteria for Membership, available at* https://ici.org/about_ici/membership/criteria (last visited Apr. 11, 2017).

236 Tamar Frankel & Lawrence A. Cunningham, *The Mysterious Ways of Mutual Funds: Market Timing*, 25 Ann. Rev. Banking & Fin. L. 235, 282 (2006).

237 *Id.* at 283.

238 Fin. Indus. Regulatory Auth., *About FINRA, available at* http://www.finra.org/about (last visited Feb. 5, 2015).

239 Rule 2090, *available at* http://finra.complinet.com/en/display/display_main.html?rbid=2403&element_id=9858 (last visited Apr. 4, 2017) (requiring brokers to "use reasonable diligence, in regard to the opening and maintenance of every account, to know (and retain) the essential facts concerning every customer and concerning the authority of each person acting on behalf of such customer"); Rule 2090, Supplementary Material, .01, *available at* http://finra.complinet.com/en/display/display_main.html?rbid=2403&element_id=9858 (last visited Apr. 4, 2017) (defining "essential facts" as "those required to (a) effectively service the customer's account, (b) act in accordance with any special handling instructions for the account, (c) understand the authority of each person acting on behalf of the customer, and (d) comply with applicable laws, regulations, and rules").

the broker-dealers' fiduciary duties concerning their advice to their customers has been the subject of a significant argument among regulators and financial brokers, dealers and, to a lesser extent, advisers. At the beginning of 2016 the Labor Department has passed a rule that imposed a limited fiduciary duty on brokers.[240] However, the issue is still subject to judicial decisions.

III. STATE SECURITIES REGULATORS[241]

States, rather than the SEC, regulate investment advisers that do not manage more than $100 million of clients' assets. Insurance companies are regulated by the States, except where federal law is expressly imposed on them.[242] Federal regulation may also be imposed on insurers that create and offer hybrid securities. Such offerings are functionally part insurance—e.g., covering the risk of premature dying, as with life insurance, or longevity, as with annuities—and part mutual funds. These hybrids, called variable annuities and variable life insurance, shift the investment risks of the policies from the insurance company to the insured.[243]

IV. THE COMMODITY FUTURES TRADING COMMISSION (CFTC)[244]

This Commission was established as the regulator of commodities trading, hence its name. However, when commodities or commodity indices began being used as a basis for securities, the CFTC and the SEC began to share regulation. For example, parties may wish to buy not the commodities themselves, but securities whose performance is tied to the price of an underlying commodity or a related index. These new financial products may have the earmarks of a security. In 2015, the SEC and the CFTC are coordinating their regulation of these hybrid financial products.[245]

---

240 Dodd-Frank Wall Street Reform and Consumer Protection Act, Pub. L. No. 111-203, § 913(g), 124 Stat. 1376, 1828-19 (authorizing SEC to establish fiduciary duty for brokers and dealers when providing personalized investment advice about securities to retail customers); U.S. SEC. & EXCH. COMM'N., STUDY ON INVESTMENT ADVISERS AND BROKER-DEALERS (2011), *available at* http://www.sec.gov/news/studies/2011/913studyfinal.pdf (last visited Feb. 5, 2016) (SEC staff study recommending that SEC adopt fiduciary standard); Dept. of Labor, Definition of the Term "Fiduciary," 81 Fed. Reg. 20,946 (Apr. 8, 2016), *to be codified at* 29 C.F.R. § 2510.3-2 (Labor Department rule).

241 North American Securities Administrators Ass'n, *Our Role, available at* http://www.nasaa.org/about-us/our-role/ (last visited Feb. 5, 2015).

242 15 U.S.C. § 1011 (2012).

243 1 TAMAR FRANKEL & ANN TAYLOR SCHWING, THE REGULATION OF MONEY MANAGERS: MUTUAL FUNDS AND ADVISERS § 5.07[E]-[F] (2d ed. 2001 & Supp. 2015).

244 U.S. Commodity Futures Trading Comm'n, *About the CFTC, available at* http://www.cftc.gov//About/Mission Responsibilities/index.htm (last visited Feb. 5, 2016).

245 *See, e.g.,* U.S. Sec. & Exch. Comm'n, *Derivatives* (last modified May 4, 2015), *available at* http://www.sec.gov/spotlight/ dodd-frank/derivatives.shtml (last visited Feb. 10, 2016).

The Commission proposes rules and invites comments before making the rules final. For example, on May 3, 2017, the Commodity Futures Trading Commission approved proposed amendments to its rules describing the obligations of the chief compliance officer (CCO) for swap dealers (SD), major swap participants (MSP), and futures commission merchants (FCM) for publication in the Federal Register.1 The CFTC noted that it proposed the amendments to harmonize its CCO rules with similar Securities and Exchange Commission rules applicable to security-based swap dealers where it believed the differences would reduce regulatory burden for market participants while continuing to provide the protections that the rules were intended to provide.[2] Comments to the proposed rule are due on July 7, 2017.

V. THE FEDERAL RESERVE BOARD (FRB),[246] THE OFFICE OF THE COMPTROLLER OF THE CURRENCY (OCC),[247] AND THE FEDERAL DEPOSIT INSURANCE CORPORATION (FDIC)[248]

The Federal Reserve Board (FRB or Fed) regulates the banking system and consequently much of the financial system that relates to money. The Office of the Controller of the Currency (OCC) regulates federal banks. The Federal Deposit Insurance Corporation (FDIC) is a government insurance company that backs up bank deposits.

How does the New York Federal Reserve Bank supervise New York banks?

The New York Fed works diligently to execute its supervisory authority in a manner that is most effective in promoting the safety and soundness of the financial institutions it is charged with supervising. To accomplish this important task, the New York Fed employs and trains a large workforce of examiners and specialists and works with the Board of Governors, which sets supervisory policy, and other experts throughout the Federal Reserve System.[249]

---

246 Federal Reserve, *The Structure and Functions of the Federal Reserve System, available at* https://www.federalreserveeducation. org/about-the-fed/structure-and-functions (last visited Feb. 5. 2016). The Federal Reserve Board "guide[s] monetary policy action" and "exercises broad supervisory control over the financial services industry" including "set[ting] reserve requirements for depository institutions." Twelve Reserve Banks act as the bank for the U.S. government and supervise commercial banks. All national commercial banks and some state-chartered commercial banks are members of the Federal Reserve System, but nonmember depository institutions are also subject to Federal Reserve regulations.

247 Ofc. of the Comptroller of the Currency, *About the OCC, available at* http://www.occ.treas.gov/about/what-we-do/ mission/index-about.html (last visited Feb. 5, 2016). The OCC regulates and supervises national banks and federal savings associations. It "ensure[s] that national banks and federal savings associations operate in a safe and sound manner" and issues rules and regulations regarding investments and lending.

248 Fed. Deposit Insurance Corp., *Who Is the FDIC?, available at* https://www.fdic.gov/about/learn/symbol/ (last visited Feb. 5, 2016). The FDIC insures deposits in banks and thrift institutions. It also examines and supervises more than half of U.S. banking institutions for safety and soundness. It is the primary federal regulator for state-chartered banks that do not join the Federal Reserve System, and the backup supervisor for other banks and thrifts.

249 Excerpted from Fed. Res. Bank of N.Y., *Statement Regarding New York Fed Supervision* (Sept. 26, 2014), *available at* http://www.newyorkfed.org/newsevents/statements/2014/0926_2014.html (last visited July 20, 2015) (Carmen Segarra's allegations). Edited.

Because the New York Fed supervises financial firms that are large and complex, it has established a dedicated examination team for each such firm. These teams review key aspects of a supervised firm's businesses and risk management functions to assess the adequacy of policies, processes and practices for identifying, measuring, monitoring, and controlling risk.

Activities identified as those likely to pose the highest risk to the firm, or areas where internal controls appear weak, receive the most scrutiny. Examiners employ the assistance of a range of experts from within the New York Fed and other areas of the Federal Reserve System with skills tailored to these specific activities, including attorneys when dealing with matters of law and regulation.

In addition to its own reviews, the New York Fed expects firms under its supervision to report issues at the firms, and firms are required by law to provide any and all information and documents that the New York Fed requests.

Examiners are required to be independent, critical and analytical thinkers, and be able to communicate confidently and accurately within their teams and when dealing with supervised institutions. Examiners do not work alone and teamwork is an important element in successful supervision. Examiners consult with and draw on the expertise, experience and seasoned supervisory judgment of their colleagues.

Examiners are encouraged to speak up and escalate any concerns they may have regarding the New York Fed or the institutions that [it] supervise[s]. The New York Fed provides multiple venues and layers of recourse to help ensure that its employees freely express their views and concerns, including the Ethics Office, employee hotline and internal ombudsman.

Because of the potential impact of our decisions and actions, we review our determinations very thoroughly to ensure that the facts are sound and the approach is reasonable and defensible. To vet ideas and conclusions, we have developed a multi-step "checks and balances" review process, in which the supervisory team and its lead supervisor play a key role. This process also involves officials from within the New York Fed, the Board of Governors and the Federal Reserve System. [The Fed reformed the prior system.]

The reform involved a restructuring to enhance our oversight of the largest financial firms and the industry more broadly, including:

• Establishing new team structures, with senior Bank officers acting as lead supervisors to increase engagement with senior leadership of the firms;

• Increasing examiner coverage of systemically important financial institutions, with dedicated supervisory teams ranging from 12 to 40 people, depending on the size of the firm, complemented by additional analytics and policy teams;

- Creating new, specialized roles to better understand firms' revenue drivers and business strategies and to evaluate the implications of these factors for a firm's risk profile; and,

- Emphasizing the importance of looking at trends, practices and risks across the financial industry, in addition to firm-specific activities. . . .

The reforms further provided a more effective structure for our supervisory organization that facilitates the sharing of insights, expertise, and data, as well as the robust exchange of diverse viewpoints. Working across teams and regularly rotating our people ensure examiner independence and provide opportunities for staff to gain experience, perspective and judgment over time.[250]

VI. THE FINANCIAL CRIMES ENFORCEMENT NETWORK (FINCEN)[251]

FinCEN is a bureau of the U.S. Department of the Treasury. The Director of FinCEN is appointed by the Secretary of the Treasury and reports to the Undersecretary for Terrorism and Financial Intelligence. FinCEN's mission is to safeguard the financial system from illicit use and combat money laundering and promote national security through the collection, analysis, and dissemination of financial intelligence and strategic use of financial authorities.

FinCEN carries out its mission by receiving and maintaining financial transactions data; analyzing and disseminating that data for law enforcement purposes; and building global cooperation with counterpart organizations in other countries and with international bodies.

FinCEN exercises regulatory functions mainly under the Currency and Financial Transactions Reporting Act of 1970, as amended by Title III of the USA PATRIOT Act of 2001 and other legislation, which legislative framework is commonly referred to as the "Bank Secrecy Act" (BSA). The BSA is the nation's first and most comprehensive Federal anti-money laundering and counter-terrorism financing (AML/CTF) statute. The BSA authorizes the Secretary of the Treasury to issue regulations requiring banks and other financial institutions to take a number of precautions against financial crime, including the establishment of AML programs and the filing of reports that have been determined to have a high degree of usefulness in criminal, tax, and regulatory investigations and proceedings, and certain intelligence and counter-terrorism

---

250 Excerpted from Fed. Res. Bank of N.Y., *Statement Regarding New York Fed Supervision* (Sept. 26, 2014), *available at* http://www.newyorkfed.org/newsevents/statements/2014/0926_2014.html (last visited Feb. 9, 2016) (Carmen Segarra's allegations). Edited.

251 Excerpted from Financial Crimes Enforcement Network, *What We Do, available at* https://www.fincen.gov/what-we-do (last visited Oct. 14, 2016). Edited.

matters. The Secretary of the Treasury has delegated to the Director of FinCEN the authority to implement, administer, and enforce compliance with the BSA and associated regulations.

Congress has required FinCEN to perform certain duties and responsibilities for the central collection, analysis, and dissemination of data reported under FinCEN's regulations and other related data in support of government and financial industry partners at the Federal, State, local, and international levels. To fulfill its responsibilities toward the detection and deterrence of financial crime, FinCEN:

- issues and interprets regulations authorized by statute;

- supports and enforces compliance with those regulations;

- supports, coordinates, and analyzes data regarding compliance examination functions delegated to other Federal regulators;

- manages the collection, processing, storage, dissemination, and protection of data filed under FinCEN's reporting requirements;

- maintains a government-wide access service to FinCEN's data, and networks users with overlapping interests;

- supports law enforcement investigations and prosecutions;

- synthesizes data to recommend internal and external allocation of resources to areas of greatest financial crime risk;

- shares information and coordinates with foreign financial intelligence unit (FIU) counterparts on AML/CFT efforts; and

- conducts analysis to support policymakers; law enforcement, regulatory, and intelligence agencies; FIUs; and the financial industry.[252]

FinCEN serves as the FIU for the United States and is one of more than 100 FIUs making up the Egmont Group, an international entity focused on information sharing and cooperation among FIUs. An FIU is a central, national agency responsible for receiving (and, as permitted, requesting), analyzing, and disseminating to the competent authorities disclosures of financial information: concerning suspected proceeds of crime and potential financing of terrorism or

---

252 FinCEN, *What We Do, available at* https://www.fincen.gov/what-we-do (last visited Oct. 16, 2016).

required by national legislation or regulation in order to combat money laundering and terrorism financing.

As one of the world's leading FIUs, FinCEN exchanges financial information with FIU counterparts around the world in support of U.S. and foreign financial crime investigations. The basic concept underlying FinCEN's core activities is "follow the money." The primary motive of criminals is financial gain, and they leave financial trails as they try to launder the proceeds of crimes or attempt to spend their ill-gotten profits. FinCEN partners with law enforcement at all levels of government and supports the nation's foreign policy and national security objectives.

Law enforcement agencies successfully use similar techniques, including searching information collected by FinCEN from the financial industry, to investigate and hold accountable a broad range of criminals, including perpetrators of fraud, tax evaders, and narcotics traffickers. More recently, the techniques used to follow money trails also have been applied to investigating and disrupting terrorist groups, which often depend on financial and other support networks.[253]

———————

VII. DEPARTMENT OF JUSTICE (DOJ)[254]

The Department of Justice (DOJ), under the Attorney General, generally has the exclusive power to conduct litigation in which the United States is a party.[255]

The DOJ, not the SEC, has the power to bring criminal actions under the securities laws. The Securities Exchange Act authorizes the SEC to transmit evidence of violations to the Attorney General, who has discretion to institute criminal proceedings.[256]

The DOJ has an effect on the regulation of financial service firms by virtue of its authority to bring criminal proceedings. As we shall see, it has established criteria for whether to

———————

253 Excerpted from Financial Crimes Enforcement Network, *What We Do, available at* https://www.fincen.gov/what-we-do (last visited Oct. 16, 2016). Edited.

254 U.S. Dep't of Justice, *About the DOJ, available at* https://www.justice.gov/about (last visited Jan. 6, 2017).

255 28 U.S.C. § 516.

256 15 U.S.C. §78u(d)(1).

bring a proceeding.[257] In addition, it has the power to set conditions for a Deferred Prosecution Agreement (DPA), under which the government agrees to defer prosecution.[258]

Problem

GS, a famous and powerful financial firm, sells certain securities, as underwriter and broker, and at the same time makes bets against the possible rising price of these securities. Does anything sound "wrong" in this practice? If so, which regulatory agency, if any, should look into this practice?

---

257 U.S. Dep't of Justice, U.S. Attorneys' Manual § 9-27.230, *available at* https://www.justice.gov/usam/usam-9-27000-principles-federal-prosecution#9-27.230 (renumbered and revised Nov. 2015) (last visited Jan. 5, 2017) (listing considerations for "determining whether prosecution should be declined because no substantial Federal interest would be served by prosecution"); *id.* § 9-28.300, *available at* https://www.justice.gov/usam/usam-9-28000-principles-federal-prosecution-business-organizations#9-28.300 (renumbered and revised Nov. 2015) (last visited Jan. 5, 2017) (listing additional factors to be considered in determining whether to charge corporations or negotiating plea or other agreements).

258 U.S. Dep't of Justice, *Assistant Attorney General Lanny A. Breuer Speaks at the New York City Bar Association* (Sept. 13, 2012), *available at* https://www.justice.gov/opa/speech/assistant-attorney-general-lanny-breuer-speaks-new-york-city-bar-association (last visited Jan. 6, 2017) (stating that in DPA government "agree[s] to defer prosecution against the corporation in exchange for an admission of wrongdoing, cooperation with the government's investigation, including against individual employees, payment of monetary penalties, and concrete steps to improve the company's behavior").

Chapter 5

COMPLIANCE CODES REQUIRED BY LAW

"The truth does not change according to our ability to stomach it."
Flannery O'Connor

"I do not want to get started if I am not in compliance."
Atish Kala

INTRODUCTION

The Sentencing Guidelines issued by the Justice Department (Guidelines) were the historical source of legally required compliance codes. After a court convicts a corporation of violating the law, the court may impose a requirement to establish and maintain a compliance code under various conditions, for example, by requiring the employment of in-house or outside monitors. Over time, other legal sources have evolved to require the imposition of compliance programs. This Chapter deals with three such additional legal sources and one voluntary movement that impose compliance codes within corporations.

Since the 1960s, broker-dealers attracted regulatory actions for failing to supervise their employees and their related organizations. In the 1960s and 1970s, the prohibition of offering clients unsuitable investments (the "suitability requirement") and the duty of "know-your-customer"[259] became more prominent. In addition to brokers' self-regulation, the Securities and Exchange Commission (SEC) began enforcing a requirement that brokers establish compliance committees comprised of independent directors.

---

[259] Rule 2090, *available at* http://finra.complinet.com/en/display/display_main.html?rbid=2403&element_id=9858 (last visited Apr. 4, 2017) (requiring brokers to "use reasonable diligence, in regard to the opening and maintenance of every account, to know (and retain) the essential facts concerning every customer and concerning the authority of each person acting on behalf of such customer"); Rule 2090, Supplementary Material, .01, *available at* http://finra.complinet.com/en/display/display_main.html?rbid=2403&element_id=9858 (last visited Apr. 4, 2017) (defining "essential facts" as "those required to (a) effectively service the customer's account, (b) act in accordance with any special handling instructions for the account, (c) understand the authority of each person acting on behalf of the customer, and (d) comply with applicable laws, regulations, and rules").

In the 1990s, the Justice Department amended the Guidelines to include mitigating factors for violators that had implemented compliance programs. Responding to changed financial conditions and to the Guidelines, the courts began to impose compliance governance duties on boards of directors. Later, the roles of legal and compliance professionals for investment advisers and mutual funds were formalized with the adoption of the compliance program rules (Rule 206-(4)-7) of the Investment Advisers Act of 1940 (Advisers Act)[260] and Rule 38a-1 of the Investment Company Act of 1940 (1940 Act),[261] (collectively, the Compliance Program Rules).[262]

However, a requirement that investment companies establish a code of ethics has never been imposed by legislation. This requirement was negotiated by the Securities and Exchange Commission and the Investment Company Institute (the Institute), the self-regulating professional organization of mutual fund investment advisers. The negotiations led to an agreement before Congress between the Institute and the SEC under which the Institute's members agreed to implement a code of ethics (Code).[263]

The Institute established a Code for the main purpose of preventing insider trading by those whose work required acquiring insider information. Similarly, the Investment Adviser Association (IAA) established a model code of ethics, prohibiting violations of general fiduciary duties (e.g., regulating conflict of interest and required disclosure). The law does not require membership in the IAA. However, all investment advisers are required by the IAA to follow fiduciary law standards, and the Supreme Court long ago held that investment advisers must comply with fiduciary rules.[264]

However, the environment does not stand still. Demands for more attentive self-regulation are rising. In the past, SEC compliance rules were quite general, requiring "policies and procedures" that are "reasonably designed" to comply with federal securities laws.[265] In 2015, however, the SEC and its different divisions required far more detailed internal rules. Experts advise institutions to review the SEC's "guidance updates," "sweep exams," statements in SEC rule releases,

---

260   17 C.F.R. § 275.206(4)-7 (2016).

261   17 C.F.R. § 270.38a-1 (2015).

262   17 C.F.R. § 270.38a-1 (2016). For a discussion of the requirements under the Rules and possible CCO liability, see Theodore J. Sawicki & Kerry K. Vatzakas, *Chief Compliance Officer Liability: Setting the Record Straight October 2008*, PRACTICAL COMPLIANCE & RISK MGMT. FOR THE SEC. INDUS., Nov.-Dec. 2008, at 25, *available at* (last visited Feb. 6, 2016) (discussing the Compliance Program Rules). *See also* LES ABROMOVITZ, THE INVESTMENT ADVISOR'S COMPLIANCE GUIDE (2012).

263   *Hearings on H.R. 9510 Before Subcomm. on Commerce and Finance of House Comm. on Interstate and Foreign Commerce*, 90th Cong., 1st Sess. 73 n.27 (1967); *see id.* at 80, 84-85 (SEC memorandum on recommended changes to provisions of S. 1659. Reflecting agreements reached between SEC staff and representatives of Investment Company Institute, both parties agreed "that the purposes intended by the proposed amendment would be more precisely delineated if the amendment prohibited insider trading in contravention of such rules as the Commission may adopt to define fraudulent, deceptive and manipulative practices and to prescribe means reasonably necessary to prevent such practices." ICI agreed that SEC would be authorized "to adopt rules with respect to minimum standards for codes of ethics governing insider trading by insiders of investment companies to prevent such practices, and the statute so specifies"); *Hearings on S. 1659 Before Sen. Comm. on Banking and Currency*, 90th Cong., 1st Sess. 41-42, 167 n.17 (1967).

264   SEC v. Capital Gains Research Bureau, 375 U.S. 180 (1963).

265   *See, e.g.*, 17 C.F.R. § 270.38a-1(a)(1) (2015); 17 C.F.R. § 275.206(4)-7(a) (2015).

as well as Commissioner and Staff speeches. The requirements and suggestions are far more specific and bulky. Most importantly, the SEC examinations reflect a focus on the details and on possible future violations, that is, on "red flags," or warning signals,[266] and "slippery slopes," or series of events that lead to worse events.[267]

The rise in the adoption of compliance programs imposed by regulation spurred consideration of various issues. These include: the role of compliance officers within an organization, their reporting process, and the structure of a more effective compliance plan. In the past, firms have organized their compliance function in different ways, reflecting the firms' size, maturity, complexity, resources, and culture. Compliance officers could report directly to the Board of Directors, Chief Executive Officer, Chief Finance Officer, Chief Operations Officer, senior management generally, or, perhaps most commonly, to the Chief Legal Officer. In some circumstances, compliance officers have had multiple direct and indirect reporting lines.

There cannot be a fixed formula for designing and implementing a successful compliance program. The years since 2000 have been an era of compliance experiments. As compliance functions evolve, so do their purposes, and relative measures of success, along with the institutional culture, power relationships, and duties and structure. While many commentators and members of the SEC offer guidance, the liabilities, duties, and sources of authority for compliance officers continue to be the subject of debates and adjustment. Therefore, the legal requirements of compliance programs continue to change and evolve as well.

This Chapter outlines select laws that impose a duty on certain financial institutions to establish a compliance code: the Investment Advisers Act of 1940, the Investment Company Act of 1940, anıd rules issued by FINRA (formerly the National Association of Securities Dealers). These laws contain detailed directives targeting particular problems that financial institutions are likely to experience. In these cases the absence of an effective compliance program is, by itself, a violation of the law. However, recognizing that institutions differ, these requirements leave flexibility in designing the programs and the codes.

Select Laws that Impose a Duty to Establish Codes of Ethics on Financial Institutions

We discuss the law that requires broker-dealers and investment advisers to establish compliance programs. The law applicable to broker-dealers is incorporated in the rules of FINRA (formerly the National Association of Securities Dealers), which is a self-regulatory organization (SRO) that regulates broker-dealers, subject to the supervision of the SEC. The laws governing

---

266 *Red Flag, available at* https://www.merriam-webster.com/dictionary/red%20flag (last visited Apr. 4, 2017) (defining "red flag:" as a "warning signal").

267 *Slippery Slope, available at* https://www.merriam-webster.com/dictionary/slippery%20slope (last visited Apr. 4, 2017) (defining "slippery slope" as "a course of action that seems to lead inevitably from one action or result to another with unintended consequences" and defining it "for English learners" as "a process or series of events that is hard to stop or control once it has begun and that usually leads to worse or more difficult things").

investment advisers are found in the Investment Advisers Act of 1940, and the Investment Company Act of 1940 (regulating investment companies and their servicers). These laws are enforced by the SEC. In addition, Rule G-44, proposed in 2014 by the Municipal Securities Regulation Board (MSRB) and approved by the SEC, requires municipal advisors to establish compliance policies and supervisory procedures.[268]

I. THE BROKER-DEALER COMPLIANCE REQUIREMENTS

A. Rule 3130 of FINRA Rules269

Rule 3130 requires each brokerage firm to designate and identify one or more principals as a chief compliance officer (CCO).[270] In addition, the chief executive officer (CEO) (or its equivalent) must certify annually that the firm has "processes to establish, maintain, review, test and modify written compliance policies and written supervisory procedures reasonably designed to achieve compliance with applicable FINRA rules, MSRB rules and federal securities laws and regulations" and that the CEO has met with the CCO in the last 12 months to discuss the processes.[271]

The certification should state that the requirements mentioned above are met. These include: (i) the processes were stated in a report reviewed by the CEO, CCO, and other officers if necessary, and submitted (or will be submitted) to the board of directors (or its equivalent) and the audit committee. In addition the certification must state that (ii) the CEO has consulted with the CCO, other officers as applicable, and other employees and parties, as appropriate, to attest to the statements.[272] Certification does not establish that the signatory has business-line

---

268 Mun. Sec. Rulemaking Bd., *SEC Approves MSRB Rule G-44 on Supervisory and Compliance Obligations of Municipal Advisors, and Amendments to MSRB Rules G-8 and G-9, MSRB Regulatory Notice 2014-19* (Oct. 24, 2014), *available at* http://www.msrb.org/~/media/Files/Regulatory-Notices/Announcements/2014-19.ashx (last visited Aug. 15, 2016).

269 Rule 3130, *available at* http://finra.complinet.com/en/display/display_main.html?rbid=2403&element_id=6286 (last visited Feb. 6, 2016).

270 Rule 3130(a), *available at* http://finra.complinet.com/en/display/display_main.html?rbid=2403&element_id=6286 (last visited Feb. 6, 2016).

271 Rule 3130(b), *available at* http://finra.complinet.com/en/display/display_main.html?rbid=2403&element_id=6286 (last visited Feb. 6, 2016).

272 Rule 3130(c), *available at* http://finra.complinet.com/en/display/display_main.html?rbid=2403&element_id=6286 (last visited Feb. 6, 2016).

responsibility,[273] and the CCO is not prohibited from holding other positions.[274] Therefore, the CCO in a brokerage firm may also engage in brokerage activities.

The CEO/CCO meetings should cover: (1) "the matters that are the subject of the certification;" (2) "the member's compliance efforts;" and (3) "significant compliance problems and plans for emerging business areas."[275] However, the CCO(s) has a unique role, namely, there should be "regular and significant interaction between senior management and the CCO(s)."[276] The heightened responsibilities of the CCO(s), do not, however, limit the responsibilities of other relevant employees.[277]

A compliance report should "document the member's processes for establishing, maintaining, reviewing, testing and modifying compliance policies" and "should include the manner and frequency in which the processes are administered, as well as the identification of officers and supervisors who have responsibility for such administration."[278]

Discussion topic

Which of the requirements above is more effective, and why?

Problem

Heron was employed as general counsel for Amkor Technology, Inc. (Amkor) at all times relevant to this appeal. Amkor is a semiconductor manufacturer that is publicly traded on the NASDAQ stock exchange. Between October 2003 and July 2004, the period of time at issue in this case, Heron served as Amkor's chief insider trading compliance officer, in addition to his duties as general counsel.

During that time period, Heron made numerous trades in Amkor securities. The dollar amounts of those trades represented a substantial investment for an individual earning

----

273 Rule 3130, Supplementary Material, para. .07, *available at* http://finra.complinet.com/en/display/display_main. html?rbid=2403&element_id=6286 (last visited Feb. 6, 2016).

274 Rule 3130, Supplementary Material, para. .08, *available at* http://finra.complinet.com/en/display/display_main. html?rbid=2403&element_id=6286 (last visited July 1, 2014).

275 Rule 3130 Supplementary Material, para. .04, *available at* http://finra.complinet.com/en/display/display_main. html?rbid=2403&element_id=6286 (last visited July 1, 2014).

276 Rule 3130 Supplementary Material, para. .05, *available at* http://finra.complinet.com/en/display/display_main. html?rbid=2403&element_id=6286 (last visited July 1, 2014).

277 Rule 3130 Supplementary Material, para. .06, *available at* http://finra.complinet.com/en/display/display_main. html?rbid=2403&element_id=6286 (last visited July 1, 2014).

278 Rule 3130, Supplementary Material, para. .10, *available at* http://finra.complinet.com/en/display/display_main. html?rbid=2403&element_id=6286 (last visited July 1, 2014).

approximately $140,000 per year. The trades included purchasing 4,000 shares of Amkor stock on October 15, 2003, for approximately $ 60,000. Two weeks later, Heron sold 75% of those shares for a profit of $115,000. Later, in April 2004, Heron sold 17,000 shares of Amkor stock and traded in bearish Amkor options; those trades resulted in benefits to Heron of approximately $141,000. From May 24 through June 23, 2004, Heron sold approximately 22,000 Amkor shares and again traded in bearish Amkor options, reaping a windfall to Heron of approximately $130,000. During the relevant time period, it appears that Heron made only one transaction involving Amkor securities that did not work to his financial benefit—a sale, on June 23, 2004, of twenty put options at a cost of $900.

Please note that the law regulating these activities is the Securities Exchange Act of 1934.[279] In addition, there may be other rules that apply to the transactions and the actors. In this context, however, we deal with the activities of the compliance officers and do not explore all other laws that might have applied to the transactions.

Discussion topic

May the general counsel trade so freely in the client corporation, as Heron did in this case?

Enforcement of compliance programs is on the rise. In March 2014, a broker-dealer firm agreed to pay $25 million to settle SEC and prosecutors' allegations that it failed to supervise its traders, who lied to customers about bond pricing. SEC officials viewed the guilty verdict against the guilty trader as strengthening their hand in pursuing Wall Street trading practices that cross the line from sharp salesmanship into outright deception. "Officials said the verdict confirmed their view that traders who choose to disclose their commissions, or the prices they paid for bond-deal slices they are selling, can't misrepresent those facts."[280]

However, some people argue that under the law, as it existed in 2015, the salespersons could avoid saying anything. That is because salespersons might become advisers if the buyers rely upon their sales talk and if the buyers are not sufficiently expert in securities' trading. A heated and continuing debate arose in 2014, and later, on the status of brokers as advisers.

Are brokers, or should they be, deemed advisers and fiduciaries of their clients with respect to their information and contacts with clients, rather than only agent fiduciaries, who merely offer certain securities to clients and execute the clients' transactions? What facts would you seek to identify in order to determine what your advice should be? What guidelines would you offer to brokers in this case? What principles should the law apply and have you follow?

---

279 17 C.F.R. § 240.10b-5 (2015).

280 Jean Eaglesham & Katy Burne, *SEC Is Probing Dealings by Banks and Companies in Loan Securities,* WALL ST. J., Mar. 24, 2014 (updated Mar. 24, 2014), *available at* http://online.wsj.com/news/articles/SB100014240527023039497045794597213 96289900?mod=WSJ_hp_LEFTTopStories&mg=reno64-wsj (login required).

Discussion topic

FINRA, a broker-dealer self-regulator, proposed a Comprehensive Automated Risk Data System (CARDS), to allow it to collect information from brokers.[281] CARDS would collect information from on a regular basis to help FINRA identify "red flags" of sales practice misconduct and other business misconduct.[282] FINRA could also use the information before on-site examinations, to possibly streamline such examinations.[283] Brokers would submit: (1) account information, (2) account activity information, and (3) security identification information, or information brokers are already required to maintain.[284]

Is this a good idea?

B. An Example of a Broker Dealer's Compliance Failure

Reading Focus

The *GunnAllen* case that follows[285] demonstrates the failure of a legally required broker-dealer compliance program. Before you begin to read the case, please choose your position as COO or CEO. Then, as you read the case, note the elements that constituted a violation of the compliance program and the elements that were necessary to achieve an effective compliance program. After you finish reading, please revisit the questions directly below.

Which laws did the defendants violate? What are the relevant facts that the SEC had to prove in this case? What precisely should any of the people involved have done or not done to avoid the violations? Please distinguish between the actions or inactions that constituted a violation of the law and those that demonstrated failure of the compliance program.

Do the facts signal the structural and/or personal relationships problems in the GunnAllen or Amkor organization?

In this case, would written detailed instructions have helped to avoid continued theft of customers' information?

GunnAllen was a registered broker dealer with its principal place of business in Florida. In April 2010, GunnAllen discontinued its operations, filed for bankruptcy, and submitted a

---

281 FINRA, Regulatory Notice 13-42, Comprehensive Automated Risk Data System (Dec. 2013), *available at* http://www.finra.org/sites/default/files/NoticeDocument/p413652.pdf (last visited Jan. 3, 2017).

282 *Id.* at 2.

283 *Id.* at 4.

284 *Id.* at 5.

285 *In re* Mark A. Ellis, Exchange Act Release No. 64,220, Adm. Proceeding File No. 3-14328 (Apr. 7, 2011).

Broker-Dealer Withdrawal Form with the SEC withdrawing its registration, effective on June 11, 2010. How did this come about?

Under Rule 30(a) of Regulation S-P,[286] every broker and dealer registered with the SEC must adopt written policies and procedures addressing administrative, technical, and physical safeguards for the protection of customer records and information. These policies and procedures should be reasonably designed to: (1) insure the security and confidentiality of customer records and information; (2) protect against any anticipated threats or hazards to the security or integrity of customer records and information; and (3) protect against unauthorized access to, or use of, customer records or information that could result in substantial harm or inconvenience to any customer.

> Between July 2005 and February 2009, GunnAllen's policies and procedures addressing the protection of customer information were contained in its Written Supervisory Procedures Manual (the "Manual"), including a short, general, and vague provision: *"Safeguarding Information."* It recited the Safeguard Rule 30(a) and provided examples of safeguards that "may be adopted" by GunnAllen without specifying what safeguards were actually adopted by the firm.

The provision failed to instruct GunnAllen's registered representatives on how to protect customer information to ensure compliance with the Safeguard Rule 30(a). The provision also contained no instructions for mitigating damage should an actual security breach transpire. The provision did repeatedly refer to a "Designated Principal" charged with (i) monitoring and annually testing the firm's safeguards and (ii) identifying reasonably foreseeable risks warranting improvements or adjustments to the safeguards. However, the "Designated Principal" was not identified by name or position and none was actually appointed.

[B]etween August 2006 and February 2008 laptop computers belonging to three GunnAllen registered representatives and the computer password credentials belonging to a fourth were misappropriated from the firm. Although no reports of misuse of customer information . . . subsequently arose, the thefts jeopardized the confidentiality and integrity of customer information maintained by the firm and placed some information at risk of unauthorized use that could have resulted in substantial harm or inconvenience to customers. The first laptop computer was stolen in August 2006 from a GunnAllen franchise office . . . The laptop contained contact records reflecting the names, addresses, and telephone numbers and, in many instances, spouses, dates of birth, and social security numbers of approximately 1,120 of the firm's customers. GunnAllen filed a report of the theft with local police and considered, but did not send, a letter to the affected customers notifying them of the theft. The firm did not take any further steps concerning the matter and the laptop was never recovered.

---

286 17 C.F.R. § 248.30 (2016).

In January 2007, a GunnAllen office in Arizona found "that a registered representative, who the firm had terminated almost a year earlier, had misappropriated another employee's computer password credentials, and was monitoring the employee's e-mails, including those exchanged with customers, from a remote location." Upon notification, GunnAllen's IT Department confirmed that the terminated representative had gained unauthorized access to the firm's e-mail system, and had been accessing the employee's e-mail for at least three months and, possibly, as long as a year.

"GunnAllen directed its employees . . . to change their computer password credentials and planned to implement an automated program, already under development, requiring employees on a firm-wide basis to periodically change their computer password credentials." No additional steps were taken; management declined to follow the IT department's recommendation to contact and notify the authorities about the thefts. In February 2008, laptop computers were stolen from two GunnAllen registered representatives in separate incidents. The representatives reported the thefts to GunnAllen and informed the firm's IT Department that the laptops did not hold any customer information. No other steps were taken and the laptop computers were never recovered.

GunnAllen's senior managers, including Mark Ellis, who was serving as the firm's CCO, and the firm's General Counsel, learned of the thefts, but no person or department directed or coordinated the firm's responses to the thefts, and no follow-up steps were taken. "After the theft of the first laptop computer, a dispute arose between GunnAllen's General Counsel and its IT Department, as to which department was responsible for sending a letter to the affected customers notifying them of the theft. A senior GunnAllen officer subsequently sent an e-mail to the General Counsel and Ellis stating that the letter should be sent to the affected customers, but it was never mailed."

From "July 2005 to February 2009, Ellis was responsible for implementing and maintaining policies and procedures ensuring the firm's compliance with Regulation S-P, including the Safeguard Rule mandating broker-dealers adopt written policies and procedures reasonably designed to protect customer records and information. Ellis was also responsible for reviewing the adequacy of GunnAllen's written supervisory procedures contained in the Manual, including those concerning the Safeguard Rule. Ellis, with the assistance of the firm's Assistant Chief Compliance Officer, directed and oversaw GunnAllen's annual reviews of its written supervisory procedures in 2007 and 2008.

Ellis was notified both by e-mail and orally in 2007 and 2008 regarding the laptop computer thefts and the misappropriated computer password credentials. The thefts and the company's limited response "revealed the inadequacy of the firm's policies and procedures for safeguarding customer information. . . Ellis failed to direct the firm to supplement the *Safeguarding*

Information provision in the Manual or to adopt additional written policies and procedures to protect customer information and ensure GunnAllen's compliance with the Safeguard Rule."[287]

FINRA Rule 4530[288] requires stockbrokers to disclose personal "red flags" on FINRA Form U4[289] or U4 amendments. FINRA then compiles the information and makes it available to the public through its online "BrokerCheck" portal. Such personal "red flags" include civil or judicial customer complaints, regulatory or criminal investigations, bankruptcy, and other relevant matters.[290] However, a 2014 *Wall Street Journal* investigation revealed that over 1,600 stockbrokers failed to disclose their personal bankruptcies and criminal backgrounds as required by the rule.[291]

Discussion topics

What does the FINRA Rule 4530 require? On whom is the rule imposed? Why, in your opinion, is it not always followed?

Where was the most obvious failure to prevent the later information theft? What could be done to prevent the first information theft? Is there a difference between the two events?

Is it fair to impose a duty to disclose error on people who erred once in a lifetime? Is it fair for a broker who "went straight" to bear the burden of those who did not?

What incentives would induce these people to disclose?

What correction by the brokers and the regulators do you suggest for this situation?

Brokers that facilitate transfer of money are subject to the laws regulating money laundering, as is demonstrated in the following *Oppenheimer & Co., Inc.* case:

Washington, D.C. – The Financial Crimes Enforcement Network (FinCEN), working closely with the U.S. Securities and Exchange Commission (SEC), assessed a $20 million civil money penalty [on January 27, 2015] against Oppenheimer & Co., Inc., for willfully violating the Bank Secrecy Act (BSA). Oppenheimer, a securities broker–dealer in New York, admitted that it failed to establish and implement an adequate anti–money laundering program, failed to conduct adequate

---

287 *In re* Mark A. Ellis, Exchange Act Release No. 64,220, Adm. Proceeding File No. 3-14328 (Apr. 7, 2011).

288 Rule 4530, *available at* http://finra.complinet.com/en/display/display_main.html?rbid=2403&element_id=9819 (last visited Dec. 6, 2016).

289 Form U4, *available at* https://www.finra.org/sites/default/files/form-u4.pdf (last visited Dec. 6, 2016).

290 Exchange Act Release No. 63,260, File No. SR-FINRA-2010-034 (Nov. 5, 2010).

291 Jean Eaglesham & Rob Barry, *Rule Breakers: Stockbrokers Fail to Disclose Red Flags to Investors*, WALL ST. J., Mar. 6, 2014, at A1, LEXIS, News Library, Wsj File.

due diligence on a foreign correspondent account, and failed to comply with requirements under Section 311 of the USA PATRIOT Act.

FinCEN and the New York Stock Exchange assessed a civil money penalty of $2.8 million against Oppenheimer in 2005 for similar violations. In 2013, the Financial Industry Regulatory Authority fined the firm $1.4 million for violations of securities laws and anti–money laundering failures.

"Broker–dealers face the same money laundering risks as other types of financial institutions," noted FinCEN Director Jennifer Shasky Calvery. "And by failing to comply with their regulatory responsibilities, our financial system became vulnerable to criminal abuse. This is the second time FinCEN has penalized Oppenheimer for similar violations. It is clear that their compliance culture must change."

Section 311 of the USA PATRIOT Act provides important protections to the U.S. financial system. Under that authority, the Director of FinCEN may determine that a foreign financial institution is of primary money laundering concern and may require domestic financial institutions to take certain special measures against that entity. These special measures can include prohibiting domestic financial institutions from opening or maintaining correspondent accounts for the named foreign financial institution. To be effective, U.S. financial institutions must conduct adequate due diligence and notify their foreign correspondent financial institutions of special measures imposed under Section 311, so that institutions of primary money laundering concern do not have improper and unfettered access to the U.S. financial system. By failing to notify its correspondents, Oppenheimer potentially placed the U.S. financial system at risk.

From 2008 through May 2014, Oppenheimer conducted business without establishing and implementing adequate policies, procedures, and internal controls reasonably designed to detect and report suspicious activity. FinCEN identified 16 customers who engaged in patterns of suspicious trading through branch offices in five states. All the suspicious activities involved penny stocks, which typically are low-priced, thinly traded, and highly speculative securities that can be vulnerable to manipulation by stock promoters and "pump–and–dump" schemes. Oppenheimer failed to report patterns of activity in which customers deposited large blocks of unregistered or illiquid penny stocks, moved large volumes of penny stocks among accounts with no apparent purpose, or immediately liquidated those securities and wired the proceeds out of the account.

In addition, Oppenheimer itself designated a customer foreign financial institution as "high risk" but failed to assess the institution's specific risks as a foreign financial institution or conduct adequate due diligence. Oppenheimer inadequately monitored the foreign financial institution's transactions and consequently did not detect or investigate numerous suspicious transactions conducted through the account, including prohibited third–party activity and illegal penny stock trading.[292]

Discussion topics

Why should brokers be responsible for the activities of their clients?
What is the difference between banks and brokers regarding the money transfer activity?
Are the cautious preventive measures that banks are using similar to those adopted by brokers?
Are the same measures appropriate?

II. INVESTMENT ADVISERS AND INVESTMENT COMPANIES: DUTY TO SUPERVISE AND PREVENT POSSIBLE INSIDER TRADING[293]

There are three main kinds of servicers that involve offering advice to investors. One advises individual investors, and is regulated under the Investment Advisers Act of 1940. Another manages mutual funds and other pools of investors' money. This adviser-manager usually offers all the management services to the investors' pool under a contract and is regulated under the Investment Company Act of 1940 in addition to the Advisers Act of 1940 (with some exceptions).

The third kind of servicer is a broker, who advises clients about trading in securities in connection with its main function of executing securities transactions. Brokers are conditionally exempt from the Advisers Act of 1940 if they are not paid for their advice. However, they are subject to a duty to offer clients only "suitable" investments. Throughout the years, brokers have expanded their advisory services in various ways. One of the unanswered and hotly debated issues since 2009—and still not fully resolved in 2016—is whether today's brokers, who offer various types of advice and receive payment in different ways, ought to be excluded from regulation under the Advisers Act of 1940[294] or be subject to the advisers' full-fledged fiduciary duties.[295] The additional, and more complex, issue is whether brokers should continue to be

---

292 Excerpted from FinCEN, *FinCEN Fines Oppenheimer & Co. Inc. $20 Million for Continued Anti–Money Laundering Shortfalls* (Jan. 27, 2015), *available at* https://www.fincen.gov/news/news-releases/fincen-fines-oppenheimer-co-inc-20-million-continued-anti-money-laundering (last visited Oct. 20, 2016).

293 Tamar Frankel, *Self-Regulation of Insider-Trading in Mutual Funds and Advisers*, 8 BROOK. J. CORP. FIN. & COM. L. 80 (2013).

294 15 U.S.C. § 80b-2(a)(11)(C) (2012).

295 Dodd-Frank Wall Street Reform and Consumer Protection Act, Pub. L. No. 111-203, § 913(g), 124 Stat. 1376, 1828-19 (authorizing SEC to establish fiduciary duty for brokers and dealers when providing personalized investment advice about securities to retail customers); U.S. SEC. & EXCH. COMM'N., Study on Investment Advisers and Broker-Dealer (2011), *available at* http://www.sec.gov/news/studies/2011/913studyfinal.pdf (last visited Feb. 5, 2016) (SEC staff study

exempt from the Employee Retirement Income Security Act of 1974 (ERISA). This is the Act that regulates services involved in managing pension funds. In 2016, after years of conflicts and arguments with organizations of broker-dealers, the Labor Department issued a rule that regulates brokers as fiduciaries.296 While a court examines the rule, brokerage firms have split, with some supporting the rule. Firms should follow developments in the implementation and interpretation of this rule. As of the beginning of 2018, the rule is not in effect. This is law in the making,

1. Advisers Act of 1940

Investment companies are required to establish Codes of Ethics (Codes) applicable to employees that have access to nonpublic, securities market information. Similar Codes proliferate in many other financial and business corporations, sometimes with poor and ineffective results.[297] In fact, employees and managers of many business corporations face similar temptation; therefore, these companies publish self-imposed Codes. Yet, as compared to mutual funds, business companies were less successful in preventing insider trading.[298]

Arguably, regulated mutual funds are less vulnerable to insider trading as compared to non-regulated funds and corporate insiders, because Codes have also influenced the mutual fund management companies' corporate culture and perhaps because of their stricter regulation and culture. These Codes have four important features:

(1) The Codes are required by law;

(2) The Codes contain general principles as well as self-enforcement mechanisms;

(3) Mutual funds, like other financial services, depend heavily on investors' trust; a hint of unfair treatment can create a "run" to cash out, thus decimating the fund's business;[299]

(4) The Investment Company Institute—the professional and trade organization of investment advisers that manage mutual funds—supported the legally required provisions of the Code. These factors may have assisted in reducing incentives for, and strengthened deterrents against, bad

---

recommending that SEC adopt fiduciary standard); *see, e.g.,* Arthur B. Laby, *Selling Advice and Creating Expectations: Why Brokers Should Be Fiduciaries,* 87 WASH. L. REV. 707 (2012).

296 Dept. of Labor, Definition of the Term "Fiduciary," 81 Fed. Reg. 20,946 (Apr. 8, 2016), *to be codified at* 29 C.F.R. § 2510.3-21.

297 DELOITTE, CODE OF ETHICS & PROFESSIONAL CONDUCT (2013), http://www2.deloitte.com/content/dam/Deloitte/us/Documents/about-deloitte/us_about_ei_coe2013_06042013.pdf (last visited Feb. 6, 2016) (accounting firm); U.S. BANK, CODE OF ETHICS AND BUSINESS CONDUCT (n.d.), https://usbank.com/hr/docs/policies/coeHandbook.pdf (last visited Feb. 6, 2016) (bank); WHIRLPOOL CORP., CODE OF ETHICS (2006), http://assets.whirlpoolcorp.com/wp-content/uploads/code_of_ethics.pdf (last visited Feb. 6, 2016) (manufacturing firm).

298 Result of LEXIS search performed Feb. 1, 2013 in "SEC Decisions, orders & releases." under Rule 17j-1 of the Investment Company Act of 1940, 17 C.F.R. § 270.17j-1 (2016).

299 15 U.S.C. § 80a-22(e) (2016) (general rule); 17 C.F.R. § 270.22e-1 to -3 (2016) (exceptions).

behavior in the mutual fund industry. Most importantly, arguably, the Codes establish a culture of compliance, and make good behavior habitual.

Investment advisers' services involve collecting information about present fund investments and evaluation of future investments. This service involves collection of nonpublic information. In addition, advisers' advice and trading may affect the market prices of the traded securities because the adviser may offer advice to many clients (including large ones) that, in the aggregate, can represent a large portion of the market for a particular security. Over the short term, such large transactions may create a "liquidity effect" that may induce a significant price movement in these securities.[300]

Yet, the laws against abusive use of non-public information may remain unenforced because outside regulators may not have the facilities to detect and prevent such violations. In 2012 the SEC alleged that a consulting firm and its manager obtained material nonpublic information and provided it to the clients, who were "portfolio managers and analysts as well as hedge fund and mutual fund advisors."[301] Therefore, financial service providers, whether advisers, brokers, or others, and their personnel, must control a strong and continuous temptation to use insider information for their own benefit. The use of such insider information is prohibited by Rule 17j-1, and Rule 38a-1 of the Investment Company Act of 1940.[302]

Compliance programs must include a duty to supervise, and therefore enforce, their dictates. Law and compliance rules may remain a dead letter, especially in large complex institutions, because outside regulators are unlikely to detect violations, or may not have the authority to prevent violations. Besides, legal sanctions may be a "blunt instrument" for thwarting violations. They can be usually exercised only after violations have been clearly found and proven, although they still have the gravity of damaging investigations. In contrast, authorities within the institution have other, perhaps more effective ways of preventing and punishing violations. In addition, these internal authorities are able to more easily prevent violations from occurring. Compliance should be sensitive to possible violations, and internal policing is the best means of achieving this.

Under Advisers Act Rule 206(4)-7, advisers are required to designate a chief compliance officer (CCO), but they are not required to hire an additional executive to serve in that capacity. Instead, they may assign the CCO role to an existing executive already in another role. For example, the general counsel may serve as a CCO as well, so long as that person has, in

---

300 *See* INVESTMENT COMPANY FACT BOOK 237 (55th ed. 2015), *available at* www.ici.org/pdf/2015_factbook.pdf (last visited Feb. 6, 2016) (at the end of 2014, mutual funds alone held over 31 trillion dollars in worldwide assets).

301 Complaint, SEC v. Kinnucan (S.D.N.Y. Feb. 17, 2012).

302 17 C.F.R. §§ 270.17j-1, .38a-1 (2016).

the language of the rule release, "sufficient seniority and authority within the organization to compel others to adhere to the compliance policies and procedures."[303]

There are investment companies and advisers that outsource their compliance function, including the CCO role. The SEC staff conducted examinations of a number of investment companies and advisers that have outsourced the CCO role and has noted issues raised by outsourced CCOs.[304]

U.S. Sec. & Exch. Comm'n, Questions Advisers Should Ask While Establishing or Reviewing Their Compliance Programs[305]

Introduction

Every investment adviser registered with the SEC is required to establish and maintain policies and procedures reasonably designed to prevent violations of the Investment Advisers Act of 1940 ("Advisers Act") and rules and regulations related to that Act as well as to detect and correct violations that occur.

The compliance policies and procedures should address the practices and risks present at each adviser. No one standard set of policies and procedures will address the requirements established by the Compliance Rule for all advisers because each adviser is different, has different business relationships and affiliations, and, therefore, has different conflicts of interest. Because the facts and circumstances (i.e., risks) that can give rise to violations of the Advisers Act are unique for each adviser, each adviser should identify its unique set of risks, both as the starting point for developing its compliance policies and procedures and as part of its periodic assessment of the continued effectiveness of these policies and procedures. This process of assessing factors that may cause violations of the Advisers Act is often called a "Risk Assessment," a "Gap Analysis," or the compilation of a "Risk Inventory."

Whatever an adviser may call its process for identifying its unique set of compliance risks, it is important that this analysis be conducted while initially establishing compliance policies and procedures and periodically thereafter to make sure that the policies and procedures are sufficiently comprehensive and robust to address all areas in which an adviser is at risk of violating the Advisers Act.

---

303 Compliance Programs of Investment Companies and Investment Advisers, Investment Advisers Act Release No. 2204, Investment Company Act Release No. 26299 (Dec. 17, 2003), 68 Fed. Reg. 74,714, 74,720 & n.74 (Dec. 24, 2003).

304 Ofc. of Compliance Inspections & Examinations, U.S. Sec. & Exch. Conn'n, *Examinations of Advisers and Funds That Outsource Their Chief Compliance Officers*, RISK ALERT, Nov. 9, 2015, *available at* https://www.sec.gov/ocie/announcement/ocie-2015-risk-alert-cco-outsourcing.pdf (last visited June 14, 2017); Chapter 12 (quoting Risk Alert).

305 U.S. Sec. & Exch. Comm'n, *Questions Advisers Should Ask While Establishing or Reviewing Their Compliance Programs* (May 2006) (modified Feb. 5, 2009), *available at* http://www.sec.gov/info/cco/adviser_compliance_questions.htm (last visited Apr. 21, 2009). Edited.

To assist advisers in conducting their risk assessments, SEC examination staff has compiled the following non-exclusive list of questions. These questions address a range of activities often present at advisers and point to possible risk areas. Based on each adviser's responses to these questions, the adviser can begin to develop a solid foundation for drafting policies and procedures that are designed to mitigate, manage, and control each risk area in ways that reflect the adviser's resources and need for assurance that violations can be prevented or, if violations occur, such violations will be detected promptly and corrected.

A. COMPLIANCE PROGRAMS

Does your compliance program comply with the requirements of the Compliance Rule?

Risk assessment

1. Have you conducted an effective "risk assessment" (i.e., evaluated how your activities, arrangements, affiliations, client base, service providers, conflicts of interest, and other business factors may cause violations of the Advisers Act or the appearance of impropriety)?

2. Did this risk assessment serve as the basis for developing your compliance policies and procedures?

3. Do you periodically re-evaluate your risk assessment to determine that new, evolving, or resurgent risks are adequately addressed?

Compliance policies and procedures

4. Are your compliance policies and procedures designed to manage and control the compliance risks identified in your risk assessment?

5. Does the implementation of your compliance policies and procedures reflect good principles of management and control?

Quality control and forensic testing

6. Do you regularly conduct transactional or quality control tests to determine whether your activities are consistent with your compliance policies and procedures?

7. Do you conduct periodic tests to detect instances in which your policies and procedures may be circumvented or where there may have been attempts to take advantage of the gaps in your policies and procedures?

8. Do these tests produce exception or other reports? Does knowledgeable staff review these reports, follow up on any exceptions, and resolve problematic items found in a timely manner?

Annual review

9. Have you planned or conducted an annual review of your compliance program? Does or did the review test the comprehensiveness of your compliance policies and procedures, taking into account any changes in your business or organization?

10. Were changes to existing policies and procedures made as a result of the annual review? Are any changes under consideration?

11. Were the findings and results of the annual review brought to the attention of senior management?

Qualities and role of the CCO and other compliance staff

12. Is your CCO knowledgeable regarding the Advisers Act, competent in regard to administering your compliance program, and empowered to enforce compliance with your policies and procedures?

13. Does your compliance staff (including operational staff with compliance responsibilities) approach compliance issues or possible compliance issues with professional skepticism and the incentive and security to ask the hard questions to get to the real issues involved in a matter?

14. When your staff, particularly compliance staff, is confronted with a set of facts and circumstances that is inconsistent with how things should be, does your compliance culture encourage them to follow-up on these matters, including bringing these matters to the attention of higher-level management and the CCO?

15. Does your compliance staff recommend necessary changes to resolve compliance issues? Do they follow-up as needed to ensure that necessary steps are being taken?

Conflicts of interest

16. Does your CCO have both compliance and organizational (operational) positions? Are the resulting conflicts of interest appropriately identified and managed?

Disclosures

17. Do disclosures regarding your compliance program fully and fairly inform clients of your practices?

Information handling

18. With respect to your annual compliance review, is documentation or other output generated to substantiate that you obtained and reviewed all related information in a timely, accurate, and complete manner as pursuant to Rule 204-2(a)(17)(ii)? How do you ensure that this information is preserved and protected from unplanned destruction, loss, alteration, compromise, or use?

B. PROVIDING INVESTMENT ADVICE

(Reference: Sections 204, 204A, 205 and 206, and the rules thereunder)
Information to make decisions

1. Do you maintain current and complete information regarding each client's financial and family circumstances, investment objectives and restrictions, and risk tolerance? Is this information used to provide clients suitable investment advice?

2. What processes, including supervisory procedures, do you have to ensure that the investment advice provided to each client is consistent with (a) the client's circumstances, expectations, restrictions, direction, and risk tolerance, and (b) the information provided to each client in brochures, marketing materials, contracts and otherwise?

3. Are your investment recommendations consistent with the disclosures made to clients? Do your investment recommendations carry a greater or lesser risk than disclosed to clients?

4. If you use an approved list of investments, how do you ensure that actual client investments are consistent with this list?

5. Do you recommend derivative instruments, such as swaps and inverse floaters? Is your client accounting system able to fully accommodate the sometimes unusual terms and conditions relating to these instruments?

Handling non-public information

6. Do you have effective processes to identify, contain, and prevent the unauthorized and/or inappropriate use of non-public information that comes into your possession?

7. If your employees come into possession of non-public information, is this information effectively identified, documented, and contained so that it is used appropriately?

8. If your employees come into possession of non-public information about an issuer as a result of a client's position in that issuer (e.g., a participation in a bank loan), is this information controlled effectively so that it is not used to unlawfully trade in other instruments of the issuer (e.g., shorting the issuer's equity if the issuer's financial condition deteriorates)?

Conflicts of interest

9. If you provide investment advice to clients regarding companies with which you have business relationships, do you have processes to prevent providing conflicted investment advice to clients and to ensure that clients receive full and fair disclosures regarding these conflicts?

10. Do you engage in "window dressing" (i.e., are decisions to effect trades in client or proprietary accounts undertaken in an attempt to manipulate the closing price of a security or to be able to present to clients a list of portfolio positions

that is consistent with their investment objectives but which is substantially different than the positions held in between reporting periods)?

11. How do you deal with conflicts in advice you give to clients (e.g., advising one client to sell a thinly traded security, while at the same time recommending that another client purchase the same security)?

12. Is portfolio turnover (frequency and amount of trading in clients' accounts) consistent with clients' investment objectives, or is it the result of decisions by employees to generate commission credits that you can use for your own purposes?

13. If you participate in soft dollar arrangements (or other arrangements dependent on the receipt of clients' business or use of clients' assets), are the sources and types of information or products and services obtained or used consistent with disclosures made to clients and with your fiduciary relationship with clients?

14. How do you prevent cherry-picking of favorable trades on behalf of favored clients or proprietary accounts? Are changes in order allocations consistent with your fiduciary relationship with clients, code of ethics, and disclosures?

15. How do you prevent scalping of investment advice provided to clients (i.e., the illegal practice of recommending that clients purchase a security and secretly selling the same security in a personal or proprietary account contrary to the recommendation)?

16. Do you have any side letters or agreements with any participant in a pooled vehicle you advise or manage? Are the terms and conditions of these agreements consistent with your disclosures to clients and fiduciary relationship with clients and pooled vehicle participants?

17. Do you vote proxies consistent with your proxy voting policies and procedures, disclosures to clients, and status as a fiduciary?

Advisory fees

18. Are advisory fees, including any incentive compensation or other fees, calculated and charged in accordance with contractual arrangements and disclosures?

19. Do clients that pay performance fees meet the requirements established in Section 205?

20. If a client terminates its advisory relationship, are the clients reimbursed fees calculated and paid in advance in accordance with contractual terms and disclosures?

Disclosures

21. Are disclosures made to clients consistent with your actual practices? Are those disclosures reviewed regularly to determine whether they remain current?

22. If you made materials changes to your disclosures, have you conveyed such information to clients?

Information handling

23. How do you ensure that your compliance policies and procedures are adequate with respect to the investment advice you provide?

24. Is documentation or other output generated to substantiate that you obtained all information related to providing investment advice in a timely, accurate, and complete manner? Do you ensure that this information is preserved for the required period of time and protected from unplanned destruction, loss, alteration, compromise, or use?

C. BROKERAGE ARRANGEMENTS AND TRADE EXECUTIONS

(Reference: Section 206; Regulation SHO, and Regulation M under the Securities Exchange Act of 1934, Banking Regulation, Regulation T)

Seeking best execution

1. Do you have policies and procedures in place designed to seek best execution of clients' orders and that are consistent with client disclosures?

2. Do you periodically evaluate your arrangements with broker-dealers to determine that those broker-dealers continue to provide best execution of clients' orders? Are clients' orders consistently placed with broker-dealers that are likely to provide best execution?

3. Based on post-trade analyses of client order execution, are the full costs incurred by clients (market impact, opportunity, spreads, and commissions) consistent with your duty to seek best execution, disclosures regarding your practices in placing orders, and your status as a fiduciary?

Regulatory issues

4. Are trades placed in ways that are consistent with all marketplace regulations in the jurisdictions in which trading takes place?

5. Are short sale trades placed consistently with applicable regulations such as Regulation SHO and Regulation M? Are appropriate levels of initial and maintenance margin maintained as required by Regulation T?

Conflicts of interest

6. If you are also registered as a broker-dealer or futures commission merchant (FCM) or are affiliated with or have a proprietary relationship with a broker-dealer or FCM, are the terms and conditions of clients' orders placed through such entities consistent with your fiduciary relationship and disclosures made to clients?

7. If trades are placed on a principal basis, are these trades consistent with the requirements of Section 206-3?

8. If trades are placed on an agency cross basis, are these trades consistent with the requirements of Section 206(3) and Rule 206(3)-2 thereunder?

9. Are trade errors identified at the earliest possible time and resolved in a manner that is consistent with disclosures made to clients and your fiduciary relationship with clients?

10. Given your current policies and procedures, is there a high probability that clearly erroneous trades or trades with "intent to defraud" will be identified and prevented from being communicated to broker-dealers for execution?

Forensic test

11. Do you periodically compare brokerage commissions paid to executing broker-dealers with the value of products and services (i.e., research) you and clients have obtained from these broker-dealers? Are the outcomes consistent with your disclosures and status as a fiduciary?

Disclosures

12. Do you disclose material issues that may impact your decision to maintain your brokerage arrangements and place clients' orders? Are these disclosures consistent with your actual practices?

Information handling

13. With respect to brokerage arrangements and the placing of clients' orders (including each subsequent modification, addition, or cancellation of an order), is documentation or other output generated to substantiate that information was obtained and reviewed in a timely, accurate, and complete manner? How do you ensure that this information is preserved and protected from unplanned destruction, loss, alteration, compromise, or use?

D. ALLOCATING INVESTMENT OPPORTUNITIES AMONG CLIENTS

(Reference: Section 206)

Fairness among clients

1. Are allocations of limited investment opportunities (e.g., hot IPOs) dispersed among clients in ways that fairly reflect clients' investment objectives and

restrictions, disclosures made to clients, and your fiduciary relationship with clients?

2. Are allocations among clients of positions acquired in blocked or bunched trades consistent with disclosures and your fiduciary relationship with clients?

3. Are proprietary accounts' and access persons' participation in investment opportunities, including blocked or bunched trades, consistent with your code of ethics, and disclosures made to clients? Also, are any staff issued interpretive guidance, such as no-action letters, applicable?

4. When changes are made to the initial decisions regarding the allocation of trades among client, proprietary, and/or access persons' accounts, are these changes supported by fully documented and approved audit trails?

5. If the allocation of block orders among clients or proprietary accounts is determined at any time after an order is placed for execution, is the allocation, including the selection of accounts to participate in such trades, consistent with disclosures and your status as a fiduciary?

Forensic test

6. Do you periodically evaluate the extent to which each client actually participated in limited investment opportunities, taking into account your trade allocation policies, disclosures, and status as a fiduciary?

7. Over relevant periods of time, is the performance among client accounts consistent with what would be expected if investment opportunities were allocated fairly and equitably among all eligible clients?

Disclosures

8. Are disclosures regarding trade allocation policies and procedures, including possible exceptions to the use of these policies and procedures, consistent with your actual practices?

9. Do disclosures of trade allocation policies and procedures, including possible exceptions to the use of these policies and procedures, fully and fairly inform

clients of your practices and enable clients to give their informed consent to all material conflicts of interest that may arise?

Information handling

10. With respect to the allocation of investment decisions among clients, is documentation or other output generated to substantiate that you obtained and reviewed all related information in a timely, accurate, and complete manner? Do you ensure that this information is preserved for the required period of time and protected from unplanned destruction, loss, alteration, compromise, or use?

E. CODE OF ETHICS AND PERSONAL TRADING

(Reference: Rule 204A-1, Section 206)

Code provisions

1. Does your code of ethics encourage an honest, open, and ethical compliance culture/ethical environment?

2. Is your compliance culture/ethical environment consistent with the description in your code of ethics?

3. Do you use specific factors (e.g., the number of compliance issues that occur) to measure the effectiveness of the ethical environment?

4. Does your compliance culture handle conflicts of interest and compliance issues in ways that are consistent with your disclosures, given your fiduciary responsibilities?

5. Is periodic training provided to your staff that effectively provides information with respect to expectations regarding ethical conduct?

6. Is your process for designating "supervised persons" consistent with the definition of such persons in Rule 204A-1 as well as the organization of your firm?

7. Is your process for designating "access persons" consistent with the definition of such persons in Rule 204A-1 and encompass those people associated with your firm that have, or may have, knowledge or access to information regarding the advice provided to clients?

8. For all access persons, do you obtain written annual acknowledgement regarding their knowledge of your code of ethics?

9. Do the provisions of your code of ethics comply with the requirements described in Rule 204A-1 regarding pre-clearance and reporting of certain access persons' trades and access persons' transaction and holdings reports?

10. If your code of ethics is more restrictive than Rule 204A-1 regarding pre-clearance and transaction reporting do you ensure that access persons adhere to your code of ethics?

11. Is the information contained in periodic reports of trading and annual holdings reports used to effectively monitor personal trading activities of access persons?

12. Are violations of the code of ethics handled appropriately and consistently across all staff, including the imposition of fines or similar sanctions for repeated violations of code provisions?

13. Is the CCO, or another designated person, responsible for administering your code of ethics? If another designated person is responsible, does this individual report directly to the CCO or upper management of your firm, in general, and with respect to the code of ethics?

Trading by insiders

14. Are personal trades and holdings of access persons, including proprietary trades and holdings, consistent with your code of ethics, disclosures to clients, and your fiduciary relationship with clients?

Forensic tests

15. Is the performance of access persons' accounts and proprietary accounts consistent with the performance of client accounts (taking into account

differences in objectives, restrictions, and amount of risk taken)? Is it consistent with your code of ethics and other disclosures made to clients?

16. Are there strong information barriers between you and affiliates regarding advice given to clients? If not, is the performance of these affiliates' proprietary accounts consistent with the performance of client accounts (taking into account differences in objectives, restrictions and amount of risk taken)? Is it consistent your code of ethics and other disclosures made to clients?

Conflicts of interest

17. Are gifts and entertainment provided by actual or potential service providers and/or broker-dealers (whether or not currently used to execute client transactions) and accepted by your officers, directors, and employees consistent with the code of ethics and disclosures made to clients?

18. Are gifts and entertainment offered to third parties by your officers, directors and employees consistent with your fiduciary relationship with clients?

19. Are business arrangements with third parties that impact the services you provide to clients (e.g., the negotiation of loans from bank custodians you recommend for client use) consistent with disclosures and your fiduciary relationship with clients?

Registration status

20. In light of the amount of assets under management and the other types of advisory services you offer, are you appropriately registered with the SEC?

21. Are all advisory representatives that have direct client contact appropriately registered with the state(s) in which each representative conducts advisory business in accordance with applicable state law?

Information handling

22. With respect to the operation of your code of ethics, is documentation or other output generated to substantiate that you obtained all related information in a timely, accurate, and complete manner? Do you ensure that this information

is preserved for the required period of time and protected from unplanned destruction, loss, alteration, compromise, or use?

F. VALUATION OF CLIENTS' POSITIONS

(Reference: Section 206)

Accuracy of prices used

1. Do you perform adequate and on-going due diligence on the methodologies used by all entities, such as pricing services, that provide pricing information used to value clients' positions?

2. Do the prices used to value clients' positions consistently reflect the price(s) that would be paid or received in a transaction with a knowledgeable and willing counter party at the time the pricing was performed?

3. Are the prices used to value clients' holdings based on the appropriate quantities of each position (i.e., match the quantities of each position as reported by the client's custodian)?

4. Do other assets (e.g., cash, receivables, and prepaid items) and liabilities (e.g., payables) used in determining the gross and net value of clients' accounts consistently reflect the current value of these items at the time of the calculation?

5. If you manage a pooled investment vehicle and move positions into a "side pocket," is the value applied to those positions consistent with your pricing policies and procedures?

6. If an error is made when calculating the gross or net value of clients' positions or the net asset value ("NAV") of pooled accounts, is the error corrected in a way that is consistent with disclosures and your fiduciary relationship with clients?

7. Is your process for calculating the NAV of pooled clients' accounts and allocating the NAV of pooled vehicles among participants consistent with the pooled vehicles' policies, disclosures, and your fiduciary relationship with clients?

Corporate actions

8. Do your (or a service provider's) procedures for identifying and recording corporate actions, such as dividends and stock splits that impact clients' positions, timely and accurately capture these actions?

9. Do your (or a service provider's) procedures for monitoring pending corporate actions ensure that appropriate follow-up is taken so that stale receivable items, such as recapture of taxes withheld, do not accumulate in clients' accounts?

10. Are your (or a service provider's) policies and procedures for following-up and causing clients to participate in class action settlement funds consistent with your disclosures and fiduciary relationships with clients?

Forensic test

11. Taking into account the volume and timing of transactions in pooled vehicles that you advise, do the valuations that make up the NAV fairly represent each participant's ownership interest?

Disclosures

12. Are your clients fully and fairly informed of your process for valuing clients' positions, including possible exceptions? Are they able to give their informed consent to all material conflicts of interest that arise from such processes?

Information handling

13. With respect to your pricing and valuation process, including the calculation of NAV for pooled vehicles, is documentation or other output generated to substantiate that you obtained all related information in a timely, accurate, and complete manner? Do you ensure that this information is preserved for the required period of time and protected from unplanned destruction, loss, alteration, compromise, or use?

G. SAFEGUARDING CLIENTS' ASSETS

(Reference: Rule 206(4)-2, Regulation S-P under the Gramm-Leach-Bliley Act)

Custody practices

1. Are client assets held in accounts maintained by qualified custodians as required by Rule 206(4)-2?

2. If you inadvertently obtain possession of clients' assets (e.g., if a client sends you stock certificates), are required actions taken within the time periods specified in Rule 206(4)-2 to dispose of those assets?

3. Does the custodian of each client's account independently monitor corporate actions (e.g., stock splits, dividends) affecting the account?

4. Does the custodian of each client's account independently determine the value of each position on a date near the date of each statement sent to the client and communicate such valuations and the total value of the account in its statements sent to clients?

5. Are securities lending practices that involve loans of clients' securities consistent with clients' contracts and disclosures made to clients?

Providing information to clients

6. Do all clients receive periodic statements directly from their qualified custodians, and do these statements describe all activity in their accounts? Are these statements accurate (i.e., fully and fairly reflect transactions in and balances of each account during the periods covered by the statements)? If not, is the information contained in account statements provided to clients regularly verified by a knowledgeable person that has no access to clients' assets to determine the truthfulness of transactional, balance and performance information?

7. If you are the only source of information provided to clients regarding activity in and balances of their accounts (i.e., no custodial statements are sent to clients), are those accounts subject to annual, unannounced surprise audits by an independent auditor? Do those audits include confirmation of account activity and balances directly with clients?

8. If one or more client's account holdings are subject to a surprise audit, does the auditor file the results of its audit with the SEC on Form ADV-E?

Forensic tests

9. Do you periodically verify the postal/e-mail addresses to which clients' account statements are sent (both by you and client custodians)?

10. Do you regularly reconcile account balances and transaction detail shown on your records with information reported by clients' custodians? Is there follow-up to resolve all reconciling items?

11. Are pooled vehicles over whose assets you have custody annually audited by an independent auditor in accordance with generally accepted accounting principles?

12. Does the auditor performing the financial statement audit of each pooled vehicle confirm with all participants in the pool the activity in and balances of their account and appropriately follow-up on any discrepancies identified (not a specific requirement)?

13. Does the auditor send a copy of the pooled vehicles' audited financial statements directly to each participant in the pooled vehicle or to a representative of the participant (not a specific requirement)?

Conflicts of interest

14. Do you or your advisory representatives maintain business or personal relationships with clients' custodians? Do you personally benefit in some way from clients' relationships with those custodians (e.g., borrowing at below market rates)? If you or your advisory representatives benefit, do you disclose this to clients and/or have you established policies and procedures to mitigate any perceived risks?

Disclosures

15. Are clients fully and fairly informed of your practices for safeguarding clients' assets, including possible exceptions to these practices, and able to give their

informed consent to all material conflicts of interest that arise from such practices?

Information handling

16. With respect to custody or safekeeping for each client asset and liability, is documentation or other output generated to substantiate that you obtained all related information in a timely, accurate, and complete manner? Do you ensure that this information is preserved for the required period of time and protected from unplanned destruction, loss, alteration, compromise, or use?

H. MARKETING AND PERFORMANCE ADVERTISING

(Reference: Rules 206(4)-1 and 206(4)-3)

Truthfulness of representations

1. Are all "communications with clients" (i.e., representations made and numbers used in advertisements, responses to requests for proposals, in other marketing literature and on web sites maintained by you or to which you maintain links) truthful, representative, complete, and not misleading?

2. Is information about past specific performance of investment advice that is contained in communications with clients and other investors consistent with Rule 206(4)-1, and your status as a fiduciary? Also, are any staff-issued interpretive guidance, such as no-action letters, applicable?

3. Are model and composite performance figures, formulas, and related disclosures contained in communications to clients consistent with your status as a fiduciary? Also, are any staff-issued interpretive guidance, such as no-action letters, applicable?

4. Are representations that composite performance shown in communications with clients is presented in conformity with a specified industry standard consistent with the requirements of that standard?

5. Are advertisements that must be cleared by the NASD before use or filed with the NASD after use done so on a timely basis?

6. Are all communications with clients provided by advisory representatives reviewed and cleared as required by your policies and the law?

Use of solicitors

7. Is your use of third party solicitors consistent with Rule 206(4)-3?

8. Do the disclosure documents used by third party solicitors comply with the requirements of Rule 206(4)-3 and your status as a fiduciary?

9. Are all payments made to third party solicitors or other compensation arrangements maintained with solicitors consistent with disclosures and your status as a fiduciary?

10. Are the solicitors used by pooled vehicles that you manage or advise required to be registered representatives of a broker-dealer (as a result of the form of compensation they received for their work) and, if so, are they appropriately registered?

11. Is the compensation received by solicitors used by pooled vehicles that you manage or advise and the relationships between you and these solicitors fully and fairly disclosed to investors and consistent with your status as a fiduciary?

12. Are advisory clients referred to you by broker-dealers fully and fairly informed of the conflicts of interest you face in placing trades for their accounts and negotiating commission rates (e.g., if you do not negotiate commission rates paid on trades placed for clients referred by broker-dealers, and the commissions paid by such clients are higher than rates paid other clients for whom you do negotiate commission rates)?

Disclosures

13. Are your marketing and performance advertising practices fully and fairly disclosed to clients, and are clients enabled to give their informed consent to all material conflicts of interest that arise from such policies and procedures?

Information handling

14. With respect to performance advertising, is all required documentation or other output generated to substantiate that you obtained all related information in a timely, accurate, and complete manner maintained pursuant to Rule 204-2(a)(16)? Do you ensure that this information is preserved for the required period of time and protected from unplanned destruction, loss, alteration, compromise, or use?

I. CREATING, RECORDING, RETAINING AND REPORTING INFORMATION

(Reference: Rule 204-2)

Information handling

1. Do you create, record, and retain all required information, including information that may be contained in e-mails and instant messages, for required periods? Is this information accurate and current as required by Rule 204-2?

2. Can you promptly produce information, whether on paper or electronic media, upon request?

3. Do you maintain the means to or does your records management program enable you to read and produce information maintained electronically or photographically or that has been encrypted for the entire period required by record retention rules (taking into account changes in software needed to access the information)?

4. Does your records management program provide for the destruction of records after the required retention periods have passed? Is the destruction automatic, or can it be suspended (e.g., when the possibility of an inspection or litigation arises)?

5. Do you ensure that all information that is deleted from files or otherwise disposed of is either not required to be kept or is beyond any required retention period?

6. Do you effectively safeguard information you are required to maintain from unauthorized access, alteration, loss, or destruction?

7. Do you have security measures to properly safeguard personal and financial information of clients, including consumer credit report information, from unauthorized access, disclosure or use? Do you ensure that the security measures of your service providers also safeguard this information?

Malicious intrusions

8. Do your electronic information systems, both internal and those supplied by third parties, effectively detect and prevent malicious intrusions from internal and external sources? Do you have effective oversight measures to protect your electronic infrastructure, operating systems, files and databases?

Disclosures and filings

9. Do you periodically provide clients with privacy policy notices, as required?

10. Are required filings (e.g., updates of Form ADV, Parts 1 and II; Form ADV-E and Form 13F) accurately and completely prepared and filed on a timely basis?

11. Do disclosures provided to clients fully and fairly describe all material conflicts of interest that you face when providing investment advice?

12. Are all required reports and information (e.g., annual offer of disclosure document) prepared accurately, completely, timely, and consistent with applicable regulations?

13. Have you reported to clients information required by Rule 206(4)-4 (e.g., an adverse financial condition or certain disciplinary events)?

14. Are complaints and concerns that you receive (either from clients or from sources that impact clients) reviewed by a person(s) that has no access to clients' assets and that is in a position to effectively act on the information?

15. With respect to the collection and retention of information, is documentation or other output generated to substantiate that you obtained all related information

in a timely, accurate, and complete manner? Do you ensure that this information is preserved for the required period of time and protect it from unplanned destruction, loss, alteration, compromise, or use?

J. ANTI-MONEY LAUNDERING PROGRAM

The anti-money laundering (AML) regulations, which are administered through the Financial Crimes Enforcement Network (FinCEN), are applicable to open-end mutual funds. To date, investment advisers have not been identified as entities that must comply with the AML regulations. However, investment advisers may be delegated to perform certain AML responsibilities on the behalf of other entities and/or may be required to comply with certain related regulations (e.g., U.S. Treasury Office of Foreign Assets Control ("OFAC") reporting requirement and Internal Revenue Code/Bank Secrecy Act reporting procedures for cash transactions). For information about possible AML requirements please see http://www.sec.gov/about/offices/ocie/amlmfsourcetool.htm#3 and www.fincen.gov.

If you conclude you are obligated to administer an AML program, you should consider the following:

1. Does your AML program contain all of the elements required by applicable regulations?

2. Do you ensure that your staff has sufficient knowledge and skills to effectively carry out their AML responsibilities?

3. Does your AML program appear to be effective in identifying suspicious cash/currency activity and reporting such activities to appropriate authorities?

4. With respect to your AML program, is documentation or other output generated to substantiate that you obtained all related information in a timely, accurate, and complete manner? Do you ensure that this information is preserved for the required period of time and protected from unplanned destruction, loss, alteration, compromise, or use?

You should also consider whether you are complying with the U.S. Treasury OFAC requirements by restricting your business transactions with certain individuals, entities, and/or countries on lists compiled by OFAC.

The SEC staff has also stated that "[a]dvisers that employ or hire supervised persons with disciplinary events should be mindful of their supervisory obligations and may want to consider heightened supervision of such individuals."[306]

2. The Investment Company Act of 1940

Rule 17j-1 under the Investment Company Act of 1940 requires investment companies, their investment advisers, and their principal underwriters to establish Codes of Ethics.[307] Rule 17j-1 also details some of the substance required in such Codes. The Codes should contain specific self-enforcing provisions that must serve to effectively *prevent*, rather than simply punish, violations of the federal securities laws. Prevention includes oversight of compliance functions by the investment adviser, principal underwriter, administrator, and transfer agent.[308] Under Rule 38a-1 of the Investment Company Act of 1940, the funds' boards of directors are required to approve the policies and procedures of the Codes.[309] Let us review just a few of a Code's required details. The Code should subject "access persons" to reporting of their personal securities transactions and holdings.[310] An "access person" is a supervised person who: has access to nonpublic information regarding clients' purchase or sale of securities; is involved in making securities recommendations to clients; or who has access to such recommendations that are nonpublic. Thus, "access persons" include portfolio management personnel and, in some organizations, client service representatives who communicate investment advice to clients (even though they did not prepare the advice). These employees gain information about investment recommendations whose effects may not yet be felt in the marketplace.

We should note that prohibited insider trading has been with us for a very long time, perhaps as long as we had active markets. In addition, the prohibition on the use of insider information applies not only to securities but also to other marketable financial obligations, such as derivatives. Thus, sometimes a securities trader is required to divest itself of a business that would give its personnel access to insider information.

The rule does not provide a definition of the word "access" to insider information. Access is measured by the organizations' controls and structures. If an organization has a large number of employees with broad responsibilities, yet imposes on them few barriers to insider information, the organization may have to consider a larger percentage of its staff to be "access persons." In

---

306 Ofc. of Compliance Inspections & Examinations, U.S. Sec. & Exch. Comm'n, *Examinations of Supervision Practices at Registered Investment Advisers*, RISK ALERT, Sept. 12, 2016, *available at* https://www.sec.gov/ocie/announcement/ocie-2016-risk-alert-supervision-registered-investment-advisers.pdf (last visited June 14, 2017).

307 17 C.F.R. § 270.17j-1(c)(1)(i) (2016).

308 17 C.F.R. § 270.38a-1(a)(1) (2016).

309 17 C.F.R. § 270.38a-1(a)(1) (2016).

310 17 C.F.R. § 270.17j-1(d) (2016).

contrast, if an organization keeps strict controls on sensitive information, it may be deemed to have fewer "access persons." Thus, the position of the employees, as well as the internal controls of the organization, plays a part in the definition of access.

Rule 17j-1 establishes a presumption that, in a firm whose primary business is providing investment advice, all its directors, officers, and partners are access persons.[311] Therefore, in many advisory firms, directors, officers and partners will be deemed "access persons" as well.

Rule 17j-1 requires that the Code provide compliance procedures and practices. These requirements apply only to firms that are registered investment advisers or those required to be registered. The Code should impose on an adviser's "access persons" a requirement to periodically report their personal securities transactions and holdings. The report should be forwarded to the adviser's chief compliance officer or other designated persons. The reports should be reviewed to ensure that the Adviser and the SEC examiner would be able to identify improper trades or patterns of trading by "access persons."[312]

*The Code should require access persons to submit initial and annual holdings and quarterly transaction reports regarding their personal trading activities,[313] with three exceptions: automatic investment plans;[314] securities held in accounts over which the access person had no direct or indirect influence or control;[315] and reporting that duplicates information contained in broker trade confirmations or account statements provided that recordkeeping requirements of these transactions are met.[316] Annual holdings and quarterly transaction reports may also be avoided if the advisory firm has only one access person and the firm maintains records of the holdings and transactions under rule 17j-1 discussed above.[317]

*An adviser's Code must require pre-approval of certain investments. The Code must require the access persons to obtain the adviser's approval before acquiring ownership in a security in an initial public offering (IPO) or a limited offering (e.g., a private placement).[318] This requirement is debated. On the one hand, because "[m]ost individuals rarely have the opportunity to invest in these types of securities; an access person's IPO or private placement purchase therefore raises

---

311 17 C.F.R. § 270.17j-1(a)(1)(i) (2016).

312 17 C.F.R. § 270.17j-1(d) (2016).

313 17 C.F.R. § 275.204A-1(b) (2016).

314 17 C.F.R. § 275.204A-1(b)(3)(i) (2016).

315 17 C.F.R. § 275.204A-1(b)(3)(ii) (2016).

316 17 C.F.R. § 275.204A-1(b)(3)(iii) (2016).

317 17 C.F.R. § 275.204A-1(d) (2016).

318 17 C.F.R. § 275.204A-1(c) (2016).

questions."[319] Yet, to what extent does the "employee . . . misappropriat[e] an investment opportunity that should first be offered to eligible clients?" Or is "a portfolio manager . . . receiving a personal benefit for directing client business or brokerage"?[320] Yet, it seems that these actions should generally be prohibited. One signal is Rule 204A-1's exception for advisory firms with only one "access person."[321] Thus, the issue is unclear and requires more attention for compliance.

The SEC also noted in the adopting release that advisory firms with codes of ethics have "commonly include[d] many of the following elements, or address[ed] the following issues, which [the SEC] believe[s] that all advisers should consider in crafting their own procedures for employees' personal securities trading":

> Prior written approval before access persons can place a personal securities transaction ("pre-clearance").

> . Maintenance of lists of issuers of securities that the advisory firm is analyzing or recommending for client transactions, and prohibitions on personal trading in securities of those issuers.

> . Maintenance of "restricted lists" of issuers about which the advisory firm has inside information, and prohibitions on any trading (personal or for clients) in securities of those issuers.

> . "Blackout periods" when client securities trades are being placed or recommendations are being made and access persons are not permitted to place personal securities transactions.

> . Reminders that investment opportunities must be offered first to clients before the adviser or its employees may act on them, and procedures to implement this principle.

> . Prohibitions or restrictions on "short-swing" trading and market timing.

> . Requirements to trade only through certain brokers, or limitations on the number of brokerage accounts permitted.

> . Requirements to provide the adviser with duplicate trade confirmations and account statements.

---

319 Investment Adviser Codes of Ethics, IA-2256, IC-26492 (July 2, 2004), 69 Fed. Reg. 41,696, 41,700 (July 9, 2004).

320 *Id.*

321 17 C.F.R. § 275.204A-1(d) (2016); 69 Fed. Reg. at 41,700; *id.* n.51 ("Firms with only one access person are generally one-person operations. It would make little sense to require the individual to pre-clear investments with himself").

. Procedures for assigning new securities analyses to employees whose personal holdings do not present apparent conflicts of interest.[322]

3. The Code should impose a duty to report violations and to educate employees

Each Code of Ethics must require prompt internal reporting of any violations of the Code. Violations must be reported to the adviser's chief compliance officer.[323] Further, the Code must require the adviser to provide each supervised person with a copy of the Code and any amendments.[324] This requirement reduces the cost of government examiners.

In October 2014 the SEC approved Rule G-44 of the Municipal Securities Regulation Board (MSRB),[325] which requires municipal advisors to establish compliance policies and supervisory procedures.[326]

Note that sanctions for violating a Code of Ethics are crucial to the Code's viability, although we later examine cultures in which punishment is not the main mover towards self-regulation. In our reality, employers must enforce the rules, and punish their violations. The SEC backs these sanctions with more severe ones, such as disqualification from engaging in the service or trade.[327] Lawyers and compliance officers play a role in enforcing the law. While legal provisions may disqualify violators from continuing to practice,[328] the provisions rarely impose termination of the violators' employment.

As we noted before, in contrast to legal sanctions, private enforcement by employers for violations of codes of conduct can involve reduced bonuses, demotion, and termination of employment, and other penalties. Thus, the employers may not only augment the government's enforcement function but carry it out with more flexibility as well.

Note also Rule 38a-1. The rule is promulgated under the Investment Company Act of 1940 pursuant to the SEC authority in sections 31(a) and 38(a) of the Act (15 U.S.C. Sections. 30(a), and 37(a)). This rule imposes compliance procedures and practices on certain investment companies (not on their advisers). It requires that the investment companies' boards of directors approve

---

322 Investment Adviser Codes of Ethics, IA-2256, IC-26492 (July 2, 2004), 69 Fed. Reg. 41,696, 41,697-98 (July 9, 2004) (footnotes omitted).

323 17 C.F.R. § 275.204A-1(a)(4) (2016).

324 17 C.F.R. § 275.204A-1(a)(5) (2016).

325 Rule G-44, *available at* http://www.msrb.org/Rules-and-Interpretations/MSRB-Rules/General/Rule-G-44.aspx (last visited Dec. 6, 2016).

326 Mun. Sec. Rulemaking Bd., *SEC Approves MSRB Rule G-44 on Supervisory and Compliance Obligations of Municipal Advisors, and Amendments to MSRB Rules G-8 and G-9, MSRB Regulatory Notice 2014-19* (Oct. 24, 2014), *available at* http://www.msrb.org/~/media/Files/Regulatory-Notices/Announcements/2014-19.ashx (last visited Aug. 15, 2016).

327 15 U.S.C. § 80a-9(b) (2012); 15 U.S.C. §80b-3(f) (2012).

328 15 U.S.C. § 80a-9(b) (2012); 15 U.S.C. §80b-3(f) (2012).

the policies and procedures of the compliance Codes.[329] Rule 206(4)-7 under the Investment Advisers Act of 1940 imposes compliance procedures and policies on investment advisers.[330]

Discussion topics

*How does a Code of Ethics differ from a statute or a regulation? What is the interplay between the Code and compliance programs?

*Why didn't the SEC prohibit insiders within the advisory organizations from securities trading? After all, such a requirement would have made the issues and enforcement simpler?

*What sanctions can the employers impose on violators of the Code?

*Rule 17j-1 requires the Code to provide compliance procedures and practices. What is the legal status of the Code under this design? If such a Code was imposed by the employer, and an employee violated the Code's provision, whom can the SEC sue, and for what violation?

*What are the relationships between NASD Rule 3013, section 38(a) of the Investment Company Act of 1940 and Rule 206(4)-7 pursuant to the Investment Advisers Act of 1940? Can you convert these rules into one rule? Is that desirable?

In the proposing release for compliance programs for investment companies and investment advisers, the SEC requested comments on other approaches involving the private sector:

1. Compliance Reviews

One approach might be to require each fund and adviser to undergo periodic compliance reviews by a third party that would produce a report of its findings and recommendations. Our examination staff could use these reports to quickly identify areas that required attention, permitting us to allocate examination resources better and, as a result, to increase the frequency with which our staff could examine funds and advisers. Funds and advisers with reports indicating that they have effective compliance programs could be examined less frequently, which would reduce the burdens on them of undergoing more frequent examination by our staff.

---

329 17 C.F.R. § 270.38a-1(a)(1) (2016).

330 17 C.F.R. § 275.206(4)-7 (2016). Rule 206(4)-7 was adopted pursuant to the authority set forth in sections 206(4) and 211(a) of the Advisers Act (15 U.S.C. §§ 80b-6(4), -11(a) (2012)).

There are many organizations that provide compliance reviews, including "mock audits" for investment advisers and funds, and have personnel that have experience in designing, implementing, and assessing the effectiveness of compliance programs. As a condition to the settlement of an enforcement action, we frequently require an adviser or fund to engage a compliance consultant. The USA Patriot Act requires financial institutions (including mutual funds), as part of their anti-money laundering programs, to have an independent audit function to test their programs.

We request comment on the advantages and disadvantages of requiring advisers and funds to undergo compliance reviews. If we adopt such a requirement, should we exclude certain types of funds or advisers? Would the cost of these reviews be prohibitive for smaller advisers? Would some fund groups or advisers hire the least expensive compliance consultant regardless of the quality of the consultant's work? If so, how could we ensure that a high quality compliance review is conducted? If we adopt such a requirement, should we require the third parties who conduct such reviews to satisfy certain minimum standards for education and experience? What criteria should be included in the rule to determine whether a third party compliance expert is independent? How frequently should we require such reviews to be conducted? What is the proper scope for third party reviews? Should we require the third party consultant to file its report with us? If so, what should the scope of the report be?

2. Expanded Audit Requirement

Another approach might be to expand the role of independent public accountants that audit fund financial statements to include an examination of fund compliance controls. Such an approach would involve the performance by fund auditors of certain of the compliance review procedures currently performed by our staff in a compliance examination.

Our rules today require fund auditors to submit internal control reports to fund boards. In these reports, the auditor must identify any material weaknesses in the accounting system, the system of internal accounting controls, and the procedures for safeguarding securities of which they become aware while planning and performing the audit on the fund's financial statements. The auditor's responsibilities could be augmented to require the identification of material weaknesses in the internal controls or a report on other aspects of the internal controls that are not required to be reviewed in planning and performing an audit of the financial statements. Expanding the auditor's responsibilities could, to some extent, serve as a substitute for staff examination or reduce the frequency of staff examination of funds with strong internal compliance programs, which would free Commission resources to focus on other areas of fund operations and permit us to examine funds with weaker internal compliance programs more often.

We request comment on this approach. Should we expand the responsibilities of the fund auditor? If so, what specific areas would it be appropriate for auditors to review? What type of assurance report should be provided?

3. Self-Regulatory Organization

The formation of one or more self-regulatory organizations (SROs) for funds and/or advisers also would be a means to involve the private sector in support of our regulatory program. An SRO would function in a manner analogous to the national securities exchanges and registered securities associations under the Securities Exchange Act of 1934 by (i) establishing business practice rules and ethical standards, (ii) conducting routine examinations, (iii) requiring minimum education or experience standards, and (iv) bringing its own actions to discipline members for violating its rules and the federal securities laws.

SROs play an increasingly important role in the regulation of financial services in the United States. SROs participate with us in overseeing the public securities markets, including broker-dealers. They also oversee the municipal bond market, and the system of clearance and settlement of securities trades. An SRO also plays an important part in the oversight of the futures markets, including futures commissions merchants, commodity pool operators, and commodity trading advisers. In the Sarbanes-Oxley Act, Congress affirmed the role of private sector regulatory organizations by establishing the Public Company Accounting Oversight Board, which is charged with overseeing the audit of public companies.

United States Supreme Court Justice Stewart stated that the purpose of the provisions of the Exchange Act creating SROs was "to delegate governmental power to working institutions which would undertake, at their own initiative, to enforce compliance with ethical as well as legal standards in a complex and changing industry." Our experience with SROs suggests that this delegation of authority can have many advantages: SROs can marshal resources not available to the Commission and can have greater access to industry expertise. They can act more nimbly than a government agency, which is subject to significant personnel, contracting, and procedural requirements. An SRO can require its members to adhere to higher standards of ethical behavior than we can require under the securities laws. Moreover, industry leaders who participate in the regulatory process acquire a greater sense of their stake in the process.

Proposals to create SROs for funds or investment advisers have been considered by Congress, the Commission, and members of the investment management industry in past years. In 1983, we requested comment on the concept of designating an "inspection-only" SRO for funds. And in 1989, we submitted legislation to Congress requesting authority to designate one or more SROs for investment advisers. Both initiatives reflected the concern of the Commission that our resources were inadequate to address the growth of investment advisers and funds. Any SRO would be subject to the pervasive oversight of the Commission. We would examine its activities, require it to keep records, and approve its rules only if we conclude that they further the goals of the federal securities laws. Disciplinary actions could be appealed to the Commission. We would expect to be vigilant in preventing SRO rules that impose a burden on competition not necessary to further a regulatory purpose. Our staff would continue to examine the activities of funds and advisers, both to ensure adequate examination coverage and to provide oversight of the SRO examination program.

We request comment on whether one or more SROs should be established for funds and/or investment advisers. Should the SROs be limited in their authority? For example, should they be limited to conducting examinations? How should the activities of an SRO be financed?

4. Fidelity Bonding Requirement for Advisers

Another means to privatize some of the compliance function would be to require investment advisers to obtain fidelity bonds from insurance companies. Fidelity bonds provide a source of compensation for advisory clients who are victims of fraud or embezzlement by advisory personnel. They result in additional oversight of advisers by insurance companies, which are unwilling to issue bonds to advisers that place their assets at risk by having poor controls or that hire employees with criminal or poor disciplinary records. The cost of that oversight is reflected in the premiums charged for the bond. High-risk advisers would be denied bonds or would be charged higher amounts to compensate the insurance company for assuming greater risk.

Investment advisers are among the only financial service providers handling client assets that are not required to obtain fidelity bonds. The Advisers Act does not require advisory firms to have a minimum amount of capital invested, and many have few assets. When we discover a serious fraud by an adviser, often the assets of the adviser are insufficient to compensate clients. The losses are borne by clients who may lose their life's savings, or be unable to afford a college education for their children or a comfortable retirement.

Should advisers be required to obtain a fidelity bond from a reputable insurance company? If so, should some advisers be excluded? Alternatively, should advisers be required to maintain a certain amount of capital that could be the source of compensation for clients? What amount of capital would be adequate?[331]

*Should one or more of such approaches be adopted?

The Financial Crimes Enforcement Network ("FinCEN") proposed amendments that would require certain investment advisers to establish anti-money laundering programs.

In the proposing release, FinCEN discussed the possible role of investment advisers in money laundering:

---

331 Compliance Programs of Investment Companies and Investment Advisers, IC-25925, IA-2107 (Feb. 5, 2003), 68 Fed. Reg. 7038, 7043-48 (Feb. 11, 2003) (footnotes omitted).

Money laundering occurs when money from illegal activity is moved through the financial system to make it appear that the funds came from legitimate sources. Money laundering usually involves three stages, known as placement, layering, and integration. In the placement stage, cash or cash equivalents are placed into the financial system. Investment advisers rarely have occasion to receive currency from or disburse it to clients. Nevertheless, in some instances, FinCEN has received reports of suspicious activities indicating that clients may attempt to use investment advisers in the placement stage. These reports include attempts by clients to structure transactions with an investment adviser to avoid reports of currency transactions, as well as attempts to fund accounts with fraudulent checks.

"Layering" describes the distancing of illegal proceeds from their criminal source through the creation of complex layers of financial transactions. A money launderer could use its client account with an investment adviser as one of many accounts in a layering scheme, frequently transferring funds to the adviser for management and then withdrawing the funds or transferring them to accounts at other institutions. Layering could also involve establishing an advisory account in the name of a fictitious corporation or an entity designed to conceal the true owner. For example, FinCEN in one instance received reports of suspicious activity involving an investment advisory client who established an account under an alias for the family of a Colombian narcotics trafficker. Investment advisory firms could also be used for integrating illicit income into legitimate assets. "Integration" occurs when illegal funds previously placed into the financial system are made to appear to have been derived from a legitimate source. For example, proceeds from investments made on a client's behalf by an investment adviser would appear legitimate to any financial institution receiving such proceeds.

The crime of money laundering also encompasses the movement of funds to support terrorism or terrorist organizations. These funds may be from illegitimate or legitimate sources. Even where the funds derive from legitimate sources, money launderers might attempt to use investment advisers to aid movement of the funds through the money laundering patterns described above, in order to disguise the identity of the originator of the funds.

Investment advisers in the United States today control over $ 21 trillion in assets. Although advisers rarely hold financial assets themselves and even more rarely accept cash, they are often in a critical position of knowledge as to the movement of large amounts of financial assets through financial markets. If some of these assets include the proceeds of illegal activities, or are intended to further such activities, an anti-money laundering program should help discover them. In some cases, an investment adviser may be the only person with a complete understanding of the source of invested assets, the nature of the clients, or the objectives for which the assets are invested. Other market participants may, for example, hold and trade assets in an account controlled by the adviser, but these parties often rely solely on an investment adviser's instructions and lack knowledge of the adviser's clients. In other cases, an adviser may be the only participant aware of the overall investment program of a client who may use multiple broker-dealers to trade securities in transactions that individually may not raise money laundering concerns. As a result, FinCEN believes that investment advisers have an important role to play in preventing the use of their services for money laundering and the financing of terrorism.[332]

*Should investment advisers be required to adopt anti-money laundering programs?

In addition, officers, directors, and other employees report their trades in a company's stock on SEC Form 4. A company announced that it would use the information in these filings as the strategy of its mutual fund, which would in effect be conducting legal "insider trading."[333]

*What other restrictions should be placed on employees' investments?

The case of Oppenheimer appears in different contesta. Here the question is how should Oppenhimer prevent the violations of the USA PATRIOT Act?

Oppenheimer & Co., Inc.

Washington, D.C. – The Financial Crimes Enforcement Network (FinCEN), working closely with the U.S. Securities and Exchange Commission (SEC), assessed a $20 million civil money penalty [on January 27, 2015] against Oppenheimer & Co., Inc., for willfully violating the Bank Secrecy Act (BSA). Oppenheimer, a securities broker–dealer in New York, admitted that it failed to establish and implement an adequate anti–money laundering program, failed to conduct adequate due diligence on a foreign correspondent account, and failed to comply with requirements under Section 311 of the USA PATRIOT Act.

FinCEN and the New York Stock Exchange assessed a civil money penalty of $2.8 million against Oppenheimer in 2005 for similar violations. In 2013, the Financial Industry Regulatory Authority fined the firm $1.4 million for violations of securities laws and anti–money laundering failures.

"Broker–dealers face the same money laundering risks as other types of financial institutions," noted FinCEN Director Jennifer Shasky Calvery. "And by failing to comply with their regulatory responsibilities, our financial system became vulnerable to criminal abuse. This is the second time FinCEN has penalized Oppenheimer for similar violations. It is clear that their compliance culture must change."

---

332 Financial Crimes Enforcement Network, Anti-Money Laundering programs for Investment Advisers, 68 Fed. Reg. 23,646, 23,647-48 (May 5, 2003) (footnotes omitted).

333 Bruce Carton, *Investment Firm Offers First 'Legal Insider Trading Mutual Fund,'* COMPLIANCE WK., June 20, 2012, *available at* https://www.complianceweek.com/blogs/enforcement-action/investment-firm-offers-first-legal-insider-trading-mutual-fund#.WH83XvkrKUk (last visited Jan. 17, 2017).

Section 311 of the USA PATRIOT Act provides important protections to the U.S. financial system. Under that authority, the Director of FinCEN may determine that a foreign financial institution is of primary money laundering concern and may require domestic financial institutions to take certain special measures against that entity. These special measures can include prohibiting domestic financial institutions from opening or maintaining correspondent accounts for the named foreign financial institution. To be effective, U.S. financial institutions must conduct adequate due diligence and notify their foreign correspondent financial institutions of special measures imposed under Section 311, so that institutions of primary money laundering concern do not have improper and unfettered access to the U.S. financial system. By failing to notify its correspondents, Oppenheimer potentially placed the U.S. financial system at risk.

From 2008 through May 2014, Oppenheimer conducted business without establishing and implementing adequate policies, procedures, and internal controls reasonably designed to detect and report suspicious activity. FinCEN identified 16 customers who engaged in patterns of suspicious trading through branch offices in five states. All the suspicious activities involved penny stocks, which typically are low–priced, thinly traded, and highly speculative securities that can be vulnerable to manipulation by stock promoters and "pump–and–dump" schemes. Oppenheimer failed to report patterns of activity in which customers deposited large blocks of unregistered or illiquid penny stocks, moved large volumes of penny stocks among accounts with no apparent purpose, or immediately liquidated those securities and wired the proceeds out of the account.

In addition, Oppenheimer itself designated a customer foreign financial institution as "high risk" but failed to assess the institution's specific risks as a foreign financial institution or conduct adequate due diligence. Oppenheimer inadequately monitored the foreign financial institution's transactions and consequently did not detect or investigate numerous suspicious transactions conducted through the account, including prohibited third–party activity and illegal penny stock trading.[334]

Problem

As a Compliance Officer, how would you prepare a preventive program to avoid violations of the USA PATRIOT Act?

To what extent does the brokerage firm have information about its clients' business and control its clients' transactions? Does the brokerage firm need to exercise control in this case?

---

[334] Excerpted from FinCEN, *FinCEN Fines Oppenheimer & Co. Inc. $20 Million for Continued Anti–Money Laundering Shortfalls* (Jan. 27, 2015), *available at* https://www.fincen.gov/news/news-releases/fincen-fines-oppenheimer-co-inc-20-million-continued-anti-money-laundering (last visited Oct. 20, 2016).

III. THE LIABILITIES OF A CONTROLLING COMPLIANCE OFFICER UNDER THE INVESTMENT COMPANY ACT OF 1940

Thomas Pritchard, the principal owner, managing director, and CCO of Pritchard Capital, was found liable for books–and–records violations and failure to supervise. Pritchard Capital had numerous offices throughout the United States. He was responsible for developing the supervisory policies and procedures of Pritchard Capital and for supervising the activities of certain associated persons.

Pritchard visited the New York office only periodically. In part, due to his infrequent trips to the office in question, Pritchard gave only a cursory look to mutual fund correspondence and trade ticket files and missed red flags. One set of important red flags that were missed took the form of tentative or contingent trade ticket files. These suggested that certain associated persons were permitting late trading in mutual funds in violation of the Investment Company Act of 1940.

Therefore, Pritchard failed to recognize or respond to these indications of wrongdoing. The SEC noted that Pritchard Capital's written supervisory procedures did not contain policies or procedures reasonably designed to prevent or detect illegal late trading. Pritchard was suspended from association, in a supervisory capacity, with any broker or dealer for a period of nine months. He was also ordered to pay a civil penalty in the amount of $50,000.[335]

Discussion Topic

Why does the law interfere to impose on some institutions but not on others a requirement to have and enforce a Code of Ethics? Does the following answer satisfy?

Some financial services can present great temptations to the firms that provide these services. These temptations include gains by trading on insider information, acting for others in conflicts of interest, and taking high and unacceptable risks with other people's money. In addition, financial services that involve networking offer opportunities for those who work in the area to exchange illicit benefits, such as insider information. These interactions make it difficult to distinguish between innocent actors and fraudulent ones.

Therefore compliance codes contain specific prohibitions and enforcement mechanisms. The following are examples of the types of financial services that the law focuses on, and the legal requirements of related compliance codes, specifically, the legal requirement that management supervises its employees and ensures compliance with the law. Failure to effectively supervise can be a legal violation regardless of whether a violation of the law occurred. The trend towards additional legislation and regulation, requiring internal compliance programs, is likely to continue, unless internal culture takes hold of the leadership of the financial professions.

----

335   *In re* Prichard Capital Ptrs., LLC, Securities Exchange Act Rel. No. 57,704, Investment Company Act Rel. No. 28,251 (Apr. 23, 2008).

Chapter 6

Imposing Compliance Codes in the Shadow of Prosecution: The Rise of Deferred Prosecution Agreements

INTRODUCTION

As noted, the requirement of corporate compliance codes began with a judicial finding of corporations' criminal liability. Recently, especially when corporations seek to avoid the publicity of criminal actions, we witness negotiations between corporations and prosecutors for strong compliance codes and enforcement, before the launch of judicial proceedings against the corporations. Thus, prosecutors have used the imposition or strengthening of compliance programs as part of the terms against suspected corporations. The trend is enforced by the recognition that there are serious cost consequences to formal prosecution for the accused corporation and for the government. These circumstances led to Deferred Prosecution Agreements ("DPAs"). Early in the process the agreements were not uniform, depending on the parties and the prosecutors. Currently, there is a tendency towards establishing a code for the regulators, providing both flexibility and directions on their negotiations with the potential accused or defendants. Yet, consistently, prosecutors have treated companies that monitor and enforce compliance more leniently.[336]

A Non-Prosecution Agreement ("NPA") is similar to a DPA. A DPA generally includes "filing of a formal charging document by the government, and the agreement is filed with the appropriate court."[337] A Non-Prosecution Agreement ("NPA") differs from a DPA in that "formal charges are not filed and the agreement is maintained by the parties."[338]

In a 2012 speech, Lanny A. Breuer, Assistant Attorney General, head of the Criminal Division of the DOJ, noted the effect of DPAs on companies and corporate culture. Until the 1990s,

---

336 *See, e.g.,* Miriam Hechler Baer, *Governing Corporate Compliance,* 50 B.C. L. Rev 949 (2009).

337 Memorandum from Craig S. Morford, Acting Deputy Att'y Gen., to the Heads of Dep't Components & U.S. Att'ys, on Selection & Use of Monitors in Deferred Prosecution Agreements and Non-Prosecution Agreements with Corporations 1 n.2 (Mar. 7, 2008), *available at* https://www.justice.gov/sites/default/files/dag/legacy/2008/03/20/morford-useofmonitorsmemo-03072008.pdf (last visited Jan. 17, 2017).

338 *Id.*

prosecutors had only the choice to "indict, or walk away"; under a DPA companies "will be answerable even for conduct that in years past would have resulted in a declination."[339]

I. FACTORS CONSIDERED

The DOJ has established a list of considerations for determining whether prosecutors should bring a proceeding:[340]

In determining whether prosecution should be declined because no substantial Federal interest would be served by prosecution, the attorney for the government should weigh all relevant considerations, including:

1. Federal law enforcement priorities;

2. The nature and seriousness of the offense;

3. The deterrent effect of prosecution;

4. The person's culpability in connection with the offense;

5. The person's history with respect to criminal activity;

6. The person's willingness to cooperate in the investigation or prosecution of others; and

7. The probable sentence or other consequences if the person is convicted.[341]

The DOJ has also established additional factors to be considered in determining whether to charge corporations or in negotiating pleas or other agreements:

In conducting an investigation, determining whether to bring charges, and negotiating plea or other agreements, prosecutors should consider the following factors in reaching a decision as to the proper treatment of a corporate target:

1. the nature and seriousness of the offense, including the risk of harm to the public, and applicable policies and priorities, if any, governing the prosecution of corporations for particular categories of crime;

---

339 U.S. Dep't of Justice, *Assistant Attorney General Lanny A. Breuer Speaks at the New York City Bar Association* (Sept. 13, 2012), *available at* https://www.justice.gov/opa/speech/assistant-attorney-general-lanny-breuer-speaks-new-york-city-bar-association (last visited Jan. 17, 2012).

340 U.S. Dep't of Justice, U.S. Attorneys' Manual § 9-27.230, *available at* https://www.justice.gov/usam/usam-9-27000-principles-federal-prosecution#9-27.230 (renumbered and revised Nov. 2015) (last visited Jan. 5, 2017) (listing considerations for "determining whether prosecution should be declined because no substantial Federal interest would be served by prosecution"); *id.* § 9-28.300, *available at* https://www.justice.gov/usam/usam-9-28000-principles-federal-prosecution-business-organizations#9-28.300 (renumbered and revised Nov. 2015) (last visited Jan. 5, 2017) (listing additional factors to be considered in determining whether to charge corporations or negotiating plea or other agreements).

341 U.S. Dep't of Justice, U.S. Attorneys' Manual § 9-27.230, *available at* https://www.justice.gov/usam/usam-9-27000-principles-federal-prosecution#9-27.230 (renumbered and revised Nov. 2015) (last visited Jan. 5, 2017).

2. the pervasiveness of wrongdoing within the corporation, including the complicity in, or the condoning of, the wrongdoing by corporate management;

3. the corporation's history of similar misconduct, including prior criminal, civil, and regulatory enforcement actions against it;

4. the corporation's willingness to cooperate in the investigation of its agents;

5. the existence and effectiveness of the corporation's pre-existing compliance program;

6. the corporation's timely and voluntary disclosure of wrongdoing;

7. the corporation's remedial actions, including any efforts to implement an effective corporate compliance program or to improve an existing one, to replace responsible management, to discipline or terminate wrongdoers, to pay restitution, and to cooperate with the relevant government agencies;

8. collateral consequences, including whether there is disproportionate harm to shareholders, pension holders, employees, and others not proven personally culpable, as well as impact on the public arising from the prosecution;

9. the adequacy of remedies such as civil or regulatory enforcement actions; and

10. the adequacy of the prosecution of individuals responsible for the corporation's malfeasance.[342]

The DOJ elaborates on the evaluation of the pre-existing compliance program.[343] In a 2012 speech, Lanny A. Breuer, Assistant Attorney General, head of the Criminal Division of the DOJ, noted that to obtain a DPA a company must demonstrate a firm commitment to compliance:

One of the reasons why deferred prosecution agreements are such a powerful tool is that, in many ways, a DPA has the same punitive, deterrent, and rehabilitative effect as a guilty plea: when a company enters into a DPA with the government, . . . it almost always must acknowledge wrongdoing, agree to cooperate with the government's investigation, pay a fine, agree to

---

342 *Id.* § 9-28.300, *available at* https://www.justice.gov/usam/usam-9-28000-principles-federal-prosecution-business-organizations#9-28.300 (revised Nov. 2015) (last visited Jan. 5, 2017) (citations omitted).

343 *Id.* § 9-28.800, *available at* https://www.justice.gov/usam/usam-9-28000-principles-federal-prosecution-business-organizations#9-28.800 (renumbered Nov. 2015) (last visited Jan. 5, 2017)

improve its compliance program, and agree to face prosecution if it fails to satisfy the terms of the agreement. All of these components of DPAs are critical for accountability.

Perhaps most important, whether or not a corporation pleads guilty, . . . or enters into a DPA with the government, the company must virtually always publicly acknowledge its wrongdoing. And it must do so in detail. This often has significant consequences for the corporation, and it prevents companies from explaining away their resolutions by continuing to deny that they did anything wrong. . . .

Another absolutely critical point is that regardless of whether we indict a company or agree to defer prosecution, individual wrongdoers can never secure immunity through the corporate resolution. . . .

. . . In reaching every charging decision, we must take into account the effect of an indictment on innocent employees and shareholders, just as we must take into account the nature of the crimes committed and the pervasiveness of the misconduct. [I] consider whether individual employees with no responsibility for, or knowledge of, misconduct committed by others in the same company are going to lose their livelihood if we indict the corporation. In large multinational companies, the jobs of tens of thousands of employees can be at stake. And, in some cases, the health of an industry or the markets are a real factor. . . .

When the only tool we had to use in cases of corporate misconduct was a criminal indictment, prosecutors sometimes had to use a sledgehammer to crack a nut. More often, they just walked away. In the world we live in now, though, prosecutors have much greater ability to hold companies accountable for misconduct than we used to—and the result has been a transformation in the culture of corporate compliance. In appropriate circumstances, large corporations, such as Siemens AG, must plead guilty for their crimes. In other cases, because the company has gone to extraordinary lengths to turn itself around, for example, or provided the government with extensive cooperation, a deferred prosecution agreement or non-prosecution agreement may be the best resolution. No matter what, individual executives and employees must answer for their conduct. And, perhaps most important of all, companies know that they are now much more likely to face punishment than they were when our choice was limited to indicting or walking away. Overall, this state of affairs is better for companies, better for the government, and better for the American people.[344]

Similarly, the Securities and Exchange Commission ("SEC"), in determining whether to open an investigation, considers factors including:

- The statutes or rules potentially violated

---

344 . U.S. Dep't of Justice, *Assistant Attorney General Lanny A. Breuer Speaks at the New York City Bar Association* (Sept. 13, 2012), *available at* https://www.justice.gov/opa/speech/assistant-attorney-general-lanny-breuer-speaks-new-york-city-bar-association (last visited Jan. 17, 2012).

- • The egregiousness of the potential violation

- The potential magnitude of the violation

- The potential losses involved or harm to an investor or investors

- Whether the potentially harmed group is particularly vulnerable or at risk

- Whether the conduct is ongoing

- Whether the conduct can be investigated efficiently and within the statute of limitations period

- Whether other authorities, including federal or state agencies or regulators, might be better suited to investigate the conduct[.][345]

The SEC also set out its criteria for evaluating cooperation:

1. What is the intent and the nature of the misconduct involved? Did it result from inadvertence, honest mistake, simple negligence, reckless or deliberate indifference to indicia of wrongful conduct, willful misconduct or unadorned venality? Were the company's auditors misled?

2. How did the misconduct arise? Was it the result of pressure placed on employees to achieve specific results, or a tone of lawlessness set by those in control of the company? What compliance procedures were in place to prevent the misconduct now uncovered? Why did those procedures fail to stop or inhibit the wrongful conduct?

3. Where in the organization did the misconduct occur? How high up in the chain of command was knowledge of, or participation in, the misconduct? Did senior personnel participate in, or turn a blind eye toward, obvious indicia of misconduct? How systemic was the behavior? Is it symptomatic of the way the entity does business, or was it isolated?

4. How long did the misconduct last? Was it a one-quarter, or one-time, event, or did it last several years? In the case of a public company, did the misconduct occur before the company went public? Did it facilitate the company's ability to go public?

---

345 Div. of Enforcement, Sec. & Exch. Comm'n., Enforcement Manual 2.3, at 13, *available at* https://www.sec.gov/divisions/enforce/enforcementmanual.pdf (last visited May 19, 2017).

5. How much harm has the misconduct inflicted upon investors and other corporate constituencies? Did the share price of the company's stock drop significantly upon its discovery and disclosure?

6. How was the misconduct detected and who uncovered it?

7. How long after discovery of the misconduct did it take to implement an effective response?

8. What steps did the company take upon learning of the misconduct? Did the company immediately stop the misconduct? Are persons responsible for any misconduct still with the company? If so, are they still in the same positions? Did the company promptly, completely and effectively disclose the existence of the misconduct to the public, to regulators and to self-regulators? Did the company cooperate completely with appropriate regulatory and law enforcement bodies? Did the company identify what additional related misconduct is likely to have occurred? Did the company take steps to identify the extent of damage to investors and other corporate constituencies? Did the company appropriately recompense those adversely affected by the conduct?

9. What processes did the company follow to resolve many of these issues and ferret out necessary information? Were the Audit Committee and the Board of Directors fully informed? If so, when?

10. Did the company commit to learn the truth, fully and expeditiously? Did it do a thorough review of the nature, extent, origins and consequences of the conduct and related behavior? Did management, the Board, or committees consisting solely of outside directors oversee the review? Did company employees or outside persons perform the review? If outside persons, had they done other work for the company? Where the review was conducted by outside counsel, had management previously engaged such counsel? Were scope limitations placed on the review? If so, what were they?

11. Did the company promptly make available to our staff the results of its review and provide sufficient documentation reflecting its response to the situation? Did the company identify possible violative conduct and evidence with sufficient precision to facilitate prompt enforcement actions against those who violated the law? Did the company produce a thorough and probing written report detailing the findings of its review? Did the company voluntarily disclose information our staff did not directly request and otherwise might not have uncovered? Did the company ask its employees to cooperate with our staff and make all reasonable efforts to secure such cooperation?[3]

12. What assurances are there that the conduct is unlikely to recur? Did the company adopt and ensure enforcement of new and more effective internal controls and procedures designed to prevent a recurrence of the misconduct? Did the company provide our staff with sufficient information for it to evaluate the company's measures to correct the situation and ensure that the conduct does not recur?

13. Is the company the same company in which the misconduct occurred, or has it changed through a merger or bankruptcy reorganization?[346]

Discussion Topic

The Department of Justice has established a policy to consider a corporation's willingness to waive its attorney-client privilege. This policy has been heatedly criticized. What in your opinion are the pluses and minuses of the criticism?[347]

II. EXAMPLES OF DPAS

A. General

As noted earlier, DPAs are generally entered into when a company has taken affirmative steps toward compliance. In addition, the government may consider the effect of prosecution on innocent employees and possibly the industry or the markets.[348]

The DOJ has approved different CCO reporting structures. The DOJ has sometimes required senior compliance officials to report directly to the board or to an appropriate board committee.[349] A recent DPA required the CCO to report directly to the CEO and reporting obligations to

---

346 U.S. Sec. & Exch. Comm'n, Report of Investigation Pursuant to Section 21(a) of the Securities Exchange Act of 1934 and Commission Statement on the Relationship of Cooperation to Agency Enforcement Decisions, Securities Exchange Act Rel. No. 44,969 ((Oct. 23, 2001), *available at* https://www.sec.gov/litigation/investreport/34-44969.htm (last visited May 25, 2017).

347 *Id.* § 9-28.710, *available at* https://www.justice.gov/usam/usam-9-28000-principles-federal-prosecution-business-organizations#9-28.710 (renumbered and revised Nov. 2015) (last visited May 25, 2017); George M. Cohen, *Of Coerced Waiver, Government Leverage, and Corporate Loyalty: The Holder,Thompson, and McNulty Memos and Their Critics*, 93 Va. L. Rev. Online 153 (2007), *available at* http://www.virginialawreview.org/volumes/content/coerced-waiver-government-leverage-and-corporate-loyalty-holder-thompson-and-mcnulty (last visited Jan. 16, 2017)..

348 U.S. Dep't of Justice, *Assistant Attorney General Lanny A. Breuer Speaks at the New York City Bar Association* (Sept. 13, 2012), *available at* https://www.justice.gov/opa/speech/assistant-attorney-general-lanny-breuer-speaks-new-york-city-bar-association (last visited Jan. 17, 2012)..

349 *E.g.*, U.S. Dep't of Justice, Re: UTStarcom, Inc. (Dec. 31, 2009), *available at* http://www.justice.gov/criminal/pr/documents/12-31-09UTSI-%20NPA-Agreement.pdf (last visited Aug. 5, 2014).

the corporate audit committee.[350] For example, in its settlement with the DOJ, Pfizer, Inc. agreed to a plea to criminal charges for off-label promotion of the drug Bextra. It agreed to a civil settlement of claims for off-label promotion of Bextra and other drugs. It agreed to a civil resolution of allegations of illegal kickbacks to physicians to induce them to prescribe certain drugs.[351] Finally, Pfizer also entered into a Corporate Integrity Agreement with the Office of Inspector General of the Department of Health and Human Services.[352] That agreement required the CCO to report directly to the CEO and make reports to the audit committee. The agreement specifically prohibited the CCO from being (or being subordinate to) the general counsel or CFO.[353]

In addition, DPAs and NPAs "help define compliance 'best practices' for particular industries."[354] For example:

(1) A bank facing anti-money laundering (AML) and trade sanctions (a) increased its compliance spending and staffing, (b) "reorganized its AML department to strengthen its reporting lines and elevate its status within the institution as a whole by (i) separating the Legal and Compliance departments; (ii) requiring that the AML Director report directly to the Chief Compliance Officer; (iii) providing that the AML Director regularly report directly to the Board and senior management about [its] program;" and (c) exiting some business relationships that heightened the risk of future AML violations.[355]

(2) A money transfer firm facing AML allegations and allegations of aiding and abetting consumer fraud by its agents (a) created "an independent compliance and ethics committee of the board of directors with direct oversight of the chief compliance officer and the compliance program;" (b) adopted a worldwide anti-fraud and AML standard to ensure all its agents adhere to U.S. standards; and (c) adopted "enhanced due diligence for agents deemed to be high risk or operating in a high-risk area."[356]

---

350 Deferred Prosecution Agreement, United States v. Pfizer H.C.P. Corp., U.S. Dep't of Justice, Attachment C.2, at C.2-1 (D.D.C. rec'd Aug. 7, 2012), *available at* https://www.justice.gov/sites/default/files/criminal-fraud/legacy/2012/08/15/2012-08-07-pfizer-dpa.pdf (last visited May 22, 2017).

351 U.S. Dep't of Justice, *Pharmaceutical Company Pfizer, Inc. to Pay $301 Million for Off-Label Drug Marketing* (Sept. 2, 2009), *available at* http://www.justice.gov/usao/pae/News/2009/sep/pfizerrelease.pdf (last visited Aug. 5, 2014).

352 Corporate Integrity Agreement Between the Office of Inspector General of the Department of Health and Human Services and Pfizer Inc., *available at* http://oig.hhs.gov/fraud/cia/agreements/pfizer_inc.pdf (last visited Aug. 5, 2014).

353 *Id.* at 4.

354 *Accountability, Transparency, and Uniformity in Corporate Deferred and Non-Prosecution Agreements: Hearing Before the Subcomm. on Commercial & Admin. Law,* 111th Cong. 75--88 (2009) (statement of Gary G. Grindler, Deputy Assistant Att'y Gen. for the Criminal Div., U.S. Dep't of Justice), *quoted in* Julie R. O'Sullivan, *How Prosecutors Apply the "Federal Prosecutions of Corporations" Charging Policy in the Era of Deferred Prosecutions, and What That Means for the Purposes of the Federal Criminal Sanction,* 51 AM. CRIM. L. REV. 29, 57(2014), LEXIS, News Lib, Curnws File.

355 Information, United States v. USBC Bank USA, N.A., No. 1:12-cr-00763-ILG (filed Dec. 11, 2012), *available at* http://www.justice.gov/opa/documents/hsbc/hsbc-info.pdf (last visited Aug. 4, 2014); Statement of Facts, United States v. USBC Bank USA, N.A., No. 1:12-cr-00763-ILG (filed Dec. 11, 2012), *available at* http://www.justice.gov/opa/documents/hsbc/dpa-attachment-a.pdf (last visited Aug. 4, 2014).

356 U.S. Dep't of Justice, *Moneygram International Inc. Admits Anti-Money Laundering and Wire Fraud Violations, Forfeits $100 Million in Deferred Prosecution* (Nov. 9, 2012), *available at* https://www.justice.gov/opa/pr/moneygram-international-inc-

(3) A manufacturing firm facing allegations that it illegally imported wood protected under environmental laws agreed to "implement a compliance program designed to strengthen its compliance controls and procedures" and "guard against the acquisition of wood of illegal origin by verifying the circumstances of its harvest and export."[357]

Other notable DPAs include those involving Bristol-Myers[358] and another involving Pfizer.[359]

B. Buckingham Research Group[360]

In *Buckingham Research Group* the SEC ordered that the respondents cease and desist from violations and violations of Section 15(f) of the Securities Exchange Act[361] and Sections 204(a), 204A and 206(4) of the Investment Advisers Act[362] and Rule 206(4)-7[363] as appropriate. Respondents agreed to remedial undertakings and other sanctions including censure and money damages.

Summary

1. From at least September 2005, BRG, a registered broker-dealer and institutional equity research firm, and its subsidiary, BCM, a registered investment adviser, failed to establish, maintain and enforce policies and procedures reasonably designed, taking into account the nature of their respective and interconnected businesses, to prevent the misuse of material, nonpublic information. For 2005, BCM also failed to conduct an annual review of the adequacy of its compliance policies and procedures and the effectiveness of their implementation, as required by the Advisers Act.

---

admits-anti-money-laundering-and-wire-fraud-violations-forfeits (last visited May 24, 2017).

357 U.S. Dep't of Justice, *Gibson Guitar Corp. Agrees to Resolve Investigation into Lacey Act Violations* (Aug. 6, 2012), *available at* https://www.justice.gov/opa/pr/gibson-guitar-corp-agrees-resolve-investigation-lacey-act-violations (last visited May 23, 2017).

358 Deferred Prosecution Agreement (June 5, 2006), *available at* http://www.law.virginia.edu/pdf/faculty/garrett/bristol-meyers.pdf (last visited Aug. 5, 2014).

Deferred Prosecution Agreement (June 15, 2005), *available at* https://www.sec.gov/Archives/edgar/data/14272/000119312505125970/dex992.htm (last visited Jan. 17, 2017).

359 Deferred Prosecution Agreement (Aug. 15, 2012), *available at* https://www.justice.gov/sites/default/files/criminal-fraud/legacy/2012/08/15/2012-08-07-pfizer-dpa.pdf (last visited Jan. 17, 2017).

360 *In re* Buckingham Res. Group, Inc., 34-63323, IC-3109 (Nov. 17, 2010).

361 15 U.S.C. § 78o(f) (2012).

362 15 U.S.C. §§ 80b-4(a), 80b-4A, 80b-6(4) (2012).

363 17 C.F.R. § 275.206(4)-7 (2016).

2. BRG and BCM's policies and procedures were deficient in a number of ways. BRG had a written procedure to address the misuse of material, nonpublic information, but did not follow its written procedure in practice. Important compliance policies and procedures were not contained in BCM's written policies and procedures. Further, in some instances, BCM's written policies and procedures were so unclear that employees did not understand their responsibilities. In other instances, the practices BCM employed varied materially from its written policies and procedures. These failures led to inadequate implementation and enforcement of the firms' written compliance policies and procedures.

3. BCM also failed to create and maintain records evidencing important supervisory authorizations and compliance reviews. In October 2006, the SEC examination staff began conducting an examination of BCM. In the course of preparing for the examination and collecting records to produce to the SEC staff, BCM discovered that certain compliance-related records were incomplete and that others were missing from its files. BCM personnel altered its records by creating compliance documents, and produced those records to the SEC examination staff without disclosing that those records included "replacements" for incomplete or missing records. This conduct prevented the examination staff from discovering BCM's failure to follow its compliance procedures and violated BCM's statutory obligation to make its records available for examination.

4. Karp was the chief compliance officer of both BRG and BCM during the relevant period and was directly responsible for establishing and administering the firms' compliance programs, including policies and procedures reasonably designed to prevent misuse of material, nonpublic information. Karp failed to discharge those responsibilities adequately, which resulted in the violations by BRG and BCM.

Respondents

5. BRG is a Delaware corporation with its principal place of business in New York City. Since 1982, it has been registered with the Commission as a broker-dealer pursuant to Section 15(b) of the Exchange Act. BRG's primary business is providing equity research to hedge funds, broker-dealers, and other institutional customers, and the firm is known for its research in retail, apparel, and footwear.

BRG obtains the majority of its revenue from executing trades for its research customers.

6. BCM is a Delaware corporation with its principal place of business in New York City. Since December 1985, it has been registered with the Commission as an investment adviser pursuant to Section 203(c) of the Advisers Act. BCM is a wholly-owned subsidiary of BRG. BCM provides discretionary investment advisory services to investors that include high net worth individuals and various entities. BCM offers its clients equity portfolio management through two groups of funds, one that invests in the retail, apparel and footwear sector and one that invests in a diversified portfolio.

7. Lloyd Karp, age 52, was the chief compliance officer of both BRG and BCM from December 2002 to May 2010. He has also been the chief operations officer of BRG since 2004, and is the corporate secretary, treasurer, and a senior vice-president of the firm. Karp has a small direct ownership interest in BRG. Karp has Series 7, Series 8 and Series 63 licenses, and has been an associated person and registered principal of BRG since December 2002.

Facts

A. Compliance Failures

8. BRG and BCM have adjoining office space, separated only by a partial glass barrier, and they share certain facilities. In addition to their parent-subsidiary relationship, BRG and BCM share a chief executive officer and, until May 2010, Karp was the chief compliance officer of both firms. BRG analysts cover, and BCM invests in, securities in a wide range of industry sectors, including the retail, apparel, and footwear sector ("RAF"). Two of the senior portfolio managers of BCM's RAF strategy are former BRG analysts. BCM is a significant brokerage customer of BRG; its trading accounts for approximately 25% of BRG's commission revenue. Taking into consideration the nature of the firms' business and relationship, BCM and BRG did not establish, maintain and enforce written policies and procedures reasonably designed to prevent misuse of material, nonpublic information.

9. In January 2005, to address the information flow risk between BRG and BCM, BRG instituted a Material Research Information ("MRI") review procedure

to detect and prevent potential misuse by BCM of BRG material research information, such as the initiation of research coverage or changes in price targets. BRG's written policy required research analysts to complete a certification form whenever there was an MRI event, attesting that they had maintained confidentiality of the material research information. The policy specifically identified two reasons for the certification: to document compliance with the firm's confidentiality policy and to remind the analyst of his/her responsibility to restrict disclosure of material research information. However, in practice, BRG did not follow its written policy. Instead, BRG required an analyst to complete a certification only if a compliance assistant determined that BCM had traded in the stock in the same direction as the research and requested the analyst certification. Nor did BRG uniformly adhere to this practice—in some instances, analyst certifications were lacking or incomplete, and some were dated long after the MRI event occurred. In February 2007, BRG changed its written policy to conform to its practice.

10. Before February 2007, BCM's written policies did not address the potential misuse of BRG material research information. In practice, if a BRG analyst was required to complete a certification, the BCM portfolio manager who directed the trade was asked afterward to provide a written explanation of the basis for his investment decision. This practice was not consistently followed. Further, prior to 2007, the compliance staff did not request back-up information to determine whether the portfolio manager's explanation was reasonable. In early 2007, BCM incorporated the BRG practice into its written policies and procedures.

11. Two of BCM's senior portfolio managers are former executives of companies in the retail, apparel, and footwear sector. They have long-standing, collegial relationships with industry insiders. In addition, some of these industry insiders are BCM investors. Until May 2009, BCM's written "Insider Trading Prohibitions" policy required that persons with access to material, nonpublic information report "all business, financial, or personal relationships that may result in access to material, non-public information" (emphasis added). However, BCM never followed its written policy. Instead, the firm required employees to report only relationships that actually did result in access to material, nonpublic information. BCM did not compile a list of its investors who are RAF insiders to use for compliance review of its trading.

12. Rule 206(4)-7(a) requires an investment adviser to adopt and implement written policies and procedures reasonably designed to prevent violations of the Advisers Act and the rules thereunder. Karp created a compliance review log form in 2005 to ensure that important compliance reviews, including best execution and observing client guidelines and restrictions, had been conducted and thereby prevent violations of the anti-fraud provisions of the Advisers Act. However, as late as June 2009, BCM had no written procedure that adequately set forth the use of the compliance review log, and, therefore, BCM's personnel had no uniform understanding of its use.

13. Rule 206(4)-7(b) requires an investment adviser to review, at least annually, the adequacy of its policies and procedures and the effectiveness of their implementation. BCM failed to conduct an annual compliance review for 2005.

14. In late 2003 and early 2004, the SEC examination staff identified deficiencies in BCM's monitoring of employees' personal trading, and documented those findings in a deficiency letter to the firm. The staff specifically stated that BCM's written policies and procedures should be updated to reflect its current policies and procedures.

15. In a written response to the staff, prepared by Karp, BCM represented that it would cure the deficiencies identified by the examination staff by adding certain documentation and review requirements. The remedial steps included: requiring all employees to use a pre-approval form to document pre-approval of their trades; requiring Karp to conduct quarterly reviews of all employee trading to determine that the pre-approval and documentation requirements had been met; and requiring Karp to initial and date a compliance log to confirm that quarterly reviews had been performed.

16. BCM and Karp failed to implement these remedial steps fully. The updates to BCM's written policies and procedures did not clearly or completely reflect these new procedures, including use and maintenance of the pre-approval forms and completion of the compliance log. Karp did not conduct the promised quarterly review of all employee trading to assure that pre-approval and documentation requirements had been met.

17. For the entire period of the conduct described above, Karp was the chief compliance officer at both firms and was responsible for establishing and

administering their compliance policies and procedures. Karp was aware of the compliance weaknesses and failures and either failed to act or failed to correct them.

B. BCM's Failures to Produce

18. When BCM began preparing for the 2006 examination by the Commission staff, BCM discovered that it was missing pre-approval forms for more than 100 employee trades in 2005. However, instead of producing the incomplete employee trading records for the exam staff, BCM altered the records produced by creating and adding forms, and produced the existing records along with the added forms to the Commission examination staff without disclosing what had been done.

19. During the 2006 exam, BCM also discovered that its compliance review logs for 2005 and 2006 were incomplete. Karp had not initialed and dated the compliance logs and had not checked them regularly. Instead of producing the incomplete compliance logs, BCM staff altered the firm's records by replacing the incomplete logs with newly-created ones that the staff had various BCM personnel initial, creating the appearance that all the reviews had been completed in a timely way, that various compliance reviews were being logged properly, and that Karp was following through on his promise to use the log to track his quarterly employee trading review. BCM produced those replacement logs to the Commission examination staff without disclosing what had been done.

20. Karp was on medical leave at the time the 2006 examination commenced and did not have primary responsibility for BCM's response to the Commission staff's examination requests.

Legal Discussion

21. Section 15(f) of the Exchange Act requires brokers and dealers to establish, maintain, and enforce written policies and procedures reasonably designed, taking into consideration the nature of such broker's or dealer's business, to prevent the misuse of material, nonpublic information by such broker or dealer or any person associated with such broker or dealer. "Person associated with a broker or dealer" is defined in Section 3(a)(18) of the Exchange Act to include

"any person directly or indirectly... controlled by, or under common control with" the broker or dealer. Accordingly, BCM is an associated person of BRG.

22. Section 204A of the Advisers Act requires investment advisers to establish, maintain and enforce written policies and procedures reasonably designed, taking into consideration the nature of such investment adviser's business, to prevent the misuse of material, nonpublic information by such investment adviser or any person associated with such investment adviser. "Person associated with an investment adviser" is defined in Section 202(a)(17) of the Advisers Act to include "any person directly or indirectly...controlling" the investment adviser. Accordingly, BRG is an associated person of BCM.

23. Taking into consideration the relationship between BRG and BCM, BRG's research and BCM's investment in the RAF sector, their overlapping senior management, and their physical proximity, the firms' policies and procedures were not reasonably designed to prevent the misuse of material, nonpublic information. Despite the need for enhanced controls to prevent the misuse of material, nonpublic information presented by the firms' relationship, BCM and BRG failed to establish adequate written policies and procedures to address those risks. BRG had a written policy to address the misuse of material, nonpublic information, its MRI review, but did not follow that written policy in practice. Important compliance procedures, such as the MRI review, were not contained in BCM's written policies and procedures until 2007. Further, in some instances, such as documenting employee trading pre-approval, BCM's written procedures were so unclear that employees did not understand their responsibilities. In other instances, such as identifying relationships that may result in access to material, nonpublic information, the practices BCM employed varied materially from its written procedures. These failures led to inadequate implementation and enforcement of the firms' written procedures. Accordingly, BRG willfully violated Section 15(f) of the Exchange Act, and BCM willfully violated Section 204A of the Advisers Act. As the chief compliance officer who was responsible for establishing and administering all compliance policies, including policies and procedures to prevent misuse of material, nonpublic information, Karp willfully aided and abetted and caused the firms' violations.

24. Section 206(4) of the Advisers act prohibits advisers from engaging in any act, practice, or course of business which is fraudulent, deceptive, or manipulative. Rule 206(4)-7 thereunder requires advisers to adopt and implement written

policies and procedures reasonably designed to prevent violation of the Act and the rules. BCM willfully violated Section 206(4) and Rule 206(4)-7 by failing to adopt and implement adequate written procedures with respect to use of the compliance log, which was designed, among other things, to monitor compliance reviews to prevent violation of the anti-fraud provisions of the Advisers Act. As the chief compliance officer who was responsible for establishing and administering all compliance policies, Karp willfully aided and abetted and caused BCM's violations.

25. Rule 206(4)-7(b) under Section 206(4) of the Advisers Act requires that an investment adviser review, at least annually, the adequacy of its policies and procedures and the effectiveness of their implementation. BCM willfully violated Advisers Act Section 206(4) and Rule 206(4)-7(b) thereunder by failing to conduct an annual compliance review for 2005. As the chief compliance officer who was responsible for establishing and administering all compliance policies, Karp willfully aided and abetted and caused BCM's violations.

26. Section 204(a) of the Advisers Act provides that all records of an investment adviser are subject to examination by the Commission. The Commission's examination authority is fundamental to its ability to protect investors by monitoring investment advisers' compliance with the federal securities laws. Regulated firms cannot undermine this crucial component of Commission oversight by producing altered records or by supplementing existing records with replacements for missing documents, even if not required records, without disclosure of the additions and alterations to the Commission examination staff. BCM was obligated under Section 204(a) to produce its records for the Commission examination staff as those records existed at the time of the exam staff's request. BCM willfully violated Section 204(a) by failing to produce to the examination staff its incomplete compliance logs and by creating records and producing them to the exam staff without disclosing what had been done.

Respondents' Remedial Efforts

27. In determining to accept the Offers, the Commission considered remedial acts undertaken by Respondents and cooperation afforded the Commission staff.

Undertakings

28. Respondents BRG and BCM have undertaken to:

A. Retain, at Respondents' expense and within 30 (thirty) days of the issuance of this Order, a qualified independent consultant (the "Consultant") not unacceptable to the staff of the Division of Enforcement (the "Staff") to conduct a comprehensive review of Respondents' policies, practices, and procedures to ensure compliance with the federal securities laws, including: (1) the prevention of the misuse of material, nonpublic information as required, for BRG, by Section 15(f) of the Exchange Act and, for BCM, by Section 204A of the Advisers Act, taking into account and consideration the nature of Respondents' businesses and the relationship between the two Respondents; and (2) BCM's policies and procedures required by Section 206(4) of the Advisers Act and Rule 206(4)-7 thereunder, and to prepare the written reports, referenced below, review-ing the adequacy of each Respondent's policies, practices, and procedures and making recom-mendations regarding how Respondents should modify or supplement their respective policies, practices, and procedures, taking into account and consideration the nature of their businesses and the relationship between them, to prevent the misuse of material, nonpublic information in compliance with Section 15(f) of the Exchange Act and Sections 204A and 206(4) of the Advisers Act. Respondents shall provide a copy of the engagement letter detailing the Consultant's responsibilities to [the Assistant Director of the Division of Enforcement];

B. Cooperate fully with the Consultant, including providing the Consultant with access to their respective files, books, records, and personnel as reasonably requested for the above-mentioned review, and obtaining the cooperation of their respective employees or other persons under their control;

C. Require the Consultant to report to the Staff on his/her/its activities as the Staff shall request;

D. Permit the Consultant to engage such assistance, clerical, legal or expert, as necessary and at a reasonable cost, to carry out his/her/its activities, and the cost, if any, of such assistance shall be borne exclusively by Respondents;

E. Within ninety (90) days of the issuance of this Order, unless otherwise extended by the Staff for good cause, Respondents shall require the Consultant to complete the review described in subparagraph A above and prepare a written Preliminary Report that: (i) evaluates the adequacy under Section 15(f) of the Exchange Act and Sections 204A and 206(4) of the Advisers Act of each Respondent's policies, practices, and procedures, taking into account and consideration the nature of their businesses and the relationship between them, to prevent the misuse of material, nonpublic information; and (ii) makes any recommendations about modifications thereto or additional or supplemental procedures deemed necessary to remedy any deficiencies described in the Preliminary Report. Respondents shall require the Consultant to provide the Preliminary Report simultaneously to both the Staff (at the address set forth above) and Respondents;

F. Within one hundred and twenty (120) days of Respondents' receipt of the Preliminary Report, Respondents shall adopt and implement all recommendations set forth in the Preliminary Report; provided, however, that as to any recommendation that Respondents consider to be, in whole or in part, unduly burdensome or impractical, Respondents may submit in writing to the Consultant and the Staff (at the address set forth above), within thirty (30) days of receiving the Preliminary Report, an alternative policy, practice, or procedure designed to achieve the same objective or purpose. Respondents shall then attempt in good faith to reach an agreement with the Consultant relating to each recommendation that Respondents consider to be unduly burdensome or impractical and request that the Consultant reasonably evaluate any alternative policy, practice, or procedure proposed by Respondents. Within fourteen (14) days after the conclusion of the discussion and evaluation by Respondents and the Consultant, Respondents shall require that the Consultant inform Respondents and the Staff (at the address set forth above) of his/her/its final determination concerning any recommendation that Respondents consider to be unduly burdensome or impractical. Respondents shall abide by the determinations of the Consultant and, within sixty (60) days after final agreement between Respondents and the Consultant or final determination by the Consultant, whichever occurs first, Respondents shall adopt and implement all of the recommendations that the Consultant deems appropriate;

G. Within fourteen (14) days of Respondents' adoption of all of the recommendations that the Consultant deems appropriate, Respondents shall certify in writing to the Consultant and the Staff (at the address set forth above) that Respondents have adopted and implemented all of the Consultant's recommendations and that Respondents have established policies, practices, and procedures as required by Section 15(f) of the Exchange Act and Sections 204A and 206(4) of the Advisers Act that are consistent with the findings of this Order;

H. Within one hundred and eighty (180) days from the date of the certifications described in subparagraph G above, Respondents shall require the Consultant to have completed a review of Respondents' revised policies and procedures and practices and submit a written Final Report to Respondents and the Staff. The Final Report shall describe the review made of Respondents' revised policies, practices, and procedures and describe how Respondents are implementing, enforcing, and auditing the enforcement and implementation of those policies, practices, and procedures. The Final Report shall include an opinion of the Consultant as to whether the revised policies, practices, and procedures and their implementation and enforcement by

Respondents and Respondents' auditing of the implementation and enforcement of those poli-cies, practices, and procedures are reasonably adequate under Section 15(f) of the Exchange Act and Sections 204A and 206(4) of the Advisers Act;

I. Respondents may apply to the Staff for an extension of the deadlines described above before their expiration and, upon a showing of good cause by Respondents, the Staff may, in its sole discretion, grant such extensions for whatever time period it deems appropriate.In addition, Respondents may not terminate the Consultant without SEC staff approval and the Consultant may not enter into certain relationships with Respondents during the engagement and for the following two years. Respondents must also certify to the SEC staff, as of calendar year 2011, that they "have established and continue to maintain policies, practices, and procedures as required by [applicable statutes] that are consistent with the findings of this Order."[364]

Discussion Topics and Exercise

Please prepare: (a) a request by BCM and BRG for an extension of the deadlines mentioned in the above order; (b) a statement by Mr. Karp to his employees in the compliance group; and (c) a statement to be issued by BCM and BRG management to the press. (d) As an external monitor, please prepare a list of the people you would speak to on your visit and the questions you would ask them. Or (e) you may choose instead to be the internal compliance officer and prepare the questions you might be asked and your expected answers.

C. Eli Lilly and Company[365]

The Securities and Exchange Commission today charged Eli Lilly and Company with violations of the Foreign Corrupt Practices Act (FCPA) for improper payments its subsidiaries made to foreign government officials to win millions of dollars of business in Russia, Brazil, China, and Poland.

The SEC alleges that the Indianapolis-based pharmaceutical company's subsidiary in Russia used offshore "marketing agreements" to pay millions of dollars to third parties chosen by gov-ernment customers or distributors, despite knowing little or nothing about the third parties beyond their offshore address and bank account information. These offshore entities rarely pro-vided any services and in some instances were used to funnel money to government officials in order to obtain business for the subsidiary. Transactions with offshore or government-affiliated entities did not receive specialized or closer review for possible FCPA violations. Paperwork

---

364 . *In re* Buckingham Res. Group, Inc., 34-63323, IC-3109 (Nov. 17, 2010).

365 U.S. Sec. & Exch. Comm'n, *SEC Charges Eli Lilly and Company with FCPA Violations* (Dec. 12, 2012), *available at* https://www.sec.gov/news/press-release/2012-2012-273htm (last visited May 23, 2017).

was accepted at face value and little was done to assess whether the terms or circumstances surrounding a transaction suggested the possibility of foreign bribery.

The SEC alleges that when the company did become aware of possible FCPA violations in Russia, Lilly did not curtail the subsidiary's use of the marketing agreements for more than five years. Lilly subsidiaries in Brazil, China, and Poland also made improper payments to government officials or third-party entities associated with government officials. Lilly agreed to pay more than $29 million to settle the SEC's charges.

"When a parent company learns tell-tale signs of a bribery scheme involving a subsidiary, it must take immediate action to assure that the FCPA is not being violated," said Antonia Chion, Associate Director in the SEC Enforcement Division. "We strongly caution company officials from averting their eyes from what they do not wish to see."

Kara Novaco Brockmeyer, Chief of the SEC Enforcement Division's Foreign Corrupt Practices Unit, added, "Eli Lilly and its subsidiaries possessed a 'check the box' mentality when it came to third-party due diligence. Companies can't simply rely on paper-thin assurances by employees, distributors, or customers. They need to look at the surrounding circumstances of any payment to adequately assess whether it could wind up in a government official's pocket."

As alleged in the SEC's complaint filed in federal court in Washington D.C.:

- Lilly's subsidiary in Russia paid millions of dollars to offshore entities for alleged "marketing services" in order to induce pharmaceutical distributors and government entities to purchase Lilly's drugs, including approximately $2 million to an offshore entity owned by a government official and approximately $5.2 million to offshore entities owned by a person closely associated with an important member of Russia's parliament. Despite the company's recognition that the marketing agreements were being used to "create sales potential" with government customers and that it did not appear that any actual services were being rendered under the agreements, Eli Lilly allowed its subsidiary to continue using the agreements for years.

- Employees at Lilly's subsidiary in China falsified expense reports in order to provide spa treatments, jewelry, and other improper gifts and cash payments to government-employed physicians.

- Lilly's subsidiary in Brazil allowed one of its pharmaceutical distributors to pay bribes to government health officials to facilitate $1.2 million in sales of a Lilly drug product to state government institutions.

- Lilly's subsidiary in Poland made eight improper payments totaling $39,000 to a small charitable foundation that was founded and administered by the head of one of the regional government health authorities in exchange for the official's support for placing Lilly drugs on the government reimbursement list.

Lilly agreed to pay disgorgement of $13,955,196, prejudgment interest of $6,743,538, and a penalty of $8.7 million for a total payment of $29,398,734. Without admitting or denying the allegations, Lilly consented to the entry of a final judgment permanently enjoining the company from violating the anti-bribery, books and records, and internal controls provisions of the FCPA. Lilly also agreed to comply with certain undertakings including the retention of an independent consultant to review and make recommendations about its foreign corruption policies and procedures. The settlement is subject to court approval.

D. Western Asset Management[366]

In *Western Asset Management* (WAM) the SEC ordered that WAM cease and desist from violations and violations of Sections 206(2) and 206(4) of the Investment Advisers Act[367] and Rule 206(4)-7 thereunder.[368] WAM agreed to remedial undertakings and other sanctions including money damages and censure.

Summary

These proceedings arise out of an investment adviser's failure to disclose its violation of an issuer-imposed restriction prohibiting plans subject to Part 4 of Subtitle B of Title 1 of the Employee Retirement Income Security Act ("ERISA plans") from participating in a private placement. Respondent was aware no later than October 2008 that it had breached this offering restriction by allocating the security to ERISA accounts that it managed, yet failed to take prompt corrective action, contrary to its disclosed error correction policy. Specifically, Respondent did not notify most of its affected ERISA clients until August 2010, more than a year after Respondent had liquidated the securities out of all client accounts.

Respondent

1. Respondent Western Asset Management Company ("WAM"), a California corporation located in Pasadena, California, is an investment adviser registered with the Commission pursuant to Section 203(e) of the Advisers Act. WAM is a wholly-owned subsidiary of Legg Mason, Inc. As of September 30, 2013, WAM

---

366 *In re* Western Asset Mgmt. Co., Investment Advisers Act Release No. 3763 (Jan. 27, 2014). Footnotes omitted.

367 15 U.S.C. § 80b-6(2), (4) (2012).

368 17 C.F.R. § 275.206(4)-7 (2016).

reported $442.7 billion in assets under management. WAM provides investment management services primarily to institutional clients such as pension plans and mutual funds. Many of WAM's clients are ERISA plans.

Background

2. WAM's compliance policies, including its error correction policy, were set forth in WAM's Form ADV and its compliance manual. A copy of the current Form ADV was sent to each client when its account was opened.

3. During the relevant period, WAM's policies and procedures required it to notify its clients of any breach or error resulting in a loss. Specifically, WAM disclosed the following Error Correction Policy in its Form ADV from 2007 through 2009:

Western Asset's general policy, except where contractual arrangement or regulatory requirements provide otherwise, is (i) to make a client account whole for any net loss associated with a breach or an error; (ii) to retain in a client's account, a net gain resulting from an error. Western categorizes breaches and errors as follows:

1. Breaches of investment guidelines and/or investment restrictions resulting from any transaction or other factor whereby a transaction and/or portfolio is not consistent with:

   a. Regulatory requirements/restrictions (examples include, but are not limited to, legally improper or prohibited transactions with affiliates; legally improper or prohibited cash/currency transactions).

   b. Client mandates (includes prospectus for a fund).

2. Operational Errors

   a. Trading errors include, but are not limited to, execution of incorrect security transaction (other than as described above for breaches of guidelines, restrictions, or regulations)

   b. Settlement errors.

If breach or error occurs in a client portfolio, it is Western Asset's policy that the error will be corrected immediately or, in the case of guideline breaches, the client will be immediately be

[sic] contacted to obtain a waiver. If a waiver is declined, the error will be promptly corrected. If the breach, after correction, results in a gain to the client, that gain is retained in the client portfolio. If the client suffers a loss as a result of the breach, Western Asset will reimburse the account.

4. WAM relied heavily on an automated compliance system from Charles River Development ("Charles River") to comply with client investment guidelines. Once the investment guidelines for a particular client were entered into Charles River, WAM could monitor pre- and post-trade compliance with client investment guidelines through the system.

5. As the portfolio managers selected a security for the clients, and before a trade was allocated to accounts, the compliance staff determined whether that security comported with client investment guidelines by running the proposed account allocations through Charles River. If a client had a restriction prohibiting the proposed trade, the system generated an alert and WAM's pre-trade compliance staff advised the trading desk that the trade had been rejected. In addition, each morning, compliance officers reviewed exception reports for their assigned accounts to identify any guideline issues triggered by the prior day's trading activity.

6. If the proposed investment was a new issue, WAM's compliance staff populated certain attributes of the security (such as coupon rate, maturity, call date, registration status, and ERISA eligibility) before the proposed trades were processed through Charles River for pre-trade review. WAM's compliance personnel used information obtained from outside providers like Bloomberg and its own trading desk to populate the data fields for a new security into Charles River. Compliance staff did not independently review any offering documents.

WAM's Coding Error

7. On January 31, 2007, WAM purchased $50 million of the initial offering of Glen Meadow, a $500 million private placement that was designed to provide subordinated debt financing to the Hartford Insurance Group ("Hartford"). Glen Meadow was designated by market data providers as a corporate security. WAM received the preliminary offering memorandum that stated on the first page that the securities could be offered or sold only to an "eligible purchaser," defined to exclude employee benefit plans subject to ERISA. The preliminary offering

memorandum also required any participant in the offering to warrant that it was an eligible purchaser and agree to transfer the security only to other eligible purchasers, noting: "Any purported purchase or transfer of the Pass-Through Trust Securities in violation of this requirement will be void and without legal effect whatsoever. The purchaser understands and acknowledges that the Pass-Through Trust may also require the sale of its Pass-Through Trust Securities held by persons that fail to provide such certifications or otherwise comply with the [eligible purchaser requirement]."

8. Glen Meadow was initially coded in WAM's automated compliance system as an asset-backed security that was non-ERISA eligible. On February 1, 2007, a portfolio compliance officer, following up on an exception report from an overnight compliance run, directed WAM's back office staff to change the security type from "asset-backed security" to "corporate debt." Charles River, however, had been configured so that slightly different fields appeared on screen depending on whether the security was designated asset-backed or corporate debt. Changing the designation of Glen Meadow from asset-backed to corporate debt resulted in Charles River automatically populating this field as ERISA eligible without any user input.

9. The trader on WAM's corporate desk who was responsible for Glen Meadow was copied on the email message directing WAM's back office staff to change the security designation thereby updating ERISA field, but he did not raise any concerns about ERISA. Portfolio compliance staff told WAM's back office staff to ignore alerts triggered by the Glen Meadow security, assuring them that according to the trader on WAM's corporate desk, this was "a corporate note and is ERISA eligible." Neither the portfolio compliance staff nor the trader recognized, and accordingly neither advised the back office, that the security was not eligible for ERISA accounts.

10. In the following months, WAM continued purchasing the Glen Meadow security for the accounts of its clients, ultimately purchasing $204 million of Glen Meadow for 233 client accounts, including more than $90 million par value for 99 ERISA client accounts.

WAM's Discovery and Failure to Disclose the Coding Error

11. On October 7, 2008, WAM received an email message from a former institutional client (the "Former Client") notifying WAM that the Glen Meadow security WAM had purchased for the Former Client's master pension trust account was not ERISA eligible. By the time WAM received this notice, eight of the original 99 ERISA accounts that had purchased the Glen Meadow security were closed, transferred, or had exited the position.

12. Initially, upon learning of the coding error, WAM compliance staff changed the ERISA field in Charles River from ERISA eligible to ERISA ineligible. Re-coding the security in Charles River allowed compliance staff to run "fallout" reports to determine the impact of the error. The first fallout report completed on October 8, 2008 indicated that 94 accounts were impacted and many of these accounts were coded "[n]o non-ERISA [securities]."

13. Even though WAM had promptly identified the affected accounts, it did not immediately correct the error or notify clients. WAM's compliance staff instead completed an internal portfolio breach compliance report to document the issue reported by the Former Client. According to this report, the issue arose because "[t]he security was improperly coded as ERISA eligible when it was in fact a non-ERISA eligible security." The report also indicated that the price at purchase was "100" or par. The report further noted that when the Former Client transferred its account to a new adviser on October 1, 2008, Glen Meadow was trading at a price of $73.78, resulting in an unrealized loss of $ 226,872.95.

14. WAM then launched a three-month investigation into the matter. Although WAM acknowledged that an internal coding issue had caused it to breach an issuer-imposed offering restriction, WAM's compliance staff first determined that there was no "error" within the meaning of WAM's error correction policy, which specifically referenced regulatory, trading, and settlement errors. WAM focused its investigation on whether there had been a violation of ERISA and whether any client guidelines had been breached. WAM staff conducted key word searches of client guidelines to determine whether any of the affected ERISA clients had guidelines forbidding investment in ERISA ineligible securities. The key word searches failed to uncover the applicable guidelines for two accounts belonging to one client. WAM compliance staff also failed to discover a guideline breach unrelated to ERISA in the account of a second

client. As a result, they incorrectly concluded that the allocation of the Glen Meadow security to ERISA accounts did not violate the investment guidelines applicable to these three accounts. WAM also confirmed that the issuer-imposed restriction against participation in the offering by ERISA plans was still in place. In addition, WAM consulted with outside counsel on legal aspects of the issue.

15. In December 2008, WAM's committee which oversaw the resolution of possible investment compliance issues met and received a summary of the Glen Meadow matter from inside counsel. The committee concluded, based on the factual investigation and legal analysis of inside and outside counsel presented at that meeting, that there had been no guideline breaches and no "prohibited transaction" under ERISA, _29 U.S.C. 1106_ (generally forbidding transactions between an ERISA plan, on the one hand, and a plan fiduciary or a party in interest, on the other) at the time of purchase, but that WAM might have potential exposure to the issuer for breaching the terms of the offering. In light of this information, the Committee did not discuss whether WAM had any obligations to notify clients of the allocation error under its Error Correction Policy.

16. Although WAM concluded there had been no guideline breaches or ERISA prohibited transactions affecting its clients, it realized that its ERISA clients might still be concerned. As a result, WAM explored selling the Glen Meadow position out of all ERISA accounts in February and March 2009. This effort met with little success. In an email dated March 6, 2009, a WAM trader advised his colleagues that although "we're still trying to find bids, the entire space is taking a hit and the liquidity for [Glen Meadow] is not particular [sic] well." During this time, the price of the Glen Meadow security continued to deteriorate. By March 10, 2009, real-time broker quotes for the Glen Meadow security had fallen to $22. These liquidity and pricing problems caused WAM to abandon its attempts to sell the security out of all ERISA accounts.

17. Because WAM concluded that no breach or error occurred, WAM did not notify its affected ERISA clients that it had allocated the Glen Meadow security to their accounts in violation of an issuer-imposed offering restriction. Nor did WAM offer to make its affected ERISA clients whole for losses attributable to the Glen Meadow security. By interpreting its error correction policy narrowly, WAM effectively exempted issues relating to the allocation of Glen Meadow to ERISA accounts from its own compliance controls.

18. In May 2009, Hartford announced it had received preliminary approval for Troubled Asset Relief Program funds, and liquidity and pricing for Glen Meadow improved. Accordingly, WAM sold all holdings in the Glen Meadow security from ERISA and non-ERISA client accounts between May and June 2009 pursuant to a decision of the investment desk. Although WAM was able to sell Glen Meadow, the sales were at prices materially lower than the purchase prices for Glen Meadow for all of WAM's ERISA and non-ERISA clients.

19. Before executing these sales, WAM did not inform its ERISA clients that the Glen Meadow security had been allocated to their accounts due to its coding error. Nor did WAM advise its clients of its error immediately after selling the Glen Meadow security out of their accounts.

20. WAM did not notify its ERISA clients that it had erroneously purchased the Glen Meadow security for their accounts until August 2010, by which time WAM was aware of the SEC investigation.

WAM's Violations of Section 206(2) of the Advisers Act

21. As a result of the conduct described above, WAM willfully violated Section 206(2) of the Advisers Act. This section prohibits any investment adviser from engaging in any transaction, practice, or course of business which operates as a fraud or deceit upon any client or prospective client. Pursuant to Section 206(2), investment advisers have a fiduciary duty that requires them to act in the best interests of their clients and to make full and fair disclosure of all material facts.

22. Although WAM's senior management was aware of the misallocation of Glen Meadow to ERISA accounts no later than December 2008, WAM did not promptly disclose it to affected ERISA clients. Instead, WAM sold the security at prices well below par in May and June 2009, resulting in substantial losses to client portfolios. More importantly, WAM did not notify its ERISA clients that Glen Meadow had been allocated to their accounts in error until more than a year after it had sold the position across all accounts. By negligently buying Glen Meadow for certain of its ERISA clients, delaying disclosure of its error, and failing to promptly reimburse its clients, WAM engaged in a transaction, practice, or course of business which operated as a fraud or deceit upon its clients.

WAM's Violations of Section 206(4) of the Advisers Act and Rule 206(4)-7 Thereunder

23. As a result of the conduct described above, WAM also willfully violated Advisers Act Section 206(4) and Rule 206(4)-7 thereunder. Rule 206(4)-7 requires investment advisers to "[a]dopt and implement written policies and procedures reasonably designed to prevent violation" of the Advisers Act and its rules. The Commission has stated that an adviser's failure "to have adequate compliance policies and procedures in place will constitute a violation of our rules independent of any other securities law violation." Compliance Programs of Investment Companies and Investment Advisers , Advisers Act Rel. No. 2204, 68 F.R. 74714, 74715 (Dec. 24, 2003) ("Compliance Release"). The Compliance Release further provides that "[t]he policies and procedures should be designed to prevent violations from occurring, detect violations that have occurred, and correct promptly any violations that have occurred." 68 F.R. at 74716. The Compliance Release also states that "[e]ach adviser, in designing its policies and procedures, should first identify conflicts and other compliance factors creating risk exposure for the firm and its clients in light of the firm's particular operations, and then design policies and procedures that address those risks." 68 F.R. at 74716.

24. WAM's compliance policies and procedures required it to notify its clients of any breaches or errors resulting in a loss and to make clients whole for such losses. WAM's error correction policy applied to allocation and coding errors. In implementing this policy, however, WAM determined that the allocation of Glen Meadow to ERISA accounts did not trigger the notification or reimbursement provisions of WAM's error correction policy. By applying a narrow definition of the term "error" under its error correction policy, WAM was able to conclude that a coding and allocation issue affecting 99 ERISA client accounts did not require disclosure. As a result, WAM did not notify its ERISA clients that it had improperly allocated Glen Meadow to their accounts for nearly two years. WAM therefore violated Rule 206(4)-7 by failing to implement policies and procedures reasonably designed to ensure that errors and breaches are promptly corrected and disclosed to affected clients.

WAM agreed to remedial efforts including retention of an Independent Compliance Consultant "to conduct a comprehensive review of [WAM's] supervisory, compliance, and other policies and procedures designed to resolve allocation and coding errors by [WAM] and its employees, including whether such policies and procedures are sufficiently detailed to constrain [WAM's] discretion to determine whether such errors are subject to [WAM's] Error Correction Policy. As part of its comprehensive review, the Independent Compliance Consultant will evaluate whether [WAM's] Error Correction Policy adequately discloses [WAM's] practices with respect to the treatment of such errors."[369]

Discussion topics

(a) How many mistakes and what kind of mistakes did WAM personnel make with awareness? Who made the mistakes?

(b) Who, if anyone, approved the mistakes? Who, if anyone, benefitted from the mistakes?

(c) In light of your answers, what should WAM management do to avoid recurrence of such mistakes?

(d) Which of the SEC orders in this case is most effective?

III. ISSUES CONCERNING DPAS

A. Consistency

One problem that surfaced when prosecutors exercised power concerning Deferred Prosecution Agreements is that their agreements lack uniformity. The United Kingdom has adopted a Deferred Prosecution Agreement Code of Practice to unify these agreements.[370]

The problem also arises when different regulators are involved. In 2012 Robert Khuzami, Director of the SEC's Division of Enforcement, noted that the policies of the SEC in a civil proceeding are different from the policies associated with a criminal proceeding:

> Following a review by senior enforcement staff that began this spring and separate discussions with the Commissioners over the last several months, last week we modified our settlement language for cases involving criminal convictions where a defendant has admitted violations of the criminal law. As explained below, the new policy does not require admissions or adjudications of

---

369 *In re* Western Asset Mgmt. Co., Investment Advisers Act Release No. 3763 (Jan. 27, 2014). Footnotes omitted.

370 SERIOUS FRAUD OFFICE & CROWN PROSECUTION SERVICE, DEFERRED PROSECUTION AGREEMENTS CODE OF PRACTICE (2014), *available at* https://www.cps.gov.uk/publications/directors_guidance/dpa_cop.pdf (last visited Jan. 17, 2017).

fact beyond those already made in criminal cases, but eliminates language that may be construed as inconsistent with admissions or findings that have already been made in the criminal cases.

Under our traditional "neither admit nor deny" approach, a defendant could be found guilty of criminal conduct and, at the same time, settle parallel SEC charges while neither admitting nor denying civil liability. This approach has reflected that the goals, objectives and other factors in the civil settlements that we and other federal and state agencies enter into often are distinguishable from those at issue in criminal proceedings. It nevertheless seemed unnecessary for there to be a "neither admit" provision in those cases where a defendant had been criminally convicted of conduct that formed the basis of a parallel civil enforcement proceeding.

The change applies to cases involving parallel (i) criminal convictions or (ii) NPAs or DPAs that include admissions or acknowledgments of criminal conduct. Under the new approach, for those settlements we will:

Delete the "neither admit nor deny" language from the settlement documents.

Recite the fact and nature of the criminal conviction or criminal NPA/DPA in the settlement documents.

Give the staff discretion to incorporate into the settlement documents any relevant facts admitted during the plea allocution or set out in a jury verdict form or in the criminal NPA/DPA.

Retain the current prohibition on denying the allegations of the Complaint/OIP or making statements suggesting the Commission's allegations are without factual basis.

The revision applies in the minority of our cases where there is a parallel criminal conviction (by plea or verdict) or criminal NPA/DPA involving factual or legal claims that overlap to some degree with the factual or legal claims set out in the Commission's complaint or OIP. . . .[371]

B. Secrecy

Arguably, one way of driving a strong compliance program is government pressure after serious corporate losses. In September 2013, the *Wall Street Journal* reported that "[s]ince 2008, J.P. Morgan has incurred more than $18 billion in legal expenses," more than any other U.S. bank. In addition, examiners from the Comptroller of the Currency and the Federal Reserve reportedly told CEO Jamie Dimon and the board "that they had lost trust in management." The "London Whale" trading scandal had cost the bank over $6 billion, and settlements with regulators could

---

371 Robert Khuzami, Director of the SEC's Division of Enforcement, U.S. Sec. & Exch. Comm'n, *Public Statement by SEC Staff: Recent Policy Change* (Jan. 7, 2012), *available at* http://www.sec.gov/News/PublicStmt/Detail/PublicStmt/1365171489600 (last visited Jan. 17, 2017).

cost $600 million. JPMorgan "acknowledged mistakes in managing the London situation" but "denied deliberately misleading investors."[372]

However, an agreement with the Department of Justice[373] did not end the affair. Better Markets Inc., a non-profit watchdog group, filed a lawsuit against the DOJ and Attorney General challenging the $13 billion agreement[374] Better Markets argued that the agreement gave JPMorgan "blanket civil immunity" for "egregious and widespread illegal conduct." Arguably, the DOJ's approval of the agreement without approval by the judicial branch violated the separation of powers doctrine. Better Markets also noted "the unique facts and circumstances of this case," including the facts that the claims related to fraud contributed to a crash and that the settlement and FIRREA penalties were the largest ever.[375] Arguably, the government should explain why it settled rather than sued, and should have publicly disclosed what it knew before it settled.

Discussion Topic

Why was secrecy important in this case? Was it justified? If secrecy was important, who was it important to? What did the leadership of JP Morgan learn about this issue, if anything?

C. Rehabilitation

An interesting view of compliance was drawn from an analogy in sentencing persons guilty of criminal activities in which judges have adopted alternatives to incarceration including alcohol and drug treatment and recognized post-offense rehabilitation as a ground for sentencing mitigation.[376] Courts have increasingly recognized judges' discretion to defer sentencing to allow rehabilitation.[377]

---

372 Monica Langley & Dan Fitzpatrick, *Embattled J.P. Morgan Bulks up Oversight*, Wall St. J., Sept. 13, 2013, at A1.

373 Settlement Agreement, JPMorgan Chase (n.d.), *available at* https://www.justice.gov/iso/opa/resources/695201311191912469 41958.pdf (last visited May 24, 2017); U.S. Dep't of Justice, Justice Department, Federal and State Partners Secure Record $13 Billion Global Settlement with JPMorgan for Misleading Investors About Securities Containing Toxic Mortgages (Nov. 19, 2013), *available at* https://www.justice.gov/opa/pr/justice-department-federal-and-state-partners-secure-record-13-billion-global-settlement (last visited May 24, 2017).

374 Better Mkts., Inc. v. United States DOJ, 83 F. Supp. 3d 250 (D.D.C. 2015) (memorandum opinion) (dismissing action for lack of standing).

375 Plaintiff's Memorandum of Points and Authorities in Opposition to Defendant's Motion to Dismiss, Better Mkts., Inc. v. United States DOJ, 2014 U.S. Dist. Ct. Briefs LEXIS 317 (D.D.C. July 7, 2014).

376 Bruce J. Winick, *Redefining the Role of the Criminal Defense Lawyer at Plea Bargaining and Sentencing: A Therapeutic Jurisprudence/Preventive Law Model*, 5 Psych. Pub. Pol. & L. 1034, 1036 (1999).

377 *Id.* at 1037 (citing cases).

Therefore, attorneys should: (1) understand the rehabilitative approach, (2) apprise clients of it, (3) help devise rehabilitative plans, and (4) advocate as appropriate to prosecutors, probation officers, and sentencing judges.[378]

Discussion topics

*Some argue that settlements do not induce change of behavior and culture.[379] What is your opinion?

Problem

The SEC is examining the investment strategy devised by an asset management company called F-Squared. The strategy is to base a portfolio only on stocks that have improved over the past 10 years. In its marketing documents, F-Squared claimed that this strategy was very profitable. However, when a different mutual fund called Virtus Premium AlphaSector employed the strategy to a particular fund, its fund ultimately underperformed the market. While no investors actually lost money, the concern is that F-Squared marketed the strategy as producing higher returns than the actual, realized returns.

Moreover, F-Squared did not disclose that its strategy's alleged success may have been due in part to F-Squared's ability to cherry pick the portfolio with 20/20 hindsight, that is, to disclose its success after it has verified the success. The SEC is concerned about this non-compliance.[380] Advise F-Squared's Chief Compliance Officer before the SEC's visit has uncovered this information.

IV. DECLINATIONS OF PROSECUTION

Please review the DOJ and SEC criteria presented earlier in the chapter for whether to bring a criminal proceeding.

---

378 *Id.*

379 *Better Markets Statement on DOJ's Latest "Slap on the Wrist" Settlement Charade for Wall Street's Too-Big-To-Fail Banks*, BETTER MARKETS, May 20, 2015, *available at* https://www.bettermarkets.com/newsroom/better-markets-statement-doj%E2%80%99s-latest-%E2%80%9Cslap-wrist%E2%80%9D-settlement-charade-wall-street%E2%80%99s-too-big (last visited May 20, 2017).

380 Stephen Gandel, *Hot Mutual Fund Promised Amazing Returns Based on 'Fake History,'* FORTUNE, Sept. 5, 2014, *available at* http://fortune.com/2014/09/05/f-squared-sec-mutual-funds/?xid=nl_termsheet (last visited May 20, 2017).

The DOJ and SEC have provided examples of past declinations, including some factors taken into consideration, in the context of the Foreign Corrupt Practices Act, which generally prohibits American corporations and businesses from bribing foreign officials:[381]

Example 1: Public Company Declination

DOJ and SEC declined to take enforcement action against a public U.S. company. Factors taken into consideration included:

The company discovered that its employees had received competitor bid information from a third party with connections to a foreign government.

The company began an internal investigation, withdrew its contract bid, terminated the employees involved, severed ties to the third-party agent, and voluntarily disclosed the conduct to DOJ's Antitrust Division, which also declined prosecution.

During the internal investigation, the company uncovered various FCPA red flags, including prior concerns about the third-party agent, all of which the company voluntarily disclosed to DOJ and SEC.

The company immediately took substantial steps to improve its compliance program.

Example 2: Public Company Declination

DOJ and SEC declined to take enforcement action against a public U.S. company. Factors taken into consideration included:

With knowledge of employees of the company's subsidiary, a retained construction company paid relatively small bribes, which were wrongly approved by the company's local law firm, to foreign building code inspectors.

When the company's compliance department learned of the bribes, it immediately ended the conduct, terminated its relationship with the construction company and law firm, and terminated or disciplined the employees involved.

The company completed a thorough internal investigation and voluntarily disclosed to DOJ and SEC.

The company reorganized its compliance department, appointed a new compliance officer dedicated to anti-corruption, improved the training and compliance program, and undertook a review of all of the company's international third-party relationships.

---

381 Foreign Corrupt Practices Act of 1977, Pub. L. No. 95-213, 91 Stat. 1494, *codified as amended at* 15 U.S.C. §§ 78dd-1 to -3, 78m(b)(2)(A), (B) (2012).

Example 3: Public Company Declination

DOJ and SEC declined to take enforcement action against a U.S. publicly held industrial services company for bribes paid by a small foreign subsidiary. Factors taken into consideration included:

The company self-reported the conduct to DOJ and SEC.

The total amount of the improper payments was relatively small, and the activity appeared to be an isolated incident by a single employee at the subsidiary.

The profits potentially obtained from the improper payments were very small.

The payments were detected by the company's existing internal controls. The company's audit committee conducted a thorough independent internal investigation. The results of the investigation were provided to the government.

The company cooperated fully with investigations by DOJ and SEC.

The company implemented significant remedial actions and enhanced its internal control structure.

Example 4: Public Company Declination

DOJ and SEC declined to take enforcement action against a U.S. publicly held oil and gas services company for small bribes paid by a foreign subsidiary's customs agent. Factors taken into consideration included:

The company's timely internal controls detected a potential bribe before a payment was made.

When company management learned of the potential bribe, management immediately reported the issue to the company's General Counsel and Audit Committee and prevented the payment from occurring.

Within weeks of learning of the attempted bribe, the company provided in-person FCPA training to employees of the subsidiary and undertook an extensive internal investigation to determine whether any of the company's subsidiaries in the same region had engaged in misconduct.

The company self-reported the misconduct and the results of its internal investigation to DOJ and SEC.

The company cooperated fully with investigations by DOJ and SEC.

In addition to the immediate training at the relevant subsidiary, the company provided comprehensive FCPA training to all of its employees and conducted an extensive review of its anti-corruption compliance program.

The company enhanced its internal controls and record-keeping policies and procedures, including requiring periodic internal audits of customs payments.

As part of its remediation, the company directed that local lawyers rather than customs agents be used to handle its permits, with instructions that "no matter what, we don't pay bribes"—a policy that resulted in a longer and costlier permit procedure.

Example 5: Public Company Declination

DOJ and SEC declined to take enforcement action against a U.S. publicly held consumer-products company in connection with its acquisition of a foreign company. Factors taken into consideration included:

The company identified the potential improper payments to local government officials as part of its pre-acquisition due diligence.

The company promptly developed a comprehensive plan to investigate, correct, and remediate any FCPA issues after acquisition.

The company promptly self-reported the issues prior to acquisition and provided the results of its investigation to the government on a real-time basis.

The acquiring company's existing internal controls and compliance program were robust.

After the acquisition closed, the company implemented a comprehensive remedial plan, ensured that all improper payments stopped, provided extensive FCPA training to employees of the new subsidiary, and promptly incorporated the new subsidiary into the company's existing internal controls and compliance environment.

Example 6: Private Company Declination

In 2011, DOJ declined to take prosecutorial action against a privately held U.S. company and its foreign subsidiary. Factors taken into consideration included:

The company voluntarily disclosed bribes paid to social security officials in a foreign country.

The total amount of the bribes was small.

When discovered, the corrupt practices were immediately terminated.

The conduct was thoroughly investigated, and the results of the investigation were promptly provided to DOJ.

All individuals involved were either terminated or disciplined. The company also terminated its relationship with its foreign law firm.

The company instituted improved training and compliance programs commensurate with its size and risk exposure.[382]

V. THE UNITED KINGDOM REGULATORS' CODE CONCERNING DEFERRED PROSECUTION AGREEMENTS

Introduction

The following is a summarized example of a Deferred Prosecution Agreement Code of Practice ("Code") in the United Kingdom.[383] The proposed Code lists the factors that a prosecutor should consider when deciding whether to prosecute or offer a DPA instead. The Code was published and became effective in February 2014.[384]

A. "Whether a Deferred Prosecution Agreement is a possible disposal of alleged criminal conduct"

The prosecutor must apply a two-stage test, including an evidential test and a public interest test.[385]

1. Evidential test. Either (a) the evidential stage of the Full Code Test in the Code for Crown Prosecutors" must be met, i.e., there must be a "realistic prospect of conviction,"[386] or (b) there must be "at least a reasonable suspicion based upon some admissible evidence that P [the organization] has committed the offence, and there are reasonable grounds for believing that a continued investigation would provide further admissible evidence within a reasonable period of time, so that all the evidence together would be capable of establishing a realistic prospect of conviction."[387]

382 CRIM. DIV., U.S. DEP'T J., & ENFORCEMENT DIV., U.S. SEC. & EXCH. COMM'N, A RESOURCE GUIDE TO THE U.S. FOREIGN CORRUPT PRACTICES ACT 77-79 (2012), *available at* https://www.justice.gov/sites/default/files/criminal-fraud/legacy/2015/01/16/guide.pdf (last visited Feb. 13, 2017).

383 SERIOUS FRAUD OFFICE & CROWN PROSECUTION SERVICE, DEFERRED PROSECUTION AGREEMENTS CODE OF PRACTICE (2014), *available at* https://www.cps.gov.uk/publications/directors_guidance/dpa_cop.pdf (last visited Jan. 17, 2017).

384 Serious Fraud Office, *Deferred Prosecution Agreements: New Guidance for Prosecutors* (Feb. 14, 2014), *available at* https://www.sfo.gov.uk/2014/02/14/deferred-prosecution-agreements-new-guidance-prosecutors/ (last visited May 18, 2017).

385 SERIOUS FRAUD OFFICE & CROWN PROSECUTION SERVICE, DEFERRED PROSECUTION AGREEMENTS CODE OF PRACTICE ¶ 1.2 (2014), *available at* https://www.cps.gov.uk/publications/directors_guidance/dpa_cop.pdf (last visited Jan. 17, 2017).

386 Crown Prosecution Service, *The Principles We Follow, available at* https://www.cps.gov.uk/about/principles.html (last visited May 18, 2017).

387 *Id.* ¶ 1.2.i.

2. Public Interest Test. The public interest must be "properly served by the prosecutor not prosecuting but instead entering into a DPA with P."[388] "A prosecution will usually take place unless there are public interest factors against prosecution which clearly outweigh those tending in favour of prosecution."[389] "Investigation and prosecution of the bribery of a foreign public official should not be influenced by considerations of national economic interest, the potential effect upon relations with another State or the identity of the natural or legal persons involved."[390]

B. Factors in favor of prosecution:

Factors in favor of prosecution include: "The offence was committed at a time when P had no or an ineffective corporate compliance programme and it has not been able to demonstrate a significant improvement in its compliance programme since then."[391] Other factors are "Failure to notify the wrongdoing within reasonable time of the offending conduct coming to light"[392] or "Reporting the wrongdoing but failing to verify it, or reporting it knowing or believing it to be inaccurate, misleading, or incomplete."[393]

C. Factors against prosecution:

Factors against prosecution include "co-operation," i.e., "a genuinely proactive approach adopted by P's management team when the offending is brought to their notice, involving within a reasonable time of the offending coming to light reporting P's offending otherwise unknown to the prosecutor and taking remedial actions including, where appropriate, compensating victims." The prosecutor must "establish whether sufficient information about the operation and conduct of P has been supplied." "Co-operation will include identifying relevant witnesses, disclosing their accounts and the documents shown to them."[394]

D. Transparency.

Negotiations must be transparent. The prosecutor must "[e]nsure that a full and accurate record of negotiations is prepared and retained"[395] and "[e]nsure that the prosecution and P

---

388 *Id.* ¶¶ 1.2.ii, 2.4.

389 *Id.* ¶ 2.5.

390 *Id.* ¶ 2.7.

391 *Id.* ¶ 1.2.

392 *Id.* ¶ 1.2. (footnote omitted)

393 *Id.* ¶ 1.2.

394 *Id.* ¶ 1.2.

395 *Id.* ¶ 3.4.i.

have obtained sufficient information from each other so each can play an informed part in the negotiations."[396]

E. Subsequent use of information.

"The use to which information obtained by a prosecutor during the DPA negotiation period may subsequently be put is dealt with at paragraph 13 of Schedule 17 to the [Crime and Courts] Act [2013]."[397]

If the DPA is approved by the court, the statement of facts in the DPA may be used in subsequent criminal proceedings as an admission.[398]

If the DPA is not concluded, certain material related to the DPA may be used in evidence only in limited circumstances.[399] This material is: "(a) material that shows that P entered into negotiations for a DPA, including in particular— (i) any draft of the DPA; (ii) any draft of a statement of facts intended to be included within the DPA; (iii) any statement indicating that P entered into such negotiations;" or "(b) material that was created solely for the purpose of preparing the DPA or statement of facts."[400] It "may only be used in evidence against P— (a) on a prosecution for an offence consisting of the provision of inaccurate, misleading, or incomplete information, or (b) on a prosecution for some other offence where in giving evidence P makes a statement inconsistent with the material."[401]

F. Unused material and disclosure.

"P should have sufficient information to play an informed part in the negotiations. The purpose of disclosure here is to ensure that negotiations are fair and that P is not misled as to the strength of the prosecution case. The prosecutor must always be alive to the potential need to disclose material in the interests of justice and fairness in the particular circumstances of any case."[402]

---

396 *Id.* ¶ 3.4.ii.

397 *Id.* ¶ 4.1.

398 *Id.* ¶ 4.4.i.

399 *Id.* ¶ 4.4.ii.

400 Crime and Courts Act 2013, Schedule 17, pt. 1, ¶ 13(6), *available at* http://www.legislation.gov.uk/ukpga/2013/22/schedule/17/enacted (last visited May 16, 2016).

401 *Id.* ¶ 13(4).

402 Serious Fraud Office & Crown Prosecution Service, Deferred Prosecution Agreements Code of Practice ¶ 5.2 (2014), *available at* https://www.cps.gov.uk/publications/directors_guidance/dpa_cop.pdf (last visited Jan. 17, 2017).

"A statement of the prosecutor's duty of disclosure will be included in the terms and conditions letter provided to P at the outset of the negotiations."[403]

"The disclosure duty of the prosecutor . . . is a continuing one and the prosecutor must disclose to P any material that comes to light after the DPA has been agreed which satisfies the test for disclosure above."[404]

G. Statement of facts.

The statement of facts must "give particulars relating to each alleged offence"[405] and "include details where possible of any financial gain or loss, with reference to key documents that must be attached."[406]

"The parties should resolve any factual issues necessary to allow the court to agree terms of the DPA on a clear, fair, and accurate basis."[407]

"There is no requirement for formal admissions of guilt in respect of the offences charged by the indictment though it will be necessary for P to admit the contents and meaning of key documents referred to in the statement of facts."[408]

H. Terms.

The terms of a DPA must be "fair, reasonable, and proportionate."[409]

A DPA must normally include the organization's warranty "that the information provided to the prosecutor throughout the DPA negotiations and upon which the DPA is based does not knowingly contain inaccurate, misleading, or incomplete information relevant to the conduct P has disclosed to the prosecutor" and a requirement that the organization "notify the prosecutor and . . . provide where requested any documentation or other material that it becomes aware of whilst the DPA is in force which P knows or suspects would have been relevant to the offences particularised in the draft indictment."[410]

---

403 *Id.*

404 *Id.* ¶ 5.8

405 *Id.* ¶ 6.1.i.

406 *Id.* ¶ 6.1.ii.

407 *Id.* ¶ 6.2.

408 *Id.* ¶ 6.3.

409 *Id.* ¶ 7.2.

410 *Id.* ¶ 7.7.ii.

A DPA must normally also state "that the DPA relates only to the offences particularised in the counts of the draft indictment."[411] "Prosecutors should not agree to a term that would prevent P from being prosecuted for conduct not included in the indictment even where the conduct has been disclosed during the course of DPA negotiations but not charged."[412]

"Any financial penalty is to be broadly comparable to a fine that the court would have imposed upon P following a guilty plea."[413] "The discount for a guilty plea is applied by the sentencing court after it has taken into account all relevant considerations, including any assistance given by P. The level of the discount to reflect P's assistance would depend on the circumstances and the level of assistance given, and the parties should be guided by sentencing practice, statute, and pre-existing case law on this matter."[414]

I. Monitors.

"An important consideration for entering into a DPA is whether P already has a genuinely proactive and effective corporate compliance programme. The use of monitors should therefore be approached with care."[415]

The organization must "pay all the costs of the selection, appointment, remuneration of the monitor, and reasonable costs of the prosecutor associated with the monitorship during the monitoring period."[416]

If monitorship is proposed, before the DPA is approved the monitor must be selected and provisionally appointed, the terms of the monitorship must be agreed by the parties, and a detailed work plan for the first year and an outline work plan for the remainder of the monitoring period must be agreed with the monitor.[417]

J. Concurrent jurisdiction.

"The draft proposed application and any supporting documents must be submitted on a confidential basis to the court before the preliminary hearing."[418]

"The application must explain why the agreement is in the interests of justice and fair, reasonable, and proportionate. In so explaining the prosecutor must address issues such as concurrent

---

411 *Id.* ¶ 7.7.i.

412 *Id.* ¶ 7.7.i n.5.

413 *Id.* ¶ 8.3.

414 *Id.* ¶ 8.4.

415 *Id.* ¶ 7.11.

416 *Id.* ¶ 7.13.

417 *Id.* ¶ 7.18.

418 *Id.* ¶ 9.3.

jurisdiction, on-going and/or subsequent ancillary proceedings, any conduct outwith the scope of the DPA which P has disclosed to the prosecutor but which does not form part of the draft indictment on account of the [two-stage test] above."[419]

Note: The UK practice is not a controlling practice in the United States. Therefore, we examine practices in foreign countries in order to observe and learn, but not necessarily to follow, unless the practice is adopted in the United States. However, our examination of foreign rules is enhanced when the institution is operating in foreign countries that apply different laws.

Discussion topic

*Why did the U.K. engage in a Code for its regulators?

*Should the U.S. adopt a code similar to the U.K. code?

---

419 *Id.* ¶ 9.4.

IDENTIFYING AND ADDRESSING "CONDUCT RISK;" COMBINING BUSINESS AND LEGAL REGULATION, AND PREPARING FOR GOVERNMENT EXAMINATIONS

INTRODUCTION

Chapter 7 deals with the definition and nature of risk, which may be posed to institutions by the conduct of their employees and related persons. Section I defines the term "conduct risk" and the nature of the risk that a conduct may pose. Section II describes the view and attitude of the regulators to conduct risk. Section III outlines an institution's preparations for SEC's examiners "visit." Section IV invites an evaluation of external supervision of conduct risk.

I. THE DEFINITION OF CONDUCT RISK AND THE NATURE OF THE RISK IT MAY POSE

A. The Meaning of Risk in Our Context

Like many events that happen to us and many actions by us, self-regulation may involve the purpose of avoiding risk. Risk has many meanings and appears in many contexts. Let us define it. A dictionary defines "risk" in part as "possibility of loss or injury" or "someone or something that creates or suggests a hazard."[420] In finance, for example, we may speak of a risky investment, meaning that we are in danger of losing some, or all, of our investment. Crossing the street may involve the risk of being run over by a car. Annoying a friend may present the risk of losing a friendship. And so on. Risk signifies an unpleasant result from a stationary situation or an activity. The unpleasant result may involve loss of money, loss of friendship, loss of freedom; in sum, loss of something that we value, more or less. Finally, risk has a very broad dimension from almost none to almost certain to be the result. It relates to future possible (not assured), results.

---

420 *Risk, available at* https://www.merriam-webster.com/dictionary/risk (last visited Jan. 9, 2017).

In our area of study, we deal with the risk of any activity that involves the law and may bring undesirable results. However, not only are the unpleasant results unpredictable, but the law may be unpredictable as well. The risk we focus on is not a risk of being found to have violated the law, although our concern includes such a risk as well. Our main risk covers a far broader area: It is a risk that an activity, which is not necessarily a violation of the law, may—although not necessarily—lead to a violation of the law, and that such a violation may result in painful consequences.

Therefore, we are dealing with a wide range of activities or intentions that (a) contemplate some other range of activities (which may be quite legitimate, or may be tolerated as legitimate) that may lead to (b) a range of other activities, which may lead to (c) possible violations of the law, which may lead to (d) a range of possible punishments. The span of unpleasant possibilities in our case is quite wide. It may be high or low or medium. For example, any investment may be considered risky, but the measure of the possible financial loss may differ greatly.

Another aspect of a risk is the ability of the risk-takers to tolerate the results. A very wealthy person may be able to bear the loss of far more money than a poorer person. On the other hand, we cannot ignore the temperament and personality of the actors. A financial loss by a very wealthy person may cause that person to "go crazy" notwithstanding his or her wealth, while a less wealthy person would not give it another thought, because that person holds different values or suffers from fewer cognitive and behavioral biases. Thus, no matter how much we seek to quantify possible losses and their gravity, they cannot be fully ascertained. In fact, quantification may be misleading and dangerous when we rely only on the quantity and do not consider other factors.

Further, risk levels are not stationary; they are changeable and often unpredictable. In our context, law changes. Yet, we cannot live in a state of constant concern about possible legal risks. Therefore, we establish guidelines as to the level of legal risks we take, and the movement from low risk to higher risk that we will watch. In addition, we establish preventive measures. We (i) learn and evaluate various types of risks; (ii) seek signals of risks; (iii) recognize conflicting drives that may lead to legal risks; (iv) attempt to balance them to create a positive non-risky environment; and (v) attempt to establish an environment—a culture—that would divert the actors from violating the law.

To be sure, we would like to maximize profits, benefits, personal well-being, and the good feeling of success. However, we may make mistakes and take steps that lead to higher risks. We may not have been prepared to compensate for losses or mistakes we have made. Along the way we learn about balancing risk with caution, and tolerance with watchfulness.

Our study involves risk to a group, and only indirectly risk to individuals. Therefore, we deal with risk to the group, but we recognize the benefit and the shelter from risk that can be shared with the group and reduced for the individual. We learn about the risks of deviant behavior, and examine risk controls within our institutions.

We learn to deal with the absence of specificity, and with trends of individual and group behavior. In these respects, the law seems to have little to say, although the specific rules are piling up in this area. However, our main purpose is to help prevent institutional violations of the law. Therefore, we aim at avoiding litigation and imposing self-regulation. That, perhaps, is the best service lawyers could offer.

B. Conduct Risk

The term "conduct risk" is used to describe many kinds of risks linked to many types of activities and behaviors. Therefore, it is difficult to offer a precise definition of this term. However, a useful test of conduct risk is to link certain kinds of behavior to certain types of risks.

Following the financial institutions' benchmarks, we note, first, that "conduct risk" covers activities that are not included in main risk categories, such as market risk, credit risk, or liquidity and operational risk. Rather, conduct risk pertains to risks posed by the behavior of employees and others. An Australian regulator defined conduct risk as "the risk of inappropriate, unethical, or unlawful behaviour (sic) on the part of an organisation's (sic) management or employees."[421] Such behavior may be intentional or inadvertent, and may be caused by inadequate company policies. "Conduct risk can have significant ramifications for an organization (sic), its shareholders, clients, customers, counter-parties, and the financial services industry."[422] As conduct risk is related to behavior, it is related to company culture. It is a group habitual behavior; we will deal with this later in detail.

II. REGULATORS' VIEW AND ATTITUDE TOWARD CONDUCT RISK

Regulators have emphasized and focused on conduct risk. For example, the Securities and Exchange Commission has emphasized that:

> [e]nhanced focus on high-risk activities at firms, including: the valuation of investments that are privately placed, thinly-traded, or otherwise difficult to value (such as securities' lending collateral investments); remuneration arrangements, especially when client monies are paid to entities

---

421 Australian Securities & Investments Comm'n, *Conduct Risk*, MARKET SUPERVISION UPDATE, Issue 57 (last updated Mar. 23, 2016), *available at* http://asic.gov.au/about-asic/corporate-publications/newsletters/asic-market-supervision-update/asic-market-supervision-update-previous-issues/market-supervison-update-issue-57/ (last visited Jan. 10, 2017).

422 *Id.*

affiliated with the adviser; and verification of the existence of client assets.[423] . . . Inherent in the remuneration point above is the risk of conflicts of interest.[424]

Conduct risk can apply to an institution. Consider the following case:

Oppenheimer & Co., Inc.

Washington, D.C. – The Financial Crimes Enforcement Network (FinCEN), working closely with the U.S. Securities and Exchange Commission (SEC), assessed a $20 million civil money penalty [on January 27, 2015] against Oppenheimer & Co., Inc., for willfully violating the Bank Secrecy Act (BSA). Oppenheimer, a securities broker–dealer in New York, admitted that it failed to establish and implement an adequate anti–money laundering program, failed to conduct adequate due diligence on a foreign correspondent account, and failed to comply with requirements under Section 311 of the USA PATRIOT Act.

FinCEN and the New York Stock Exchange assessed a civil money penalty of $2.8 million against Oppenheimer in 2005 for similar violations. In 2013, the Financial Industry Regulatory Authority fined the firm $1.4 million for violations of securities laws and anti–money laundering failures.

"Broker–dealers face the same money laundering risks as other types of financial institutions," noted FinCEN Director Jennifer Shasky Calvery. "And by failing to comply with their regulatory responsibilities, our financial system became vulnerable to criminal abuse. This is the second time FinCEN has penalized Oppenheimer for similar violations. It is clear that their compliance culture must change."

Section 311 of the USA PATRIOT Act provides important protections to the U.S. financial system. Under that authority, the Director of FinCEN may determine that a foreign financial institution is of primary money laundering concern and may require domestic financial institutions to take certain special measures against that entity. These special measures can include prohibiting domestic financial institutions from opening or maintaining correspondent accounts for the named foreign financial institution. To be effective, U.S. financial institutions must conduct adequate due diligence and notify their foreign correspondent financial institutions of special measures imposed under Section 311, so that institutions of primary money laundering concern do not have improper and unfettered access to the U.S. financial system. By failing to notify its correspondents, Oppenheimer potentially placed the U.S. financial system at risk.

---

423 U.S. Sec. & Exch. Comm'n, Fiscal Year 2012 Agency Financial Report 19 (2012), *available at* http://www.sec.gov/about/secafr2012.shtml (last visited Mar. 4, 2016).

424 *Id.*

From 2008 through May 2014, Oppenheimer conducted business without establishing and implementing adequate policies, procedures, and internal controls reasonably designed to detect and report suspicious activity. FinCEN identified 16 customers who engaged in patterns of suspicious trading through branch offices in five states. All the suspicious activities involved penny stocks, which typically are low–priced, thinly traded, and highly speculative securities that can be vulnerable to manipulation by stock promoters and "pump–and–dump" schemes. Oppenheimer failed to report patterns of activity in which customers deposited large blocks of unregistered or illiquid penny stocks, moved large volumes of penny stocks among accounts with no apparent purpose, or immediately liquidated those securities and wired the proceeds out of the account.

In addition, Oppenheimer itself designated a customer foreign financial institution as "high risk" but failed to assess the institution's specific risks as a foreign financial institution or conduct adequate due diligence. Oppenheimer inadequately monitored the foreign financial institution's transactions and consequently did not detect or investigate numerous suspicious transactions conducted through the account, including prohibited third–party activity and illegal penny stock trading.[425]

We note that the U.K. Financial Conduct Authority has no "master definition of 'conduct risk' for all firms" but looks first to a firm's business model and strategy. It also assesses culture, focusing on governance.[426]

The U.K. Financial Conduct Authority (FCA) model for supervision is built around "three clear pillars": (1) "Proactive Firm Supervision (Firm Systematic Framework)": assessment of how the firm is being run, currently and prospectively, through a "firm-specific assessment"; (2) "Event-driven work": regarding "issues that are emerging or have happened and are unforeseen in their nature" and are "frequently of high importance"; and (3) "Issues and products" (i.e., "thematic supervision"): "to address [the FCA's] key conduct priorities at the issue and product level" based on "sector risk assessments."[427]

Similarly, the Australian Securities and Investments Commission (ASIC) conducted a survey of investment banks on conduct risk. As a result, the ASIC set out a "3 C's message on conduct risk," i.e., "communication," "challenge," and "complacency."

---

425 Excerpted from FinCEN, *FinCEN Fines Oppenheimer & Co. Inc. $20 Million for Continued Anti–Money Laundering Shortfalls* (Jan. 27, 2015), *available at* https://www.fincen.gov/news/news-releases/fincen-fines-oppenheimer-co-inc-20-million-continued-anti-money-laundering (last visited Oct. 20, 2016).

426 Speech by Linda Woodall, Director of Mortgages and Consumer Lending, FCA, at the Council of Mortgage Lenders (CML) - Mortgage Industry Conference and Exhibition, Building a Common Language in the Mortgage Market (June 11, 2013), *available at* http://www.fca.org.uk/news/building-a-common-language-in-the-mortgage-market (last visited Mar. 4, 2016).

427 Fin. Conduct Authority, FCA Factsheet: How The FCA Will Supervise Firms, *available at http://www.fca.org.uk/ static/fca/documents/factsheet.pdf* (last visited Mar. 4, 2016). See also FDIC, Compliance Examination Manual (Mar. 2016), *available at* https://www.fdic.gov/regulations/compliance/manual/ComplianceExaminationManual.pdf (last visited Dec. 6, 2016).

- Communication of conduct expectations needs to be *clear, concise, proactive, and regularly reiterated* across all levels of the organization, to ensure it is 'front of mind'.

- Organizations' communication strategies should identify meaningful bottom-up validation to ensure the message is embedded (i.e. the message is *clear, concise, and effective*).

- Messaging needs to be linked to the importance of the reputation of the individual, organization, and broader financial markets.

Challenge

Organizations should:

- challenge existing practices to determine whether current conduct and behaviors are appropriate, and

- foster an environment where employees are encouraged to escalate concerns and consider rewarding staff for speaking up.

Complacency

- There is a danger in thinking that because something hasn't happened yet, it won't happen.

- Conduct risk should be continually reviewed, enforced, and validated the same way as other key risks are (such as market, credit, liquidity and operational risks).

- Conduct risk is avoidable! It is every organization's responsibility to provide frameworks to empower its employees to recognize, prevent, escalate, and respond to conduct risks.[428]

---

428 Australian Securities & Investments Comm'n, *Conduct Risk*, MARKET SUPERVISION UPDATE, Issue 57 (last updated Mar. 23, 2016), *available at* http://asic.gov.au/about-asic/corporate-publications/newsletters/asic-market-supervision-update/asic-market-supervision-update-previous-issues/market-supervison-update-issue-57/ (last visited Jan. 10, 2017).

In light of the directives to the examiners, how should the compliance officers prepare for the visit? Here is a list of suggestions:

The FDIC Compliance Examination Manual[429] provides as follows:

Overview of Compliance Examinations

Introduction

***

This section provides a general overview of the FDIC compliance examination. The purposes of compliance examinations are to:

- assess the quality of an FDIC-supervised institution's compliance management system . . . for implementing federal consumer protection statutes and regulations;
- review compliance with relevant laws and regulations; and
- initiate effective supervisory action when elements of an institution's compliance management system are deficient and/or when violations of law are found.

Examination Approach

FDIC compliance examinations blend risk-focused and process-oriented approaches. Risk-focusing involves using information gathered about a financial institution to direct FDIC examiner resources to those operational areas where compliance errors present the greatest potential risks of having a negative impact on bank customers, resulting in consumer harm . . . . .)

Concentrating on the institution's internal control infrastructure and methods, or the "process" used to ensure compliance with federal consumer protection laws and regulations, both acknowledges that the ultimate responsibility for compliance rests with the institution and encourages examination efficiency.

Determining Risk

Risk-focusing involves:

---

429 FDIC, Compliance Examination Manual (Mar. 2016), *available at* https://www.fdic.gov/regulations/compliance/manual/ComplianceExaminationManual.pdf (last visited Dec. 6, 2016).

- developing a compliance risk profile for an institution using various sources of information about its products, services, markets, organizational structure, operations, and past supervisory performance;
- assessing the quality of an institution's compliance management system in light of the inherent risks associated with the level and complexity of its business operations and product and service offerings; and
- testing selected transactions based on risk such as when an operational area is determined to have a high risk of consumer harm and institution's compliance management efforts appear weak.

Evaluating the Compliance Management System

Compliance examinations start with a top-down, process-oriented, risk-focused, comprehensive review and analysis of an institution's compliance management system. The compliance examiner considers:
- the knowledge level and attitude of management and personnel;
- management's responsiveness to emerging issues and past or self-identified compliance deficiencies;
- compliance organizational structure such as reporting relationships and recent experiences with staff turnover;
- accuracy of management information systems;
- adequacy of policies and procedures;
- effectiveness of monitoring and training programs;
- handling of consumer complaints and response procedures; and
- effectiveness of the audit function (if applicable).

Based on the results of this review, the examiner may conclude that weaknesses in the institution's compliance management system may result in current or future noncompliance with federal consumer protection laws, regulations, or policy statements, thereby resulting in potential consumer harm. The examiner must determine, based on this analysis, whether transaction testing is warranted to further study particular risk in an entire operational area or regulation, or only a limited aspect of an area or regulation.

The FDIC examination approach appropriately recognizes that the Board of Directors and management of a financial institution are responsible for complying with all federal consumer protection laws and regulations. While the formality and complexity of compliance management systems will vary greatly among institutions, the FDIC expects the Board of Directors and management of each institution to have a system in place to effectively manage its compliance risk, consistent with its size and products, services, and markets.

Managing the examination based on risk maximizes examiner efficiency and may reduce the on-site examination presence, while emphasizing areas requiring elevated supervisory attention. By focusing on compliance management systems, examiners will be able to identify the root causes of deficiencies and suggest appropriate corrective actions designed to address the problem.

Applicability and Adaptability to Large and Small Institutions

In order to provide as much relevant and useful guidance as possible, the procedures detailed in this Manual include instructions for reviewing various likely elements of a compliance management system (CMS), such as written policies and procedures, monitoring, training, and audit. When these elements are in place at an institution being examined, the examiner will use the guidance to evaluate their effectiveness. However, the fact that certain elements of a CMS are described in these examination procedures is not intended to suggest that all institutions must maintain a CMS that includes such elements. Many institutions do not. There is no reason for them to, if their operations do not warrant it. Conclusions about the adequacy of a bank's CMS must be based on the effectiveness of those elements that are in place, taken as a whole, for that bank's particular operations.

For example, assume two institutions—a large, complex bank and a small, non-complex bank—and each has a record of strong compliance with all regulations that apply to the products and services it offers. Because of the complex nature of its operations, the large bank's CMS includes comprehensive external audits and formalized training from third-party vendors. The smaller bank's CMS includes no internal or external audits and no formalized training except for the compliance officer, who trains bank staff individually when needed. After reviewing all relevant material available, the examiner finds no significant deficiencies in the small bank's CMS and no reason to believe that the adoption of an audit function or formalized training is necessary to ensure ongoing compliance. The examiner would not criticize the small bank for the absence of audit (or training.) Nor should the examiner feel obliged to assign a higher rating to the larger bank simply because its CMS has more elements than the smaller bank. This is because each bank has a CMS that is adequate for the compliance responsibilities that are incumbent upon it due to its operating environment.

The descriptions of CMS elements provided in the Manual will assist the examiner in evaluating the element if one exists and in suggesting content if he or she determines that management should consider adopting an element.

Role of the Compliance Examiner

Compliance examiners play a crucial role in the supervisory process. The compliance examination, and follow-up supervisory attention to an institution's compliance program deficiencies and violations, helps to ensure that consumers and businesses obtain the benefits and protections afforded them under federal law. To this end, an examiner's efforts should help the financial institution improve its compliance posture and prevent future violations.

Primarily, examiners must:

- establish an examination scope focused on areas of highest consumer harm risk;
- evaluate an institution's compliance management system;
- conduct transaction testing where risks intersect with weaknesses in the compliance management system or uncertainties about aspects of that system; and
- report findings to the Board of Directors and management of the institution.

As part of the examination process, examiners are expected to:

- take a reasoned, common sense approach to examining and use sound judgment when making decisions;
- maintain ongoing communication with financial institution management throughout an examination;
- assist an institution to help itself improve performance by providing management with sound recommendations for enhancing its compliance management system;
- share experiences and knowledge of successful compliance management systems; and
- provide guidance regarding the various consumer protection and fair lending laws and regulations.

Overview of the Examination Process

Compliance examinations primarily involve three stages: pre-examination planning; review and analysis, both off-site and on-site; and communicating findings to institution management via meetings and a report of examination.

Pre-examination Planning

Pre-examination planning involves gathering information available in FDIC records and databases, contacting the financial institution to review and narrow the draft request for information and documents, and delivering a letter to the institution requesting specific information and documents for detailed analysis by the examination team . . . Proper examination preparation and planning maximizes an examination team's time and resources.

Review and Analysis

During the review and analysis phase of an examination, an examiner thoroughly evaluates an institution's compliance management system to assess its quality and effectiveness, and documents system weaknesses and violations of federal consumer protection laws and regulations, if any. The EIC starts by analyzing information about the type, level, and complexity of the institution's operations, and begins to develop the scope of the examination and plan for resource deployment to areas of highest risk. The EIC also preliminarily assesses the potential risk of consumer harm based upon the information available at the time of pre-examination planning.

The scope of an examination will be preliminarily established prior to entering the financial institution, and should be refined through the results of examiner discussions with senior management, the compliance officer (or staff assigned), and the internal auditor. Consistent with the FDIC's approach, examination resources are focused on addressing the areas of highest risk of consumer harm. Additionally, there may be some cases where the EIC may include additional areas in the examination scope even though risk of consumer harm is not exhibited.

While on-site at an institution, an examiner may limit the scope of the compliance review based on reliable procedures and controls in place. Similarly, the examiner may expand the review based on, for example, management's view about compliance, a lack of necessary procedures or controls, the presence of violations, the identification of potential or actual consumer harm, or the presence of new or significantly amended regulations. The compliance review continues with an evaluation of the:

- commitment of the Board of Directors, management, and staff to compliance;
- qualifications of the compliance officer or designated staff;
- scope and effectiveness of compliance policies and procedures;
- effectiveness of training;
- thoroughness of monitoring and any internal/external reviews or audits;
- responsiveness of the Board and management to the findings of internal/ external reviews and to the findings of the previous examination.

An examiner must consider the size, level, and complexity of an institution's operations when evaluating the adequacy of an institution's compliance management system.

The examination procedures outlined in this Manual are designed to enable an examiner to identify and measure compliance risk; make an assessment of an institution's compliance infrastructure and methods for identifying, monitoring, and controlling compliance risk and potential consumer harm; and determine the transaction testing needed to assess the integrity of the compliance management system. The number of transactions selected and the type of sampling used should be relative to the perceived risk of consumer harm and the need to assess the level of compliance in an activity or function.

At the conclusion of the review and analysis phase, an examiner:

- summarizes all findings regarding the strengths and weaknesses of an institution's compliance management system;
- determines the cause(s) of programmatic deficiencies or Level 3 or Level 2 violations and relates them to the underlying root causes as well as specific weakness(es) in the institution's compliance management system; and
- identifies actions necessary to address deficiencies or violations.

Determining the cause(s) of a program deficiency or violation is critical to recommending solutions that will successfully address problem areas and strengthen an institution's compliance posture for the future.[430]

Discussion topics

In light of the FDIC Manual:

*What do you learn about conduct risk?

*What should you prepare before the examination of the FDIC?

*What should senior management prepare?

*How should the institution avoid being surprised by unexpected risks?

*How should you treat the government examiners?

*Should you make copies of everything? If so, why?

---

430 FDIC, Compliance Examination Manual II-1.1 to .4 (Mar. 2016), *available at* https://www.fdic.gov/regulations/compliance/manual/2/II-1.1.pdf (last visited Jan. 9, 2017).

*What disagreements among the staff do you expect?

*How would you react to these disagreements?

*Should the legal counsel be active or passive in the government examinations, or should legal counsel avoid being present?

*Should you get professional help relating to conduct risk? What kind of help would you seek? If not always, then when?

V. MANAGEMENT OF CONDUCT RISK

A. Evaluation of Internal Controls

Federal securities laws require public companies to evaluate internal controls.

Rules 13a-15(c) and 15d-15(c) under the Securities Exchange Act of 1934, adopted under Section 404 of the Sarbanes-Oxley Act of 2002,[431] generally require issuers required to file annual reports under Section 13(a) or 15(d) of the Securities Exchange Act (other than registered investment companies) to evaluate internal control over financial reporting on an annual basis.[432]

The SEC published guidance that "sets forth an approach by which management can conduct a top-down, risk-based evaluation of internal control over financial reporting [("ICFR")]."[433] Compliance with this guidance "is one way to satisfy the evaluation requirements of Rules 13a-15(c) and 15d-15(c) under the Securities Exchange Act of 1934."

The guidance covers (1) the evaluation of ICFR and (2) reporting considerations.

The purpose of the evaluation process is "to provide management with a reasonable basis for its annual assessment as to whether any material weaknesses in ICFR exist as of the end of the fiscal year." This process includes (A) "the identification of financial reporting risks and the evaluation of whether the controls management as implemented adequately address those risks" and (B) "making judgments about the methods and procedures for evaluating whether the operation of ICFR is effective."

First, management should identify financial reporting risks and controls.

---

431 15 U.S.C. § 7262 (2012 & Supp. III 2015).

432 17 C.F.R. §§ 240.13a-15(c), .15d-15(c) (2016).

433 Commission Guidance Regarding Management's Report on Internal Control over Financial Reporting Under Section 13(a) or 15(d) of the Securities Exchange Act of 1934 (June 20, 2007), 72 Fed. Reg. 35,324 (June 27, 2007). Edited.

Identification of financial reporting risks generally begins with evaluating the application of the financial statements and GAAP to the company. [434]

Management uses its knowledge and understanding of the business, and its organization, operations, and processes, to consider the sources and potential likelihood of misstatements in financial reporting elements. Internal and external risk factors that impact the business, including the nature and extent of any changes in those risks, may give rise to a risk of misstatement. Risks of misstatement may also arise from sources such as the initiation, authorization, processing, and recording of transactions and other adjustments that are reflected in financial reporting elements. Management may find it useful to consider "what could go wrong" within a financial reporting element in order to identify the sources and the potential likelihood of misstatements and identify those that could result in a material misstatement of the financial statements. . . .

Management's evaluation of the risk of misstatement should include consideration of the vulnerability of the entity to fraudulent activity (for example, fraudulent financial reporting, misappropriation of assets and corruption), and whether any such exposure could result in a material misstatement of the financial statements. The extent of activities required for the evaluation of fraud risks is commensurate with the size and complexity of the company's operations and financial reporting environment.

Management should recognize that the risk of material misstatement due to fraud ordinarily exists in any organization, regardless of size or type, and it may vary by specific location or segment and by individual financial reporting element. For example, one type of fraud risk that has resulted in fraudulent financial reporting in companies of all sizes and types is the risk of improper override of internal controls in the financial reporting process. While the identification of a fraud risk is not necessarily an indication that a fraud has occurred, the absence of an identified fraud is not an indication that no fraud risks exist. Rather, these risk assessments are used in evaluating whether adequate controls have been implemented.[435]

In identifying controls that adequately address financial reporting risks, management must judge "whether the controls, if operating properly, can effectively prevent or detect misstatements that could result in material misstatements in the financial statements. If management determines that a deficiency in ICFR exists, it must be evaluated to determine whether a material weakness exists. . . ." [436]Management may consider the comparative efficiency of controls.

In addition to identifying controls that address the financial reporting risks of individual financial reporting elements, management also evaluates whether it has controls in place to address the entity-level and other pervasive elements of ICFR that its chosen control framework prescribes as necessary for an effective system of internal control. This would ordinarily include, for example, considering how and whether controls related to the control environment, controls

---

434 *Id.*

435 *Id.*

436 *Id.*

over management override, the entity-level risk assessment process and monitoring activities, controls over the period-end financial reporting process, and the policies that address significant business control and risk management practices are adequate for purposes of an effective system of internal control. The control frameworks and related guidance may be useful tools for evaluating the adequacy of these elements of ICFR.

In addition, management must have evidential matter to support its assessment.

Second, management should evaluate evidence of the operating effectiveness of ICFR, considering "whether the control is operating as designed and whether the person performing the control possesses the necessary authority and competence to perform the control effectively." "Evidence about the effective operation of controls may be obtained from direct testing of controls and on-going monitoring activities." Sufficiency of evidence depends on its quantity (e.g., sample size) and qualitative characteristics (e.g., the nature of the evaluation procedures performed, the relative period of time, the objectivity of the evaluation, and (for on-going monitoring) "the extent of validation through direct testing of underlying controls." [437]

Management must determine the evidence needed to support the assessment:

Management should evaluate the ICFR risk of the controls [that adequately address financial reporting risks] as adequately addressing the financial reporting risks for financial reporting elements to determine the evidence needed to support the assessment. This evaluation should consider the characteristics of the financial reporting elements to which the controls relate and the characteristics of the controls themselves. . . .

Management's consideration of the misstatement risk of a financial reporting element includes both the materiality of the financial reporting element and the susceptibility of the underlying account balances, transactions, or other supporting information to a misstatement that could be material to the financial statements. As the materiality of a financial reporting element increases in relation to the amount of misstatement that would be considered material to the financial statements, management's assessment of misstatement risk for the financial reporting element generally would correspondingly increase. In addition, management considers the extent to which the financial reporting elements include transactions, account balances or other supporting information that are prone to material misstatement. For example, the extent to which a financial reporting element: (1) involves judgment in determining the recorded amounts; (2) is susceptible to fraud; (3) has complex accounting requirements; (4) experiences change in the nature or volume of the underlying transactions; or (5) is sensitive to changes in environmental factors, such as technological and/or economic developments, would generally affect management's judgment of whether a misstatement risk is higher or lower.

---

437 *Id.*

Management's consideration of the likelihood that a control might fail to operate effectively includes, among other things:

- The type of control (that is, manual or automated) and the frequency with which it operates;
- The complexity of the control;
- The risk of management override;
- The judgment required to operate the control;
- The competence of the personnel who perform the control or monitor its performance;
- Whether there have been changes in key personnel who either perform the control or monitor its performance;
- The nature and materiality of misstatements that the control is intended to prevent or detect;
- The degree to which the control relies on the effectiveness of other controls (for example, IT general controls); and
- The evidence of the operation of the control from prior year(s).

For example, management's judgment of the risk of control failure would be higher for controls whose operation requires significant judgment than for non-complex controls requiring less judgment.[438]

Management must also implement procedures to evaluate evidence on the operation of ICFR:

> Management should evaluate evidence that provides a reasonable basis for its assessment of the operating effectiveness of the controls identified . . . . Management uses its assessment of ICFR risk . . . . The evaluation methods and procedures may be integrated with the daily responsibilities of its employees or implemented specifically for purposes of the ICFR evaluation. Activities that are performed for other reasons (for example, day-to-day activities to manage the operations of the business) may also provide relevant evidence. Further, activities performed to meet the monitoring objectives of the control framework may provide evidence to support the assessment of the operating effectiveness of ICFR.
>
> The evidence comes from direct tests of controls, on-going monitoring, or a combination of both. Direct tests of controls are tests ordinarily performed on a periodic basis by individuals with a high degree of objectivity relative to the controls being tested. Direct tests provide evidence as of a point in time and may provide information about the reliability of on-going monitoring activities. On-going monitoring includes management's normal, recurring activities that provide information about the operation of controls. These activities include, for example,

---

438 *Id.*

self-assessment procedures and procedures to analyze performance measures designed to track the operation of controls.

As the ICFR risk increases, management will ordinarily adjust the nature of the evidence that is obtained. For example, management can increase the evidence from on-going monitoring activities by utilizing personnel who are more objective and/or increasing the extent of validation through periodic direct testing of the underlying controls. Management can also vary the evidence obtained by adjusting the period of time covered by direct testing. When ICFR risk is assessed as high, the evidence management obtains would ordinarily consist of direct testing or on-going monitoring activities performed by individuals who have a higher degree of objectivity. In situations where a company's on-going monitoring activities utilize personnel who are not adequately objective, the evidence obtained would normally be supplemented with direct testing by those who are independent from the operation of the control. In these situations, direct testing of controls corroborates evidence from on-going monitoring activities as well as evaluates the operation of the underlying controls and their continuing ability to adequately address financial reporting risks. When ICFR risk is assessed as low, management may conclude that evidence from on-going monitoring is sufficient and that no direct testing is required. Further, management's evaluation would ordinarily consider evidence from a reasonable period of time during the year, including the fiscal year-end. [439]

Management evaluates the evidence and determines whether there is a deficiency; if so, the deficiency is evaluated to determine if it is a material weakness. Management's assessment must be supported by evidential matter as well.

Second, the guidance discusses reporting considerations. Management must evaluate the severity of each control deficiency. Material weaknesses must be disclosed in the annual report, and significant deficiencies must be reported to the audit committee and external auditor. Multiple deficiencies in combination may constitute a material weakness.

Risk factors affect whether there is a reasonable possibility that a deficiency, or a combination of deficiencies, will result in a misstatement of a financial statement amount or disclosure. These factors include, but are not limited to, the following:
- The nature of the financial reporting elements involved (for example, suspense accounts and related party transactions involve greater risk);
- The susceptibility of the related asset or liability to loss or fraud (that is, greater susceptibility increases risk);
- The subjectivity, complexity, or extent of judgment required to determine the amount involved (that is, greater subjectivity, complexity, or judgment, like that related to an accounting estimate, increases risk);

---

439 *Id.*

- The interaction or relationship of the control with other controls, including whether they are interdependent or redundant;
- The interaction of the deficiencies (that is, when evaluating a combination of two or more deficiencies, whether the deficiencies could affect the same financial statement amounts or disclosures); and
- The possible future consequences of the deficiency.

Factors that affect the magnitude of the misstatement that might result from a deficiency or deficiencies in ICFR include, but are not limited to, the following:
- The financial statement amounts or total of transactions exposed to the deficiency; and
- The volume of activity in the account balance or class of transactions exposed to the deficiency that has occurred in the current period or that is expected in future periods.

Management should also consider the mitigating effect of compensating controls.

In determining whether a deficiency or a combination of deficiencies represents a material weakness, management considers all relevant information. Management should evaluate whether the following situations indicate a deficiency in ICFR exists and, if so, whether it represents a material weakness:
- Identification of fraud, whether or not material, on the part of senior management;
- Restatement of previously issued financial statements to reflect the correction of a material misstatement;
- Identification of a material misstatement of the financial statements in the current period in circumstances that indicate the misstatement would not have been detected by the company's ICFR; and
- Ineffective oversight of the company's external financial reporting and internal control over financial reporting by the company's audit committee.

When evaluating the severity of a deficiency, or combination of deficiencies, in ICFR, management also should determine the level of detail and degree of assurance that would satisfy prudent officials in the conduct of their own affairs that they have reasonable assurance that transactions are recorded as necessary to permit the preparation of financial statements in conformity with GAAP. If management determines that the deficiency, or combination of deficiencies, might prevent prudent officials in the conduct of their own affairs from concluding that they have reasonable assurance that transactions are recorded as necessary to permit the preparation of financial statements in conformity with GAAP, then management should treat the deficiency, or combination of deficiencies, as an indicator of a material weakness.[440]

In addition, the Securities and Exchange Commission noted that management should not qualify its expression assessment of effectiveness of ICFR (e.g., "the company's controls and procedures are effective except to the extent that certain material weakness(es) have been identified").

Management should consider disclosing, in addition to the existence of a material weakness, (1) its nature, (2) its impact on the company's financial reporting and ICFR, and (3) any future plans or past actions to remediate the weakness.

If there is a restatement of previously issued financial statements due to a material misstatement, management should consider revising its original disclosures regarding the effectiveness of ICFR.

If management is unable to assess certain aspects of ICFR (e.g., if a process is outsourced), it must determine whether the inability is significant enough to conclude that ICFR is not effective.

B. Identifying and restricting risk

As we shall see, the design of a compliance system involves identifying and restricting risk. For example, the U.K. Financial Stability Board set out four non-exhaustive indicators of a sound risk prevention culture: (i) the "tone from the top," that is, the behavior of the board and senior management; (ii) accountability of employees at all levels; (iii) effective communication and challenge, that is, "an environment of open communication and effective challenge, in which decision-making processes encourage a range of views; allow for testing of current practices; stimulate a positive, critical, attitude among employees; and promote an environment of open and constructive engagement," and (iv) incentives to "encourage and reinforce maintenance of the financial institution's desired risk management behavior" and "support the core values and risk culture at all levels of the institution".[441] To be sure, the possible punishment also plays a role in many institutions, which reflects the law of the land.

C. Key drivers of conduct risk include the following:

*Structures and behaviors: "[s]tructures, processes, and management (including culture and incentives) that have been designed into and become embedded in the financial sector, allowing firms to profit from systematic consumer shortcomings and from market failures."

---

440 *Id.*

441 Fin. Stability Board, Guidance on Supervisory Interaction with Financial Institutions on Risk Culture: A Framework for Assessing Risk Culture 3-4 (Apr. 7, 2014), *available at* http://www.fsb.org/wp-content/uploads/140407.pdf?page_moved=1 (last visited Mar. 4, 2016).

*The environment: "[l]ong-running and current economic, regulatory, and technological trends and changes that affect the factors [above] and are important drivers of firm and consumer decisions."

*Inherent factors: information asymmetries, biases and heuristics, and inadequate financial capability.

*Behaviors, such as conflicts of interest, culture and incentives, and ineffective competition.

*Environmental factors, such as economic and market trends, technological developments, and regulatory and policy changes.[442]

*The Firm Systematic Framework: Is it designed to assess a firm's conduct risk? This design generally involves "[a]ssessment of how the firm embeds fair treatment of customers and ensures market integrity," which includes an assessment of "governance and culture," "to assess how effectively a firm identifies, manages, and reduces conduct risks."[443]

*Fair treatment and market integrity assessment, including assessment of "product design," "sales or transaction processes," and "post/sales services and transaction handling."[444]

Arguably, if risk-taking were a value-adding activity, roulette players would contribute disproportionately to global welfare. And if government subsidies were the route to improved well-being, today's growth problems could be solved at a stroke. Typically, this is not the way societies keep score. But it was those very misconceptions that caused the measured contribution of the financial sector to be overestimated ahead of the crisis.

For banks, risk management is a legitimately value-adding activity. It lies at the heart of the services banks provide. Today's debate around banking and bankers has usefully rediscovered that key fact, amid the rubble of broken balance sheets and wasted financial and human capital. Investors, regulators, and statisticians now need to adjust their measuring rods to ensure they are not blind to risk when next evaluating the return to banking.

---

442 FIN. CONDUCT AUTHORITY, FCA RISK OUTLOOK 10 (2013), *available at* http://www.fca.org.uk/your-fca/documents/fca-risk-outlook-2013 (last visited Mar. 4, 2016).

443 FIN. SERVICES AUTHORITY, JOURNEY TO THE FCA 27 (Oct. 2012), *available at* http://www.fsa.gov.uk/static/pubs/other/journey-to-the-fca-standard.pdf (last visited Mar. 4, 2016).

444 *Id.*

VI. THE NEW LEGAL VIEW AND FOCUS ON CONDUCT RISK

A. The Volcker Rule and the CFPB Nonbank Supervision Program

There are new risk-management demands imposed on banks and other financial institutions. In 2009 the former chair of the Federal Reserve Board proposed a rule now known as The Volcker Rule, which restricted the bank holding companies' issuance and trading in their own shares.[445]

The banks that had failed and were bailed out by taxpayers were mostly "bank holding companies" that owned and managed a variety of financial intermediation units. These holding companies are in fact "financial malls" that engage in various financial intermediation services. Like other businesses, the bank holding companies issued their own shares, and reported quarterly performance. Arguably, one reason for the 2008 market crash and the failure of large banks was the pressure to increase profits, which may cause, and did cause, bank holding companies to take greater market risks. After all, risk and return usually go together.

The Volcker Rule may have contributed to an interesting and important development in the regulatory attitude toward banking. Regulators have often spoken about culture as a method of controlling bank risks. However, their focus used to be on economic or financial risks. Recently, the regulators began to speak about risk somewhat differently. The emphasis today is also on a culture in non-economic terms—a culture of appropriate risk avoidance by the actors. The emphasis is not only on the extent of financial risk taken by the actors, but also and more on the actors' degree of risk avoidance.

In addition, the Dodd-Frank Wall Street Reform and Consumer Protection Act of 2010 authorizes the Consumer Financial Protection Bureau (CFPB) to supervise certain nonbank entities "engaging, or has engaged, in conduct that poses risks to consumers with regard to the offering or provision of consumer financial products or services."[446]

B. Recent Attention to Conduct Risk

After the market 2008 crash, there was a rising focus on the actors' risky habits and behavior, apart from economic and business risks. We ask:

(i) How do the employees actually behave?

---

445 Dodd-Frank Wall Street Reform and Consumer Protection Act, Pub. L. No. 111-203, § 619, 124 Stat. 1376, 1620-31 (2010) (codified at 12 U.S.C. § 1851 (2012))..For a general description and background of the Volcker rule and its pluses and minuses, *see Much Ado About Trading,* THE ECONOMIST, July 25, 2015 at 60, *available at* http://www.economist.com/news/finance-and-economics/21659671-next-great-regulation-tame-banks-now-place-much-ado-about-trading (last visited Feb. 18, 2016).

446 Pub. L. No. 111-203, § 1024, 124 Stat. at 1987-1990 (codified as amended at 12 U.S.C. § 5514 (2012 & Supp. III 2015)); Steve Antonakes & Peggy Twohig, *The CFPB Launches Its Nonbank Supervision Program* (Jan. 5, 2012), *available at* http://www.consumerfinance.gov/about-us/blog/the-cfpb-launches-its-nonbank-supervision-program (last visited Jan. 10, 2017).

(ii) What drives behavior within the organization?

(iii) What incentives are provided to induce behavior?

(iv) What are the rewards and advances within the organization? Are the compensation and punishment policies aligned with risk culture?

(v) How are the activities within the organization aligned with risk avoidance policies?

(vi) Notwithstanding government and corporate written policies, the important question is: "Do the boards, the managements, and the employees really mean it?" "Do they mean it on a day-to-day regular basis? Do they mean it when no one is watching?" What should boards do?

Consider the root problem and document it. An unhelpful but a truthful answer is: You know a risk management culture when you see it! Regulators will expect the institutions to develop their own programs and focus on the issues. To find out the answers to these questions, we ask:

*Does the behavior of the actors within the enterprise follow the written policies?

*Do they follow the policies even if they are not exposed to enticement or coercion?

*Do they like to behave in this fashion? Are they proud of behaving in this way?

*Do the enterprise conduct a self-assessment when it sees its own red flags? Are there patterns of behavior that have to be addressed? For example, how long did it take to resolve a risk problem or a supervision problem?

*Recognize the internal conflict of "risk appetite." The enterprise, its leaders, its management and its employees face a conflict, described as an institutional or personal "risk appetite." We may call it "financial returns appetite."

* Justifying Conduct Risk. There are many temptations and justifications for people to take risks, especially if (i) they risk other people's money, (ii) the government is backing at least some of the risk, and (iii) the people hope to be rewarded by higher returns. After all, returns are more tangible and positive. Here are suggestions for mediating between the business and restrictive law:

*Business: What is the monetary difference between taking and not taking the risks? Should we slow or terminate the activity all at once? Is it a long term-short term issue? Does the rule affect the business as a whole or only part of it?

*Law: What is the chance that we will do the business? What is the chance of reaching the violation stage? What is the chance of being caught? How serious is the violation going to be?

*Test: What is the nature and extent of (i) the harm to society? (ii) The harm to the business? (iii) The harm to the growth of the business? (iv) The harm to the group? And (v) The harm as compared to benefit to ME?

*How could enterprises, their management, and other employees be induced to curb their "risk appetite"? Would numbers help in this case? One suggested key to the answer is judgment, based on experience.

C. The Institutional Leadership.

Regulators have begun to pay far more attention to the activities and leadership of the boards of directors and their impact on the business managers. Regulators expect the board of directors to (i) distinguish between the various departments in the organizations with respect to the legal risk they may pose; (ii) identify the impact of the departments on the choice of personnel, and (iii) evaluate personnel behavior.

For example, regulators pay more attention to (i) HR hiring policies and to personnel activities outside the policies; (ii) the personnel's response to the occurrence of lapses; and (iii) attendance and assessment of consultants and survey of third-party assessments.

D. Introducing a Law-Abiding Culture.

Unlike active supervision, culture involves internal value guidelines and self-regulation. The more policing one imposes on employees, the less they might feel obligated to follow the rules on their own initiative. Therefore, there should be a balance between policing and respectful trust that would induce employees to behave as expected and be proud of being trusted rather than fearful of being caught in violation. At the same time, supervision and awareness of supervision, is necessary.

There is a proposal for "changing and refocusing future government examinations of market intermediaries." The proposal suggests "focusing on bubbles and crashes and viewing them as dangerous to the financial system and the economy." The proposal points to the "undesirable effect[s]" of "[p]rior substantive regulation" "on innovations and freedom of the markets" and the equally undesirable, and perhaps ineffective results of regulating activities "after a crash (when the 'horse has left the barn')." Therefore, the proposal suggests a closer examination of a kind that is somewhat different from the current ones.[447]

(1) "Examine more frequently when market prices rise (not only when they have fallen)." A rise in prices might precede the crash;

(2) "Examine entities that are too large to fail; those that are highly leveraged; those whose [share prices] rise steadily with . . . no fluctuation; and [those] that have obtained exemptions from [regulatory laws]";

(3) "Examiners should search for violations of the law ([or] the spirit of the law), but not [for] economic or financial rationalizations"; and

(4) "Examiners should be experts, highly paid and incentivized to remain in government employ. Expert information about the markets will hopefully reduce the impact of bubbles and inevitable crashes and [mostly:] the loss of [investors'] trust [in] the financial system."[448]

E. The Impact of Unfair Competition on Risk Taking.

Competition may drive risk taking, especially if the competition is unfair. Here is an example of a regulation aimed at fair competition. The California Unfair Competition Law (UCL) defines "unfair competition" as "any unlawful, unfair, or fraudulent business act or practice and unfair, deceptive, untrue, or misleading advertising" and any of a number of specific acts prohibited by the Business and Professions Code.[449] Therefore, the Law prohibits an act that is (a) "unlawful," (b) "unfair," or (c) "fraudulent."

An "unlawful" act can be one prohibited by "[v]irtually any state, federal, or local law."[450] The "unfairness" prong is "intentionally broad" and involves a balancing test.[451] The test "involves an examination of [that practice's] impact on its alleged victim, balanced against the reasons, justifications, and motives of the alleged wrongdoer." Stated differently, the Act balances "the utility of

---

447 Tamar Frankel, *Chapter 9: Regulating the Financial Markets by Examinations, in* THE PANIC OF 2008;

CAUSES, CONSEQUENCES AND IMPLICATIONS FOR REFORM (Lawrence E. Mitchell & Arthur E. Wilmarth, Jr. eds., 2010), *summarized at* https://www.elgaronline.com/view/9781849802611.00018.xml (last visited Jan. 13, 2017).

448 Tamar Frankel, *Chapter 9: Regulating the Financial Markets by Examinations, in* THE PANIC OF 2008;

CAUSES, CONSEQUENCES AND IMPLICATIONS FOR REFORM (Lawrence E. Mitchell & Arthur E. Wilmarth, Jr. eds., 2010), *summarized at* https://www.elgaronline.com/view/9781849802611.00018.xml (last visited Jan. 13, 2017).

449 CAL. BUS. & PROF. CODE § 17200 (2014) (LEXIS version).

450 Podolsky v. First Healthcare Corp., 50 Cal. App. 4th 632, 647, 50 Cal. Rptr. 2d 89, 98 (Cal. Ct. App. 1996).

451 *Id.*

the defendant's conduct against the gravity of the harm to the alleged victim."[452] "An unfair business practice occurs when the practice 'offends an established public policy or when the practice is immoral, unethical, oppressive, unscrupulous or substantially injurious to consumers.'"[453] The "fraud" prong is broader than common law deception. It does not require actual deception, reliance, or damage, only that "members of the public are likely to be deceived."[454]

The case of *Podolsky v. First Healthcare Corp.* is instructive. It demonstrates the limits to unfair treatment and competition under contract laws. The Defendant, First Healthcare Corporation (FHC), operator of nursing homes, pressured relatives of nursing home patients to sign admission agreements. The agreements required the relatives to co-sign as "responsible parties" with little opportunity to examine the agreements or ask questions.[455]

The Court found the agreements "deceptive" because they did not contain information about the protections that the guarantors, who signed the agreements, had under federal and state law.[456] While the court based its decision on the legal rationale described above, the Court also stated that there was a triable issue as to whether FHC deceptively induced, or in effect required, such guarantees. The Court noted the stress involved in admitting a family member to a nursing home,[457] and a triable issue as to whether the guarantees lacked consideration.[458]

Discussion Topic

What were the areas of the law on which this decision was based?
Why did the court choose to discuss one area (Unfair Competition) but mention other legal areas as well?

---

452 *Id.*

453 *Id.*

454 *Id.* at 647-48, 50 Cal. Rptr. 2d at 98.

455 *Id.* at 638-42, 50 Cal. Rptr. 2d at 92-95.

456 *Id.* at 649-51, 50 Cal. Rptr. 2d at 100-01.

457 *Id.* at 652-54, 50 Cal. Rptr. 2d at 101-03.

458 *Id.* at 654-55, 50 Cal. Rptr. 2d at 103-04.

Chapter 8

IT IS ALL ABOUT PEOPLE AND RELATIONSHIPS: THE INTERACTION BETWEEN INSTITUTIONAL LEADERSHIP, THE ENVIRONMENT AND SELF-REGULATION (COMPLIANCE)

"Doing it right is no excuse for not meeting the schedule."

"I love mankind ... it's people I can't stand!!"

Charles M. Schulz, The Complete Peanuts,
Vol. 5: 1959-1960.

INTRODUCTION

This chapter revisits in more detail the interaction between the institutional environment, corporate business processes, internal self-regulation (compliance), and the law. Internal structures raise issues involving personalities and power relationships. These pressures arise when the law limits the actors' freedom and may foreclose opportunities for profit, competitive advantages, or societal influence and other satisfactions of other desires.

Therefore, to evaluate the efficacy of a self-regulatory program, we should understand the personal makeup of the institution's actors and their role within the institution. Self-regulation poses conflicting pressures. It may result in limiting the freedom of management and employees to act for short-term or long-term gains. Limits may be good, constraining wrongful behavior. Limits can also be bad, adversely affecting useful creative innovations. To be sure, limits accompany us throughout life, including not only the limits imposed by the law.

We encounter limits imposed by the disapproval of the people and the groups with whom we interact, and the culture of the groups to which we belong. Disapproval or approval occurs in all social interactions, be it in the family, school, the workplace, and in society at large. Yet, who does not have an occasional strong desire to rebel against limits?

In addition, we find that not all people comply with orders that are backed by threats of punishment. Many people might react in just the opposite way to assert their personal importance and independence. Some, and perhaps many, people may comply far more readily to requests and rewards. Thus, limits on desired activities produce external and internal conflicts. Many of these conflicts are resolved within the institution. Because institutions differ by size, type of business, and objectives, the ways they resolve these conflicts differ as well. These differences should be recognized, accounted for, and reacted to in order to assure appropriate internal regulation and achieve compliance with the law.

Similarly, individuals differ. Not all fit into the same workplace environment. Some individuals may be more sensitive than others, both to personal relationships and to the institutional culture. These differences may bring about legal compliance issues. What kind of rule would be more effective to the most people? More importantly, how would treatment of individuals induce compliance? Therefore, personal characteristics should be recognized and watched as well. Finally, institutional violations of the law do not usually arise all at once. There are situations and signals that send a warning of tendencies to violations. We call a one-time signal a "red flag" and a pattern of such signals a "slippery slope." These constitute our guidelines. We deal with these signals at length because they are most effective means for self-regulation.

As noted in Chapter 7, we emphasize the risk that emanates from people's behavior or conduct risk. The same concerns are expressed in a different, perhaps a more "monitoring" way. Conduct risk is broad, covering the actors who may harm as well as benefit the institution, and who may violate as well as follow the law. For example, an over-enthusiastic employee may cross the boundaries of the law, just a little bit, to bring greater profits for the institution. This employee may be ambitious not to receive monetary rewards but to gain the approval of his boss.

Section I examines the individual actor, noting personal characteristics that may raise problems of compliance with the law within the institution and the impact of its culture.

Section II offers a lesson derived from self-regulation failure, which resulted in illegal activities and the demise of the institution. This failure reflects the personalities and ambitions of the actors. We learn about the reasons for the breakdowns of self-regulation, and highlight the actors' degree of sensitivity to past and present problems.

Section III discusses two danger patterns to self-regulation. One is failing to recognize red flags, signals of tendencies toward violations of the law. The other danger is failing to recognize slippery slopes, small step-by-step activities on the road towards violations of self-regulation and the law. We start this part with a story of "market timing" in mutual funds. We learn the role of lawyers in interpreting the law by focusing on specific words rather than the principles that led to the specific legal directives.

Section IV deals in conduct risk and to some extent might duplicate the prior discussion. However, the questions regarding this risk might be different and should be asked.

A. People and their actions and interaction in the wrong environment: The wrong atmosphere.

We start by examining individual actors, and personal characteristics that may undermine not only self-regulation but may pose managerial problems as well. Our purpose is to learn the reasons for breakdown of self-regulation, recognize the pressures on the system, and be aware of the actors' degree of sensitivity to serious past and current problems. Breakdowns demonstrate the crucial importance of recognizing red flag signs. Small malfunctions of self-regulation programs may start a slippery slope, leading to serious violations of the law. Thus, as we read the stories of failed self-regulation, let us pay attention to whether any red flags, and of what kind of red flags, were waving, yet not heeded.[459] We deal with these patterns of behavior in Section IV.

Experts recognize that managers must deal with "negativity," i.e., "pessimistic, hostile, or uncooperative behavior," and that negativity "can quickly infect an entire department (or a whole company) if the manager doesn't rein it in quickly."[460] They note that one "bad apple" can demoralize the entire workplace "basket."[461]

How does negativity lead to fraud rather than to merely decreased productivity? Fraud and "positivism" are not mutually exclusive. Many of the recent "Wall Street types" were very positive, while arguably engaged in less than socially optimal business behavior. In fact, financial prosperity, positivism, and enthusiasm may also bring about irrational risk-taking. This risk taking is related to a "contagion of enthusiasm" in the corporate culture. Further, competition may drive additional risk taking, partly because of unrealistic goals. Expectations of others (i.e., investors) may drive risk taking as well.

---

459 Joann S. Lublin, *Do You Know Your Hidden Work Biases?*, WALL ST. J., Jan 10, 2014, at B1, LEXIS, News Library, Wsj File (employees may be unjustifiably biased with respect to race, sex, and various other employees' traits, such as quieter colleagues who do not speak much at meetings. Big businesses are struggling to overcome these hidden biases, in order to highlight talent and other features which the businesses need and value. There are training sessions for this issue. The recommendation is not to feel guilty but to recognize the biases).

460 Business Management Daily, *10 Ways to Overcome Negativity Among Staff*, HAMILTON SPECTATOR *(Hamilton, Ont.), May 14, 2016, at C7, LEXIS, News Library, Curnws File.*

461 Francesca Gino et al., *Contagion and Differentiation in Unethical Behavior: The Effect of One Bad Apple on the Barrel*, 20 PSYCHOLOGICAL SCI. 393, *available at* http://people.duke.edu/~dandan/Papers/Cheating/contagion.pdf (last visited Feb. 16, 2016).

B. Of Human Behavior[462] and Human Nature

How should we balance bright lines with vague values? In law, we struggle to determine the balance between bright-line rules and general values: How much is too much? To what extent should courts interfere in managers' decisions, when management has been vested with decision-making power? How about constructive v. toxic competition? Each individual faces similar issues. For instance, while food is crucial to our survival, too much food can kill us. Similarly, the extent to which a lawyer should interfere in a client's business decisions is a matter of degree.

Fraud and dishonesty can be addictive, although addiction is not necessarily the exclusive province of fraud. Like compulsive gamblers, addicts may "live in a fantasy world and deny reality."[463] Both managers and clients seem to share the gamblers' joys and weaknesses: a study in 1990 found that many white-collar criminals were repeat offenders,[464] making the compliance record of a potential hire so important.

The hunger for money can drive fraudulent activities. So can the enjoyment of the "game." The thrill associated with the risk of being caught and punished may be a feature of the addiction. For example, one fraudster spent years in prison for "bilking investors out of tens of millions of dollars through a phony carpet-cleaning company called ZZZZ Best" and then spent ten years as a stock fraud investigator, but a few years later pleaded guilty to a stock fraud conspiracy.[465] Another fraudster, who operated a pyramid scheme, had been in the Better Business Bureau's files for several years.[466]

Law does not necessarily create nor affect addictive habits. The very act of taking a legal risk does not induce illegal activity. Lotteries are legal, when operated by the State; gambling and betting is legal, when approved and licensed for casinos. One court explained "the basic distinction between the illegal gambling transaction and the legitimate speculative investment turns on the nature of the stake."[467] If the money is used in a speculative venture, the profits are deemed a return on an investment. But, of course, there must be a legitimate venture, from which the return is drawn, rather than a fraudulent one.

---

462 *See* TAMAR FRANKEL, THE PONZI SCHEME PUZZLE, chs.3-4 (2012).

463 "Compulsive gamblers live in a fantasy world and deny reality ... ." The problem of gambling is similar to drug addiction. John G. Edwards, *Former Broker Warns About the Dangers of Gambling Addiction*, LAS VEGAS REV. J., Nov. 9, 1999, at 3D (listing the results of investor addiction, including attempted suicides which are double those of drug addicts, and resort to crime, including violent crime).

464 David Weisburd et al., *White-Collar Crime and Criminal Careers: Some Preliminary Findings*, 36 CRIME & DELINQUENCY 342, 349 (1990).

465 Robbie Whelan, *Guilty Plea Ends Tale of Redemption*, WALL ST. J., Apr. 5, 2011, at C1, LEXIS, News Library, Wsj File.

466 Jim Henderson, *Preacher Has Faith in Pitch*, HOUSTON CHRON., May 26, 2002, at 33.

467 *Liss v. Manuel*, 58 Misc. 2d 614, 617, 296 N.Y.S.2d 627, 631 (Civ. Ct. 1968).

Discussion topics

Where should the line to be drawn between a legitimate and illegitimate venture?
Are government lotteries materially representing the odds of winning?

Let us evaluate the following case:

The Financial Crimes Enforcement Network (FinCEN) [on December 18, 2014] issued a $1 million civil money penalty (CMP) against Mr. Thomas E. Haider for failing to ensure that his company abided by the anti-money laundering (AML) provisions of the Bank Secrecy Act (BSA) and implementing regulations. This CMP is the product of a joint investigation by FinCEN and the SDNY.

From 2003 to 2008, Mr. Haider was the Chief Compliance Officer for MoneyGram International Inc. Mr. Haider oversaw MoneyGram's Fraud Department, which collected thousands of complaints from consumers who were victims of fraudulent schemes. Mr. Haider also headed MoneyGram's AML Compliance Department, which was charged with ensuring compliance with requirements under the BSA designed to protect the financial system against money laundering and terrorist finance.

. . . .

Mr. Haider was responsible for monitoring MoneyGram's worldwide network of agents, and through the information he received from complaints to the Fraud Division, he could have suspended or terminated any agents that were participating in illicit activity. His inaction led to thousands of innocent individuals being duped out of millions of dollars through fraud schemes that funneled, and sometimes laundered, their illicit profits through MoneyGram's money transmission network.

The schemes relied on a variety of tales and false promises aimed at misleading and persuading unsuspecting victims to send money through the participating MoneyGram agents and outlets. The often elderly victims were solicited through the mail, e-mail, and telephone, and told, among other things, that they had won a lottery, had been hired for a "secret shoppers" program, had been approved for a guaranteed loan, or had been selected to receive an expensive item or cash prize. The victims were told that to receive the item or winnings, they had to pay the perpetrators money in advance. For example, in situations where the victims were promised lottery winnings or cash prizes, they were told that they had to pay taxes, customs' duties, or processing fees up front and were directed to send the advance payments to fictitious payees using MoneyGram's money transfer system.

Mr. Haider also failed in his responsibility to ensure the filing of suspicious activity reports (SARs) on agents who he knew or had reason to suspect were engaged in fraud, money laundering, or other criminal activity. By failing to file SARs, despite having extensive information regarding complicit MoneyGram outlets and the evident victimization of MoneyGram's customers, he denied critical information to law enforcement which could have been used to combat the fraud and dismantle the criminal networks.[468]

Haider (1) willfully violated the requirement to implement and maintain an effective anti-money laundering program and (2) willfully violated the requirement to report suspicious activity. . . .

Haider's failures included the following:

Failure to Implement a Discipline Policy. Haider failed to ensure that MoneyGram implemented a policy for disciplining agents and outlets that MoneyGram personnel knew or suspected were involved in fraud and/or money laundering.

Failure to Terminate Known High-Risk Agents/Outlets. Haider failed to ensure that MoneyGram terminated agents and outlets that MoneyGram personnel understood were involved in fraud and/or money laundering, including outlets that Haider himself was on notice posed an unreasonable risk of fraud and/or money laundering.

Failure to File Timely SARs. Haider failed to ensure that MoneyGram fulfilled its obligation to file timely SARs, in part because Haider maintained MoneyGram's AML program such that the individuals responsible for filing SARs were not provided with information from MoneyGram's Fraud Department that should have resulted in the filing of SARs on specific agents or outlets.

Failure to Conduct Effective Audits of Agents/Outlets. Haider failed to ensure that MoneyGram conducted effective audits of agents and outlets, including outlets that MoneyGram personnel knew or suspected were involved in fraud and/or money laundering.

Failure to Conduct Adequate Due Diligence on Agents/Outlets. Haider failed to ensure that MoneyGram conducted adequate due diligence on prospective agents, or existing agents seeking to open additional outlets, which resulted in, among other things, MoneyGram (1) granting outlets to agents who had previously been terminated by other money transmission companies and (2) granting additional outlets to agents who MoneyGram personnel knew or suspected were involved in fraud and/or money laundering.[469]

Discussion topics

*What are MoneyGrams? Who is likely to use them and why?

---

468 Excerpted from FinCEN, *FinCEN Assesses $1 Million Penalty and Seeks to Bar Former MoneyGram Executive from Financial Industry* (Dec. 18, 2014), *available at* https://www.fincen.gov/news/news-releases/fincen-assesses-1-million-penalty-and-seeks-bar-former-moneygram-executive (last visited Oct. 20, 2016).

469 Excerpted from FinCEN, *In re* Haider (Dec. 18, 2014), *available at* https://www.fincen.gov/news_room/ea/files/Haider_Assessment.pdf (last visited Oct. 20, 2016).

*Is it difficult or costly for a money intermediary to examine MoneyGrams and their use?

*What induced Haider to be so "sloppy" in monitoring this case?

*What were the main drivers of the violation in the Haider case?

II. SPECULATION

Speculation may or may not be addictive. Investors may become addicted through "the excitement of trading and the "You can do it!" atmosphere created by online brokerage advertisements and the financial media."[470] Arguably, speculative activities in which the trader or gambler can control the timing of the activity are more likely to be addictive (e.g., video poker, day trading) as are those in which the participant has less control (e.g., lottery, roulette).[471] From 1% to 4% of investors are "habitual gamblers," as are at least 1% of traders on the NASDAQ exchange.[472]

Con artists may crave to present the image of persons who are risk-averse,[473] attract the attention and admiration of others,[474] and feel superior and condescending to others.[475]

III. MONEY, ADDICTION, AND THE EXCITEMENT OF "CONNING"

Not surprisingly, many fraudsters' obsession and addiction is money. It feeds their egos to get it, spend it, and use it to exercise and experience power.[476] They are proud to have money and not to have to budget their money, like their victims,[477] yet they want more money, may spend money, and crave making more.[478] They are drawn to the excitement of "conning" itself and the

---

470 Liz Pulliam Weston, *Talk Is Vital in Planning Family Finances*, L.A. TIMES, Apr. 28, 2000, pt. C, at 1.

471 TAMAR FRANKEL, THE PONZI SCHEME PUZZLE 154 (2012).

472 David Ferrell, *Some Use Financial Markets to Invest in Addiction: Going for Broke* (pt. 1 of 3), L.A. TIMES, Dec. 13, 1998, *available at* http://articles.latimes.com/1998/dec/13/news/mn-53756 (last visited Nov. 3, 2016).

473 Lisa Davis, *Jamba Liar,* SF WKLY., Oct. 27, 1999, LEXIS, News Library, Arcnws File; Peter Byrne, *Double Injustice,* SF WKLY., July 12, 2000, LEXIS, News Library, Arcnws File.

474 Michael Benson & Francis T. Cullen, *The Special Sensitivity of White-Collar Offenders to Prison: A Critique and Research Agenda,* 16 J. CRIM. JUSTICE 207, 211-12 (1988).

475 MALIN AKERSTROM, CROOKS AND SQUARES 176 (1995).

476 CHARLES PONZI, THE RISE OF MR. PONZI 96, 99 (1935), *available at* http://www.pnzi.com (last visited Mar. 6, 2012).

477 MALIN AKERSTROM, CROOKS AND SQUARES 156-57 (1995).

478 *Id.* at 168.

feeling of being smarter than others.[479] However, they also lie to themselves[480] and seem to lack the capacity for self-condemnation, which is a necessary component of feeling guilty.[481]

IV. JUSTIFYING FRAUDULENT ACTIONS.

Con artists justify fraudulent actions by blaming the laws or the regulators: It is the regulators, not the con artists, who caused the investors' losses; the laws are unjust in some way; and enforcement is ineffective in any event.[482] In addition, the markets are adequate to solve most problems without regulation.[483] And besides "everyone does it,"[484] and in addition, fraud is justifiable or necessary to protect oneself.[485]

Fraudsters may desire to maintain their status or advance within their organizations.[486] For example, the company may be experiencing difficulties, but the fraudster believes the company will turn around and consequently may use accounting tricks or misstatements in the short term. The fraudster then must take further steps to conceal the tricks or misstatements.[487]

Risk becomes less serious with experience and repetition that does not produce adverse result. In the United States, investment risk, just like the risk of traffic accidents, is far less frightening as compared to the risk in some other countries. That is because we experience these risks often. In other countries the experience may differ. In Israel, for example, the risk of being hurt by a terrorist bomb is far less frightening than the perception of such a risk in countries that have not been exposed to terrorist attacks for long periods. Thus, the social environment, especially when it persists long-term, shapes people's perception, fear, and worry, and their attitudes towards many kinds of risks, including fraud.[488]

Professor Langevoort discusses the sale of an exceptionally novel and risky financial instrument by Goldman Sachs to a bank, IKB, and a portfolio manager, ACA. IKB may have ignored or underestimated the risk. IKB had bought this type of security as part of a routine, and may have

---

479 TAMAR FRANKEL, THE PONZI SCHEME PUZZLE 152 (2012).

480 TAMAR FRANKEL, THE PONZI SCHEME PUZZLE 155-56 (2012), *citing* http://www.answers.com/topic/calculating. (expired link).

481 ROBERT H. FRANK, PASSIONS WITHIN REASON 159 (1988).

482 MARSHALL B. CLINARD & PETER C. YEAGER, CORPORATE CRIME 67-73 (1980).

483 TAMAR FRANKEL, THE PONZI SCHEME PUZZLE 129 (2012).

484 Gary Johns, *A Multi-Level Theory of Self-Serving Behavior in and by Organizations,* 21 RES. IN ORGANIZATIONAL BEHAVIOR 1, 14 (1999).

485 MARSHALL B. CLINARD & PETER C. YEAGER, CORPORATE CRIME 67 (1980).

486 Ezra Stotland, *White Collar Criminals,* 33 J. SOCIAL ISSUES 179, 186 (1977).

487 TAMAR FRANKEL, THE PONZI SCHEME PUZZLE 136 (2012).

488 *See* TAMAR FRANKEL, THE PONZI SCHEME PUZZLE 136-46 (2012) (discussing victims' risk tolerance).

had no reason to change the routine with this transaction. Regarding Goldman, it may have rationalized and justified its actions because of its role as a "market maker" acting in the belief that the markets are generally accurate even for esoteric and novel transactions.[489] Besides, investment risk promises investment returns. Therefore, it may be attractive to some people.

How does the American public view fraudsters? The general view of abusers of our trust differs from the general view of thieves and robbers, who abuse our privacy and property. In the famous comic strip "Little Orphan Annie," con artists (abusers of trust) were portrayed as the good people and the government officials as the villains.[490] There are reasons for public sympathy towards fraudsters.[491] Many fraudsters are creative, clever, fascinating, and charismatic persons.

"Corporations are seldom referred to as lawbreakers and rarely as criminals in enforcement proceedings. Even if violations of the criminal law, as well as other laws, are involved, enforcement attorneys and corporation counsels often refer to the corporation as 'having a problem'; one does not speak of the robber or the burglar as 'having a problem.'"[492] "Since the 1980s, this attitude changed somewhat, but was later revived. After the debacle of 2008, the attitude changed somewhat again."[493]

Arguably, this discussion has nothing to do with self-regulation (compliance). And yet, self-regulation is affected by the business atmosphere and by the relationship among the employees themselves as well as their relationship with their leaders and outsiders with whom they do business. Therefore, we should note these relationships as well.

V. LEADERSHIP STYLE AND THE GENERAL ATMOSPHERE IN THE INSTITUTION.

Leadership sets the tone for the organization. Employees follow their leaders and react to them. Leadership has a major effect on the culture of the organization and that affects the organization's self-regulation. Therefore, leadership requires behavior that would be followed mostly willingly and identified with it.[494]

For example, in the *Urban* case, discussed later, a high-level employee in a brokerage firm called the firm's compliance officer "Nazi and Gestapo" in front of a laughing crowd of

---

489 Donald C. Langevoort, *Essay: Chasing the Greased Pig Down Wall Street: A Gatekeeper's Guide to the Psychology, Culture, and Ethics of Financial Risk Taking*, 96 CORNELL L. REV. 1209, 1234-40 (2011).

490 *E.g.*, Alice T. Carter, *The Con is On*, PITT. TRIB. REV., Jan. 21, 2007, LEXIS, News Library, Arcnws File (noting that in Broadway and film versions, con artists posing as Annie's long-lost parents are among "con artists who have wormed their way into our hearts").

491 *Id.* (noting "charisma" of movie and stage con artists and that real-life con artists "have much in common" with them).

492 MARSHALL B. CLINARD & PETER C. YEAGER, CORPORATE CRIME 21 (1980).

493 TAMAR FRANKEL, THE PONZI SCHEME PUZZLE 163 (2012).

494 *See* Chapter 14 (meaning and role of culture in institutional self-regulation).

employees. The CEO did not reprimand the high level employee. Instead he viewed his behavior as a good-humored joke. The compliance officer was in fact rendered ineffective and finally resigned. The fact that the officer was a woman did not help.

VI. EFFECTS OF LEADERSHIP'S PERSONAL TENDENCIES AND ATTITUDE TOWARD RISKS ON INSTITUTIONAL RISK-TAKING

A. Who would be the perfect leader?

The leaders' knowledge, familiarity, position, and personal preferences affect their decisions involving institutional risk taking. Firms took on more debt when they had bankers on their board; firms were more prone to making contributions to local nonprofits when their leaders had network ties to nonprofit leaders. Firms relied less on shared directorships for information about acquisitions when the CEO had access to other relevant sources of high-level intelligence. In short, corporations were embedded in a network of information flows via the pervasive practice of sharing directors.

Board members' personal ties can act as devices for promoting cohesion among elites as well. For instance, corporations with well-connected board members were less likely to receive an unwanted takeover bid in the 1960s, although more likely to during the 1980s. And States with densely connected local corporate elites were quicker to adopt antitakeover laws during the 1980s than states with sparse local elite networks.[495]

There is a recently developing view of team leadership that is aimed not only at enforcing compliance with the law but mainly at creating a more productive group. Instead of commanding a way of behavior and encouraging competition among the employees, the leader develops a practice of group cooperation that involves the commander as well. The leader seeks the opinion of the group members, rather than directing them. The managers teach rather than command. This system creates a sense of "ownership" by members of the group and at the same time raises the level of their responsibility as well. After all, they were not told what to do but participated in the decision. The commander's skills in this case are far more complex and few managers are used to this model. However, we might witness the rise of this form of leadership in corporations and should watch out for it.[496]

---

495 *See, e.g.,* Marcel Kahan & Ehud Kamar, *The Myth of State Competition in Corporate Law,* 55 Stan. L. Rev. 679, 703 (2002) (noting that all commentators conclude that antitakeover statutes were adopted to protect local firms; many were passed to protect specific companies).

496 *See* Kimball Fisher, Leading Self-Directed Work Teams, A Guide to Developing New Team Leadership Skills (2000).

Most importantly, this leadership style can be used to enforce compliance with the law. It is being used in other countries and creates a "group think"[497] which makes it easier to admit mistakes, correct them, and learn from negative reactions and events, thereby producing far more positive results. It has been noted that this form of leadership is more successful in privately held corporations where the investors are not following markets and trading daily or even more often. Thus, the pressure of minute-to-minute performance does not exist.

Discussion topic:
- Which leadership style is more productive? Does the answer depend on the kind of business?
- Do you agree that the type of leadership described above is suitable only for privately held corporations? If so, why?
- In general, does competition produce better results than cooperation? On what details would your answer depend?
- Personally, which form of leadership would you choose?

In establishing the corporate risk attitude, note the corporate leadership's attitude to risk. When financial markets "bubbled" JPMorgan Chase did not take excessive risk. This conservative attitude may have been due in part to its conservative culture, and in part to its CEO, who believed that risk-taking should be justified. In contrast, AIG's London affiliate aggressively issued CDSs that were linked to exceptionally risky securities (collateralized debt obligation tranches), possibly because the individual, who became head of that division, took the risks to drive his own financial prosperity.[498]

Professor Donald C. Langevoort suggests that over-confidence and over-commitment to a particular way of operating are problems related to cognitive biases that can distort rational judgment. Overconfidence may lead to arrogance, over-optimism, and an escalation of commitment to choices that might turn out to be wrong.[499] Consequently, decision makers "may ignore or suppress dissent, overestimate their ability to rectify adverse consequences, and cover up mistakes." These attitudes may begin the "slippery slope" into bad conduct.[500] It seems that even success may drive fraud. "Once you've tasted the rewards of innovation, the temptation to continue to drink at that well is so large that when economics are against you, you lie."[501]

---

[497] See, Eli P. Cox, III , Seeking Adam Smith, Finding The Shadow Curriculum if Business 149-195 (2017).

[498] Donald C. Langevoort, *Essay: Chasing the Greased Pig Down Wall Street: A Gatekeeper's Guide to the Psychology, Culture, and Ethics of Financial Risk Taking*, 96 Cornell L. Rev. 1209 (2011).

[499] *Id.*

[500] Deborah L. Rhode, *Legal Ethics: Moral Counseling*, 75 Fordham L. Rev. 1317, 1321 (2006).

[501] Greg Farrell, *Bright Ideas Gone Bust Can Lead to Corporate Fraud*, USA Today, July 31, 2006, at 1B, *available at* http://usatoday30.usatoday.com/money/companies/management/2006-07-31-innovation-usat_x.htm (July 31, 2016) (last visited Feb. 17, 2016) (quoting Columbia professor Bruce Greenwald).

B. The Fall of Bear Stearns in March 2008 Offers a Lesson[502]

Bear Stearns CEO James Cayne

> was known for leaving the office early on Thursday to catch a chartered helicopter ride to various golf courses, taking multiple extended vacations each year to compete in bridge tournaments, and habitually smoking marijuana . . . . But, worst of all, he purportedly had neither any interest in, nor knowledge of, risk management. And it was for this reason that Bear's real estate traders were able to accumulate nearly $50 billion in mortgage-related assets on the bank's balance sheet by the time the housing market began to hemorrhage.[503]

This is a question of balance. Each of the items may be fine so long as it is not excessive. A combination of all these items, even if each is not excessive, may signal serious trouble.

In 2007, some hedge funds nearly collapsed. Hedge funds are investment vehicles that generally invest in illiquid assets.[504] Hedge fund managers are generally compensated by an annual management fee (usually 1-2% of the client's investment) and a share of the net profits of the long-term investments (often 30% or more).[505] Therefore, managers may have had an incentive to take risks, for example, by using borrowed money, or leverage, to increase returns. The two Bear Stearns hedge funds that nearly collapsed (the High-Grade Structured Credit Strategies Fund and the High-Grade Structured Credit Strategies Enhanced Leverage Fund) were leveraged, and their leverage was a cause of their losses.[506]

The Bear Stearns CEO's handling of the crisis raised issues:

> As Bear's fund meltdown was helping spark this year's mortgage-market and credit convulsions, Cayne at times missed key events. At a tense, August conference call with investors, he left after a few opening words and listeners didn't know when he returned. In summer weeks, he typically left the office on Thursday afternoon and spent Friday at his New Jersey golf club, out of touch for stretches, according to associates and golf records. In the critical month of July, he

---

502 John Maxfield, The Motley Fool, *A Timeline of Bear Stearns' Downfall*, Houston Chron., Mar. 15, 2013, *available at* http://www.chron.com/business/fool/article/A-Timeline-of-Bear-Stearns-Downfall-4275736.php (last visited Oct. 19, 2016).

503 *Id.*

504 Justin Lahart & Aaron Lucchetti, *Wall Street Fears Bear Stearns Is Tip of an Iceberg --- Near-Collapse of Funds Stokes Broader Concerns over Murky Investments*, Wall St. J., June 25, 2007, at A1, LEXIS, News Library, Wsj File.

505 John Steele Gordon, *'Carried Interest' Is Not a Capital Gain*, Wall St. J., Apr. 3, 2013, at A15, LEXIS, News Library, Wsj File.

506 Justin Lahart & Aaron Lucchetti, *Wall Street Fears Bear Stearns Is Tip of an Iceberg --- Near-Collapse of Funds Stokes Broader Concerns over Murky Investments*, Wall St. J., June 25, 2007, at A1, LEXIS, News Library, Wsj File.

spent 10 of the 21 workdays out of the office, either at the bridge event or golfing, according to golf, bridge, and hotel records.[507]

In sum, failed leadership plays an important contributing role in the failure of institutions.

_____

507 Kate Kelly, *Bear CEO's Handling Of Crisis Raises Issues --- Cayne on Golf Links, 10-Day Bridge Trip Amid Summer Turmoil*, WALL ST. J., Nov. 1, 2007, at A1, LEXIS, News Library, Curnws File.

Chapter 9

THE STORY OF E.F. HUTTON'S SLIDE INTO OBLIVION[508]

Reading focus

*What triggered the changes in E.F. Hutton's practices?

*What law applied to E.F. Hutton's general practice?

*What is the point of delineation between aggressive but responsible maximization of shareholder value and deceptive business practices?

*How can employees respond when they believe that their company has crossed the line?

*What actions can reverse a slide into deceptive business practices?

Use the questions above and the material that follows to hone your skill in identifying the slippery slope and persuasively arguing for appropriate countermeasures.

INTRODUCTION.

The case of E.F. Hutton illustrates a slippery slope, and how, in hindsight, it could have been avoided. Most importantly, it demonstrates the pitfalls of failing to adjust correctly to changed circumstances, including changes in the law.

E.F. Hutton, a financial services powerhouse in the 1980s, fell into oblivion by the end of the decade. Ironically, the slide began when Hutton adopted an otherwise prudent cash management strategy in the 1970s. The strategy was initially intended to assure that the corporation put its cash balances to use overnight and over weekends. From this textbook strategy evolved

---

508 Footnotes omitted. *E.F. Hutton's Slide into Oblivion: The Slippery Slope, in* Mark Fagan & Tamar Frankel, Trust and Honesty In the Real World: A Joint Course for Lawyers, Business People, and Regulators (2007) (case study companion to Tamar Frankel, Trust and Honesty, America's Business Culture at a Crossroad (2005)).

a deceptive practice whereby the company periodically over-drafted its cash accounts to gain more interest income.

By 1980, and through 1982, the company was consistently over-drafting tens of millions of dollars daily. Ultimately, this practice resulted in the company pleading guilty to 2,000 counts of fraud. Despite a management turnover and new strategies, E.F. Hutton never regained the trust of its customers or its financial footing. In 1987, it was sold to Shearson Lehman Brothers for only $965 million, substantially less than the company's market capitalization only a year earlier.[509]

In 2006, 30 graduate students between the ages of 25 and 35 were asked if they knew of E.F. Hutton. The results: 90% of the respondents never heard of the company. Had the survey been of those ages 50 and older, they would have immediately recognized the name. E.F. Hutton's 1970s and 1980s television advertising campaign showed a noisy crowded restaurant where an E.F. Hutton broker is dining with a customer. When the Hutton broker begins to speak, the restaurant becomes silent and everyone turns toward the broker because: "When E.F. Hutton talks, people listen." The ad was wildly successful and was a major contributor to the growth of E.F. Hutton's retail brokerage business. During that period: E.F. Hutton was "a financial powerhouse in America; they were founded at the turn of the century and have one of the strongest reputations for trust and honesty in the business."[510]

A decade later, on May 2, 1985, the president of E.F. Hutton & Co. pled guilty, on behalf of the corporation, to 2,000 counts of wire and mail fraud[511] related to the over-drafting of checking accounts with E.F. Hutton's banks. The fraud had cost E.F. Hutton's banking partners millions of dollars. With the guilty plea, the company agreed to pay a fine of $2 million, compensate the government $750,000 for the cost of its investigation, and make restitution to the banks that E.F. Hutton defrauded. The direct financial impact of the plea bargain was trivial for a billion dollar company. However, the reputational damage to the company was so great that it never regained its own financial viability. In December 1987, the company was sold at a fire sale price to a competing brokerage firm.

I. BUILDING A BROKERAGE BUSINESS

E.F. Hutton was the picture of success entering the 1980s. The company's revenues in 1980 were $1.1 billion and its profits totaled $82 million. Hutton offered products across the financial services spectrum from stock and bond trading to tax advisory services. The flagship product was its retail brokerage services for which Hutton employed over 6,000 brokers. From the date of

---

[509] *Id.*

[510] *Id.*

[511] 18 U.S.C. § 1341 (2012) (mail fraud); 18 U.S.C. § 1343 (2012) (wire fraud).

its founding, in 1904, buying and selling stocks and bonds on behalf of retail customers was the foundation of the company. Hutton's success in brokerage was a result of innovation, aggressive management, and a decentralized operational structure. In 1905, Hutton was the first West Coast broker with a direct wire to New York, enabling its customers to eliminate timing risks resulting from slow communications between the two coasts. Another example of the company's innovation was its practice of using seasonal offices—Palm Beach and Miami, Florida in the winter and Saratoga, New York in the summer—to best access its well-heeled customers. Management also realized that broad geographic coverage would leverage the firm's strong brand equity. Thus, Hutton acquired regional brokerage firms to build a national network.

The founder, Edward Francis Hutton, was bold and aggressive. After several unsuccessful positions at financial houses in New York, he married well and launched his career on his father-in-law's coattails. He saw the potential of California's exploding growth at the beginning of the 20th century and had the courage to open up shop in this emerging market. From his first office in San Francisco, Hutton rapidly expanded over the next several years opening offices in Los Angeles, Hollywood, Santa Monica, and San Diego. The aggressive tone he set became the firm's culture.

Hutton died in 1962 but his legacy continued. The culture he established was reinforced by Bob Fomon, who was Hutton's CEO from 1970 to 1986 and its chairman from 1977 to 1987. He, too, was forceful and directive in his management style. He supported the company's hiring of aggressive salespeople for the brokerage business. The culture of the Hutton team was that, when Hutton competed for business, it won.

II. MANAGEMENT PHILOSOPHY AND ORGANIZATIONAL STRUCTURE

"The world consisted of winners and losers in the Darwinian creed he adopted, and he would devote himself to winning at all costs," as *New York Times* correspondent James Sterngold described Fomon's philosophy. The aggressive style was paying off. *Institutional Investor* magazine wrote: "Hutton has surged into second place among US brokers—and very probably leads the pack when it comes to sheer aggressiveness."

Hutton adopted a decentralized management model. The brokers, not the managers at headquarters, generated the firm's revenues. Hutton's idea was to tap the brokers' entrepreneurial spirit. Thus, the brokers defined the processes for managing their own business to maximize profits. This decentralized model enabled Hutton to attract successful brokers; individual deals could be cut to recruit "superstars" without upsetting predetermined organizational hierarchies. For example, Joe Sales was one of Hutton's most productive salesmen. He generated $2 to $3 million in commissions for the firm every year. In order to minimize the bureaucracy Sales had to face, Hutton built a separate organizational branch for him, which enabled Hutton to cut a special profit-sharing deal with Sales without changing the profit-sharing split for the rest of the brokers in the branch. Moreover, "[w]hen the designation 'N53,' (the code for Sales' Houston office), showed up on a document, no questions were asked."

Headquarters' role was to track performance. As Fomon adopted a hands-off approach, he was complemented by George Ball, president of the holding company, who watched branch profitability with an eagle eye. Ball "had a prodigious appetite for the facts and details Fomon abhorred. A branch did not change a light bulb without his [Ball's] noticing." On a monthly basis, Ball ranked the branches according to profitability. He rewarded the winners with gifts and chided the losers to improve. Despite his aggressive drive for profits, he was liked by the branch managers and brokers because he had a very human side as well. By knowing the brokers personally (and their spouses and children's names and birthdates) and treating them as the real heroes of the company, he earned their unwavering support. Greater-than-industry-average pay packages for successful brokers also built broker loyalty. However, while Ball was very focused on the bottom line, he did not examine the processes that generated these results.

The organizational structure at headquarters mirrored the laissez-faire approach to management permitted in the branches. Hearings held by the House Judiciary Committee Subcommittee on Crime, which followed the company's guilty plea, revealed that this billion-dollar company did not have an organizational chart. "Its lack of that traditional management tool speaks volumes about the way the firm was run. More than eighty years after its founding and with 17,000 employees, Hutton still operated as if it were an entrepreneurial enterprise." From Hutton's founding until the 1970s, making money in the brokerage business was relatively easy. The firm earned commissions on each buy and sell transaction. The fees were set by the SEC and the stock exchanges to enable even the inefficient houses to make money. The secret to success was obvious: grow the number and value of trades, keep expenses under reasonable control, and watch the profits soar.

III. THE CHANGE: MOBILIZING FUNDS.

The Hutton model underwent dramatic changes in 1975 with the Securities Acts Amendments of 1975. Under this law, brokerage fees formerly fixed at 1% of the value of the trade were deregulated. A brokerage firm could now charge any fee. The objective was to create competition in the brokerage sector and it worked. Although the average commissions by full service brokers did not fall for individuals, "no frills" brokers that charged reduced fees emerged. For example, in 1979, E.F. Hutton charged a retail customer $85 to purchase 100 shares of IBM. The discount broker Charles Schwab charged $40 for the same transaction.

The transition to a deregulated and competitive marketplace was not easy for Hutton. The company's culture of special arrangements for key brokers and Bob Fomon's flamboyance did not make it easy for the company to be a low-cost provider. In fact, to hire and retain aggressive brokers, Hutton shared a larger portion of its commissions with its sales staff than most of its competitors. To maintain profits amid falling commission rates, greater competition and higher sales costs, branch offices looked to other sources of income. Cash management was identified as a particularly promising new tool.

Any financial management textbook includes a chapter on cash management, noting that prudent management requires "putting the firm's funds to work" at all times. Idle money is equal to lost profits. In the 1970s and 1980s, two main techniques were often cited to maximize the productivity of cash for corporations with operations across large geographic areas. One was "concentration banking" in which checks collected from customers were deposited at local banks to speed the availability of funds. The second strategy was "money mobilization." This concept encompassed bringing excess cash balances into a centralized bank location(s) for either disbursement or investment.

Another related approach was to use geographically dispersed banks to "play the float," which allowed an institution to earn interest on checks that were still in the clearing process. This strategy took advantage of time lags between the time when a check was sent by mail and the time it was cleared by the Federal Reserve System. Firms, including Hutton, exploited and purposefully exacerbated the natural delays in the check clearing process. For example, if a Hutton customer in Maine was due a check for $10,000, the firm could write the check on a bank in Arizona. The geographic separation of the banks lengthened the time for the check to clear. During this "travel" time, Hutton had the use of the funds, enabling the company to reduce its borrowing or earn interest on surplus cash. Of course, the company's gain was a loss to the customer and the process also imposed added administrative costs on the banks. The company's gain could be the loss to the bank. That is, if the bank paid to the company amounts that were not yet in the company's account, then it really gave the company an interest free loan, which the company can use to its benefit. These activities are referred to as "check kiting."

Three factors made playing the float particularly attractive to Hutton in the late 1970s and early 1980s. First, deregulation of the brokerage business and the subsequent competition from discount brokers reduced Hutton's profits. Consequently the company sought new sources of income. Second, large sums of money are received and disbursed in the brokerage business, thus even small percentage gains on these sums could significantly improve the bottom line. Third, interest rates, including those paid on the float, were at historically high levels during this time period. For example, the prime rate averaged 9% in 1978 and exceeded 20% in December 1980. Funds that could be invested rather than paid to customers were a further boost to otherwise sagging profits. The magnitude of the gain could be substantial. Increasing Hutton's daily cash balance by $10 million on an annual basis could lead to $2 million in interest income at the December 1980 interest rate levels.

In 1974, Hutton hired a '"Money Mobilizer" to help the company better manage its cash. The Mobilizer realized that cash concentration was leaving excess funds at local banks used by various Hutton branches. Moving money quickly from local banks to Hutton's main banks in Los Angeles and New York would enable the firm to earn interest on the otherwise unproductive funds. After implementing these changes, the Mobilizer realized that he could exploit delays in the check clearing system to draw down twice the value of the funds in the local bank accounts. The additional funds drawn were then put to work earning more interest income for Hutton.

For example, if a local Hutton branch deposited $100,000 per day with its local bank, this branch could then write a check on the account for $200,000 and send it to Hutton's main New York bank. Because of the strong relationship between Hutton and its New York bank, Hutton would be credited with the $200,000 immediately in New York. By the time the $200,000 check cleared back in the local branch bank that it was written on, another day's deposit of $100,000 would cover the original shortfall. Thus, Hutton earned interest income on $200,000 during the time the check was being processed. In sum, a check clears when the money leaves the bank of the writer and goes to the bank of the recipient of the check. Thus, if it takes a few days for the money to leave the check-writer's account the money continues to earn interest until it does.

In 1980 a new Money Mobilizer adopted two new cash management techniques: Hutton overdrew local bank accounts by increasingly large amounts. According to an internal investigation conducted by former U.S. Attorney General Griffin Bell, someone in the Alexandria, VA office inadvertently wrote a $9 million overdraft check rather than the intended $900,000 check. "When the overdraft went through without a complaint from the bank, the $9 million overdraft was repeated."

The second technique was "chaining" (or check kiting) where Hutton branches would write checks greater than the funds they had on deposit at their local bank and then cover the balance deficiency with checks drawn on banks in other cities. Thus, Hutton had the use of the funds in both accounts until all the checks cleared. In fact, it had the equivalent of an interest free loan.

The branches had a strong incentive to participate in these practices. First, under the decentralized company philosophy, local managers shared directly in their branches' profits. For branch managers, this usually amounted to approximately 10% of local net earnings. Thus, if a particular branch had interest earnings of $124,000 for one month, the managers would gain a bonus of $12,400. Second, headquarters "encouraged" the practice. Ball wrote memos to the branches "praising branches with high profits from over-drafting and encouraged others to learn the process." Third, the strongest selling point for the over-drafting scheme was that it worked!

By the end of 1980, Hutton had reduced its working cash borrowing from $383 million to $192 million. The estimated reduction in Hutton's debt servicing costs was about one-third of the company's profits that year. 1980 also marked the start of an aggressive push by Ball to generate interest expense savings (or outright profits) firm wide. "Within a year, a third of Hutton's branches were engaged in at least one of the two abusive practices. . . . Ball exhorted his troops to use over-drafting to boost their income, while leaving the precise method vague." In 1981, an estimated 70% of profit earned by the retail sales area was from interest income. Ball and the branch managers most extensively involved in the over-drafting later stated to internal auditors and the House Judiciary Committee that they had thought they were using a generally accepted business practice.

IV. THE LEGAL MEANING OF CHECK KITING.

The Comptroller of the Currency defines "check kiting" as "a method whereby a depositor . . . utilizes the time required for checks to clear to obtain an unauthorized loan without any interest charge." Similarly, the FBI defines the practice as a scheme which: (1) "artificially inflates bank account balances... (2) in accounts that are under common control... (3) for the purposes of obtaining unauthorized use of bank funds... (4) through the systematic exchanging or swapping of checks between these accounts... and (5) in a manner which is designed to misuse the float that exists in the banking system."

A. The E.F. Hutton Check Kiting Scheme

Check kiting is illegal in the United States and can be prosecuted under several bank fraud laws. The penalties include fines up to $1 million and 30 years in prison. The manager of the Genesee Country Bank in Batavia, New York, watched with delight as its newest customer, E.F. Hutton, deposited a steady stream of funds into its account during December 1981. On December 1, two checks totaling $334,000 were deposited. On December 2, two additional deposits raised the Hutton balance to $1.2 million. On December 3, a $2.6 million deposit boosted the Hutton account to $3.8 million. The account build-up continued on Friday, December 4 when Hutton deposited a check for $8 million bringing the balance to almost $12 million. On Monday, the deposits continued but three checks written on the bank also arrived; these totaled $11 million. The bank honored the checks but a bank auditor noticed that Genesee had paid $8 million before the Hutton deposits were cleared through the Federal Reserve System.

The Genesee officials realized that the magnitude of deposits was far greater than the banking requirements of Hutton's four-person Batavia office. They also realized that the deposited checks were written by Hutton to Hutton and drawn from two separate Pennsylvania banks. Genesee contacted the banks and learned that Hutton had insufficient funds to cover the checks written. By Thursday, December 10, Genesee refused to honor any more Hutton checks.

The bouncing of Hutton checks continued on Friday, December 11, and Monday, December 14. Further conversations between the banks revealed that Hutton was just moving money between them. On December 18, one of the Pennsylvania banks, United Penn Bank, contacted the Federal Deposit Insurance Corporation (FDIC) to investigate. Genesee reported its concerns to the New York State Banking Department. In January 1982 the FDIC investigator wrote: "At first glance it could appear that Hutton was 'playing the float,'... but further investigation revealed evidence of an apparent deliberate kiting operation almost 'textbook' in form."[512]

E.F. Hutton's immediate responses failed to defuse the problem. First, when the checks bounced, the Hutton manager told Genesee that it would take its business elsewhere. The bank said: "fine." Second, Hutton offered $5,000 to United Penn Bank to drop the matter; the bank refused. Within a few months, Hutton's New York leadership was involved in the investigation. Fomon opted to retain a high-profile lawyer to solve the problem based on his "reputation for being tough." The Hutton strategy appeared at first to be "drag your feet." The information requests submitted by the Pennsylvania prosecutor went largely unanswered. When this prosecutor showed no signs of backing down, Hutton dumped 7 million documents at his office.[513]

By early 1984, the Pennsylvania prosecutor had become convinced that Hutton's practices were "illegal, fraudulent, and criminal." On April 20, the government sent letters to the Hutton executives at the center of the probe stating: "This is to advise you that you are a target of a Federal Grand Jury investigation being conducted in the Middle District of Pennsylvania into possible violations of Federal law." At this point, Fomon realized that the over-drafting issue was not going away. He attempted one last effort to solve the problem — he went to Washington and dined with William French Smith, the U.S. Attorney General. When the meal was over, Fomon stated: "I don't know if you're aware but the U.S. Attorney in the Middle District of Pennsylvania has been investigating our banking practices for two years. . . . Our lawyers have been having trouble with your lawyers. Will you look into it?" Smith was not happy about the request and never got involved.[514]

The discovery of a smoking gun in February 1985 changed the Hutton approach. A memo written in 1982 by a vice president responsible for several branches in the DC area stated: "Specifically, we will from time to time draw down not only deposits plus anticipated deposits, but also bogus deposits. I know of at least a dozen managers at Hutton who do precisely the same thing." Based on this memo, and the fact that it was not produced in response to prior requests, Hutton's defense counsel changed his strategy and began a plea bargaining process. On May 2, 1985, E.F. Hutton pled guilty to 2,000 counts of mail and wire fraud.

The financial community was shocked that a financial pillar had fallen into disrepute. The press was shocked that only the firm, not individuals, had been required to plead guilty. In turn, Congressmen "wrote a letter to the Attorney General, demanding to know why he didn't hang everybody at Hutton by their toes." The House Subcommittee on Crime took up the issue. The U.S. Attorney General's Pennsylvania prosecutor testified that the law around cash management

---

512 Footnotes omitted. *E.F. Hutton's Slide into Oblivion: The Slippery Slope, in* Mark Fagan & Tamar Frankel, Trust and Honesty In the Real World: A Joint Course for Lawyers, Business People, and Regulators (2007) (case study companion to Tamar Frankel, Trust and Honesty, America's Business Culture at a Crossroad (2005)).

513 *Id.*

514 *Id.*

was unclear. He testified further that many banks must have known that the practice was being used and accepted it as a cost of doing business with Hutton. He concluded that it was the corporation, not the individuals, that committed the crime. Beyond this, he stated that he thought it would have been difficult proving the case against the individuals involved. The plea bargain allowed him to achieve his core objective — helping to stop fraudulent banking practices. As it turns out, the prosecutor probably did actually have a greater impact because of his strategy of pursuing the corporation rather than a handful of individuals.

B. The Decline and Fire Sale of Hutton

Hutton faced minimal short-term impact from the actual guilty plea. Hutton's stock price barely moved and senior management took steps to regain positive footing. One of their first actions was to conduct an internally sponsored investigation of the over-drafting affair to understand what went wrong and how to prevent it, or similar problems, in the future. Former U.S. Attorney General Griffin Bell was retained to conduct the investigation. Bell's investigators interviewed hundreds of Hutton employees as well as bank and regulatory officials. They also reviewed 40,000 pages of documentation. Bell concluded that Hutton had inadequate internal controls and a loose decentralized management structure that permitted employees to overdraft at will. The report directly blamed the CFO, the Money Mobilizer, Hutton's CLO, and three regional managers. At the branch level, Griffin found that six branch managers "participated in patterns of intentional over-drafting" that "were so excessive and egregious as to warrant sanctions."

A second step Hutton took was to hire Robert Rittereiser, the former Chief Administrative Officer at Merrill Lynch, to improve Hutton's operations. Shortly after he joined Hutton the *Wall Street Journal* ran a story headlined: "Battered Broker: E.F. Hutton Appears Headed for Long Siege in Bank-Draft Scheme." Hiring Rittereiser, however, was too little, too late. The Board and Fomon were also slow to act on the Bell report. Hutton's combative style was leading to more House hearings and this kept Hutton under a negative spotlight. The publicity led existing customers to rethink their relationships with Hutton. Rittereiser discovered that Hutton's culture had spawned problems in other areas outside of the current scandal, for example, that Hutton had marketed tax-exempt securities with potentially misleading descriptions.

In late 1986, Shearson and Hutton held merger discussions. The Shearson offer was in the $50 per share range. Hutton's Board demanded $55 and Shearson walked away. One year later, after continued struggles, Hutton agreed to an acquisition by Shearson for $29.25 per share.

What caused E.F. Hutton's change of business fortune? Why did E.F. Hutton look for other sources of income? Were the duties of broker dealers violated in the case of Hutton? Should Hutton's broker-dealer registration have been suspended or even revoked? Why was its registration not touched? Why did not the SEC or the National Association of Securities Dealers (now FINRA) attempt to prevent the violations at Hutton? Did E.F. Hutton's lawyer do his or her job?

What are the duties of the directors and controlling shareholders of a broker-dealer?

What is the role of corporate counsel in setting management policies? Is one of these roles the proactive monitoring of compliance in light of the fact that the corporations did not have a compliance officer?

In this case, what were the early warning signs of fraudulent behavior?

Where was the dividing line between prudent cash management and fraud? How could the dividing line be established?

Could the directors or the CEO of Hutton have prevented the violations that actually transpired? How could the branch managers have stopped the violations? How could they have limited or prevented the precursors to these violations?

Why was hiring Rittereiser arguably too little, too late? What would have been different had Hutton acted sooner, and why?

Why did the Hutton stock price move so little after the corporation's guilty plea?

If Hutton did not practice check kiting, what were Hutton's prospects in the 1980s?

Was the prosecutor justified in prosecuting only the corporation and not the culpable individuals?

What message did it send to the individuals involved? Were there any extenuating circumstances in this case?

How, if at all, could regulations prevent violations such as those at Hutton from ever occurring again?

Were there any red flags that the regulators could or should have discerned?

———————

Chapter 10

Monitoring to Prevent Violations of the Law

"A person may cause evil to others not only by his actions but by his inaction, and in either case he is justly accountable to them for the injury."

John Stuart Mill, "On Liberty"

"So it is carved in stone but still open to interpretation, right?"

Moses, upon receiving the Ten Commandments

"People who are willing to lie about small things have no problem lying about big things"

David Einhorn, "Fooling SOME of the people
ALL of the Time at 64" (2008).

In other [than the American colonies] countries, the people ... judge of an ill principle in government only by an actual grievance; here they anticipate the evil, and judge of the pressure of the grievance by the badness of the principle. They augur misgovernment at a distance and snuff the approach of tyranny in every tainted breeze.

Edmund Burke, "On Moving His Resolutions
for Conciliation with the Colonies," speech to
Parliament, Mar. 22, 1775.

INTRODUCTION

In this chapter we discuss a preventive measure that an institution should establish to ensure its compliance with the law. As we view the various forms of such a preventive measure, we might also consider which of the forms would be more effective and under what circumstances. We should note that the system-structure of self-regulation affects the institutional culture.

A crucial preventive measure in any institution is culture: the habitual members' self-limitation of possible wrongs. Participants in this culture have a "knee jerk" reaction to any move towards a legal violation or dishonest behavior, saying with pride: "We do not do this here!"

They disdain those who behave differently. In such a social culture the members might enforce legal behavior.

Compliance does not wait for full-blown violations. It seeks to nip them in the bud. To learn about the preventive systems that institutions should install, we draw, on the directives to government-examiners, among other sources. These directives are important for three reasons. First, the tasks of compliance officers are, to some extent, similar to those of government examiners and auditors. Like regulators, compliance officers should be alert to red flags: pointing to possible future violations. Second, it is helpful for corporate law officers (CLOs), and chief compliance officers (CCOs) to understand what government examiners are looking for when they visit the corporation: what the government examiners are looking for is what internal self-regulation should be looking for as well. Third, government examinations offer experience, which all of us can learn from. For example, the reaction of the corporate employees and management to the government examiner may reveal information the CCO should pay attention to.

Section I of Chapter 10 explores the meaning and function of monitoring and investigation and draws on the directives that the SEC and the FDIC give to their investigators. We will deal with investigations in more detail in Chapter 11.

Section II examines the thorny issue of monitoring the activities and messages of the institution's employees. In this context, we discuss the legal rights of employers and employees, and the human and ethical issues involved.

Section III deals with the problem of employee theft.

Section IV describes the issues that arise in connection with securities market brokerage activities. It lists possible, and sometimes probable, regulated brokers' activities that are difficult to monitor and difficult to prevent.

Section V deals with monitoring the laws. Rules that govern and regulate the functions we are dealing with can be complex. That is because these functions are usually composed of many activities. Each activity may be used well or abused. This complexity requires simplification, which can usually be achieved only by a cooperative effort of experts. In addition, the rules that regulate these functions may be changed relatively often. Therefore, the rules governing certain functions should be monitored for change. In addition, as rules change, the activities, and the way they were conducted, may have to change as well. Monitoring the rules, and the changes in the affected functions, can be very time-consuming and require expertise in various areas.

Section VI notes the conditions under which monitoring may lead to investigations

A. What is the meaning of monitoring?

One definition of the act of monitoring is: "[o]bserve and check the progress or quality of (something) over a period of time; keep under systematic review."[515] A definition of a monitor is: "One that admonishes, cautions, or reminds, especially with respect to matters of conduct."[516] Another view of monitoring is: "[t]o keep track of systematically with a view to collecting information."[517] Together, these definitions aptly describe monitoring by compliance officers or managers. In fact, there is little, if any, difference between monitoring required by law and monitoring imposed by good compliance practices.

In our context, we seek answers to the following questions:

(i)   What is the danger that monitoring prevents? This danger is defined in terms of possible violations of legal requirements or prohibitions.

(ii)   What danger signals is monitoring looking for?

(iii)   How should monitoring be conducted to detect danger signals that might lead to violations?

(iv)   How does a compliance officer "monitor" activities within a small or a large institution?

(v)   What steps should be taken to uncover the true facts, and yet protect the rights of those who are investigated?

B. What are the main systems by which the risk of fraud and other violations are uncovered?

The main systems used to uncover violations of the law within an institution are monitoring, investigating, and reporting. These systems should be backed by verification of the uncovered facts, and by the overall supervisory system. For example, FINRA requires member firms to establish and maintain a supervisory system over each associated person, including written procedures, to achieve compliance with laws and regulations, and FINRA rules.[518] In addition, each member firm should designate principals to establish, maintain, and enforce a system of supervisory control. This system should contain policies and procedures that test and verify

---

515   *Monitor, at* http://www.oxforddictionaries.com/us/definition/american_english/monitor (last visited Feb. 29, 2016).

516   *Monitor, at* https://ahdictionary.com/word/search.html?q=monitor (last visited Feb. 29, 2016).

517   *Monitor, at* http://www.thefreedictionary.com/monitor (last visited Feb. 29, 2016).

518   FINRA, Rule 3110 (last amended July 31, 2015), *available at* http://finra.complinet.com/en/display/display_main.html?rbid=2403&element_id=11345 (last visited Mar. 10, 2016).

(i) the supervisory procedures and (ii) the need to amend these procedures.[519] Thus, the FINRA system includes both "checks" and "double-checks." Other organizations may adopt similar approaches.[520]

A similar definition of monitoring is offered by H. David Kotz:[521]

Monitoring differs from auditing. According to the Federal Deposit Insurance Corporation (FDIC) staff monitoring is "a proactive approach to identifying problems before they are identified by an audit." In addition, monitoring is generally performed by in-house personnel. Auditing is "less frequent, more formal, and more comprehensive than monitoring," and may be conducted either in-house or by an outside firm, and includes a written report to the board of directors or a board committee.[522]

For example, how should a bank manage the risks posed by a third party that the bank has a relationship with? Here are a number of suggestions: "A bank should adopt risk-management processes commensurate with the level of risk and complexity of its third-party relationships. . . . A bank should ensure comprehensive risk-management and oversight of third-party relationships involving critical activities. . . . An effective risk management process throughout the life cycle of the relationship includes plans that outline the bank's strategy, identify the inherent risks of the activity, and detail how the bank selects, assesses, and oversees the third party."[523]

Discussion topic

How should a bank monitor its relationship with an outsourced cleaning service as compared to an outsourced auditing service?

---

519 FINRA, Rule 3120 (last amended eff. Dec. 1, 2014), *available at* http://finra.complinet.com/en/display/display_main.html?rbid=2403&element_id=11346 (last visited Mar. 10, 2016).

520 Jason Lunday, *Monitoring for Compliance: A Strategic Approach,* CORP. COMPLIANCE INSIGHTS, July 29, 2010, *available at* http://corporatecomplianceinsights.com/compliance-monitoring-strategic-approach/ (last visited Feb. 29, 2016).

521 *See also* H. DAVID KOTZ, FINANCIAL REGULATION AND COMPLIANCE, HOW TO MANAGE COMPETING AND OVERLAPPING REGULATORY OVERSIGHT 182-183 (2015) (describing monitoring in the context of Foreign Corrupt Practices Act); HARRY CENROWSKI, JAMES P. MARTIN, & LOUIS W. PETRO, THE HANDBOOK OF FRAUD DETERRENCE 137 (2007).

522 DIV. OF COMPLIANCE & CONSUMER AFFAIRS, U.S. FED. DEPOSIT INS. CORP., FDIC DCA EXAMINATION MANUAL, IV app. B (n.d.) (LEXIS) (last visited May 3, 2017).

523 OFC. OF COMPTROLLER OF CURRENCY, RISK MANAGEMENT GUIDANCE (Oct. 30, 2013) (OCC Bulletin 2013-29), *available at* http://occ.gov/news-issuances/bulletins/2013/bulletin-2013-29.html (last visited Mar. 10, 2016).

C. What Is the Purpose of Monitoring?

"The purpose of monitoring is to demonstrate actual compliance."[524] That is, monitoring is useful because it helps demonstrate what individuals and groups actually do. Their actions might be good or bad, supportive of or dangerous to the enterprise. The resulting monitored information about what is actually being done in the institution can offer a useful signal. Such signals can identify changes that should be made to restrain the dangerous and undesirable results and encourage the good ones. Finally, monitoring can provide documented evidence of what is actually being done, although this type of proof involves costs.

In sum, a good monitoring system provides an effective information system that assists supervision, which may detect possible or actual problems and lead to remedial actions. To some extent monitoring becomes a good habit, like a person who automatically looks left and right before crossing the street or rereads the drafted letter for errors and for assurance that the letter says what it was meant to say.

D. What Processes Are Used in Monitoring?

The following describes the monitoring process in the context of bank monitoring of third parties:

- plans that outline the bank's strategy, identify the inherent risks of the activity, and detail how the bank selects, assesses, and oversees the third party.

- proper due diligence in selecting a third party.

- written contracts that outline the rights and responsibilities of all parties.

- ongoing monitoring of the third party's activities and performance.

- contingency plans for terminating the relationship in an effective manner.

- clear roles and responsibilities for overseeing and managing the relationship and risk management process.

- documentation and reporting that facilitates oversight, accountability, monitoring, and risk management.

---

524 Pinkhame v. State of Fla. Dep't of Environmental Regulation, 1986 Fla. ENV LEXIS 48, ay *17 (Apr. 18, 1986).

- independent reviews that allow bank management to determine that the bank's process aligns with its strategy and effectively manages risks. 525

Similarly, the Office of the Inspector General (OIG) issues guidance for hospitals for compliance with federal and state law, the requirements of government and private health plans, and hospital policies.[526]

The OIG guidance includes "[t]he use of audits and/or other evaluation techniques to monitor compliance and assist in the reduction of identified problem area[s]" as one element of a comprehensive compliance program.[527]

The OIG guidance elaborates on the monitoring process:

F. Auditing and Monitoring

An ongoing evaluation process is critical to a successful compliance program. The OIG believes that an effective program should incorporate thorough monitoring of its implementation and regular reporting to senior hospital or corporate officers. Compliance reports created by this ongoing monitoring, including reports of suspected noncompliance, should be maintained by the compliance officer and shared with the hospital's senior management and the compliance committee.

Although many monitoring techniques are available, one effective tool to promote and ensure compliance is the performance of regular, periodic compliance audits by internal or external auditors who have expertise in Federal and State health care statutes, regulations and Federal health care program requirements. The audits should focus on the hospital's programs or divisions, including external relationships with third-party contractors, specifically those with substantive exposure to government enforcement actions. At a minimum, these audits should be designed to address the hospital's compliance with laws [and procedures related to the industry]. In addition, the audits and reviews should inquire into the hospital's compliance with specific rules and polices that have been the focus of particular attention on the part of [certain entities including] and law enforcement . . . . In addition, the hospital should focus on any areas of concern that have been identified by any entity, i.e., Federal, State, or internally, specific to the individual hospital.

---

525 Ofc. Of Comptroller of Currency, Risk Management Guidance (Oct. 30, 2013) (OCC Bulletin 2013-29), *available at* http://occ.gov/news-issuances/bulletins/2013/bulletin-2013-29.html (last visited Mar. 10, 2016).

526 Ofc. of the Inspector General, Dep't of Health & Human Servs., Publication of the OIG Compliance Program Guidance for Hospitals, 63 Fed. Reg. 8987 (Feb. 23, 1998).

527 *Id.* at 8989.

Monitoring techniques may include sampling protocols that permit the compliance officer to identify and review variations from an established baseline.[528] Significant variations from the baseline should trigger a reasonable inquiry to determine the cause of the deviation. If the inquiry determines that the deviation occurred for legitimate, explainable reasons, the compliance officer, hospital administrator or manager may want to limit any corrective action or take no action. If it is determined that the deviation was caused by improper procedures, misunderstanding of rules, including fraud and systemic problems, the hospital should take prompt steps to correct the problem. Any overpayments discovered as a result of such deviations should be returned promptly to the affected payor, with appropriate documentation and a thorough explanation of the reason for the refund.

. . .

An effective compliance program should also incorporate periodic (at least annual) reviews of whether the program's compliance elements have been satisfied, e.g., whether there has been appropriate dissemination of the program's standards, training, ongoing educational programs and disciplinary actions, among others. This process will verify actual conformance by all departments with the compliance program. Such reviews could support a determination that appropriate records have been created and maintained to document the implementation of an effective program. However, when monitoring discloses that deviations were not detected in a timely manner due to program deficiencies, appropriate modifications must be implemented. Such evaluations, when developed with the support of management, can help ensure compliance with the hospital's policies and procedures.

As part of the review process, the compliance officer or reviewers should consider techniques such as:
- On-site visits;
- Interviews with personnel involved in management, operations, . . . ;
- Questionnaires developed to solicit impressions of a broad cross-section of the hospital's employees and staff;
- Reviews of medical and financial records and other source documents . . . ;
- Reviews of written materials and documentation prepared by the different divisions of a hospital; and
- Trend analysis, or longitudinal studies, that seek deviations, positive or negative, in specific areas over a given period.

---

528 The OIG recommends that when a compliance program is established in a hospital, the compliance officer, with the assistance of department managers, should take a "snapshot" of their operations from a compliance perspective. This assessment can be undertaken by outside consultants, law or accounting firms, or internal staff, with authoritative knowledge of health care compliance requirements. This "snapshot," often used as part of benchmarking analyses, becomes a baseline for the compliance officer and other managers to judge the hospital's progress in reducing or eliminating potential areas of vulnerability. . .

The reviewers should:

- Be independent of physicians and line management;
- Have access to existing audit and health care resources, relevant personnel and all relevant areas of operation;
- Present written evaluative reports on compliance activities to the CEO, governing body and members of the compliance committee on a regular basis, but no less than annually; and
- Specifically identify areas where corrective actions are needed.

With these reports, hospital management can take whatever steps are necessary to correct past problems and prevent them from reoccurring. In certain cases, subsequent reviews or studies would be advisable to ensure that the recommended corrective actions have been implemented successfully.

The hospital should document its efforts to comply with applicable statutes, regulations and Federal health care program requirements. For example, where a hospital, in its efforts to comply with a particular statute, regulation or program requirement, requests advice from a government agency (including a Medicare fiscal intermediary or carrier) charged with administering a Federal health care program, the hospital should document and retain a record of the request and any written or oral response. This step is extremely important if the hospital intends to rely on that response to guide it in future decisions, actions or claim reimbursement requests or appeals. Maintaining a log of oral inquiries between the hospital and third parties represents an additional basis for establishing documentation on which the organization may rely to demonstrate attempts at compliance. Records should be maintained demonstrating reasonable reliance and due diligence in developing procedures that implement such advice.[529]

A monitor must not only observe, but also act by reacting to any unusual situation. For example, when a committee was expected to monitor the performance of stock investments in a pension fund, but established no system to review and evaluate the performance of fund managers or to verify whether "potential breaches were otherwise going unaddressed," the Court held that these failures are sufficient to state a claim against the committee members for violating their fiduciary duty to monitor. "[T]he Monitoring Defendants," wrote the Court "are alleged to have simply stood by and watched the value of [the] stock decline precipitously. Based on such statements this Court cannot help but conclude that monitoring fiduciaries failed to provide sufficient attention, if any, to the risks of the continued purchase and retention of AMBAC stock."[530] Noticing without reacting is not monitoring.

---

529 63 Fed. Reg. at 8996-97 (some footnotes omitted).

530 Veera v. Amback Plan Admin. Comm., 769 F. Supp. 2d 223, 231 (S.D.N.Y. 2011).

Discussion topics

Please summarize the parts used to build a new monitoring system, explaining the reason for and evaluating the importance of each part for uncovering and preventing possible.

What would be the difference between monitoring a bank cashier and monitoring students taking an exam? How would monitoring the exam of an applicant seeking a driving license differ from monitoring an exam by a law school student?

Is the timing of monitoring important? What type of activity should be conducted before, during, or after a business activity?

Should a supervisor approve a risky activity before it happens, after the event, or during an activity?How comprehensive should monitoring be? Should each transaction be monitored? Should some transactions be monitored by random sampling? Should some transactions be selected for monitoring through systematic sampling, and if so, what criteria should be used?[531]

Who are the monitors? Should management perform the monitoring or delegate monitoring to staff?[532]

Should an employee or group of employees monitor itself? What advantages could this provide? How would management monitor such monitoring?[533] This form of self-monitoring is discussed in greater detail in the next Chapter 11.

"Continuous monitoring . . . relies on software to monitor transactions and not only identify transactions for testing, but especially to test 100% of the processed transactions for compliance with selected parameters. An example would be a test that identifies purchase orders issued in excess of approved requisitions."[534] The advantages of continuous monitoring, in addition to the fact that it tests 100% of the transactions, include a "[s]ubstantial reduction in time required to test and assess internal controls" and "[i]mmediate notification of control deficiencies to both management and audit."[535]

In sum, as noted earlier, monitoring demonstrates what an individual actually does, so that management can determine whether compliance is achieved. One example of a monitoring process is school examinations. Some learning results may be checked by everyday classroom questions. Others, which demonstrate more general and comprehensive learning, should be

---

531 Jason Lunday, *Monitoring for Compliance: A Strategic Approach,* Corp. Compliance Insights, July 29, 2010, *available at* http://corporatecomplianceinsights.com/compliance-monitoring-strategic-approach/ (last visited Feb. 29, 2016).

532 *Id.*

533 Jason Lunday, *Monitoring for Compliance: A Strategic Approach,* Corp. Compliance Insights, July 29, 2010, *available at* http://corporatecomplianceinsights.com/compliance-monitoring-strategic-approach/ (last visited Feb. 29, 2016).

534 Letter of David A. Richards, President, Inst. of Internal Auditors (Sept. 18, 2006) (SEC comment on rulemaking).

535 Letter of John Verver, CA, CISA, CMC, Vice President - Professional Services of ACL Services Ltd., Vancouver, British Columbia (Oct. 10, 2006) (SEC comment on rulemaking).

checked by examinations after a longer period. The ability to analyze and write coherently is monitored by drafts that culminate in a final paper. All these systems are part of monitoring.

_____

Problems

What would catch your attention as a monitor studying the following facts?

*You are a monitor in a bank. One of the tellers, aged 35, a nice person, appears in a new very expensive car wearing very expensive clothes. How would you act? Would your reaction change if the employee is 55 years old?

*One of the employees in the accounting department hands you a report prepared by another employee. The report is covered with red marks showing mistakes. How would you react?

II. MONITORING EMPLOYEES: LITTLEBROTHER IS WATCHING YOU

A number of programs are available for employers to monitor employees' Internet use, such as "LittleBrother," a program that reports to employers what sites are being used and allows employers to block or limit access to specific sites.[536] As of 2016 there are at least ten employee monitoring software packages available.[537] In addition, for years employers have had the capability of monitoring employees' e-mails.[538]

Workplace electronic monitoring raises two sets of issues; whether it is legal, and whether it is ethical or justifiable.

The first legal issue is whether electronic monitoring violates the Electronic Communications Privacy Act of 1986. The Act generally prohibits interception of electronic communications.[539] However, there is a general exemption for a service provider "while engaged in any activity which is a necessary incident to the rendition of his service or to the protection of the rights or property of the provider of that service."[540] Therefore, presumably there would generally be no violation where the employer provides the service.

_____

536 Sami Menefee, *LittleBrother Is Watching You*, NEWSBYTES, July 15, 1997, LEXIS, News Library, Arcnws File.

537 Whitney Sanchez, *The Best Employee Monitoring Software Packages of 2016*, Mar. 9, 2016, *available at* http://www.toptenreviews.com/business/software/best-employee-monitoring-software/ (last visited Dec. 7, 2016).

538 Katie Johnston, *From Afar, the Boss Can Follow Every Step*, BOSTON GLOBE, Feb. 19, 2016, at A,1,1, LEXIS, News Library, Curnws File.

539 18 U.S.C. § 2511 (2012).

540 18 U.S.C. § 2511(2)(a)(i) (2012).

Second, there is an issue of the employee's common law right to privacy. Generally, courts have not recognized an employee's legally protectable expectation of privacy in the employer's system, and additionally have recognized an employer's legitimate interest in monitoring. For example, an employee whose employment was terminated for "transmitting. . . inappropriate and unprofessional comments over [the employer's] e-mail system despite the employer's assurances of confidentiality." The court held that the employee had "no reasonable expectation of privacy" on his employer's system, even though the employer assured its employees that their e-mail communications would be confidential and privileged. The court noted that the employee communicated the comments over an e-mail system used by the entire company, and that the company did not force the employee to disclose the information. In addition, even if there is a reasonable expectation of privacy, the employee's behavior is subordinated to the company's interest in preventing "inappropriate and unprofessional" conduct.[541] Therefore, presumably employers should have a legitimate reason for monitoring.

An employer may be able to defeat a privacy claim if the employee had advance notice of the employer's policy and agreed to the policy. In a case where an employee signed a policy statement agreeing to use the computers for business purposes only and agreed that the computers could be monitored, the Court found no reasonable expectation of privacy.[542]

Employers that monitor employee communications (including telephone calls, e-mails, and Internet connections) do so for reasons including: (1) legal compliance (e.g., in telemarketing), (2) legal liability for employees' acts,[543] (3) "performance review," (4) "productivity measures," and (5) "security concerns" (i.e., "protection of trade secrets and other confidential information."[544] Companies that monitor their employees' electronic activities do so for a number of reasons. Employers are concerned about their employee productivity because labor is the employers' major expense.[545] Other reasons for the employers' concerns include legal liability for an employee's offensive material in the workplace, and disclosure of trade secrets or other confidential information.[546] _____

---

541 Smyth v. Pillsbury Co., 914 F. Supp. 97, 101 (E.D. Pa. 1996).

542 TBG Ins. Services Corp. v. Superior Court, 96 Cal. App. 4th 443, 453 (Cal. Ct. App. 2002).

543 *E.g.*, Owens v. Morgan Stanley & Co., No. 96 Civ. 9747 (DLC), 1997 U.S. Dist. LEXIS 20493 (S.D.N.Y. Dec. 23, 1997) (employees filed action against employer where employee sent other employees e-mail with racist jokes, claiming racial discrimination and existence of hostile work environment).

544 TBG Ins. Services Corp. v. Superior Court, 96 Cal. App. 4th 443, 451 (Cal. Ct. App. 2002) (citing. AMERICAN MANAGEMENT ASSN., 2001 AMA SURVEY, WORKPLACE MONITORING & SURVEILLANCE, SUMMARY OF KEY FINDINGS (April 2001) [as of Feb. 13, 2002]).

545 Katie Johnston, *From Afar, the Boss Can Follow Every Step*, BOSTON GLOBE, Feb. 19, 2016, at A,1,1, LEXIS, News Library, Curnws File.

546 TBG Ins. Services Corp. v. Superior Court, 96 Cal. App. 4th 443, 451 (Cal. Ct. App. 2002).

Discussion topics

Please offer one example of a justified invasion of employees' privacy and one example of an unjustified invasion of employees' privacy.

Is your choice guided by: (i) The employees' tasks? (ii) The extent of their power and impact on the corporation's activities? (iii) Their character and behavior? (iv) Other conditions? How would you balance these considerations in a fairly consistent way?

Is contract agreement an appropriate test in this case? What about lower-income workers, who have little, or no, bargaining power?

What about an agreement embodied in the company's policies, which apply to everyone (including the sophisticated employees that agreed to it)? What about companies that do not disclose to employees that they are being monitored in a particular way?

Does it make sense to impose a rule that e-mail monitoring should be disclosed to employees?

What about involving the employees in creating a monitoring policy? Would that enable both parties to reach an acceptable policy? In such a case, what should the employers explain to their employees? Should they explain the reasons for their policies? What limits should the employers impose on their ability to "snoop" by LittleBrother or by "Big Brother"?

How would you argue for the employees? How would you argue for the employer? Would you recommend a general rule on this subject, for example by the ALI? If so, how would you phrase it?

III. THE PROBLEM OF EMPLOYEE THEFT

Employee theft is estimated to cost businesses $40 billion per year, and is responsible for "one of every three business failures."[547] The retail industry alone lost $15 billion in 2014 to employee theft.[548]

---

547 Ursula Watson, *Southfield Author Covers the How, Why People Steal*, DETROIT NEWS, Mar. 8, 2016, at 6U, LEXIS, News Library, Curnws File; T.K. Keanini, *Why Insider Threats Are Succeeding*, DATABASE & NETWORK J., at 16(2). LEXIS, News Library, Curnws File. June 1, 2015 (noting that $40 billion estimate is for "most recent year on record").

548 *Employee Theft Costs Retailers Billions*, US OFFICIAL NEWS, July 29, 2015, LEXIS, News Library, Curnws File, *available at* https://www.shrm.org/ResourcesAndTools/hr-topics/risk-management/Pages/Employee-Theft-Costs-Retailers-Billions.aspx (last visited Nov. 29, 2016); *see also* JACK L. HAYES INT'L, INC., 28TH ANNUAL RETAIL THEFT SURVEY (June 2016), *available at* http://hayesinternational.com/news/annual-retail-theft-survey/ (last visited Nov. 29, 2016) (noting that "75,947 dishonest employees were apprehended in 2015, up 1.0% from 2014" in a study of 25 large retailers).

Related to the issue of theft is the more general issue of fraud, including embezzlement. According to a 2014 report, "it is estimated that a typical organization loses 5% of revenues each year to fraud."[549]

Employee theft can include theft of physical property[550] or theft of intangible property, such as trade secrets.[551] Suggestions for preventing employee theft include various types of monitoring, such as pre-employment screening, continuous employee screening (e.g., credit checks), physical surveillance, and electronic surveillance.

Other suggestions list the use of codes of ethics or anti-theft policies and agreements. Still other suggestions include the establishment of an ethical culture, or the recognition and elimination of circumstances that may motivate theft.

Discussion Topic

In your opinion, of all the suggestions mentioned above, what suggestion is the most effective? Why?

What effect of monitoring the employees' honesty have on the employees' honesty?

IV. MONITORING TRADERS' PRACTICES

Monitoring securities traders requires high-level expertise. The following are examples provided by a compliance officer, who was formerly a trader. He called the problems "holes," in the sense that they are vacuums in the regulatory and practice realities. Here are a number of such examples.

A. Trade-Amendment Processes.

An amendment of trades allows traders, salespeople, portfolio managers and others, to "work out" trade changes after execution without a second and independent line of oversight. These persons might have different levels of legal duties. They may have fiduciary or contractual obligations to the owners of the money they control, or they may have more limited duties or none at all.

---

549 Tom Cooney & Crystal Faulkner, *To Prevent Fraud and Theft, Think like a Thief,* Cincinnati Enquirer, Aug. 21, 2014, sec. A, at 18, LEXIS, News Library, Arcnws File (citing Association of Certified Fraud Examiners, Report to the Nations on Occupational Fraud and Abuse (2014)).

550 *E.g.,* Young v. UAW-Labor Empl. & Training Corp., 95 F.3d 992 (10th Cir. 1996) ("pilfering" and resale of materials from nonprofit).

551 *E.g.,* Beach v Touradji Capital Mgt., LP, 144 A.D.3d 557 (N.Y. 2016) (proprietary research, etc. from hedge fund).

For example: a trader at a broker-dealer group (i) makes a trade mistake, or (ii) receives a bribe in order to execute a transaction at less than a market price. Later the trade is noticed, and the trader is concerned that he or she might be caught. How could the trader act? The trader might simply amend the trade details to a proper price or quantity. The news carries countless similar examples each year: a trader buys instead of sells, or buys 10X as much as he or she should, etc., or "helps" a "buddy" out of a bad trade, or does a trade at a bad price for a friend, etc.

The trader's motive may be to hide a mistake that would require compensating the client, or having to compensate a colleague by doing the same favor in the future (a quid pro quo). If it is a "quid pro quo arrangement," the compensation can be anything, such as cash, gifts and entertainment, a good trade or tip (information) down the road, or a new job with the person who has received the favor. The cost of the favor or the bad trade is borne by the client or by the trader's employer. There may be thousands of variations of this practice, some of which might surprise the unwary. These days the practices are not as blatant, but there are those who believe that the events "almost definitely" occur.

B. Examples of Manipulative Trade Schemes

1. Valuation Systems or Liquidity Calculations

These systems provide the interested party—usually the trader or the portfolio manager—a key position and participation in marking or evaluating the interested party's own book of trades; that is, in supervising themselves. This was especially a problem in the past, and especially regarding complex derivative securities.

The traders and portfolio managers were, and still are often, the only people with both the quantitative skills and market intelligence to put a value on their holdings or assess the liquidity of these holdings. A recent example is "Tier 3" assets at the investment banks that were "marked to model." Lawyers and regulators usually are forced to accept the word of the market experts as to the value of the assets because neither has the requisite modeling and finance skills to evaluate the assets. Often, however, the market experts, who perform the valuation, have conflicts of interest because their incentives are compensation based. Catching these "holes" requires a "fox hunting the fox," and the foxes rarely are working for Compliance.

2. Drawer Trades

That is hiding a trade in the drawer to wait for a sunny market day. A bad trade, such as a mistaken price or execution quantity (e.g., buying instead of selling, or getting "picked off" by a counter-party) can be hidden from the client until market results become favorable for the trader. Similar to the risk described above, this action uses a technological flaw in the operational processing of the trade that the trader can take advantage of in order to hide the trade. This flaw may also occur in the case of collusion between the trader and the operations staff that is processing the trade. This too is a potential disaster. It is a risk that can manifest itself in as many permutations as the trader's imagination and intelligence allows. It will probably always be a problem, especially at less sophisticated or poorly managed banks or asset managers. Arguably, such a risk may exist at smaller institutions that receive less regulatory scrutiny and have less litigious clients.

3. Information Leakage Regarding "Soft or Real" Insider Information

Insider information was classically a typical corporate-action type of information, such as mergers and acquisitions, earnings announcements, and Central Bank announcements. Increasingly, the real risk on which such information is focused (some say correctly), is what we would call "liquidity information," for example, information that a trader or a portfolio manager intends to buy or sell a market-moving volume of financial product at a specific date and time.

A party that receives this information can easily "front run" the information. "Front run" means that this party will execute the same order earlier than the larger transaction will be executed. When the leaking party then enters the market to transact, that party will have to "pay up" (buy high) or "hit down" (sell low) to have its order completed, because the normal supply and demand for that product has already been exhausted by the front-runner (tippee): the "front-runner" knows what securities the "leaked party" is holding. This situation may be common, and is, in practice, hard to identify and catch. In fact, this is, in part, the reason why banks and brokers monitor their traders' communications and personal brokerage accounts. However, there are always ways of communicating surreptitiously: hand signals, dead drops, burner phones, etc., etc. It is "basic espionage" and has been going on, in some form, for centuries.

How can employers provide incentives that counteract this practice? The employers may conduct Trade Cost Analysis and impose penalties on poor execution. In addition, Codes of Conduct may prohibit this activity and lay down a labor law basis for harsh deterrents (termination or docked pay) for any violations. The alternative is to compensate middle management for monitoring and correcting such violations.

4. Spoofing or Order Book Layering

This practice is mainly a sell-side problem that regulators pay intense attention to. Basically, spoofing covers any injection into the market of misleading information, for example, information regarding liquidity or pricing.

This is somewhat similar to spreading and trading on false rumors, for example, that a Central Bank is examining your bank: "I just got asked by the Bank of Japan for a bid on 10 billion dollar/yen." Currently, spoofing refers to actual orders that are publicly visible to the market, where the party that placed the order has no intention to execute the order, but wishes to push the market in a favorable direction.

A typical example could occur in the futures market, or in the equity markets. In both these markets the "order book" is visible, and one can put in "bids below" or "offers above" current prices. That means a "sell" or "buy" order near, but different from, the direction of current market trading. This notice gives other market participants an impression of selling or buying pressure that is not really there. The "spoofer" will then place his own order on the other side of the fictitious order, and hope that the misinformation will create a "squeeze in his direction" allowing him to get a better execution than he otherwise would.

The regulatory guidance in 2016 allows a real buyer or seller to misrepresent the order size but not to enter a completely false order. Thus, it is a prohibited felony in many markets to offer, or bid for, something you have no intention of buying or selling. However, it is permissible to show only 1 (one) share on the offer or bid, even if the true amount of your interest is much greater. In either case, the information flowing to the market is inaccurate and, consequently, efficient capital allocation decisions are impaired. "Currently intent" is proved by a forensic analysis of "fills" to order placement, that is, how much you actually execute as compared to how much you place in a visible order book.

An interesting question is whether a central bank could be guilty of "spoofing" or manipulation when the bank, for instance, intervenes in equity or bond markets, as Central Banks increasingly do.

5. Window Dressing

Window dressing means any tactic in which a trader or an investor dresses up reported holdings immediately before the reporting period. For instance, an advisor may, shortly before statements connect with the client, buy and sell securities in the client's portfolio demonstrating the winners.

This action may defraud unsophisticated investors. Sophisticated investors will care less about their holdings. Rather they focus on the change in their investment return. But with retail investors, rather than institutional investors, this form of window dressing may still raise an issue.

6. Portfolio Pumping, High-Ticking, and Painting the Screens

This is a variation of "window dressing," except that the trader or portfolio manager buys or sells a large, and market-moving, volume of securities, just before the "marking" or valuation of the "book" (held assets). The trader or portfolio manager will adopt this approach: (i) in a period of market illiquidity to maximize the movement caused by the action; or (ii) right before the official close of the market; or (iii) use a market order (pay any price until the order is filled) or purposefully pay the highest price available, rather than bid a fixed price. Consequently, the prices of the securities or products they own (or short) are temporarily moved in a favorable direction immediately before the valuation of the "book."

This activity typically takes place immediately before a broker's performance-based compensation award is to be made, and is not uncommon. The compliance risk increases with the opacity of the market: the more illiquid and opaque the market is, the easier it is to manipulate it, up or down, over the short term. High-yield bonds and emerging market equities are most susceptible to this kind of manipulation, but even large and very liquid markets like LIBOR or T-bills can be subject to this type of manipulation, if the traders have enough capital to play it. Despite its name, which implies that it is limited to portfolio managers, "pumping" may be used by both broker-dealers and investment managers.

7. Broker Favoritism

This issue is "tricky." The magnitude of the problem depends on whether or not the actors are fiduciaries and act as fiduciaries. In the broker-dealer context, the issue can be a matter of degree and amount to what brokers simply call "a relationship," i.e., dealing with friends. If the execution is not optimized and the client suffers, a trader has arguably breached a duty of loyalty to his or her employer. This breach remains an internal matter. However, if the actions constitute a breach of a fiduciary duty, resulting in poor execution for a client, then legally, the trader has violated his or her duty of loyalty to the client and should compensate the client for the difference between market price and traded price or even have to pay punitive damages. This is a gray area because "Best Execution" law is an unclear concept (and is seldom litigated).

The quality of execution is judged not merely by price but also by liquidity, market intelligence and information, speed of execution, and many other factors. Like "information leakage" or "front-running," it is also very hard to uncover because "catching the culprit" requires identification of the suspect broker relationships in advance. Nevertheless, patterns in broker-dealer practices as compared to execution quality over time can be used to "sniff out" such malfeasance after or during the fact.

8. Allocation Malfeasance

This violation is related to "cherry picking." It occurs when a trader or portfolio manager follows an allocation methodology that prefers some clients to others. The reason for this violation can be that one client pays a performance fee while another does not, or because one client is doing more trading business than another.

Consequently, most sophisticated broker-dealer entities have a hard-coded black-box allocation system that squeezes any manager discretion out of the process. However, some of these systems can be "gamed" and result in one portfolio manager or trader putting a fellow trader or portfolio manager at a disadvantage.

9. Internal Crossing

Here money managers cross trade in-house rather than trading with outsiders to avoid paying some costs and clearing fees associated with a market transaction. Normally, this is a good thing, because it saves costs to the clients. However, cross trades may not be done without prior conditions. First, the client must approve cross trading in-house in the client's investment management agreement. Second, the actual "crossing" must be done in a manner that does not disadvantage one client as against another.

Improper crossing could occur for the same reasons as any allocation malfeasance would, such as different compensation, or performance payments paid to the trader or portfolio manager. As with allocations, this is typically hard-coded into a black box system to avoid the use of any potentially improper discretion. To the extent that these systems can be overridden or manipulated, the problem will rise again.

10. Churning and Washing

This violation occurs when a trader or portfolio manager continuously buys and sells a financial product for a purpose other than gaining trading profits for their employer or client. Instead, the trades are made for the purpose of generating commission or bid-offer spreads for the broker's friends or associates, who are employed by other broker-dealers. A classic "wash trade" is a trade of the same security or product, at the same price, at nearly the same time, with no residual risk position left on the book.

In addition, a "wash trade" profile will be seen where a fiduciary is attempting to cover a mistake made in a client account. However, in that situation the goal is not to generate commission but to hide a trading error, which the fiduciary should disclose and compensate the client for.

In practice, wash trades are hard to identify, because identification requires Compliance Officers to independently reverse-engineer the trade and its rationale. This difficulty becomes more serious with the greater discretion that the client or employer has vested in the trader or portfolio manager. For instance, if the client has given the trader full (100%) discretion, the trader can claim that he or she is engaging not in wash-trading but in high frequency speculation.

When the client mandate is restricted to a pre-determined passive strategy—for instance matching the S&P 500 basket—it is easier to identify the wrong, however that may be difficult if the client's account is commingled with those of other clients. In that case there are many intra-day cash flows in and out, because of clients' redemptions, investments, and dividend reinvestment or currency hedging. In quantitative terms, the likelihood of a wash trade rises as a function of: (i) temporal proximity of offsetting trades; (ii) similarity in notional capital involved in each side of the offsetting transaction; and (iii) similarity in prices in each offsetting transaction.

11. Model-Gaming

Here the trader or portfolio manager takes advantage of a mark-to-model valuation system. This violation occurs almost exclusively with complex illiquid securities, with loans, or with over-the-counter derivatives. In this case, the trader identifies and exploits a gap in the client or employer's valuation and risk management system.

For instance, for financial call and put options, less sophisticated systems often assume that security prices are normally distributed. In practice, however, they are not. As a result, the institution's system will systemically under- and over-value certain trades and the trader or portfolio manager will stock up on these mispriced securities.

12. The Price of Trading in Junk Bonds

When friends become competitors, the "market solution" should be considered. Drexel Burnham Lambert (Drexel) was one of the great commodity traders. In the mid-1980s it became the preeminent pioneer of "junk" bond issuance and trading. The term "junk" referred to the bonds' lower credit rating. Companies that issued such bonds had formerly been either locked out of the debt financing markets altogether, or forced to turn to more costly commercial bank loans. Developing a market in junk bonds (also known as "high yield" bonds) effectively dis-intermediated the commercial banks involved in the corporate lending. This also lowered the debt financing costs for the corporate borrowers.

Usually, trading partners give credit to each other. However, Drexel experienced trouble when savings and loan institutions that had invested in these junk bonds sustained severe losses. As the scandal broke, the trading community quickly cut Drexel's lines of credit. Other competing institutional traders exacerbated Drexel's situation by reversing, and thus closing out, existing trades with Drexel. The closing of trades required Drexel to come up with new cash to settle these trades, when its ability to access cash through credit lines with other banks had been cut off. Drexel's forced selling of securities to meet its liquidity needs also depressed the prices of its junk bond inventories. This combination of factors resulted in Drexel severe losses. The company eventually filed for Chapter 11 bankruptcy protection.

Discussion topic

How different is the Drexel story from any of the examples outlined above?

Should the law have prohibited the Drexel "invention"?

What was the competitors' reaction to Drexel's trouble? To what extent is this reaction "fair competition"?

Can free market forces, such as those that undid Drexel, be viewed as a type of compliance regulator?

C. Other Examples

Other examples of manipulation have been described in court opinions and enforcement actions.

1. Marking the Close

A hedge fund traded natural gas futures contracts, i.e., agreements to buy or sell natural gas for delivery in the future. The buyer (who will accept delivery in the future) holds a long position; the seller (who promises delivery in the future) has a short position. A party may, in effect, cancel its obligation by acquiring the opposite position in another contract. Because the fund could not actually deliver or accept natural gas, it had to have a "flat position" at the close of trading, i.e., offset its position before the expiration date or continue its position for the next month. Contracts expire on a specified expiration day each month when settlement must be made on open contracts. The settlement price is based on an average of trades made during a period late in the settlement day (the "closing range"). The fund also traded natural gas swaps, i.e., instruments in which the payout to one party is based on the settlement price of natural gas futures.

The fund held large short positions on natural gas swaps and would profit from a high settlement price. The fund purchased a substantial number of natural gas futures contracts in the period leading up to the closing range and sold them in the closing range just before the close of trading. This is called "marking the close," i.e., trading near the close of trading to change the closing price, and was prohibited in the fund's compliance manual.[552]

---

552 CFTC v. Amaranth Advisors, L.L.C., 554 F. Supp. 2d 523 (S.D.N.Y. 2008).

2. Improper Short Sales

A short sale is "any sale of a security which the seller does not own [the security] or any sale [that] is consummated by the delivery of a security borrowed by, or for the account of, the seller."[553]

The SEC noted problems with "abusive 'naked' short selling," "generally . . . selling short without having stock available for delivery and intentionally failing to deliver stock within the standard three day settlement cycle."[554] The SEC settled a case in which the defendants allegedly "profited from engaging in massive 'naked' short selling that flooded the market with [the] stock, and depressed its price."[555] The SEC noted other problems with "naked" short selling.[556]

Generally, a broker-dealer implementing a short sale must first "locate" the security to be borrowed, i.e., borrow the security (or arrange to do so), or at least have reasonable grounds to believe the security can be borrowed for delivery, and document the location.[557]

There is an exception to the locating requirement for "[s]hort sales effected by a market maker in connection with bona-fide market making activities in the security for which this exception is claimed."[558]

A "market maker" is "any specialist permitted to act as a dealer, any dealer acting in the capacity of block positioner, and any dealer who, with respect to a security, holds himself out (by entering quotations in an inter-dealer communications system or otherwise) as being willing to buy and sell such security for his own account on a regular or continuous basis."[559] The SEC has also defined a "bona fide market maker" as "a broker-dealer that deals on a regular basis with other broker-dealers, actively buying and selling the subject security as well as regularly and continuously placing quotations in a quotation medium on both the bid and ask side of the market."[560]

The SEC issued guidance to define bona-fide market making. Factors that indicate bona-fide market making activities include: (1) "whether the market maker incurs any economic or market

---

553 17 C.F.R. § 242.200(a) (2016).

554 Amendments to Regulation SHO, 34-58775 (Oct. 14, 2008), 73 Fed. Reg. 61,690, 61,691 n.5 (Oct. 17, 2008).

555 *Id.* at 61,691 n.6 (citing enforcement actions).

556 *Id.* at 61,691 (noting that (1) failure to deliver may deprive shareholders of benefits of ownership; (2) failure to deliver in effect converts contract into "futures-type contract"; (3) "sellers . . . may enjoy fewer restrictions than if they were required to deliver the securities in a timely manner, and . . . may attempt to use this additional freedom to engage in trading activities that are designed to improperly depress the price of a security"; (4) seller avoids cost of borrowing).

557 17 C.F.R. § 242.203(b)(1) (2016).

558 17 C.F.R. § 242.203(b)(2)(iii) (2016).

559 15 U.S.C. § 78c(a)(38) (2012).

560 Self-Regulatory Organizations; National Association of Securities Dealers, Inc.; Order Approving Proposed Rule Change Relating to Close-Out Requirements for Short Sales and an Interpretation on Prompt Receipt and Delivery of Securities, 34-32632 (July 14, 1993), 58 Fed. Reg. 39,072, 39,074 (July 21, 1993).

risk with respect to the securities (e.g., by putting their own capital at risk to provide continuous two-sided quotes in markets)"; (2) "[a] pattern of trading that includes both purchases and sales in roughly comparable amounts to provide liquidity to customers or other broker-dealers"; and (3) "[c]ontinuous quotations that are at or near the market on both sides and that are communicated and represented in a way that makes them widely accessible to investors and other broker-dealers."561

In contrast, activities that do not qualify as bona fide market making include: (1) an "activity that is related to speculative selling strategies or investment purposes of the broker-dealer and is disproportionate to the usual market-making patterns or practices of the broker-dealer in that security"; (2) "post[ing] continually at or near the best offer, but ... not also post[ing] at or near the best bid"; and (3) "continually execut[ing] short sales away from [the market maker's] posted quotes."562

In an enforcement action, the SEC alleged that a broker-dealer applied the market maker exception to the "locate" requirement for short sales. The head of the broker-dealer's proprietary trading group allegedly did not adequately review the traders' activities nor make other efforts to determine whether the short sales were part of bona-fide market making activity.563

3. Improperly Calculating Advisory Fees and Overcharging Clients

Transamerica Financial Advisors (TFA), a registered broker-dealer and investment adviser, offered clients programs with advisory fees based on the amount of assets under management. These fees included an administrative fee component, also based on assets under management, and including reductions or "breakpoints" as the assets increased. TFA offered clients the opportunity to aggregate related accounts to qualify for the discounts and informed clients of the opportunity in account opening documents. To qualify, clients had to request aggregation and identify the accounts to be aggregated. However, the SEC staff found that TFA did not properly aggregate some of the accounts.

The SEC noted a number of compliance failures: (1) two teams were involved in establishing new accounts but the company's policies and procedures did not clearly designate one team for reviewing new account forms; (2) clients did not always receive the mailing insert on the aggregation policy because the company used a third-party mailing service; (3) account forms did not ensure that a client's reasons for not wanting aggregation be documented, in violation of policies and procedures; (4) representatives did not always reduce total advisory fees when clients chose aggregation because representatives sometimes set total fees to negate the breakpoint

---

561 *Id.* at 61,699.

562 *Id.*

563 *In re* Barkley, 34-79578, Admin. Proc. File No. 3-17731 (Dec. 16, 2016), *available at* https://www.sec.gov/litigation/admin/2016/34-79578.pdf (last visited Jan. 26, 2017).

discount, in violation of policies and procedures; and (5) two policy and procedure manuals (one for advisers, one for adviser representatives) conflicted on whether the representative is actually required to pass on the discount.[564]

4. Manipulation of Interest Rates

The London Interbank Offered Rate ("LIBOR") is a benchmark interest rate used for futures, options, swaps, and other derivatives. LIBOR is calculated for ten currencies and fifteen maturities. A panel of banks for each currency submits its rates on a daily basis and the daily setting is determined from the average of the middle quartiles. A bank's submission "must be the rate at which members of the bank's staff primarily responsible for management of a bank's cash, rather than a bank's derivative trading book, consider that the bank can borrow unsecured interbank funds in the London money market," and a bank "may not contribute a rate based on the pricing of any derivative financial instrument"; i.e., it should not be influenced by its own transactions tied to LIBOR.

Barclays, a bank that was one of the LIBOR submitter banks, employed derivatives traders who traded instruments tied to LIBOR. Some Barclays traders requested LIBOR settings that would benefit their trading positions to the Barclays LIBOR submitters, and some accommodated them. In addition, some Barclays traders communicated with traders at other LIBOR submitter banks. The manipulation of the rates benefited Barclays traders. Further, Barclays management sometimes directed that its submitters submit unrealistically low rates, to create the impression that its borrowing costs were lower than the real borrowing costs, and these submissions sometimes affected the computed rates.[565]

V. MONITORING THE LAW

Law has become increasingly complex and more often changing. Regulations are more detailed than ever. As the range of activities grows with the variety of financial obligations and organizations, it is harder to follow precisely what rules apply and the range of their application. Therefore, organizations use the Unified Compliance Framework (UCF) to simplify compliance. "UCF acts as the cornerstone of IT compliance, mapping hundreds of regulations [including the Sarbanes-Oxley Act] into a master hierarchal framework."

---

564 *In re* Transamerica Fin. Advisors, Inc., Admin. Proc. File No. 3-15822, 34-71850, IC-3808 (Apr. 3, 2014).

565 App. A, *available at* https://www.justice.gov/iso/opa/resources/9312012710173426365941.pdf (last visited Jan. 31, 2017), *incorporated in* U.S. Dep't of Justice, Barclays Bank PLC (June 26, 2012), *available at* https://www.justice.gov/iso/opa/resources/337201271017335469822.pdf (last visited Jan. 31, 2017),

"The UCF harmonizes IT controls from over 400 international regulatory requirements, standards, and guidelines from both technical and legal perspectives. Rather than testing and asserting compliance for each individual regulation, organizations use the UCF to save time and money by distilling compliance requirements to their essence and asserting compliance across multiple authority documents simultaneously."[566]

A convicted fraudster asserted that despite the antifraud provisions of the Sarbanes-Oxley Act of 2002 and the more recently enacted Dodd-Frank Wall Street Reform and Consumer Protection Act, it remains as easy today for both internal and external bad guys to loot corporate coffers as it was during the Enron and WorldCom days, and authorities note increasing fraud.[567]

There are abundant varieties of fraud. In addition to embezzlement and theft (including information theft) there is running a fraudulent business, i.e., purposely selling poor products, and running a business fraudulently, such as avoiding environmental or safety laws or using fraudulent accounting practices.[568]

How should companies respond? We will explore the issues time and again in the next chapters. But let us just mention a few suggestions right now: "Most fraud today is uncovered by whistle-blowers, or by accident—a tip, a rogue piece of mail, or by happenstance" even though companies, especially if publicly traded, are expected to internally impose adequate controls. But at many companies there is no self-enforcement or "oversight." "Many companies have no compliance or risk management at all," and those who do may not be effective. "It's not a job that wins friends and influences fellow workers. . . . ' 'The compliance officer is the most hated person in the company,' . . . 'Companies often retaliate against them' . . . 'Compliance staff [is] pushing paper [and] not effective.'"[569]

Here are some suggestions: "Start at the board and executive management; educate employees, change the culture." And as noted before, check the employees' backgrounds.[570]

Discussion Topic

What are the problems you might encounter in achieving each of the items in the list of suggestions outlined above?

---

566 *Unified Compliance Framework Licensed by Compliance Spectrum; Compliance Spectrum's Spectra Uses the UCF to Dramatically Reduce Costs and Risks Associated With Compliance Management,* Business Wire, Apr. 7, 2008, LEXIS, News Library, Arcnws File.

567 Laton McCartney, *Where There's Smoke, There's Fraud,* CFO Mag., Mar. 2011, LEXIS, News Library, Arcnws File, *available at* http://www.cfo.com/printable/article.cfm/14557373 (last visited Oct. 10, 2014).

568 *Id.*

569 *Id.*

570 *Id.*

Throughout the next chapters we will continue to examine the same issue: what does and does not work to affect compliance with the law. The answer may depend on the circumstances, the nature of the institution, its people, history, and power structure. Some of these issues will appear in many contexts, and one of the purposes of our study is to identify and single them out of the "mess." Because institutions do not act and react in an orderly manner, our study may go back and forth to uncover new insights and deepen our understanding of the materials we have already studied.

Problem

Suppose an adviser was found to have imposed an ineffective compliance program in its practice. The adviser has a subsidiary that is a registered broker. One of the employees of the subsidiary shared his brokerage fees with an outside broker. Neither the adviser nor its subsidiary firms have discovered this practice, but a customer, who realized how high the fees were, complained to the SEC. The SEC sent an examiner to review the firm's practices.

As a CCO, how would you conduct an internal examination in the future, to avoid this situation?

What would the CCO and the firm do in preparation of the examiner's "visit"?

Discussion Topics

*How different would monitoring be under the top-down system as compared to the bottom-up system that we reviewed?

*What problems would arise under each of these systems, and what solutions could be offered in each case?

VI. NOTES ON MONITORING THAT MAY LEAD TO INVESTIGATIONS

An observation about a suspicious event may require further investigation, that is, the process that narrows the inquiry and seeks information about the more specific event. This information is needed in order to determine whether, and to what extent, a violation has occurred or is about to occur very soon. There are activities, such as accounting, or dealing with cash, which call for an investigatory approach continuously because of their very nature.

Further, there are personal histories or events or activities in a particular corporation that may require more attention, in order to avoid undesirable repetition. Monitoring such events or activities may reach the level of an investigation. Thus, at the beginning of a monitoring design, one might focus on the facts that require additional attention and information, depending on the nature of the activities and the history of the institution and its personnel.

Some information may require investigation, and some investigation may require remedial actions. These actions include notifying the authorities and punishing wrongdoing or changing existing patterns of the business, among others.

_____

Reading focus

What are the reasons for each of these directives? Please distinguish a very large brokerage firm, such as Merrill Lynch, that has international, as well as American, securities trading facilities, from a small brokerage firm that employs ten brokers and specializes in one type of U.S. securities.

Please prepare the questions you would ask in order to determine the answers to the directives outlined below.

Please identify the persons whom you would approach, and the documents you would require.

_____

A. The Directive of the U.S. Sentencing Guidelines: Continuous Revisions and Evaluations

The Federal Sentencing Guidelines requirements for an effective compliance and ethics program include requirements for monitoring.

(5) The organization shall take reasonable steps— (A) to ensure that the organization's compliance and ethics program is followed, including monitoring and auditing to detect criminal conduct;

(B) to evaluate periodically the effectiveness of the organization's compliance and ethics program . . . .

(7) After criminal conduct has been detected, the organization shall take reasonable steps to respond appropriately to the criminal conduct and to prevent further similar criminal conduct, including making any necessary modifications to the organization's compliance and ethics program.[571]

_____

[571] U.S. SENTENCING GUIDELINES MANUAL § 8B2.1(b)(5), (7) (eff. Nov. 1, 2015), *available at* http://www.ussc.gov/sites/default/files/pdf/guidelines-manual/2015/GLMFull.pdf (last visited Mar. 14, 2016).

In addition, the Technical Committee of the International Organization of Securities Commissions set out principles for compliance, including monitoring.[572] These principles apply to market intermediaries. However by analogy, and careful examination and appropriate adjustments, these elements might be followed by organizations that engage in other activities.

A select number of directives are the following:

(1) "Each market intermediary should periodically assess the effectiveness of its compliance function." (2) "[T]he compliance function should be subject to periodic external review," e.g., by external auditors, self-regulatory organizations, or regulators. (3) "As part of an assessment, a market intermediary should determine whether it has assigned responsibility for all necessary compliance functions, and in addition, that the compliance function overall is coordinated and operates effectively . . . ."[573]

B. Means for Implementation.

(1) "The policies and procedures and controls put in place to identify, assess, monitor, and report on compliance with regulatory requirements should be evaluated." (2) "The effectiveness of the compliance function should be reported to the governing authority and/or senior management, by either the designated senior officer responsible for compliance or by individuals, independent from the compliance function." (3) Any deficiencies should be addressed. (4) The scope of the review may be extended based on findings during the review.[574]

After a triggering event and a determination that an investigation is necessary, a preliminary action may be necessary. For example, if the situation poses risk to the company or the company has to pursue an investigation in order to uncover additional facts. Further, the company may take preventive measures by suspending the possible offender or transferring that person to another location.[575]

For example, in November 2014 FINRA "fined Citigroup Global Markets Inc. $15 million for failing to adequately supervise communications between its equity research analysts and its clients as well as Citigroup sales and trading staff, and for permitting one of its analysts to participate indirectly in two road shows promoting IPOs to investors."[576]

---

[572] TECHNICAL COMM. OF INT'L ORG. OF SEC. COMM'NS, COMPLIANCE FUNCTION AT MARKET INTERMEDIARIES — FINAL REPORT 15-16 (2006), *available at* https://www.iosco.org/library/pubdocs/pdf/IOSCOPD214.pdf (last visited Mar. 14, 2016).

[573] *Id.*

[574] *Id.*

[575] DEWEY POTEET , HOW TO CONDUCT AN EFFECTIVE WORKPLACE INVESTIGATION 16 (Akin, Gump, Strauss, Hauer & Feld, L.L.P., April 2001), *available at* http://www.readbag.com/akingump-docs-publication-293 (last visited Mar. 14, 2016).

[576] *Id.*

"FINRA found that from January 2005 to February 2014, Citigroup failed to meet its supervisory obligations regarding the potential selective dissemination of non-public research to clients and sales and trading staff. During this period, Citigroup issued approximately 100 internal warnings concerning communications by equity research analysts. However, when Citigroup detected violations involving selective dissemination and client communications, there were lengthy delays before the firm disciplined the research analysts and the disciplinary measures lacked the severity necessary to deter repeat violations of Citigroup policies."[577]

(i) Failure to supervise involves equity research analysts that hosted "idea dinners." "One example of Citigroup's failure to supervise certain communications by its equity research analysts involved "idea dinners" hosted by Citigroup equity research analysts that were also attended by some of Citigroup's institutional clients and sales and trading personnel. At these dinners, Citigroup research analysts discussed stock picks, which, in some instances, were inconsistent with the analysts' published research. Despite the risk of improper communications at these events, Citigroup did not adequately monitor analyst communications or provide analysts with adequate guidance concerning the boundaries of permissible communications."[578]

"Brad Bennett, FINRA Executive Vice President and Chief of Enforcement, said 'The frequent interactions between Citigroup analysts and clients at events like 'idea dinners' created a heightened risk that views inconsistent with research would selectively be disclosed to clients. Citigroup failed to effectively police these risks.'"[579]

(ii) In addition, one analyst, an employee of a Citigroup affiliate, in "Taiwan selectively disseminated research information concerning Apple Inc. to certain clients, which was then selectively disseminated to additional clients by a Citigroup equity sales employee."[580]

(iii) Further, "in 2011 a Citigroup senior equity research analyst assisted two companies in preparing presentations for investment banking road shows. Between 2011 and 2013, Citigroup did not expressly prohibit equity research analysts from assisting issuers in the preparation of road show presentation materials."[581]

"Citigroup also failed to have procedures in place expressly prohibiting equity research analysts from assisting issuers in the preparation of road show presentations, and allowed one of its

---

577 *Id.*

578 *Id.*

579 FINRA, *FINRA Fines Citigroup Global Markets Inc. $15 Million for Supervisory Failures Related to Equity Research and Involvement in IPO Roadshows* (Nov. 24, 2014), *available at* https://www.finra.org/newsroom/2014/finra-fines-citigroup-15-million-failures-related-equity-research (last visited Mar. 10, 2016). "In settling this matter, Citigroup neither admitted nor denied the charges, but consented to the entry of FINRA's findings."

580 *Id.*

581 *Id.*

analysts to participate indirectly in two road shows promoting IPOs to investors. FINRA found that from January 2005 to February 2014, Citigroup failed to meet its supervisory obligations regarding the potential selective dissemination of nonpublic research to clients and sales and trading staff."[582]

Discussion topic

How could Citicorp enforce its admonitions to the analysts?

Legal Audits

Legal audits may be part of a compliance program. In a legal audit, a compliance entity (either internal or external) obtains information and advises managers regarding the potential liability for possible acts. John Calvin Conway suggests that legal audits can lead to fewer violations, and thus less liability, but can also detect otherwise undetected violations, leading to greater liability. Therefore, Conway suggests that legal audits may be more effective if they are granted a privilege similar to the attorney-client privilege in litigation.[583]

Discussion Topics

*What would you advise the head of the department to do under the following scenarios?

*One of the employees asks to see you and tells you that the head of the department has suddenly begun to act in a "funny" manner. He comes to the office very late, he sways a bit, like a drunken person; he cusses a lot. "He was never like that" says the employee. "I worry about him."

*What if the employee adds that the head of the department is also taking a number of the people in the department to the new resort? Suppose the department accountant, at lunch, expresses concern about some mistakes in the numbers that he has received?

*In light of the facts described above, how should the compliance officer act? How should the head of the department act? Should the information be brought to the attention of the higher

---

582 *Id.*

583 John Calvin Conway, Note, *Self-Evaluative Privilege and Corporate Compliance Audits,* 68 S. Cal. L. Rev. 621, 622-23 (1995) (footnotes omitted).

echelon in the organization? Who is the higher echelon? How should the information be presented?

* Why not make a cost/benefit analysis of the violation and decide if it is worth doing?

C. Did Internal Audit Failures Contribute to the Financial and Economic Crisis?

This question should cause every practitioner to step back and think about his or her own practice. In many cases internal audits could have detected the board and management governance and risk management processes. Arguably, these situations were few. Yet, numerous internal audit functions had failures that in turn may have allowed process failures to go undetected.[584]

Discussion topics

Please evaluate the following: How should the performance of the internal audit function be evaluated?

Assess: (i) risk management and reporting to the board and management; (ii) governance processes (including board oversight); (iii) the risks relating to the control environment (e.g., risks related to compensation), ... including risks related to executive compensation and bonuses; (iv) reporting to management and the board on the adequacy of internal controls; (v) addressing major risks, including not delegating addressing of the risks to others without sufficient oversight or review; (vi) addressing risks related to the extended enterprise, including outsourced services; (vii) updating of the risk assessment and audit plan at least quarterly; (viii) evaluating internal auditing based on coverage of risks rather than completion of the audit plan, including updating the audit plan as necessary; (ix) prioritizing of assurance over relevant processes over cost savings; (x) providing information to the audit committee on any assurance gaps due to inadequate internal audit resources.[585]

---

584 Norman Marks, *Did Internal Audit Failures Contribute to the Financial and Economic Crisis?*, INTERNAL AUDITOR, May 27, 2009, *available at* https://iaonline.theiia.org/blogs/marks/archive/Pages/Did-Internal-Audit-Failures-Contribute-to-the-Financial-and-Economic-Crisis.aspx (last visited Apr. 7, 2016).

585 *Id.*

Investigations to Prevent Violations of the Law

In other [than the American colonies], countries, the people... judge of an ill principle in govern-
ment only by an actual grievance; here they anticipate the evil, and judge of the pressure of the
grievance by the badness of the principle. They augur misgovernment at a distance and snuff the
approach of tyranny in every tainted breeze.

INTRODUCTION

In Chapter 11 we examine preventive supervision through investigations. As with the case of monitoring, we learn much from the directives to government examiners and investigators. These directives are important for similar reasons. Government examination and investigation offer experience we can all learn from.

Section I of this chapter explores the meaning and requirements of investigations. Here we analyze the concept of investigation. We draw on the directives of the Securities and Exchange Commission (SEC) and legal requirements of President Obama's Executive Order No. 13694 (E.O. 13694).

Section II offers examples of the activities that trigger investigation, referring to the legal requirements of E.O. 13694.

Section III deals with the art and science of investigations. Investigations are required in areas that present risk by their inherent nature. These are the obvious risks that raise red flags by their very nature, and should be routinely examined. Investigations are also required after disturbing or suspicious facts that red flags have been uncovered. A compliance officer or an independent lawyer might be engaged to establish all the relevant true facts. The choice of an outside investigator is sometimes desirable to protect the confidentiality of the information held by the inside lawyer.[586]

Section IV describes how to conduct an investigation within a large corporation. What steps should be taken to uncover the truth, and yet protect the rights of those who are investigated?

Section V notes how regulators raise concern about risk culture.

---

586 *See* Chapter 18 discussing the lawyer's confidentiality.

1. In Chapter 10, we studied monitoring. Monitoring does not necessarily produce new results, show risky patterns of behavior, or highlight suspicious new facts. However, when such patterns and facts appear in the monitoring process, they might call for an investigation. The investigation narrows the inquiry and seeks addition information about more specific events. This information is needed to determine whether and to what extent a violation has occurred or is about to occur. Investigation may lead to required remedial actions, such as notifying the authorities, punishing wrongdoing, or changing existing patterns in the business.

There are a number of reasons for conducting close examinations routinely. Therefore, at the beginning of a monitoring design one might focus on the situations that require continuous additional attention and information, depending on the nature of the activities and the history of the institution and its personnel. These situations would be treated at the outset and continuously as investigations. In addition, investigations are triggered by signals that point to the need for more information before taking action.

Here are a number of examples:

(i) There are activities, such as accounting, or dealing with cash, that call for an continuous investigatory approach. That is because these activities by their very nature pose a high risk of violations.

(ii) Regulators may require investigations of third parties. For example, FINRA requires that member firms supervise third-party service providers.[587] The SEC holds firms to be responsible for compliance by third-party vendors.[588] Note that notwithstanding these requirements, problems concerning outside third parties may continue and persist. According to an April 2015 report by the New York State Department of Financial Services, "[t]hirty percent of the banking organizations surveyed do not appear to require their third-party vendors to notify them in the event of an information security breach or other cyber security breach."[589] Thus, supervision of vendors may reach an ongoing format of investigation.

(iii) There was a time when a brokerage firm conducted its business in one state, subject to one set of laws, enforced by one regulator. The same inquiries were therefore limited to a less

---

587 Fin. Indus. Regulatory Auth., FINRA, Notice to Members 05-48 (July 2005), *available at* http://www.finra.org/file/notice-members-05-48 (last visited Mar. 17, 2016).

588 *See* Lori A. Richards, *Speech by SEC Staff: The Next Phase: Implementing the Patriot Act*, Director, Ofc. of Compliance Inspections & Examinations, U.S. Sec. & Exch. Comm'n (Mar. 27, 2003), *available at* https://www.sec.gov/news/speech/spch032703lar.htm#P142_24335 (last visited Mar. 17, 2016).

589 N.Y. State Dep't of Fin. Servs., Update on Cyber Security in the Banking Sector: Third Party Service Providers 5 (Apr. 2015), *available at* http://www.dfs.ny.gov/reportpub/dfs_rpt_tpvendor_042015.pdf (last visited Oct. 21, 2016).

complex environment. This is no longer the case: presently, we have far more than one inquiry with respect to one item. For example, with respect to an activity we must focus on (a) the activity; (b) where and when the activity occurred; (c) who was impacted by the activity; and (d) who regulated the activity and where. Needless to say, we should make these inquiries after the suspicious story is told and before the story ends in violation.

(iv) A closer investigation is required if a unique arrangement is made for one employee, which enables the employee to avoid closer supervision, for example, when the employee is allowed to live and work in two places and thereby avoids supervision by either.

(v) There are employees' situations that should raise attention. For example, if an employee, who was known to live at a certain level of spending, begins to spend larger amounts, without any explanation as to the source of the funds. Similarly, sometimes the people involved have not done anything wrong, but their very involvement in the enterprise raises red flags. Thus, the rise of unusual situations can raise red flags in light of past experience and trigger investigations.

(vi) An example of a significant attention-raising change is the quick and enormous 2014 rise of stock prices of small companies. For example, PwC, an accounting firm, changed its report regarding a foreign bank dealing with Iran and other countries that were subject to economic sanctions by the U.S. In its final report the auditor "softened" the statements it made in its preliminary report.[590] The firm was fined $25 million and banned for two years from some consulting work, to settle the regulators' allegations that it mishandled its work for a foreign bank. This change was not detected nor investigated until it was too late. In this case the investigation was triggered by a specific legal provision or issue.

On August 26, 2016, the *Financial Times* noted that PwC, "[t]he world's biggest professional services firm by annual revenues," settled a case for giving a bank a "clean audit opinion for six years until it collapsed in 2009, when it emerged that huge chunks of its loans" [presumably $5.5 billion] to a bank "were secured against assets that did not exist."[591] Being the world's largest professional auditor it is not surprising that the problems and settlements in which this auditor [was] involved [were] very large as well. Thus, auditors play a significant role in compliance, especially when they do not uncover significant problems. A similar failure let to the ultimate collapse of Arthur Anderson, one of the big five accounting firms of its time. In February 2001, "Arthur Anderson, Enron's auditor, discusse[d] whether to retain Enron as

---

590 Michael Rapoport, *State to Fine PwC in Japan Bank Case*, WALL ST. J., Aug. 18, 2014, at C6.

591 Ben McLannahan, *PwC Settles $5.5bn Fraud Detection Lawsuit*, FIN. TIMES, Aug. 26, 2016, *available at* https://www.ft.com/content/befa9e50-6ba4-11e6-a0b1-d87a9fea034f (last visited Oct. 21, 2016) (the amount of the settlement was not disclosed).

a client amid concern over Enron's use of special partnerships to disguise debt," but decided to do so. By December 2, 2001, "Enron file[d] for bankruptcy, the biggest in US history," as a result of its risky activities and accounting manipulation practices. By March 2002 "Arthur Anderson [was] indicted for obstruction of justice" in connection with evading its auditing duties and allegedly destroying evidence relating to Enron's accounting practices. By August 2002, "Arthur Anderson surrender[ed its] license to practice in the U.S." and "85,000 people los[t] their jobs."[592]

> (vii) In a particular corporation, there may be problematic personal histories, events, or activities that may require more attention, in order to avoid repetition. The monitoring of such situations may reach the level of an investigation if signals of problematic past events reappear in the horizon.

> (viii) Generally, an investigation may be triggered by any activity that raises the need for additional facts.

2. Regulators may outline which items investigations may or should include.[593]

3. New legal rules and sanctions may trigger investigations as well. For example, in April 2015 President Obama issued Executive Order No. 13694 (E.O. 13694), which imposes sanctions against persons involved in certain malicious cyber-enabled activities from outside the United States.[594] The Order directs the Secretary of the Treasury, in consultation with the Attorney General and the Secretary of State, to impose sanctions on those persons determined responsible. The Treasury's Office of Foreign Assets Control (OFAC), in coordination with other agencies, will identify and designate persons for sanctions.[595] Persons so designated will be listed on OFAC's list of Specially Designated Nationals and Blocked Persons (SDN List).[596]

Consequently, the Order requires that "U.S. persons (and persons otherwise subject to OFAC jurisdiction) must ensure that they are not engaging in trade or other transactions with persons

---

592 *Timeline: Enron.* GUARDIAN.COM, Jan. 30, 2006, at C1, LEXIS, News Library, Guardian Unlimited File.

593 Jennifer Cummings, *Checking Your Vendors' Cyber-Security Practices*, REUTERS, June 5, 2015, *available at* http://www.reuters.com/article/us-advisers-cybersecurity-comply-idUSKBN0OL1JS20150605 (last visited Apr. 27, 2017).@@@

594 Executive Order 13694, Blocking the Property of Certain Persons Engaging in Significant Malicious Cyber-Enabled Activities (Apr. 1, 2015), *available at* https://www.whitehouse.gov/the-press-office/2015/04/01/executive-order-blocking-property-certain-persons-engaging-significant-m (last visited Mar. 16, 2016).

595 U.S. DEP'T OF TREAS., *OFAC FAQs: Other Sanctions Programs*, question 444 (last updated May 22, 2015), *available at* https://www.treasury.gov/resource-center/faqs/Sanctions/Pages/faq_other.aspx#cyber (last visited Mar. 16, 2016).

596 U.S. DEP'T OF TREAS., *OFAC FAQs: Other Sanctions Programs*, question 444 (last updated May 22, 2015), *available at* https://www.treasury.gov/resource-center/faqs/Sanctions/Pages/faq_other.aspx#cyber (last visited Mar. 16, 2016); U.S. DEP'T OF TREAS., *Specially Designated Nationals List* (SDN) (Mar. 10, 2016), *available at* https://www.treasury.gov/resource-center/sanctions/SDN-List/Pages/default.aspx (last visited Mar. 16, 2016).

named on OFAC's SDN List pursuant to E.O. 13694 or any entity owned by such persons."[597] U.S. persons under E.O. 13694 include "any United States citizen, permanent resident alien, entity organized under the laws of the United States or any jurisdiction within the United States (including foreign branches), or any person in the United States."[598]

Thus, an investigation can be triggered by a clear sign of potential danger. Outside companies that help manage the advisers' businesses, such as payroll companies and computer repair firms, are a weak link in many financial advisers' cyber-security plans. Because advisers wish to focus on delivering great service to customers, they often trust their vendors to protect their clients' interests, and this trust may be mistaken and costly. For example, the risk is high if the service giver should, but does not, inform customers about a breach of security. Yet, protections against security violations may be weak because they are costly, involving payments to credit monitoring services, lawyers, and technology experts.

Finally, investigation may have extraneous consequences. Sometimes an investigation requires a preliminary action, for example, suspending a probable offender[599]

II. AN EXAMPLE OF ACTIVITIES LEGALLY TARGETED FOR INVESTIGATION

One example of activities targeted for investigation is outlined by E.O. 13694, and includes the following:

(1) "harming, or otherwise significantly compromising the provision of services by, a computer or network of computers that support one or more entities in a critical infrastructure sector";[600]

---

597 U.S. DEP'T OF TREAS., *OFAC FAQs: Other Sanctions Programs,* question 446 (last updated May 22, 2015), *available at* https://www.treasury.gov/resource-center/faqs/Sanctions/Pages/faq_other.aspx#cyber (last visited Mar. 16, 2016).

598 Executive Order 13694, Blocking the Property of Certain Persons Engaging in Significant Malicious Cyber-Enabled Activities (Apr. 1, 2015), *available at* https://www.whitehouse.gov/the-press-office/2015/04/01/executive-order-blocking-property-certain-persons-engaging-significant-m (last visited Mar. 16, 2016).

599 DEWEY POTEET , HOW TO CONDUCT AN EFFECTIVE WORKPLACE INVESTIGATION 16 (Akin, Gump, Strauss, Hauer & Feld, L.L.P., April 2001), *available at* http://www.readbag.com/akingump-docs-publication-293 (last visited Mar. 14, 2016)..

600 Executive Order 13694, Blocking the Property of Certain Persons Engaging in Significant Malicious Cyber-Enabled Activities (Apr. 1, 2015), *available at* https://www.whitehouse.gov/the-press-office/2015/04/01/executive-order-blocking-property-certain-persons-engaging-significant-m (last visited Mar. 16, 2016) (defining "critical infrastructure sector" as "any of the designated critical infrastructure sectors identified in Presidential Policy Directive 21[.]");. Presidential Policy Directive 21, Critical Infrastructure Security and Resilience (Feb. 12, 2013), *available at* https://www.whitehouse.gov/the-press-office/2013/02/12/presidential-policy-directive-critical-infrastructure-security-and-resil (last visited Mar. 16, 2016) (designating the following as critical infrastructure sectors: chemical, commercial facilities, communications, critical manufacturing, dams, defense industrial base, emergency services, energy, financial services, food and agriculture, government facilities, healthcare and public health, information technology, nuclear reactors, materials, and waste, transportation systems, waste and wastewater systems).

(2) "significantly compromising the provision of services by one or more entities in a critical infrastructure sector";

(3) "causing a significant disruption to the availability of a computer or network of computers";

(4) "causing a significant misappropriation of funds or economic resources, trade secrets, personal identifiers, or financial information for commercial or competitive advantage or private financial gain";

(5) "to be responsible for or complicit in, or to have engaged in, the receipt or use for commercial or competitive advantage or private financial gain, or by a commercial entity, outside the United States of trade secrets misappropriated through cyber-enabled means, knowing they have been misappropriated, where the misappropriation of such trade secrets is reasonably likely to result in, or has materially contributed to, a significant threat to the national security, foreign policy, or economic health or financial stability of the United States"; or

(6) "to have attempted to engage in any of the activities described [above]."[601]

It was noted, however, that E.O. 13694 will not apply to legitimate cyber-related activities. The Order is "directed against significant malicious cyber-enabled activities that have the purpose or effect of causing specific enumerated harms." The order is not directed at legitimate activities, such as "academic, business, or non-profit activities," "activities to ensure and promote the security of information systems, such as penetration testing and other methodologies," "activities undertaken to further academic research or commercial innovation as part of computer security-oriented conventions, competitions, or similar 'good faith' events," "network defense or maintenance activities performed by computer security experts and companies as part of the normal course of business." The program is also not aimed at individuals whose devices are used in activities without their knowledge or consent.[602]

(7) E.O. 13694 imposes specific compliance obligations on U.S. persons. U.S. persons must ensure that they are not engaging in transactions with persons named on the SDN List pursuant to E.O. 13694 or any entity owned by such persons.

---

601 Executive Order 13694, Blocking the Property of Certain Persons Engaging in Significant Malicious Cyber-Enabled Activities (Apr. 1, 2015), *available at* https://www.whitehouse.gov/the-press-office/2015/04/01/executive-order-blocking-property-certain-persons-engaging-significant-m (last visited Mar. 16, 2016).

602 U.S. Dep't of Treas., *OFAC FAQs: Other Sanctions Programs,* questions 448-50 (last updated May 22, 2015), *available at* https://www.treasury.gov/resource-center/faqs/Sanctions/Pages/faq_other.aspx#cyber (last visited Mar. 16, 2016).

"As a general matter, U.S. persons, including firms that facilitate or engage in online commerce, are responsible for ensuring that they do not engage in unauthorized transactions or dealings with persons named on any of OFAC's sanctions lists or operate in jurisdictions targeted by comprehensive sanctions programs. Such persons, including technology companies, should develop a tailored, risk-based compliance program, which may include sanctions list screening or other appropriate measures. An adequate compliance solution will depend on a variety of factors, including the type of business involved, and there is no single compliance program or solution suitable for every circumstance."

The names of individuals and entities on the SDN list are publicly available through OFAC's free online search engine. OFAC also offers data file versions of its lists for automated screening. Companies may wish to consider a screening software package.[603]

III. HIDDEN ACTIVITIES

As noted, the need for an investigation is triggered by evidence of highly probable risks. There are activities that send signals of risk by their very existence, such as payroll payments. For example, in 2002 it was reported that "check fraud ranks second, behind embezzlement, on the list of crimes that hurt the nation's top 1,000 companies the most."[604]

Discussion topics:

*How can people use electronic devices to hide and obscure their activities?[605]

*How can earnings be manipulated? [606]

*Are check frauds easy or hard to uncover; if so, why?[607]

---

603 U.S. Dep't of Treas., *OFAC FAQs: Other Sanctions Programs,* question 446 (last updated May 22, 2015), *available at* https://www.treasury.gov/resource-center/faqs/Sanctions/Pages/faq_other.aspx#cyber (last visited Mar. 16, 2016).

604 *American Payroll Association Offers Tips on Minimizing Payroll Check Fraud,* Bus. Wire, Jan. 7, 2003, LEXIS, News Library, Arcnws File, *available at* https://www.thefreelibrary.com/FEATURE%2fAmerican+Payroll+Association+Offers+Tips+on+Minimizing...-a096198040 (last visited Oct. 21, 2016).

605 Dawn Lomer, *How to Find Digital Evidence in an Investigation,* i-Sight, *available at* http://i-sight.com/resources/how-to-find-digital-evidence-in-an-investigation/ (last visited Mar. 16, 2016).

606 Matthew Argersinger, *4 Signs a Company is Fudging Its Quarterly Earnings Results,* Aol.Fin., July 19, 2011, *available at* http://www.aol.com/article/2011/07/19/4-signs-a-company-is-fudging-its-quarterly-earnings-results/19993765/?gen=1 (last visited Oct. 21, 2016),@@@ *discussing* Howard Schilit, Financial Shenanigans: How to Detect Accounting Gimmicks & Fraud in Financial Reports (2010); Goldstein v. MCI WorldCom, 340 F.3d 238 (5th Cir. 2003).

607 *American Payroll Association Offers Tips on Minimizing Payroll Check Fraud,* Bus. Wire, Jan. 7, 2003, LEXIS, News Library, Arcnws File, *available at* https://www.thefreelibrary.com/FEATURE%2fAmerican+Payroll+Association+Offers+Tips+on+Minimizing...-a096198040 (last visited Oct. 21, 2016).

Court decisions may point to the need for reinvestigating issues that produced no results in the past. In *In re Zappos.com, Inc. Customer Data Security Breach Litigation*[608] the issue was the extent to which the corporation was liable for the cyber theft of 24 million customers' data, including customers' names, account numbers, passwords, email addresses, billing and shipping addresses, phone numbers, and the last four digits of their credit cards. The plaintiffs alleged damages, including decreased value of their personal information and higher risk of financial fraud and identity theft, increased threat of future harm, and costs to mitigate damages (i.e., purchase of credit monitoring services).

The court granted Zappos's motion to dismiss, finding lack of standing. First, the Court rejected the "decreased value" argument, stating that plaintiffs did not allege facts explaining how their personal information became less valuable (as a result of the theft), or that they were unable to sell the information because the breach lowered the price of their personal information. Second, the court rejected the "increased threat of future harm to the plaintiffs" argument. To confer standing, such a threat must be "certainly impending" or "immediate." The future possibility of such harm is insufficient. The Court noted further that no plaintiff has alleged misuse of data even though the breach occurred over three years ago. Third, the Court rejected the "costs to mitigate" argument, stating that plaintiffs cannot "manufacture standing" by mitigating damages where the injury is otherwise speculative.[609]

The Court granted the plaintiffs leave to amend their complaints, in the event of an occurrence of actual misuse of the stolen data. The Court agreed that class members, who have suffered damages as a result of the breach, would have standing to sue. However, the named plaintiffs would not be their proper representatives because the named plaintiffs did not allege that they suffered such damages.[610]

Discussion topics

What is the effect of a court's holding regarding representation of a putative class?

In light of the decision noted above, what should the corporation do? What should the monitor do? What should the board of directors do?

---

608 *In re* Zappos.com, Inc., 108 F. Supp. 3d 949 (D. Nev. 2015).

609 *Id.*, citing Clapper v. Amnesty Int'l USA, 133 S. Ct. 1138, 1151 (2013).

610 *Id.; see also* S. Kasim Razvi, Comment, *To What Extent Should State Legislatures Regulate Business Practices as a Means of Preventing Identity Theft?*, 15 Alb. L.J. Sci. & Tech. 639 (2005).

Thomas E. Haider

The Financial Crimes Enforcement Network (FinCEN) [on December 18, 2014] issued a $1 million civil money penalty (CMP) against Mr. Thomas E. Haider for failing to ensure that his company abided by the anti-money laundering (AML) provisions of the Bank Secrecy Act (BSA) and implementing regulations. This CMP is the product of a joint investigation by FinCEN and the SDNY.

From 2003 to 2008, Mr. Haider was the Chief Compliance Officer for MoneyGram International Inc. Mr. Haider oversaw MoneyGram's Fraud Department, which collected thousands of complaints from consumers who were victims of fraudulent schemes. Mr. Haider also headed MoneyGram's AML Compliance Department, which was charged with ensuring compliance with requirements under the BSA designed to protect the financial system against money laundering and terrorist finance.

. . . .

Mr. Haider was responsible for monitoring MoneyGram's worldwide network of agents, and through the information he received from complaints to the Fraud Division, he could have suspended or terminated any agents that were participating in illicit activity. His inaction led to thousands of innocent individuals being duped out of millions of dollars through fraud schemes that funneled, and sometimes laundered, their illicit profits through MoneyGram's money transmission network.

The schemes relied on a variety of tales and false promises aimed at misleading and per-suading unsuspecting victims to send money through the participating MoneyGram agents and outlets. The often elderly victims were solicited through the mail, e-mail, and telephone, and told, among other things, that they had won a lottery, had been hired for a "secret shop-pers" program, had been approved for a guaranteed loan, or had been selected to receive an expensive item or cash prize. The victims were told that to receive the item or winnings, they had to pay the perpetrators money in advance. For example, in situations where the victims were promised lottery winnings or cash prizes, they were told that they had to pay taxes, customs' duties, or processing fees up front and were directed to send the advance payments to fictitious payees using MoneyGram's money transfer system.

Mr. Haider also failed in his responsibility to ensure the filing of suspicious activity reports (SARs) on agents whom he knew or had reason to suspect were engaged in fraud, money laundering, or other criminal activity. By failing to file SARs, despite having extensive informa-tion regarding complicit MoneyGram outlets and the evident victimization of MoneyGram's customers, he denied critical information to law enforcement which could have been used to combat the fraud and dismantle the criminal networks.[611]

---

611 Excerpted from FinCEN, *FinCEN Assesses $1 Million Penalty and Seeks to Bar Former MoneyGram Executive from Financial Industry* (Dec. 18, 2014), *available at* https://www.fincen.gov/news/news-releases/fincen-assesses-1-million-penalty-

Haider (1) willfully violated the requirement to implement and maintain an effective anti-money laundering program and (2) willfully violated the requirement to report suspicious activity. . . .

Haider's failures included the following:

Failure to Implement a Discipline Policy. Haider failed to ensure that MoneyGram implemented a policy for disciplining agents and outlets that MoneyGram personnel knew or suspected were involved in fraud and/or money laundering.

Failure to Terminate Known High-Risk Agents/Outlets. Haider failed to ensure that MoneyGram terminated agents and outlets that MoneyGram personnel understood were involved in fraud and/or money laundering, including outlets that Haider himself was on notice posed an unreasonable risk of fraud and/or money laundering.

Failure to File Timely SARs. Haider failed to ensure that MoneyGram fulfilled its obligation to file timely SARs, including because Haider maintained MoneyGram's AML program so that the individuals responsible for filing SARs were not provided with information possessed by MoneyGram's Fraud Department that should have resulted in the filing of SARs on specific agents or outlets.

Failure to Conduct Effective Audits of Agents/Outlets. Haider failed to ensure that MoneyGram conducted effective audits of agents and outlets, including outlets that MoneyGram personnel knew or suspected were involved in fraud and/or money laundering.

Failure to Conduct Adequate Due Diligence on Agents/Outlets. Haider failed to ensure that MoneyGram conducted adequate due diligence on prospective agents, or existing agents seeking to open additional outlets, which resulted in, among other things, MoneyGram (1) granting outlets to agents who had previously been terminated by other money transmission companies and (2) granting additional outlets to agents who MoneyGram personnel knew or suspected were involved in fraud and/or money laundering.[612]

Discussion topics

*What are MoneyGrams? Who is likely to use them and why?

*Is it difficult or costly for a money intermediary to examine MoneyGrams and their use?

*What induced Haider to be so "sloppy" in monitoring this case?

---

and-seeks-bar-former-moneygram-executive (last visited Oct. 20, 2016).

612 Excerpted from FinCEN, *In re* Haider (Dec. 18, 2014), *available at* https://www.fincen.gov/news_room/ea/files/Haider_Assessment.pdf (last visited Oct. 20, 2016).

A. The SEC has announced the creation of the Office of Risk Assessment within its Division of Economic and Risk Analysis (DERA).

The press release states, in part:

Since its creation in 2009, DERA has collaborated with market experts throughout the SEC to develop risk assessment tools. One example, the Aberrational Performance Inquiry, launched in 2009 to proactively identify atypical hedge fund performance, led to eight enforcement actions and is one of the tools used by the Division of Enforcement to assess private funds. Similarly, DERA developed a broker-dealer risk assessment tool that helps SEC examiners allocate resources by assessing a broker-dealer's comparative riskiness relative to its peer group. It also is working closely with the Enforcement Division's Financial Reporting and Audit Task Force and the Division of Corporation Finance on developing a tool to assist in identifying financial reporting irregularities that may indicate financial fraud and help assess corporate issuer risk.

"The Office of Risk Assessment will build on the existing expertise of DERA's staff, which includes economists, accountants, analysts, and attorneys, to provide sophisticated assessments of market risks. The establishment of this new office reflects the Commission's ongoing focus on deploying data-driven analytics to assist in routing scarce resources to areas of the greatest risks to the market," said DERA Deputy Director Scott W. Bauguess, who oversees the division's risk assessment activities."

Initial staffing of the new Office of Risk Assessment will be drawn from across DERA and the division will seek a new assistant director to head the office. The office will continue to develop and use predictive analytics to support supervisory, surveillance, and investigative programs involving corporate issuers, broker-dealers, investment advisers, exchanges, and trading platforms. In addition, the office will support the SEC's ongoing work related to the Financial Stability Oversight Council.[613]

What steps should be taken to uncover the truth, and yet protect the rights of those who are investigated? When a government examiner visits a financial institution and meets with one or more of the employees, both need to learn some basic lessons. An examiner may pay attention to the way the person behaves and reacts to questions.

---

613 U.S. SEC. & EXCH. COMM'N, *SEC Announces Creation of New Office Within its Division of Economic and Risk Analysis* (Sept. 11, 2014), *available at* http://www.sec.gov/News/PressRelease/Detail/PressRelease/1370542914800 (last visited Feb. 18, 2016).

The first step for an internal examiner is to pose questions to herself, similar to those of the external and government examiner.

- What are you looking for?
- Do the persons whom you examine understand your questions? Do they know the meaning of words they use that are "a professional expression"?
- Do these persons answer instinctively or seem to think hard and long before they answer?
- Are these persons cooperative or hostile to the examination?
- When the examiner meets with a group, how do group members react to each other? Are they cooperative or competitive?
- How do the employees treat their own compliance officer? How does the "boss" treat the compliance officer?
- Do you meet with the legal counsel or is he or she too busy or otherwise unavailable?
- As an examiner roams around the corporate premises or shares lunch with its employees, how do they treat the examiner?
- When you ask for a file, do the persons choose the file carefully or automatically? Is there any sign that some files are not for your perusal? Do the persons suggest that you look at another, selected files?

Discussion topics

What do the answers to these questions reveal?

What does the following tell you? (a) The examination is carried together with the local compliance employees; (b) the examined persons let the visiting examiners wait for half an hour; (c) the examined personnel treat the visiting examiners with arrogance bordering on disrespect?

Please add the questions that would help your examination?

Some examinations are "surprise" visits; some are planned in advance. How would you determine what type of an examination you should choose?

What are the suspicious activities in the following two cases?

North Dade Community Development Federal Credit Union

The Financial Crimes Enforcement Network (FinCEN) [on November 25, 2014] assessed a $300,000 civil money penalty against North Dade Community Development Federal Credit Union in Miami Gardens, Florida, for significant Bank Secrecy Act (BSA) violations. North Dade's anti-money laundering (AML) failures exposed the United States financial system to significant opportunities for money laundering and terrorist financing from known high-risk jurisdictions.

The credit union consented to the assessment and admitted that it willfully violated BSA program, reporting, and recordkeeping requirements. Included within these lapses, the credit union failed to comply with Section 314(a) of the USA PATRIOT Act, a program requiring financial institutions to search their records to locate accounts and transactions of persons that may be involved in terrorism or money laundering.

North Dade, a small credit union with $4 million in assets and only five employees, contracted with a third-party vendor and money services business (MSB) to provide services and sub-accounts to 56 MSBs located in high-risk jurisdictions far outside its field of membership, including locations in Central America, the Middle East, and Mexico. The revenue generated from these accounts constituted 90% of North Dade's annual revenue. In 2013 alone, the total transaction volume through North Dade by MSBs included $1.01 billion in outgoing wires and $984 million in remotely captured deposits.

. . . .

. . . [According to FinCEN Director Jennifer Shasky Calvery.] "This case raises pretty obvious questions that no one seems to have asked. Why would MSBs located all over the world choose a small Florida credit union to conduct close to $2 billion in transactions? Credit unions pride themselves on close and low-risk relationships with known neighborhood customers. However, North Dade welcomed customers far beyond its field of membership, without adequate policies and procedures to ensure AML compliance."

. . . .

From 2009 through 2014, North Dade had significant deficiencies in all aspects of its AML program, including its internal controls, independent testing, training, and failure to designate an appropriate BSA compliance officer. North Dade also had a systemic failure in meeting its 314(a) obligations. North Dade did not provide any meaningful risk assessment for its size and type of business and blindly relied on a third-party vendor to conduct due diligence for all 56 MSBs that held sub-accounts at North Dade. Without knowing or understanding its customers or risks, North Dade was unable to adequately monitor, detect, or report significant suspicious transactions and other activities taking place through the credit union, including those related to money laundering and drug trafficking. When the credit union did file suspicious activity reports, the reports were often late and insufficient. [614]

---

614 Excerpted from FinCEN, *FinCEN Penalizes Florida Credit Union for Failures in Managing High-Risk International Financial Activity* (Nov. 25, 2014), *available at* https://www.fincen.gov/sites/default/files/shared/20141125.pdf (last visited Oct. 20, 2016).

Associated Bank, N.A., Green Bay, Wisconsin

The Comptroller of the Currency of the United States of America (Comptroller), through his examiners and other staff of the Office of the Comptroller of the Currency (OCC), has conducted an examination of Associated Bank, N.A., Green Bay, Wisconsin (Bank), specifically to determine the adequacy of the Bank's Bank Secrecy Act and Anti-Money Laundering (BSA/AML) compliance program. The OCC identified BSA/AML deficiencies in the Bank's internal controls, independent testing, day-to-day monitoring and coordination, and training. These BSA/AML deficiencies occurred primarily during the period 2010–2012 and were addressed by a Consent Order issued by the OCC on February 23, 2012 (Consent Order), which in part required the Bank to undertake remedial actions with respect to its BSA/AML program. The OCC terminated the Consent Order on March 11, 2014. The Bank . . . has executed a Stipulation and Consent to the Issuance of a Consent Order for a Civil Money Penalty (Stipulation) that is accepted by the Comptroller. . .

(1) The Comptroller finds, and the Bank neither admits nor denies that, primarily during the period of 2010-2012:

(a) the Bank failed to (i) conduct adequate risk assessments, (ii) conduct sufficient customer due diligence, (iii) properly identify high-risk customers, and (iv) implement an adequate suspicious activity monitoring system;

(b) the Bank's independent testing of the Bank's BSA/AML compliance program was inadequate;

(c) the Bank's BSA officer and staff lacked the necessary resources and expertise, including knowledge of regulatory requirements;

(d) the Bank's BSA training efforts for staff were inadequate; and

(e) after conducting a lookback, the Bank filed 670 new Suspicious Activity Reports (SARs).

(2) In light of the findings of paragraph (1) of this Article, the OCC determined that the Bank violated the following BSA laws and regulations:

(a) 12 C.F.R. § 21.21, including specifically that the Bank (i) lacked a system of internal controls to ensure ongoing compliance with the BSA, (ii) failed to provide for independent testing for compliance with the BSA, (iii) lacked a qualified BSA officer, and (iv) failed to provide adequate training to Bank personnel on the requirements of the BSA; and

(b) 12 C.F.R. § 21.11, by failing to file SARs in a timely manner.[615]

. . . .

---

[615] Excerpted from OCC, *In re* Associated Bank, N.A., (June 26, 2014), *available at* http://www.occ.gov/static/enforcement-actions/ea2014-094.pdf (last visited Oct. 20, 2016).

New Millenium Cash Exchange, Inc.

The Financial Crimes Enforcement Network has determined that grounds exist to assess a civil money penalty against New Millenium Cash Exchange, Inc. (NMCE or MSB) and its President and Owner, Flor Angella Lopez (Ms. Lopez), pursuant to the Bank Secrecy Act and regulations issued pursuant to that Act.

. . .

The Financial Crimes Enforcement Network conducted an investigation and determined that, since at least February 2008, NMCE and Ms. Lopez willfully violated the Bank Secrecy Act's program, reporting, and recordkeeping requirements.

These violations included:

(A) Failure to register as a money service business, including submission of filings with inaccurate information regarding the services rendered by the MSB;

(B) Violations of the requirement to establish and implement an effective written anti-money laundering program; including

(1) Lack of adequate AML programs for its check cashing and money order activities as well as its currency exchange transactions;
(2) Inadequate policies, procedures and internal controls (a) to verify the identities of persons conducting transactions; (b) to monitor for suspicious activities; (c) to identify currency transactions exceeding $10,000; and (d) to ensure that NMCE filed the required currency transaction reports (CTRs);
(3) Inadequate internal controls for creating and retaining adequate Bank Secrecy Act records related to currency exchange;
(4) Failure to conduct a Bank Secrecy Act/AML risk assessment of the MSB and failure to include "red flags" in the MSB's procedures for each type of business;
(5) Failure to recognize the potential conflicts of interest in establishing a relationship with a consultant that: (a) created NMCE's written AML program, (b) performed the only independent testing of the AML program, and (c) provided the only source of Bank Secrecy Act training for the MSB; such training used a generic module that was provided by the consultant that also created its written AML program; the training was not comprehensive and was not tailored to the MSB's specific business lines and associated risk.

(C) Violations of the reporting and recordkeeping requirements; including (1) filing 51 CTRs significantly late and (2) failure to file at least 149 CTRs for exchanges of currency with other financial institutions.[616]

B. The New Risk Management Rules for U.S. Banks and Other Financial Institutions.

In 2009 the former chair of the Federal Reserve Board proposed a rule now known as The Volcker Rule, which restricted the bank holding companies' issuance and trading in their own shares.[617]

The banks that had failed and were bailed out by taxpayers were mostly "bank holding companies" that owned and managed a variety of financial intermediation units. These holding companies are in fact "financial malls" that engage in various financial intermediation services. Like other businesses, the bank holding companies issued their own shares, and reported quarterly performance. Arguably, one reason for the 2008 market crash and the failure of large banks was the pressure to increase profits, which may cause, and did cause, bank holding companies to take greater market risks. After all, risk and return usually go together.

The Volcker Rule may have contributed to an interesting and important development in the regulatory attitude toward banking. Regulators have often spoken about culture as a method of controlling bank risks. However, their focus used to be on economic or financial risks. Recently, the regulators began to speak about risk somewhat differently. The emphasis today is also on a culture in non-economic terms—a culture of appropriate risk avoidance by the actors. The emphasis is not only on the extent of financial risk taken by the actors, but also and more on the actors' degree of risk avoidance.

C. The Role of Culture.

Culture involves rules of behavior that are accepted and imposed by the group or group leaders. It is the attitude of: "we do not do this here!" So what does culture in non-economic terms mean? It seems to include business behavior: (1) fair treatment of the customers; (2) maintaining the institution's reputation for trustworthiness; and (3) legal behavior or compliance with the law. This view focuses on the actors' approach, habits, and behavior. In short, it focuses on people.

---

616 Excerpted from *In re* New Milenium Cash Exchange, Inc. (Apr. 23, 2014), *available at* https://www.fincen.gov/sites/default/files/shared/NMCE%20Assessment.pdf (last visited Oct. 20, 2016).

617 Dodd-Frank Wall Street Reform and Consumer Protection Act, Pub. L. No. 111-203, § 619, 124 Stat. 1376, 1620-31 (2010) (codified at 12 U.S.C. § 1851 (2012))..For a general description and background of the Volcker rule and its pluses and minuses, *see Much Ado About Trading*, THE ECONOMIST, July 25, 2015 at 60, *available at* http://www.economist.com/news/finance-and-economics/21659671-next-great-regulation-tame-banks-now-place-much-ado-about-trading (last visited Feb. 18, 2016).

For example, risk avoidance culture in non-economic terms, seeks to establish:

- How do employees actually behave?
- What drives behavior within the organization? What incentives, rewards, and advances are provided to induce behavior? Are the compensation and punishment policies aligned with risk culture?
- How are the activities within the organization aligned with risk avoidance policies?
- Notwithstanding government and corporate written policies, the important question is: "Do the board, management and employees really mean it—on a day-to-day, consistent basis—and even when no one is watching?How do the bottom-up and top-down structures contribute to risk management? Do the board and the CEO focus mostly on profits, regardless? Or do they also ask how the profits were made? (i) State most of the recent requirements of behavior, including self-regulation in face of temptation. Put in place and develop the culture to enforce it: How do you create this culture? (ii) How do you inculcate a process restricting "risk appetite" especially when risk is linked to higher returns and rewards? (iii) Do decisions that are too profit driven fail to evaluate not only short-term but also long-term risk, considering the reputational harm and loss of trust? (iv) Do compensation policies balance producing profits with these risks? Regulators aim at considering the root problem and documenting it. An unhelpful but truthful answer about compliance is: You know risk management culture when you see it. Regulators will expect institutions to develop their own programs and focus on the issues that might result in violations of the law. To find out the answers to these questions, we ask:
  - Do the actors within the enterprise follow the written policies?
  - Do they follow the policies, even if they are exposed to enticement or coercion? Do they like to behave in this fashion?
  - Are they proud of behaving in this way?
  - Does the firm conduct a self-assessment when it sees a red flag?
  - Are there patterns of behavior that have to be addressed? For example, how long did it take to resolve a risk problem or a supervision problem?
  - Recognize the internal conflict raised by "risk appetite." The firm and its leaders, management, and employees face a conflict, described as an institutional or personal "risk appetite." We may call it "financial returns appetite."

There are many temptations and justifications for people to take risks, especially if (i) they risk other people's money, (ii) the government is backing at least some of the risk, and (iii) there is a reasonable probability of higher returns. After all, returns are more tangible and positive. As previously noted in Chapter 7, here are suggestions for mediating between the business and the restrictive law:

- Business: What is the dollar difference between acting and not acting? Should we slow or terminate the activity all at once? Is it a long-term or short-term issue? Does the rule affect the business as a whole or only part of it?
- Law: What is the chance of action? What is the chance of its reaching the legal violation stage? What is the chance of the actors being caught? What is the chance of their being held responsible for a violation? How serious is the violation going to be?
- Test: What is the nature and extent of (i) the harm to society, the firm, the growth of the firm, and (ii) the actor?

How could firms, their management and employees, be induced to curb their "risk appetite"? Numbers do not help in this case. One suggested key to the answer is judgment, based on experience.

Regulators have begun to pay far more attention to the activities and leadership of the boards of directors and their impact on business managers. The regulators expect the board of directors to (i) distinguish between the various departments in the organizations with respect to risk, (ii) identify the impact of the departments on the choice of personnel, and (iii) evaluate personnel behavior.

For example, regulators pay more attention to (i) HR hiring policies and personnel activities outside of the policies; (ii) the personnel's response to the occurrence of lapses; (iii) attendance and assessment of consultants and surveys of third-party assessments.

Unlike active supervision, culture involves internal value guidelines and self-regulation. The more employees are policed, the less they might feel obligated to behave as they should on their own. Therefore, there must be a balance between policing and respectful trust that would induce employees to behave as expected and be proud of being trusted rather than fearful of being caught.

At the same time, supervision, and awareness of supervision, is necessary. There was a case of a small bank that hired three people from a very large bank. They were granted authority to trade in securities, placed in a separate building, and hardly supervised. They brought this small bank down. What was wrong with this arrangement? Was their background checked? Why did they leave the large bank? What were their ambitions? When they were hired, what facilities were given to them and how much supervision was imposed on their activities?

The regulators' new approach is not free of criticism. First, if the small or big banks do not take any risk or very little risk, they open the door to "shadow banking," which may not be regulated, and may harm investors. Second, smaller institutions are not expected to impose the same level of formality as large ones do, and yet there is a concern that these small organizations can expose investors to unfair predatory services. They present unfair competition for regulated institutions.

One response to this criticism is that shadow banks, which are small, do not pose risk to the entire economy or financial system. In addition, large banks can publicly demonstrate their tighter regulation in ways that small institutions cannot. Therefore, large institutions can compete by demonstrating their trustworthiness. Arguably, business partners of large banks may have greater "risk appetite" with the support of the large banks. They may pose risk for the system as the banks themselves do. Therefore, the banks should choose their partners with great care and ensure their reliability.

The harm of bank failures is borne by the financial system as well as unsophisticated investors. However, banks that practice investment management must comply with the Investment Company Act of 1940 as well as the regulation of broker-dealers to give investors suitable advice. If they fail to do so, investors suffer.

It is impossible and undesirable to impose the same rules on each of the bank holding company's varied activities, yet they are all performed under the same roof. It is difficult to keep different cultures under the same roof as well.

As we already noted, the liabilities of the boards of directors are very difficult to define. The boards must set the risk parameters and expectations, but by definition, range is not specific and is subject to judgment. Management must execute a business plan that meets the parameters. The regulators do not require boards to ensure compliance yet have not found the appropriate word for the degree of the board's responsibilities. The words used may be "oversee" or "responsible for an appropriate culture" or "execute an appropriate culture"—all of which are just short of "ensure." But the Board can pick up some signals: if managers are resentful of constraints, employees will be; if management delays responsibility, so will other employees.

V. HOW DO REGULATORS INDUCE CONCERN ABOUT RISK CULTURE?

Currently regulators give lectures and symposiums about the right way to achieve compliance. They watch and sometimes follow the compliance steps taken in the UK and Europe. In this respect, regulators conduct an international quest for understanding culture. How do they understand the meaning of culture? How varied are different cultures?

Banks are subject to an overall risk assessment. Regulators increasingly include in their assessment the weaknesses in the banks' internal systems, and frame such weakness as a "risk culture" issue. Risk assessment includes rating management, because management's attitude is part of the entire risk context. Thus, non-bank risk culture, e.g., at mutual funds and insurance subsidiaries, may affect the banks' risk evaluation. Unfortunately, a stricter and more reliable risk context does not, then, necessarily apply to the banking activities.

Risk culture has become an important fact in the overall rating of banking institutions. Although this approach is result oriented, it is not quantifiable. Rather it is qualitative. It is suggested that bank management as well as managers of other financial institutions should take a deep breath and learn to comply with directives that are far less specific. These non-specific directives are the future.

There is a proposal to change future government examinations of market intermediaries. It suggests focusing on bubbles and crashes as dangerous to the financial system and the economy. The proposal points to the undesirable effects of prior substantive regulation on innovations and freedom of the markets and on the equally undesirable, and perhaps ineffective, results of regulating activities after a crash (when the "horse has left the barn"). Therefore, the proposal advocates closer examinations of a kind somewhat different than the current ones.

* Examine more frequently, when market prices rise (not when they have fallen);

* Examine entities that are too large to fail or highly leveraged; those whose share prices rise steadily with no fluctuation; and those that have obtained exemptions;

* Examiners should search for violations of the law or the spirit of the law, but not of economic or financial rationalizations; and,

* Examiners should be experts, highly paid and incentivized to remain in government employ. Expert information about the markets will hopefully reduce the impact of bubbles and inevitable crashes and mostly the loss of investors trust in the financial system.[618]

* Note The California Unfair Competition Law (UCL). This Act defines "unfair competition" as "any unlawful, unfair or fraudulent business act or practice and unfair, deceptive, untrue or misleading advertising" and any of a number of specific acts prohibited by the Business and Professions Code.[619] Therefore, this Law prohibits an act that is (a) "unlawful," (b) "unfair," or (c) "fraudulent." An "unlawful" act can be one prohibited by "[v]irtually any state, federal, or local law."[620] The "unfairness" prong is "intentionally broad" and involves a balancing test.[621] The test "'involves an examination of [that practice's] impact on its alleged victim, balanced against the reasons, justifications and motives of the alleged wrongdoer." Stated differently, it balances

---

618 Tamar Frankel, *Chapter 9: Regulating the Financial Markets by Examinations, in* THE PANIC OF 2008; CAUSES, CONSEQUENCES AND IMPLICATIONS FOR REFORM (Lawrence E. Mitchell & Arthur E. Wilmarth, Jr. eds., 2010).

619 CAL. BUS. & PROF. CODE § 17200 (2014) (LEXIS version).

620 Podolsky v. First Healthcare Corp., 50 Cal. App. 4th 632, 647, 50 Cal. Rptr. 2d 89, 98 (Cal. Ct. App. 1996) (citing case).

621 *Id.* (quoting case).

"the utility of the defendant's conduct against the gravity of the harm to the alleged victim."[622] "An unfair business practice occurs when the practice 'offends an established public policy or when the practice is immoral, unethical, oppressive, unscrupulous or substantially injurious to consumers.' . . . "[623] The "fraud" prong is broader than common law deception. It does not require actual deception, reliance, or damage, only that "members of the public are likely to be deceived."[624]

In one case the Defendant, First Healthcare Corporation (FHC), operator of nursing homes, pressured relatives of nursing home patients to sign admission agreements that required them to cosign as "responsible parties" with little opportunity to examine the agreements or ask questions.[625]

The Court found the agreement "deceptive" because it did not contain information about the protections that the guarantors have under federal and state law.[626] While the decision of the court was based on this rationale, the Court also stated that there was a triable issue as to whether FHC deceptively induced or in effect required such guarantees, noting the stress involved in admitting a family member to a nursing home,[627] and a triable issue as to whether the guarantee lacks consideration.[628]

Discussion topic

What problems might be encountered in achieving the list of suggestions outlined above? An ex-bank executive allegedly received a free bathroom remodel for insider tips.[629] How, in your opinion, was this fact uncovered?

---

622 *Id.* (quoting case).

623 *Id.* (quoting case).

624 *Id.* at 647-48, 50 Cal. Rptr. 2d at 98 (citing cases).

625 *Id.* at 638-42, 50 Cal. Rptr. 2d at 91-94.

626 *Id.* at 649-51, 50 Cal. Rptr. 2d at 100-01.

627 *Id.* at 652-54, 50 Cal. Rptr. 2d at 101-03.

628 *Id.* at 654-55, 50 Cal. Rptr. 2d at 103-04.

629 Nicole Hong,, *Did a Plumber Swap Tiles for Insider Tips?*, WALL ST.. J., June 1, 2016, at C1, C3.

The Office of the Inspector General ("OIG") issued guidance for hospitals for compliance with federal and state law, the requirements of government and private health plans, and hospital policies.[630]

The guidance includes "[t]he investigation and remediation of identified systemic problems and the development of policies addressing the non-employment or retention of sanctioned individuals" as one element of a comprehensive compliance program.[631]

G. Responding to Detected Offenses and Developing Corrective Action Initiatives

1. *Violations and Investigations.* Violations of a hospital's compliance program, failures to comply with applicable Federal or State law, and other types of misconduct threaten a hospital's status as a reliable, honest and trustworthy provider capable of participating in Federal health care programs. Detected but uncorrected misconduct can seriously endanger the mission, reputation, and legal status of the hospital. Consequently, upon reports or reasonable indications of suspected noncompliance, it is important that the chief compliance officer or other management officials initiate prompt steps to investigate the conduct in question to determine whether a material violation of applicable law or the requirements of the compliance program has occurred, and if so, take steps to correct the problem. As appropriate, such steps may include an immediate referral to criminal and/or civil law enforcement authorities, a corrective action plan, a report to the Government, and the submission of any overpayments, if applicable.

. . .

Depending upon the nature of the alleged violations, an internal investigation will probably include interviews and a review of relevant documents. Some hospitals should consider engaging outside counsel, auditors, or [industry] experts to assist in an investigation. Records of the investigation should contain documentation of the alleged violation, a description of the investigative process, copies of interview notes and key documents, a log of the witnesses interviewed and the documents reviewed, the results of the investigation, e.g., any disciplinary action taken, and the corrective action implemented. While any action taken as the result of an investigation will necessarily vary depending upon the hospital and the situation, hospitals should strive for some consistency by utilizing sound practices and disciplinary protocols. Further, after a reasonable period, the compliance officer should review the circumstances that formed the basis for the investigation to determine whether similar problems have been uncovered.

If an investigation of an alleged violation is undertaken and the compliance officer believes the integrity of the investigation may be at stake because of the presence of employees under investigation, those subjects should be removed from their current work activity until the

---

630 Ofc. of the Inspector General, Dep't of Health & Human Servs., Publication of the OIG Compliance Program Guidance for Hospitals, 63 Fed. Reg. 8987 (Feb. 23, 1998).

631 *Id.* at 8989.

investigation is completed (unless an internal or Government-led undercover operation is in effect). In addition, the compliance officer should take appropriate steps to secure or prevent the destruction of documents or other evidence relevant to the investigation. If the hospital determines that disciplinary action is warranted, if should be prompt and imposed in accordance with the hospital's written standards of disciplinary action.

2. Reporting. If the compliance officer, compliance committee or management official discovers credible evidence of misconduct from any source and, after a reasonable inquiry, has reason to believe that the misconduct may violate criminal, civil or administrative law, then the hospital promptly should report the existence of misconduct to the appropriate governmental authority within a reasonable period .... Prompt reporting will demonstrate the hospital's good faith and willingness to work with governmental authorities to correct and remedy the problem. In addition, reporting such conduct will be considered a mitigating factor by the OIG in determining administrative sanctions (e.g., penalties, assessments, and exclusion), if the reporting provider becomes the target of an OIG investigation.

When reporting misconduct to the Government, a hospital should provide all evidence relevant to the alleged violation of applicable Federal or State law(s) and potential cost impact. The compliance officer, under advice of counsel, and with guidance from the governmental authorities, could be requested to continue to investigate the reported violation. Once the investigation is completed, the compliance officer should be required to notify the appropriate governmental authority of the outcome of the investigation, including a description of the impact of the alleged violation on the operation of the applicable health care programs or their beneficiaries. If the investigation ultimately reveals that criminal or civil violations have occurred, the appropriate Federal and State officials should be notified immediately. . . . [632]

VI. THE TALMUDIST STORY

Both monitoring (Chapter 10) and investigations are systems of inquiry. The following story highlights an analysis in a very different context:

A Beautiful Talmudic Mind

After months of negotiation with the authorities, a Talmudist from Odessa was finally granted permission to visit Moscow.

He boarded the train and found an empty seat. At the next stop, a young man got on and sat next to him. The scholar looked at the young man and he thought: This fellow doesn't look

---

632 *Id.* at 8997-98 (footnotes omitted).

like a peasant, so if he is no peasant he probably comes from this district. If he comes from this district, then he must be Jewish, because this is, after all, a Jewish district.

But on the other hand, since he is a Jew, where could he be going? I'm the only Jew in our district who has permission to travel to Moscow.

Ahh, wait! Just outside Moscow there is a little village called Samvet, and Jews don't need special permission to go to Samvet. But why would he travel to Samvet? He is surely going to visit one of the Jewish families there. But how many Jewish families are there in Samvet? Aha, only two: the Bernsteins and the Steinbergs. But the Bernsteins are a terrible family, so such a nice looking fellow like him, he must be visiting the Steinbergs.

But why is he going to the Steinbergs in Samvet? The Steinbergs have only daughters, two of them, so maybe he's their son-in-law. But if he is, then which daughter did he marry? They say that Sarah Steinberg married a nice lawyer from Budapest, and Esther married a businessman from Zhitomer, so it must be Sarah's husband. Which means that his name is Alexander Cohen, if I'm not mistaken.

But if he came from Budapest, with all the anti-Semitism they have there, he must have changed his name.

What's the Hungarian equivalent of Cohen? It is Kovacs. But since they allowed him to change his name, he must have special status to change it. What could it be? Must be a doctorate from the University. Nothing less would do.

At this point, therefore, the Talmudic scholar turns to the young man and says, "Excuse me. Do you mind if I open the window, Dr. Kovacs?"

"Not at all," answered the startled co-passenger. "But how is it that you know my name?"

"Ahhh," replied the Talmudist, "It was obvious."[633]

Discussion topic

What method did the Talmudist use to reach his conclusion?

What are the differences between fact-finding and conclusions; and how are they connected in this story?

---

633 *A Beautiful Talmudic Mind, available at* http://www.aish.com/j/j/51475187.html (last visited Apr. 27, 2017).

Chapter 12

GAINING INFORMATION FROM WHISTLEBLOWERS AND OUTSIDE ADVISORY SERVICES

In this chapter, we examine two sources of information that may help to prevent and uncover corporate misdeeds, whistleblowers and outsourced advisory services, discussing their roles and the issues they raise.

I. THE WHISTLEBLOWERS

A whistleblower is a person who points to wrongful activities by or within an institution.

Usually a whistleblower becomes aware of the wrongful activities because he or she is an employee of the institution or has ongoing relationships with the institution. Whistleblowing by alerting the government to a wrongful act is an old tradition in the United States, and is usually encouraged by compensation.[634]

Because whistleblowers have information about the institution by virtue of their ongoing relationships, their assistance and information about the details of institutional wrongdoing can be among the most powerful weapons in the law enforcement arsenal. Whistleblowers' knowledge of the details can help SEC and DOJ, as well as other government regulators, identify potential violations far earlier than might otherwise have been possible. This allows the law enforcement agencies to minimize the harm caused to investors and national interests, better preserve the integrity of the U.S. capital markets, and more swiftly hold accountable those responsible for unlawful conduct.[635] Similarly, FINRA encourages whistleblowers to come forward with evidence of violations or potential violations.[636]

---

634 *See* TAMAR FRANKEL, TRUST AND HONESTY: AMERICA'S BUSINESS CULTURE AT A CROSSROAD 164-65 (2006) (the issue of "snitching").

635 *See also* Lee H. Rubin & Anne M. Selin, *Self-Disclosure to the SEC in the Age of the Whistleblower*, INV. LAW., Apr. 2016, at 1, 4.

636 FINRA, *FINRA Announces Creation of "Office of the Whistleblower,"* available at http://www.finra.org/newsroom/2009/finra-announces-creation-office-whistleblower (last visited Apr. 4, 2017). FINRA's Office of the Whistleblower, within its Office of Fraud Detection and Market Intelligence, reviews tips from whistleblowers "on an expedited basis," although FINRA does not offer rewards. FINRA, *Office of Fraud Detection and Market Intelligence (OFDMI)*, available at http://www.finra.org/industry/ofdmi (last visited Apr. 4, 2017).

There are laws that require "whistleblowing" by institutions. For example, banks may be required or encouraged to report financial abuse of older adults.[637] The Gramm-Leach-Bliley Act generally prohibits a bank from disclosing nonpublic personal information to a third party without notice,[638] but reporting suspected financial abuse of older adults would generally fall within the exceptions.[639]

Regulators assure banks that they won't violate privacy laws by coming forward, and that reporting violations to the government doesn't violate federal restrictions on sharing personal information. Yet, financial institutions have voiced concerns about their ability to report wrongful behavior, in light of the right-to-privacy laws. Regardless of the law, privacy rights have a strong public backing in the U.S. Privacy is protected not only by damages, but also by punitive damages, as they are awarded in common law torts, rooted in corrective justice. Therefore, whistleblowers are doubly valuable to law enforcement agencies.

II. WHISTLEBLOWERS' CONFLICTED POSITIONS AND THEIR NEED FOR PROTECTION

A. The Employee's Problems.

An employee who "blows the whistle" on a wrongful act within the organization does a good thing by preventing or punishing the wrongful act. However, this employee faces two serious issues. First, if the employee has received the information in an illegal manner, or if the employee took part in the violation, then this employee is exposed to liability. Second, even if the employee was not a party to the wrongful actions, as an employee of the organization, the whistleblower is exposed to a conflict of interest. He or she has a fiduciary duty to the employer. This duty has its limits, but these limits are unclear. When does an employee become disloyal?[640]

There are employees and managers who will view a whistleblower as a traitor. And the whistleblower or other employees might partially agree with them. Therefore, employers do not

---

637 Bd. of Governors of the Fed. Res. Sys., Commodity Futures Trading Comm'n, Consumer Fin. Protection Bureau, Fed. Deposit Ins. Corp., Fed. Trade Comm'n, Nat'l Credit Union Admin.., Ofc. of the Comptroller of the Currency, & Sec. & Exch. Comm'n, *Federal Regulators Issue Guidance on Reporting Financial Abuse of Older Adults* (Sept. 24, 2013), *available at* https://www.federalreserve.gov/newsevents/pressreleases/bcreg20130924a.htm (last visited June 13, 2017).

638 15 U.S.C. § 6802(a) (2012).

639 15 U.S.C. § 6802(e)(8) (2012) (disclosure to comply with law); id. § 6802(e)(3)(B) (disclosure to prevent fraud); *id.* § 6802(e) (3)(B) (disclosure to law enforcement agency or certain regulators); Bd. of Governors of the Fed. Res. Sys., Commodity Futures Trading Comm'n, Consumer Fin. Protection Bureau, Fed. Deposit Ins. Corp., Fed. Trade Comm'n, Nat'l Credit Union Admin.., Ofc. of the Comptroller of the Currency, & Sec. & Exch. Comm'n, Federal Regulators Issue Guidance on Reporting Financial Abuse of Older Adults (Sept. 24, 2013).

640 *See* TAMAR FRANKEL, TRUST AND HONESTY: AMERICA'S BUSINESS CULTURE AT A CROSSROAD 164-65 (2006) (the issue of "snitching").

always gratefully reward whistleblowers. And if they leave the employer, they may have difficulties in getting a job with other employers, who prefer loyalty to the employer over loyalty to the law.

Whistleblowing employees may pose similar issues within government regulators. For example, a former examiner in the New York Federal Reserve Bank was pressured by her superiors to "weaken" her reports concerning Goldman Sachs, which had become a bank holding company, subject to bank regulators. After she refused to change her evaluation she was fired.[641] Yet, bank regulators may have all sorts of justifications for being discreet about wrongful activities of a bank, for example, to avoid a run on the bank. In sum, whistleblowers need protection.

B. Legislation and Rules Concerning Whistleblowers

The provisions of the Sarbanes-Oxley Act of 2002 (SOX) affect whistleblowers who report Foreign Corrupt Practices Act violations. SOX prohibits issuers from retaliating against whistleblowers and provides that employees who are retaliated against for reporting possible securities law violations may file a complaint with the Department of Labor. Upon proof of violations these employees would be eligible to be reinstated, and entitled to receive back pay and other compensation.[642] Thus, the Sarbanes-Oxley Act prohibits retaliation against employee whistleblowers under the obstruction of justice statute. Nonetheless, retaliation may have continued.

In 2010, the Dodd-Frank Act added Section 21F to the Exchange Act, addressing whistleblower incentives and protections. Section 21F authorizes the SEC to provide monetary awards to eligible individuals who voluntarily come forward with high quality, original information that leads to an SEC enforcement action in which over $1,000,000 in sanctions is ordered.[643] The awards range is between 10% and 30% of the monetary sanctions recovered by the government. The Dodd-Frank Act also prohibits employers from retaliating against whistleblowers[644] and creates a private right of action for employees who are retaliated against.[645] Furthermore, employers should be aware that retaliation against a whistleblower may also violate state, local, and foreign laws that provide protection of whistleblowers.

---

641 Julie Steinberg & Dan Fitzpatrick, *New York Fed Is Sued by Ex-Staffer*, WALL ST. J., Oct. 11, 2013, at C3.

642 18 U.S.C. § 1514A (2012).

643 15 U.S.C. § 78u-6(a)(3) (2012). The new provision defines "original information" to mean information that: "(A) is derived from the independent knowledge or analysis of a whistleblower; (B) is not known to the Commission from any other source, unless the whistleblower is the original source of the information; and (C) is not exclusively derived from an allegation made in a judicial or administrative hearing, in a governmental report, hearing, audit, or investigation, or from the news media, unless the whistleblower is a source of the information."

644 18 USCS § 1514A(a)(1) (2012).

645 15 U.S.C. § 78u-6 (2012); *see also* Dodd-Frank Wall Street Reform and Consumer Protection Act, Pub. L. No. 111-203, § 922, 124 Stat. 1376, 1841-49 (2010).

The Act has not always been protective. The *Wall Street Journal* reported the request of a lawyer who blew the whistle for help from the SEC. In response, the employer company argued that the lawyer violated the state law of professional conduct and company policy. The employer demanded the return of the documents that the lawyer had used to demonstrate the employer's violations.[646]

In another case an employee sued his former employer Siemens AG (Siemens), alleging retaliation against him for his disclosures of alleged corrupt conduct within the corporation. The United States District Court for the Southern District of New York granted Siemens's motion to dismiss with prejudice, holding that the anti-retaliation provision does not apply extraterritorially. The plaintiff was not a citizen and was employed abroad by a foreign company; all the events allegedly giving rise to liability occurred outside the United States. Therefore, applying the anti-retaliation provision to these facts would constitute an extraterritorial application of the statute. Because a statute is presumed, in the absence of clear congressional intent to the contrary, to apply only domestically, and because there is no evidence that the anti-retaliation provision is intended to have extraterritorial reach, the court concluded that that provision does not apply extraterritorially.[647]

On August 12, 2011, the final rules for the SEC's Whistleblower Program became effective. These rules set forth the requirements for whistleblowers to be eligible for award consideration, the factors that the SEC will use to determine the amount of the award, and the categories of individuals who are subject to limitations in or excluded from award considerations.[648] The final rules strengthen incentives for employees to report the suspected violations internally through internal compliance programs when appropriate, although it does not require an employee to do so in order to qualify for an award.[649]

Individuals with information about a possible violation of the federal securities laws, including Foreign Corrupt Practices Act violations, should submit that information to the SEC either online through SEC's Tips, Complaints, and Referrals (TCR) Intake and Resolution System[650] or by mailing or faxing a completed Form TCR to the Commission's Office of the Whistleblower.

---

646 Kirsten Grind & Jean Eaglesham, *Lawyer Who Blew the Whistle Seeks Help*, Wall St. J., Aug. 9, 2014, at B2.

647 Meng-Lin Liu v. Siemens A.G., 978 F. Supp. 2d 325 (S.D.N.Y. 2013).

648 For detailed information about the program, including eligibility requirements and certain limitations that apply, *see* Dodd-Frank Wall Street Reform and Consumer Protection Act, Pub. L. No. 111-203, § 922, 124 Stat. 1376, 1841-49 (2010), *available at* http://www.sec.gov/about/offices/owb/dodd-frank-sec-922.pdfhttp://www.sec.gov/about/offices/owb/dodd-frank-sec-922.pdf (last visited Mar. 8, 2016), (last visited Mar. 8, 2016), and the final rules on eligibility, Exchange Act Rule 21F-8, 17 C.F.R. § 240.21F-8 (2016).

649 *See* Exchange Act Rule 21F, 17 C.F.R. § 240.21F (2015).

650 *Available at* https://denebleo.sec.gov/TCRExternal/disclaimer.xhtml (last visited Mar. 8, 2016).

C. Whistleblowers Can Submit Information to the SEC Anonymously

To be considered eligible for a reward under SEC's whistleblower program, an attorney must submit the information on behalf of the anonymous whistleblower.[651] However, this process is expensive and may be risky for the employee if the number of employees in the group where the problem has occurred is small. For instance, a whistleblower on a broker-dealer desk of four people is easily identified when an investigation begins.

Regardless of whether a whistleblower reports anonymously, the SEC is committed to protecting the identity of a whistleblower to the fullest extent possible under the statute.[652] For example, the rules: (1) make a whistleblower eligible for an award if the whistleblower reports original information internally, and the company informs the SEC about the violations; (2) give whistleblowers 120 days to report information to the SEC after first reporting internally and still be treated as if he or she had reported to the SEC at the earlier reporting date, thus preserving the "place in line" for a possible whistleblower award from the SEC; and (3) provide that a whistleblower's voluntary participation in an entity's internal compliance and reporting system is a factor that can increase the amount of an award, and that a whistleblower's interference with an internal compliance and reporting system is a factor that can decrease the amount of an award.

The SEC staff will not disclose a whistleblower's identity in response to requests under the Freedom of Information Act.[653] However, there are limits on the SEC's ability to shield a whistleblower's identity, and in certain circumstances the SEC must disclose it to outside entities. For example, in an administrative or court proceeding, the SEC may be required to produce documents or other information that would reveal the whistleblower's identity. In addition, as part of ongoing SEC investigatory responsibilities, the SEC staff may use information provided by a whistleblower during the course of the investigation. In appropriate circumstances, the SEC may also provide information, subject to confidentiality requirements, to other governmental or regulatory entities.[654]

The SEC sued an employer under this rule, when the employer caused an employee-whistleblower to resign. The decision is important for two reasons. First, the wrongful act of the employer did not cause injury to its clients and investors. Nonetheless, its actions were conducted in conflict of interest, as the employer also benefited from the arrangement. Second, the

---

651 *See* Exchange Act Rule 21F-7(b), 17 C.F.R. § 240.21F-7(b) (2015).

652 The SEC's Office of the Whistleblower administers SEC's Whistleblower Program and answers questions from the public regarding the program. Additional information regarding SEC's Whistleblower Program, including answers to frequently asked questions, is available online at http://www.sec.gov/whistleblower (last visited Oct. 23, 2016).

653 5 U.S.C. § 552 (2012).

654 Exchange Act Rule 21F-7(a), 17 C.F.R. § 240.21F-7(a) (2016).

employer was fined for pressing the whistleblower hard to protect its interests, which ended in the employee's resignation.[655]

Employers have started asking employees to sign confidential agreements to ward off whistle blowing. On April 1, 2015, in connection with charges that KBR, Inc. violated Rule 21F-17, the SEC announced its "first enforcement action against a company for using improperly restrictive language in confidentiality agreements with the potential to stifle the whistleblowing process."[656]

Interestingly, the Dodd-Frank Act called for creating an office of the Investor Advocate. The Office would appoint an ombudsman, who will act as a liaison in resolving problems that retail investors may have with the Commission or self-regulatory organizations. The ombudsman also will establish safeguards to maintain the confidentiality of communications with investors.[657]

D. The Objections to Protecting Whistleblowers

Not surprisingly, there are objections to whistleblowing for a number of reasons. First, arguably, efficient market forces might encourage violations and breach of integrity rules. For example, expected profits from violating the law may exceed expected costs. In addition, the expected profit may be larger for some people than the harm done to those who will be injured. When considering costs and benefits, economics does not take into account the bearers of the cost and benefit. Therefore, such legal violations may be justified. Whistleblowers should not prevent these economically justified activities.[658]

Second, arguably, under the common law, deterrence undermines democratic values if it focuses on the harm to a particular plaintiff, rather than on moral outrage concerning the wrong. Further, it seems that the Supreme Court has moved the rationale of punitive damages from moral retribution and corrective justice to results. Besides, protecting whistleblowers is contrary to the values and beliefs imbedded in American culture: that freedom from harm is primary, that institutions are corruptible, that power should be separated, and that humans are sometimes irrational.

---

655 *In re* Paradigm Cap. Mgmt., Admin. Proc. File No. 3-15930, Securities Exchange Act Rel. No. 72,393, Investment Advisers Act Rel. No. 3857 (June 16, 2014).

656 U.S. Sec. & Exch. Comm'n, *SEC: Companies Cannot Stifle Whistleblowers in Confidentiality Agreements* (Apr. 1, 2015), *available at* https://www.sec.gov/news/pressrelease/2015-54.html (last visited Apr. 27, 2017).

657 Dodd-Frank Wall Street Reform and Consumer Protection Act, Pub. L. No. 111-203, § 915, 124 Stat. 1376, 1830-32 (2010) (codified at 15 U.S.C. § 78d(g) (2012)). The first ombudsman was named in September 2014. U.S. Sec. & Exch. Comm'n, *Tracey L. McNeil Named as SEC's First Ombudsman* (Sept. 5, 2014), *available at* http://www.sec.gov/News/PressRelease/ Detail/PressRelease/1370542869949 (last visited Mar. 8, 2016).

658 Paul J. Zwier, *The Utility of a Nonconsequentialist Rationale for Civil-Jury-Awarded Punitive Damages,* 54 Kan. L. Rev. 403, 440 (2006).

In addition, under this view, if only economic costs and benefits are considered, whistleblowing regarding some activities would not be justified even though the activity is illegal and may be morally reprehensible to some members of society (*e.g.,* production of alcoholic beverages during a period of "prohibition" in the United States where such activity was prohibited).

Punishing and preventing bad corporate behavior is a difficult task. Effective punishment depends on sending a message of moral condemnation and economic pain, especially where the market blurs the lines of morality and values profit above all else. Where the institutional conduct is particularly egregious, the most effective way to punish in civil law is to simulate incarceration. In some ways, bankruptcy, which limits a company's freedom and taints its reputation, serves this purpose.

Third, an international perspective supports a non-result argument as well. Arguably, individual freedom and liberty support jury-awarded punitive damages. Societies value the individual according to different beliefs, as when valuing a cause or a religion more than human life, or believing that the collective good takes precedence over an individual's happiness. Punitive damages in international law may enable each society to maintain its values in the global arena.

Fourth, arguably, according to Paul J. Zwier, jurors should determine punitive damages, considering community values.[659]

Fifth, arguably, according to the National Association of Corporate Directors, rewards for whistleblowers may damage companies' own internal compliance programs, as they may provide an incentive for employees to go to the SEC rather than reporting through companies' own programs.[660]

Discussion Topics

To what extent is a whistleblower's employment protected after taking the employer's documents to hand them over to the regulators?

What arguments for encouraging whistleblowers do you support? What arguments against encouraging whistleblowers would you adopt?

Is the situation of whistleblowers really that bad? If it could be improved, what would you suggest?

Which of these theories and approaches would help reduce fraud in the U.S.?

---

659 Paul J. Zwier, *The Utility of a Nonconsequentialist Rationale for Civil-Jury-Awarded Punitive Damages,* 54 KAN. L. REV. 403, 440 (2006).

660 Laton McCartney, *Where There's Smoke, There's Fraud,* CFO Mag., Mar. 2011, LEXIS, News Library, Arcnws File, *available at* http://www.cfo.com/printable/article.cfm/14557373 (last visited Oct. 10, 2014).

The following case deals with the issue of reinstating employees whose employment was terminated for refusal to obey a suspected illegal order or support an illegal action.

This is an action for equitable relief brought in connection with a failed employment relationship. The plaintiffs, John Bechtel and Willie Jacques, assert that the defendant, Competitive Technologies, Inc. (CTI), terminated their employment in retaliation for conduct protected by § 806 of the Corporate and Criminal Fraud Accountability Act of 2002 (Sarbanes-Oxley Act), 18 U.S.C. § 1514A. The plaintiffs, joined by the intervening plaintiff United States Secretary of Labor, sought an injunction enforcing a preliminary order of the Secretary requiring CTI to reinstate the plaintiffs to their previous positions.

The issues presented were: (1) whether the court has subject matter jurisdiction to enforce a preliminary order of reinstatement under the *Sarbanes-Oxley Act*; and (2) whether enforcement requires the plaintiffs to prove the material elements required for a preliminary injunction. The court concluded that it had subject matter jurisdiction to enforce the Secretary's preliminary order and, further, the plaintiffs are entitled to this relief regardless of whether they have also met the standard for awarding injunctive relief. The application was therefore granted.[661]

On three separate occasions before their job terminations, Bechtel and Jacques raised concerns with several members of CTI's management concerning CTI's financial reporting and whether certain oral agreements entered into by the CEO John Nano with consultants were material and should be disclosed on the SEC reports and to the shareholders. The plaintiffs were told that any oral agreements were not material.

The materiality of these oral agreements was later . . . verified by their inclusion in the SEC 10-K report in July 2004. Following a disclosure meeting, the plaintiffs refused to sign off on the report because their concerns that the oral agreements had not been addressed. The CEO held a meeting with the plaintiffs and assured them that their concerns would be addressed by the next disclosure meeting and they finally signed off on the report. After the meeting the CEO's attitude towards the plaintiffs changed. He criticized and attempted to embarrass them at staff meetings and in front of co-workers. His hostility continued until they were terminated on June 30, 2003.

After the termination the plaintiffs filed the complaint with the Secretary of Labor pursuant to the Sarbanes-Oxley Act, *18 U.S.C. § 1514A(b)(1)(A), alleging* that CTI terminated their employment because of issues they raised at quarterly disclosure committee meetings. After CTI had responded to the allegations the Secretary issued a preliminary order finding that CTI violated the Sarbanes-Oxley Act, *18 U.S.C. § 1514A(b)(1)(A)*, and ordered CTI to "reinstate [Bechtel and

---

661 Bechtel v. Competitive Techs., Inc., 369 F. Supp. 2d 233 (D. Conn. 2005), *vacated, remanded,* 448 F.3d 469 (2d Cir. 2006). The legal issues in this case do not pertain to our topic, but the facts demonstrate the possible problems that arise in our context. Therefore, the case is mentioned.

Jacques] to the same positions and provide them with salaries and all other benefits commensurate with the position of vice president." CTI objected to the Secretary's preliminary finding and, pursuant to *C.F.R. § 1980.107*, requested a hearing before an administrative law judge. With this request, all provisions of the preliminary order [were] stayed, *except for the portion requiring preliminary reinstatement.* The portion of the preliminary order requiring reinstatement will be effective immediately upon the [defendant's] receipt of the findings and preliminary order, regardless of any objections to the order.

Although the rule required CTI to immediately reinstate [Bechtel and Jacques], CTI did not do so. Instead, CTI filed a motion to stay the reinstatement order. On May 29, 2005, the administrative law judge denied the motion. CTI has refused to comply with the preliminary order of reinstatement. In April 18, 2005, the plaintiffs filed suit in this court seeking enforcement of the preliminary order of reinstatement with an application for injunctive relief. On April 27, 2005, the court heard argument on the application.

"The plaintiffs, John Bechtel and Willie Jacques, joined by the United States Secretary of Labor, have applied for a preliminary injunction to enforce a preliminary order of the Secretary requiring CTI to reinstate them to their former positions. In response, CTI maintains that the court does not have subject matter jurisdiction to hear this case and that, even if it does, Bechtel and Jacques have failed to show entitlement to injunctive relief. The court considers each contention below.

A. Jurisdiction

The Sarbanes-Oxley Act "provides that no company subject to the *Securities Exchange Act of 1934* may retaliate against an employee who lawfully cooperates with an investigation concerning violations of the Act or fraud on the shareholders." An employee "who alleges discharge or other discrimination by any person in violation of [the Act] may seek relief . . . by (A) filing a complaint with the Secretary of Labor; or (B) if the Secretary has not issued a final decision within 180 days of the filing of the complaint and there is no showing that such delay is due to the bad faith of the claimant, [the claimant may] bring[] an action at law or equity for de novo review in the appropriate district court. . . . Under this provision, the Secretary of Labor conducts an investigation and determines whether reasonable cause exists to believe that a violation has occured. . . . "If the Secretary of Labor concludes that [such cause exists], the Secretary shall accompany the Secretary's findings with a preliminary order providing the relief prescribed by paragraph (3)(B) [i.e., the section governing final orders]."[662] The Act requires the defendant to reinstate the complainant to his former[663] position (including backpay) with the

---

662   49 U.S.C. § 42121(b)(2).

663   49 U.S.C. § 42121(b)(2)(A).

same compensation, terms, conditions, and privileges associated with his employment.[664] The employer has the right to file objections to the preliminary order and to a hearing before an administrative law judge on the merits of the retaliation claim. However, the filing of objections does not operate to stay any reinstatement remedy contained in the preliminary order.[665]

Although the court agreed with CTI that the agency has not issued a final order, the statute explicitly authorizes jurisdiction in this court to enforce a preliminary order as if it were a final order.[666] A finding to the contrary would negate the plain words of the statute that preliminary orders of reinstatement may not be stayed pending an appeal of the Secretary's order. Accordingly, the court concluded that it had jurisdiction to enforce the order of reinstatement of the plaintiffs.

B. Injunctive Relief.

CTI next argues that Bechtel and Jacques are not entitled to a preliminary injunction because they have failed to demonstrate the material elements for such relief. In response, Bechtel and Jacques, and the Secretary of Labor, argue that the elements for a preliminary injunction are not relevant here as they are entitled to an injunction based exclusively on the Secretary's findings. The court agrees with the plaintiffs.

The Sarbanes-Oxley Act makes it clear that the Secretary of Labor, and not the court, is authorized to make the determination of whether an order of reinstatement is appropriate. The statutory scheme is similar to the whistleblower protections under the Surface Transportation Assistance Act (STAA), now codified at 49 U.S.C. § 31105. Like the Sarbanes-Oxley Act, the STAA provides preliminary orders to protect whistleblowers. An employer under the STAA can obtain a hearing by filing objections to the reasonable cause finding.[667] Like Sarbanes-Oxley, however, the filing of objections does not result in a stay of the reinstatement order. In *Brock*, the Supreme Court observed that Congress could invest the Secretary of Labor with the authority to order reinstatement on the basis of an investigation, provided that the investigation met minimum due process standards that are not at issue in this case.[668] Accordingly, the court concludes that the plaintiffs are entitled to an injunction enforcing the Secretary's preliminary order regardless of whether the elements for preliminary injunctive relief have also been established.

---

664 49 U.S.C. § 42121(b) (3)(B) (ii).

665 *Id. See also* 29 C.F.R. § 1980.105 (c) ("the portion of any preliminary order requiring reinstatement will be effective immediately upon receipt of the findings and preliminary order[.]").

666 *See 49 U.S.C. § 42121(b)(2).*

667 49 U.S.C. § 31105(b)(2)(B).

668 *Brock v. Roadway Express, Inc., 481 U.S. 252, at 259 (1987). See id.* (the "statute reflects a careful balancing of the relevant interests of the Government, employee, and employer").

The Court granted the application for preliminary injunction and orders CTI to immediately reinstate Bechtel and Jacques to their former positions of employment with CTI. Further, the court orders CTI to pay Bechtel and Jacques all salary, benefits and other compensation that would have been earned had CTI complied with the preliminary order issued on February 2, 2005. It is so ordered this 13th day of May, 2005 at Hartford, Connecticut.

IV. PROFESSIONS IN SUPPORT OF COMPLIANCE

Two professions have an impact on the corporations' internal compliance: auditors and lawyers. Preeti Choudhary and other authors noted the role of public accounting firms in ensuring that financial and other information is prepared appropriately, accounting standards are applied, and financial statements are audited, and the role of attorneys in preparing and reviewing disclosure documents.[669] In addition, there are professional outside monitors that can act as compliance supervisors.

A. Privatizing the Monitoring of Banks and Investment Advisers

The Office of the Comptroller of the Currency (OCC) "uses its supervisory and enforcement authorities to ensure that national banks and federal savings associations (banks) operate in a safe and sound manner, provide non-discriminatory access to financial services, treat customers fairly, and comply with applicable laws and regulations. [T]he OCC and the other federal banking agencies (FBAs) have a broad range of supervisory and enforcement tools to achieve this purpose."[670] However, the OCC expects banks to outsource monitoring and use outside private entities. One such larger monitor is owned and managed by a former head of the OCC. Similarly, New York State's top regulator seeks to expand the use of independent monitors. The outside monitors may have skills that the regulators might not possess, as the complexity of large bank operations has risen in recent years.[671]

Using a tool that was employed traditionally for companies in financial trouble,[672] the New York regulator plans to utilize independent outside monitors as part of settlements with accused

---

669 Preeti Choudhary et al., *Boards, Auditors, Attorneys and Compliance with Mandatory SEC Disclosure Rules,* 34 MANAGERIAL & DECISION ECON. 471, 474 (2013), *available at* http://onlinelibrary.wiley.com/doi/10.1002/mde.2623/pdf (last visited Mar. 8, 2016).

670 *Outsourcing Accountability? Examining the Role of Independent Consultants: Hearing before the Subcomm. on Financial Institutions and Consumer Protection of the S. Comm. on Banking, Housing, and Urban Affairs, 113th Cong.* (2013), CONG. DOCUMENTS & PUBLICATIONS, LEXIS, News Lib, Arcnws File (testimony of Daniel Stipano, Deputy Chief Counsel, Office of the Comptroller of the Currency).

671 James Sterngold, *Regulator Wants Greater Use of Bank Monitors,* WALL ST. J., Nov. 6, 2014, at C1, LEXIS, News Library, Wsj File.

672 *Id.*

institutions. The regulator admitted that it lacks the skills of professional monitors. In the past, monitors were not as frequent visitors to the institutions as they are today. In addition, the monitors today focus not merely on past violations but also on how to prevent future violations, and on high-risk international relationships. The resort to expert monitors has been strengthened with the discovery of "holes" in compliance programs of defendant institutions. However, financial institutions spokespersons expressed doubts about the new use of outside monitors. After all these monitors would like to please those who hired them.[673] Unfortunately, outside monitors may have conflicts of interest and may conflict with the regulators. The monitors might be accused of providing a shield for the banks they monitor.

A conflict of this sort flared up between an outside monitor of banks. The CEO of this monitor headed a banking regulator in the past. The argument involved disclosure to the bank regulators of information that the private monitor had. After a few weeks of confrontation, the monitor "settled by paying $15 million to the Department of Financial Services," and "acknowledged that it did not follow the regulator's requirements for consultants." It also agreed to a voluntary six-month abstention from new consulting engagements that would require the use of confidential reports . . . ."[674] The liable bank settled for $340 million. The violation consisted of "hiding $250 billion of [prohibited] transactions for Iranian customers."[675]

––––––––––––

Discussion topic

How do you evaluate the new trend of outside monitors of banks?

B. The Role of Outsourced Compliance Programs for Investment Advisers

Rule 206(4)-7 under the Investment Advisers Act requires a registered investment adviser to designate an individual to administer its compliance policies and procedures (i.e., a Chief Compliance Officer (CCO)).[676]

In the Adopting Release, the SEC stated that the CCO "should be competent and knowledgeable regarding the Advisers Act and should be empowered with full responsibility and authority to develop and enforce appropriate policies and procedures for the firm." The SEC also noted

––––––––––

673 *Id.*

674 Christopher M. Matthews, *Promontory, State, Reach Pact, in About-Face,* Wall St. J., Aug. 19, 2015, at C2, LEXIS, News Library, Wsj File.

675 *Id.*

676 17 C.F.R. § 275.206(4)-7(c) (2016).

that the CCO "should have a position of sufficient seniority and authority within the organization to compel others to adhere to the compliance policies and procedures."[677]

The SEC clarified that "[t]he rule does not require advisers to hire an additional executive to serve as compliance officer, but rather to designate an individual as the adviser's chief compliance officer."[678]

Some firms provide outsourced compliance services for investment advisers. According to one firm's press release, the firm describes itself as "a full-service consultancy providing outsourced compliance programs and solutions to U.S. and offshore investment advisers."[679]The following is an excerpt from a Risk Alert issued by the SEC in November, 2015.

Examinations of Advisers and Funds That Outsource Their Chief Compliance Officers[680]

OCIE staff (the "staff") have noted a growing trend in the investment management industry: outsourcing compliance activities to third parties, such as consultants or law firms. Some investment advisers and funds have outsourced all compliance activities to unaffiliated third parties, including the role of their chief compliance officers ("CCOs"). Outsourced CCOs may perform key compliance responsibilities, such as updating firm policies and procedures, preparing regulatory filings, and conducting annual compliance reviews.

The staff conducted nearly 20 examinations as part of an Outsourced CCO Initiative that focused on SEC-registered investment advisers and investment companies (collectively, "registrants") that outsource their CCOs to unaffiliated third parties ("outsourced CCOs"). The purpose of this Risk Alert is to share the staff's observations from these examinations and raise awareness of the compliance issues observed by the staff.

1. Staff Examinations

CCOs are integral participants in OCIE's examinations of registrants. For example, each examination typically includes interviews with the CCO and other senior officers. During these interviews, the staff assesses the registrants' tone at the top and culture of compliance. These

---

677 Compliance Programs of Investment Companies and Investment Advisers, IA-2204, IC-26299 (Dec. 17, 2003), 68 Fed. Reg. 74,714, 74,720 (Dec. 24, 2003).

678 *Id.* at 74,720 n. 74.

679 EisnerAmper, *Experienced Compliance Team to Offer Wide Range of Services to SEC-Registered Investment Advisers and Broker-Dealers* (June 16, 2014), *available at* http://www.eisneramper.com/compliance-regulatory-services-0614/ (last visited Jan. 27, 2017).

680 Ofc. of Compliance Inspections & Examinations, U.S. Sec. & Exch. Conn'n, *Examinations of Advisers and Funds That Outsource Their Chief Compliance Officers*, RISK ALERT, Nov. 9, 2015, *available at* https://www.sec.gov/ocie/announcement/ocie-2015-risk-alert-cco-outsourcing.pdf (last visited June 14, 2017). Footnotes omitted.

assessments are important factors in the staff's review of the effectiveness of the registrants' compliance programs in which a CCO plays an important role.

As part of the Outsourced CCO Initiative, the staff evaluated the effectiveness of registrants' compliance programs and outsourced CCOs by considering, among other things, whether:

- the CCO was administering a compliance environment that addressed and supported the goals of the Advisers Act, Investment Company Act, and other federal securities laws, as applicable (i.e., compliance risks were appropriately identified, mitigated, and managed);
- the compliance program was reasonably designed to prevent, detect, and address violations of the Advisers Act, Investment Company Act, and other federal securities laws, as applicable;
- the compliance program supported open communication between service providers and those with compliance oversight responsibilities;
- the compliance program appeared to be proactive rather than reactive;
- the CCO appeared to have sufficient authority to influence adherence with the registrant's compliance policies and procedures, as adopted, and was allocated sufficient resources to perform his or her responsibilities; and
- compliance appeared to be an important part of the registrant's culture.

2. Staff Observations

During these examinations, the staff observed instances where the outsourced CCO was generally effective in administering the registrant's compliance program, as well as fulfilling his/her other responsibilities as CCO. The staff observations regarding effective, outsourced CCOs generally involved: regular, often in-person, communication between the CCOs and the registrants; strong relationships established between the CCOs and the registrants; sufficient registrant support of the CCOs; sufficient CCO access to registrants' documents and information; and CCO knowledge about the regulatory requirements and the registrants' business. More specifically, the staff observed the following.

- Communications: Outsourced CCOs who frequently and personally interacted with advisory and fund employees (in contrast with impersonal interaction, such as electronic communication or pre-defined checklists) appeared to have a better understanding of the registrants' businesses, operations, and risks. As a result, at these registrants the staff noted fewer inconsistencies between the compliance policies and procedures and the registrants' actual business practices. The staff also noted that these CCOs were typically able to effectuate compliance changes that they deemed to be necessary.

- Resources: More significant compliance-related issues were identified at registrants with an outsourced CCO that served as the CCO for numerous unaffiliated firms and that did not appear to have sufficient resources to perform compliance duties, especially given the disparate and dispersed nature of the registrants that the CCO serviced.

- Empowerment: Annual reviews performed by outsourced CCOs, who were able to independently obtain the records they deemed necessary for conducting such reviews, more accurately reflected the registrants' actual practices than annual reviews conducted by CCOs, who relied wholly on the firm to select the records subject to their review. In some instances, the registrants' employees had discretion to determine which documents were provided to the outsourced CCOs. In these cases, the registrants' ability to selectively provide records to the outsourced CCO may have affected the accuracy of these registrants' annual reviews.

The staff's observations with respect to the strength and effectiveness of the registrants' compliance programs are described in further detail below.

3. Meaningful Risk Assessments

The staff observed that an effective compliance program generally relies upon, among other things, the correct identification of a registrant's risks in light of its business, operations, conflicts, and other compliance factors. The compliance policies and procedures should then be designed to address those risks. The staff observed that certain outsourced CCOs could not articulate the business or compliance risks of the registrant or, to the extent the risks were identified, whether the registrant had adopted written policies and procedures to mitigate or address those risks. In some instances, the risks described to the staff by the registrant's principals were different than the risks described by the outsourced CCO. In these instances, the staff identified several areas where the registrant did not appear to have policies, procedures, and/or disclosures in place necessary to address certain risks.

- Standardized checklists: The staff notes that some outsourced CCOs used standardized checklists to gather pertinent information regarding the registrants. While the use of questionnaires or standardized checklists may be a helpful guide to identify conflicts and assess risks at registrants, the staff observed the following:

- Some standardized risk checklists utilized by outsourced CCOs were generic and did not appear to fully capture the business models, practices, strategies, and compliance risks that were applicable to the registrant.
- Some of the responses to the standardized questionnaires completed by the registrants included incorrect or inconsistent information about the firms' business practices. The outsourced CCOs did not appear sufficiently knowledgeable about the registrant to identify or follow-up with the registrant to resolve such discrepancies.

- Policies, procedures, and disclosures: Several registrants did not appear to have the policies, procedures, or disclosures in place necessary to address all of the conflicts of interest identified by the staff. These issues were identified in critical areas that affect the registrants' clients, such as compensation practices, portfolio valuation, brokerage and execution, and personal securities transactions by access persons.

4. Compliance Policies and Procedures

Although the Compliance Rules do not expressly require compliance policies and procedures to contain specific elements, the Commission stated in the Adopting Release that it expects an adviser's policies and procedures, at a minimum, to address ten core areas to the extent that they are relevant to the adviser's business. The staff observed certain instances where the registrants did not appear to have adopted, implemented, and/or adhered to policies and procedures that were reasonably designed to prevent the violation of applicable regulations or that were relevant in light of the registrant's business and operations, such as the following.

- Compliance policies and procedures were not followed. The staff observed instances in which compliance policies and procedures were not followed or the registrants' actual practices were not consistent with the description in the registrants' compliance manuals. These practices were observed in areas that are required to be reviewed by regulations (e.g., reviews required for the payment of cash for solicitation activities and personal securities transactions) and in areas that registrants included in their policies and procedures, but that are not expressly required to be reviewed by regulations (e.g., quarterly review of employees' e-mails). In many instances, the outsourced CCOs were designated as the individuals responsible for conducting the reviews.
- Compliance policies and procedures were not tailored to registrants' businesses or practices. Several of the compliance manuals that the staff reviewed were created using outsourced CCO-provided templates. However, some of these templates

were not tailored to registrants' businesses and practices and, thus, the compliance manuals that had been adopted contained policies and procedures that were not appropriate or applicable to the registrants' businesses or practices. Examples include:

- Critical areas were not identified, and thus certain compliance policies and procedures were not adopted, such as reviewing third-party managers hired to manage client money, or safeguarding client information.
- Policies were adopted, but were not applicable to the advisers' businesses and operations, such as: monitoring of account performance composites when in practice the adviser did not monitor composites because it did not advertise performance; collecting management fees quarterly in advance when in practice clients were billed monthly in arrears; and referencing departed employees as responsible parties in performing compliance reviews or monitoring.
- Critical control procedures were not performed, or not performed as described, including: oversight of private fund fee and expense allocations; reviews of solicitation activities for compliance with the Advisers Act; trade allocation reviews for fairness of side-by-side management of client accounts with proprietary accounts; oversight of performance advertising and marketing; personal trading reviews of all access persons; and controls over trade reconciliations.

5. Annual Review of the Compliance Programs

For the registrants examined, the outsourced CCOs were typically responsible for conducting and documenting registrants' annual reviews, which included testing for compliance with existing policies and procedures. The staff, however, observed a general lack of documentation evidencing the testing.

In addition, the staff notes that certain outsourced CCOs infrequently visited registrants' offices and conducted only limited reviews of documents or training on compliance-related matters while on-site. Such CCOs had limited visibility and prominence within the registrants' organization, which appeared to result in the CCOs also having limited authority within the organization to, among other things, improve adherence to the registrants' compliance policies and procedures. Limited authority also appeared to affect the outsourced CCOs' ability to implement important changes in disclosure regarding key areas of client interest, such as advisory fees.

During these examinations, the staff observed certain compliance weaknesses associated with registrants that outsourced their CCOs, as described in this Risk Alert. Advisers and funds with outsourced CCOs should review their business practices in light of the risks noted in this Risk Alert to determine whether these practices comport with their responsibilities as set forth in the Compliance Rules. The staff anticipates that, by sharing these examination observations, it will assist registrants in assessing whether their compliance programs have weaknesses, particularly with respect to identifying applicable risks and ensuring that the firm's compliance program encompasses all relevant business activities.

A CCO, either as a direct employee of a registrant or as a contractor or consultant, must be empowered with sufficient knowledge and authority to be effective. Each registrant is ultimately responsible for adopting and implementing an effective compliance program and is accountable for its own deficiencies. Registrants, particularly those that use outsourced CCOs, may want to consider the issues identified in this Risk Alert to evaluate whether their business and compliance risks have been appropriately identified, that their policies and procedures are appropriately tailored in light of their business and associated risks, and that their CCO is sufficiently empowered within the organization to effectively perform his/her responsibilities. The staff observed fewer compliance-related issues at the registrants examined that had developed appropriate controls in each of the areas identified in this Risk Alert.

Discussion Topics

Which would you prefer: outsourcing the function of monitoring or having the institution establish a monitoring system? What are the advantages and disadvantages in each of the systems? What are the conditions that might help determine the type of system that a particular institution should install?

How do you evaluate the new trend?

Chapter 13

Assessing Compliance in Light of Failures

In this chapter, we learn about four significant failures of institutional self-regulation. Our main focus is on the laws that were violated and the compliance failures. Focusing on the failures, we seek the source of the failures: were they legal, business, financial, or human? And as is our practice, we ask how these failures could have been avoided.

I. THE COLLAPSE OF BARINGS BANK IN 1995[681]

In 1995 the Barings Bank was the oldest and most venerable investment bank in Great Britain, listing the Queen of England among its clients. The bank's pedigree was so distinguished that it did not have a logo: it had a crest! But to survive in the late 20th century, Barings called upon young, ambitious traders who knew the instruments of global finance, such as derivatives. Among these hungry young climbers was Nick Leeson, the son of a plasterer. Starting out in Barings' back office, he proved to be adept at understanding the derivatives market and soon was stationed in Singapore, betting on market shifts around the world. At one point, his speculations accounted for 10% of Barings profits. He was a star!

But Leeson knew how to manipulate the internal system as well. He created a secret Barings account, whose losses the bank automatically covered. He could do that because his girlfriend was working in the back-office that booked, oversaw, and specified the value of Leeson's trades. Thus, Leeson was able to cover his increasing losses. His girlfriend may have been instrumental in effectuating the fraud. A properly enforced relationship policy, and perhaps an insurance against such risk, may have mitigated or avoided the scandal.

Leeson started risking huge amounts of money on Japan's stock market, the Nikkei, betting that the price of stocks would rise. Instead, the Kobe earthquake on January 17, 1995 sent prices crashing down. Leeson's losses mounted quickly until he realized they would swamp not only himself but all of Barings as well. Indeed, the losses were more than $1 billion, an amount the bank could not cover. The bank collapsed that March and was bought by a Dutch financial company for GBP 1. Leeson fled Singapore but was captured and extradited back to Singapore,

---

681 Howard Chua-Eoan, *The Collapse of Barings Bank, 1995*, Time, Mar. 01, 2007, *available at* http://content.time.com/time/specials/packages/article/0,28804,1937349_1937350_1937488,00.html (last visited Oct. 23, 2016).

where he served six and a half years in jail for fraud. He is now the manager of a soccer team in Scotland.

_____

Discussion Topics and Reading Focus

What were the flaws in the Barings Bank compliance system? How could they have been remedied?

Could purchasing insurance against such a risk mitigate or avoid the fall of Barings Bank? To answer this question, view the following description of an examination process concerning a bank's compliance adequacy.[682]

As you read through these examination directives, how, if at all, could these directives have changed the result of the Barings case disaster? The following directives apply to different laws that require banks to be vigilant. After all, they are the pathways of money throughout the world.

_____

II. THE JPMORGAN CASE: SIGNALS OF FAILURE

The banking firm JPMorgan Chase (JPMorgan) had officers in charge of risk, legal, and compliance functions under the authority of other business officers. The chief compliance officer reported to general counsel. In addition to the supervisors of the trader, who managed to cause the banks a loss of about $6 billion, there were other active traders engaged in similar activities as well.

An investor action against JPMorgan includes the following description:

> This action arises from JPMorgan's [the "Company's"] representations about the risk-management role of [the Chief Investment Office (CIO)] and the trading losses incurred by CIO's SCP in 2012. CIO is a business unit within JPMorgan that is primarily responsible for managing the risks arising from imbalances between JPMorgan's loans (assets) and deposits (liabilities). During the financial crisis, JPMorgan's excess deposits increased significantly due to the bank's perceived financial stability. By the beginning of 2012, CIO's investment-securities portfolio was a significant component of JPMorgan's overall assets and held more than $350 billion of assets, up from $76 billion at the end of 2007. Plaintiffs allege that JPMorgan's representations concerning the

_____

682 FED. FIN. INSTITUTIONS EXAMINATION COUNCIL, BANK SECRECY ACT ANTI-MONEY LAUNDERING EXAMINATION MANUAL, _available at_ https://www.ffiec.gov/bsa_aml_infobase/pages_manual/manual_online.htm (last visited Apr. 27, 2017).

risk management activities of CIO were false and that by the start of the Class Period, Defendant [CEO James "Jamie"] Dimon had "secretly transformed the CIO from a risk management unit into a proprietary trading desk whose principal purpose was to engage in speculative, high-risk bets designed to generate profits."Plaintiffs allege that in order to facilitate "the aggressive trading required to meet Dimon's profit objectives," CIO removed some of the risk limits on the SCP. In particular, the Company removed the "stop loss limits" that previously required CIO traders to exit positions when losses reached $20 million, and allegedly did not impose any risk limits on the SCP—despite public assurances to the contrary. Plaintiffs allege that Defendants took additional steps to keep CIO's aggressive trading a secret, such as excluding executives from CIO's risk meetings and terminating executives who pushed for risk controls.

Plaintiffs' primary allegations concern the [synthetic credit portfolio ("SCP")], the London-based portfolio that was managed by CIO and incurred significant losses in 2012. The "primary purpose" of the SCP was "to provide a partial offset to losses [JPMorgan] would suffer elsewhere in CIO, and the Company in a stressed credit environment." The SCP was a multi-billion dollar portfolio managed by a London-based trader named Bruno Iksil. The SCP eventually became CIO's "largest position" during the Class Period, and constituted such a large part of the market for synthetic-credit derivatives that, by the end of 2009, Iksil's positions were illiquid. By the start of the Class Period in early 2010, the illiquidity risk presented by the SCP was so severe that a senior JPMorgan executive allegedly prepared a report documenting the need for a $2 to $4 billion reserve to guard against losses in CIO. JPMorgan did not establish such a reserve for CIO, and Plaintiffs allege that, as a result, the Company's net income was overstated by billions of dollars throughout the Class Period. The SCP continued to grow during the Class Period and so did the risk for the portfolio. The Company's model for measuring risk, known as "value at risk" or "VaR," which measured how much money a trade could lose on a given day, showed that at one point during the Class Period the SCP could lose as much money in a single day as the hundreds of positions in the Company's Investment Bank.

Plaintiffs allege that by no later than mid-2011, JPMorgan knew that the SCP portfolio had grown to a "perilous size" such that the Company's publicly reported VaR would spike if accurately calculated and reported. Plaintiffs allege that in order to conceal the true purpose of and risk associated with CIO, JPMorgan developed a new VaR model that was designed to artificially lower CIO's VaR. Plaintiffs allege that Defendant Dimon personally approved the development of this new model, and its implementation in January 2012. Plaintiffs further allege that using the new model, JPMorgan reported in the first quarter of 2012 that CIO's VaR was virtually unchanged from the prior quarter when, in truth, the original VaR model showed that the risk of loss had doubled. Defendants did not disclose that CIO's VaR model had been changed in either JPMorgan's 2011 annual report or when announcing results for the first quarter of 2012, after the changes were made.

In the spring of 2012, the media first reported that CIO had amassed a portfolio of credit derivatives so large that Bruno Iksil, a London-based trader who helped manage the portfolio, had been nicknamed the "London Whale" by credit derivatives traders. Plaintiffs allege that although losses in the SCP had already reached $1.2 billion, and internal JPMorgan reports were warning that the SCP could lose as much as $9 billion, Defendants mounted a public relations campaign to falsely assure investors and downplay concerns about proprietary trading in CIO. CEO [Jamie] Dimon famously called the news reports about the portfolio a "tempest in a teapot" during an April 13, 2012 earnings call.[683].

Following the housing crisis, J.P. Morgan faced regulatory enforcement actions and investigations regarding allegations concerning, e.g., improper trading, mortgage bond sales practices, and overseas hiring.[684] [T]op examiners from the Office of the Comptroller of the Currency and the Federal Reserve told [the top executive of J.P. Morgan] and his board that they had lost trust in management."[685]

Regulators charged JPMorgan with maintaining inadequate controls in connection with the "London Whale" trades. "[A] massive trading bet in London . . . had gone wrong" and "[t]he losses . . . stemmed from bad bets in [the bank's] Chief Investment Office, which manages risk for the bank."[686] The SEC examined a number of individuals who might have been responsible for failed internal controls, whether due to negligence or outright fraud.[687] Internally, however, there may have been no negligence or fraud. If leadership was knowingly accepting or outright ignoring the high-risk brokers' activities in order to pursue profits, it may be a case of failed compliance.

During 2013, JPMorgan negotiated with the U.S. and other governments about the $6 billion losses resulting from one of its traders' activities, and other failures that were very costly to the investors of the bank and, to some extent, to the U.S. Government. The next step was to reserve anticipated payments for the legal fees, judgments, and fines that were bound to come.[688] As noted by Monica Langley, after the tremendous losses at JPMorgan the bank planned "to spend an additional $4 billion and commit 5,000 extra employees this year to clean up its risk and compliance problems," according to sources. JPMorgan "is spending an additional $1.5 billion

---

683 *In re* JPMorgan Chase & Co. Sec. Litig., No. 12 Civ. 03852 (GBD), 2014 U.S. Dist. LEXIS 44050, at *7-11 (S.D.N.Y. Mar. 31, 2014) (citations omitted).

684 Monica Langley & Dan Fitzpatrick. *Embattled J.P. Morgan Bulks Up Oversight,* Wall St. J., Sept. 13, 2013, at A1, LEXIS, News Library, Wsj File.

685 Monica Langley & Dan Fitzpatrick, *Embattled J.P. Morgan Bulks Up Oversight,* Wall St. J., Sept. 13, 2013, at A1, LEXIS, News Library, Wsj File.

686 Robin Sidel et al., *J.P. Morgan Faces a Hard-Line SEC,* Wall St. J., Sept. 20, 2013, at C1, LEXIS, News Library, Wsj File.

687 Scott Patterson & Jamila Trindle, *Pact Unveils New Details on 'Whale' Trades,* Wall St. J., Oct. 17, 2013, at C3, LEXIS, News Library, Wsj File.

688 Dan Fitzpatrick & Saabira Chauhjuri, *Buffer for Legal Tab Batters J.P. Morgan,* Wall St. J., Oct. 12, 2013, at B1

on managing risk and complying with regulations, including a 30% increase in risk-control staffing" and "expects to add $2.5 billion to its litigation reserves in the second half of the year," according to sources.[689]

The result was a far tighter compliance program within the bank. This included assigning responsibility to many top management people, and allocating significant funds to the compliance program. First, the CEO put the "most senior executives in charge of separate elements of the regulatory problems," establishing "some 50 meetings per month between those executives and various regulators." Hearing the same story from the regulators may have been an important and helpful lesson for the executives.[690] Yet, perhaps meetings or more meetings alone may not solve problems. Perhaps in addition to meetings there is a need for actions, and what is said in the meetings might be given weight and lead to actions. In sum, it depends on what happens not only at the meetings but also as a result of the meetings.

Second, JPMorgan had officers in charge of risk, legal, and compliance functions under the authority of other business officers. The chief compliance officer reported to the general counsel. When JPMorgan faced regulatory enforcement actions and investigations,[691] the executives in charge of risk controls, legal decisions, and compliance were granted greater authority: they could no longer be overruled by the heads of the business groups. JPMorgan's risk and internal controls managers were vested with greater autonomy than similar managers in other banks. For example, JPMorgan shifted the reporting lines so that its top compliance officer reports to the bank's chief operating officer, not the general counsel, in contrast to the power structure in other banks.

Third, there was heightened recognition of the importance of compliance. "Fixing our controls issues is job No. 1," Chief Executive Officer James Dimon said in an interview. "This is a huge investment of people, time, and money . . . but it will make us stronger in the long run."[692]

Fourth, the issue of the status of compliance officers was raised.[693] Needless to say, the chances of preventing trading losses are lower if risk managers don't report to conflicted executives.

Fifth, the responsibilities for compliance were reallocated. "Mr. Dimon has assigned each major executive a companywide 'control initiative,' such as anti-money-laundering and an annual regulatory assessment of the bank's ability to weather a future crisis. The executives are accountable for the results of each initiative." "A turning point came earlier this summer at a

---

689 Monica Langley & Dan Fitzpatrick, *Embattled J.P. Morgan Bulks Up Oversight*, WALL ST. J., Sept. 13, 2013, at A1, LEXIS, News Library, Wsj File.

690 *Id.* ("In April top examiners from the Office of the Comptroller of the Currency and the Federal Reserve told Mr. Dimon and his board that they had lost trust in management, said people familiar with the meeting.").

691 Monica Langley & Dan Fitzpatrick. *Embattled J.P. Morgan Bulks Up Oversight*, WALL ST. J., Sept. 13, 2013, at A1, LEXIS, News Library, Wsj File.

692 *Id.*

693 Scott Patterson et al., *J.P. Morgan 'Whale' Hunt Isn't Over*, WALL ST. J., Sept. 18, 2013, at C1, LEXIS, News Library, Wsj File. See the discussion in Chapter 2.

two-day executive-strategy retreat in Martha's Vineyard. Business chiefs invited their control managers for briefings. Compliance and controls groups came away empowered as equals to their business counterparts."[694]

What specific actions were taken? "While grappling with how to fix its internal-control breakdowns, JPMorgan's senior management broke a cardinal rule of corporate governance and deprived its board of critical information it needed to fully assess the company's problems and determine whether accurate and reliable information was being disclosed to investors and regulators . . . . Among the lapses JPMorgan admitted to as part of its settlement with the SEC was keeping its board, particularly its independent audit committee, in the dark about the status of the trades even as losses mounted."[695] Arguably, boards must rely on the corporation's operational officers. In fact, the board members cannot or would not seek the details of the issues. They receive the broad picture. However, board members should be able to sense when something may be wrong and ask the right questions that lead to particular relevant details.

Mr. Dimon shook up his management team as he had noticed "which executives ran to the fire, and which ones ran from it." In fact, on February 23, 2016 the *Wall Street Journal* published an article entitled: "J.P. Morgan Is Quietly Testing Blockchain Technology." The purpose of this mechanism is to test read trades and allay the investors' concerns.[696]

JPMorgan dedicated large sums of money to improving compliance. The most "'controls-related expenses' stem[med] from new staffing." J.P. Morgan planned to add thousands of people to the bank's control staff to work on legal and regulatory matters, including an additional 2,000 employees to supervise inside their business units.[697] "J.P. Morgan also has provided 750,000 hours of training on regulatory and control issues. The bank hired consultants from McKinsey & Co., Ernst & Young, and other firms."[698]

Fines added to the price of the compliance failure. JPMorgan admitted to wrongdoing. Two former traders have been indicted, and Bruno Iksil, the "London Whale," signed a non-prosecution agreement. The CFTC (Commodity Future Trading Commission) investigation focused on price manipulation, as JPMorgan held a large position in one index of derivatives. Arguably "J.P. Morgan's big move into the index . . . effectively manipulated prices by dramatically increasing the demand."[699]

---

694 Monica Langley & Dan Fitzpatrick. *Embattled J.P. Morgan Bulks Up Oversight,* WALL ST. J., Sept. 13, 2013, at A1, LEXIS, News Library, Wsj File.

695 Robin Sidel et al., *J.P. Morgan Faces a Hard-Line SEC,* WALL ST. J., Sept. 20, 2013, at C1, LEXIS, News Library, Wsj File.

696 Emily Glazer, *J.P.Morgan Is Quietly Testing Blockchain Technology,* WALL ST. J., Feb. 23, 2016, at C3, LEXIS, News Library, Wsj File.

697 Monica Langley & Dan Fitzpatrick, *Embattled J.P. Morgan Bulks Up Oversight,* WALL ST. J., Sept. 13, 2013, at A1, LEXIS, News Library, Wsj File.

698 *Id.*

699 Scott Patterson et al., *J.P. Morgan 'Whale' Hunt Isn't Over,* WALL ST. J., Sept. 18, 2013, at C1, LEXIS, News Library, Wsj File.

Prosecutors agreed not to charge Bruno Iksil, the "London Whale," in exchange for his cooperation. Two other former traders were indicted.[700] Iksil avoided prosecution by providing incriminating evidence about his superiors. Ask whether granting the trader immunity may "prevent incidents in the future, as firms already have controls in place but traders may still be able to conceal losses."[701] After all, traders have an incentive to take risks that may pay off. If they are granted immunity, traders will have an incentive but no disincentive to take risks as management will be blamed.[702]

JPMorgan agreed to pay a fine to settle with U.S. and U.K. regulators over the "London Whale" scandal. In addition, the SEC is investigating individual employees, and "refused to negotiate the amount of the fine," according to sources, which "represents an unusually tough stance by the SEC." The consent order "contained uncommonly strong language" and made many references to "senior management."[703]

Discussion topics

In your opinion, how effective are board meetings? In light of the compliance steps it has taken, do you believe that in the future JPMorgan would avoid disasters of the sort that it has experienced?

To what extent can the board of directors be effective in preventing similar disasters? What precisely can it do to be effective?

Are there any other elements that might make compliance difficult to achieve?

What in your opinion would change the behavior of personnel and management within JPMorgan?

The New Millenium Cash Exchange Inc.

The Financial Crimes Enforcement Network has determined that grounds exist to assess civil money penalty against New Millenium Cash Exchange, Inc. (NMCE or MSB) and its President and Owner, Flor Angella Lopez (Ms. Lopez), pursuant to the Bank Secrecy Act and regulations issued pursuant to that Act.

---

700 *Id.*

701 Stephen R. Etherington, *The 'London Whale' vs. the Big-Fish Strategy*, WALL ST. J., Sept. 20, 2013, at A15, LEXIS, News Library, Wsj File.

702 *Id.*

703 Robin Sidel et al., *J.P. Morgan Faces a Hard-Line SEC*, WALL ST. J., Sept. 20, 2013, at C1, LEXIS, News Library, Wsj File.

. . .

The Financial Crimes Enforcement Network conducted an investigation and determined that, since at least February 2008, NMCE and Ms. Lopez willfully violated the Bank Secrecy Act's program, reporting, and recordkeeping requirements.

These violations included:

(A) Failure to register as a money service business, including submission of filings with inaccurate information regarding the services rendered by the MSB;

(B) Violations of the requirement to establish and implement an effective written anti-money laundering program; including

> (1) Lack of adequate AML programs for its check cashing and money order activities as well as its currency exchange transactions;
> (2) Inadequate policies, procedures and internal controls (a) to verify the identities of persons conducting transactions; (b) to monitor for suspicious activities; (c) to identify currency transactions exceeding $10,000; and (d) to ensure that NMCE filed the required currency transaction reports (CTRs);
> (3) Inadequate internal controls for creating and retaining adequate Bank Secrecy Act records related to currency exchange;
> (4) Failure to conduct a Bank Secrecy Act/AML risk assessment of the MSB and failure to include "red flags" in the MSB's procedures for each type of business;
> (5) Failure to recognize the potential conflicts of interest in establishing a relationship with a consultant that: (a) created NMCE's written AML program, (b) performed the only independent testing of the AML program, and (c) provided the only source of Bank Secrecy Act training for the MSB; such training used a generic module that was provided by the consultant that also created its written AML program; the training was not comprehensive and was not tailored to the MSB's specific business lines and associated risk.

(C) Violations of the reporting and recordkeeping requirements; including (1) filing 51 CTRs significantly late and (2) failure to file at least 149 CTRs for exchanges of currency with other financial institutions.[704]

---

704 Excerpted from *In re* New Milenium Cash Exchange, Inc. (Apr. 23, 2014), *available at* https://www.fincen.gov/sites/default/files/shared/NMCE%20Assessment.pdf (last visited Oct. 20, 2016).

Discussion topics

Are the steps taken to prevent such violations in the future similar to the steps taken by JPMorgan? How would you distinguish the wrongs committed and the steps taken?

M&T Bank Corporation (M&T), a bank holding company, and a subsidiary, Manufacturers & Traders Trust Company (Bank), a state-chartered bank, entered into a Written Agreement with the Federal Reserve Bank of New York (the "Reserve Bank") on June 17, 2013. M&T also owns nonbank subsidiaries including Wilmington Trust Company (WTC).

The Agreement followed an inspection by the Reserve Bank which identified deficiencies in M&T's firm-wide compliance risk management program with respect to compliance with anti-money laundering laws, rules, and regulations including the Bank Secrecy Act (BSA/AML Requirements), the Bank's internal controls, customer due diligence procedures, and transaction monitoring processes with respect to compliance with BSA/AML Requirements; and WTC's due diligence practices for foreign correspondent accounts.

Under the Agreement, M&T adopted a firm-wide compliance risk management program for its subsidiaries, including the Bank, designed to identify and manage compliance risks related to BSA/AML Requirements. M&T also agreed to conduct customer due diligence and transaction monitoring on behalf of its subsidiaries.

M&T agreed to submit to the Reserve Bank an acceptable revised written firm-wide BSA/AML compliance program that describes the specific actions that will be taken, including time-lines for completion, to ensure compliance with applicable BSA/AML Requirements. The revised program shall, at a minimum, among other requirements, include the findings and recommendations of the consultant recently engaged by M&T to assist in matters related to compliance with the BSA/AML Requirements.

In addition, the Bank agreed to engage an independent consultant, acceptable to the Reserve Bank, to conduct a review of account and transaction activity associated with any high-risk customer accounts conducted at, by, or through the Bank and WTC from July 1, 2012 to December 31, 2012 to determine whether suspicious activity involving high risk customer accounts or transactions at, by, or through the Bank or WTC was properly identified and reported in accordance with applicable suspicious activity reporting regulations (the "Transaction Review"). Based on the Reserve Bank's evaluation of the results of the Transaction Review, the Reserve Bank may direct the Bank to engage the independent consultant to conduct a review of account and transaction activity associated with any high risk customer accounts for additional time periods.[705]

---

705 Excerpted from Bd. of Governors of Fed. Reserve Sys., Written Agreement by and Among M&T Bank Corp. et al. (June 17, 2013), *available at* http://www.federalreserve.gov/newsevents/press/enforcement/enf20130617a1.pdf (last visited Mar. 3, 2016).

Discussion topics

What violations did M&T commit? What changes did it agree to install?

Do these changes match the past wrongs?

Would you recommend other changes instead of or in conjunction with the newly installed changes?

III. THE JEROME KERVIEL CASE

In 2008 the headlines noted: "'Rogue' French trader must pay $6.7 billion for fraud." "Jerome Kerviel will also serve a minimum three-year jail term." "This French trader was accused of masterminding one of history's biggest trading frauds and costing one of France's largest banks billions in losses."[706]

Kerviel, a former index futures trader at Societe Generale SA, was convicted of "charges related to the claim that he covered up bets worth nearly EUR 50 billion, or more than the bank was worth." Kerviel held "a job on the futures desk where he invested the bank's money by hedging on European equity market indices."

"During the proceedings, both sides admitted to mistakes but Kerviel insisted his bank superiors knew what he was doing." "Societe Generale's former chairman acknowledged there were problems in monitoring the trader's work." Yet Kerviel bet in amounts that were higher than the bank's total market value. He bet on futures contracts on three European equity indices. But he balanced his real trades with fictitious transactions, so his net position was "unremarkable."

"Societe Generale's former chairman acknowledged there were problems in monitoring the trader's work, and an internal report by the bank found managers failed to follow up on 74 different alarms about Kerviel's activities."[707]

The court held that "Kerviel acted without the bank's knowledge"; "it was 'obvious' none of his bosses would have allowed him to bet sums exceeding the bank's capital." The court also stated that he "endangered the solvency" of the bank. No one else was charged in the case. The bank's CEO Daniel Bouton and its head of investment banking Jean-Pierre Mustier resigned.[708] Yet, this part of the decision was not closed. On June 8, 2016 the *Wall Street Journal* reported that a labor court ordered Societe Generale to pay Jerome Kerveil $511,000 because he was "fired without real or serious cause." The judge held that the bank "could not pretend it hadn't long

---

[706] Greg Keller, *'Rogue' French Trader Must Pay $6.7 Billion for Fraud*, SALON, .Oct. 5, 2010, *available at* http://www.salon.com/2010/10/05/eu_france_trader_on_trial/ (last visited Mar. 21, 2016).

[707] *French Trader Hit with $6.7 Billion Fraud Fine*, CBS NEWS, Oct. 5, 2010, *available at* http://www.cbsnews.com/news/french-trader-hit-with-67-billion-fraud-fine/.

[708] *Id.*

been aware of the unauthorized trades conducted by Mr. Kerviel." Needless to say, the bank contested this finding.[709]

_____

Discussion Topic

Kerviel was accused of making enormous bets on three European equity indexes, and masking the size of his bets by recording fictitious offsetting transactions. Yet, hedging against an internal position is what brokers sometimes do. How do you distinguish one such transaction from the other?

Do you believe that Kerviel acted without management's knowledge?

_____

Discussion topics

*Compare the London Whale case with the Kerviel and Leeson cases. The London Whale was hedging; were the other two hedging as well? Why would anyone trade like this?

*In terms of compliance, how are these cases similar and how are they different? If they are similar, do losses, per se, mean wrongful behavior?

*What precisely did either of these traders do wrong?

Saddle River Valley Bank

[On September 24, 2013] The Financial Crimes Enforcement Network (FinCEN) announced the assessment of a $4.1 million civil money penalty against Saddle River Valley Bank in Saddle River, New Jersey. FinCEN has determined that the bank violated several provisions of the Bank Secrecy Act (BSA) from 2009 through May 2011. The Bank has consented to the assessment.

Working with the Office of the Comptroller of the Currency (OCC) and the U.S. Attorney's Office for the District of New Jersey, FinCEN concluded that the bank willfully violated aspects of the BSA's program, recordkeeping, and reporting requirements by lacking an effective anti-money laundering (AML) program reasonably designed to manage the risks of money laundering and other illicit activity, failing to conduct adequate due diligence on foreign correspondent accounts, and failing to detect and adequately report in a timely manner suspicious activities in the accounts of foreign money exchange houses, also known as "casas de cambio." The Bank

_____

709 Noemie Bisserbe, *SocGen Ordered to Pay Rogue Trader*, WALL ST. J., June 8, 2016, at C1, C2.

executed $1.5 billion worth of inadequately monitored transactions on behalf of Mexican and Dominican casas de cambio despite publicly available information, such as a FinCEN advisory, that provided ample notice of the heightened risks of dealing with these institutions.

"It's pretty remarkable that a small community bank in suburban New Jersey was attracting more than a billion dollars in transactions with customers in Mexico and the Dominican Republic, and nobody thought it was too good to be true," FinCEN Director Jennifer Shasky Calvery said. "Banks of all sizes, in any part of the country, may be tempted by such lucrative ventures. However, banks must use common sense in evaluating customer risk or seemingly lucrative business could become quite the opposite."

FinCEN's penalty is concurrent with a $4.1 million civil money penalty assessed by the OCC, and will be satisfied by one payment of $4.1 million to the U.S. Department of the Treasury. In addition, the U.S. Attorney's Office for the District of New Jersey will collect $4.1 million from the bank through civil asset forfeiture. The bank ceased operations in 2012 and the combined collection amount of $8.2 million represents the majority of its remaining assets.[710]

[Further,] Saddle River Valley Bank (SRVB) agreed [on September 24, 2013] to resolve civil claims brought by the U.S. Department of Justice in connection with violations of the Bank Secrecy Act (BSA), which requires financial institutions to maintain programs designed to detect and report suspicious activity that might be indicative of money laundering and other financial crimes. In addition to the combined monetary penalty of $8.2 million, the bank has agreed to a number of related regulatory actions.

The complaint alleged that the bank failed to maintain an effective anti-money laundering program and processed transactions involving at least $4.1 million in violation of federal money laundering laws. While a joint investigation by the U.S. Attorney's Office and the Office of the Comptroller of the Currency (OCC) was underway, the majority of the bank's assets were acquired by another financial institution. The proceeds of that acquisition, plus all other assets of the bank, which are currently valued at approximately $9.2 million, were held pending the outcome of the investigation. The bank has agreed to settle the government's allegations with a combined penalty of $8.2 million of the remaining $9.2 million and has separately agreed with the OCC to cease operation and to dissolve its charter.

[According to the complaint:]

Beginning at least as early as 2000, numerous federal agencies, including the Department of State, the Department of the Treasury, the Federal Reserve Bank, and the IRS, began issuing public warnings to United States financial institutions about the increased money laundering threat present in Mexico. These warnings were also available through industry-wide advisories.

---

710 FinCEN, *FinCEN Penalizes New Jersey Community Bank for Risky Dealings with Foreign Money Exchanges* (Sept. 24, 2013), *available at* https://www.fincen.gov/news/news-releases/fincen-penalizes-new-jersey-community-bank-risky-dealings-foreign-money (last visited Oct. 20, 2016).

It was believed that the proceeds of narcotics sales in the United States were being disproportionately laundered and transferred through banking institutions in Mexico. Many of these
warnings also discussed the specific money laundering risks associated with "casas de cambio,"
(CDCs), which are non-bank currency exchange businesses located in Mexico and elsewhere.

Beginning in June 2009, SRVB began servicing what would ultimately become four CDCs,
including three CDCs in Mexico and one in the Dominican Republic. SRVB voluntarily severed its relationship with the CDCs by May 2011, but only after processing at least $1.5 billion
in transactions on behalf of the CDCs. SRVB's anti-money laundering program related to the
CDCs was deficient in several key areas

SRVB failed to:

- appropriately monitor at least $1.5 billion in transactions conducted on behalf of the
  CDCs;
- properly detect and report suspicious activity occurring within the CDC accounts
  and file Suspicious Activity Reports on a timely basis;
- conduct sufficient enhanced due diligence on the CDCs;
- have a BSA officer or other personnel with sufficient experience to operate an AML
  program;
- provide adequate training to its employees concerning anti-money laundering;
- retain qualified periodic independent testers for its anti-money laundering program,
  as required by the BSA.[711]

Discussion topics

*What drew the regulators attention to this small bank?

*Are the required corrections adequate?

IV. CASE STUDY: WORLDCOM'S REBIRTH AS THE TRUSTWORTHY MCI

The jury foreman read the verdict: Guilty on all counts. Judge Barbara S. Jones polled each
member of the jury who concurred that Bernie Ebbers, the former WorldCom CEO, was guilty
of one count of conspiracy, one count of securities fraud and seven counts of false regulatory
filings. For his misdeeds at WorldCom, he faced a maximum prison sentence of 85 years. On
July 13, 2005 Ebbers was sentenced to 25 years in a Yazoo City, Mississippi prison for his role

---

711 Dep't of Justice, *Saddle River Valley Bank Agrees To $8.2 Million Penalty for Money Laundering Violations* (Sept. 24, 2013),
     available at https://www.justice.gov/usao-nj/pr/saddle-river-valley-bank-agrees-82-million-penalty-money-laundering-
     violations (last visited Oct. 20, 2016).

in the scandal. Only a few years earlier, Ebbers had been celebrated as the "telecom cowboy" for spurring on the telecom revolution, and had an estimated net worth of more than a billion dollars. By the time of his sentencing, his personal financial fortune was lost, as was the value that had been created for WorldCom's shareholders and employees. In total, the scandal resulted in a $7.7 billion income restatement, an $80 billion write-off of the stated book value of assets, the company's filing for Chapter 11 bankruptcy protection, and the loss of $180 billion in shareholder value.

Ebbers rose from a milkman to one of the richest men in America by riding the telecommunications bubble of the 1990s. Beginning in the early 1980s, AT&T's long distance monopoly was being opened to competition. Ebbers decided to enter the market in 1983 as a long distance telephone service provider. His business model was to buy long distance service at bulk rate discounts and resell the service to smaller users at rates that were lower than the traditional rates but high enough for CEO Ebbers' Long Distance Discount Carriers ("LDDC") to make a profit. He did make money through this model and took the company public in 1989 in conjunction with a merger. Wall Street (the "Street") was impressed with his business and his stock appreciated rapidly.

The Street wanted growth and Ebbers responded by buying other industry players using his strong share price to fund the acquisitions. As the telecommunications industry evolved during the 1990s to focus on a single integrated carrier providing one stop shopping, Ebbers expanded his acquisition targets to include MFS, which provided local service. The renamed WorldCom, reflecting Ebbers' vision for the company, went global in 1994 when it acquired IBD Communications Group. WorldCom's revenue growth throughout the 1990s drove its stock price up, which in turn funded the acquisitions. Its acquisition of MCI in 1997 made WorldCom the second largest telecom provider in the U.S. The Street was thrilled with the company. Its share price soared from $8.17 in 1994 to $47.91 in 1999 surpassing the performance of its rivals, AT&T and Sprint.

Ebbers' special skill appeared to be his ability to do deals that consolidated the fragmented telecom industry. As the industry consolidated, his model began to run out of steam. In 1999, he attempted to complete a $100 billion transaction with Sprint. Citing antitrust concerns, the Department of Justice turned down the deal. At the same time, the telecommunication bubble began to burst. The 1990s excitement over cable, broadband, and the Internet resulted in a flood of capacity on the market. Despite the expectations to the contrary, supply began to outstrip demand and as a result prices began to fall, taking with them the revenues and profits of the Internet service providers.

During the successful period of acquisitions, Ebbers was able to meet Street expectations by simply buying more companies. In the pricing downturn, however, WorldCom needed to consolidate and fully integrate its acquisitions to extract synergies and reduce costs. This was not a skill that Ebbers seemed to possess. The Special Investigative Committee of the Board of Directors of

WorldCom that analyzed how the eventual fraud took place concluded: "WorldCom's continued success became dependent on Ebbers' ability to manage the internal operations of what was then an immense company, and to do so in an industry-wide downturn. He was spectacularly unsuccessful in this endeavor."[712] As the business environment became more challenging, Ebbers made it clear to his team that the Street expected double-digit revenue growth and so did he. "But he did not provide the leadership or managerial attention that would enable WorldCom to meet those expectations legitimately."[713]

Perhaps due to pressure from the top, WorldCom's financial team delivered for Ebbers by fraud what they could not deliver by business acumen. The beginning of the financial engineering malfeasance came in 1999 when the financial team met Wall Street targets by reversing accruals for line costs. Line costs are the fees WorldCom paid local operators at each end of a call for the use of their lines. For long distance carriers, line costs represent the largest cost category and are closely watched by management and the Street.

Since there was a lag in ascertaining the actual costs, WorldCom booked estimated accruals for the costs. If the actual costs were lower than expected, the excess accrual would be reversed by reducing the expenses reported on the income statements in the next period. This practice was not wrong. However, in WorldCom's case, the reversals were manipulated to meet financial targets rather than to reflect actual costs that were lower than expected. When it needed to meet the Street's targets, the company reversed and shifted accruals regardless of whether or not there was an excess that needed to be realized. . . . During those two years, the total shifted accruals amounted to $3.3 billion.

Once the accrual strategy ran out of juice, the WorldCom financial team began to capitalize the line costs. The capitalization, which was done in 2001 and 2002 inappropriately, shifted $3.5 billion from the income statement to the balance sheet thus postponing costs to the future, even though the costs were incurred in the present. This manipulation exaggerated WorldCom's income over the short term. Eventually these capitalized assets must be depreciated, thus resulting in a future expense. Thus the process overstates actual current profits and understates actual future profits. Line costs are operating expenses and thus should have been recorded on the income statement as an expense. However the business downturn, combined with the long term take or pay contracts for line capacity, led the company's line expenses to move from 42% of revenue to 50%. In 2001 and 2002, "Ebbers . . . put pressure on many groups responsible for WorldCom's network . . . to reduce line costs. One former executive in Network Financial

---

712 Mark Fagan & Tamar Frankel, Trust and Honesty in the Real World a Teaching Course in Law, Business and Public Policy 217 (Fathom Publishing Company 2009). Some changes were made in the text and the footnotes were omitted.

713 Id.

Management described the pressure as unbearable, [as] greater than he had ever experienced in his fourteen years with the Company."[714]

WorldCom had not capitalized line costs in the past. The company's policies prohibited it from doing so. However, an accounting manager came up with a rationale for capitalizing the line expenses: since the problem of line costs stemmed from underutilized capacity, why not consider the line capacity as inventory, and pay for it when it was used? Other members of the finance team rejected the suggestion because it could not be supported under Generally Accepted Accounting Principles (GAAP). Nevertheless, the CFO adopted the capitalization strategy to "make the numbers." The evidence that the capitalization scheme was designed to meet Street expectations is that the capitalization entries were made after the end of the quarter, just before the earnings release, and were generally large, round-dollar amounts. It should be noted that implementing the capitalization program could not have been a secret since it impacted numerous departments including Property Accounting, Capital Reporting, and General Accounting.

Controlling expense was certainly important but Ebbers also focused his team on revenue growth. "WorldCom marketed itself as a high-growth company, and revenue growth was clearly a critical component of WorldCom's early success. . . . As market conditions deteriorated in 2000 and 2001, WorldCom . . . nevertheless continued to post impressive revenue numbers, and Ebbers and [his CFO] continued to assure Wall Street that WorldCom could sustain that level of growth." The growth was particularly noteworthy since WorldCom's major competitors were experiencing substantially lower growth rates. "Not surprisingly, management's promises of double-digit revenue growth and the expectations created thereby translated into intense pressure within WorldCom to achieve those results. No single measure of performance received greater scrutiny within WorldCom generally, and by Ebbers personally, than revenue growth . . . . [T]he focus on revenue was 'in every brick in every building' . . . ."[715]

When actual revenue was insufficient to meet targets, the company made one-time/unusual adjustments to the revenue figures at the end of the quarter in order to achieve targets. One such adjustment was minimum deficiencies. These charges were billed to WorldCom's customers if they did not meet threshold volumes of billings. In the industry, these charges were rarely collected. Under GAAP, these charges may not be recognized until actually collected. Yet, WorldCom recognized $312 million in deficiencies—which had not been collected—as revenue in order to make financial goals at the end of 1999 and 2001. In total, the Special Investigative Committee found $958 million in improper revenue entries, and an additional $1.1 billion in questionable entries.

Ebbers' need to maintain the WorldCom stock price extended beyond his role as a steward to the company. Ebbers' financial success at WorldCom enabled him to build an empire ranging from a rice farm in Louisiana to a cattle ranch in Canada, and even a luxury yacht maker. His

714 *Id.*

715 *Id.*

WorldCom stock secured the bank loans and/or margins that often funded his investments. A drop in WorldCom stock price could lead to margin calls on these investments and the need for Ebbers to sell shares. Of course insider selling of WorldCom shares in a down market would call into question the artificially rosy outlook that Ebbers continued to project for his company. A question about the company's outlook could start a vicious downward spiral of its stock price. When WorldCom stock finally did decline enough to result in a margin call from the banks, Ebbers' solution was to obtain a loan from WorldCom to cover it.

Ebbers ran the company as his own fiefdom; an approach that included his relationship with the board of directors. Although the chairman of the board was an outside director, Ebbers established the agenda and ran the meetings. Most board members joined the board as WorldCom acquired their companies. They received a director's retainer of $35,000 and modest additional payments of committee membership. In addition these members received stock options. For example, in 1999 the members were provided with options to buy 15,000 shares. The combination of option grants and shares, previously obtained when WorldCom acquired their companies, resulted in eight of the 15 board members each owning more than a million WorldCom shares.

The board met 4-6 times per year. The sessions provided high-level, one-way communications from the management team to the board. Over time it became clear to the members that their responsibilities were limited; many simply deferred to Ebbers, who was hailed by the corporate world as a great executive. The Investigative Committee's synopsis of board governance practices, described below, is instructive.

Boards rely on "information they receive from others," yet should "create the environment and the opportunities" that maximize their "chance of learning of issues [that require board] attention." "The WorldCom Board and the Audit and Compensation Committees were distant and detached from the company's operation. Ebbers controlled the Board's agenda, its discussions, and its decisions. The Board did not function as a check on Ebbers. He created a corporate environment in which the pressure to meet the numbers was high, the departments that served as controls within the Company were weak, and the word of senior management was final and not to be challenged."[716]

The board had three committees. The Nominating Committee rarely met and had no real mandate. The Compensation Committee focused on Ebbers and a few other senior executives. Ebbers' compensation was allegedly set at the median level, obtained by a compensation survey, for similarly situated industry executives. Despite this claim, Ebbers was often reported in the press as being one of the highest paid CEOs in the country. The committee also approved the bonus programs that provided both cash and options to senior management. The compensation committee was also especially active as it related to Ebbers' personal finances. For instance, the committee approved loans to Ebbers that he used to cover margin calls on his investments

---

716 *Id.*

outside of the company. "In making these loans and guaranties, WorldCom assumed risk that no financial institution was willing to assume. The Company did not have a perfected security interest in any collateral for the loans for most of the time period during which they were outstanding."[717] The committee chair helped Ebbers work through his difficulties. For example in 2000 as the WorldCom stock slipped below $31, the chair authorized a $50 million loan for Ebbers. The cash was transferred to Ebbers before other board members were even notified. Ultimately, the company's total outstanding loans to Ebbers exceeded $400 million.

During the period in which the fraud was committed, the audit committee met 3 to 5 times per year for an hour each time. Nominally the committee was responsible for overseeing the internal audit department, the external auditors, and management's financial reporting. While the Special Investigator did not find evidence that the audit committee knew of the fraud or found red flags, they did conclude that "the audit committee—played so limited a role in the oversight of WorldCom that it is unlikely that any but the most flagrant and open financial fraud could have come to their attention."[718] The fraud continued for 13 quarters before it finally came to light.

A core reason for the fraud was the corporate culture that Ebbers instilled. "Organizational culture refers to the values, norms, beliefs, and practices that govern how an institution functions. At the most basic level, organizational culture defines the assumptions that employees make as they carry out their work." The culture that Ebbers encouraged "emphasized making the numbers above all else; kept financial information hidden from those who needed to know; blindly trusted senior officers even in the face of evidence that they were acting improperly; discouraged dissent; and left few, if any, outlets through which employees believed they could safely raise their objections." The Special Investigative Committee found that this culture began with Ebbers who "created the pressure that led to fraud. He demanded the results that he had promised [the Street] . . ." and appears not to have been concerned with how they were achieved. Ebbers purportedly said, in response to the proposed implementation of a corporate code of conduct, that it would be "a colossal waste of time."[719]

While the number of people who actually committed fraud was small, a much larger number of employees knew or suspected that that company was being dishonest. In order to reverse the accruals and capitalize the line costs, the General Accounting group, the Property Accounting group, and the Capital Reporting group made adjustments to the financial statements. The Ebbers culture appears to have prevented the employees from "blowing the whistle." Individual employees reported to the Investigative Committee that questioning senior management was a risk too great to take. For example, "When an employee in Wireless Accounting started asking questions about a $150 million corporate reduction in line costs, Yates [Director of General

717 *Id.*

718 *Id.*

719 *Id.*

Accounting] asked Walter Nagel, the General Tax Counsel, to stop the inquiry because 'the entry he asks about is one of the 'I'll need to kill him if I tell him' [ones], even though the employee was [just] trying to determine whether the adjustment affected one of the Company's state tax returns.'" In another instance, an employee who appropriately budgeted for actual costs and appropriate corporate adjustments was told by the CFO: "This is complete, complete garbage . . . . What am I supposed to do with this? What have we been doing for the last six months? This is a real work of trash."[720] In short, the risk of being fired from one of the Street's most admired companies was more than most employees would take.

Where was the internal audit group, one of the critical backstops against malfeasance, during this period? WorldCom's internal audit department was largely chartered to conduct operations-oriented assessments, not to confirm the veracity of the company's financial statements. As early as 1999, the head of Internal Audit requested the monthly revenue report. The CFO wrote in a memo: "Do not give her the total picture—i.e. she does not need international, other revenues, etc." Moreover, Internal Audit reported directly to the CFO who was a key participant in the fraud. Further, the audit committee of the board, which should have used Internal Audit to confirm management's numbers, simply lacked any interest in doing so. Ironically, it was the dogged determination of the internal auditor, who sensed there was a problem and kept pursuing it, which ultimately exposed the fraud.

Upon the revelation of fraud, the board fired Ebbers, but gave him severance payments of $1.5 million per year for life. In June 2002, WorldCom announced a $9.2 billion restatement of its financials. The Street finally woke up to the WorldCom fiction. In rapid succession, the company's debt was downgraded to junk bond status, the share price collapsed, and the company sought Chapter 11 protection. Soon after the filing of Chapter 11 the SEC filed suit against the corporation for fraud. To the credit of the bankruptcy court, emphasis was placed on saving the operations of the company (under the MCI banner) and the jobs of thousands of employees. The starting point of this restoration process was appointing a Corporate Monitor.

---

720 *Id.*

Chapter 14

THE MEANING AND ROLE OF CULTURE IN INSTITUTIONAL SELF-REGULATION

"There are no societies, only individuals who interact with each other"
Jon Elster 1989.

We studied the laws that we should comply with, and the institutional rules and mechanisms designed to avoid violation of the laws. Laws are accompanied by punishments because we believe that the threat of punishment deters violators. Similarly, institutional rules are accompanied by deterrent punishments, such as reduced bonuses and salaries, or removal to less desirable positions or locations or termination of the employment. Yet, the enforcement of the law and its self-regulation can be supported or undermined by group culture.

That is why along the way we kept reading time and again about the importance of the culture of self-regulation. In that context we also noted "ethics" and "morality," as well as the power structure within institutions. Here we examine these concepts and their practical impact. We recognize that culture is not limited to institutions; it encompasses any community of humans. Yet, here we focus on the culture within institutions and its effect on the legality of the institutional activities and its self-regulation.

Some fundamental ideas take time to be recognized and followed. In 1975, Christopher D. Stone wrote a book: *Where the Law Ends, The Social Control of Corporate Behavior.* The author suggests that in a certain group culture people may do what they would not do had they been on their own,[721] and therefore a group should adopt a compliance model that goes beyond compliance with the law to voluntary behavior, sensitive to social needs.[722]

This chapter is divided into four sections. Section I inquires into the meaning and role of culture. Section II deals with the role of culture in institutional self-regulation. Section III outlines the symptoms of a deteriorating culture of honesty. Section IV discusses how to reform a faulty culture.

---

721 CHRISTOPHER D. STONE , WHERE THE LAW ENDS, THE SOCIAL CONTROL OF CORPORATE BEHAVIOR 235-36 (1975).

722 *Id.* at 239-42.

I. THE MEANING AND ROLE OF INSTITUTIONAL CULTURE

A. What does culture mean?

Like many words, the term "culture" has multiple meanings, yet the different meanings are connected by similar features. In one use of the word, we speak about a culture of bacteria, or other growing microorganisms. We develop more of the organisms in the laboratory—putting the few together and feeding them, and then over a certain period they multiply and create an entire culture of many. In this description the microorganisms are very similar, and perhaps identical. The word "culture" in this context denotes the creation of identical units. While no one bacteria can develop light, when these bacteria are fed together they can develop light. Information contact among the bacteria and cooperation (rather than competition) produces what neither can produce alone.

A similar image, although in a far more complex context, applies to the social culture of humans: the continuously repeated binding relationships, manners of behavior, preferred food, and other aspects of life that are shared by a group of people constitutes their culture. Some cultures can be benevolent and provide support to their members and to others; some can be cruel, dishonest, and corrupt. The feature that ties the members of a culture together is "sameness." It is the product of behavior that becomes entrenched by rewards, punishment, repetition, and pressure to conform.

Habitual group behavior consists mainly of acceptable, repeated behavior. It is the behavior of group members that share a psychological common ground, stimulating confidence and relief from decision-making by each group member. It results in the same assurance and confidence that: "everyone does this, and we always do this, and therefore it is good." This is what makes habits and "group-think" both enduring and difficult to change. A culture of compliance can become a long-term, reassuring, and self-reinforcing group habit. Thus, culture consists of rules followed and enforced by a group. We may call it self-regulation.

Cultures evolve, but not necessarily quickly nor easily. They may evolve in reaction to a change in environment, such as the introduction of a new technology.[723] But that, of course, depends on the nature of the culture.

Culture affects and is affected by the personality of the group members. And because it is composed of many items it is very hard to accurately generalize. To some extent you know culture when you see it, and experience it. [724]

---

[723] P. Barroso, Proceedings for CEPE 2003 and Sixth Annual Ethics and Technology Conferences, Boston College, June 25-28, 2003, at 3.

[724] ANTHONY F.C. WALLACE, CULTURE AND PERSONALITY (1961).

An Example: The following is a "scoreboard"[725] for a Chief Technology Officer of a corporation:

Mission: The mission of the Chief Technology Officer (CTO) is to understand the strategy and portfolio of the [corporation's] [I]nformation services, and lead the selection, architecture, and governance of technologies required to execute against the portfolio and achieve the strategies. The CTO is responsible for knowing about all relevant technologies, running experiments, enterprise architecture, defining the technology standards . . . and managing relationships throughout the organization to ensure unity of technical vision.

Outcomes: Within the first thirty (30) days the CTO will: 1. Familiarize [himself] with the current list of [I]nitiatives and technological landscape and systems at . . .. 2. Establish relationships with the Technology leadership and gain an understanding of the competencies, systems, and technical challenges of each Technology team. 3. Establish relationships with business/ product management leadership and gain an understanding of their business operations/ product functionality as well as their future needs. 4. Establish relationships with the product Owners across the organization as well as gain an understanding of their respective backlogs. 5. Familiarize [himself] with the product development life cycle in place at [the corporation].

Within the first ninety (90) days the CTO will: Establish a schedule for assessments of . . .technological environment, identifying Strengths, Weaknesses, Opportunities, and Threats with go forward plans. Areas to be covered include (but are not limited to): . . .

Produce the first Assessment outlined above; Contribut[e] to the identification of Technology enabler epics; Establish [himself] as the primary Technology expert;

Job Competencies:

Strategic Thinking/vision: Able to see and communicate the big picture in an inspiring way. Determines opportunity and threats through a comprehensive analysis of current and future trends.

Intelligence. Learns quickly. Demonstrates ability to quickly and proficiently understand and absorb new information.

Drive: Is goal-oriented and relentless in pursuit. Perseveres or pivots with decisiveness.

Analytical skills. Able to structure and process qualitative or quantitative data and draw insightful conclusions from it. Exhibits a probing mind and achieves penetrating insights.

Attention to detail. Does not let important details slip through the cracks or derail efforts.

Listening skills. Lets others speak and seeks to understand their viewpoints.

---

725 *Chief Technology Officer (CTO) Ability To Work Remote, Relocation Assistance Available, available at* http://www. americasjobexchange.com/job-detail/Chief-Technology-Officer-CTO-Ability-To-Work-Remote-Relocation-Assistance-Available-Ipswich-MA-573916272 (last visited Dec. 28, 2016).

Teamwork: Reaches out to peers and customers and fosters a collaborative working relationship personally and within the team.

Creativity/innovation: Generates new and innovative approaches to problems.

Communication skills: Communicates clearly and articulately without being overly verbose or talkative. Listens to others, and is open to and solicits feedback. Reacts calmly to criticism or negative feedback.

Follow-through on commitments: Lives up to verbal and written commitments.

Proactivity: Acts without being told what to do. Brings new ideas to the company.\

Negotiating and Consensus Building: Is effective at finding common ground in negotiations with others. Works to achieve Win-Win when possible, and strives to find the optimal solution given diverse or conflicting goals. Shows leadership in building consensus.

Efficiency: Able to produce significant output with minimal wasted effort.

Honesty/integrity: Does what is right even when no one is watching. Earns trust and maintains confidences. Always behaves in a manner that holds the highest ethical standards.

Organization and planning: Plans, organizes, schedules, and prioritizes in an efficient, productive manager, focusing on key priorities.

Cultural Competencies: [The Corporation] has a set of principles that define how we operate culturally.

We expect employees to embrace these principles:

1. Commit to sustained profit growth
2. Have a defined Vision and Operate with a Bias for Action
3. Be Customer Focused and Sales Driven
4. Understand that Change is Necessary
5. Recognize that you can't manage what you can't measure
6. Foster creativity and continuous improvement
7. Insist on Quality
8. Do what you say you will do
9. Cultivate passion
10. Realize that business is a long-run game
11. Improve the foundation
12. Be humble

Being successful in this role will require fitting into a work environment that is fast paced, creative, diverse and demanding. The teams are talented and the bar is high for all who work with us. We want collaborative, non-political, non-territorial people who are comfortable challenging the status quo. We want to work with nice people. We want people who are respectful of their co-workers and people that enjoy what they do. We want people who like to get things done, efficiently, and demand that of those around them. Thinking outside the box is encouraged. We like to solve hard problems and push ourselves to high standards.

Experience Requirements. . . Preferred qualifications: . . .[726]

Group self-regulation is not unusual. To a greater or lesser extent, most people are taught early in life to control their actions and sometimes their feelings, and to obey the rules of the group, such as the rules within the family. Some lessons come from the reaction of others. A child learns to control his or her screaming by experiencing the parents' reactions. In school, other rules of behavior are imposed and followed. A group's self-regulation is "group culture." It is a similar behavior of the units within a group, enforced by the members of the group.

Culture includes socially required behavior. For example, some cultures frown on people who eat while walking in the street. In other countries everyone eats while walking on the street. In some cultures the question: "How is your spouse doing?" is considered polite. In other cultures asking the same question is incredibly rude. "What my wife is doing is none of your business," may be the reply.

B. Humans Cannot Survive Alone.

Humans must live in a group. Culture involves the rules and the power structure of the group and rules of behavior within the group. It identifies who commands and establishes the rules of behavior, and who must obey. The rules can be backed by supervision to ensure compliance, as well as by sanctions and expulsion for misbehavior. Thus, a golf club, a lawyers' association, and a medical organization are mostly ruled by their culture.

Who established the rules that shape culture? Usually social groups have leaders that formulate and impose rules. These social groups may be family, the church, a school, a club or Congress and courts. Accordingly, the leader or a group of leaders could be parents, priests, teachers, political party leaders, and judges. The rules they formulate and impose create the basis on which habits grow. These habits serve to fill in and automate the implementation of a culture's internal rule system that members follow.

C. How Is Culture Enforced?

One of the more powerful enforcement features of a culture is habit: "We have always done it this way." A social habit can be efficient and beneficial; it produces a "knee-jerk reaction" rather than an evaluation of the pros and cons of a particular action.[727] It creates a framework

---

[726] *Chief Technology Officer (CTO) Ability To Work Remote, Relocation Assistance Available, available at* http://www.americasjobexchange.com/job-detail/Chief-Technology-Officer-CTO-Ability-To-Work-Remote-Relocation-Assistance-Available-Ipswich-MA-573916272 (last visited Dec. 28, 2016).

[727] *See* TAMAR FRANKEL, TRUST AND HONESTY 190 (2005).

of formal and informal rules. Habits are efficient because they require little thought and invoke little argument. However, a changing environment may make strong static habits destructive. Therefore, as we shall see, effective organizations introduce and practice the habit of evaluating their habits from time to time.

Needless to say, group culture may depend on various factors such as activities, group size, history, and personnel. Paradoxically, strict controls might undermine culture. Angela L. Colletti et al. noted in their paper that while prior research shows that controls may have a negative effect on trust (because of the perception they create of the work environment and employees), their paper shows that controls may increase trust; "trust-induced cooperation" may increase trust and the increased trust may increase cooperation.[728]

D. The Accepted Rules of a Culture May Be Based on Many Justifications for Permissions or Prohibitions.

There are benefits in following the rules of law and in gaining the approval of professional colleagues and managers. There are benefits in winning public reputation by acting in a trustworthy manner, and being loyal and devoted to investors and employees' interests. If, for example, insider-trading violations threaten these benefits, such trading should be prohibited. And the best way to prevent these actions is to make clear to all actors, from top management down the hierarchal ladder, that these actions will not be tolerated. With time, the prohibited behavior becomes unimaginable.

There are cultures in which an offended party is expected to kill the offending party, and there is no alternative if the offended member wishes to continue living in the community. However, even in such a culture there are respected leaders who may avoid a blood feud by using their prestige and power to bring the parties to agree and avoids the slaughter. But if such leaders do not exist, or do not act in time, a blood feud may spiral and lead to the annihilation of the families of both parties.

E. What Are The Benefits of Culture?

A culture can promote collaboration.[729] If the group's rules are directed towards institutional rather than personal success, if trustworthiness is a valued objective, and if service provides a feeling of achievement, regardless of reward, then the group as a whole receives the benefit.

---

728 Angela L. Colletti et al., *The Effect of Control Systems on Trust and Cooperation in Collaborative Environments*, 80 Accounting Rev.477, 478 (2005).

729 Terrence E. Deal & Kent D. Peterson, Shaping School Culture: The Heart Of Leadership 7-8 (1999), *cited in* Craig D. Jerald, *School Culture: "The Hidden Curriculum,"* Issue Brief (Center for Comprehensive School Reform and Improvement), Dec. 2006, at 1, 2, *available at* http://files.eric.ed.gov/fulltext/ED495013.pdf (last visited Jan. 28, 2016).

Culture can change to spawn competition. It may provide increased benefits to particular members but not to others and sometimes may or may not enrich the institution.

One lawyer described the changing culture in law firms 21st century. There was a time when salaries and benefits were determined by seniority. Those who contributed earlier in life were rewarded later. Now, in some firms, the rewards are relative to the financial contribution by each member. The more money the member brings in, the higher the member's salary will be. The effect of this change is to produce a competitive environment marked by a lack of communal support and sometimes by envy and arguments about the value of the member's clients, contribution, and financial success. In addition, it renders the evaluation of the members to be far more short-term, which renders the contributors' view to be short-term as well.[730] Yet there are also firms that have continued to practice past culture.

Discussion topic

What, in your opinion, led to the changed culture in at least some law firms?

Which practice would you prefer? Which practice is beneficial to the legal profession and to most law firms? Why?

II. THE ROLE OF CULTURE IN INSTITUTIONAL SELF-REGULATION

A. Ethics and Culture

David Gebler suggests that "an effective ethics and compliance program . . . serves double duty as the process to create a more profitable and sustainable culture overall." But "changing a culture is not accomplished by merely working through a checklist. Culture is determined by what people *actually* do, not what they *should* do. Yet, many organizations do not identify and manage the underlying behaviors that actually promote an ethical culture. They identify improper behavior once it occurs, but rarely identify the behavior that generates the risks in the first place."[731]

Rules, says Gebler, do not create culture. It is the workplace environment that creates the culture. While leaders can influence culture, they cannot mandate it. It exists whether or not corporate management acknowledges it. Thus, culture dictates behavior, in a positive or negative way.

---

730 Conversation with Tamar Frankel.

731 David Gebler, *The Start of the Slippery Slope: How Leaders Can Manage Culture to Create a Sustainable Ethics and Compliance Program, in* Corporate Culture and Ethical Leadership Under the Federal Sentencing Guidelines: What Should Boards, Management, and

Policymakers Do Now? 43, 43 (Michael D. Greenberg ed., 2012), *available at* http://www.rand.org/content/dam/rand/pubs/conf_proceedings/2012/RAND_CF305.pdf (last visited Mar. 28, 2016).

Culture is what is really happening. Guidelines to encourage ethical behavior will be effective only if the employees are convinced that the guidelines reflect their everyday reality. If management does not follow the program, neither will the employees.[732] When the core elements of culture are out of alignment with each other, frustrations occur. When the principles are not in alignment with the assigned goals, employees disengage and have a less vested interest in their work. They lose commitment. When goals move out of sync with standards, unfairness arises as managers and employees "do what they *have* to do" rather than what they have said they would do. And when standards are out of alignment with values, employees see that the organization's actions are not consistent with its principles. When employees hold this perception, it becomes very difficult for management to extract honest feedback from them, and transparent lines of communication in the firm are lost.

B. Natural Tendencies Can Be Translated into Compliance.

For example, rendering the position of a compliance officer or a compliance person unique and hard to get, may not only draw employees to the job, but also enhance the prestige associated with this role. Joseph Murphy suggests that government may give a compliance and ethics program no credit in an enforcement action if the program is only a code and the compliance officer is a junior lawyer with a title.[733] Murphy also suggests that if the regulatory agency examiners find the corporation, or a particular unit thereof, to be absolutely "clean" and praise it for its performance, that might also enhance the prestige and value associated with good behavior.[734]

Another factor that helps encourage compliance is the "rule of reciprocity." If management expects and rewards compliance, rules are more likely to be followed.[735] It is well known that in many cultures people tend to reciprocate: those who receive a free lunch from a salesperson are more likely to buy from the salesperson. Apparently, according to Douglas Rushkoff, most people feel uncomfortable in receiving something "free" and not "paying" for it.[736] People who accept gifts but do not reciprocate are often socially condemned. In sum, the behavior of group members relies heavily on established expectations within the group and on fulfilling those expectations.

---

732 *Id.* at 44.

733 *See* Joseph Murphy, *Over 20 Years Since the Federal Sentencing Guidelines: What Government Can Do Next to Support Effective Ethics and Compliance Programs, in* Corporate Culture and Ethical Leadership Under the Federal Sentencing Guidelines: What Should Boards, Management, and

Policymakers Do Now? 59, 61 (Michael D. Greenberg ed., 2012), *available at* http://www.rand.org/content/dam/rand/pubs/conf_proceedings/2012/RAND_CF305.pdf (last visited Mar. 28, 2016).

734 *Id.*

735 *See* Tamar Frankel, The Ponzi Scheme Puzzle 135 (2012) (social rule of reciprocity).

736 Douglas Rushkoff, Coercion: Why We Listen to Whet "They" Say 33-35 (1999).

Inculcating a culture of sound ethics and compliance is not only good practice but may have legal consequences. As we noted, when a compliance officer has been lax, she may become liable. The SEC filed an Enforcement Action against a former Wells Fargo Advisors Compliance Officer. According to the SEC, the Compliance Officer, Judy K. Wolf, was responsible for performing trading surveillance reviews to identify potential insider trading activity. Wolf's September 2010 surveillance review of a particular employee's trading found no issues. Apparently, in December 2012, after the SEC charged Wells Fargo Advisors with insider trading, Wolf revised her September 2010 surveillance review.

In this case the SEC alleged that by altering the document, the officer made it appear that she performed a more thorough review in 2010 than she actually had. Chief of the SEC Enforcement Division's Market Abuse Unit declared: that "regardless of her motivation, her conduct was inconsistent with what the SEC expects of compliance professionals and what the law requires."[737]

Discussion topics

Suppose your client is a demanding person who takes much of your time and continuously complains about the high fees. This client feels that he has always been overcharged and under-served. How would you react to and treat such a client? What facts would you seek to find out before you make the decision on how to treat the client?

Are these questions and this situation related to ethics?

. What is the Nature of a Market Culture?

Dan Awrey and other authors argue that neither markets nor law are totally effective in encouraging socially optimal behavior and that culture and ethics can help to encourage such behavior."[738]

_____

Discussion Topics

Where does the binding force of a culture come from? Why is it difficult to establish a culture and difficult to change it?

_____

[737] U.S. Sec. & Exch. Comm'n, *SEC Announces Enforcement Action Against Former Wells Fargo Advisors Compliance Officer for Altering Document,* Oct. 15, 2014, *available at* http://www.sec.gov/News/PressRelease/Detail/PressRelease/1370543175814 (last visited Jan. 29, 2016).

[738] Dan Awrey, *Between Law and Markets: Is There a Role for Culture and Ethics in Financial Regulation?*, 38 DEL. J. CORP. L. 191, 191 (2013).

When the benefits of a culture are recognized by the institutional leadership, there is a good chance that something like insider trading can be severely curtailed, if not eradicated. Do you agree that a Code of Ethics in a financial advisory firm may demonstrate its defining culture?

Please comment on the following statements:

"My main purpose is to win everything that benefits me – especially money. I aim at winning regardless of the harm that I may cause to others while pursuing this goal. In fact, if my methods cause harm to others or deprive them of the means to challenge me, so much the better. After all, they are potential competitors."[739]
What would you do when a certain behavior is legal but not ethical?
What do you do when a certain behavior "may be" legal but not quite clearly so?
What would you do when a negative behavior or standard is not punished internally within the institution or by regulators?

Problem

The SEC requires that a Certified Financial Planner (CFP) avoid holding itself out as "fee only" if the CFP works for a firm that charges commissions, even if the CFP does not itself charge commissions. The CFP Board Standards of Conduct allow a CFP to hold itself out as "fee only" only if its compensation is derived solely from fees and if no related party receives commissions. Yet, it seems that many CFPs who work for banks and brokerage firms incorrectly hold themselves out as "fee only."

In response, the Chief Executive of the CFP Board agreed to correct the problem. Member banks and brokerage firms argued that "they urge their advisers to comply with the CFP Board rules." Still, one firm spokesperson stated that "it seems logical that some advisers who use the firm only as a custodian, would call themselves 'fee only.'" Additionally, a non-CFP adviser, that describes itself as "fee only," discloses in its brochure that it may receive commissions.[740]

Discussion topic

*How should a compliance officer address the concerns of the SEC and the apparent "push-back" by the employer?

---

739 Miriam Hechler Baer, *Governing Corporate Compliance*, 50 B.C. L. Rev. 949, 949, 954 (2009); Chapter 17 (discussing Enron).

740 Jason Zweig, *'Fee-Only' Financial Advisers Who Don't Charge Fees Alone*, Wall St. J., Sept. 21, 2013, at B1.

Please comment and explain: Goldman Sachs, as well as other banks, declined to join the U.K. Bank Standards Council. In part, the reason for avoiding membership was a concern that failure to meet the standards of the Council could lead to legal repercussions.[741]

III. THE SYMPTOMS OF A DETERIORATING CULTURE OF HONESTY

A. Not Every Dishonest Person Views Himself or Herself as Dishonest.

According to David Gebler, there are a number of ways that people can embellish their view of themselves. Here are a number of examples.

1. Self-deception, .i.e., believing that what we are doing is right, e.g., where we have a desired outcome or goal and ignore facts that conflict with the outcome.

2. Rationalization, i.e., telling oneself that there is a valid reason for what we are doing, e.g., that it is in the best interests of the company.

3. Disengagement, i.e., knowing that we are doing is wrong but not caring, e.g., because "it's not my problem" or management will not listen to the employee or appreciate what she does. Traditional rewards and punishments such as raises, or promotions are not sufficient to keep employees engaged; management should show that it listens to its employees.[742]

4. Unfair Legal Requirements. If people believe that the legal requirements are unfair, or that the associated compliance measures taken are onerous, wasteful, or unreasonable, then the chances of compliance with these requirements are far lower. If, however, they believe that the legal restrictions or directives are fair, they will tend to adopt and follow them. For example, compliance rules should reflect the work burden and environment. People usually have their own moral compass that tells them what is right or wrong. If this compass is drastically out of sync with that of the employer, then one or the other requires change or removal. In such a case general concepts of right and wrong in the community should be examined. If the compliance program is far removed from the moral compass of the surrounding community, it may be time for its writers to go back to the drawing board.

---

741 David Wighton, *Goldman Sachs Declines to Join U.K. Bank-Standards Council,* WALL ST. J., Oct. 20, 2014, at C3.

742 David Gebler, *The Start of the Slippery Slope: How Leaders Can Manage Culture to Create a Sustainable Ethics and Compliance Program, in* CORPORATE CULTURE AND ETHICAL LEADERSHIP UNDER THE FEDERAL SENTENCING GUIDELINES: WHAT SHOULD BOARDS, MANAGEMENT, AND

POLICYMAKERS DO NOW? 43, 47-48 (Michael D. Greenberg ed., 2012), *available at* http://www.rand.org/content/dam/rand/pubs/conf_proceedings/2012/RAND_CF305.pdf (last visited Mar. 28, 2016).

B. Conflicting Cultures in Different Countries

A serious problem may arise when an institutional culture is not compatible with the culture that prevails in other countries where the institution does business. One solution is to hire local personnel as the offshore employees. However, when the home office CCO reviews offshore activities, he or she must undertake the difficult task of ensuring that offshore compliance still meets the minimum standards of the home office. Where the standards are very different or incompatible, the CCO must also be wary of polluting the culture of the home office. Such reviews and decisions involve judgment, and may have to be brought to senior management or the board of directors for consideration. In some cases the issues may perhaps be brought to regulators for advice.[743]

Therefore, rules that are applicable to everyone in the institution should be imposed and enforced on everyone in the institution. If no one is permitted to help himself to the institutional property—and that means any institutional property—then top management must follow the rule, especially if the rule concerns, for example, the use of the institutional transportation availability. If top management uses the corporate jet to travel with friends and family, employees are not likely to respect a rule that restricts the use of other institutional property for private use. To be sure, the institution may allow such practices to some degree. Others believe the rule should be applied equally to all employees.[744]

In the United States, the assumption, among other things, is that whatever a person has decided to do, the person aims at benefiting from the decision and will benefit from the decision. For instance, people who bet at the racetrack have the most confidence in their decision immediately after placing their bets (but before the ultimate outcome of the race). This spike in confidence immediately after a decision may be related to the process of reaching a decision, as well as to classical conditioning. Reaching a decision may require facing and evaluating uncertain information. The process may also be difficult and mentally taxing. To be sure, not everyone agrees.[745]

Attitudes towards compliance may start with the source of the compliance plans.[746] As Martin T. Beigelman and Joel T. Bartow wrote, if the employees are aware that the top echelon in the corporation is violating the law, the employees are likely to follow.[747] The authors

---

743 U.S. Sec. & Exch. Comm'n, *SEC Announces Enforcement Action Against Former Wells Fargo Advisors Compliance Officer for Altering Document*, Oct. 15, 2014, *available at* http://www.sec.gov/News/PressRelease/Detail/PressRelease/1370543175814 (last visited Jan. 29, 2016).

744 The approach was influenced by Margaret Levi et al., *The Reasons for Compliance with Law, in* Understanding Social Action, Promoting Human Rights 70 (Ryan Goodman, Derek Jinks & Andrew K. Woods eds., 2012).

745 *Id.* ch. 3.

746 *Id.* ch. 3.

747 Martin T. Beigelman & Joel T. Bartow, Executive Roadmap To Fraud Prevention And Internal Control 38-39 (2d ed. 2012).

note that frauds are usually discovered because the fraudsters make mistakes. Removal of the defrauding employee might be most effective.[748] That is because memories are short-term. Ponzi schemes have persisted even though they have been around for decades and the con artists are repeat performers.[749] Therefore, sometimes discharging an employee that has demonstrated traits of a con artist may save the company from losses and perhaps even annihilation.

Discussion topic

What do you think?

C. Conflicting Corporate Roles.

1. The Five Types of Groups Within the Corporate Entity

Charles Handy outlines five types of groups within the corporation: entrepreneurial, machine, professional, innovative, and missionary.[750]

Discussion Topics

*Brokers and their organizations have fought long and hard against the Labor Department's proposed requirement that brokers disclose to investors the sources of their fees and thereby their conflicting interests. That is, the brokers' "sales talk" is not un-conflicted advice. Why are the brokers so adamantly against this type of disclosure?

*Can the method of compensating salespeople change their behavior? If you were charged with designing the compensation scheme for your institution's sales force what would its defining features be?

*Do different subcultures within an organization affect the firm's overall culture of compliance?

*Suppose the organization is engaged in developing and selling medicines? Some of the employees work on possible new medicines; some of the employees market such medicines.

----

748 *Id.* at 40-41.

749 *Id* at 42. *See also generally* TAMAR FRANKEL, THE PONZI SCHEME PUZZLE (2012).

750 CHARLES HANDY, UNDERSTANDING ORGANIZATIONS 203-05 (4th ed. 1993).

2. We Recognize Multiple and Conflicting Power Holding and Power Exercise

In most countries and institutions, vested power is not absolute. In fact, even in a family power is not absolute. Yet, abusive exercise of power might lead to rebellion of the abused. Thus, power-holders seek to gain the trust of those over whom they wish to gain power and then exercise it. However, just as we reject absolute power, we also do not advocate absolute trust, except by those who cannot have any independence. We ask people to trust us on the one hand, and yet expect those who are able to trust to verify this trustworthiness to the extent they can.

In sum, we can't live without trusting but we can't trust blindly either. This discussion suggests that power should be balanced. The balance depends on a variety of circumstances, and is not always determined and fixed. The balance usually depends on the sense of fairness that people and institutions and society have. Fairness then directs the power holders. On the other side of the equation, the more independent the power givers are, the less limits are imposed on the power holders. The search for specificity and certainty in this case might be disappointing. The way we gain a measure of coherence is by seeking the measure of the balance: to what extent were the subjects of the power holders able to fend for themselves?

3. Should Violations of Compliance Rules Be Deemed Criminal?

Arguably, the trend toward criminalizing violations of some acts, e.g., the Securities Act of 1933, is bad. If many people follow a certain trend, their behavior should not be criminalized because it would render too many people criminals. A higher degree of criminal sanction dilutes the shock value of criminal sanctions. Pervasive wrongful financial activities should not be criminalized, especially so long as the violations fall in a gray area of the law. This view is also supported by the argument that laws and regulations should be clear, and capable of being well understood prospectively. Even though members of the financial community may wish to leave gray areas of the law free from prosecution, this wish is unlikely to be unacceptable in law, and especially not in connection with the concept of compliance.

Problem

The SEC charged a private equity fund with acting as an unregistered broker by acquiring and arranging acquisition of securities for the fund. There is a wide range of activities between advising and executing the advised actions, especially if the proposed advice involves pooling of securities that are then pooled again.

Does the second tier of pooling involve double execution (buying or selling the first tier securities) or does the last tier involve only buying or selling? After all, every mutual fund adviser buys securities for the fund. On the other hand if the same adviser presents itself as a master trader, and if the main cost imposed on the clients is the trading costs which the so-called adviser charges the investors for its so-called advice, then the combined charges and activities may require this adviser to register as a broker and be subject to the limitations imposed on brokers. The test might indeed be who collects the fees for the activities, even if the payment is combined with many, if not all, regulated activities.

4. If You Aim at Reviving a Culture of Compliance, Where Do You Start?

According to David Gebler, determine whether it is necessary to change behavior in order to change culture, or to change culture in order to change behavior. Culture drives behavior, and behavior drives culture.[751]

a. Behavior Driving Culture

If the culture of a group is strong—it has clear goals and consistent enforcement of practices—the different behavior of a few individuals within the group will have little effect on the culture. But if the group culture is weak or inconsistent, then the behavior of a few individuals can influence the culture. Society will witness "personality cults," especially if their actions are condoned by other leaders. The culture of a company's norms can change as well.[752] While behavior can drive culture, culture can also drive behavior. Employees will look to the norms of peers and leaders and behave accordingly.[753] Students will look to the norms of the teachers, and children will look to the norms of the parents.

Discussion topic

*Do you agree with the ideas stated above?

*How should the culture in an academic environment be established and directed?

---

751 David Gebler, *The Start of the Slippery Slope: How Leaders Can Manage Culture to Create a Sustainable Ethics and Compliance Program, in* Corporate Culture and Ethical Leadership Under the Federal Sentencing Guidelines: What Should Boards, Management, and

Policymakers Do Now? 43, 45 (Michael D. Greenberg ed., 2012), *available at* http://www.rand.org/content/dam/rand/pubs/conf_proceedings/2012/RAND_CF305.pdf (last visited Mar. 28, 2016).

752 *Id.*

753 *Id.* at 45-46.

*What guidelines would you adopt for looking for a job? Do you focus on what you want to get from the job? Do you focus on what the potential future employer wishes to get from your performance?

*Are these two desires and drives conflicting?

*Do you agree with the following statements: Most people "are neither completely good nor completely bad." However, they are influenced by social norms.[754] Thus, to some extent social norms or culture dictate whether the group members are good or bad.

b. The Varied Meanings of Right and Wrong

Our sense of right and wrong can change with the circumstances, including the organizational culture.[755] Employees who "feel honest" may be influenced by the company's culture to do things they would not do elsewhere. The three behavioral switches that can influence us to do this are: i) self-deception, ii) rationalization, and iii) disengagement.[756]

5. Instilling a Corporate Culture That Invites the Best: Switching Off Self-Deception, Rationalization, and Disengagement

To prevent these switches, in an "unhealthy culture" leaders should focus on influencing social norms rather than on influencing the individual.[757] Leaders may be tempted to ignore risk factors and red flags in the face of more immediate, short-term goals. Risks and benefits of preventative action should be framed in such a way that they can be compared appropriately to the risks and benefits of short-term action and inaction, and risk factors and red flags should be treated as seriously as actual misconduct.[758]

---

754 *Id.* at 47.

755 *Id., citing* Nina Mazar et al., *The Dishonesty of Honest People: A Theory of Self-Concept Maintenance,* 45 J. MARKETING RES. 633 (2008).

756 *Id.* at 47-48.

757 *Id.* at 48.

758 *Id.*

A. How Can Leaders and Organizations Adopt Better Means of Highlighting the Risks and Benefits of Preventative Action?

David Gebler suggests the following:

First, the risks and benefits should be concrete rather than vague, to compete with short-term risks and benefits. The risk factors themselves may not necessarily be illegal or unethical.

Similarly, the use of the employer's computer after work hours might not be considered a violation of the law, and yet, it if continues and especially if it breeds an attitude of comfort in using other's property for one's own, that may be the beginning of a slippery slope that might lead to violation of the law.[759]

1. Get to the Start of the Slippery Slope.

Policies and rules do not change behavior but can create expectations for behavior. "What will dictate actual behavior is whether the social and cultural norms of the organization are aligned with the expected behavior."[760]

2. Accountability is Necessary to Strengthen Integrity.

Integrity links goals with standards of behavior. The organization should align goals and behavior with standards of behavior, and insist that leaders and employees be held accountable for their actions.[761] You have to know what is right and wrong; you have to then act pursuant to values of right and avoid the values of wrong. You have to draw the line far away from the minimal line of wrong. And then you must inculcate this reaction as a habit.

3. Consistency and Predictability

There must be consistency and predictability in the processes so that employees may be able to gauge their performance and to avoid feelings of unfairness, which may lead to rationalization.

---

759 David Gebler, *The Start of the Slippery Slope: How Leaders Can Manage Culture to Create a Sustainable Ethics and Compliance Program, in* CORPORATE CULTURE AND ETHICAL LEADERSHIP UNDER THE FEDERAL SENTENCING GUIDELINES: WHAT SHOULD BOARDS, MANAGEMENT, AND POLICYMAKERS DO NOW? 43, 48-49 (Michael D. Greenberg ed., 2012), *available at* http://www.rand.org/content/dam/rand/pubs/conf_proceedings/2012/RAND_CF305.pdf (last visited Mar. 28, 2016).

760 *Id.* at 49.

761 *Id.*

Managers must watch their own behavior so as not to negatively impact the culture. Leaders should avoid being unapproachable, and should have a mentor or small group to speak "truth to power."[762] Habits of power can be corrosive if they are not contained. That is why someone who tells the power person the truth is so crucial.

4. Incentives Have a Tremendous Influence on Behavior.

Incentives are necessary. Employees may not do the right thing "because they should." Ethical behavior should be incentivized.[763] The issue is how.

a. Speaking Up and Boosting Transparency.

Transparency is necessary. Employees should be free to speak up so that the company can discover where standards and principles are in conflict.[764] If they do not do that openly, they might do that within a close circle and have no contradiction to straighten their beliefs or to make them review and think over their views.

b. How Should a Bank Manage Risks Posed by Third-Party Relationships?

- A bank should adopt risk management processes commensurate with the level of risk and complexity of its third-party relationships.

- A bank should ensure comprehensive risk management and oversight of third-party relationships involving critical activities.

- An effective risk management process throughout the life cycle of the relationship includes
    - plans that outline the bank's strategy, identify the inherent risks of the activity, and detail how the bank selects, assesses, and oversees the third party.
    - proper due diligence in selecting a third party.
    - written contracts that outline the rights and responsibilities of all parties.
    - ongoing monitoring of the third party's activities and performance.
    - contingency plans for terminating the relationship in an effective manner.

---

762 *Id.*

763 *Id.* at 50.

764 *Id.*

- clear roles and responsibilities for overseeing and managing the relationship and risk management process.
- documentation and reporting that facilitates oversight, accountability, monitoring, and risk management.
- independent reviews that allow bank management to determine that the bank's process aligns with its strategy and effectively manages risks.[765]

In addition, or perhaps, alternatively:

*Find out more about the third party's culture, its leaders, their ambition, their employees' loyalty.

*Find out about the culture of the country or state in which the bank is operating. Find out about its reputation.

B. Making It Happen.

According to David Gebler, "To change, behavior leaders need to focus on the social norms that prevent cultural alignment and what influences them." The most important types of interventions are accountability, incentives, and "speaking up" above.[766]

Discussion topic

*Are social drive and business drive compatible?

*Can social culture and business culture merge?

C. Use of the Code of Ethics

As noted, ethics is not necessarily linked to culture. Rather it is linked to values that need not be shared by others but are driving particular individuals and enforced by their own behavior. A

---

765 Ofc. Of Comptroller of Currency, Risk Management Guidance (Oct. 30, 2013) (OCC Bulletin 2013-29), *available at* http://occ.gov/news-issuances/bulletins/2013/bulletin-2013-29.html (last visited Mar. 10, 2016).

766 David Gebler, *The Start of the Slippery Slope: How Leaders Can Manage Culture to Create a Sustainable Ethics and Compliance Program, in* Corporate Culture and Ethical Leadership Under the Federal Sentencing Guidelines: What Should Boards, Management, and

Policymakers Do Now? 43, 49 (Michael D. Greenberg ed., 2012), *available at* http://www.rand.org/content/dam/rand/pubs/conf_proceedings/2012/RAND_CF305.pdf (last visited Mar. 28, 2016).

code, however, is a collection of rules that apply to those who are subject to the rules, whether or not they choose to adopt the ethics that the code represents and is used to enforce.

Thus, one purpose of a code of ethics is to maintain or to change the culture of an institution in order to establish and retain good ethical values. While values of right and wrong, truthfulness and trustworthiness are the foundation of the institutional culture, the details to achieve these values may change with the changing environment. The ability to adjust and change institutional culture is crucial for any institution. That is because in a changing environment, formerly good habits can become toxic.

A code should contain guiding principles as well as details designed to enforce these principles. The habit of evaluating habits must be part of the same Code of Ethics, but the review must distinguish between the principles that should be followed and the details that may differ in order to follow the principles in light of environmental changes.

Thus, the code must include a habit, which facilitates the desire to re-evaluate rules of behavior and ensure that they are guided by principles of ethics. The very nature of ethics is sensitivity to the environment and, by definition, requires changing behavior to follow the same principles.[767]

Therefore, a habit of periodically reviewing the "way we do it" is crucial to avoid continued and strong habits that may have become harmful in a changing and changed environment. After all, whatever has been a fair and honest culture in a small community engaged in a specialized business may cease to be such a culture in a highly diversified and interwoven community that is engaged in various functions requiring different expertise. A Code of Ethics is helpful because it aims at and can be used for establishing habits. But far more is required to change a group's culture.

As noted earlier, Angela L. Colletti et al. wrote that while prior research shows that controls may have a negative effect on trust, because of the perception they create of the work environment and employees, their paper shows that controls may increase trust: "trust-induced cooperation" may increase trust and the increased trust may increase cooperation.[768]

Discussion topic

*Do you agree with the statement above?

*To what extent and how is a Code effective in shaping and maintaining institutional culture?

---

767 John C. Lere & Bruce R. Gaumnitz, *Changing Behavior by Improving Codes of Ethics*, Am. J. Bus., Fall 2007, at 7, 7.

768 Angela L. Colletti et al., *The Effect of Control Systems on Trust and Cooperation in Collaborative Environments*, 80 Accounting Rev.477, 478 (2005).

*Is anything else needed to maintain institutional culture?

Speech by SEC Staff: Working Towards a Culture of Compliance: Some Obstacles in the Path by Lori Richards, Director, Office of Compliance Inspections and Examinations
U.S. Securities and Exchange Commission[769]

What is a Culture of Compliance?

First, some background—what is a Culture of Compliance? We at the SEC have often talked about the need to instill a strong Culture of Compliance within firms—this means establishing, from the top of the organization down, an overall environment that fosters ethical behavior and decision-making. Simply put, it means instilling in every employee an obligation to do what's right. This culture will underpin all that the firm does, and must be part of the essential ethos of the firm, so that when employees make decisions, large and small, and regardless of who's in the room when they make them, and whether or not lawyers or regulators or clients or anyone else is looking, they are guided by a culture that reinforces doing what's right. Importantly, a firm's Culture of Compliance exists *outside* the compliance department—it exists throughout the firm.

It is of great interest to me that compliance programs exist outside the securities industry in companies of every type. After all, organizations of all types are asked to comply with a pretty diverse body of laws and regulations, as well as with ethical standards. A significant paradigm for compliance programs is contained in the Federal Sentencing Guidelines, which sets forth criteria for courts to follow in sentencing organizations for criminal offenses. Having an effective compliance program may allow an organization to mitigate punishment under criminal laws. To provide guidance, the Sentencing Guidelines set forth underlying core elements of an effective compliance program. Importantly, the Guidelines state that, to have an effective compliance and ethics program, an organization shall "promote an *organizational culture* that encourages ethical conduct and a commitment to compliance with the law" (emphasis added).

SEC Chairman Christopher Cox recently spoke about best practices in establishing an ethical culture in U.S. companies. He said that:

"Without a doubt, the best practice of all in any company is to set the right tone at the top. Over and over again, commissioners and staff at the SEC observe that the tone at the top is a major factor in determining the effectiveness of internal controls to prevent fraud, in treating customers, employees, investors and other stakeholder fairly, and in contributing to the long-term

---

[769] Working Towards a Culture of Compliance: Some Obstacles in the Path: Speech by Lori Richards, Director, Office of Compliance Inspections and Examinations, U.S. Sec. & Exch. Comm'n, Before the National Society of Compliance Professionals 2007 National Membership Meeting, Washington, D.C. (Oct. 18, 2007) (modified Oct. 31, 2007), *available at* http://www.sec.gov/news/speech/2007/spch101807lar.htm (last visited Apr. 21, 2017).

success of the organization. Leadership by example, good communication, and ongoing ethics education and training are all vital."

How Do You Measure Effectiveness?

At this point, most securities firms have a compliance program. Now, measuring its results and determining whether it is *effective* is your challenge. Today, some years after industry scandals, business leaders may be asking if the resources they had dedicated to compliance programs in past years are still worth maintaining, or maintaining at the same levels. In this environment, it's critical that compliance professionals be able to clearly demonstrate the effectiveness of their programs.

I think it's important to realize that firms can technically have all the elements of a compliance program—the policies, the procedures, the training—but not actually have an effective compliance program. Let's face reality here—if you have all the bells and whistles but still have violations, or are at least not seeing declining levels of violations—what's the use? In 2004, in recognition of this, the Sentencing Guidelines were modified to put more emphasis on not just having a compliance program, but having an *effective* compliance program.

In measuring the effectiveness of your program, I would strongly suggest that you think about measurements that include not just output, but that also include outcomes. That is, that you not just measure the number of new surveillance reports, new training programs, new guidance provided to firm employees, but that you also seek to measure the reduction or elimination of violations.

In that spirit, and with my experience as an examiner in seeing both the best and the worst in compliance programs at firms, I've been giving some thought to why some compliance programs fail, or are at least not fully effective.

Why do some Compliance Programs Fail?

I believe that the most common reason why compliance programs fail or are not fully effective is that they don't operate within a larger Culture of Compliance within the firm. We've all heard the management truism that a firm's culture will beat its change agents every time. What that means is that a firm's cultural norms will be stronger than any new contrary policy that a manager develops. This was borne out in the 2005 *National Business Ethics Survey*—which found that employees in organizations with a weak ethical culture reported observing much higher levels of misconduct than employees in organizations with strong ethical cultures (70% compared to 30%). And, employees in organizations with a strong ethical culture were more likely to report the misconduct than those in weak-culture organizations (79% compared to 48%).[2]

So, with this in mind, it's imperative to think about how a firm's culture can be influenced to achieve a strong Culture of Compliance. There are some obstacles and pitfalls in improving a firm's Culture of Compliance. I'd like to talk about 5 of them: 1) Lack of Real Management

Support; 2) Valuing Risk-Taking Over All Else; 3) Employees Who Don't Understand the Value or Purpose of Compliance Obligations; 4) Lack of Resources; and 5) Lack of Constancy.

Lack of Real Management Support

Lack of real support by senior management is far and away the fastest and most destructive retardant to an effective compliance program. It's pretty easy for employees to see when the firm's leaders are paying lip service to the importance of compliance.

Here's an example—a private lawyer friend of mine told me about a newly-registered investment adviser that asked him for legal advice about a transaction, and he gave it—that the transaction was clearly illegal. The manager called back awhile later and asked what dollar amount of penalty he would pay in an enforcement action if he went ahead with the transaction and got caught—he was doing a cost-benefit analysis to determine whether he should go ahead with the transaction. He was weighing his likely profits from the transaction against the dollar amount of the enforcement penalty! This story stunned me—because it was so brazen, and so clearly showed a lack of any real management support for compliance.

I hope nothing about this anecdote rings familiar to you. But if it does, what do you do? My CCO friends would say that this is a situation in which their placement within the organization might really make a difference—if they have a seat at the table, along with other senior managers, they might be able to bring their perspective to bear. They would use their "C" status within the organization to maximum effect. In this regard, they are most likely to be heard and respected by management if they can articulate the connections between the firm's "brand" and its trust with its clients and investors and its compliance with high ethical standards. In other words, be able to convince senior managers that good compliance is good business. One CCO friend said that he'd work hard to make clear that he understands and supports the business, he would strive to be seen as a member of team, and not a naysayer or an obstacle—that he'd work to find compliant solutions to problematic practices or proposals.

Another CCO said that this is a situation in which she might bring in an outside expert to educate senior management and make clear their legal and fiduciary obligations, and the serious legal, reputational and business risks that exist in violating the law—drawing a clear connection between the firm's compliance and its bottom-line profitability. Another CCO said that it's useful to find a member of senior management or the board who "gets it" and can champion the cause of compliance to his/her peers.

Valuing Risk-Taking Over All Else

Sometimes, cultural values can clash. A value that may clash with a Culture of Compliance is one that values risk-taking without limits. I call this the "everyone loves a cowboy" culture.

And we do—don't we? The rebel, the contrarian, the James Dean, the Cool Hand Luke, the Jack Bauer. All good, but placing excessive value on risk-taking can minimize the importance of compliance—because compliance efforts may be seen only as box-checking inhibitors to profit-making, rather than as healthy assurance that risk-taking is occurring within the limits of the law, and the firm's policies and risk appetite.

A common example of this is firms that allow excessive deference to their big producers, and to avoid alienating the big producer, managers don't really want to know how he got that way. In this environment, a compliance person who reaches in to find out why the big producer is such a big producer may face pushback and even hostility.

What do you do to overcome this obstacle? I think some education may help—to emphasize that compliance isn't about stifling risk-taking or profit-making, but about helping to ensure that risks are taken within the firm's tolerance for risk, and it may help to remind people that the firm and its franchise are bigger and more important than any one individual producer.

Employees Don't Understand the Value or the Purpose of Compliance Obligations

If the firm's employees don't affirmatively buy in to the value and the purpose of compliance, the compliance program won't be effective. We all know that compliance people don't "do" compliance, they set up the infrastructure within which it happens. If employees don't get what you do or why you do it, they're a lot more likely not to think to come to you for advice when a vexing situation arises, and also not likely to report possible problems to you. And, if employees don't understand why they are required to do certain things, they're less likely to do them.

I read a recent survey that found that one in five firm employees never read their firms' compliance manual. To me, this indicates that these employees didn't see either the need or the value in doing so. Perhaps the policy manual was poorly written and didn't really speak in plain English. I don't know. Firms that grab their employees' attention with real world examples of compliance issues—using video, Q &A, and other techniques—seem to have a better chance at getting employees to understand and thereby to value compliance efforts. And, firms that explain the underlying reasons for the compliance policies, and why they're good for the firm, do even better.

For example, one firm was having a very hard time getting its employees to comply with the various anti-money laundering rules. When the firm's compliance staff provided employees with clear explanations about the purpose of these requirements, and their own role in possibly stopping terrorist financing, they were much more willing to comply with them. This is an example of how simply telling employees to do something, without explaining the larger reasons why—will undercut strong compliance.

A sidebar on training—we've seen training programs for firm employees that were very engaging—even entertaining—and that really focused on how compliance guidelines applied to employees in the specific context of their work. I've also seen compliance programs that are "branded" within firms using ad campaign-like tactics—to get the word out to employees that compliance is an easy resource to use, and a part of the team.

Lack of Resources

We all know that ensuring compliance costs money. Hiring and retaining good people, and in sufficient numbers, and obtaining and implementing technological tools has costs. Implementing new technology solutions may have up-front costs. And, because compliance is an ongoing requirement, it has steady-state costs. Inadequate and variable funding can cause compliance programs to be unable to effectively plan and implement long-term solutions to issues.

Let me give you an example. One large firm invested heavily in its compliance program a few years back—it spent *a lot* of money on its human and technological resources (and it complained loudly about doing so!). It did so only after it was sanctioned in a serious enforcement action. The firm could not effectively comply with regulatory obligations, or implement any new rules, because it lacked the compliance infrastructure within which to do so. Because it had been so behind in funding its compliance program, when it did decide that it needed an effective compliance program, this effort required a lot more money than it would have, had the firm been investing steadily in compliance along the way.

What can you do to help ensure that compliance efforts are adequately funded? My CCO friends say that you will need to carefully determine if you need additional compliance resources. If you do, you will need to make the case clearly and credibly, and be willing to take it up the chain of command.

You may also want to refer to regulators' expectations. I will be clear with you about what those expectations are. Simply put, under the securities laws, securities firms need to have adequate compliance and supervisory programs to ensure that they are operating within the law. OCIE examines securities firms' compliance and supervisory programs for adequacy — and if there are weaknesses, those are the very areas that examiners will probe most deeply for possible violations. We determine the relative risk of each firm we examine in part, based on whether the firm has a healthy compliance program, such that it is likely to identify and head off any compliance problems in the future. A firm that has a strong compliance program should be predictably more compliant, and thus not as deserving of our examination. In addition, if violations exist and the firm is found to have an inadequate supervisory or compliance program, the firm may be held responsible in an enforcement action by the SEC or another securities regulator.

Lack of Constancy

Another obstacle to embedding a culture of compliance in a firm is lack of constancy. Compliance education may be once a year, or may involve a big push in one area—such as when new rules come out—and then employees may never hear about the issue again. I think that this is a common phenomenon—we assume that if we tell people something important once, they will know it forever. This is just not true. In fact, repetition is key.

In a different context, academic literature suggests that compliance that requires behavioral changes—as opposed to a technological fix—requires more constant vigilance by management. And this makes obvious sense doesn't it? If you've programmed your trading system not to accept certain types of violative trades, you don't need to rely on individuals remembering and supervisors ensuring that employees don't place violative trades into the system. In contrast, for those provisions that rely entirely on behavioral compliance, you need to be very, very constant in your message.

And, to ensure a Culture of Compliance, constancy is needed at all levels, from the CEO down. The best example of this is the firm with senior managers who often speak about the firm's culture and emphasize that doing what's right is what is expected. They repeat, repeat, repeat this message in many different ways—in written messages to the firm's employees, to its service providers, to its shareholders. And, perhaps most importantly, in meetings and in private conversations, they make clear that the decision-making process will be guided by this philosophy.

What can you do to ensure constancy of message? You might inventory compliance obligations that rely on behavioral compliance and focus your ongoing message on those areas. And, develop ways to get the message out in an interesting way, again and again and again, as part of a long-term plan.

Discussion topic

How different is the Commission's view from other views of culture, if at all? Why is it difficult for the regulators to inculcate the culture of compliance with the law?

Chapter 15

CREATING INSTITUTIONAL CULTURES; TWO MODELS

Team unity is a competitive advantage. The most important step in building a team is the establishment of trust.

Trust is reliance on the character ability, strength, or truth of someone or something. A team without trust is not really a team at all.

A lot of maturity takes place between "it fell" and "I dropped it." Pepper ... and Salt.
                                    The *Wall Street Journal.*

"A company can't buy true emotional commitment from managers no matter how much it's willing to spend; this is something too valuable to have a price tag. And yet a company can't afford not to have it."

                                    — Stan Slap

A "[c]ompliance officer can think about incentives, power structures, ethical culture—and all of these things are more macro-level. But, in addition, a compliance officer can also think about how to take advantage of individual psychology and [the] heuristic biases of individual traders to frame the ethical question in a way that they may be more likely (due to their internal biases or framing) to choose the ethical choice or comply." Baxter Schooly, 2nd year Student, Boston University School of Law. 2013.

INTRODUCTION

We studied the laws, with which we should comply, and the institutional rules and mechanisms designed to avoid violation of the laws. But along the way we kept reading, time and again, about the importance of the culture of self-regulation. In that context we also noted "ethics" and "morality," as well as the power structure within institutions. In this chapter we examine to these concepts.

How could anyone within an institution that has hundreds of thousands of employees around the globe control the employees' activities and assure their compliance with the laws?

How could violations be prevented and uncovered, especially if employees face temptations to benefit from illegal activities? Much depends on persuading the employees to comply with the law. Much depends on the way in which institutions, their employees, and related entities conduct their activities, and how trustworthy they are to avoid violations of the law.

The design of an institutional compliance plan and its form and ways of enforcement may make a difference. Honesty is hard to buy. Attempts to pay for honesty are not usually successful. How much should be paid to a person who does not violate the law, or who does not gamble with the institution's assets, or does not risk its reputation? Some rewards are not expressed in money: they may satisfy peoples' desire for distinction. But they are hard to measure and gratify continuously. Usually, these rewards do not match up to financial rewards. So how can honesty be financially compensated?

This chapter examines three types of compliance programs.

Section I discusses group enforcement by the culture and the habits it produces. In fact, this aspect of group rule-enforcement exists in most, if not all, groups and institutions. Group culture may include a power structure, required rules of behavior, the habits the rules produce, the punishment that the group can impose on violators and the reward system in the group.

Section II summarizes the design of most compliance programs in the United States, and in other countries as well. However, these programs are evolving and their changes ought to be followed. Most compliance programs in the United States as well as in other states are fashioned in a "top-down" structure: the rules are imposed by the power holders in the institution. The rules involve codes of behavior, dictated by the institutions' boards and management on the rest of the employees, as well as on other subordinates and outside contractors. To ensure compliance, the programs include methods of policing the employees: monitoring activities, investigating problem situations more closely, and other methods to uncover violations and activities that might result in violations, as well as incentives to avoid violations.

Section III describes another form of a compliance program, which is fashioned in a "bottom-up" structure and interactive group operation. That is, the middle managers in the institution, rather than the board and the management, design the compliance program. The middle managers organize the monitoring activities. They are in fact the monitors and enforcers of the program within their jurisdiction. The middle managers gain bonuses for the enforcement of compliance and self regulation in their group.[770]

---

770 These materials are derived from a 2015 conversation with a former student of Tamar Frankel, at Boston University Law School, who is currently the Chief Compliance Officer of Clal, an Israeli insurance company.

Self-regulation is not unusual. To a greater or lesser extent, most people are taught early in life to control their actions and sometimes their feelings. Some lessons come from the reaction of others. A child learns to control his or her screaming by experiencing the parents' reactions.

Groups impose self-regulation on their members as well. We may call group self-regulation "group culture." It is a similar behavior of the units within a group enforced by the members of the group. Culture may include the power structure in the group: who commands and who must obey? Culture involves rules of behavior that the group imposes on its members: "Here we do not do this" or "here we do that." The rules can be backed by supervision to ensure compliance, as well as by sanctions and expulsion for misbehavior. Thus, a golf club, a lawyers' association, and/or a medical organization are mostly ruled by their culture. Similarly, hunting and fishing/outdoor clubs are governed by their rules of culture.[771]

One of the more powerful features of culture is its enforcement mechanism by habit: "We have always done it this way." Habits are efficient, requiring little thought and invoking little argument. However, group members might act without paying much attention to the changing environment and the impact of their actions in the new environment. Thus, many organizations introduce the habit of evaluating habits from time to time.

Needless to say, group culture may depend on various factors such as functions, size, history, and personnel. The two institutional cultures, which we compare, aim at ensuring that the institutions and their personnel will comply with the laws of the land. Thus, cultural rules of behavior may aim at enforcing conflicting rules of behavior. Yet, the two systems demonstrate two different ingredients of culture: institutional power structures and internal institutional rules.

One crucial difference between the legal rules system and compliance system with these rules is that "enforcer rules" involves detecting "red flags," that is, activities that might point to possible violations in the future. Therefore, the programs involve, to a greater extent, policing and sensitivity to activities that might but not necessarily will, result in violation of the law. Yet, the umbilical cord between compliance rules and the laws remains strong when the laws not only require institutions to establish compliance programs but also guide the substance of these rules and the power structure of the institutions. To this extent the laws determine the compliance culture of the institutions.

Self-regulation by institutions mirrors the law to a great extent. Self-regulation is established by a code of rules, and imposes enforcement (power) structures, but leaves space for the institutions to adapt to their special design and uniqueness. Compliance Codes express and

---

771 E.g., Clarke Canfield, *Lobster Wars Rock Remote Maine Island*, SAN DIEGO UNION-TRIB., Sept. 4, 2009, *available at* http://www.sandiegouniontribune.com/sdut-lobster-wars-090409-2009sep04-story.html (last visited June 13, 2017) (Maine lobster fishing self-regulation).

demonstrate fundamental principles of the particular corporation and of society's culture.[772] The Codes integrate not only the rules of law and related market regulations, but also acceptable rules of the marketplace, such as fair business practices, and, most importantly, the principles on which all types of rules are based in the relevant society. These principles express the society's aspirations.

An example of failing to consider the three systems was demonstrated by the Deepwater Horizon oil spill.[773] It can be argued that in that case the democratic accountability by Congress and the regulators was missing, and their accountability shifted to reliance on the industry. Industry followed "a narrow focus on profit maximization through time and cost reduction at the expense of professional best practices."[774] These are some of the reasons for the failure, though not all of them. There are random reasons for failures as well, and from the past experiences, we might learn to prevent them in the future.

Much has been written about the style and design of Codes and how they affect the readers. Our focus is on the culture that enforces the dictates of the codes and on the power structure in the institutions, compliance, and insider supervision.

What is the best method to create an institutional culture and habits of compliance? What communicating rules of behavior could become a self-enforcing culture, achieving compliance? Experience demonstrates that two main conditions might affect the voluntary compliance with the law: the power structure within the institution that would produce the cultural behavior rules, and the rewards for complying with the law. The following are two forms of institutional compliance that might worth comparing.

---

772 A "Code of Ethical Conduct:" is typically the centerpiece of an effective ethics and compliance program. A good code will include a statement of values and the commitment of the organization's leadership to ethics and compliance. The Code will also cover the organization's key legal and ethical obligations, the employees' obligation to comply with these legal obligations and possible disciplinary sanctions for non-compliance. The Code should also provide a mechanism for reporting compliance concerns and a clear policy of non-retaliation for good faith reports. U.S. Sentencing Guidelines Manual §8B.2.1 (2015), *available at* http://www.ussc.gov/sites/default/files/pdf/guidelines-manual/2015/CHAPTER_8.pdf (last visited Dec. 16, 2015); Criminal Div., U.S. Dep't of Justice, & Enforcement Div., U.S. Sec. & Exch. Comm'n, A Resource Guide to the U.S. Foreign Corrupt Practices Act 56-65 (2012), *available at* http://www.sec.gov/spotlight/fcpa/fcpa-resource-guide.pdf (last visited Dec. 17, 2015).

773 Russell W. Mills & Christopher J. Koliba, *The Challenge of Accountabilities in Complex Regulatory Networks: The Case of the Deepwater Horizon Oil Spill*, 9 Reg. & Governance 77 (2015), *available at* http://onlinelibrary.wiley.com/doi/10.1111/rego.12062/pdf (first published online Sept. 9, 2014) (last visited Dec. 15, 2015).

774 *Id.* at 89.

1. In the United States[775] and other international professional[776] and business organizations[777] the predominant design of compliance mirrors the design of the legal system. The first level of self-regulation is the law of the state. In addition, there are laws that require self-regulatory programs or codes, and regulators may come to visit and require information from the regulated institutions.[778] The second level of self-regulation is composed of internal rules designed to detect, prevent, and punish violations of the law.

Because the objective of self-regulation is to enforce the law, compliance involves the enforcement of rules that back up and support the restrictions imposed by the legal rules. Because preventing violations of the law often takes the form of policing (e.g., monitoring), we follow the policing model as well. Thus, the main model of self-regulation reflects the model of the law's regulation and enforcement.

The institution has high-echelon lawgivers—the issuers of the Codes, supervisors and detectors of violations, compliance officers, and their in-house and outside monitors and investigators. It includes deterrent measures such as termination of membership.[779] The Code contains the rules of behavior. It is sent, periodically, to the employees, to read and be trained. In addition, the management establishes a monitoring system to watch the employees' activities, and ensure their compliance with the Code. Failing employees are punished. In sum, this "top to bottom" process follows, to a great extent, the model of the democratic legal system.[780]

2. In the U.S. system, most Code outlines contain elements similar to the following:

The Federal Sentencing Guidelines outline general guidance on the writing of a Code: in determining what specific actions are necessary to meet the requirement of the Guidelines,

---

775 U.S. SENTENCING GUIDELINES MANUAL §8B.2.1 (2015), *available at* http://www.ussc.gov/sites/default/files/pdf/guidelines-manual/2015/CHAPTER_8.pdf (last visited Dec. 16, 2015); CRIMINAL DIV., U.S. DEP'T OF JUSTICE, & ENFORCEMENT DIV., U.S. SEC. & EXCH. COMM'N, A RESOURCE GUIDE TO THE U.S. FOREIGN CORRUPT PRACTICES ACT 56-65 (2012), *available at* http://www.sec.gov/spotlight/fcpa/fcpa-resource-guide.pdf (last visited Dec. 17, 2015).

776 TECHNICAL COMMITTEE, INT'L ORG. SEC. COMM'NS, COMPLIANCE FUNCTION AT MARKET INTERMEDIARIES: FINAL REPORT (2006), *available at* http://www.iosco.org/library/pubdocs/pdf/IOSCOPD214.pdf (last visited Dec. 16, 2015).

777 *See, e.g.,* NITISH SINGH & THOMAS J. BUSSEN, COMPLIANCE MANAGEMENT 59-72 (2015) (suggesting elements of compliance program).

778 15 U.S.C. § 78s (2012) (authorizing SEC oversight over self-regulatory organizations); 15 U.S.C. § 78q(b)(1) (2012) (authorizing SEC examination of records); 15 U.S.C. § 78d(h) (2012) (authorizing SEC Divisions of Trading and Markets and Investment Management to have staffs of examiners to perform compliance inspections and examinations).

779 U.S. SENTENCING GUIDELINES MANUAL §8B.2.1 (2015), *available at* http://www.ussc.gov/sites/default/files/pdf/guidelines-manual/2015/CHAPTER_8.pdf (last visited Dec. 16, 2015) (providing requirements for "Effective Compliance and Ethics Program"); *id.* at .Application Note 1(defining "compliance and ethics program" as "a program designed to prevent and detect criminal conduct").

780 *See* U.S. CONST. art. I, § 1 (vesting legislative powers in Congress); id. art. I, § 2, cl. 1 (providing that House of Representatives be composed of members chosen by the people); id. amend. XVII (providing that Senators be elected by people).

"factors that shall be considered include: (i) applicable industry practice or the standards called for by any applicable governmental regulation; (ii) the size of the organization; and (iii) similar misconduct." These are the general provisions.[781]

Element One of the sample Code outline describes the high-level company personnel who exercise effective oversight. An organization's governing authority should "be knowledgeable about the content and operation of the compliance and ethics program" and "exercise reasonable oversight with respect to the implementation and effectiveness" of the program.[782] "Governing authority" means "(A) the Board of Directors; or (B) if the organization does not have a Board of Directors, the highest-level governing body of the organization."[783] "[U]ltimately the governing authority is responsible for the activities of the organization. It can only perform this function if its members are actively involved in compliance reviews and reasonably educated about the business of the organization and the legal and fiduciary duties of governing authority members."[784]

A governing authority should have knowledge of "practical management information about compliance risks faced by the organization and others with similar operations, and the primary program features aimed at counteracting those risks. The governing body will typically obtain this information through reports from senior organization managers. Governing authorities are expected to be proactive in seeking and evaluating information about their organization's compliance programs, evaluating that information when received, and monitoring the implementation and effectiveness of responses when compliance problems are detected."[785]

"[H]igh-level personnel of the organization" means "individuals who have substantial control over the organization or who have a substantial role in the making of policy within the organization. The term includes: a director, an executive officer, or an individual in charge of a major business or functional unit of the organization, such as sales, administration, or finance." The term "substantial authority personnel" means "individuals who within the scope of their authority exercise a substantial measure of discretion in acting on behalf of an organization."[786]

---

781 *See* U.S. Sentencing Guidelines Manual §8B.2.1 Application Note 2 (2015), *available at* http://www.ussc.gov/sites/default/files/pdf/guidelines-manual/2015/CHAPTER_8.pdf (last visited Dec. 16, 2015).

782 U.S. Sentencing Guidelines Manual §8B2.1(b)(2)(A), *available at* http://www.ussc.gov/sites/default/files/pdf/guidelines-manual/2015/CHAPTER_8.pdf (last visited Dec. 16, 2015).

783 *See* U.S. Sentencing Guidelines Manual §8B.2.1 Application Note 1 (2015), *available at* http://www.ussc.gov/sites/default/files/pdf/guidelines-manual/2015/CHAPTER_8.pdf (last visited Dec. 16, 2015).

784 Report of the Ad Hoc Advisory Group on the Organizational Sentencing Guidelines 58 (Oct. 7, 2003), *available at* http://www.ussc.gov/sites/default/files/pdf/training/organizational-guidelines/advgrprpt/AG_FINAL.pdf (last visited Dec. 22, 2015) (citing *In re* Caremark Int'l Inc. Deriv. Litig., 698 A.2d 959 (Del. Ch. 1996)) (footnote omitted).

785 Robert F. Roach, Compliance at Larger Institutions 6 (Nov. 11-13, 2009), *available at* http://www.higheredcompliance.org/compliance/resources/larger-institutions.pdf (last visited Dec. 22, 2015).

786 U.S. Sentencing Guidelines Manual §8A.1.2 Application Note 3 (2015), *available at* http://www.ussc.gov/sites/default/files/pdf/guidelines-manual/2015/CHAPTER_8.pdf (last visited Dec. 16, 2015).

High-level personnel of the organization should "ensure that the organization has an effective compliance and ethics program" and specific individual(s) who are high-level personnel should "be assigned overall responsibility" for the program.[787] Specific individual(s) within the organization should "be delegated day-to-day operational responsibility" for the program.[788] Specific individual(s) within the organization should "be delegated day-to-day operational responsibility" for the program.[789]

High-level personnel and substantial authority personnel should "be knowledgeable about the content and operation of the compliance and ethics program," "perform their assigned duties consistent with the exercise of due diligence," and "promote an organizational culture that encourages ethical conduct and a commitment to compliance with the law."[790]

The reward system should be established by rules. The employees' rank, range of production, or evaluation by clients and superiors, can be linked to a range of compensation. This compensation may include pay, bonuses, or stock options. Non-monetary rewards can be used as well. These include, for instance, the allocation of the symbolic "corner office," or the use of exclusive corporate dining rooms and bathrooms. Access to these perks signifies rank and authority. Rewards or honors bestowed to individual employees may also be effective. Rewarded employees may benefit socially from being associated with a well-regarded and prestigious institution. In addition, social benefits may translate into financial benefits, if they increase the employee's job prospects with the firm's competitors.

As noted, punishment can include termination of employment, and refusal to provide recommendation, as well as removal to another undesirable location and demotion. In the United States punishments have slowly reached the high level management as well as the corporations. As of July 22, 2004, according to *Wall Street Journal Online*, of a group of 27 officers of firms involved in eight noted corporate scandals (including also a broker and brokerage assistant for two officers) who have faced criminal charges, seven have been sentenced. Nine others have been found guilty or pled guilty, and 11 others have been indicted (including three who pled not guilty); two of those indicted were acquitted and mistrials were declared in the case of three others.[791]

---

787 U.S. Sentencing Guidelines Manual §8B2.1(b)(2)(B), *available at* http://www.ussc.gov/sites/default/files/pdf/guidelines-manual/2015/CHAPTER_8.pdf (last visited Dec. 16, 2015).

788 U.S. Sentencing Guidelines Manual §8B2.1(b)(2)(C), *available at* http://www.ussc.gov/sites/default/files/pdf/guidelines-manual/2015/CHAPTER_8.pdf (last visited Dec. 16, 2015).

789 U.S. Sentencing Guidelines Manual §8B2.1(b)(2)(C), *available at* http://www.ussc.gov/sites/default/files/pdf/guidelines-manual/2015/CHAPTER_8.pdf (last visited Dec. 16, 2015).

790 *See* U.S. Sentencing Guidelines Manual §8B.2.1 Application Note 3 (2015), *available at* http://www.ussc.gov/sites/default/files/pdf/guidelines-manual/2015/CHAPTER_8.pdf (last visited Dec. 16, 2015).

791 *Executives on Trial,* Wall St. J. Online, *available at* http://online.wsj.com/page/0,,2_1040,00.html?mod=home_in_depth_reports (last modified July 22, 2004) (last visited July 24, 2004).

How is self-regulation imposed within the U.S. institutions? As noted, the first level of self-regulation may be the law that requires the establishment of self-regulatory programs. There is a second level that is provided by regulators.[792] Within the institutions, the usual model establishes a "compliance program," dictated by the institutional leadership. The directives of the program are sent to the employees, to read or be trained in, once or periodically. In addition, the management establishes a monitoring system to monitor the employees' activities, and expects them to comply with the program rules. Failure to comply with the rules results in punishment (light or severe) depending on the nature of the violation.

The possible violations of the laws as well as violations of customer and investor expectations are recognized in the U.S. and are often deemed to be "conduct risks." Even though the term is hard to define, there are suggested benchmarks, which we studied.

Following the financial institutions' benchmarks, we note, first, that "conduct risk" covers activities that are not included in main risk categories, such as market risk, credit risk, or liquidity and operational risk. Rather, conduct risk pertains to risks posed by employee and others' behavior.

3. An Australian regulator defined conduct risk as "the risk of inappropriate, unethical, or unlawful behaviour (sic) on the part of an organisation's (sic) management or employees."[793] Such behavior may be intentional or inadvertent, and may be caused by inadequate company policies. "Conduct risk can have significant ramifications for an organization (sic), its shareholders, clients, customers, counter-parties, and the financial services industry."[794] As conduct risk is related to behavior, it is related to company culture.

4. In the United States the importance of culture is recognized. Some of the factors examined include: (i) the "tone from the top" (the behavior of the board and senior management); (ii) accountability (of employees at all levels); (iii) effective communication and challenge; ("an environment of open communication and effective challenge, in which decision-making processes encourage a range of views; allow for testing of current practices; stimulate a positive, critical, attitude among employees; and promote an environment of open and constructive engagement"), and (iv) incentives (incentives to "encourage and reinforce maintenance of the

---

792 *See* 17 C.F.R. § 270.17j-1(c) (2015) (requiring Code of Ethics for investment companies and their investment advisers and principal underwriters regarding personal investment activities); 17 C.F.R. § 270.38a-1 (2015) (requiring investment companies to adopt compliance practices and procedures including oversight of compliance by investment advisers, principal underwriters, administrators, and transfer agents); 15 U.S.C. § 78o(b)(4)(E) (2012) (providing that broker, dealer, or associated person is liable for aiding and abetting violation for failure to supervise supervised person, but is not liable if there are reasonable compliance procedures and person acted reasonably under such procedures).

793 Australian Securities & Investments Comm'n, *Conduct Risk*, MARKET SUPERVISION UPDATE, Issue 57 (last updated Mar. 23, 2016), *available at* http://asic.gov.au/about-asic/corporate-publications/newsletters/asic-market-supervision-update/asic-market-supervision-update-previous-issues/market-supervison-update-issue-57/ (last visited Jan. 10, 2017).

794 *Id.*

financial institution's desired risk management behavior" and "support the core values and risk culture at all levels of the institution").[795]

A 2012 Agency Financial Report in the United States stated that some of its risk-focused efforts would include "enhanced focus on high-risk activities at firms."[796] The U.K. Financial Conduct Authority has no "master definition of 'conduct risk' for all firms" but looks first to a firm's business model and strategy. It also assesses culture, looking closely at governance.[797]

Risk has raised and tightened supervision both within firms and by regulators.[798] It has become a value-added and debated activity. Regulators, such as the SEC, have created a risk management unit.[799] Some risk restrictions have raised arguments, for example, the Volcker Rule restricts bank holding companies' investments, which creates an incentive to take higher risks.[800]

The role of culture is recognized as well, even in non-economic terms. For example, risk avoidance culture seeks to establish: (1) How employees actually behave; (2) The drivers and incentives, rewards and punishments of the organization; (3) How the activities within the organization are aligned with risk-avoidance policies. Thus, notwithstanding government and corporate written policies, the important question is recognized: "Do the boards, management, and employees really mean it?" "Do they mean it on a day-to-day basis, even when no one is watching?"

What should be done? (i) State most of the new requirements. (ii) Put in place and develop the culture to enforce the new requirements, including: (iii) Establish a process for "risk appetite." (iv) Notice the decisions that are too driven by dollars and are not balanced; (v) Establish compensation policies that are balanced.

What questions should be asked: Does the actors' behavior within the institution follow the written policies even if they are not exposed to enticement or coercion? Do the employees

---

795 Fin. Stability Board, Guidance on Supervisory Interaction with Financial Institutions on Risk Culture: A Framework for Assessing Risk Culture 3-4 (Apr. 7, 2014), *available at* http://www.fsb.org/wp-content/uploads/140407.pdf?page_moved=1 (last visited Mar. 4, 2016).

796 *Id.*

797 Speech by Linda Woodall, Director of Mortgages and Consumer Lending, FCA, at the Council of Mortgage Lenders (CML) - Mortgage Industry Conference and Exhibition, Building a Common Language in the Mortgage Market (June 11, 2013), *available at* http://www.fca.org.uk/news/building-a-common-language-in-the-mortgage-market (last visited Mar. 4, 2016).

798 Jane Walshe, *Conduct Risk: An Overview*, Reuters, Mar. 19, 2014, *available at* http://blogs.reuters.com/financial-regulatory-forum/2014/03/19/conduct-risk-an-overview/ (last visited Feb. 18, 2016).

799 U.S. Sec. & Exch. Comm'n, *SEC Announces Creation of New Office Within its Division of Economic and Risk Analysis* (Sept. 11, 2014), *available at* http://www.sec.gov/News/PressRelease/Detail/PressRelease/1370542914800 (last visited Feb. 18, 2016).

800 Dodd-Frank Wall Street Reform and Consumer Protection Act, Pub. L. No. 111-203, § 619, 124 Stat. 1376, 1620-31 (2010) (codified at 12 U.S.C. § 1851 (2012)). For a general description and background of the Volcker rule and its pluses and minuses see *Much Ado About Trading*, Economist, July 25-31, 2015, at 60, *available at* http://www.economist.com/news/finance-and-economics/21659671-next-great-regulation-tame-banks-now-place-much-ado-about-trading (last visited Feb. 18, 2016).

like to behave in this fashion? Are they proud of behaving in this way? Are there patterns of behavior that have to be addressed? For example, how long did it take to resolve a risk problem or a supervision problem?

These directives recognize that there are many temptations and justifications for people to take risks at the expense of others. The directives offer suggestions for mediating between the business, which might involve a measure of risk, and the restrictive law. The assumption is that the business can be induced to behave legally by talking business language: What is the difference between doing and not doing the actions? Should we slow or terminate the activity all at once? Is it a long-term or a short-term issue? Does the rule affect the business as a whole or only part of it? What is the opportunity to take risks, and the probability of violating the law and/or of getting caught? How serious is the violation going to be?

The proposed test is: What is the nature and extent of the (i) harm to society, the business, the growth of the business, and/or the group? Then, how does the harm compare to benefit to ME?

How could firms, management, and other employees be induced to curb their "risk appetite"? Numbers do not necessarily help in this case. But perhaps the following might be helpful: (i) judgment, based on experience; (ii) the activities and leadership of the boards of directors and their impact on management to distinguish between the various departments in the organizations with respect to risk; and (iii) the impact of the departments on the choice of personnel (e.g., HR), and personnel behavior.

In the U.S., regulators recognize that unlike active supervision, culture involves internal value guidelines and self-regulation. The more employees are policed, the less they might feel obligated to behave as they should on their own. Therefore, there must be a balance between policing and trusting that would induce employees to be proud of being trusted rather than fearful of being caught. However, supervision, and awareness of supervision, is necessary.[801]

The regulators' new approach is not free of criticism. First, if the small or big banks do not take any risk or very little risk, they open the door to "shadow banking," which may not be regulated and may harm investors. Second, smaller institutions are not expected to impose the same level of formality as large ones do, and yet there is a concern that these small organizations can expose investors to unfair predatory services and the like. They become unfair competition for regulated institutions.

One answer to this criticism is that shadow banks, which are small, do not pose risk to the entire economy or financial system. In addition, large banks can publicly demonstrate their tighter regulation as small institutions cannot. Therefore, large institutions can fight unfair

---

801 For example, the case noted in Chapter 11 of a small bank that hired three persons from a very large bank. They were granted authority to trade in securities, placed in a separate building, and hardly supervised. They brought this small bank down. What was wrong with this arrangement? Was their background checked? Why did they leave the large bank? What were their ambitions? When they were hired, what facilities were given to them and how much supervision was imposed on their activities?

competition by demonstrating their trustworthiness. Arguably, business partners of large banks may have higher "risk appetite" with the support of the large banks. They may pose risks for the system as the banks themselves do. Therefore, the banks should choose their partners with great care and ensure their reliability.

How do regulators introduce concern and drive to a culture of low risk? Currently they give lectures and symposiums about true compliance. They also watch and sometimes follow the steps taken in the UK and Europe. In this respect regulators join an international quest to understand culture. How do they define culture? How variable are different cultures?

There is a proposal to change and re-focus future government examinations of market intermediaries. It suggests paying attention to bubbles and crashes as dangerous to the financial system and the economy. However, it points to the undesirable effects of prior substantive regulation on market innovations and freedom and the equally undesirable, and perhaps ineffective results of regulating activities after a crash (when the "horse has left the barn"). Therefore, the proposal suggests closer examinations of a kind that is somewhat different: (i) more frequent examinations when market prices rise (not when they have fallen); (ii) examination of entities that are too large to fail and those that are highly leveraged; (iii) examination of entities whose share prices rise steadily with no fluctuation, and those that have obtained exemptions. Examiners should search for violations of the law or the spirit of the law, but not for economic or financial rationalizations.[802]

There is also a legislative drive to reduce unfair competition. The California Unfair Competition Law ("UCL") defines "unfair competition" as "any unlawful, unfair or fraudulent business act or practice and unfair, deceptive, untrue or misleading advertising" and any of a number of specific acts prohibited by the Business and Professions Code.[803] Therefore, the California Law prohibits an act that is (a) "unlawful," (b) "unfair," or "fraudulent." An "unlawful" act can be one prohibited by "[v]irtually any state, federal, or local law."[804]

The "unfairness" prong is "intentionally broad" and involves a balancing test.[805] The test "'involves an examination of [that practice's] impact on its alleged victim, balanced against the reasons, justifications and motives of the alleged wrongdoer." Stated differently, it balances "the utility of the defendant's conduct against the gravity of the harm to the alleged victim."[806] "An unfair business practice occurs when the practice 'offends an established public policy or when the practice is immoral, unethical, oppressive, unscrupulous or substantially injurious

---

802 Tamar Frankel, *Chapter 9: Regulating the Financial Markets by Examinations, in* The Panic of 2008; Causes, Consequences and Implications for Reform (Lawrence E. Mitchell & Arthur E. Wilmarth, Jr. eds., 2010).

803 Cal. Bus. & Prof. Code § 17200 (2014) (LEXIS version).

804 Podolsky v. First Healthcare Corp., 50 Cal. App. 4th 632, 647, 50 Cal. Rptr. 2d 89, 98 (Cal. Ct. App. 1996) (citing case).

805 *Id.* (quoting case).

806 *Id.* (quoting case).

to consumers.' . . . "[807] The "fraud" prong is broader than common law deception. It does not require actual deception, reliance, or damage, only that "members of the public are likely to be deceived."[808]

Notwithstanding the better understanding of internal institutional regulation, the "top to bottom" regulatory process follows the model of the legal system in a democracy to a great extent. However, there is a fundamental difference between enforcing a country's laws and enforcing compliance with these laws within institutions.

When legislators and regulators pass laws, they seek to gain the direct or indirect acceptance of most of the country's citizens. The "people" choose their representatives and, indirectly, their regulators. The "people" can observe the reasons and consideration that lead to the passage and enforcement of the laws, both in the legislature and by the courts. The "people" can protest if the laws or their enforcement conflict with the people's judgments and objectives. The "people" can force the legislators and the law enforcers to change the substance of the laws and the behavior of law enforcers.

Thus, in a democratic regime, we believe that the rules are not only made for the people but that the rules are also made by the people. Therefore, the more people accept their country's rules as their own, the greater their conformity and compliance with the rules is likely to be. People are likely to follow the laws because these are their laws.

Because this model of self-rule legislation and self-enforcement works in democratic societies, we assume that the same model should work within most institutions. After all, like law enforcement, self-regulation requires compliance with the law. In the self-regulatory-compliance model, the law dictates the prohibited and required activities and the institution and its employees, from the top echelon to the bottom, are required to follow and obey the law.

Yet, does the model of the legislation and punishment in a democracy reflect the model of insider-supervision and prevention of employees' violations? The answer: "Not entirely." There are fundamental differences between political and institutional realities. In institutions, the power structure is different than in the state. The top echelon is not chosen by the employees, whereas the reverse may be correct. Unlike the voters, who, in a democracy, ultimately elect and therefore control the legislators, employees may depend more heavily on the boards and top management that establish the rules and the punishments within the institutions. Likewise, top management depends less on employees. In some sense, however, the top echelon in institutions depends on the employees more than the government depends on its citizens: one or a few employees could cause the imposition of legal punishment on the entire institution. And this punishment may injure the country's interests and its citizens as well as the "citizens and inhabitants" of the institution.

---

807 *Id.* (quoting case).

808 *Id.* at 647-48, 50 Cal. Rptr. 2d at 98 (citing cases).

In addition, supervision of the institution's personnel by outside regulators may be more difficult and costly as compared to internal supervision. This difference may depend not only on the size and scope of the institution and the nature of its operations, but also on the purpose of the supervision within the institution. Arguably, because the purpose of compliance supervision is to prevent, rather than punish, violations, insiders can be far more effective enforcers than outsiders. The culture of the institution may be more powerful than the culture of the larger group, such as the entire nation.

Most important is the difference between supervising, monitoring, and investigating the activities of the employees (as well as the management's tendencies and beliefs). Self-regulation does not aim at proving and punishing wrongful activities. It aims at the detection, investigating, and preventing the activities from ever becoming full-fledged violations of the law, that is, it aims at prevention. Waiting until wrongful tendencies mature into full-fledged violations of the law constitutes and demonstrates the failure of self-regulation. Mimicking the structure of the legal system within an institution has failed to achieve this purpose. The hiring of thousands of "compliance officers" and bestowing on them a higher and more threatening status does not seem to have produced a law-abiding institutional society.

Therefore, a search for the reasons of the costly failures should continue. It is not surprising that among the emerging forms of compliance requirements is a system that differs significantly from the model of state law creation and enforcement.

III THE MODEL OF BOTTOM-UP COMPLIANCE STRUCTURES

1. A system adopted by an insurance company offers an alternative to the current model designed to achieve institutional compliance.[809] This system has been in practice and seems to have overcome not only the usual compliance problems but also the whistleblower's stigma and harm as well. How should the compliance plan induce, and provide incentives for, employees to follow its directives, and reduce the instances of violations? Here is a model to consider.This model follows three principal guidelines. The guidelines focus on the elements that create the culture that the company aspires to establish and retain. The company has adopted a bottom-up compliance approach.

a. First and foremost, the middle managers are the legislators, the code writers. These managers do not receive directives, nor are they given a compliance Code. Instead, these managers receive a questionnaire. They are provided with the legal background to create their rules of behavior. To some extent the foundation of this design is similar to a democratic political structure. The people may not actually write the law but they are the ones to choose the lawmakers.

---

809 Conversation with Hila Conforti, Chief Compliance officer of Clal, Ins. Co.

In the institution, the board of directors is similar to the lawmakers, while the executives reflect the lawgivers. However, because they do not receive their mandate from the low level, these managers become similar to the legislators.

How do the middle-level managers become lawmakers? The process starts with a questionnaire, and the first step in the questionnaire is discussing the law. Compliance officers should know the legal prohibitions or requirements. Other managers should receive information about the conditions imposed by the applicable laws, as well as the historical reasons that caused the passage of these laws. Middle-level managers should understand and recognize the problems that current law addresses. For example, middle managers in a mutual fund advisory service should know about the history of the Investment Company Act of 1940, and about the 1929 market crash, and its reasons and drivers. They should understand why the law was imposed and why it continues to be imposed.

b. Second, middle-level managers should understand the price their institution, including themselves, might pay for legal violations. They should realize that even one newspaper story about an investigation of their institution can cause a very serious problem to the institution and to their own interests—their own reputations and their chances of gaining other positions both within the institution and elsewhere. They may be tainted with a violation, in which they had no say and took no part.

c. Third, rather than directives, the middle-level managers should be asked to answer questions and make suggestions. The questions should be answered by the middle managers instead of regulators, compliance officers, or business managers. While compliance officers and lawyers may provide information to these issues, they should not interfere in the process of the managers' responses.

d. How are compliance rules delivered? Compilations of compliance rules carry different names, such as "Code," "Code of Ethics," "Compliance Code," and "Program." All these compilations share two features. They are not rules of law—although they may be required by law—but are imposed only on operations within the institution. Second, they apply to particular groups.

e. What distinguishes Compliance Codes from other codes of conduct, such as the rules in a boarding house? The main purpose of these Codes is to prevent violations of the law in the corporate context, rather than in other contexts. Similarly, the line between the various groups within the boarding house is not hermetically drawn. To be sure, the boarding-house rules may include rules of behavior that are legally imposed. The boarding-house owners are in the business of renting and perhaps serving food. Our main focus is on enterprises that are fairly large, and in most of our examples deal with financial activities. The demarcation line in compliance is not only legal. In fact, it is mainly contextual.

f. Here are a number of proposed questions for the middle managers:

*Because you know the prohibited activities under the law: What questions should you ask to determine a danger or risk of violation? To whom would you address the questions?

*If a problem existed, what supervision is inadequate?

*What kind of reporting is too general and insufficiently accurate?

*Which of the inadequate information existed in the past as well?

*Which inadequacy has appeared now, or would appear in the future?

*How can you ensure that these problems, and the risks that these problems posed, will not occur again?

*Where and how would you expect to uncover problems?

*How would you prevent these problems and violations from ever occurring again?

g. This process and design enable and require middle management to write their own compliance code. They think about the ways in which the prohibited activities might occur and establish ways in which these activities can be prevented.

Thus, the message to these managers, whether explicitly or impliedly, is: "You are the experts; you should be treated as such. You know the answers and prevention methods better than anyone else, including your supervisors." The managers should ask the questions and offer the answers rather than merely receive orders, and report on what should have been done, or whether they did it.

When middle managers view themselves as the legislators, there is a higher probability that they will avoid violating the law or allow legal violations in their groups. They may feel pride in self-regulation. They will retain the power over their activities, and that gives them an incentive to avoid failing. This power carries with it the burden of enforcement. The pride of having this power may be more forceful enforcement than any threats of punishment and any tempting benefits.

In addition, middle managers have an important financial stake in the effectiveness of their compliance system. The system should provide them with incentives to be involved in the compliance decisions . Whistleblowers are usually deemed traitors and "snitches." But in this system they may be viewed as legitimate enforcers, authorized by the entire group and top management.

2. How should middle managers be rewarded for doing well on the compliance issue? Following the law leaves a negative or a vacuum—nothing wrong happened—rather than a positive landmark of a violation—something terrible has happened. Therefore, it is easier to punish than to reward for events that did not happen. Yet, there may be a solution to this inadequacy. One company has established the following system:

a. How is performance measured?

(i) Managers receive points, which they may gain or lose, depending on the compliance performance of their group. The points are granted to managers that: (i) notice a problem, (ii) react by notifying the superior of the problem, and (iii) suggest solutions.

(ii) The issues are ongoing: Reporting is insufficient, for example, if a report was incorrect; or was not prepared on time, or the reporting in one automatic format was not similar to another report in another format, or the two reports did not complement each other as they should have. Thus, the managers are expected to monitor, to correct mistakes, and to check whether the correction was effective. They should check and re-check to prevent the problem from ever happening again. In sum, the program provides for managers' self-monitoring.

b. The rewards. Once per year, the compliance division provides each middle manager with a certificate. The certificate evaluates the manager's compliance performance and grants points for good compliance service. The evaluation is not in words but in points. Therefore, it is harder to evaluate differently the same activity or lack of activity. This format makes it harder to reward on the basis of personal bias rather than on objective activity or lack of activity.

The managers' bonuses are linked to the points in this certificate. In addition, those who grant the points have little or no discretion. Points are awarded for positive behavior and reduced for negative behavior. There is a method of point calculation for good as well as bad behavior. Thus, even though there may have been a compliance failure, if the manager reported the failure and suggested and sometimes implemented the right changes, the manager may lose points for the failure, but gain points for the desirable behavior. This system offers managers incentives to contribute to compliance and to its enforcement by entitling them to bonuses.

Needless to say, top management must fully support this form of incentives to avoid legal violations. Without this support, the system is unlikely to be successful.

3. As noted in Part One, one of the most important issues in any program is to include mechanisms for change. The question is: how do managers change the program to adapt to outside changes? Internally and externally, whether we want it or not, these changes occur. Individuals change with age, with knowledge, with experience, with sickness. They also become locked in to habits. Whether good or bad, a habit that is entrenched may be harmful, because it might conflict with changes in the environment that pose new issues and resolve old ones. Therefore, as the environment changes, an institution, as well as its internal structure and its employees' behavior, might have to change. How should this change be introduced?

a. Business managers might recognize, or be alerted to, changes in the environment. To address change, they should be asked the same questions they answered before. That is, with the changed environment, where are the potential dangers of legal violations? How can these violations be prevented from occurring?

b. Alertness to change should be continuous. The actors should notice the signal that might point to the direction of the change, and then address this signal. They should do so by notifying their supervisors, suggesting changes in the direction of the examinations and suggesting how the changes should be introduced.

c. The scale for grading the members is purposely set at an even number, such as four (4), to avoid the easy choice of the middle grade. The scale includes an option of "strong" (that is better than "adequate") in order to encourage workers and managers to be innovative, to challenge their own processes, and to go beyond the basic requirements to ensure the quality of the activities under their responsibility. These criteria form the basis for the grading by the managers (and the internal controllers). The grades become part of the employees' compensation. Grading "is set in a mid-year review, to highlight the areas the actors need to improve, and encourage them to take action." In the experience of the chief compliance officer of this company, "it works like magic."[810]

d. How to evaluate internal control-compliance?[811] The criteria to evaluate the employees' contribution to compliance are also aimed to create the culture that the company aspires to maintain. These criteria form the basis for grading by the managers and internal controllers. It is used as part of their compensation. The grading is set in a mid-year review to highlight the areas the actors need to improve, and encourage them to take action. In the opinion of the chief compliance officer of this company, "it works like magic."[812]

---

810 Conversation with Hila Conforti, Chief Compliance officer of Clal, Ins. Co.

811 *Id.*

812 *Id.*

e. Attention is paid to:

(i) The compliance unit, and the methodology of evaluating the compliance atmosphere. The evaluation focuses on the unit's work program, the extent of the program's active initiative, and sensitivity of the unit's members to these issues. The evaluation considers the degree of the unit's dependence on outside help, and the effective use of the compliance findings' results.

(ii) The grades the compliance unit receives on each of these items are: Weak/Needs improvement/Satisfactory/Strong.

(iii) The status of the compliance unit involves "its participation in various forums to continue self-education, as well as educating outsiders, the sufficiency of its resources, and its independence."

(iv) The involvement of the unit's management should be guided by the extent to which top management considers the substantive compliance reports and management's involvement in the periodic evaluation of compliance, and the extent to which it has followed the actions after the findings were made.

f. Cooperation is a crucial support for this process. Martin A. Nowak noted in *Science* magazine that among others, the following mechanisms help create and maintain cooperation: direct and indirect reciprocity, "network reciprocity, and group selection."[813]

(i) The process of reaching solutions should be based on a communal level, within a group. Thus, instead of blaming each other, managers would build a culture of interaction and mutual support, in which the problems are viewed as the problems of all employees, and the solutions are probably rewarded with points in the certificate to all employees.

(ii) While competition among the managers and employees may depend on the nature of each member in the group, the culture of the group ought to be "group think." The managers' and employees' pride should be based on membership in the group, which each participant can enjoy, both psychologically and financially. Arguably, a more competitive institutional culture can reward some members more, relative to others in the group. However, some say that a collaborative culture, which provides pride of belonging to the group, might be more satisfying and enriching. As a group, it may achieve more than the competitive group.

---

813 Martin A. Nowak, *Five Rules for the Evolution of Cooperation*, 314 SCIENCE 1560 (2006), *available at* https://www.sciencemag.org/content/314/5805/1560.full.pdf (last visited Dec. 15, 2015).

To a great extent, the bottom-up system is similar to a legitimized form of "whistleblowing." However, many consider whistleblowing a violation of employee fiduciary duties and a breach of commitment to the employer. Therefore, statutes have specifically authorized the employees' disclosure of the employer's wrongful acts. However, getting paid for such disclosures is a must. The "disloyal" actions by the employees create "career suicide"[814] and make it very difficult for the employee to then get a job. The bottom-up system is in fact a self-whistleblowing system, which is both approved and is compensated by the employer. It rewards self-regulation.

Discussion topics

In "Understanding Organizations" Charles Handy highlights some of the features that help in designing compliance programs and assuring their enforcement. First, he reminds us that people are different in different roles. A person may behave differently towards a spouse, parents, older children or younger ones, friends, mutual friends, and neighbors. Obviously, we should also add the relationships between employees and employers. The roles people play may change their view of themselves and of their behavior. The point that author Handy makes, however, is that these roles can be ambiguous.

. . .

Charles Handy outlines five types of groups within the corporation: entrepreneurial, mechanical, professional, innovative, and missionary. In his opinion, one of the challenges of corporate management is to encourage and continue the groups' cooperation without eliminating either their unique contributions or subcultures. Some subcultures within an institution may be highly strict, precise, and predictable, while others might be loose, freewheeling, and erratic. Yet, each group's subculture feeds its productivity.

> How similar is this comment to the bottom-up approach? How different? What other facts do
> the desired approaches depend on?
> Can social culture and business culture merge? Is the social drive compatible with the business
> drive? How would the bottom-up design answer this question?

Conclusion: Comparing the Two Self-Regulation Models

In both models of self-regulation the actors in the institutions face occasional temptations to violate the laws, especially when the laws restrict highly beneficial and profitable activities and are not clear and specific. Sometimes the laws conflict with the beliefs of the actors and their view of the financial system, and this conflict may tend to induce a rebellion against the laws

---

[814] S. Rep. No. 111-176 at 111 (2010), derived from Eli Ol paper, Boston University Law School, Fiduciary Law Seminar, Spring, 2015.

and justification of violation. In top-down and middle or bottom-up self-regulatory designs the assumed potential wrongdoers are the numerous employees, perhaps with their supervisors and even with top management. In both cases the top management must fully support the design for it be effective. Further, the assumption is that top management is honest. We assume that this is the case as well. Therefore, the focus of compliance is on the employees, and they are the targets of the compliance rules. We must, however, remember that top management is not always as innocent as it is presumed. What top management does not do, it may direct or signal others to do. Assuming that the law applicable to the institutions in both models is the same, the issue narrows down to the culture of the institution and its employees and the effectiveness of the models. However, the two models pose significant conflicts. The bottom-up model may conflict with the legal and business model of most U.S. institutions, with business and compliance structures and cultures that are usually top-down. Most difficult would be an adjustment of the corporate culture from competitive to cooperative. The idea of "group think" or "self-directed work-teams" has been practiced elsewhere and is slowly being introduced in the United States. Currently, the U.S. practice is for the manager to dictate a certain action and its implementation. The alternative is for the manager to bring the goal or objective. Group members may then bring new ideas, projects, and arguments to the discussion. Thus, while the manager of the group may start the discussion, the purpose is for the group as a whole to create the positive results. The focus is on the group's achievements, rather than one or more specific members of the group. This format leads to a cooperative effort rather than a competitive one: (i) The members have identical or very similar objectives; (ii) the satisfaction of the group members is in completing the project successfully, and (iii) each member's contribution is usually acknowledged. In addition, the group may have received some bonuses as a group.

This model does not imply that a group does not need a manager. It does. As Kimball Fisher noted in his marvelous book *Leading Self-Directed Work-teams*, the managers of the group have important management roles. First, the leaders should recognize the nature and character of their group-members and learn to create the atmosphere that would lead to "group think" and "group performance." They should identify "group members who try to lead and those who try to complete and those who talk too much and those who are masters of intrigue and constrain them." Group managers have a significant role in creating the atmosphere within the group. That is why coaches should refrain from judgment statements like: "That won't work."[815] In sum, the manager leads in terms of the objective, the focus, a timetable and other constraints, including the objective of efficiency to bring down costs and bring up profitability as well as good service to the clients.

The group should develop a culture of information sharing. For example "the employees of a firm that has more than 100 full-time knowledge managers and 65,000 employees are expected

---

815 KIMBALL FISHER, LEADING SELF-DIRECTED WORK TEAMS, A GUIDE TO DEVELOPING NEW TEAM LEADERSHIP SKILLS 160-163 (2000); *see also id.*at 162.

to share their knowledge and keep their group current. They are rewarded in doing so. The most useful reports are being elevated and this behavior is crucial to support and encourage sharing."[816]

The physical environment can affect and be affected by the employees' work. In a research group, for example, the manager provided a very large hall where each researcher had a connected bench and research tools. There were no walls among the researchers and that physical environment helped establish a culture of teamwork, information sharing, and problem solving.[817]

Among brokers, however, competition as well as cooperation may present problems. Brokers' cooperation may be at the expense of their clients, but so may be competition among them. Competition has driven management to allocate to specific brokers specific functions and types of securities trading. On the other hand, to reduce competition, some employers, such as Vanguard mutual funds, pay brokers salaries.

Discussion topics

*Which corporation is more likely to adopt the group culture: A privately owned corporation or a publicly owned corporation?

*Suppose you joined a group of compliance officers in a bank. You met only two of the group members. Now is the first "business" meeting of the group, led by a group manager.

*How would you react to the following? (i)Your manager makes a statement about the law that you know for sure is wrong. (ii) A member of the group makes a statement about the law that you know for sure is wrong.

* Please comment: The Fourteen Paradoxes

1. Is listening effective? Is a lecture more effective than questioning?

2. How important is a feeling of safety to making a change or taking a risk? Do gamblers feel differently from others?

3, How often do we doubt ourselves? What causes the doubt? Does doubt affect our performance?

4. Does our strength come through serving or by dominating?

5. How does a person gain respect from others? Does it depend only on the person or also on the others?

6. We might have to make mistakes in order to get it right.[818]

---

816 *Id.* at 290-91.

817 Recounted by a friend.

818 Charles R Edmunson, Paradoxes of Leadership: Reflections from Twenty Years of Managing a Highly Participative Ccompany (1999).

Chapter 16

INSTITUTIONAL SUBVERSIVE CULTURE, ETHICS, POWER, AND BEHAVIOR

I do have strong moral values but I do not let them rule my life.

Pepper ... and Salt. The Wall Street Journal.

A lot of maturity takes place between "it fell" and "I dropped it."

Pepper ... and Salt. The Wall Street Journal.

"A company can't buy true emotional commitment from managers no matter how much it's willing to spend; this is something too valuable to have a price tag. And yet a company can't afford not to have it."

Stan Slap

INTRODUCTION

Section I of this Chapter examines subversive cultures and weak self-regulatory compliance cultures. In this connection we inquire about the leadership of the institution: how does it rise and what is its impact?

Section II examines the stages in the evolution of personal slippery slopes.

Section III explores what drives honest people and organizations to fraudulent activities.

Section IV inquires: What triggers the first step of a sliding slope towards fraud?

Section V poses the question of how a slippery slope works.

Section VI tells the story of the Enron Corporation's slide to oblivion.

I. SUBVERSIVE AND WEAK COMPLIANCE CULTURES

Wrongful acts do not necessarily start with a planned, large-scale scheme. Wrongs can flourish through small incremental violations. The seeds of fraud may sprout from a strong desire or a belief that the wrongful act will resolve problems, and then disappear. "It will work out! . . . Somehow!" But a small step that can (not even does) go in the wrong direction may result in changing a person's or a firm's cultural orientation. This change may then lead to far more serious violations that metastasize over time into horrendously wrongful activities. A supervisor's pressure and high expectations may add to the temptation to take the first wrong step. For example, according to Jon Elster, a supervisor in a law firm or in an accounting firm may suggest it, if he says to an assistant (half jokingly?): "Have a good weekend Doug, and don't forget to spring ahead a few billable hours."[819]

A. What are the Ways to a Subversive Corporate Culture?

There are "bad apples" that prefer and prepare fraudulent plans from the start. If their plans result in failure, they may stop, or take a deep breath, and start again. They will continue in the hope that "something will work out later." And in a number of cases it does. But in other cases it does not. The actors continue, until they find themselves trapped in their own schemes. The fraudulent practice then continues until it is discovered.

This process can lead to the best and the most innovative fraudsters. In fact, the more innovative they are, the higher their risk of failure may be. At some point there is a greater risk, not only of failure, but also of beginning the slippery slope towards violating the law and ending with no escape. There are numerous contexts in which such a slippery slope can begin. Here we discuss fraud in two areas: financial frauds and inventors and researchers fraud. These two types of frauds are hard to commit and hard to detect.

B. A Number of Pressures Can Lead a Person to Commit Fraud.

We exclude a situation in which the person not only is ignorant of the illegality, but also would in all probability admit failure. We focus on examining the person who is aware of his failure, hopes "for the best," and slips into illegal actions, searching for a way to avoid being caught.

For example, a young beginning lawyer in an aggressive law firm is required to produce 3,000 billable hours per year. He works very hard. He pulls "all-nighters." But at the end of the year, he finds that he has still missed his target by 12 billable hours. He promises himself that next year he will become more efficient and meet the quota, plus 12 hours. In the meantime he adds 12 fictitious billable hours and his report meets the 3,000-hour quota. He tells himself, that, after all, he is merely borrowing a paltry 12 hours from the next reporting period.

However, at the end of the next year he comes up short a few hours again. And again he promises himself to make up the deficit the next year, and reports the full quota. At the end

---

819 Jon Elster, The Cement Of Society: A Study Of Social Order (1989) (reprinted 1990).

of the third year, he realizes that he will never fill in the missing hours—there are not enough hours in the day to do that! At that point he again reports the full quota.

This time, he no longer promises himself to make up the missing hours. At this point he might look around and realize that others in his position are doing precisely the same thing. Perhaps he also realizes that his superiors do not actually care whether he meets the quota or not, so long as the clients pay. What he is doing is "what everyone is doing," and as such, he fits into the culture of the place. That is, until something happens! The clients sue the firm for overpayment or they may leave, because competitors charge less.

––––––––––––

Discussion Topics

*What caused the dishonest behavior by the young lawyers with respect to billable hours?

*How does the lawyer's experience shape his future behavior?

What role did the supervisors' expectations and subtle pressures play?

*What was the acceptable behavior within the firm? What was the expected reaction of the lawyer's supervisors? How were lawyers rewarded? Who determined whether a lawyer at the firm was successful?

*What role did the clients play in this example?

*Could you predict the future of this young lawyer? What scenarios would you envision?

*How could the temptation posed to the young lawyer be avoided? How could a rule be formulated to avoid over-billing?

*Should we revert to past practices and prohibit internal competition based on billable hours?

*Should we revert to the prohibition on lawyers' advertising?

––––––––––––

A. Often, the First Stage of a Slippery Slope is the Recognition of Failure.

The researcher tries for years, and finds (i) that his hypothesis was wrong, or (ii) that his hypothesis has failed to be proven by the research he has done, or (iii) that it has been proven or disproven by a third party. The temptation to insist on being right and reporting somewhat incorrect results may become too great to resist.

A broker may (i) have discretion to invest clients' money in risky securities or (ii) to advise clients to invest. If the clients lose money, the broker may begin reporting somewhat untruthfully.

An investment banker may have for years practiced close to the "hot-line" hoping to gain significant returns. As no one has complained, and the regulators did not react (perhaps they did not know, or when they knew they believed that the market will solve any problem that arose), the broker continues on this path, and becomes bolder in his interpretations of the law, and in further similar "innovations."

At some point the broker's lawyer may begin to search for ways to hide the client's activities. One way is to find a corporate or other form of subterfuge. Another way is to direct the banker or broker to act in an ambiguous way that might be interpreted as legally justified. The third is to avoid looking closely into the clients' decisions and activities.

B. What happens if you do not "nip it in the bud" at the beginning of the slippery slope?

Tamar Frankel's friend Michael told her the following story. He said: "I once owned and managed a small brokerage firm. We had several stockbrokers who managed accounts for private investors, and one of my duties was to go through all the trade reports at the end of each day, looking for possible inaccuracies or potential rule-violations. On one occasion I came across a trade ticket that reflected the purchase of $500,000 worth of a municipal bond issued by a large school district."

"Two things jumped out at me: 1) the broker had added a commission of 5% to the purchase price, and 2) the client was the broker's mother-in-law, a very wealthy widow."

"Under the regulations, the maximum commission permitted on any trade was, in fact, 5% of the amount traded. Therefore, technically this broker was not overcharging the client; the charge was permissible within the rule. However, in industry practice, a 5% charge was limited to transactions involving securities that were very thinly traded or transaction that were very difficult to effect. In contrast, most bond traders charged 0.5% in normal transactions."

"Rather than accusing this broker of inappropriate action, I decided to assume that he had mistakenly miswritten the commission, intending to reflect a charge of 0.5% rather than 5%. I called him into my office and showed him the 'ticket,' asking him to correct the mistake. He told me that it was no mistake; he had fully intended to add the 5% commission onto the purchase price. In his defense, he stated the NYSE rule quoted above, and said that he was operating within the constraints of that rule. I expressed my great discomfort with this action, both because it contradicted the 'best practices' of the industry, and even more so because the client was a close member of his family. He smiled at me in a condescending manner, and said: 'Hey, who can you gouge other than family members and close friends? They are the only ones who wouldn't question anything you do.'"

Michael concluded: "I fired him on the spot, and told him to leave immediately. Had I been able to report him to higher authorities I would gladly have done so, but he was technically in no violation of the rules, so I could only hope that his amoral behavior would one day be his undoing. That did happen less than one year later, when he traded on inside information, and was barred from the industry."

Discussion topic

Was Michael's reaction justified?

*Would the following readings change your mind?

According to a study by business school professors, "7 percent of financial advisers have been disciplined for misconduct that ranges from putting clients in unsuitable investments to trading on client accounts without permission. . . . And some large, well-regarded firms have misconduct records that far exceed the average." "About half of advisers found to have committed misconduct are fired—although 44 percent of advisers who leave a job due to misconduct are hired by another firm within a year." Significantly, "[m]any fired advisers end up moving to firms that have higher rates of misconduct than their previous employer did, and they become repeat offenders." According to law professor John Coffee, "[t]his . . . suggests not only that some firms have a high tolerance for misconduct on the part of their employees, but that their very business model is to attract the broker who can generate high revenue at the cost of repetitive disciplinary violations."[820]

---

820 Suzanne Woolley, *Study Finds Widespread Misconduct by Financial Advisers*, Patriot Ledger (Quincy, Mass.), Mar. 19, 2016, at 20, LEXIS, News Library, Curnws File.

There are cases in which car manufacturers, such as GM and Toyota, have intentionally manufactured faulty cars to save on the production costs. These faulty cars resulted in the drivers' death and injury. The money ruled. In September 2015 came the story of Volkswagen. The company admitted that "as many as 11 million cars contained software alleged to have duped emissions tests and were possibly subject to a global recall."[821]

Even before that, the automobile industry . . . had a well-known record of sidestepping regulation and even duping regulators."[822] A former Volkswagen executive noted "the company's isolation, its clannish board, and a deep-rooted hostility to environmental regulations among its engineers." Volkswagen "is governed through an unusual hybrid of family control, government ownership, and labor influence." Ordinary shareholders have little influence; the controlling families own over half the voting stock, and a number of board seats are held by representatives of the controlling families, government, and labor. "Volkswagen is seen as having a national mission to provide employment to the German people."[823] In addition, until the European Union adopted new tests after the scandal, "car companies had legal ways to cheat on emissions tests," such as the use of a "golden vehicle," a model specially outfitted for the tests.[824] After the scandal, it was suggested that "Volkswagen now needs to clean up its corporate culture."[825]

Discussion topics

*Who determined to insert the software to allegedly cheat emission tests?

*What were the justifications of the decision-makers?

*What do "isolation" and "clannish" mean? How did the management of VW view the law?

*How did they view the lawmakers? How did they view themselves?

*What does it mean to "clean up a culture?"_____

----

821 William Boston, *VW Tries To Stem Growing Scandal*, WALL ST. J., Sept. 24, 2015, at A1, LEXIS, News Library, Wsj File.

822 Danny Hakim & Hiroko Tabuchi, *An Industry with an Outlaw Streak Against Regulation*, N.Y. TIMES, Sept. 24, 2015, at B1, LKEXIS, News Library, Curnws File.

823 James B. Stewart, *Problems at VW Start at the Boardroom*, N.Y. TIMES, Sept. 25 2015, at B1, LEXIS, News Library, Curnws File, *available at* http://www.nytimes.com/2015/09/25/business/international/problems-at-volkswagen-start-in-the-boardroom.html?_r=0 (last visited Sept. 2, 2016) . .

824 Associated Press, EU *Nations Agree on Stricter Emissions Testing for Diesel*, QUAD-CITY TIMES (Davenport, Iowa), Oct. 29, 2015, at A5, LEXIS, News Library, Curnws File. .

825 Hirohisa Sakamoto, *Behind the Scenes; VW Tarnished Image of Pure Invention*, JAPAN NEWS (S edition), Oct. 21, 2015, at 5, LEXIS, News Library, Curnws File. .

III. WHAT DRIVES HONEST PEOPLE AND ORGANIZATIONS TO FRAUDULENT ACTIVITIES?

A. The Road Slide: Sliding from honesty to fraud

We have a general idea of honesty on the one hand, and fraud on the other. Honesty and fraud are viewed here as two extremes, one good and one bad. We focus on the movement from the good to the bad and the power or inertia that may lead to the acceleration of this movement.

Is it important to identify the starting point? And if so, why? The main answer is: people rely on other people. Few people can meet all their needs. Not only children, but also adults in their prime and old persons rely on others. The more developed societies become, the more their members rely on each other for what they consider to be "basic needs." In fact, the quality of life in any society is anchored in interactive dependence.

Dependence also vests commanding power in those on whom other people must depend (Others), whether individuals, or small or large associations. This power of "Others" may be openly shown as the power to withdraw support that dependents need. This power may also take the form of coercion, whether physical or psychological. To be sure, dependents may have alternative sources to rely on. However, dependence may also appear as fraud: hiding the truth about the extent and the quality of the satisfaction of need that is offered.

In a society that developed exchange mechanisms, dependence may take the form of extracting compensation by fraud or coercion. The degree of honesty of those on whom others depend differs. It may depend on the dependents' ability to satisfy their needs themselves, or to find alternative support, or to uncover the fraudulent faults of the power holders, in terms of the quality and quantity of the needs of others, and the alternatives available to them. For our purpose, it is sufficient to note that the degree of dependence rises with the power and expertise of the trusted persons and with the inability of the dependents to fend for themselves. In our discussions, we limit the disparity of power to the instances in which the dependents do not have, and cannot easily obtain or understand, the use of power by those on whom they depend. In all cases we call it fiduciary relationships. They can range from fiduciaries' unintentional mistakes to intentional fraud.

B. Why Is Fraud Itself Harmful to Society?

One answer to this question is that generally, dependent members in society do not receive the full support that they should have in order to prosper. Therefore, they cannot support others, sooner or later. The solution to this issue becomes increasingly difficult to achieve when a supporting institution operates in entire communities that lack the interest or ability to demand conformity with the principles of fair play. Thus, when an honest institution becomes vulnerable to competition, which is unfair, this honest institution may be driven to protect itself by following "what everyone does." Like many other desirable and contributing activities competition can be destructive. The destruction and its extent depend on whether the competition is based on quality or on unfair or fraudulent behavior. Needless to say, persons and institutions that are brought up or develop strong competitive drives might be driven to "win at any cost" and one of the "costs" might be defrauding others, or generally, violating the law.

IV. HOW DOES THE "SLIPPERY SLOPE TO FRAUD" WORK??

According to Professor Diego Gambetta, there are people and organizations that are established and designed for fraudulent activities.[826] There are many others that act honestly and aim to act honestly, and yet fall into fraud slowly, step by step. At the bottom of the pit, having slipped all the way down, they believe that the way they act is the natural way to act. Then they attempt to justify their actions in many different ways.

A. The Technique—the "Art" or "Science" of Influencing Others—Need Not Be a Dishonest Mechanism.

Even though the method by which we could influence others need not be dishonest, the relationship can enhance the ability of trusted persons to cheat. Dale Carnegie's book *How to Win Friends and Influence People* has spawned a training center advertising the book as "the most influential business book of the twentieth century."[827] The training in this center is based on the book's principles. There is nothing wrong in attempting to influence and convince other people. For example, our court system is based on influencing judge and jury. Lawyers learn to be effective for just that purpose. Congressional arguments and presentations seek to convince the other parties and the voters. Arguments among congressional members and presentations by lawyers before judges seek to convince others of the speakers' points of view. The elections of the president and the members of Congress are based on influencing the voters.

Indirectly, "truthful" statements can be misleading. One example is the way many items are priced. Why do we see the price of $1.99? Does it represent the true, closest price of $2.00? It seems to highlight the less accurate price, which is $1.00. The price of $1.99 is accurate because that is what we are charged, but the description is misleading because it gives the impression of a lower price, $1.

---

826 Diego Gambetta, The Sicilian Mafia: the business of private protection 20 (1993).

827 Dale Carnegie, How to Win Friends & Influence People (1998). .

The skills used to influence people may be abused. Just as a sales organization can help sell goods that are useful to the buyers at fair prices, such an organization could create fraudulent pyramid schemes that produce not only sales but also dishonest salespersons.

B. Honest People May Succumb to Temptations

For example, through the Internet people sent an e-mail that seems to have been intended for someone else, sent in great confidence. The message contained a stock recommendation, which the recipients were led to believe was a real "tip!" Some recipients of the message rushed to buy the stock. Once more recipients bought, and the price of the stock rose, the con artist, who held the stock before sending the message, sold the stock at a profit. The tempted investors, that misappropriated information that did not belong to them, lost.[828] Which of the parties was dishonest? Who should have benefited, if anyone? Does the law have a role in this case?

C. The Slippery Slope to Influencing People

It is difficult to identify the pressures that lead an institution or its members to violate the law. That is especially so when the institution operates in communities that lack the interest, ability, and will to demand that their action conforms with the principles of fair play. Thus, because the institution becomes vulnerable to violation of the law, it is driven to protect itself by following "what everyone does." A balance of power and competition can reduce the power of one or more of the competitors. However, the balance retains less of the individuals' interests and maintains less accountability to them. This is the balance between powerful people striving to retain their power against other powerful people. Other, less powerful people, do not play a role, and are not counted in this struggle.

The stories of con artists might suggest that many Ponzi schemes started in businesses that (i) have experienced financial difficulties, or (ii) were driven by ambition to expand the business and influence beyond capacity, or (iii) had an unexpected bad turn of events.

At the same time, the fraudsters did not try to resolve their difficulties by new inventions or reduced scope. In fact, they tried to continue to do what they had been doing, sometimes for many years. They borrowed from new investors, and paid dividends to their earlier investors with their new investors' money. The fundamental change from a legitimate business to fraud was not clear cut. It was not about how one raises money; it was about a shrinking business that slowly vanished and turned into a story that helped raise money.

---

828 Dan Seligman, *The Mind of the Swindler,* FORBES, June 12, 2000, at 426, LEXIS, News Library, Arcnws File;.Kalpana Srinivasan, *Pyramid Schemes in Cyberspace: Same Old Deal,* ONLINEATHENS (Athens (Ga.) Banner-Herald), Mar. 11, 1999, *available at* http://onlineathens.com/stories/031199/new_scams.shtml#.VqeeqFJXxYU (last visited Apr. 1, 2016) (emphasizing fraud on the Internet in the form of pyramid schemes).

D. A Drastic Change in the Business Environment.

Other reasons might drive a legitimate business into a fraudulent one. As we saw in more detail, E.F. Hutton, a leading renowned and respected brokerage firm, ended up violating banking laws. But the trigger for this honorable, though aggressive, brokerage firm was a drastic change in the environment. The reaction of its brokers and management to the new environment was to use a known technique that was legal. Yet, this technique was slowly extended to cross to the realm of the illegal.[829]

Prior gain and failure can trigger the first step on the slippery slope towards fraud. Much may depend on what can be gained by the wrongful act. In one experiment a bus driver gave passengers the "wrong amount of change." Most people returned the difference if the "mistaken" amount was small; fewer people returned the difference if the "mistaken" amount was higher. There were many justifications to collect the change. After all the bus company is wealthy and the passenger may be in need of money. Besides, the bus driver should be more careful handling change and it is his fault that the passenger received more than was due. In sum, the circumstances enhanced the abilities of fundamentally honest people to cheat.

Similarly, if the opportunity to gain is a "one-time great opportunity," it may be taken by an employee. A cost-benefit calculation might show that the chances of being caught are low and the benefits are high, especially if the deal involves money and is buried in mounds of data that is not checked daily. The attitude then is: "who will notice? Who will understand how it worked? The risk for the violator is low. The only risk is that the amount is large and may be noticed. Well. . . it is worth taking the chance."

Failure can trigger fraud, including failures produced by good ideas that were poorly implemented. The initiators may lack the persistence and ability to put these ideas into practice, to plan their projects carefully, and to bring them to fruition. They may have little patience to tend to the details and no endurance to wait for the eventual rewards. Thus, they lose the opportunity to create a legitimate business, even when this opportunity exists. When they launch their enterprise they may be truthful; but as their enterprises develop and begin to falter, some may turn to fraudulent solutions and slowly venture into illegal money-raising and fraud.

There is no precise measure for the starting point of the slippery slope. But we might consider some cases. The slippery slope is likely to start with activities that are similar to a legitimate business. Some businesses start legitimately and only when they fail is the owner or operator faced with the painful choice of closing up and admitting failure. At that point the owner may engage in wishful thinking and hope that something will come up and the mess will clear up. Charles Ponzi made this decision when he collected $5 million from investors and concluded that he could not possibly meet his obligations. He wrote in his biography that he

---

829 DONNA SAMMONS CARPENTER & JOHN FELONI, THE FALL OF THE HOUSE OF HUTTON (1989).

decided to continue and hope that something would come up to resolve the inability to meet the obligations.[830]

V. HOW DOES THE PROCESS OF SLIDING DOWN THE SLIPPERY SLOPE BEGIN AND HOW DOES IT CONTINUE?

A. It Seems Easier to Begin and Difficult to Stop.

It is difficult to identify the point at which a slippery slope starts. Almost every step taken could be the beginning of a slippery slope. The slide is not an even process; it does not proceed at the same pace or in the same depth if it continues to be practiced. The longer the slide is practiced, the more pernicious it becomes and the faster it is likely to move towards more conscious and bold fraud. In fact the more it continues, the more the actions become a habit, and the less likely they are to weigh on one's conscience.

A habit develops. Habits relieve people from evaluating the pros and cons of their actions. People greet each other in the same way without weighing advantages and disadvantages, unless these become unique and important. Thus, the repeated act of taking something from the office and using it at home, without recording the taking, can become a habit; it becomes less painful every time. If the activity produces benefits, and is not discovered, there is a chance that it will be done again and later without giving it a thought. The next step, however, is likely to be an activity that involves a greater amount, or a faster action. That may require a more conscious decision, but less than the first step. The new activity, however, may add speed and quantity of the sliding.

Further, habits can be good just as they can be destructive. Yet, in contrast to the habit of picking one's nose or slurping one's soup, there are habits that can destroy life. Red wine is good for you. It has antitoxins. But if it reduces the anxieties of the day or the hurt feeling of the moment, that relaxation can bring a craving that may end as alcoholism. Thus, habits can be destructive, if they are deeply embedded to prevent changes with the changing environment. But learning and knowing too many alternatives can prevent people from taking any action. Institutions are structured, and, by definition, cannot change easily with a fast changing economy and external circumstances. Then they might have to change their size, to break down some large units, but there are pressures against doing that for personal and cost reasons. Yet, continuing to do "what we have always done" in a changing environment can be very difficult.[831].

---

830 CHARLES PONZI, THE RISE OF MR. PONZI (1935), *available at* https://pnzi.com/ (last visited Sept. 3, 2016).

831 *See* Darrell Delamaide, *Rules Push Big Banks to Shrink,* USA TODAY, Apr. 8, 2015, at 2B, *available at* http://www.usatoday.com/story/money/business/2015/04/07/delamaide-rules-downsizing-big-banks/25413163/ (last visited Sept. 4, 2016) (higher restrictive requirements are pressuring banks to downsize and focus on particular lines of business or markets).

B. One Starting Point—Our Own Personality

We may wish to learn more about people's dreams, personalities, preparedness for hardships and the way hardship is addressed, and their environment. Sometimes the changing environment brings about the beginning of a slippery slope. As noted, E. F Hutton, the renowned brokerage firm, faced a relatively sudden change in its environment. First, fixed trading fees were eliminated and then competitive fees arose. E.F. Hutton became too expensive, but its management and its brokers did not wish to change their positions and sought the easier way to maintain earnings. In fact, the danger today could be greater than in the past because today's environment may change even faster and in an unexpected way.

C. What Solutions are Available?

If individuals organize, they must choose reliable representatives. The representatives are subject to the same temptations as governing representatives are. They may coalesce with the other representatives rather than represent their constituencies. This system becomes a vicious circle.

Balance of power and competition can reduce the power of one or more of the competitors. However, the system then retains less of the individuals' interests and maintains less accountability to them. This is the balance between the powerful against the powerful in retaining power. The individuals do not play a role and are not counted in this struggle.

However, the individuals retain some power as well: They can exit, they can raise their voice in tandem and overrule the existing power holders, and they have the power to organize and create a true strong counter-power. This image may involve an exchange of power. However, this solution is problematic because exchange without constraints may lead to the same problems.

One suggestion is that the crucial part of trust is trusting the system rather than the people. In fact, the suggestion is: never trust people. Expose the people who hold public power, and leave them with as little protection as possible. Expose them to the media as well as to other transparencies. Will this exposure lead to public lynching? If so, limit this power by other protective mechanisms to retain their power.[832]

Discussion Topics

Is a broker, who offers advice to a prospective buyer, an adviser? Could the broker's advice be the beginning of a slippery slope that can lead to defrauding other potential buyers? After

----

832 *Miners Speak on Safety Violations at Upper Big Branch Mine, available at* http://www.youtube.com/watch?v=9iT-WH6lZUU (last visited Jan. 29, 2015).

all, the broker is paid to sell (or buy) and his advice to a potential party is sales talk. What would eliminate any possibility of such a misleading impression?

There are those who search for a balance as the solution. A bit of fraudulent benefit is fine, so long as the harm is balanced. Is a balance of just a bit of fraud useful? Would it work long-term? Where would it lead?

Can we seek a moving balance? After all, we cannot factor in every variant and every possibility that might feed fraud. But we are able to recognize changes and learn. We can learn about a changing environment, listen to conflicting opinions and try new risks or change the risk we have already taken.

The issue of a slippery slope has appeared in various legal contexts. We deal with the nature and use of rules v. principles. The courts struggle with bright lines v. general values in their own process of reasoning and judging. They pose the questions: To what extent should the courts interfere in decisions of others to whom the decision making was assigned, such as individuals and managers, legislatures and the government executive branch? What are the benefits and weaknesses of specific rules? What are the benefits and weaknesses of general rules?[833]

If success is a red flag, in and of itself, how can a compliance officer approach the problem? To whom would a CCO go, if he or she encountered such a red flag? How would such a CCO present these concerns?

———————

One study found four attributes that usually accompany corporate fraud, particularly large-scale corporate fraud: (i) moral turpitude; (ii) "cooperation among a small group of conspirators"; (iii) "payoffs that create a weak-link coordination game"; and (iv) "a leadership structure that may facilitate unethical behavior."[834]

Corporate culture is built on the relationships among the various actors. An example of a criticism about such relationships is Pope Francis's talk concerning the Vatican's bureaucracy in his message before Christmas 2014.

The Pope listed 15 points of "diseases" from which the Vatican's bureaucracy suffers. It turns out that not only the Vatican but also other religious institutions may have similar "sicknesses." A partial list included "lack of self-criticism;" "mental and spiritual hardening; and those who, along the way, lose their inner serenity, vivacity, and boldness."

He listed: "Ailments of rivalry and vainglory; when appearances, the color of one's robes, insignia and honors become the most important aim in life." The curia should be a model of the

---

833 Dan Seligman, *The Mind of the Swindler*, FORBES, June 12, 2000, at 426, LEXIS, News Library, Arcnws File; Kalpana Srinivasan, *Pyramid Schemes in Cyberspace: Same Old Deal*, ONLINEATHENS (ATHENS (Ga.) BANNER-HERALD), Mar. 11, 1999, *available at* http://onlineathens.com/stories/031199/new_scams.shtml#.VqeeqFJXxYU (last visited Apr. 1, 2016) (emphasizing fraud on the Internet in the form of pyramid schemes).

834 Michael D. Guttentag, *Brandeis' Policeman: Results from a Laboratory Experiment on How to Prevent Corporate Fraud.*, 5 J. EMPIRICAL LEGAL STUDIES 239, 243 (2008).

entire church: "'one priest who falls may cause' harm to the whole church." An important starting point in reforming the curia, said the Pope, is financial management. Another starting point is to diversify the cardinals' origins to represent more parts of the world.

One reaction to the Pope's list was that reforming the bureaucracy requires "a strong man." Another reaction was a note of admiration: "He is opening a dialogue that never existed before." The same observer considered the dialogue to be "a very healthy thing."[835]

The following is a sentence contained in Raytheon Corporation's Annual Report in 2015. "Our values . . . begin with trust, which is fundamental and is reinforced by our ethical culture of integrity."[836]

Discussion topic

How effective is the Pope's behavior announcement and that of Raytheon's? Are they different? If so, how?

Why are criminal legal deterrents not very effective in preventing fraud?

Discussion topics

Please reread the *Caremark* Case in Chapter 2.

What elements of the corporate structure supported good compliance in *Caremark?* What elements did not? What effect, if any, does a decentralized business structure have on compliance?

List the compliance programs that Caremark revised through the years. Why were they ineffective? When did the last program become effective?

In *Caremark,* what was the salespersons' main incentive for violating the rules? As a board member, what suggestions would you make to reduce or eliminate this incentive? How was this incentive eventually recognized and blocked?

In *Caremark,* who benefitted from the misconduct? Who sustained losses as a result of the misconduct?

Please describe the culture of Caremark's board and employees. Was the compliance program of Caremark "ethical"?

------

835 Deborah Ball & Tammy Audi, *Pope Rebukes Curia as 'Ailing Body.'* WALL ST. J., Dec. 23, 2014, at A7, LEXIS, News Library, Wsj File.

836 RAYTHEON, 2015 ANNUAL REPORT, *available at* http://investor.raytheon.com/phoenix.zhtml?c=84193&p=irol-reportsannual (last visited Sept. 25, 2015).

A. On December 2, 2001, Enron Corporation Filed for Bankruptcy.

While large companies do occasionally fail, Enron's collapse was spectacular. When it failed, Enron was the seventh largest corporation in the U.S. by revenue ($100.8 billion in 2000), just behind Citigroup and General Electric. Before its failure "*Fortune* magazine hailed Enron as the country's most innovative company for five years in a row, and included Enron in the top quarter of its list of the 'Best 100 Companies to Work for in America.'" Ken Lay, Enron's CEO, was regarded as a business visionary and power broker. The company's CFO, Andy Fastow, was included in CFO Magazine's 1999 cover story about the Finest in Finance with the tag line "Capital Structure Management."

Enron was established against a turbulent market background, in the process of moving from regulated to market pricing. One of the company's innovations was to introduce and engaged in a market in oil. Its division (Enron Oil) was a New York oil-trading group. In the early 1980s, trading in crude oil futures began on the New York Mercantile Exchange. As this market became more liquid, oil trades offered an opportunity to profit from trading oil paper, rather than oil product: instead of buying and storing the oil, buyers received a paper that entitled them to claim oil from those who had it. To some extent this distinction resembles the difference between holding cash and having an IOU entitling the holder to claim cash. In the 1980s, the head of Enron Oil described the opportunity to Enron's board: Oil trading by professionals, using sophisticated tools, could generate substantial earnings with virtually no fixed investment and relatively low risk.

"Enron Oil" participated in this new business and was profitable. Its financial success enabled the trading unit to operate quite independently. However, the "low risk" described by the unit's head to Enron's board was a relative term.

In fact, Enron faced two types of risks. The first risk was fraud. Its signs were flickering. A New York bank contacted Enron's internal auditor expressing concern about millions of dollars that moved between Enron Oil and the personal accounts of some of its executives as well as some questionable trading companies. Enron asked its outside auditor, Arthur Andersen, to examine the issue. Arthur Andersen reported that they "were unable to verify ownership or any other details' regarding Enron Oil's supposed trading partners." When confronted with this statement, the unit's executives explained that they had "created" trading partners to smooth earnings and demonstrate to Wall Street Enron's strong business model. The executives would shift the money back into Enron the next year.

---

837 This is an edited version of a "case study" in Mark Fagan and Tamar Frankel, Trust and Honesty in the Real World (2d ed. 2009) (footnotes omitted).

At a board meeting in which this issue was discussed, Enron's president stated: "While there appear to have been some errors in judgment, there are no indications that anything was done for personal gain." Although there was some board discussion of dismissing the executives involved, CEO Ken Lay had the last word: "I hear your concerns, and I understand them. But I've made the decision." Considering how important the trading operations were to Enron's financial performance he decided not to fire anyone. Later, several of the executives involved were convicted of fraud.

The second risk facing Enron was its large wagers on predicted future movements in the price of oil. As a safeguard, the company had established trading risk limits, but there were rumors that Enron Oil routinely exceeded these limits. The issue came to a head in October 1987 when the trading group could not hide a $1 billion trading exposure. This happened when Enron Oil bet that oil prices would fall and when they did not, Enron traders continued betting that the prices would fall. In trading parlance, instead of exiting the trade, Enron's traders "doubled down" on their losing position. If prices did not fall, Enron faced potential failure. Even though he had received warnings about the risky trading from his traders in Houston and from his auditors, Ken Lay was shocked at the gravity of the situation. In the end, hard work and luck enabled a trader and troubleshooter to reduce the associated after-tax trading losses to only $85 million. After this write-off, Lay stated: "We became involved in a business with risks that we did not appreciate well enough. And I promise you, we will never again risk Enron's credibility in business ventures without first making sure we thoroughly understand the risks." If only he had kept his word.

Manufacturing Revenues and Profits. The Enron team produced not products but ideas; what Jeff Skilling called "intellectual capital.'" This strategy, for a time, made Enron the world's leading energy company. In 1990 Skilling introduced Enron's executives to the idea of a gas bank. Skilling was a management consultant for McKinsey & Co. tasked with developing a long-term strategy for Enron. Studying changes in gas regulation he realized that the new environment had created increased uncertainty for producers and consumers. The deregulation of the industry thus offered Enron an opportunity to create a market for hedging this uncertainty through a gas bank.

The gas bank would accept gas from producers at an established price and sell to consumers at known prices for the long term. As a market maker or intermediary, Enron's gas bank would profit from the spread between the buy and sell prices. The key to success was insuring long-term supply at a known price by buying the future production of wells for cash up front.

A second innovation that Skilling brought to Enron was mark-to-market accounting. In traditional accounting, revenues are recognized at the date of an actual sale, even under a long-term contract. Under mark-to-market, the revenues for the entire contract period can be recorded in the first year. To the extent that the underlying value of the contract changes during its life, an adjustment would be made to the financial statement. Skilling believed that mark-to-market best portrayed Enron's actual value creation. Trading creates value and completes its earning process when the transactions are finalized; other analogous commodity trading businesses used market-to market accounting. Andersen agreed, and the Securities and Exchange Commission did not oppose the idea. The new accounting methodology enabled Enron to report substantial revenues from long-term gas sale contracts in the first year of the deal, thus putting itself on the growth fast track.

This accounting approach had a side effect, however: because all the revenue from a long-term contract was recognized in the first year, new and larger deals were needed each year to demonstrate sustained growth. The solution was to use cash to buy more gas and sell it with mark-to-market contracts. But where would the cash come from? While Enron was able to book the entire revenue of the long-term contracts in the first year, the cash would actually flow in year by year. Thus, cash from operations was not enough to support growth. Debt was not an alternative either because Enron was already highly leveraged.

Andy Fastow, the corporation's CFO, had a solution: special purpose entities (SPEs). This third innovation enabled Enron to raise investment funds but keep the liability for these funds off its own books. That liability, if any, appeared in the financial statements of another corporation, the SPE. Enron's outside accountants and lawyers established the requirements to create these SPEs. First, ownership of the assets had to shift to the independent investors and losses could not be made whole by Enron. Second, at least 3% of the SPE's capital had to be invested by entities that were independent of Enron.

The independent investors, not Enron, had to control strategic decisions. The investor in the first SPE (Jedi) was California Public Employees Retirement System (Calpers). Calpers made up to $500 million available for Enron investments. Enron's capital contribution was in the form of its own stock. The Jedi deal worked very well. Enron bought gas with the cash provided by Jedi and in turn sold the gas to customers generally under long-term contracts. For Enron the combination of Jedi cash and mark-to-market accounting produced rapid revenue growth. Calpers liked the arrangement as well because it received an attractive rate of return on its investment.

Because the initial commitment of cash was invested, Enron sought to establish another SPE modeled on Jedi. Calpers was interested in participating in a new SPE, but demanded, first, repayment of its initial investment in Jedi. Enron agreed, and Jedi II was born. But how would Enron buy out the Calpers portion of Jedi? If Enron itself purchased Calpers' share, Jedi would no longer meet the requirements of an SPE and would legally have to be consolidated with Enron on its financial statements. This would have the undesirable effect of highlighting Enron's added debt, taken on indirectly through Jedi.

Fastow's solution to this dilemma was the creation of another SPE known as Chewco. (The entitities were named for Star Wars characters, this one for Chewbacca.) Fastow could not find new independent investors to meet the legal 3% requirement needed to establish an SPE. To get around this, he manufactured an "outside investor" known as Big River. Actually, Big River's investment came from a loan from Barclays Bank. But that loan— backed by Enron's $6.6 million cash collateral and a guarantee of repayment—was a thinly disguised loan to Enron.

Thus, the "outside investor" was, in fact, Enron itself. The general partner of Chewco was Michael Kopper, an Enron finance department employee, reporting to Fastow. Through Big River and Chewco the buyout of Calpers was accomplished, and the new Calpers capital from Jedi II flowed into Enron. This enabled the company to make additional investments in long-term contracts and show new mark-to-market profits from them.

The need to find "3% investors" to make Enron's SPEs legal was proving difficult and time consuming. Therefore, Fastow proposed a new fund to provide the independent equity; this new entity would be named LJM, after Fastow's wife and children. The outside funding funneled through LJM would be his money and that of related investors. LJM would henceforth serve as the 3% investor whenever Enron wanted to create a new SPE to move a transaction off its books. Recognizing the potential conflict of interest—Fastow might be negotiating on behalf of LJM to buy an Enron asset that was the property of his employer—Enron's board granted a waiver from the company's Code of Ethics and LJM was born.

To protect itself from mark-to-market losses at Chewco, Jedi II, and another SPE, Enron used more SPEs, called Raptors, with which a number of assets were hedged..[838]

The value of a position that is hedged should, for the most part, be unaffected by subsequent fluctuations in the market price for that asset. Thus, Enron should realize the Raptor's hedged price, that is, the sales value for Enron, regardless of current market price for the SPE's assets. In the case of Enron the Raptors were generally backed with Enron stock. Therefore, the SPE's ability to transfer profits to Enron was being insured with Enron stock. However, if the SPE encountered financial difficulty and could not transfer profits to Enron, this would cause Enron's earnings and stock price to decline. Any decline in Enron's price would thus further weaken the SPE's ability to transfer profits to Enron.

There was thus a potentially mortal flaw inherent in the Raptor's capital structure caused by the fact that, in essence, Enron was hedging itself with itself. A combination of declining asset values and lower Enron Stock price doomed Enron. Then came an unrelated accounting error applicable to the Raptors in the form of an increase to shareholder equity rather than a decrease. This alerted investors.

---

838 The principle of boosting investment performance by augmenting investable capital with borrowed funds is called "leverage." Leverage is present in nearly every balance sheet whether corporate or personal. For instance, when you take out student loans to partially pay for your education you are leveraging your personal balance sheet. The decision on how much to finance a project from debt and how much from savings (a/k/a retained earnings or equity) is called a "capital structure" decision. This decision is a complex one and hinges on many factors including: whether the interest on the debt is tax deductible (as it is with a home mortgage); the relative market prices of equity and debt; the entity's ability to repay the debt; and the amount of existing debt the entity may already have. The problem is not with leverage itself, but with the degree of its use, and whether it is properly disclosed to investors and other stakeholders. While some corporations push certain debt financing off of their balance sheet in order to clarify core versus non-core financial activity, others have abused so called "off-balance sheet" debt. Enron for instance used SPE's abusively in order to hide the presence of dangerous levels of debt financing (or leverage) from investors and stakeholders.

B. Revelations and Responses.

1. The People

A number of Enron insiders foresaw the company's eventual problems. Vince Kaminski, Vice President of Research in the Risk Management group, was an econometrician with "a mathematician's passion for absolutes—in his mind, numbers never lied." Skilling asked him to value a "put option" to hedge Enron's investment gains, so that an SPE would enable Enron to recognize the gain on its financial statements. Kaminsky thought the idea "crazy" yet he and his team did come up with a number. He recognized that Fastow-run SPE's would create a serious conflict of interest and that the arrangement was "skewed against Enron shareholders." Therefore he recommended avoiding the deal. But the deal went forward and Kaminski was reassigned. Skilling didn't like his attitude; he was killing too many deals.

Jordan Mintz, general counsel in the Finance Division, became concerned about Fastow's and other employees' conflicts of interest. He raised the issue with the chief accounting officer and the chief risk officer and proposed presenting it to Skilling. The chief accountant's response was "I wouldn't stick my neck out. . . . Jeff [Skilling] is very fond of Andy [Fastow]. . . . Don't go there." When Mintz ignored the advice and sought a meeting with Skilling, he was unsuccessful. He tried to raise the issue with Enron's chief counsel, and failed. Finally, he retained an outside law firm to review the LJM2 conflict issues. The outside counsel confirmed his concerns.

Carl Bass, a partner at Arthur Andersen, served as an advisor to the Financial Accounting Standards Board. The Andersen lead at Enron brought Bass to work on the LJM entities. He did not favor the structure: "This whole deal looks like there is no substance. . . . The only money [at risk] here appears to be provided by Enron." His concerns were not heard inside Anderson. In fact, he was taken off the Enron account, perhaps because Enron's chief accountant complained about him.

2. The Fall and Fallout

The media ultimately succeeded in uncovering Enron's hidden reality. Enron decided to report losses and restate its equity in the third quarter of 2001. Reporters for the *Wall Street Journal* learned about Fastow's relationship with the SPEs, and revealed that Fastow had made millions from the questionable arrangement. The negative media attention led to a decline in Enron's share price, driving many of the SPEs into covenant violations. On November 8, 2001, Enron issued a financial restatement. But the *Wall Street Journal* persisted, stating that "Enron Restatements Do Not Go Far Enough." The stock price sank below $9.

3. Enron Management Sought a "White Knight," to Acquire Enron and Infuse $1.5 Billion

The cash hemorrhage and sliding price at Enron led Moody's to downgrade Enron to junk bond status. That led the white knight to end the merger discussion. The downgrade also triggered $3.9 billion in off-balance sheet debt to be repaid in 30 days. Enron's share price dropped to 27 cents and the company filed for bankruptcy.

4. Legal and Political Investigations Followed

As of March 2007, 16 people had pleaded guilty with respect to the Enron affair. Fastow entered into a bargain with prosecutors, pleading guilty to conspiracy to commit wire and securities fraud. He forfeited more than $20 million and agreed to cooperate with the prosecution before his sentencing. Fastow was sentenced to six years in prison, a light sentence that reflected his cooperation with prosecutors in building their case against Skilling and Lay. Skilling was convicted of insider trading, securities fraud, and conspiracy and sentenced to more than 20 years in prison. After a long legal fight the term was reduced. Ken Lay was found guilty of conspiracy to commit wire fraud, perpetrating wire and bank fraud, and making false and misleading statements to his employees, banks, securities analysts, and corporate credit-rating agencies. Ken Lay was never sentenced; he died of a heart attack six weeks after the verdict.[839]

Discussion Topics

Please list the problems that Enron faced, and the ways in which these problems could be addressed in an effective compliance program.

Is mark-to-market accounting appropriate for long-term contracts that require physical delivery of oil or other commodities?

What actions could Kaminski have taken while in his risk management position and after his reassignment?

How should management respond to the pressure from Wall Street to deliver smooth earnings when the underlying business model includes earnings volatility?

Who within the corporation enabled the corporation to commit the fraud?

Was Mintz justified in seeking the guidance of outside counsel on the LJM2 conflict issue? Should he have reported the study findings?

Was the board of directors alerted to what was going on? Did the board members understand it?

839 Mark Fagan & Tamar Frankel, Trust and Honesty in the Real World (2d ed. 2009).

Who else among the employees or outsiders was alerted to what was going on? Did they act? Were they effective? If not, why not?

At what point did Enron Corporation break the law? Were there any legitimate actions that could have served as a red flag for future actions that crossed the line into illegality?

Why were the regulators ineffective in detecting and preventing Enron fraud?

In light of this case, what steps should a corporation take to avoid criminal liability for its employees' actions?

———————

Chapter 17

CHIEF LAW OFFICER, CHIEF COMPLIANCE OFFICER, AND AUDITOR:
COMPARING THEIR FUNCTIONS AND LIABILITIES;
DEFINING THEIR RELATIONSHIP

*"Every man to whom salvation is offered has an inalienable natural right to say 'No, thank you:
I prefer to retain my full moral responsibility: it is not good for me to be able to load a scape-
goat with my sins: I should be less careful how I committed them if I knew they would cost me
nothing.'"*

George Bernard Shaw, Androcles and the Lion

In recent years, the status and relation of CLOs with CCOs have raised a fundamental question: Should legal and compliance services be combined, as they were in the recent past? Currently, there is a movement to separate the two positions and recognize their different duties and authority. Therefore, we inquire: What is the function of each? How do their services differ? Section I of this Chapter examines the nature and views of CLOs and CCOs. Section II evaluates the CCO as a profession. Consequently, we might evaluate their appropriate future roles and positions.

I. THE FUNCTIONS AND RELATIONSHIP OF CLOS AND CCOS

A. The Slight, but Important, Distinctions between the CLO and CCO and Their Similarities

1. The nature of the CLO's and CCO's advice, functions, and services

It is generally accepted that the CLO's function is to provide legal advice to the institutional client. The CCO's function is to prevent violations of the law by the institutional client. Thus, the CLO is charged not only with evaluating the institutional client's activities before they take place but also with defending its client-corporation that may have or has committed a wrong. The CCO is charged with detecting and preventing corporate violations, avoiding the need to defend the corporation because it will not have committed any wrong. These functional differences may manifest themselves in the different kinds of advice which a CCO and CLO offer their institutional management.

2. The different focus of the CLO's and the CCO's services

We may view the CLO's service as discovering and uncovering legal gaps, through which a corporation can act and escape the wrath of the law. The CLO is also charged with protecting the corporate client after it has violated the law. In contrast, a CCO will determine the law, analyze it, and recommend that the institutional client avoid behavior that may currently fall within a legal gap, but may potentially lead to violations in the future. In providing this advice, the CCO might render the corporation's business interests secondary, and make avoiding red flags that might lead to violations, primary.

The CCO and CLO offer management somewhat different services borne of different concerns. The effect of the concern with legal risks requires the CCO to tell management what it should not do, while the CLO tells management what it can do. Thus, the service of the CLO can be viewed as enabling, while the services of the CCO can be viewed as more limiting the freedom to act.

In sum: "The lawyers tell you whether you can do something, and compliance tells you whether you should," and "upper management should hear both arguments," according to the Office of Inspector General of the Department of Health and Human Services.[840]

3. Arguably, a CLO's and CCO's allegiance to the institution differs to some extent

A CLO must act in the best interests of the client.[841] Under the Model Rules, a lawyer for an organization represents that organization.[842] Indirectly, the CLO represents other constituents (e.g., officers, directors, employees, and shareholders), who benefit from the well being of the client company.[843] However, the company's interest may be adverse to that of a constituent's, in which case the lawyer may not represent that constituent.[844]

The CCO's responsibility to other constituencies is less clear. The SEC compliance- program rules applicable to investment companies and advisers only require a CCO to administer a firm's

---

840 ETHISPHERE, THE BUSINESS CASE FOR CREATING A STANDALONE CHIEF COMPLIANCE OFFICER POSITION 6-7 (n.d.), *available at* http://m1.ethisphere.com/resources/whitepaper-separation-of-gc-and-cco.pdf (last visited Feb. 3, 2017).

841 *See* MODEL CODE OF PROF'L RESPONSIBILITY EC 7-9 (1981).

842 MODEL RULES OF PROF'L CONDUCT Rule 1.13(a) (2011).

843 *See* MODEL RULES OF PROF'L CONDUCT Rule 1.13(a) cmt. 1 (2011).

844 *See* MODEL RULES OF PROF'L CONDUCT Rule 1.13(a) cmt. 10 (2011).

compliance policies.[845] However, the SEC and SEC personnel have suggested some measure of the CCO's responsibility to other constituencies as well.

The SEC stated that the CCO's duties are "designed to protect investors by ensuring that all funds and advisers have internal programs to enhance compliance with the federal securities laws."[846] One SEC Commissioner stated, "the [SEC] views the role of in-house compliance personnel as being critical to the maintenance of the integrity of our securities markets."[847] In the words of an SEC staff member, "[c]ompliance personnel are the customer's advocates."[848] The SEC Chairperson noted that compliance professionals "have the obligation to provide investors with an added measure of security above and beyond that which a regulator provides."[849] Thus, while the lawyer has one client, the corporation, the compliance officer may have responsibility to society as well. To be sure, there is no statutory provision for this opinion. A speech by an SEC Chairperson implies that CCOs are not, in effect, SEC agents.[850]

Discussion topic

What is your opinion of the views discussed above regarding the CLO and CCO? Where does the CCO fit in the corporate organization? Where should the CLO fit? What should be the relationship of the CCO with the CLO?

4. The Professions of Law and Compliance

The professions of law and compliance are viewed differently. They occupy different positions in the corporation's power structure. However, these positions and views are slowly changing.

---

845 17 C.F.R. § 270.38a-1(a)(4) (2016) (investment companies); 17 C.F.R. § 275.206(4)-7(c) (2016) (investment advisers).

846 Compliance Programs of Investment Companies and Investment Advisers, IA-2204, IC-26299 (Dec. 17, 2003), 68 Fed. Reg. 74,714, 74,714 (Dec. 24, 2003) (emphasis added).

847 Richard Y. Roberts, *The Role of Compliance Personnel* (National Regulatory Services 10th Anniversary Investment Adviser & Broker-Dealer Compliance Conference, Paget Parish, Bermuda, Apr. 7, 1995), *available at* http://www.sec.gov/news/speech/speecharchive/1995/spch030.txt (last visited Apr. 9, 2016).

848 John H. Walsh, *Speech by SEC Staff: What Makes Compliance a Profession?* (NRS Symposium on the Compliance Profession, Miami Beach, Apr. 11, 2002), *available at* http://www.sec.gov/news/speech/spch558.htm (last visited Apr. 9, 2016).

849 Mary L. Schapiro, *Speech by SEC Chairman:Remarks at the CCOutreach National Seminar* (Washington, D.C., Jan. 26, 2010), *available at* https://www.sec.gov/news/speech/2010/spch012610mls.htm (last visited Sept. 25, 2016).

850 William H. Donaldson, *Speech by SEC Chairman: Remarks Before the Mutual Fund and Investment Management Conference* (Palm Desert, Cal., Mar. 14, 2005), *available at* https://www.sec.gov/news/speech/spch031405whd.htm (last visited Feb. 2, 2017) (stating that new CCO outreach program "is not an effort to 'deputize' CCOs as agents of the SEC").

a. The Difference

Law has long been respected as a profession, with minimum educational and licensing requirements and subject to a formal ethical code.[851] Even if not all lawyers enjoy good reputations, all lawyers belong to a special profession. There was a time when lawyers acted cautiously and limited the clients' ambitious but legally problematic proposed actions. Then came a period of "can do" lawyers, who seek to meet the clients' desires within the parameters of the law, and limit the client's ambitions less frequently and less emphatically.

On the other hand, compliance is an emerging profession that has been recognized only recently.[852] Unlike lawyers, and especially "can do" lawyers, that work hard to find a legal way to do what the client wishes to do, compliance advice is not sought as much by the corporate client. Rather, the service of the CCO was, at a certain point, required by the law, and perhaps imposed by the courts and regulatory agencies. In the financial services profession (which some call an "industry"), a CCO is a position expressly required by the rules, or by the courts in enforcement actions, or after the regulators' examinations and inspections. Such a requirement is not imposed on CLOs.

Discussion Topics

Is compliance a new profession? Why were CCOs part of the CLOs' office in the recent past and even in many cases today? Should CCOs be part of the CLO's office?

Why were there no compliance officers in the past? Was there no need for compliance officers then? If such a need did exist in the past, who performed the compliance officers' functions? Historically, were the lawyers serving as compliance officers? If so, did the lawyers' service change? If the lawyers' service did change how did it change?

----

b. The Unclear Difference.

While the need for compliance experts is recognized, compliance has not yet become a fully accepted special and distinct profession, and its relationship with the lawyers in the institution

---

851 *See, e.g.,* Roscoe Pound, *The Professions in Society Today,* New England J. of Medicine, Sept. 8, 1949, at 351-53, *cited in* Tamar Frankel, Trust and Honesty 136-37 (2005); Roscoe Pound, The Lawyer from Antiquity to Modern Times 4-5, 9, 10 (1953), *cited in* Tamar Frankel, Trust and Honesty 137 (2005).

852 Kara M. Stein, *Keynote Address at Compliance Week 2014* (Washington, D.C., May 19, 2014), *available at* https://www.sec. gov/News/Speech/Detail/Speech/1370541857558 (last visited Feb. 2, 2017) ("The CCO is a relatively new position, and the role has evolved significantly over time").

has not become clear. The CCOs should be knowledgeable in the law.[853] However, they should also focus on "Should I do this?" rather than "Can I do this?" and "constantly challeng[e] [themselves] and [their] colleagues to identify potential risks."[854]

The CLO and CCO relationship is not yet clearly established. In light of the different views of their own services to the corporation, CLOs that manage a compliance program may be conflicted. The CCO's objective to improve the compliance program might ultimately benefit the corporation by reducing its legal risks, the financial risks of its investors, and perhaps the risks to any stakeholder.

c. The CCO's growing autonomy.

The SEC and SEC staff have noted the importance of CCO autonomy. The SEC stated in its adopting release regarding its compliance rules for investment companies and advisers that a "[CCO] should be empowered with full responsibility and authority to develop and enforce appropriate policies and procedures for the firm. Thus, the compliance officer should have a position of sufficient seniority and authority within the organization to compel others to adhere to the compliance policies and procedures."[855]

According to an SEC staff member, "CCOs will usually be a member of the senior management of a firm."[856] In addition, this SEC staff member noted that while the CCO is not explicitly required to report to the CEO, "if other 'C' level executives (e.g., CFO, CIO) report directly to the CEO and the CCO does not, . . . [the SEC] staff may interpret this difference in reporting structure to mean that compliance is not as important as those other functions and the ability of the CCO to compel compliance may be weakened." In addition, the staff member noted the possibility of conflicts if the positions of CCO and CLO are combined, or if the CCO reports to the CLO.[857] The CCO reporting to the CEO eliminates, or at least reduces, the proverbial problem of having the fox monitor the chicken coop.

An example of the expanding authority and independence of the CCO is the Corporate Integrity Agreement entered into between Pfizer, Inc., and the Office of Inspector General of

---

853 Andrew J. Donohue, *Remarks at NRS 30th Annual Fall Investment Adviser and Broker-Dealer Compliance Conference* (San Diego, Cal., Aug. 14, 2015), *available at* https://www.sec.gov/news/speech/donohue-nrs-30th-annual.html (last visited Feb. 2, 2017).

854 *Id.*

855 Compliance Programs of Investment Companies and Investment Advisers, IA-2204, IC-26299 (Dec. 17, 2003), 68 Fed. Reg. 74,714, 74,720 (Dec. 24, 2003) (footnote omitted).

856 Gene Gohlke, *Speech by SEC Staff: Managed Funds Association Educational Seminar Series 2005: Practical Guidance for Hedge Fund CCOs Under the SEC's New Regulatory Framework* (New York, N.Y., May 5, 2005), *available at* https://www. sec.gov/news/speech/spch050505gg.htm (last visited Feb. 2, 2017).

857 *Id.*

the Department of Health and Human Services.[858] This agreement required the CCO to report directly to the CEO and the board of directors' Audit Committee. In addition, the agreement specifically prohibited the CCO from being subordinate to the CLO or the CFO.[859] Under the agreement the CCO should be on the same level as the CLO. In connection with the agreement, OIG Chief Counsel Lewis Morris noted that the separation of the CLO and CCO would "eliminate conflicts of interest, and prevent Pfizer's in-house lawyers from reviewing or editing reports required by the agreement."[860] This type of strict division may not reflect the general situation in 2017; yet it might point to the possible near-future establishment of the CCO as independent from the CLO, as well as the increased management attention to the CCO.

Discussion Topics

Many CLO's assert that they should fill the role of CCO. Do you believe that the two functions should be combined, or should they be separate? What are the pluses and minuses of combining or separating the two roles?

What is the source of the disagreement about the precise role of law officer and compliance officer? Is it the meaning of the law? Is it the measure of the risk of violating the law? Is it the impact on the corporation's culture? Is it any other reason? If the two functions were combined, how would our perception of the CLO's or CCO's functions and power change?

Do you agree with the distinction between compliance and legal advice? Are the services conflicting? If so, precisely how, and to what extent, do they conflict?

Should disagreements between legal and compliance departments be resolved by compromise? Should they be resolved by a third party, and, if so, by whom?

What guidelines should be used to determine legal risk? How should legal risk be weighed against business risk? How should corporate legal risk management, and corporate business risk management functions be harmonized, if both co-exist and are within the CLO's office?

What are the possible problems if the two offices and functions are separated?

How could those problems be remedied?

5. Who Should Have the Final Say?

When the facts in a particular transaction are unclear and controversial, how should a decision be made? Rules can be vague as well, especially when applied to new situations. Yet such

---

858 Corporate Integrity Agreement Between the Office of Inspector General of the Department of Health and Human Services and Pfizer Inc., *available at* http://oig.hhs.gov/fraud/cia/agreements/pfizer_inc.pdf (last visited Aug. 5, 2014).

859 *Id.* at 4.

860 Ethisphere, The Business Case for Creating a Standalone Chief Compliance Officer Position 6 (n.d.), *available at* http://m1.ethisphere.com/resources/whitepaper-separation-of-gc-and-cco.pdf (last visited Feb. 3, 2017).

situations often arise, especially as a result of innovations and entry into international relationships. In such a situation, how will the CCO's advice differ from that which might be likely to be offered by the CLO?

The "market timing" scandal that erupted in mutual fund services in early 2000 is instructive. Under the law, the price where investors could buy or redeem mutual fund shares was determined once per day at a certain time. The purpose of this rule was to prevent insiders, who would have access to information about the funds' investments and their prices, from benefitting from this information at the expense of investors who had no way of knowing the price of the fund shares. In such a case the knowledgeable investors could know when to redeem or purchase the funds' shares at an advantageous price, while outsiders, who did not know the content of the funds' portfolios, could not.

Then advisers of a number of funds allowed select investors (who were not insiders) to buy and redeem mutual fund shares based on price information that other investors did not receive. The informed investors cashed out their shares at higher prices and at the expense of the poorly informed investors. This preferential treatment of investors occurred when senior mutual fund managers knowingly allowed it and often profited from it.

At the outset, the practice of providing special useful information to preferred investors was not clearly and specifically prohibited by law. To be sure, insiders were prohibited from benefiting for insider information in purchasing and redeeming their funds' shares. But in this case the traders were outsiders, who received the information from the insiders. If fund management benefited from providing the information to outsiders, the actions involved the extension of two violations: to put it crassly, outsiders bribed management for the information at the expense of the remaining investors. Thus, one violation consisted of the insiders' acceptance of payments for dispensing the insider information. The other violation consisted of the actual trading on insider information and benefitting from it at the expense of the other investors.

Nowhere in the applicable Act and regulation was this particular form of relationship and benefit explicitly prohibited.[861] Yet, two aspects of the process were arguably impliedly wrongful. The managers-advisers of the funds violated their duty of loyalty to the funds and to the other investors, by receiving benefits, which could be described as hidden bribes. In addition, the beneficiaries of the information were outsiders, who became insiders by these indirect bribes. There was a high probability that these activities would eventually be expressly outlawed, as they actually were, later on.

Although the specific activities were not initially explicitly illegal, at the outset the practice violated general principles of fairness by fiduciaries, and created a conflict of interest between the advisers-managers and investors. The vagueness of the situation stemmed from a clear rule

---

861 *See* Disclosure Regarding Market Timing and Selective Disclosure of Portfolio Holdings, Investment Company Act Release No. 26,287 (Dec. 11, 2003), 68 Fed. Reg. 70,402, 70,405 (Dec. 17, 2003) (noting that regulation prohibiting selective disclosure did not apply to mutual funds).

that investors can redeem their mutual fund shares. However, the rule, while clear on the general right of redemption, provided no guidance on the permissible information about the content of the investments in the funds. Because the rule was vague, it was unclear whether some mutual fund shareholders could use information about the fund's investments to redeem or purchase shares at a gain while other fund shareholders who lacked this information could not. If we allow every act that is not explicitly prohibited to be permissible, then this approach would render market timing legal.

At that point, those who followed the "dictionary meaning" of the rule would not have found that this opportunistic and essentially corruptive activity was explicitly prohibited. The issue became: whether, and at what stage, fund managers would be liable for failing to prevent the practice. It turned out that the first step of the practice was not clearly banned as a violation of the law, but it was just as clear that this first permissible step (informing the select bribing investors about the content of the fund's investments) led to subsequent impermissible acts.

Thus, the first steps in this arrangement waved red flags. Some mutual fund managers understood this issue and refused to allow investors to profit from timed redemptions and purchases, based on information that not every investor had. Other mutual fund managers, focusing instead on the technically legal first step, allowed it and sometimes benefitted from it. Thus, the more amenable mutual fund managers focused narrowly on the first step of the transaction rather than the transaction as a whole. This latter category of mutual fund managers eventually paid dearly for this approach.

Discussion Topics

As a CCO at a mutual fund management company: (a) how would you persuade senior management to refuse an offer of "sticky assets," i.e., "long-term investments,"[862] from a hedge fund manager in return for inside information regarding the investment holdings of the mutual fund?
(b) Who in the mutual fund's management structure would you seek as an "ally" on this issue?
(c) How would you deal with the mutual fund's CLO?
As the head of the trading division at the same mutual fund management company, how would you respond to the CCO arguments made in the prior question?
As either the CLO or CCO, would you advocate seeking a no-action letter from the SEC?
Whose arguments are more persuasive in this case and why?
Should the CLO have adopted the CCO's view?
May a CLO or a CCO serve in both capacities in such a case? Should the lawyer have the same approach as the CCO?

---

862 *SEC v. Treadway*, 354 F. Supp. 2d 311, 313 (S.D.N.Y. 2005).

6. The Issue of Confidentiality

Adding to the complexity of the CLO-CCO relationship is the fact that CCOs do not have the ability to shelter their clients' information behind the veil of confidentiality, as do CLOs.

To be sure, the lawyer's duty to keep client information confidential is not absolute. In the case of an in-house attorney, the client is the corporation. The Model Rules of Professional Conduct (Model Rules) for lawyers provide that the private client's information should be disclosed only in very limited circumstances. However, where an attorney knows, or has good reason to suspect, that the client has violated the law, and yet fails to disclose this information to the proper authorities, the lawyer may be subject to personal liability.[863]

In addition, a lawyer may not assist a client in a conduct that the lawyer knows is criminal or fraudulent.[864] Further, unless ordered to continue representation by an appropriate tribunal, a lawyer must withdraw from representing a client if continuing to represent the client would result in a violation of the Model Rules or other laws.[865]

If a client plans to commit a crime associated with the lawyer's representation, the lawyer may withdraw from representation.[866] In some circumstances, the lawyer may disclose confidential information regarding the client's plans to commit a crime. A lawyer may disclose confidential information relating to the representation of a client in limited circumstances, including: (1) "to prevent reasonably certain death or substantial bodily harm"; (2) "to prevent the client from committing a crime or perpetrating fraud that is reasonably certain to result in substantial injury to the financial interests or property of another and in furtherance of which the client has used or is using the lawyer's services"; (3) "to prevent, mitigate or rectify substantial injury to the financial interests or property of another that is reasonably certain to result or has resulted from the client's commission of a crime or fraud in furtherance of which the client has used the lawyer's services."[867]

In addition, a lawyer must disclose a material fact if necessary to avoid assisting a criminal or fraudulent act by a client, unless disclosure is otherwise prohibited by the confidentiality rules.[868]

---

863 MODEL RULES OF PROF'L CONDUCT Rule 1.6 (2011).

864 MODEL RULES OF PROF'L CONDUCT Rule 1.2(d) (2011).

865 MODEL RULES OF PROF'L CONDUCT Rule 1.16(a) (2011).

866 A lawyer may withdraw from representation if "the client persists in a course of action involving the lawyer's services that the lawyer reasonably believes is criminal or fraudulent" (unless ordered to continue representation by a tribunal). MODEL RULES OF PROF'L CONDUCT Rule 1.16(b)(2) (2011). Similarly the lawyer may withdraw if "the client has used the lawyer's services to perpetrate a crime or fraud" (unless ordered to continue representation by a tribunal). MODEL RULES OF PROF'L CONDUCT Rule 1.16(b)(3) (2011). *See also* Jean Eaglesham, *Wide Net Is Cast in Probe of Microcap*, WALL ST. J., Aug. 15, 2014, at C1 ("The SEC is looking at whether some lawyers and accountants are liable for helping to enable penny-stock frauds, either by signing off on phony information or simply not asking the right questions . . . ").

867 MODEL RULES OF PROF'L CONDUCT Rule 1.6(b)(1)-(3) (2011).

868 MODEL RULES OF PROF'L CONDUCT Rule 4.1(b) (2011).

Under what circumstances is a corporate counsel, and particularly a CLO, ethically obligated to "blow the whistle" on a corporate client's misconduct? Ethical considerations under the Model Code provide that "[t]he attorney-client privilege is more limited than the ethical obligation of a lawyer to guard the confidences and secrets of his client"[869] and that "[t]he obligation of a lawyer to preserve the confidences and secrets of his client continues after the termination of his employment."[870] "Ethical obligations" mentioned in this paragraph include prohibitions of conflicts of interest as well as duties to offer qualified advice.

Discussion Topics

Should lawyers adopt an approach that is similar to that of compliance officers?

If the CLO lacks sufficient subject-matter expertise to properly address a legal problem faced by his employer and needs advice, what should the CLO do?

When a CLO seeks another lawyer's advice, or when the CLO believes that disclosure must be made to the authorities, does this CLO violate his duties to the client?

Are lawyers preaching unethical conduct? What would be a CLO's advice regarding a proposed transaction that is ethically or legally on shaky ground? How might a CCO advise on the same proposed transaction? What is the difference between legal advice and compliance advice?

Why should a CCO be more concerned with ethical issues than a CLO?

---

7. Compliance is a Profession

Mr. John Walsh, when he served as Chief Counsel, Office of Compliance Inspections and Examinations at the SEC, expressed the following:[871] while compliance is similar to litigation, as well as to in-house counseling, it is a different and separate profession.[872] Mr. Walsh defined a profession by three features. First, a profession is "an occupation, for which the necessary training is intellectual, involving knowledge and learning as distinguished from skill." Second, a profession is "pursued largely" in the service of others. Third, the amount of financial rewards for the service is "not the accepted measure of success." Compliance meets all three features.

---

869 MODEL CODE OF PROFESSIONAL RESPONSIBILITY EC 4-4 (1980); H. Lowell Brown, *The Dilemma of Corporate Counsel Faced with Client Misconduct: Disclosure of Client Confidences or Constructive Discharge*, 44 BUFF. L. REV. 777, 795 (1996).

870 MODEL CODE OF PROFESSIONAL RESPONSIBILITY EC 4-6 (1980); H. Lowell Brown, *The Dilemma of Corporate Counsel Faced with Client Misconduct: Disclosure of Client Confidences or Constructive Discharge*, 44 BUFF. L. REV. 777, 795-96 (1996).

871 John H. Walsh, *Speech by SEC Staff: What Makes Compliance a Profession?* (NRS Symposium on the Compliance Profession, Miami Beach, Apr. 11, 2002), *available at* https://www.sec.gov/news/speech/spch558.htm (last visited Apr. 12, 2016).

872 *See also* TERRANCE J. O'MALLEY & JOHN H. WALSH, INVESTMENT ADVISER'S LEGAL AND COMPLIANCE GUIDE (2d ed. 2015).

a. Compliance Requires Much Learning and Creativity

This service poses real and demanding intellectual challenges. Business regulation is complex and changing. It applies to unpredictable situations. Compliance rules are usually stated as general duties, rather than bright-line directives. Therefore, they require interpretation and application to particular situations, often in unpredictable circumstances.

In addition, understanding continuous changes that are taking place in the area of expertise is crucial to any profession. In the financial area, for example, the laws since the 1940s were based on separate regulation of various species of intermediaries. These include: banks, credit unions and similar organizations, brokers, exchanges, and other securities markets, mutual funds, and advisers. The regulations of these various servicers and intermediaries addressed the characteristic problems that they posed. Throughout the years the functional boundaries between these intermediaries have been loosened. Functionalities and services were often combined or merged, and new intermediation (or disintermediation) structures have appeared. Most of these changes took place during the 1980's and 1990's. But they had effects for years thereafter.

As a result of these changes, being a competent navigator of today's regulatory systems is a far more complex task than it was in the past. Today's compliance office requires a high level of expertise as well. Compliance is a crucial and expanding profession.

Mr. Walsh also noted the importance of compliance in the United States system of securities regulation. He noted that President Roosevelt took office during an economic crisis. However, instead of controlling the securities industry, Roosevelt "wanted the securities industry to be governed by 'a simple code of ethics'" and "wanted to elevate its character, honesty, and honor." "Only when business was conducted in this fashion, only when the public's trust was morally justified, would confidence and prosperity return." According to Mr. Walsh, "if there is any group in the modern securities industry that is ready to meet this ethical challenge, that is ready to establish and enforce a simple code, simple enough for the public to understand, it is compliance."[873]

Discussion Topics

Did dishonesty produce the crash of 1929? Or did a culture of gambling and speculation cause it? Who was to blame?

Should we blame the purveyors of leverage, risky investments, and other means of speculation?

Or is the blame shared between the investor-speculators and gamblers? Perhaps neither answer

---

[873] John H. Walsh, *Speech by SEC Staff: What Makes Compliance a Profession?* (NRS Symposium on the Compliance Profession, Miami Beach, Apr. 11, 2002), *available at* https://www.sec.gov/news/speech/spch558.htm (last visited Apr. 12, 2016).

is entirely correct. Could you list the components of a market bubble and a crash? Who feeds them? Who benefits? Who loses? And for how long?

Have the securities and banking acts of the 1930s and 1940s reduced fraud? Arguably, they did not, and what reduced the fraud was the investor caution triggered by the memory of the 1929 crash. Arguably, as the memory of the Great Depression has worn off so has the related caution. To be sure, the restrictive laws of the 30's and 40's have also been relaxed. Perhaps both reflected the national mood and fading memory.

b. Like Medicine, Compliance Aims at Preventive Measures.

Most compliance situations do not deal with violations that have occurred but with possible situations that may culminate in violations. While lawyers learn the law by focusing on specific cases that have already taken place, the compliance officer turns the process around, and looks at a rule to determine: How could "knowledgeable, imaginative, [and] creative people" attempt to violate this standard? As you read the law, you can imagine all the possible violations. Therefore, one must draw on expert judgment to find an effective answer. This is one feature of a professional.

Compliance is similar to modern quality management: be "right the first time," rather than catch and correct errors. In compliance you need to take preventive actions, "designing and implementing preventive systems." In enforcement actions that present failure to supervise, "waiting for problems" is not an adequate approach. Both quality management and compliance must focus on becoming an integral part of the institution's routine and everyday operations: "training line employees" to "understand the difference" between "conforming and nonconforming output." "Education, training, and awareness are key elements." These elements as well are the fundamental features of a profession.[874]

c. A Profession Consists of Providing Service to Others.

As Justice Brandeis noted, a profession meets the needs of others: "Lawyers have clients. Doctors have patients."[875] Mr. Walsh suggested that compliance officers are the advocates of the business' customers, noting their complaints, and examining and monitoring the advertising that targets them. Compliance officers can spot the danger and stop it before the customers suffer harm.

---

874 John H. Walsh, *Speech by SEC Staff: What Makes Compliance a Profession?* (NRS Symposium on the Compliance Profession, Miami Beach, Apr. 11, 2002), *available at* https://www.sec.gov/news/speech/spch558.htm (last visited Apr. 12, 2016).

875 *Id., citing* LOUIS DEMBITZ BRANDEIS, BUSINESS: A PROFESSION (1914).

The focus of a profession is service, said Mr. Walsh; a measure of success in having achieved these objectives, and not merely having made money. For compliance, this success is "quality" and "ethics." In the law, such services are in fact the service by fiduciaries. The two main duties of fiduciaries are the duty of care—expert performance—and the duty of loyalty—avoiding conflicts of interest. In essence, it means identifying with those you serve, putting yourself in their place.

Compliance must focus on flaws in the institutional structure and patterns of behavior. Like most management problems, most compliance failures have systemic causes. The more common causes include "misguided compensation," "unrealistic performance goals," and "uneven supervision." "By carefully monitoring for recurrent red flags, compliance can identify the firm's [underlying] structural flaws and fix them before serious harm [results]." "Every form of monitoring system, from sophisticated [suspicious activity] reports, to good old-fashioned customer complaints, can serve this purpose."[876]

"Finally, there is another way in which quality management and compliance are similar," but this similarity is "less fortunate than the others." Some business managers may treat "quality management" and compliance as "unproductive cost centers." "The literature [offers] examples of businesses that slashed quality [management] in an effort to [increase] short-term profits, only to find that they had [ultimately] destroyed the firm's long-term franchise." "Compliance is often in a similar predicament. If [viewed as a regulatory cost center and nothing else] it is a ready victim when the downsizing begins. For both quality [management] and compliance, part of [the] mission is to convince management that [they] add [significant and] substantial value to the competitiveness of the firm." Unfortunately, such convincing may take a "negative tone," recalling the significant problems that follow failures in quality management or compliance. Evaluating risk is difficult because it promises returns, rather than losses.[877]

d. As Noted, it is Compliance Rather than Management that Recognizes Risk.

Mr. Walsh suggests that management should also "recognize the [risk] it is running." To be sure, risk cannot be measured with precision. It should be balanced. For example, management "should define customer satisfaction to include confidence in [the institutional] honesty and trustworthiness." Compliance and regulators "should ensure that full compliance is within the design specifications of the products and services [that the institution sells]."[878]

This purpose leads to ethics. Legally, ethics translates into the fiduciary duty of loyalty; avoiding conflicting interests that undermine the relationship and trust of the customers. In this context, the duty of loyalty is far stricter than the same duty under corporate law. Here the duty

---

876 *Id.*

877 *Id.*

878 *Id.*

prohibits the service providers from accepting any benefit from a client without first disclosing any conflicts of interest and receiving the clients' consent for these conflicts. This heightened duty of loyalty is one of the foundational pillars of federal securities industry regulation. Mr. Walsh describes this duty in the same words as those who introduced it into the regulatory regime for U.S. securities markets. We may add that expert professional service is a service whose objective is to leads to long-term success. This success is defined as clients' satisfaction and avoiding as well as eliminating defects to secure customer satisfaction.

e. A Profession Should Be Aware of Its Status

Mr. Walsh expressed the belief that "compliance satisfie[s] Justice Brandeis's definition of a profession." "Moreover, in these characteristics, we can see some of the professional standards that it should meet. The practice of compliance is an intellectual challenge that should be met through the exercise of expert judgment. Compliance should make sure the customer's interests, and the customer's perspective, are not forgotten."

Mr. Walsh "disagree[d] with Justice Brandeis in one respect: The Justice's "definition is incomplete," Mr. Walsh said. "In addition to [the Justice's three elements,] a profession should be aware of its status." "To be truly professional, compliance's special status must be recognized by its practitioners, by those who employ them, and by the members of the public who deal with them. All should respect the public interest that fills this work. Earning compliance that recognition and respect is part of our mission."[879]

8. What Kind of People Are Compliance Officers?

John Walsh suggests that compliance officers have the characteristics of entrepreneurs.[880]

They have the "what next" mentality. They are excited about change and interested in the unknown; perhaps because the unknown is where their opportunities lie. They are not afraid of what they do not know and are eager to learn. With continuous learning comes recognizing problems and ideas for solutions. They focus on creating and implementing new ways of doing things. They often are more interested in the future than in the present or the past, particularly if the future promises better methods and results. This process and the ideas it brings, are the exciting moments for entrepreneurs. Thus, in this respect compliance officers and those who work in the area are similar to entrepreneurs.

Yet, even though compliance officers are similar to entrepreneurs; the objectives of the two groups differ. Compliance officers' aim is prevention. In this respect they may differ from entrepreneurs. However, the ways compliance officers may achieve their purpose can be creative,

---

879 *Id.*

880 *Id.*

and their awareness of changing reality leads to addressing the same problem in different ways. Trying a new method or solution or anything new does not ensure success, and there is no past to verify it. In addition, like entrepreneurs, compliance personnel must be keenly aware of what is happening around them.

_____

Discussion Topic

There are many lawyers who serve as compliance officers. How different are these lawyers-compliance officers from other lawyers who are not compliance officers: in a top-down compliance structure or in a bottom-up compliance structure (described in Chapter 15)?

II. PROBLEM: THE "DUAL-HATTED" CLO/CCO CONFIDENTIALITY PRIVILEGE

A senior research analyst, holding several securities licenses, traded ahead of the firm's clients on ten separate occasions over a two-month period. The analyst made a profit of $50,000 on the trades. The "dual-hatted" CLO/CCO investigated the front-running allegations and concluded that the analyst did in fact engage in this conduct. The CLO/CCO recommended to the firm's management committee that the employee be asked to resign or be terminated. The management committee agreed with the recommendation, but the employee refused to resign and was subsequently terminated. In the U-5 filing required by the SEC to deregister the employee, the CLO/CCO described front running as the reason for termination.

The employee sued the firm for wrongful dismissal. During discovery, the CLO/CCO claimed that his discussions with others in the firm were subject to the attorney-client privilege. The analyst objected and the court found that the CLO/CCO had been acting as a compliance officer in that particular instance rather than as a lawyer. Therefore none of the CLO/CCO's conversations were privileged.

Discussion topics

What was the official position and function of the CLO/CCO? Was he a compliance officer or the firm's attorney?

Does the answer depend on whether he was investigating the front-running allegations, or recommending the termination of the employee? At the time of the investigation, was potential litigation with the employee foreseeable? Obviously, it is difficult to answer these questions in hindsight.

How much more difficult would it be to determine the issue in the heat of the moment?

What is your opinion regarding proper classification and functionality of the dual-hatted CLO-CCO discussed above?

Are there any guidelines that you would recommend implementing in order to make the distinctions between the two functions clearer?

 Do you think these guidelines would have any effect on a court's willingness to extend the attorney-client privilege discussions held by the CLO/CCO?

———————

Chapter 18

THE DUTIES OF THE COMPLIANCE OFFICER: THE URBAN CASE AND ITS IMPLICATIONS

The following case demonstrates the legal, business, compliance, and power structure within a brokerage firm. It unveils the effects of these structures and of the relationships among the actors on the firm's self-regulation and its demise.[881] In this case the CCO liability issue was raised but left unclear, and yet we can learn a great deal from this case.

Section I of this chapter tells the story of FBW's demise. Section II deals with the legal proceedings after the sale of the firm. Section III describes how each of the main actors fared after the firm's downfall. Section IV discusses the legal issues concerning the identity of the responsible actors. Section V presents the SEC's views, at the time of the *Urban* case. Section VI summarizes the discussion. And Section VII reviews the distinction between a business operations supervisor and a compliance supervisor.

I. THE STORY OF FBW'S DEMISE

FBW was a relatively small brokerage firm, where everyone knew each other.[882] Although informality is common and may even be regarded as necessary for success in small firms, lack of or even outright resistance to formalized compliance measures signals a red flag or slippery slope.

The legal and business power structure in FBW was as follows: Calvert was the firm's CEO; Akers was a former CEO and the current Director of Retail Accounts; Usry was the Director of Institutional Accounts; Urban was the CLO, responsible for Compliance; Centeno was the CCO reporting to Urban. Glantz was a broker and the person who brought FBW down. He joined FBW on Akers' recommendation.

---

881 *In re* Urban, Initial Decision Release No. 402, Administrative Proceeding File No. 3-13655 (Sept. 8, 2010) (edited and citations omitted). *See also* Theodore J. Sawicki & Kerry K. Vatzakas, *Chief Compliance Officer Liability: Setting the Record Straight October 2008*, PRACTICAL COMPLIANCE & RISK MGMT. FOR THE SEC. INDUS., Nov.-Dec. 2008, at 25, *available at* http://www.alston.com/files/Publication/0fc10566-9d41-4b3f-bcbc-282461f3b09b/Presentation/PublicationAttachment/f8089bea-0b6f-4c65-a944-4645089220f1/Sawicki-Vatzakas_PCRM_05-08.pdf (last visited Feb. 6, 2016).

882 "Gordon, who joined FBW in 1983, testified that, '[w]e were small enough that everyone knew each other pretty well, so you pretty much knew what was going on.'"

How could one person destroy a brokerage firm? The activities of Glantz raised a number of related issues. First, he engaged in illegal stock manipulation and mishandled his customers' investments. Second, he managed to escape supervision by the firm's supervisors in three ways.

FBW had offices in Baltimore (Retail Accounts Unit), and in Beachwood (Institutional Accounts Unit). Unlike other traders, Glantz was permitted to trade in both offices. Each trading office had a different supervisor and different reporting lines. Glantz "slid" between the two. Third, he worked under the Institutional rather than the Personal group, where supervision of the brokers would be closer. And fourth, he had the very strong support of the "inner circle" headed by Akers.

Two entities were involved in the trading that brought the brokerage firm down. One was Innotrac, a respectable corporation. The other was the IPOF Fund, a partnership that invested heavily in Innotrac. The partnership held the investments of Glantz's clients. Even though Glantz traded sometimes under the Institutional accounts, his accounts did not look "institutional," but "retail."[883] Its investors were individuals. In addition, Glantz used the clients' investments to borrow on margin (as the clients were allowed to do). He borrowed up to 50% of the value of the clients' shares. The borrowed money was also invested in Innotrac shares.[884]

Later, when FBW prohibited Glantz from using IPOF to trade in Innotrac shares, Glantz circumvented the prohibition by buying the shares through a new account. The new account, named Advest, was set up not at FBW but at an unrelated broker-dealer named Advest Corporation. The new account at Advest was used for trades that manipulated the share price of Innotrac though "wash sales" between Glantz's various clients.[885] Thus, the sales conflicted with each other and ended up at zero, except for the commissions that were charged.

Urban, the lawyer, directed an examination to uncover any correlation between the trading activities in the IPOF Fund accounts at FBW and Advest. Urban told CEO Calvert that Compliance was planning to communicate directly with the Glantz customers—whose money was invested in IPOF, and then in Advest—in order to make sure that the customers consented to the trading. He asked Calvert not to inform Akers of this plan. The firm's Credit Committee reacted with respect to the margin (borrowing) at IPOF. It limited the borrowing and required

---

[883] Most Institutional Accounts placed large orders, which FBW executed. The IPOF Fund, which invested in Innotrac, placed many small orders, accompanied by many phone calls and instructions to traders on the Institutional Sales desk — not typical of institutional accounts.

[884] When Urban requested from Glantz the IPOF Fund's partnership agreement and a list of IPOF Fund investors he was concerned when Glantz told him that the information was confidential. Later, it transpired clients were not directly contacted regarding their accounts' activities nor the borrowing and purchasing of more shares on margin. They trusted Glantz. Further, Urban was "dumbfounded" that Glantz's supervisor had not communicated with these retail customers. Glantz said that Urban told him that the IPOF Fund "could not continue to sell to Glantz's other clients at FBW and that FBW would have to file a Form RE-3 to disclose Glantz's unauthorized trading."

[885] A "wash sale" is the purchase and sale of a security, where each transaction is in close temporal proximity with the other. The net effect of purchasing and selling is zero or colloquially a "wash."

FBW's Margin Department to monitor the margin maintenance requirements, but on April 7, 2004, the maintenance margin account was increased again.[886]

For two years Centeno, the CCO, questioned the suitability of Glantz's trading in several of his clients' accounts. She doubted whether certain trades in these accounts were authorized. For example, one investor's account, an unsophisticated young widow, with no other substantial assets, was classified as an Institutional Account. Her account "had a high concentration of Innotrac stock and a high margin balance" (i.e., the account used borrowed money to increase its holding of Innotrac stock). Other accounts held questionable investments as well.

Many accounts had been overactive, appearing regularly on the brokerage firm's Activity Report.[887] For example, Glantz had trading authority over the account of Mr. Gilbert, who was 84 years old. The account's objectives were "growth and income." Yet, "in July 2003, the Irwin Gilbert Trust (Gilbert) account had a turnover [rate] of [595%] [for the year]," and a high commission-to-equity ratio. Generally, an account with growth and income objectives should make conservative long-term investments in stock whose price is over $5.00 per share. Another account "had a turnover [rate] of [1,044%] [per annum], and a commission-to-equity ratio of 6.4." This turnover rate indicated that the portfolios were aggressively traded, changing the composition of the entire portfolio 6-10 times per year. Such high frequency trading also resulted in high trading commissions, as indicated by the commission-to-equity ratio. By contrast, a typical conservative equity index fund has a turnover rate of 3-5% per year. The SEC refers to this manipulative and deceptive practice as referred to as "churning."[888]

Glantz had personal financial troubles. In early 2003, Glantz lied that CEO Calvert had permitted him to trade in the IPOF Fund. In fact, Calvert refused permission. Further, "[i]n January 2003, Glantz admitted that he signed his wife's name to an option agreement for a joint account," and lied that she had granted him power of attorney over the account. In fact, on that very day "FBW received a copy of a temporary restraining order that Glantz's wife had obtained against him." Glantz represented that he had discussed the IPOF Fund issues and investments in detail with a firm's compliance officer, and that fact was denied by the officer.

Centeno believed Glantz was in a "desperate financial condition." She resigned from her position in FBW on March 30, 2004, partially because Akers would not follow her requests

---

886 "Maintenance margin" is the minimum amount of equity needed in an account that borrows and buys on margin. Increasing the maintenance margin on an account effectively reduces the amount of margin borrowing.

887 For January 2003, Glantz's first month with FBW, he had sixteen of the twenty-five accounts listed on the Activity Report. Glantz's accounts that appeared on Activity Reports from June 2003 through March 2004 had very high turnover and commission-to-equity ratios, and many, if not most, of the accounts had conservative investment objectives.

888 "Churning occurs when a broker engages in excessive buying and selling of securities in a customer's account chiefly to generate commissions that benefit the broker. For churning to occur, the broker must exercise control over the investment decisions in the customer's account, such as through a formal written discretionary agreement. Frequent in-and-out purchases and sales of securities that don't appear necessary to fulfill the customer's investment goals may be evidence of churning. Churning is illegal and unethical. It can violate SEC Rule 15c1-7 and other securities laws." SEC, *Fast Answers, Churining*. Jan. 15, 2013, *available at h*ttps://www.sec.gov/fast-answers/answerschurninghtm.html (last visited Feb. 19, 2017)

regarding Glantz' behavior and the IPOF Fund investments. She had lost confidence in the ability of FBW to handle the Glantz situation. The new "risk profile of FBW . . . presented risks to her career."

On January 29, 2004, one employee characterized the IPOF Fund as a "ticking time bomb." Even though Innotrac was a respectable company, the manipulation of its shares could render its share prices unreliable and in fact worthless. Because IPOF Fund invested most of its securities in Innotrac stock, IPOF's stock "would likely be diminished by over a half a million dollars." Yet, in November 2003, Glantz collected "$200,000 commission advance on the recommendation of Akers and Vaughan" (Akers' assistant). Because of this advance and others, "[w]hen he left FBW . . . Glantz owed the firm $ 430,000."

Centeno, the compliance officer, believed that the IPOF Fund was manipulating the price of Innotrac stock, and that the fund's "accumulation of shares in small lots almost daily" artificially raised the price of Innotrac shares. It was "noted that FBW customers owned approximately 40% of Innotrac's total float,[889] and 19% of the outstanding shares." At least seven Glantz customer accounts had very large holdings of Innotrac stock. Some respected FBW brokers held Innotrac stock, but no other account came close to the amount of Innotrac shares held in the IPOF Fund.[890]

Finally, CEO Calvert woke up! He became aware that the assurances he had received from Akers and others—that the Retail Sales Unit would address concerns about Glantz's supervision—had not materialized. He noted that the plans to transfer Glantz to Baltimore, where he could be more effectively supervised, had not materialized.891 Urban informed Glantz in writing that, effective February 5, 2004, and pending a review of the IPOF Fund by FBW's Credit Committee, no additional orders for Innotrac stock should be made.[892] Nonetheless, the unclear supervision continued, and later, supervision was further reduced. Urban requested additional restrictions, which were imposed on trading in Innotrac by the IPOF Fund. Yet, neither Baltimore nor Beachwood supervised Glantz, who considered Akers his supervisor.

Then the compliance officers at the Baltimore branch became concerned about Glantz's accounts.[893] They were concerned because Glantz purchased predominantly low-priced

---

889 "Float" refers to the total number of shares publically available for trading in a particular company.

890 "Innotrac's 52-week low per share price was $ 1.50 on October 11, 2002, and the 52-week high was $ 6.65 on May 6, 2003. Innotrac's price rose in 2003. Innotrac had traded higher than $ 6.65 prior to 2002." "[T]he IPOF Fund account had a $ 9.381 million margin debit balance, which continued to increase while the account purchased the stock of Innotrac." The IPOF Fund's holdings in Innotrac were so large that IPOF qualified as a controlling shareholder.

891 On a daily basis, in the period November 3, 2003, through February 3, 2004, the IPOF Fund owned an average of 34.59% of the shares of Innotrac in the market. Before the Credit Committee meeting, Urban informed Glantz in writing that, per their discussion, Glantz would not accept any additional orders for Innotrac effective February 5, 2004, until the Credit Committee reviewed the IPOF Fund account.

892 "The memorandum date is suspect because it describes a meeting that allegedly was held on February 9, 2004." "In January 2004, the Gilbert account had a turnover ratio of 467 and a commission-to-equity ratio of 12.02. Weaver did not contact any of Glantz's clients to determine if trading was in line with their investment objectives." "Urban knew that Akers was to meet with Dadante on February 9, 2004, to convey the Credit Committee's concerns."

893 "[S]pecifically Vinocur, the Orchen Pension Plan, Fabrizi Trucking, and Ziemba & Thatcher."

securities and engaged in high commission short-term trading. They noted that "[these] investments appeared to be more speculative than the accounts' growth and income objectives would justify." They claimed to have never seen such trading activity by a broker, and "considered Glantz a top compliance concern."

The officers suspected that the trading was executed for the purpose of artificially inflating the price of Innotrac stock. Glantz also stated "everyone, including Calvert, was aware of his trading of Innotrac in the IPOF Fund." Nonetheless, nothing changed. This lack of supervision continued because "Glantz had a direct line to . . . Akers and went over [his direct supervisor's] head." Even though Glantz was trading the Institutional Accounts, the director of that unit did not actually see Glantz's trades. In sum, the compliance concerns regarding Glantz went unresolved. Glantz told sufficient lies to escape supervision.

II. ENTER THE SEC

The SEC Proceedings. "In January 2004, [the SEC's] Philadelphia Regional Office . . . conducted a regularly-scheduled examination of FBW's internal controls . . ." "Urban . . . recommended that Glantz be terminated."[894] Akers "vehemently opposed" the proposal and angrily screamed at Urban when they met. He complained about the fact that Glantz's customers were contacted directly, and "accused Compliance of conducting a 'witch-hunt'" to harm Glantz. Akers blamed Urban for "driving a 'good producer' out of the firm." "Urban got visibly angry at Akers's verbal attack and shouted in defense of Compliance."[895] Akers asserted "that he would not terminate Glantz" and "appealed for a different resolution," such as special supervision. "Glantz and Akers signed a Special Supervision Memorandum, . . . on January 11, 2005 . . ." It contained a long list of restrictions and a warning that "failure to conform would result in immediate termination."[896]

---

894   *In re* Urban, Initial Decision Release No. 402, Administrative Proceeding File No. 3-13655 (Sept. 8, 2010) (edited and citations omitted). *See also* Theodore J. Sawicki & Kerry K. Vatzakas, *Chief Compliance Officer Liability: Setting the Record Straight October 2008*, Practical Compliance & Risk Mgmt. for the Sec. Indus., Nov.-Dec. 2008, at 25, *available at* http://www.alston.com/files/Publication/0fc10566-9d41-4b3f-bcbc-282461f3b09b/Presentation/PublicationAttachment/ f8089bea-0b6f-4c65-a944-4645089220f1/Sawicki-Vatzakas_PCRM_05-08.pdf (last visited Feb. 6, 2016).

895   Calvert testified that he had no knowledge of the December 14, 2004 meeting until October 2006 even though the raised voices must have reached his office. He claimed he was away at that date and there is a disagreement about the date.

896   1. No further purchases of Innotrac allowed in any account, only liquidations; 2. [Some clients' accounts] were changed to retail accounts; 3. Glantz [will] work exclusively from Hunt Valley, but not on the Institutional Sales desk. Akers is his supervisory manager; 4. No discretion allowed in any account without written authorization received from Akers and Compliance; 5. Margin debit in [one client's] account will be reduced to zero within the next thirty days and provide Akers and Compliance with a written plan by January 15, 2005, to reduce margin debit in the other clients' accounts within three months; 6. Maintain well balanced and diversified portfolios for [specified accounts] consistent with their account objectives; 7. Glantz will give Akers a daily client contact log; 8. Glantz cannot wire funds from FBW accounts into which a personal check has been deposited for three days; 9. All client demographic, investment objectives, and financial information will be updated on Account Applications and Agreements as required within thirty days with an updated copy sent to each client for signature; 10 Glantz will appropriately mark orders as solicited or unsolicited; 11. Akers must approve in advance all IPO and secondary offering purchases; 12. Glantz will send all clients with margin

"Urban testified that he told CEO Calvert . . . that Glantz lied about . . . his trades," and that Akers refused to terminate Glantz and was "committed to performing special supervision." But Calvert blamed Urban, and decisions to supervise Glantz followed without effect.[897] On November 16, 2005, Calvert informed Hartman that Akers had authority to grant Glantz a second $200,000 advance against salary, but, in the future, Calvert did not want new advances until old advances had been paid. Prior to November 3, 2005, Guerrini and his mother, Eleanor Klemm (Klemm), complained to Akers informally about Glantz. On December 8, 2005, Glantz submitted his resignation to FBW.

The administrative judge held that (i) Calvert, the CEO, falsely "alleged he had no knowledge of events." The evidence showed that he "knew about or should have known about" these events. The judge concluded that Calvert was not credible[898] and that he acted with a conflict of interest.

(ii) "Glantz agreed to pay FBW $430,000 owed on his forgivable loans and other obligations," and to "give an exit interview." "Glantz needed a clean Form U-5 to receive a . . . bonus from another firm." He "left FBW at the end of 2005 and joined Sanders, Morris, Harris."

(iii) Lawsuits filed after Glantz left FBW cost the firm $7.2 million, paid to the receiver of the IPOF Fund and "about $1.285 million to Glantz's customers." The SEC instituted "Administrative and Cease-and-Desist Proceedings," "FBW was ordered to cease and desist from committing or causing any violations, or any future violations."

"Glantz claimed to have effectively left FBW in November 2005 and to have made $1.2 million [in] each of the last two years he was at the firm." He was censured under Section 17(a) of the Exchange Act and Exchange Act Rule 17a-8, and "ordered to pay disgorgement and prejudgment interest of $300,656, and a civil money penalty of $500,000."

III. HOW DID THE PARTIES FARE IN THIS CASE?

A number of lessons can be learned from the fortunes of the actors.

---

balances relevant FBW and NYSE information; 13. Akers will have direct contact with at least three of Glantz's clients each month and record the notes of his discussions.

897 On November 16, 2005, Calvert informed Hartman that Akers had authority to grant Glantz a second $ 200,000 advance against salary, but, in the future, Calvert did not want new advances until old advances had been paid. Prior to November 3, 2005, Guerrini and his mother, Eleanor Klemm (Klemm), complained to Akers informally about Glantz. On December 8, 2005, Glantz submitted his resignation to FBW.

898 Calvert testified that he did not know that Akers was hostile to compliance until the investigation of Glantz in 2006, yet he knew that Akers insulted the Compliance staff publicly and dismissed it as good fun and attempted humor by Akers. Calvert did not recall a conversation in early 2003, in which [he was told] that Glantz lied and represented that Calvert gave Glantz authority to trade in the IPOF Fund before the account was transferred to FBW. Calvert did not remember any conversation with Ferris about Centeno's concerns about Glantz, the IPOF Fund, Innotrac, Centeno's problems with Akers, or any compliance-related issue. However, in March 2004, Centeno had a lengthy exit interview with Ferris and told him that Glantz was a broker out of control, that the IPOF Fund was going "to blow up" on FBW, and concerns about Innotrac stock. Ferris questioned Calvert about Centeno's concerns, and Calvert told Ferris that everything was under control and was being handled properly.

CEO Calvert. In 2007, Calvert received a "Golden Parachute" that "guaranteed him [2.5] million dollars if FBW was acquired."[899] FBW was indeed acquired and merged into RBC. "On May 21, 2008, RBC filed a Form F-4 Registration Statement . . . indicating it had entered a letter agreement with Calvert to provide him with a base salary of $150,000, quarterly bonuses of $50,000, and a one-year transition bonus of $250,000 prorated for the period between the effective date of the merger and the integration of FBW into RBC." RBC "gave Calvert an approximately half a million dollar benefit." In addition, Calvert "received $257,989 over a five-year period," and "at least a twenty dollar premium on the sale of his vested FBW shares."

Attorney Urban. In the opinion of the Judge: "[T]he overwhelming evidence is that Urban was not responsible and had no authority for hiring, assessing performance, assigning activities, promoting, or terminating employment of anyone, outside of the people in the department he directly supervised."

"Urban went on administrative leave on November 14, 2006, and resigned from FBW on March 1, 2007." "FBW officials signed Urban's Form 5 on March 12, 2007 . . ." The form "state[d] that he had resigned voluntarily and he: (1) was not under internal review for violating investment-related statutes, regulations, rules, or industry standards of conduct; (2) did not voluntarily resign after allegations were made that he violated investment-related statutes, regulations, rules or industry standards of conduct; and (3) was not permitted to resign after he was accused of failure to supervise in connection with investment-related statutes, regulations, rules or industry standards of conduct." Glantz later testified that he had "encountered Urban in early 2006 and Urban said, 'I really don't blame you . . . I dropped the ball.'" Thus, Urban admitted responsibility, even though he was not responsible for the demise of the firm.

"Separating from FBW, under these circumstances, caused Urban serious personal and financial loss." "His professional opportunities were damaged, and he estimated that he lost between $800,000 and $1.3 million in terms of his [FBW] ownership interests because of the timing and conditions of his separation from FBW." Specifically, "Urban was required to forfeit unvested stock options and he sold, or was required to sell, most of his FBW shares before the merger with RBC." "Those shares could have been sold at a higher price if he had continued to work at FBW longer than his twenty-three years."[900]

Glantz. The culprit got off fairly lightly. Glantz was eventually "sentenced to thirty-three months in prison," for his activities at FBW, "followed by three years of supervised release, and

---

899 *In re* Urban, Initial Decision Release No. 402, Administrative Proceeding File No. 3-13655 (Sept. 8, 2010) (edited and citations omitted). *See also* Theodore J. Sawicki & Kerry K. Vatzakas, *Chief Compliance Officer Liability: Setting the Record Straight October 2008*, PRACTICAL COMPLIANCE & RISK MGMT. FOR THE SEC. INDUS., Nov.-Dec. 2008, at 25, *available at* http://www.alston.com/files/Publication/0fc10566-9d41-4b3f-bcbc-282461f3b09b/Presentation/PublicationAttachment/f8089bea-0b6f-4c65-a944-4645089220f1/Sawicki-Vatzakas_PCRM_05-08.pdf (last visited Feb. 6, 2016).

900 "At the [SEC's] direction, FBW calculated that, for fiscal years 2003 through 2005, Urban received $ 13,706.82 as a bonus from the revenue pool created by Glantz's activities at FBW." "However, the calculation is suspect because the bonus pool component, 'Innotrac Commission Revenues,' include[d] commissions earned by [other] FBW brokers [besides] Glantz."

was ordered to pay $110,000 in restitution." "He served approximately twelve months of [the] thirty-three month sentence with time off for good behavior and drug treatment." "He was released on March 10, 2009." "Judge Kathleen M. O'Malley remarked that Glantz's lawyer had negotiated the deal of the century."[901]

His collaborator, who had helped manipulate Innotrac stock prices, eventually pled guilty to two counts of securities fraud for managing a $50 million Ponzi scheme, and for participating in the scheme to manipulate Innotrac stock. He "was sentenced to 156 months in prison followed by three years of supervised release, and ordered to pay over $28 million in restitution on August 6, 2007." "The [Securities and Exchange] Commission barred [him] from association with any investment adviser."

IV. THE LEGAL ISSUES

A number of legal issues raised in this case remained unclear. First, what is supervision, and who is a supervisor? "Urban did not believe he was Glantz's supervisor or that he had authority to hire, fire, discipline, or direct the conduct of the Retail Unit's sales personnel without the concurrence of Akers or someone in Retail Sales management." "Compliance could recommend that a broker be placed on special supervision but someone else had to agree to exercise special supervision."

Second, who decides? Who recommends? Who is a supervisor? The FBW case is not particularly helpful in answering these questions. FBW, and its compliance personnel, directed, rather than recommended, placing a broker under special or heightened supervision, or limiting the broker's activities. However, this was a singular instance. We may conclude that facilities and financing can signal responsibility. "Throughout the 2003-05 period, the FBW Legal and

---

901 "Glantz admitted committing federal securities fraud and lying about his actions to the SEC and the FBI before July 5, 2007." "He acknowledged that, from about August 2002 through in or about November 2005, he and others artificially inflated and maintained the market price of Innotrac stock." "In May 2007, a psychiatrist, who allegedly was treating Glantz, submitted a statement to the Commission that Glantz was in no condition for a deposition. An attached facsimile from a doctor was written in all capital letters, which is the style that Glantz uses. Glantz admitted that he might have typed the statement for the doctor to sign, but denied that he signed the doctor's signature." "The Commission issued an Order pursuant to an Offer of Settlement, barring Glantz from association with any broker or dealer."

Compliance functions were lightly staffed."[902] "FBW's Legal Department was busy in 2003."[903] "There is no dispute" that Urban had an enormous amount of work and limited help.[904]

"Urban has worked with Calvert since 1988" and "they talked directly on [various] subjects from two to ten times each day." Urban's practice was "to keep Calvert informed about problems with registered representatives who were big producers." Yet, this contact was not sufficient to impose on Urban the burden of supervision and render him responsible for the behavior of Glantz.

───────────

Discussion Topics

*What was the formal power structure in FBW? What was the real power structure?

*What was wrong with the supervision of Glantz?

*Which transactions caused the brokerage firm to go bankrupt?

*Who is a "supervisor?"

The following are summaries of expert testimony, offered by the SEC and Urban. As you read these opinions, identify the different and contrasting views of a dual-hatted CLO-CCO's

───────────

902 When FBW had about 700 employees and about 275 brokers, the Legal Department had two lawyers: Urban and Dana Gloor, and Compliance had about seven or eight people. Urban was a hands-on manager and was involved in all significant Legal and Compliance actions. It was not unusual for co-workers to get emails from Urban sent at 2:00 or 3:00 a.m. Teel believed that the Legal Department took on huge responsibilities and workload without the necessary resources, so that often results were not timely.

903 In September 2003, just as Centeno began three months maternity leave, the New York State Attorney General announced a market timing investigation. Urban estimated that in the fall of 2003, he spent from 20 to 50% of his time handling allegations of market timing by four individuals at FBW. As the point-person on changes to FBW's Employee Stock Ownership Plan (ESOP), Urban was required to spend considerable time working with consultants. Centeno recalled that 2003 was a particularly hectic period because, in addition to changes in the ESOP plan, Legal and Compliance had to deal with a NYSE investigation of a broker, several arbitration cases, implementation of several new rules applicable to the securities industry, a joint NYSE/NASD examination, and several litigated matters being handled with outside counsel...

In 2004, Urban worked at the Baltimore headquarters, but most of the Compliance staff was in D.C. until space was found in Baltimore. Besides location, Compliance had major staff changes in 2004. FBW was without a Compliance Director for over two months as Centeno left on March 30, 2004, and Haas was hired in June 2004. Also, in 2004, Del Buono left and Silbert and Sraver joined Compliance. FBW was the subject of an unprecedented number of regulatory examinations in 2004. The Commission conducted a broker-dealer examination, focusing on Hunt Valley and the Annapolis branch office, and an investment adviser examination. The NYSE conducted a Financial/Operational exam and reviewed FBW's research and Investment Banking departments.

904 The minutes of the Executive Board meeting on September 12, 2005, show Urban reporting on five of ten topics. Urban and outside counsel were working with another firm on litigation against two major financial institutions, and a disgruntled former Compliance employee had raised allegations about Compliance to the Executive Committee. Urban assured the Executive Committee that Compliance was operating in a reasonably effective manner given FBW's growth and significant expansion in regulation in recent years.

liability in the event of a failure. On what basis and rationale has the Commission rejected the staff's experts? Keeping in mind the structure of the corporation, how do these experts view the structure?

_____

V. EXPERT TESTIMONY OFFERED BY THE SEC

The *Urban* decision should follow the decision reached in the matter of *Salomon Brothers* because the evidence and circumstances in both cases are similar. Urban was Glantz's supervisor. He had a senior level position at FBW, and he had knowledge and involvement in compliance matters related to Glantz's activities. It is irrelevant that, in some instances, he did not have exclusive supervisory power over Glantz.

Urban failed to supervise Glantz. He did not adequately and effectively respond to "red flags" presented by either "Glantz's conduct," or "deficiencies in Glantz's supervision." In addition, Urban failed to "insist that Akers," or anyone else, "supervise Glantz, or that Akers perform special supervision."

In response to the red flags, Urban should have made inquiries into Glantz's background, position, authority, and job duties. Urban proved himself to be Glantz's supervisor when he provided directives to Compliance to call Glantz's customers, or raised related concerns with the FBW Credit Committee. In contrast, the FBW Compliance Director was not Glantz's supervisor "because he was operating at Urban's direction." As Glantz's supervisor, Urban's responses to the "red flags" (outlined below) were insufficient.

What did Urban fail to do? He:

(1) did not "address the concerns raised" by the compliance officers;

(2) did not "take decisive action" to address investment suitability or trading concerns related to some of Glantz's accounts;

(3) did not "initiate an inquiry" when he became aware that Glantz had opened an external brokerage account for the IPOF Fund;

(4) did not address the risk to FBW associated with large, increasing, and margin financed holdings of Innotrac stock in the IPOF Fund;

(5) did not "inquire as to why and how [the compliance officer] had concluded that the [Innotrac buy order executed by Advest] was related to the IPOF Fund";

(6) did not "act on the November 2004 report from the Baltimore [SEC] branch examiners," which among other things, was "Urban's fourth written notice that Glantz was not being adequately supervised";

(7) did not "ensure that special supervision of Glantz was carried out";

(8) did not "take definitive action regarding [additional problematic] trading in [the stock of] ATC Healthcare";

(9) did not "act on information that, in December 2004, Glantz's customers bought Innotrac shares through [a second] personal account at Advest";

(10) did not "act on concerns" regarding manipulative trading in Innotrac; and

(11) "allow[ed] Glantz to return to Beachwood right after the special supervision provisions [of the SEC agreement] required that [Glantz] work in Hunt Valley or [did not] object[] strongly that Akers was allowing Glantz to do so."

Urban had the power to perform these duties. He could have prevented the problematic trading by "personally conduct[ing] follow-up monitoring," when the issues were first raised, or when "similar concerns" were subsequently voiced. Urban failed to take "definitive action on reports that Akers was not carrying out his obligations under the special supervision provisions."

When does a person become a supervisor? When a person gets involved in a compliance problem, this person becomes a supervisor. A registered principal that has authority has a duty to act to solve a problem.

The *Salomon Brothers* [905] case principles apply: the lawyer in that case was held to be a compliance officer, and so should Urban.

VI. EXPERT TESTIMONY OFFERED ON BEHALF OF URBAN

The governing principle is that "a supervisor, for the purposes of Exchange Act Section 15(b)(4)(E), [is] a person who knows, or reasonably should know, that he or she has been given the authority and responsibility for exercising control over one or more activities of a supervised person."

In contrast to the SEC's expert recommendation, a person cannot become a supervisor without knowingly accepting the position. "Urban testified that he never approved Glantz working out of Beachwood" during the special supervision period. "Urban never knew, or reasonably should have known, that he was Glantz's supervisor." [906]

"Even assuming that Glantz was subject to Urban's supervision, Urban was [neither] negligent [nor] careless in [concluding] that he was not Glantz's supervisor." "Urban understood that

---

905 *See* below.

906 *In re* Urban, Initial Decision Release No. 402, Administrative Proceeding File No. 3-13655 (Sept. 8, 2010) (edited and citations omitted). *See also* Theodore J. Sawicki & Kerry K. Vatzakas, *Chief Compliance Officer Liability: Setting the Record Straight October 2008*, Practical Compliance & Risk Mgmt. for the Sec. Indus., Nov.-Dec. 2008, at 25, *available at* http://www.alston.com/files/Publication/0fc10566-9d41-4b3f-bcbc-282461f3b09b/Presentation/PublicationAttachment/f8089bea-0b6f-4c65-a944-4645089220f1/Sawicki-Vatzakas_PCRM_05-08.pdf (last visited Feb. 6, 2016).

he had authority to recommend [action regarding] Glantz, but he did not understand" that he may have also had the authority to actually implement disciplinary measures.

Urban's "role was to advise and consult with Glantz's supervisors," not to supervise directly. "[I]n situations where [Urban] did take action concerning Glantz, [he] did so in his role as [in-house] counsel (CLO) or agent of the [FBW] Credit Committee." Urban's belief that he was not Glantz's supervisor is supported by the testimony of his colleagues at FBW.

Urban acted more as a CLO in a brokerage firm, "mak[ing] sure," for instance, "that the IPOF Fund made the necessary filings with respect to [its] Innotrac stock acquisitions." The following activity was also more consistent with the duties of a CLO: "order[ing] letters [to be] sent to Glantz's clients, authorizing contact by Compliance personnel . . . drafting Glantz's Special Supervision Memorandum [with the SEC], and "determining that Glantz's trading without written authorization was reportable . . . ."

A lawyer's advice is not a binding order, but rather the recommendation of an agent, using his legal expertise. Urban reasonably believed "that Akers was part of an atmosphere at FBW that was hostile to Compliance and that Akers was the only [person] at the firm with power to supervise or [terminate] Glantz." Calvert's belief about violations of Exchange Act Sections 15(b)(4)(E) and 15(b)(6) and negligence does not show that "Urban had authority to discipline or fire a registered representative." Any such claims are "unsupported" especially as "Calvert purportedly knew little about the . . . facts involving Glantz and the IPOF Fund account."

Liability must be matched with actual authority. "Urban did not have the degree of responsibility, ability, or authority to affect Glantz's conduct . . . *Gutfreund* can be distinguished on its facts." Unlike Feuerstein, Urban did not direct FBW's collective response to Glantz's conduct and the IPOF Fund." "Urban's role" was "as legal counsel, provid[ing] advice, consultation, and input."

The allegations aimed at Urban concerned performance outside the scope of the duties typically undertaken by a lawyer. Attorneys remain unprotected only if they move out of their legal realm. Therefore, "[these proceedings depart] from established policy and [are] contrary to [established views regarding] an attorney's non-public advice to its clients."[907]

A role in a back office differs from the role of an advisor. Business operators are the supervisors. Supervised persons must know to whose supervision they are subject, and any appointed supervisor must accept that responsibility. FBW "employed [this] traditional supervisory structure with clear identification of supervisors." Urban was not identified as a supervisor.

"[C]ompliance departments were intended to support and advise." Such departments "were never intended to replace supervisors or managers in the business departments." Management in a securities firm, not Compliance, should "supervise business units" and order that "firm and employee[s] activities [comply with applicable laws]." Only business managers have the authority to approve the activities of the people in their department. A compliance department "may . .

---

907 *Citing* William R. Carter, 47 S.E.C. 471, 504 (1981) *and* Scott G. Monson, SEC Docket 7517 (June 30, 2008).

. direct business activities" only after the firm has expressly given it authority to do so, and "the compliance department knowingly agrees to undertake that responsibility."

The authority or ability to directly affect an employee's behavior is a "unique" and "fact-specific" arrangement. No such arrangement was in place with respect to Urban and Glantz. Therefore, the business managers, rather than Urban, were Glantz's supervisors.

Urban "could [not] have successfully [caused] Advest to identify its customers as part of an inquiry into possible manipulation" of Innotrac stock. "[M]aking calls to Glantz's customers" did not make Urban a supervisor. Likewise, when Urban "accept[ed] responsibility from the Credit Committee to speak to Glantz" regarding heightened margin requirements, this responsibility did not transform him into a supervisor.

"Compliance was doing its job, and . . . Urban was a messenger from the Credit Committee." Urban and the compliance personnel "served [in] an advisory role and they performed their advisory duties reasonably." Urban was not Glantz's supervisor. In reality "revenue-generating business people have the ability to affect the conduct of registered representatives, but, absent special circumstances, legal and compliance personnel do not."

Urban's actions were consistent with the "traditional advisory role of Compliance." "[Urban] was not Glantz's supervisor, and he acted reasonably in voicing [concerns] so that Glantz's supervisors could address them." "Compliance's role in approving Glantz's hiring [was] quintessential advisory." "Urban's conclusion, in the May to June 2003 period, that the activities in the IPOF Fund were not necessarily manipulative, was reasonable." "Innotrac was a real company," and "Urban's senior management position did not imbue him with the requisite ability, authority, or responsibility to affect Glantz's conduct."

"Glantz was not subject to [Urban's] supervision." "[Urban's] actions were reasonable under the circumstances, and the Division is not entitled to the relief it seeks." "[T]he actions [Urban] took were reasonably designed to prevent Glantz's illegal conduct."[908]

"No FBW manager asked Urban to supervise Glantz himself." "Urban recommended to Akers, in late summer 2003 through early 2004, that Glantz needed closer supervision and Akers assured him Glantz would be transferred to Baltimore, where he would be under a seasoned

---

908 Urban maintains that the following actions he took were reasonably designed to prevent Glantz's illegal conduct: encouraging Compliance to inquire into the IPOF Fund and ensuring that the Credit Committee considered the IPOF Fund; recommending that the Credit Committee restrict credit to the IPOF Fund and that the IPOF Fund make required Commission filings; urging increased vigilance of Glantz by Retail Sales and other business managers; instructing Compliance to perform additional diligence on Glantz; advocating strongly for Glantz's termination and causing Compliance to make a NYSE filing as to Glantz; and advocating for strict terms of special supervision after senior business managers refused to terminate Glantz.

Urban contends that a failure to supervise cannot be found where his reasonable actions were frustrated by Glantz's consistent lies, the failure of FBW business executives to fulfill their responsibilities, and Akers's and Vaughan's refusal to accept his advice, including terminating Glantz. Finally, Urban argues that consideration of the public interest factors show[s] that no sanctions are warranted. The alleged errors were ones of omission and Urban did not seek personal gain or to disadvantage any investor. Urban did not act with a high degree of scienter, reckless disregard, or willful blindness. Urban's alleged violations are one incident in a life of honorable activities in the securities industry. There is no evidence that he was unjustly enriched to any material amount and there is no realistic likelihood that he will violate the securities laws in the future. Urban is semi-retired and his registrations have lapsed.

supervisor." "It was reasonable for Urban to rely on Akers' assurances that they would implement his recommendations . . . ."

"[I]f Urban had the power to terminate Glantz, he would have done so in December 2004, rather than write a memorandum recommending that Akers and Vaughan do so." Akers' signature on Glantz's Special Supervision Memorandum supports this view. When Akers refused to fire Glantz, Urban had no choice but to have Compliance monitor Glantz's activities . . ." However, "Urban reasonably left Glantz's future to the discretion of the business managers." What else could he do?

VII. THE SEC'S RESPONSE

Proof of a legal violation by others imposes a supervisory duty on the CLO (the law officer of a firm). A duty was imposed when Urban (i) knew that Glantz violated the antifraud provisions of the federal securities laws, (ii) had supervisory responsibility over Glantz, and (iii) failed to supervise him with a view to preventing those violations.

The SEC emphasizes that Urban comes within the scope of Section 15(b) of the Securities Exchange Act of 1934 and Section 203(f) of the Advisers Act of 1940 because he failed to reasonably respond to red flags suggesting that Glantz's conduct was illegal. Once Urban became involved in addressing the red flags, he was obligated to respond vigorously, and he failed to do so.[909] He was required to bring his concerns to FBW's Board or Executive Committee, and, if they did not act, to resign and report to the SEC. Instead he "acted recklessly and has provided no assurances against future violations and has denied any wrongdoing."

As compared to the *Salomon Brothers* case, the SEC argued in *Salomon Brothers* that "the CLO was not a line supervisor" especially when "others shared supervisory responsibility." The CLO only entered the picture "when senior management informed him of the [employee-Mozer's] misconduct," and sought "his advice and guidance . . . as part of management's collective response to the problem."[910] "[S]till," the SEC argued, "he was a supervisor because he had the requisite degree of responsibility, ability, or authority to affect the person's conduct . . . ." Indeed, the SEC "maintains that there is a long line of cases showing that individuals with less authority than Urban have been found to have failed to supervise."

---

909 Centeno's concerns about Glantz and the IPOF Fund trading in Innotrac in the spring of 2003; the Del Buono Memo on May 23, 2003; the Credit Committee meeting on the Del Buono Memo; involvement in FBW's response to the Del Buono Memo and other events; the Leatherbarrow email on January 29, 2004; turnover of Compliance personnel; findings in connection with the Baltimore examination in November 2004; Urban's December 15, 2004 memorandum and meeting with Akers and Vaughan; allowing Akers to be Glantz's special supervisor; heightened obligations after Glantz was placed on special supervision; failure to react reasonably to red flags in 2005; submission to Calvert of false assurances about FBW's compliance efforts; and negotiations that resulted in a clean Form U-5 for Glantz on his resignation.

910 "The Division notes that, in Kirk Montgomery, the Commission declared a chief compliance officer a supervisor because it was sufficient if the person plays a significant, even if shared, role in the firm's supervisory structure and that his authority was subject to countermand at a higher level."

How would Professor James Fanto's article, cited in Chapter 1, reflect on the power structure of FBW? Note that while Calvert was the CEO of FBW, he deferred to Akers, the former FBW CEO, who was removed from that position for certain unsavory behavior. After being replaced as CEO, Akers remained as the Director of the Retail Unit. Akers also continued to hold significant control power within FBW, a title change notwithstanding. The relationship between CEO Calvert, former CEO Akers, and CLO Urban (who was also responsible for compliance) was "somewhat complicated," but they all "got along reasonably well, most of the time."[911]

Although Urban was very important to the firm's activities, he was not considered the strongest member of its inner circle. For instance, he had been recommended for board membership a number of times, but never received it. CCO Centano's office was small, and had only two lawyers, even as the number of employees had increased considerably. In addition, compliance was not held in high esteem at FBW. Akers used to make fun of compliance before other employees. Calvert, the CEO, reportedly considered this to have been done in "good fun and attempted humor." Another lawyer at FBW "left FBW employment in 2005 and stopped doing contract work for FBW in 2007 because she was dissatisfied with FBW's treatment of compliance issues."[912]

IX. SALOMON BROTHERS CASE

Reading Focus: When reading this case, please take special note of the following issues.

*What was the main factual basis on which the SEC based liability for each charged member of Salomon's senior management team? As you read through the case please diagram or otherwise note the authority and responsibilities of each of the relevant senior managers.

*How was the CLO situated in Salomon's management hierarchy? What were his relevant job responsibilities and for what failings was he eventually held liable? Also, who was his supervisor?

*How did the SEC define compliance supervision in this case?

---

911 *In re* Urban, Initial Decision Release No. 402, Administrative Proceeding File No. 3-13655 (Sept. 8, 2010) (edited and citations omitted). *See also* Theodore J. Sawicki & Kerry K. Vatzakas, *Chief Compliance Officer Liability: Setting the Record Straight October 2008*, PRACTICAL COMPLIANCE & RISK MGMT. FOR THE SEC. INDUS., Nov.-Dec. 2008, at 25, *available at* http://www.alston.com/files/Publication/0fc10566-9d41-4b3f-bcbc-282461f3b09b/Presentation/PublicationAttachment/f8089bea-0b6f-4c65-a944-4645089220f1/Sawicki-Vatzakas_PCRM_05-08.pdf (last visited Feb. 6, 2016).

912 *Id.*

*Is the enforcement of a program different from the preparation and update of a compliance program? If so, how is it different?

*When is a CCO liable for the deficient design, implementation, or enforcement of a compliance program? Under what conditions is a CCO responsible for a business breakdown in the role of a supervisor (as defined by the securities laws)?

*Is a compliance program defective because a breakdown occurs? How does one show a causal relationship (or no causal relationship) between the program and its failure?

*How is the enforcer of a compliance program identified?

*Does a compliance program that does not identify a particular breach of law or rule, deficient per se? If a single failure does not render a compliance program deficient, where is the threshold to deficiency?

*How can we distinguish a failure of a compliance program from the failure of the CCO?

The following is the edited consent agreement between the SEC and John H. Gutfreund, Thomas W. Strauss, and John W. Meriwether regarding violations of Section 15(b) of the Securities Exchange Act of 1934 (Exchange Act).[913] These three individuals constituted the senior management team at Salomon Brothers at the time of the relevant scandal. These managers did not admit or deny the facts, findings, or conclusions. Salomon's CLO, Donald M. Feuerstein, also agreed to the SEC's decision.

A. The Brokerage Firm

Salomon Brothers, Inc ("Salomon") was a venerable underwriting[914] firm registered with the SEC as a broker-dealer. "Salomon ha[d] been a government-designated dealer in U.S. Treasury securities since 1939 and a primary dealer since 1961."

John H. Gutfreund was the Chairman of the Board and CEO of Salomon. Thomas W. Strauss was the President and reported to Gutfreund. John W. Meriwether was a Vice Chairman in charge of all fixed-income trading activities and reported to Strauss. Paul W. Mozer was the managing director and the head of the Government Securities Trading Desk; he reported to

---

913 *In re* John H. Gutfreund, Securities Exchange Act Rel. No. 34-31554, Administrative Proceedings File No. 3-7930, (Dec. 3, 1992) (footnotes omitted).

914 An underwriter is a firm that distributes securities for an issuer. The issuer can be a corporation or a financial institution, such as a bank or the government, that issues and distributes treasury bonds.

Meriwether. Donald M. Feuerstein was Salomon's CLO. The head of Salomon's compliance department reported directly to Feuerstein.

B. The Story

In late April of 1991, Treasury bonds were in high demand at underwriters and broker-dealers like Salomon. The Treasury imposed a limit on the amount of the number of bonds that any broker-dealers could bid. The Treasury's objective was to prevent brokers' monopolistic behavior and to encourage price competition on the bonds.

During that period Gutfreund, Strauss, and Meriwether were informed that Mozer had submitted to the Treasury a false bid in the amount of $3.15 billion in a recent auction of U.S. Treasury securities. Mozer had achieved this fraudulent bid by disguising his own bids under the name of two of Salomon's customers. He did that without the customers' knowledge. When Mozer successfully received the additional bonds in the auction, he immediately, and without knowledge of the customers, directed that a purchase and sale order be recorded. This order officially transferred the securities from the customer accounts to Salomon's.

However, Moser did not realize that the customers had become qualified to bid and had made their own bids for the same securities. When the U.S. Treasury discovered the duplication of the customer bids in the auction it notified the customers and sent a query to Mozer. Mozer called the customers and apologized for the "mistake." Nonetheless, he continued to employ this duplicitous tactic in subsequent U.S. Treasury auctions using the names of other unqualified customers. He notified his supervisors only with respect to false customer bids that were uncovered by the customers and the authorities.

When the lawyer Feuerstein was informed of Mozer's false bidding, he made it clear to his superiors that this was a criminal act, and needed to be reported to the government. Gutfreund and Strauss agreed to report the activity to the Federal Reserve Bank of New York. "Mozer was told that his actions 'might threaten his future with the firm' and would be reported to the government." Yet, the decisions did not produce action. For three months there was no further investigation, Mozer was not disciplined. Mozer's authority was not restricted, and the executives did not notify the government.

But news trickled out to the public. Agents of the FBI and Department of Justice requested an audience with the firms' representatives about the "mistaken" auction bid. An investigation followed and all the facts were uncovered. A few days later "Salomon issued a press release stating that it had 'uncovered irregularities and rule violations in connection with its bids in certain auctions of Treasury securities.'" On Sunday, August 18, 1991, at a special board meeting of Salomon Inc., Gutfreund, Strauss and Meriwether resigned. On August 23, 1991, Feuerstein resigned as Chief Legal Officer of Salomon.

C. The SEC acted on May 20, 1992

"[T]he Commission filed a complaint in U.S. District Court for the Southern District of New York charging Salomon . . . with . . . violations of the federal securities laws, "including circumventing the Treasury auction per-customer bidding limitations. Salomon consented to the judgment, "without admitting or denying the allegations of the complaint." "The judgment required, among other things, that Salomon pay [a fine in] the amount of $290 million . . . "The SEC "instituted and settled . . . an administrative proceeding against the firm pursuant to Section 15(b) of the Exchange Act [of 1934]." "[T]he Commission found that Salomon had failed [to reasonably supervise] a person subject to its supervision with a view to preventing violations of the federal securities laws."

D. Legal Principles.

Section 15(b)(4)(E) of the Securities Exchange Act authorizes the SEC to sanction a broker-dealer if it has: "failed reasonably to supervise, with a view to preventing violations [of federal securities laws), another person who commits such a violation, if such person is subject to his supervision." "Section 15(b)(6) of the Exchange [Act] incorporates Section 15(b)(4)(E) by reference and authorizes the [SEC] to impose sanctions for deficient supervision on individuals associated with broker-dealers." "The [SEC] has long emphasized that the responsibility of broker-dealers to supervise their employees is a critical component of the federal regulatory scheme."

"Many of the Commission's cases involving a failure to supervise arise [when] supervisors [are] aware only of 'red flags' or 'suggestions' of irregularity, rather than [explicit information about the actual performance of] an illegal act." Yet, knowledge of "red flags" or "suggestions" of irregularity must trigger, in the words of the SEC, "adequate follow-up and review." And "if more than one supervisor is involved in considering the actions to be taken in response to possible misconduct, there must be a clear definition of the efforts to be taken and a clear assignment of those responsibilities to specific individuals within the firm."

In the *Salomon* case, the wrongful act consisted of bidding for treasury bonds above the limited amounts that the Treasury allocated. The limit to each underwriter was imposed in order to encourage competitive underwriters' bids. Mozer breached this limit in various underhanded ways.

"[T]hree supervisors of Paul Mozer_John Meriwether, Thomas Strauss, and John Gutfreund":

(i) Learned in late April of 1991 "that Mozer had submitted a false bid in the amount of $3.15 billion in an auction of U.S. Treasury securities."

(ii) They also learned that "Mozer had said that the bid had been submitted to obtain additional securities for another trading area of the firm." "They also learned that Mozer had contacted an employee of the customer whose name was used on the bid and falsely told that individual that the bid was an error."

(iii) "The supervisors also learned that the bid had been the subject of a letter from the Treasury Department to the customer . . . ."

(iv) They also learned that "Mozer had attempted to persuade the customer not to inform the Treasury Department that the bid had not been authorized."

(v) "The supervisors were also informed by Salomon's chief legal officer that the submission of the false bid appeared to be a criminal act."

Thus, Salomon supervisors learned that "a high level employee of the firm with significant trading discretion had engaged in extremely serious misconduct." This information required an investigation, increased supervision of Mozer, and a limitation of his activities pending an investigation. The supervisors failed to do that for over three months. "The need to take prompt action was all the more critical in view of the fact that the potential unlawful conduct had taken place in the market for U.S. Treasury securities." Gutfreund, Strauss, Meriwether and Feuerstein (CLO and CCO) were not charged with participating in the violations but with deficient supervision, "compounded by the delay in reporting the matter to the government."

E. What Should Have Been Done?

"To discharge their obligations, the supervisors should at least have taken steps to ensure that someone within the firm questioned other employees on the Government [Treasury Securities] Trading Desk, such as the desk's clerk or the other managing director on the desk." "Since the supervisors were informed that Mozer had said that he submitted the false bid to obtain additional securities for another trading desk of the firm, they should also have specifically investigated any involvement of that area of the firm in the matter."

"The supervisors . . . should have reviewed, or ensured that others reviewed, the documentation concerning the February 21, 1991 auction." "Such a review would have revealed, at a minimum, that a second false bid had been submitted in the auction and that false trade tickets and customer confirmations had been created in connection with both false bids."[915]

---

915 Those facts would have raised serious questions about the operations of the Government Trading Desk, and inquiries arising from those questions might well have led to discovery of the additional false bids described above. For instance, two of the other false bids, those submitted in the December 27, 1990 and February 7, 1991 auctions, involved the same pattern of fictitious sales to and from customer accounts and the suppression of customer confirmations used in

"Each of the three supervisors apparently believed that someone else would take the supervisory action necessary to appropriately respond to Mozer's misconduct." They did not discuss "what action should be taken or who would be responsible for taking action." "Instead, each of [them] assumed that another would act."

"[When] supervisors are aware of wrongdoing," they should "take 'prompt and unequivocal action' to define the responsibilities of those who are to respond to the wrongdoing." In this case they "failed to do that." Consequently, "although there may have been varying degrees of responsibility, each of the supervisors [bore] [a] measure of responsibility for the collective failure of the group to take action."

In addition, "[a]fter the disclosure of one unauthorized bid to Meriwether," his direct boss, "Mozer committed additional violations." "Had limits been placed on his activities after the one unauthorized bid was disclosed, these violations might have been prevented." "While Mozer was told by Meriwether that his conduct was career-threatening and that it would be reported to senior management and to the government, these efforts were not a sufficient supervisory response." Thus, the failure "to take action to discipline Mozer or to limit his activities constituted a serious breach of their supervisory obligations."

"As Chairman and [CEO] of Salomon, Gutfreund bore ultimate responsibility for ensuring that a prompt and thorough inquiry was undertaken and that Mozer was appropriately disciplined." "He failed to ensure that this was done." "Gutfreund also undertook the responsibility to report the matter to the government, but failed to do so," despite being urged by other senior Salomon executives to do so.[916] "Once improper conduct came to the attention of Gutfreund, he bore responsibility for ensuring that the firm responded in a way that recognized the seriousness and urgency of the situation." In [the view of the SEC], Gutfreund did not discharge that responsibility."

Strauss, as the President of Salomon, was the official within the firm to whom Meriwether first took the matter of Mozer's misconduct for appropriate action. Moreover, as its president, Strauss was responsible for Salomon's brokerage operations. Though he arranged several meetings to discuss the matter, Strauss failed to direct Meriwether, Feuerstein, or others within the firm to take the steps necessary to respond to the matter. Even if Strauss assumed that Meriwether or Feuerstein had taken over the responsibility of addressing the matter, he still failed to follow up, and ascertain whether appropriate action had in fact been taken. When

---

connection with the February 21, 1991 auction. Inasmuch as Mozer had admitted to committing one apparently criminal act, the supervisors had reason to be skeptical of Mozer's assurances that he had not engaged in other misconduct.

916 The disclosure was made only after an internal investigation prompted by other events. Gutfreund's failure to report the matter earlier is of particular concern because of Salomon's role in the vitally-important U.S. Treasury securities market. The reporting of the matter to the government was also the only action under consideration within the firm. The failure to actually make the report thus meant that the firm failed to take any action to respond to Mozer's misconduct.

it became clear that no meaningful action was being taken, Strauss' supervisory responsibilities as the president of the brokerage firm were reactivated, and he failed to discharge those responsibilities.

Meriwether was Mozer's direct supervisor and the head of all fixed-income trading activities at Salomon. Meriwether was responsible for supervising the firm's fixed-income trading activities, including the activities of the Government Securities Trading Desk. When he first learned of Mozer's misconduct, Meriwether promptly took the matter to senior executives within the firm. That was appropriate. However, Meriwether's responsibilities did not end with this communication "[to the senior executives. As the direct supervisor of Mozer, telling Mozer that the "misconduct would be reported to the government [was] insufficient under the circumstances to discharge his supervisory responsibilities." He had to do more and failed.

"Donald Feuerstein, Salomon's chief legal officer, was informed of the submission of the false bid by Paul Mozer in late April of 1991. He was present at the meetings in late April and did advise Strauss and Gutfreund that the submission of the bid was a criminal act and should be reported to the government, and he urged them on several occasions to make disclosure when he learned that the report had not been made. He did not direct that an inquiry be undertaken, and he did not recommend that appropriate procedures, reasonably designed to prevent and detect future misconduct, be instituted, or that other limitations be placed on Mozer's activities. Feuerstein also did not inform the Compliance Department, for which he was responsible as Salomon's chief legal officer, of the false bid."

"Unlike Gutfreund, Strauss, and Meriwether, however, Feuerstein was not a direct supervisor of Mozer at the time he first learned of the false bid." "[The SEC did not name] him as a respondent in this proceeding." "Instead, [the SEC was] issuing this report of investigation concerning the responsibilities imposed by Section 15(b)(4)(E) of the Exchange Act under the circumstances of this case."

"Employees of brokerage firms who have legal or compliance responsibilities do not become 'supervisors' for purposes of Sections 15(b)(4)(E) and 15(b)(6) solely because they occupy the positions of legal and compliance officers. Rather, determining if a particular person is a 'supervisor' depends on whether, under the facts and circumstances of a particular case, that person has a requisite degree of responsibility, ability, or authority to affect the conduct of the employee whose behavior is at issue."

"Thus, persons occupying positions in the legal or compliance departments of broker-dealers have been found by the Commission to be 'supervisors' for purposes of Sections 15(b)(4)(E) and l5(b)(6) . . . ." "In this case, serious misconduct involving a senior official of a brokerage firm was brought to the attention of the firm's [CLO]. That individual was informed of the misconduct by other members of senior management in order to obtain his advice and guidance, and to involve him as part of management's collective response to the problem. Moreover, in other instances of misconduct, that individual had directed the firm's response and had made recommendations concerning appropriate disciplinary action. In these prior instances management had relied on him to perform those tasks."

"Given the role and influence within the firm of a person in a position such as Feuerstein's and the factual circumstances of this case, such a person shares in the responsibility to take appropriate action to respond to the misconduct. Under those circumstances, we believe that such a person becomes a 'supervisor' for purposes of Sections 15(b)(4)(E) and 15(b)(6). As a result, that person is responsible, along with the other supervisors, for taking reasonable and appropriate action. It is not sufficient for one in such a position to be a mere bystander to the events that occurred."

"Once a person in Feuerstein's position becomes involved in formulating management's response to the problem, he or she is obligated to take affirmative steps to ensure that appropriate action is taken to address the misconduct. For example, such a person could [(i)] direct or monitor an investigation of the conduct at issue; [(ii)] make appropriate recommendations for limiting the activities of the employee. The person could make appropriate recommendations for the institution of appropriate procedures, [(a)] reasonably designed to prevent and detect future misconduct, and [(b)] verify that his or her recommendations, or acceptable alternatives, are implemented. If such a person takes appropriate steps but management fails to act and that person knows or has reason to know of that failure, he or she should consider what additional steps are appropriate to address the matter."

"These steps may include disclosure of the matter to the entity's board of directors, resignation from the firm, or disclosure to regulatory authorities." "These responsibilities cannot be avoided simply because the person did not previously have direct supervisory responsibility for any of the activities of the employee. Once such a person has supervisory obligations by virtue of the circumstances of a particular situation, he must either discharge those responsibilities or know that others are taking appropriate action."

F. The Result

John H. Gutfreund was "ordered to comply with his undertaking not to associate in the future in the capacity of Chairman or CEO with any broker, dealer, municipal securities dealer, investment company, or investment adviser regulated by the Commission"; and "ordered to pay to the United States Treasury a civil penalty in the amount of $100,000 pursuant to Section 21B(a)(4) of the Exchange Act."

Thomas W. Strauss was "suspended from associating with any broker, dealer, municipal securities dealer, investment company or investment adviser for a period of six (6) months"; and "ordered to pay to the United States Treasury a civil penalty in the amount of $75,000 pursuant to Section 21B(a)(4) of the Exchange Act."

John W. Meriwether was "suspended from associating with any broker, dealer, municipal securities dealer, investment company, or investment adviser for a period of three (3) months"; and "ordered to pay to the United States Treasury a civil penalty in the amount of $50,000 pursuant to Section 21B(a)(4) of the Exchange Act."

Donald Feuerstein was not sanctioned, and agreed to the decision.

_____

Discussion Topics

How do the duties of a CCO differ under the *Salomon Brothers* case and the *Urban* case?

Under what conditions does a person become a supervisor? Can you become a supervisor without your consent? Can you become a supervisor without the awareness of those who are subject to your supervision? To become a supervisor does this individual need not only the awareness but also the consent of those to be supervised?

Is a CCO the supervisor of everyone in the entity? Does the answer depend on whether the entity is big or small? Does the duty to supervise a particular action or person depend on whether there is more than one supervisor?

What precisely is the function of the CCO? Is it limited to fact finding? Does it also include the authority to punish and reward employees? What facts would you seek to determine the answer? Is the CCO the only decision maker in a case? To whom is the CCO responsible and accountable?

Compare the position of the CCO to that of a regulating examiner. Should the government examiner know the law? Is it true that government examiner just collects and uncovers information? Is the examiner a judge?

What was the real root cause of malfeasance at the Salomon Brothers and FBW?

Do you agree with the distinction made by the SEC between Urban and Feuerstein in the *Salomon Brothers* case?

What do you think was the Judge's central motivation in relieving Urban from any liability?

Why did Urban not resign from FBW when he saw sufficient red flags?

_____

CCO's Liability for failure to establish, maintain, and enforce compliance policies and procedures

(i) Chanin Capital Partners ("Chanin"), a broker-dealer, had policies and procedures in place to prevent insider trading. The policies required that certain forms be signed by the employees to acknowledge receipt of the policies and to disclose the employees' purchases or sales of securities for their own account. In addition, the policies required that the firm prevent the misuse of material nonpublic information in violations of Section 15(f) of the Securities Exchange Act of

1934. However, the company and its sole compliance officer, Carlos Martinez ("Martinez"), had no consistent practice of either obtaining the employee- signed forms or of tracking employee compliance with the policies. The company did not maintain a watch list of restricted list of securities and did not track or monitor employee trading for their own account.

In 2003, the company revised its policies by adding a restricted list. This list contained the names of corporations Chanin might possess inside information on. Consistent with the Securities and Exchange Act of 1934, Chanin employees were prohibited from trading in the securities of such corporations for their personal accounts. This restricted list was to be maintained by Martinez. The company also imposed a requirement that employees identify all their personal trading accounts and release copies of their monthly account statements for review by Martinez. The company also began related mandatory training for its employees and associated persons.

Despite these improved policies, the company had no policy or procedure for continued training of its personnel regarding the insider trading prohibitions, or for tracking the personnel's trading accounts after their initial certifications. There was no continuous assurance of compliance by the employees. According to the SEC "broker-dealers must take seriously their responsibilities" to establish, to maintain, and to enforce, "sufficiently robust policies and procedures to prevent the misuse of material nonpublic information." The company failed to establish, maintain, and enforce procedures to prevent insider trading.

The decision: Martinez was held liable for aiding and abetting in the failure of Chanin to establish the compliance program. He was the only compliance officer at Chanin and had the sole responsibility for maintaining and enforcing these policies and procedures. Martinez was found to have willfully aided and abetted the company's violation of Section 15(f) of the Exchange Act. Martinez was: (1) censured; (2) ordered to cease and desist from further violations of Section 15(f); and (3) ordered to pay a fine of $25,000.[917]

(ii) Robert E. Strong was the CCO of Jesup & Lamont Securities Corp., ("J&L"). Strong was ordered to pay a fine of $10,000 for failing to supervise a research analyst whose personal securities trading violated the association's compliance with former NASD Rule 2711 (now FINRA Rule 2241)[918] and others.[919] When Strong was hired as CCO, he prepared written supervisory procedures that assigned the compliance officer—Strong himself—the following responsibilities:

---

917 *In re* Martinez, Securities Exchange Act Rel. 57,755 (May 1, 2008).

918 Rule 2241, *available at* http://finra.complinet.com/en/display/display.html?rbid=2403&element_id=11946 (last visited June 14, 2017).

919 Strong was also found to have violated former NASD Rules 2110, now FINRA Rule 2010, *available at* http://finra.complinet.com/en/display/display.html?rbid=2403&element_id=5504 (last visited June 14, 2017) and former NASD Rule 3010, now FINRA Rules 3110 and 3170, *available at* http://finra.complinet.com/en/display/display.html?rbid=2403&element_id=11345 (last visited June 14, 2017) (Rule 3110), *and* http://finra.complinet.com/en/display/display.html?rbid=2403&element_id=11348 (last visited June 14, 2017) (Rule 3170). *In re* Strong, Securities Exchange Act Rel. No. 57,426 (Mar. 4, 2008).

reviewing and approving (or disallowing) personal trading activity in the accounts of research personnel; collecting and recording personal trading activity of research personnel (e.g., account statements and trade confirmations); and reviewing research personnel's trading activity to ensure compliance with Rule 2711's personal trading restrictions.[920] Strong, however, failed to: (1) pre-approve all personal trades by analysts; (2) monitor daily trading to identify restricted transactions; (3) take any action even after he learned of misconduct by one of the research analysts; and (4) alert the regulators to the misconduct. [921]

"The [CCO's] unreasonable inaction effectively nullified the supervisory system related to the Firm's compliance with Rule 2711 that he himself had designed and was responsible for enforcing." J&L's procedures also assigned the CCO the responsibility for verifying that J&L research reports contained the appropriate disclosures, which he failed to do with reasonable diligence. Thus, Strong was held responsible for the firm's failure to include the required disclosures. Further, Strong violated NASD Rule 2711(i) because he filed an attestation regarding J&L's procedures two months late.

The sanctions were reduced from $15,000 to $10,000 based on a number of mitigating factors, including: (i) Strong was the sole compliance person in a 40-person firm whose negligent compliance activities had pre-dated Strong's appointment as CCO; (ii) the misconduct at issue occurred within months of Strong joining the firm thus potentially giving him inadequate time to implement his policies; and (iii) Strong had not personally benefited in any way from his misconduct.[922]

(iii) Thomas Pritchard, the principal owner, managing director, and CCO of Pritchard Capital, was found liable for books and records violations and failure to supervise.[923] Pritchard Capital had multiple offices throughout the United States.[924] Pritchard was responsible for developing the supervisory policies and procedures of Pritchard Capital and for supervising the activities of certain associated persons.

Pritchard visited the New York office only periodically. In part, due to his infrequent trips to the office in question, Pritchard gave mutual fund correspondence and trade ticket files only a cursory look, missing red flags. One set of important red flags that was missed took the form of tentative or contingent trade ticket files. These suggested that certain associated persons were permitting late trading in mutual funds in violation of the Investment Company Act of 1940.[925]

---

920 *In re* Strong, Securities Exchange Act Rel. No. 57,426 (Mar. 4, 2008).

921 *Id.*

922 *Id.*

923 *In re* Prichard Capital Ptrs., LLC, Securities Exchange Act Rel. No. 57,704, Investment Company Act Rel. No. 28,251 (Apr. 23, 2008).

924 *Id.*

925 *Id.*

Therefore, the Pritchard failed to reasonably recognize or respond to these indications of wrongdoing. The SEC noted that Pritchard Capital's written supervisory procedures did not contain policies or procedures reasonably designed to prevent or detect illegal late trading. Pritchard was suspended from association, in a supervisory capacity, with any broker or dealer for a period of nine months. He was also ordered to pay a civil penalty in the amount of $50,000.[926]

Discussion topics

*Please compare and contrast the behavior of Carlos Martinez and Robert Strong.

The SEC's Responses to Frequently Asked Questions[927]

Question 1. Is a CCO or any other compliance or legal personnel a supervisor of broker-dealer business personnel solely by virtue of the compliance or legal position?

Answer: No. Compliance and legal personnel are not "supervisors" of business line personnel for purposes of Exchange Act Sections 15(b)(4) and 15(b)(6) solely because they occupy compliance or legal positions. Determining if a particular person is a supervisor depends on whether, under the facts and circumstances of a particular case, that person has the requisite degree of responsibility, ability, or authority to affect the conduct of the employee whose behavior is at issue.

Question 2. What does it mean to have the requisite degree of responsibility, ability, or authority to affect the conduct of another employee?

Answer: A person's actual responsibilities and authority, rather than, for example, his or her "line" or "non-line" status, determine whether he or she is a "supervisor" for purposes of Exchange Act Sections 15(b)(4) and 15(b)(6).

Among the questions to consider in this regard are: has the person clearly been given, or otherwise assumed, supervisory authority or responsibility for particular business activities or situations?

Do the firm's policies and procedures, or other documents, identify the person as responsible for supervising, or for overseeing, one or more business persons or activities? Did the person have the power to affect another's conduct? Did the person, for example, have the ability to hire, reward or punish that person?

---

926 *Id.*

927 Div. of Trading & Markets, *U.S. Sec. & Exch. Comm'n, Frequently Asked Questions about Liability of Compliance and Legal Personnel at Broker-Dealers under Sections 15(b)(4) and 15(b)(6) of the Exchange Act* (Sept. 30, 2013), *available at* https://www.sec.gov/divisions/marketreg/faq-cco-supervision-093013.htm (last visited May 8, 2017).

Did the person otherwise have authority and responsibility such that he or she could have prevented the violation from continuing, even if he or she did not have the power to fire, demote or reduce the pay of the person in question? Did the person know that he or she was responsible for the actions of another, and that he or she could have taken effective action to fulfill that responsibility? Should the person nonetheless reasonably have known in light of all the facts and circumstances that he or she had the authority or responsibility within the administrative structure to exercise control to prevent the underlying violation?

Question 3. Can compliance and legal personnel provide advice and counsel to business line personnel without being considered supervisors of the business line personnel for purposes of the Exchange Act?

Answer: Yes. Compliance and legal personnel play a critical role in efforts by broker-dealers to develop and implement an effective compliance system throughout their organizations, including by providing advice and counsel to business line personnel. Compliance and legal personnel do not become "supervisors" solely because they have provided advice or counsel concerning compliance or legal issues to business line personnel, or assisted in the remediation of an issue. If their responsibilities or authorities extend beyond compliance and legal functions such that they have the requisite degree of responsibility, ability, or authority to affect the conduct of business line personnel, additional inquiry may be necessary to determine if they could be considered supervisors of the business line personnel.

Question 4. Can a broker-dealer establish and implement a robust compliance program without its compliance and legal personnel being considered to be supervisors for purposes of the Exchange Act?

Answer: Yes. Broker-dealers have a duty to build effective compliance programs that are reasonably designed to ensure compliance with applicable laws and regulations. Among the things that firms should consider including in their programs are robust compliance monitoring systems, processes to escalate identified instances of noncompliance to business line personnel for remediation, and procedures that clearly designate responsibility to business line personnel for supervision of functions and persons.

Broker-dealers should consider clearly defining compliance and advisory duties and distinguishing those duties from business line duties in order for persons who perform only compliance and legal functions to avoid becoming supervisors of business line employees. Management at broker-dealers can greatly benefit from the participation and input of compliance and legal personnel.

Question 5. Can compliance or legal personnel participate in a management or other committees without being considered supervisors of business activities or business personnel for purposes of the Exchange Act?

Answer: Yes. Compliance and legal personnel play a critical role in efforts by broker-dealers to develop and implement an effective compliance system throughout their organizations, including by participating in management and other committees. Compliance and legal personnel do not become "supervisors" solely because they participate in, provide advice to, or consult with a management or other committees. As explained above, the determination whether a particular person is a supervisor depends on whether, under the facts and circumstances of a particular case, that person has the requisite degree of responsibility, ability, or authority to affect the conduct of the employee whose behavior is at issue.

Question 6. Can compliance or legal personnel provide advice to, or consult with, senior management without being considered supervisors of business activities or business personnel for purposes of the Exchange Act?

Answer: Yes. Compliance and legal personnel play a critical role in efforts by broker-dealers to develop and implement an effective compliance system throughout their organizations, including by providing advice and counsel to senior management. Compliance and legal personnel do not become "supervisors" solely because they provide advice to, or consult with, senior management. In fact, compliance and legal personnel play a key role in providing advice and counsel to senior management, including keeping management informed about the state of compliance at the broker-dealer, major regulatory developments, and external events that may have an impact on the broker-dealer. In this regard, compliance and legal personnel should inform direct supervisors of business line employees about conduct that raises red flags and continue to follow up in situations where misconduct may have occurred to help ensure that a proper response to an issue is implemented by business line supervisors. Compliance and legal personnel may need to escalate situations to persons of higher authority if they determine that concerns have not been addressed.

Question 7. What is the current status of the initial decision in the Theodore W. Urban matter?[11]

Answer: Under the SEC's rules of practice, if a majority of the SEC Commissioners do not agree on the merits (as was the case in Urban), the initial decision "shall be of no effect."

Question 8. What responsibilities does a person working in a compliance or legal capacity have if he or she is also a supervisor for purposes of the Exchange Act?

Answer: Once a person has supervisory obligations, he or she must reasonably supervise with a view to preventing violations of the federal securities laws, the Commodity Exchange Act, the rules or regulations under those statutes, or the rules of the Municipal Securities Rulemaking

Board. That person must reasonably discharge those obligations or know that others are taking appropriate action. It is not reasonable for a person with supervisory obligations to be a mere bystander to events that occurred, or to ignore wrongdoing, "red flags" or other suggestions of irregularity.

Exchange Act Section 15(b)(4)(E) provides an affirmative defense to potential liability for failure to supervise if the following conditions are satisfied: a firm has established procedures and a system for applying those procedures that would reasonably be expected to prevent and detect, insofar as practicable, a violation; the supervisor has reasonably discharged his or her duties pursuant to the procedures and system; and is without reasonable cause to believe that the procedures and system were not being complied with.

Discussion topic

*Has the SEC staff changed the position it took in the *Salomon Brothers* and *Urban* cases? If so, how, and why?

Chapter 19

RESTORING AND REGAINING TRUST AFTER MALFEASANCE

The worst thing in your own development as a leader is not to do it wrong. It's to do it for the wrong reasons.

Stan Slap

I can calculate the motions of heavenly bodies, but not the madness of people.

Sir Isaac Newton

In this chapter we deal with institutions that have violated the law, yet succeeded in restoring their business, reputation, and public trust. Section I introduces the problem of reforming an institutional culture. Section II demonstrates the issue or restoring public trust with the story of WorldCom's rebirth as MCI Communications. Section III describes how NASA's culture was changed after a disastrous failure. Section IV ends on a more cautious note describing two cases in which violations continued and, as usual, we ask why.

I. HOW TO REFORM A PROBLEMATIC CULTURE?

As already noted, within the organization, culture is crucial. For example, management expert Peter Drucker wrote that "culture eats strategy for breakfast" and another expert, Edgar Schein, said that leaders are the "architects of culture." Professor Jim Ludema declared: "culture starts and ends with people."[928]

A. The Success Stories

Many corporations that slide into a culture of crime and malfeasance do not survive, but some have resurrected themselves. We examine these success stories to better understand how they achieved their transformations.

---

928 Jim Ludema, *3 People Practices for Driving Results in Your Culture*, CHI. DAILY HERALD, July 25, 2016, at 20, LEXIS, News Library, Curnws File..

As with individual human beings, no corporation can live, let alone flourish, in isolation. Therefore, when considering a culture of self-regulation, one must examine not only the institution, but also the broader competitive landscape that it conducts its affairs in. This landscape is shaped not only by competing corporations but also by the local, national, and international communities where the institution coexists.

In *Blue Ocean Strategy*, two authors, W. Chan Kim and Renee Mauborgne, wrote that even though managers have power to introduce changes in their organization, changing culture is viewed as a tough task.[929] To change culture the manager "must win the hearts and minds of the people" he or she works with. The authors note four obstacles for a manager changing culture: (1) cognition, i.e., employees must know the reasons for the change; (2) limited resources; (3) motivation, i.e., employees must be motivated to change; and (4) institutional politics.

Another suggestion is a "'tipping point' approach." First, begin with influential employees and highlight their commitment to change, in order to influence others. Second, have employees experience the circumstances that create a need for change, e.g., requiring police to ride the subways themselves to understand why residents are frightened, or requiring managers to take customer complaint calls. Third, focus on "hot spots" where few resources can result in large change. Fourth, appoint a "consigliere" or respected insider who knows that the manager needs to implement change.[930]

Alan Murray suggests considering changes in the personnel structure, such as work groups or a task force with employees with varied talents or experience levels. Consider "an egalitarian culture, flexible schedules, few meetings, and interdisciplinary project teams" and allow employees to feel trusted, for example by allowing them to work at home occasionally. In addition, consider changes in the office set-up, i.e. "eliminate exclusive-looking private office suites and assign everyone work stations in close proximity" and use the space saved for office amenities.[931] Yes. It is all about people.

B. Changing Habits

Peter Bregman suggests changing a culture through "stories" rather than through changes in formal procedures. The author pointed to the importance of peer pressure, noting a study in

---

929 *How to Change Your Organization's Culture*, WALL ST. J., *available at* http://guides.wsj.com/management/innovation/how-to-change-your-organizations-culture/ (last visited Sept. 24, 2016), *adapted in part from* ALAN MURRAY, THE WALL STREET JOURNAL ESSENTIAL GUIDE TO MANAGEMENT (2010), *citing* W. CHAN KIM & RENÉE MAUBORGNE, BLUE OCEAN STRATEGY (2005)..

930 *How to Change Your Organization's Culture*, WALL ST. J., *available at* http://guides.wsj.com/management/innovation/how-to-change-your-organizations-culture/ (last visited Sept. 24, 2016), *adapted in part from* ALAN MURRAY, THE WALL STREET JOURNAL ESSENTIAL GUIDE TO MANAGEMENT (2010), *citing* W. CHAN KIM & RENÉE MAUBORGNE, BLUE OCEAN STRATEGY (2005).

931 *How to Change Your Organization's Culture*, WALL ST. J., *available at* http://guides.wsj.com/management/innovation/how-to-change-your-organizations-culture/ (last visited Sept. 24, 2016), *adapted in part from* ALAN MURRAY, THE WALL STREET JOURNAL ESSENTIAL GUIDE TO MANAGEMENT (2010).

which children were motivated to eat vegetables they disliked by seating them at a table with children who liked them.[932]

The crucial part of trust is trusting the system rather than the people. In fact, the suggestion is: Never trust people. Expose people who hold public power, and leave them as little protection as possible. Expose them to the media. Will this exposure lead to public lynching? If so, limit this power by other protective mechanisms to retain their power.

Jon Elster concluded that "scientific, technical, economic, and social development tends to erode the ability to make credible threats and promises, by undermining social norms and reducing the scope for long-term self interest. . . [Mobility tends to weaken social norms which are affected by] incessant change in the modern world."[933]

C. What Enables People to Predict Each Other's Behavior?

A partial answer by Jon Elster is: "Altruism, envy, social norms, and self-interest all contribute, in complex, interacting ways to order, stability, and cooperation." And some elements may work for positive and negative pressures.[934]

Arguably the aggregate judgment of the crowd is the wisest.[935] Other people believe in the wisdom of select individuals, such as Warren Buffett. It may well be that both are correct. When the markets can be affected not by the anonymous crowd but by a small network of self-interested individuals or organizations, the wisdom of the crowd no longer exists. Besides, market runs suggest that, from time to time, there is not only crowd wisdom but crowd madness as well.

Cultures differ in different places. In a 1971 book, *The Anatomy of Dependence, The Key Analysis of Japanese Behavior*, Takeo Doi described how Japanese children are taught to have a deep dependence on elders and the community. This may not be the case today. However, it is still important to realize how such a culture produces dependence on the community and how its judgments may substitute for a death sentence of a person who is ostracized. In the culture Doi describes, sin and shame meant ostracization, and by the family as well.[936] If the community passed judgment on the individual, he was expected to—and did in fact—commit suicide.

Have you ever seen how a buyer in the bazaar looks for a purchase? The buyer finds the one item she likes, and shows great attention to one that she does not like. She asks for the price of that undesirable item. Then she asks for the price of both that item and the desirable one. She

---

932 Peter Bregman, *Changing Your Corporate Culture*, BLOOMBERG BUS., June 26, 2009, *available at* http://peterbregman.com/articles/a-good-way-to-change-a-corporate-culture/#.V-cqylJXxYU (last visited Sept. 27, 2016).

933 JON ELSTER, THE CEMENT OF SOCIETY: A STUDY OF SOCIAL ORDER 284-86 (1989) (reprinted 1990).

934 *Id.* at 287.

935 JAMES SUROWIECKI, THE WISDOM OF CROWDS (2004).

936 TAKEO DOI, M.D., THE ANATOMY OF DEPENDENCE 48 (1971).

can thus find the price of the desirable one without asking for it. The seller watches her carefully, to determine her true preference and prices the items accordingly.

Would this be the American way? Why not? What values underlie the two systems? In some cultures asking how the wife is doing raises true fury: "None of your business!" In another culture not asking the same question shows that you lack good manners.

Discussion Topics

What do you do when your manager asks you to do something you are uncomfortable doing? What questions should you ask yourself before taking on such projects? Should you analyze the positive consequences of just refusing? Should you identify external and internal threats to your personal integrity? Should you seek to evaluate the possible effect on your career?

What if others in the organization are doing it? What if everyone in the practice is doing it?

What does the top manager do when he or she wishes to change the corporate culture?

Are the markets effective in encouraging socially optimal behavior?

D. Summary

I. People follow their views about the legitimacy of compliance rules and the laws that require compliance.

If people believe that the legal requirements are unfair or that the associated compliance measures taken are onerous, wasteful, or unreasonable, then the chances of compliance with these requirements are far lower. Employees usually have their own moral compass that tells them what is right or wrong. If this compass is drastically out of sync with their employer's, then one or the other requires change or removal. In such a case, general concepts of wrong and right in the appropriate community should be examined. If the compliance program is far removed from the moral compass of the surrounding community, it may be time for its writers to go back to the drawing board.

Issues of compliance cover law firms as well. The larger the firms are the more difficult these issues may become. Lawyers are recognized fiduciaries and as such they must remember and be sensitive to conflicts of interests. We must remember that professional responsibility is based on personal self-regulation—ethical behavior of the individuals as reflected in the firm's culture. The same arguments against self-limitation, especially when significant amounts of money are at stake, can be used by lawyers. If money is the most satisfactory reward, then the search for nooks and crevices through which conflicts may squeeze will be the norm. They may be successful or fail for different reasons. It is worthwhile following a certain pattern of thinking that might lead to behaving in an ethical or unethical behavior. You should outline these questions and potential answers.[937]

II. THE PROBLEM OF RESTORING TRUST

For a corporation, it is easier to lose the public's trust and a good reputation than to maintain it. It is especially hard to restore trust after it has been lost. A fall from grace may result from the actions by "a few bad apples," a pervasive culture of dishonesty, or the result of external events. In all cases, restoring trust is very difficult. In the case of E.F. Hutton, which we studied, the company was never able to regain the public's confidence, even after it adopted dramatic personnel and policy changes. Ultimately, it was sold in a fire sale. The Hutton experience is the rule rather than the exception. History demonstrates that there is no simple recipe for restoring trust. Rather, there are various actions that have, in some cases, contributed to the restoration of trust. Even then, there is no guarantee of success.

The starting point for determining how to regain trust is to understand why the trust was lost. A corporation loses the trust of its stakeholders (employees, customers, regulators, communities, shareholders, etc.) when they no longer believe that it tells the truth or will honor its promises. Failure to communicate openly and honestly has been a frequent "trust buster." Dishonest communication is particularly insidious. If a company is found to have lied about its revenue accounting, for example, not only the shareholders but also other stakeholders might immediately ask what else the corporation said that was untrue. Another cause of lost trust is an action that casts doubts on whether the corporation will honor its obligations. A steel producer that refuses to deliver product to its customer, in violation of its contract, because the product's price rose beyond the contract price, may never regain that customer's trust. Short-term unethical profit optimization, even if not clearly illegal, can often lead to long-term problems. So does abuse of power and failure to accept responsibility (especially by senior management). These, too, are reasons for loss of trust in a corporation.

Often, a wrongdoer blames others rather than accepting personal responsibility. "Everyone else does it." "The investors should have read the fine print." Or "I did it for the shareholders." These are all-too-common explanations and justifications for dishonest actions.

As noted, understanding how trust is lost provides the framework for beginning the process of restoring trust. What actions should be taken? First, always communicate both the good and the bad. Management must provide transparent, truthful and, if at all possible, verifiable information to all stakeholders. The information should project both the company's values and its true performance. Even the most successful corporations may have to report bad news occasionally. Whether it is failing to meet a profit target, has product quality issues, or experiences

---

937 *See* Anthony V. Alfieri, *The Fall of Legal Ethics and the Rise of Risk Management*, 94 Geo. L.J. 1909 (2006).

low employee morale, the corporation's leaders must disclose the bad news together with the good, if any. Proactively sharing negative news restores credibility. In fact, such disclosure may eliminate outsiders' speculations, which are often far worse than the reality.

The way mutual fund giant Fidelity responded to discovering that a number of its employees accepted improper gifts illustrates the power of openly and directly communicating bad news. The company found out that some of its traders received lavish gifts from brokers seeking to do business with Fidelity. The alleged gifts included a trip to the Super Bowl and vacations in Florida.

The trustees of Fidelity Investments responded by retaining a retired judge as a special investigator. He conducted an internal investigation of the alleged improprieties. The resulting report did find that some Fidelity employees received inappropriate gifts. An economic analysis was conducted to assess whether the gifts resulted in decisions that added costs to the funds or otherwise negatively impacted shareholders. While the investigators were unable to establish harm statistically, the report does state: "the conduct at issue was serious, is worthy of redress and . . . any uncertainty should be resolved in favor of the funds."[938] The rationale for this position includes a finding that "inadequate supervision and other shortcomings exposed the funds to the potential risks of adverse publicity, loss of credibility with their principal regulators, and loss of fund shareholders."[939]

Fidelity's chairman reacted to the report by acting swiftly and publicly. First, he recognized the gravity of the issue and made "a rare public apology." "On behalf of Fidelity and myself, I extend an apology for this improper behavior. Although there was no proof of diminished execution quality, there is no question that the funds were put at potential risk" of inappropriate investments. Fidelity paid the funds $42 million as recommended by the special investigator—a large payment given the lack of proof of harm. Yet, the payment ended the controversy and began to repair the damage to Fidelity's reputation for trustworthiness. After the Chairman's letter of apology, the company posted a formal *mea culpa* on its website and reiterated its commitment to high ethical standards. More than a dozen traders were disciplined, and eight left the company.[940]

A powerful action that helps restore trust is a true apology. The word "true" is operative. Words are cheap and an apology can begin the process of restoring trust only if it is sincere and backed by actions that involve some personal risk and sacrifice for the institution asking forgiveness.

---

938 Mark Fagan & Tamar Frankel, Trust and Honesty in the Real World a Teaching Course in Law, Business and Public Policy 217 (Fathom Publishing Company 2009). Some changes were made in the text and the footnotes were omitted.

939 *Id.*

940 *Id.* at 218.

For example, Johnson & Johnson Company (J&J) management had to explain to the world why its trusted product was suddenly killing people.[941] J&J executives took bold, immediate actions, which demonstrated that the company's primary concern was customer safety, not company profits. The company immediately advised the public, through the media, not to buy or use Tylenol capsules,[942] withdrawing all Tylenol capsules from the market.[943] The company recalled 31 million bottles of Tylenol, at a cost of $100 million, which it absorbed, and ceased its advertising of Tylenol products except for a brief television campaign asking consumers to "trust" Tylenol.[944] The rapid and responsible actions taken by J&J showed that the company was not willing to take a risk with the public's safety, even if it cost the company millions of dollars. The end result was that the public viewed Tylenol as the unfortunate victim of a malicious crime.

Nevertheless, J&J was faced with extensive negative publicity—over 100,000 news stories that ran during the crisis.[945] To overcome the adverse image of its product, the company designed a process of rebuilding trust in the Tylenol brand. The features of the program included compensating the victims' families (even though the company was not liable)[946] and developing a triple sealed package to prevent future tampering.[947] At the time of the crisis, an advertising guru was quoted saying: "There may be an advertising person who thinks he can solve this, and if they find him I want to hire him, because then I want him to turn our water cooler into a wine cooler."[948] The advertising Houdini was actually a forthright, contrite, and action-oriented management team that succeeded in rebuilding sales to pre-crisis levels in only six months.

---

941 During 1982 seven individuals were killed in the Chicago area as the result of drug tampering in which the victim took Tylenol brand capsules that had been laced with potassium cyanide, a highly toxic substance.

942 Jennifer Ladson, *How Poisoned Tylenol Became a Crisis-Management Teaching Model*, Time, Sept. 29, 2014, *available at* http://time.com/3423136/tylenol-deaths-1982/ (last visited Nov. 2. 2016).

943 Mark L. Mitchell, *The Impact of External Parties on Brand-Name Capital: The 1982 Tylenol Poisonings and Subsequent Cases*, 27 Econ. Inquiry 601, 603 (1989).

944 Philip J. Hilts, *Tylenol Is Reintroduced in Triple-Sealed Package*, Wash. Post, Nov. 12, 1982, at A3, LEXIS, News Library, Acnes File.

945 A.C. Fernando, Corporate Governance 184 (2006).

946 *Settlement Ends Legal Action Over Tainted Tylenol*, N.Y. Times, May 19, 1991, sec. 4, at 7, LEXIS, News Library, Acnes File.

947 N.R. Kleinfield, *Tylenol's Rapid Comeback*, N.Y. Times, Sept. 17, 1983, sec. 1, at 33, LEXIS, News Library, Arcnws File.

948 N.R. Kleinfield, *Long, Uphill Odds for Tylenol*, N.Y. Times, Oct. 8, 1982, sec. D, at 1, LEXIS, News Library, Arcnws File.

Please review the WorldCom case in Chapter 13. In the WorldCom case, after the scandal, the company continued operations under the MCI name and a Corporate Monitor was appointed.

Richard Breeden, a lawyer and the former Chairman of the SEC, was appointed Corporate Monitor of the new MCI. In this role, Breeden was "initially directed at preventing corporate looting and document destruction." Over time, his responsibilities evolved to defining a program to restore the trust that WorldCom had lost. His vision for the new MCI was a company "built around a commitment to create a corporate culture based on transparency and integrity and to establish a model of excellence in governance to replace the odious practices of the past." Breeden recognized that there was no silver bullet to restore trust at MCI or to prevent dishonest practices in the future.

Consequently, his task was to define actions that would encourage a culture of trust, put a governance structure in place to support that culture, and establish follow-up processes to assure that management actually "walked the talk." He drafted a document titled "Restoring Trust" to serve as the blueprint for the new MCI. In his words, "Hopefully these recommendations, coupled with the strong efforts of the new management team . . . will enable MCI to succeed in its goal of becoming a model of excellence in corporate governance."

Breeden identified 78 individual actions that MCI needed to take in order to build a culture of trustworthiness. He recognized the challenge that implementing so many recommendations represented but argued that a successful restoration required the totality of his proposed changes. The actions are grouped into ten focus areas covering the composition of the board of directors, executive compensation, risk management, and ethics training. His general philosophy appears to be captured in the following: "In seeking excellence in governance, it is critical . . . to establish and to maintain the most healthy balance among the legitimate interests of management, the board, shareholders, and other stakeholders, including employees, that balance has to be struck in a manner that encourages a strong and high quality board, and an outstanding management team that can pursue business success . . . but not at the price of diluting the present unrelenting commitment of management to operating with the highest standards of integrity."

The first set of recommendations centers on the board of directors. The Report of Investigation by the Special Investigative Committee illustrates how the board failed to safeguard the shareholders' interests. Several members of the board were close personal friends of Ebbers, and the board rarely inquired into or considered the substance of the business. In fact, many did not have the experience or expertise to do so. Consequently, the board deferred to Ebbers and did nothing to restrain the "nearly imperial reign [of Ebbers] over the affairs of the Company."

---

949 Mark Fagan & Tamar Frankel, Trust and Honesty in the Real World a Teaching Course in Law, Business and Public Policy 217 (Fathom Publishing Company 2009). Some changes were made in the text and the footnotes were omitted.

Ironically, WorldCom did have in place many board-governance best practices. For instance, 80% of the board membership was independent, and the chairman of the board was not the CEO. "Unfortunately, WorldCom satisfied the form of governance and not its substance."

Based on the failures of the board and the resulting lessons learned at WorldCom, Breeden prescribed 13 recommendations for the new board. The suggested size of the new board was 8 to 12 members: a number small enough to allow for its members to build personal relationships, but large enough to encompass the range of skills and expertise needed to steer a large global technology company.

With respect to outside directors, Breeden recommended that all directors, other than the CEO, be independent of the company. His rationale was that inside board members could readily form a coalition that could dominate the external members. If internal expertise was needed, senior management could be brought to board meetings to provide the substantive expertise.

His definition of independence included a prohibition on those: (1) having close family relationships with employees; (2) receiving compensation as an employee (he actually proposed material compensation for board members based on the level of involvement outlined below); (3) interlocking board membership; and (4) having any commercial relationship with MCI.

The Corporate Monitor placed great emphasis on the members' expertise and time commitment to the company. He proposed qualification standards for some of the members, including prior board membership of a publicly traded company, financial expertise, and knowledge of the telecommunications industry. To increase the competence of MCI's board, an annual two-day strategy retreat was required. This retreat was in addition to a separate training session/briefing for new board members. He suggested 8-10 meetings per year, three of which would be held at company facilities other than corporate headquarters. Members would also be required to visit a company facility at least once a year, independent of board meetings. Term limits and rolling membership were also established. Finally, to insure that management could not independently alter his recommendations, the board requirements were incorporated in the Articles of Incorporation.

A second group of recommendations addressed the roles of the board and CEO. Breeden recommended a non-executive chairman of the board. He supported the separation of the two positions thereby allowing the CEO to focus on the company's business and the chairperson on governance issues. The chairperson was vested with the power to establish the board's agenda, coordinate the work of the board committees, distribute information to the members, and supervise the annual review of the CEO. The chairperson's qualifications included having served on the boards of three other publicly traded companies, at least one of which had a market capitalization of more than $5 billion. The chairperson would be supported by company resources as needed.

The Corporate Monitor devoted a separate section of recommendations to the compensation of board members. The recommendations were designed to compensate directors for the real time commitment they were expected to make to the company and also to avoid conflicts of interest. "The level of annual board retainer should be substantial, with a recommended level of not less than $150,000 per year." Conflicts of interest were to be minimized by prohibiting equity grants, options, or trading in related derivatives. To align board and shareholder interests the Corporate Monitor required that members invest not less than 25% of their retainers in MCI stock through open market purchases (or fixed periodic purchases at market prices), and that this stock be held for at least six months after any departure from the board. This was a stricter requirement than the requirement under Section 16 of the Securities Exchange Act of 1934.

"The executive compensation practices of the old WorldCom made a mockery of shareholder interests and eroded the legitimacy of the Company's governance practices. Both CEO Ebbers and CFO Sullivan were lavishly compensated, and both individuals were regularly among the most highly paid corporate officers in the U.S. . . . [T]he Company's compensation practices with regard to Ebbers and Sullivan were so corrosive of responsible behavior that they may have implicitly created a climate conducive to the fraud that occurred." The quote taken from the Corporate Monitor's report clearly indicated that executive compensation practices needed an overhaul. Breeden's philosophical starting point was that compensation should be linked to performance and should benefit both corporate management and shareholders. He made this operational by establishing higher base salaries and cash bonuses "tied to serious performance targets" such as profitability, tangible company net worth, balance sheet ratios, ROE, ROA, EBITDA growth, market share growth, or even cost reductions. He targeted 60-75% of total compensation to be in cash with the remainder in restricted stock with long-term holding periods. The new MCI was restricted from offering stock options for five years and thereafter only with shareholder permission.

Perhaps in reaction to Ebbers' former habit of paying his team multi-million dollar retention bonuses, the new MCI was restricted from offering such incentives except in cases of acquisitions, plant closings, etc. Breeden also addressed severance fees for executives. "It is not the function of severance programs to continue an executive's lifestyle forever." He capped future severance payments at a maximum of $10 million for the CEO and $5 million for any other employee. A maximum of 50% of those amounts could be paid if the termination was for cause. Only a vote of the shareholders could increase compensation exceeding beyond the stated caps.

The board serves the shareholders in part by providing a check and balance on management actions. The Audit Committee of the board is the facilitator of this governance process. The Corporate Monitor established that the committee would consist of not less than three independent directors who "possess substantial experience with financial reporting issues associated with large and complex companies." The qualifications for Audit Committee membership must have been earned as a senior financial officer, CEO of a financial institution, senior regulator, or senior partner of a public accounting firm.

Breeden also wanted an experienced Audit Committee, whose members would have a minimum of three years' service at other public companies. The committee would meet eight times per year. In light of their time commitment and responsibility, committee members would receive an additional retainer of $50,000. The integrity of the audit committee requires a zero tolerance of conflicts of interest. The audit committee was vested with the responsibility to annually review the CFO's performance and monitor the activities of the internal company audit department.

The importance of governance led the Corporate Monitor to create a board committee directly focused on this issue. The responsibilities of the governance committee included nominations for board members, compensation for board members, and the charter for the other board committees. The committee would also consider and approve any changes to the company's articles or by-laws.

Another new board group was the risk management committee. This committee would review management's assessment of risks and priorities. The risks included those in "technology and network operations, finance and accounting, legal, environmental, personnel, treasury, capital budgeting, or any other issues that could create significant risks to the Company's results, reputation, or capacity to serve customers." Of note, the group is to be concerned with not only financial outcomes but also with "brand equity."

A set of recommendations falls under the heading of general corporate issues. The first issue addresses cash flow reporting. WorldCom's fraudulent financial reporting led to the company's failure. Thus, Breeden required greater transparency in financial reporting, especially cash flow, to enable investors to better track and evaluate the company's future performance. Although the specifics are left somewhat ambiguous, he recommends that "the Company . . . develop standards of transparency in financial reporting that exceed minimum legal requirements, and that avoid entirely attempts to hype or manage reported balance sheets or income."

Also under the heading of general corporate issues, the Corporate Monitor addresses issues of change of control. He seeks the balance between avoiding raiders yet permitting the shareholders to benefit from an acquisition of the company. He recognizes that "shark repellant" measures could insulate management from having to seriously consider external takeover attempts. To this end, Breeden prohibits the company's management from adopting poison pill devices. However, shareholders could independently choose to adopt such protective devices if they came to believe that investors might use an acquisition to depress the stock price of MCI and thus later acquire its assets at a bargain price (thus shortchanging existing shareholders).

The Corporate Monitor's final set of recommendations centers on the legal and ethics programs at MCI. The foundation for ethical conduct articulated by Breeden is a statement of values and principles. This Code becomes "an opportunity for a company to express important values, and in this manner to reflect both the norms of society generally, and the standards of behavior that the company wishes to set for itself." These words would be meaningful only if the executives embody these values every day through their actions.

The guiding principles of MCI's Code are intended to direct the way business is conducted by everyone in the company. The first principle is "Build Trust and Credibility." Others include "Create a Culture of Open and Honest Communications" and "Set Tone at the Top." The last perhaps wraps the ten principles into one: "Do the Right Thing." The principles have been incorporated into an Ethics Pledge that all employees must agree to, starting with the CEO and senior management team. The actions taken by the company to rebuild trust were successful. When the court approved the monetary settlement, it noted that: "The Court is aware of no large company accused of fraud that has so rapidly and so completely divorced itself from the misdeeds of the immediate past and undertaken such extraordinary steps to prevent such misdeeds in the future. . . . [T]he Court is satisfied that the steps already taken have gone a very long way toward making the company a good corporate citizen."

MCI emerged from the ashes of WorldCom in April 2004. As part of the bankruptcy settlement, MCI paid the SEC $750 million to compensate investors impacted by the fraud. In the words of the new MCI CEO: "MCI's turnaround is a tribute to the human spirit and the amazing will of our 50,000 dedicated employees. . . . We are emerging with a new board and management team, a sound financial position, unmatched global assets, a strong customer base, and industry-leading service quality." His optimism about the strength of MCI was borne out in the marketplace. Within a year, a bidding war ensued for MCI. Verizon's initial bid was $6.7 billion. A rival offer from Qwest forced Verizon to up the ante to $8.44 billion. The transaction closed in January 2006. The CEO that led MCI through its revival and sale left the company with a severance package of almost $40 million.

Discussion Topics

What is the balance of power between the board of directors and management that Commissioner Breeden established in this case?

Is an ethics pledge a reasonable term of employment or is it too onerous, impractical, or ineffective?

Does the bankruptcy court have a role in actively seeking to restore the trust of a corporation?

A major law firm's commentary on Breeden's recommendations states: "Taken as a whole, Breeden's recommendations would straightjacket and enfeeble boards of directors and undermine their ability to effectively guide their corporations." Do you agree?

What steps can be taken to ensure that a Code has teeth?

Should the reporting relationship between the internal auditor and the board be direct or through a corporate executive?

Who is responsible for the veracity of the financial statements? What is the backup plan if the responsible person fails?

Was MCI's new CEO's severance fee consistent with the Monitor's report?

While aggressively handling the Tylenol tampering incident, was J&J acting in society's interest, in the interest of its own self-preservation, or both? Is there a conflict between these interests?

What benefit, if any, did Fidelity's "aberration and commitment" web posting provide? If there was a benefit, to whom did it accrue?

Were the pre-qualifications for the new MCI board members so rigorous that they might sometimes prevent the roles from being filled if applied to other companies?

How does management convey a sense of urgency about achieving results without implying an "achieve at any cost" mentality?

What actions can a management team take to create an environment in which employees are comfortable raising red flags?

Public Policy

Would a tort award limit reduce the incentives for corporate trust and honesty?

Does bankruptcy protection provide an unfair advantage to those who might be tempted to take high risks when seeking profits?

Would executive compensation limits restrict corporate performance?

IV. CHANGING NASA'S CULTURE[950]

"The organizational causes of this accident are rooted in the Space Shuttle Program's history and culture . . . . Cultural traits and organizational practices detrimental to safety were allowed to develop, including: reliance on past success as a substitute for sound engineering practices . . . ; organizational barriers that prevented effective communication . . . and stifle professional differences of opinion; lack of integrated management across program elements; and the evolution of an informal chain of command and decision-making processes that operated outside the organization's rules."

With those words, the thirteen eminent military, academic, and aerospace industry experts of the Columbia Accident Investigation Board described a primary cause of the failed re-entry of the Columbia space shuttle (mission STS 107) into earth's atmosphere on February 1, 2003.

The Board's mission included identifying both the proximate and root causes of the accident. The rationale for this dual objective is captured in the Board Statement: "Our aim has been to improve Shuttle safety by multiple means . . . . With that intent, the Board conducted not only

---

950 Mark Fagan & Tamar Frankel, Trust and Honesty in the Real World 240-241 (2007) (footnotes omitted).

an investigation of what happened to Columbia, but also—to determine the conditions that allowed the accident to occur . . ." The Board determined that the proximate cause was damage to the leading edge of the spacecraft's left wing. That resulted from a piece of insulating foam from the external tank that was stuck in the leading edge of the left wing during liftoff. After completing its 16-day mission, Columbia re-entered the atmosphere when the breach "caused by the foam strike on ascent, was of sufficient size to allow superheated air (probably exceeding 5,000 degrees Fahrenheit) to penetrate the cavity behind the panel. The breach widened, destroying the insulation protecting the wing's leading edge support structure, and the superheated air eventually melted the thin aluminum wing spar." The shuttle completely broke up shortly thereafter.

As to the root-cause of the accident the Board's focus centered on organizational culture. This culture was the primary cause of the accident. "In the Board's view, NASA's organizational culture and structure had as much to do with this accident as the External Tank foam." The group cited four critical failures from an organizational and cultural perspective.

First, NASA relied on its past success in lieu of strong scientific and engineering analysis. Second, the lines of communication, vertically and horizontally, in the agency were weak. Third, although a very complex system, the NASA's Shuttle management was not well integrated across its component elements. Finally, actual decision making failed to follow established process; rather, informal chains of command came into place. The following quotes from the accident report provide a flavor of the Board's findings:

- Given that today's risks in human space flight are as high . . . as they have ever been, there is little room for overconfidence. Yet the attitudes and decision-making of Shuttle Program managers and engineers during the events leading up to this accident were clearly overconfident and often bureaucratic in nature.

- In briefing after briefing, interview after interview, NASA remained in denial: in the agency's eyes, "there were no safety-of-flight issues" . . . . A pattern of acceptance prevailed throughout the organization that tolerated foam problems without sufficient engineering justification for doing so.

- NASA does not have a truly independent safety function with the authority to halt the progress of a critical mission element.

- The Shuttle Program's complex structure erected barriers to effective communication and its safety culture no longer asks enough hard questions about risk.

- [T]he practice of 'buying' safety services establishes a relationship in which programs sustain the very livelihoods of the safety experts hired to oversee them. These idiosyncrasies of structure and funding preclude the safety organization from effectively providing independent safety analysis.

- NASA's only guidance on hazard analysis is outlined in the Methodology for Conduct of Space Shuttle Program Hazard Analysis, which merely lists tools available. Therefore, it is not surprising that hazard analysis processes are applied inconsistently across systems . . .

- When managers in the Shuttle Program denied [the Debris Assessment Team's] request for imagery, the [Team] was put in the untenable position of having to prove that a safety-of-flight issue existed without the very images that would permit such a determination. . . . Organizations that deal with high-risk operations must always have a healthy fear of failure_operations must be proved safe, rather that the other way around. NASA inverted this burden of proof.

Assignment

You have been charged with defining a specific program to transform NASA's flawed safety culture into one that is robust and will minimize the likelihood of another Shuttle accident. Using the observations of the Accident Board and the lessons learned in the prior modules, describe the changes that NASA should implement and how the change should be accomplished. Address the following:

- What specific changes should be put in place?
- How should they be institutionalized?
- What is the timetable for effecting the changes?
- How would you monitor the progress and assure success?

V. REPEAT PERFORMANCE THAT WAS NOT CHANGED: TWO CASES[951]

New Millenium Cash Exchange, Inc.

The Financial Crimes Enforcement Network has determined that grounds exist to assess a civil money penalty against New Millenium Cash Exchange, Inc. (NMCE or MSB) and its President and Owner, Flor Angella Lopez (Ms. Lopez), pursuant to the Bank Secrecy Act and regulations issued pursuant to that Act.

   . . .

The Financial Crimes Enforcement Network conducted an investigation and determined that, since at least February 2008, NMCE and Ms. Lopez willfully violated the Bank Secrecy Act's program, reporting, and recordkeeping requirements.

---

951 MARK FAGAN & TAMAR FRANKEL, TRUST AND HONESTY IN THE REAL WORLD 240-241 (2007) (footnotes omitted).

These violations included:

(A) Failure to register as a money service business, including submission of filings with inaccurate information regarding the services rendered by the MSB;

(B) Violations of the requirement to establish and implement an effective written anti-money laundering program; including

(1) Lack of adequate AML programs for its check cashing and money order activities as well as its currency exchange transactions;
(2) Inadequate policies, procedures, and internal controls (a) to verify the identities of persons conducting transactions; (b) to monitor for suspicious activities; (c) to identify currency transactions exceeding $10,000; and (d) to ensure that NMCE filed the required currency transaction reports (CTRs);
(3) Inadequate internal controls for creating and retaining adequate Bank Secrecy Act records related to currency exchange;
(4) Failure to conduct a Bank Secrecy Act/AML risk assessment of the MSB and failure to include "red flags" in the MSB's procedures for each type of business;
(5) Failure to recognize the potential conflicts of interest in establishing a relationship with a consultant that: (a) created NMCE's written AML program, (b) performed the only independent testing of the AML program, and (c) provided the only source of Bank Secrecy Act training for the MSB; such training used a generic module that was provided by the consultant that also created its written AML program; the training was not comprehensive and was not tailored to the MSB's specific business lines and associated risk.

(C) Violations of the reporting and recordkeeping requirements; including (1) filing 51 CTRs significantly late and (2) failure to file at least 149 CTRs for exchanges of currency with other financial institutions.[952]

TCF National Bank

"The Office of the Comptroller of the Currency (OCC) today announced a $10 million civil money penalty (CMP) against TCF National Bank, Sioux Falls, S.D., for violations of the Bank Secrecy Act (BSA)."[953]

---

952 Excerpted from *In re* New Milenium Cash Exchange, Inc. (Apr. 23, 2014), *available at* https://www.fincen.gov/sites/default/files/shared/NMCE%20Assessment.pdf (last visited Oct. 20, 2016).

953 Excerpted from OCC, *OCC Assesses $ 10 Million Civil Money Penalty Against TCF National Bank, Bank Secrecy Act Violations Cited* (Jan. 25, 2013), *available at* https://occ.gov/news-issuances/news-releases/2013/nr-occ-2013-18.html (last visited Sept. 23, 2016).

The CMP follows a cease and desist order issued in July 2010 that directed the bank to correct deficiencies in its BSA and anti-money laundering programs and required an independent examination of BSA reports filed between November 2008 and July 2010. [954]

[Under the 2010 order,] the bank retained a consultant to conduct [an Account/Transaction Activity Review (look-back)] to review certain account and transaction activity specified by the OCC for the period November 2008 through July 2010. The look-back resulted in the Bank's late-filing 2,357 SARs addressing suspicious activities with a transaction amount of approximately $70 million. The suspicious activities primarily consisted of cash transactions indicative of structuring, wire transfers where the source and purpose of the funds was unknown, and of other activity out of the ordinary for the particular customer. This resulted in [Suspicious Activity Report violations.]

Later, as a result of a follow-up BSA exam commenced in November 2011, the OCC found 13 instances of the Bank's failure to properly file SARs related to transactions indicative of possible terrorist financing. The OCC determined that the Bank's systems and processes had identified and alerted on these suspicious transactions and the activity was properly investigated and determined to be suspicious. However, the SARs filed by the Bank to report the activity to law enforcement were not adequate and of poor quality. Specifically, the "terrorist financing" box on the SAR had not been checked even though the narrative section of the SAR made reference to possible terrorist financing, and in some cases the narrative section of the SAR did not clearly communicate the nature of the suspicious activity that was identified by the Bank. This resulted in Suspicious Activity Report violations. Management agreed to re-file the 13 SARs addressing suspicious activity in the amount of about $7.2 million and conduct appropriate employee training.[955]

Discussion topic

Why did punishment fail to induce better legal performance? What elements induced continued violations?

What steps would help ensure compliance with the law?

---

954 *Id.*

955 *In re* TCF Nat'l Bank (Jan. 25, 2013), *available at* http://www.occ.gov/news-issuances/news- releases/2013/nr-occ-2013-18a.pdf (last visited Sept. 27, 2016).

Chapter 20

WRITING THE CODE

INTRODUCTION

How should we write a Compliance Code in light of the background of corporation's business? This task poses three fundamental issues.

First, how should the Code require and demonstrate following society's belief in good behavior?

Second, how should the Code express the experience and position of society's leadership and decision-makers?

And third, how should the Code describe the nature of the activities and decisions that compliance is designed to persuade and induce? In sum, how could the Code facilitate voluntary law enforcement? As noted, a number of laws require financial institutions to write compliance codes (Codes of Ethics). Yet they do not provide the text of the Code. Rather, they offer directions to the writers of the text, who then create the Code from these directions.

Section I discusses the purpose of a Code.

Section II deals with the style of the document. How should the Code require and demonstrate following society's belief in good behavior?

Section III offers a Code outline.

Section IV lists suggested compliance duties of persons in the corporation, reflecting the views of the Code's enforcers.

I. THE PURPOSE OF A CODE OF BEHAVIOR

1. A Code of Behavior, or, as it is sometimes called a Code of Conduct, is part of a self-regulation and compliance program. A good code will include a statement of values and the commitment of the organization's leadership to self-regulation and compliance with the law. In sum, it explains its purpose, which is to induce its employees and related persons and institutions to adopt a certain behavior and, if at all possible, to adopt it voluntarily.

A code of behavior can be crudely analogized to a dress code, signifying both the equivalence of and the differences between different institutional participants. It identifies the duties of each group. One of the purposes of any code of behavior is to maintain the values and enforce the rules that govern the institution by establishing or changing the culture at the institution. While values of right and wrong, truthfulness and trustworthiness are the foundation of the corporate culture, the achievement of these values may change with different people from within the corporation or the outside environment. The ability to adjust and alter institutional culture is crucial for any institution; because the environment and people change, both inside and out. Therefore, with change, even good habits can become toxic.

2. Recognize and understand the habitual culture of the organization. "The way we do things around here" is often accepted with little consideration and argument. Habits are efficient. They require no evaluation and no grappling with conflicting considerations or concepts. Therefore, good habits are valuable. They are what we aim to teach our children. However, when the environment changes, fixed and entrenched habits may become harmful and sometimes even disastrous. Then, they are no longer good habits.

A Code helps establish habits, including the habit of reevaluating habits. A Code can help link the direction of the institutional behavior to the values that should guide it. As we noted, values are crucial to institutional survival. That is why we focus on the content of codes of behavior and the "design of [their] enforcement mechanisms."[956].

II. THE STYLE AND SUBSTANCE OF THE CODE

1. Codes of behavior should be brief.

Not everyone has the patience to go through, let alone remember, long documents. Besides, it is not possible to specify all activities that might lead to violations. As we know, even laws focused on specific actions leave gray areas. Therefore, Codes should be relatively short. Second, compliance codes should avoid "positions that are generally held in society." Words such as "be honest" and "obey the law" are unnecessary. People have already heard these words, sometimes more than they would have wished. Repetition turns people off.[957]

Codes should be fairly clear and more specific rather than general. For example, while one code may state: "Avoid actual or apparent conflicts of interest and advise all appropriate parties of any potential conflict," another code is more complex and verbose: "Realtors shall not undertake to provide professional services concerning a property or its value where they have

---

956 John C. Lere & Bruce R. Gaumnitz, *Changing Behavior by Improving Codes of Ethics*, AM. J. BUS., Fall 2007, at 7, 7.

957 *Id.* at 9.

a present or contemplated interest unless such interest is specifically disclosed to all affected parties."[958]

Balance the generality and specificity of the Code rules. Generalized expressions do not help to guide everyday specific activities. But too many specific rules can be both mind-numbing and enable circumvention. The key is a balanced approach, such as providing a general statement and one specific example, noting that this is only an example. The Code may also include some questions and possible answers. For example, insider information can be characterized as the kind of information that induces a desire to buy or sell a security. Yet, this definition is flawed because some people might be more risk averse than others, and some people may fail to notice how many investors already are aware of the information.

Discussion topic

Please evaluate the Code's statement: "be honest." If you aim at insider trading, what would you add to make the message effective?

Is the identity of the person or group that sends the message important?

2. Deterrence. How can the Code help deter unethical behavior?

a. One possible way to deter wrongful behavior is to introduce a threat of a meaningful penalty. For example, in a voluntary-membership organization, a code can provide that misbehavior may lead to expulsion. The loss of a bonus or a position may involve a significant monetary loss. While a threat of terminating employment may be severe, if the employee has another offer, the penalty can be far less threatening. On the other hand the proposed bonus for coming forward with information about one's own mistake may be effective as well.

b. The experience and position of the readers may be important. Thus, one may send different messages depending on the recipients. For example, compare a recently-hired, 22-year-old accounting graduate with a recently-hired CEO reading about confidentiality: "Anything you learn about the company while working here, that you know only because you work here, should not be told to anyone who does not work for the company unless you are required to do so by law."

Discussion topic:

Who may be more affected by the statement in the previous section: a new accounting graduate or an experienced CFO? How can you then express the Code prohibition to each?

---

958 *Id.* at 10-11.

3. The nature of decisions to be made

a. There are various decisions that involve integrity, yet the decisions that specific individuals make will differ with the individuals. Therefore, another way to improve the effectiveness of a code is to select and highlight positions applicable to decisions made by individuals subject to the Code.

b. The Code of the Management Accountants Institute offers an example of linking honesty to the decision by managerial accountants regarding what information to disclose. The Code provides: "Disclose all relevant information that could reasonably be expected to influence an intended user's understanding of the reports, analyses, or recommendations."[959] Relevance may depend on the types of decisions made by members of a professional organization or as individuals in their role as employees of a company.

c. These decisions are often different from those made by members of the general public, by different professional organizations, or by individuals in different positions and levels within the company. Different professional organizations may face different types of decisions.

d. The code of ethics of the American Marketing Association deals with risks associated with product or service usage, product component substitution, extra cost-added features, advertising, sales promotions, the full price, selling or fundraising under the guise of conducting research, research data, and plagiarism.[960]

4. Who makes the statement?

a. A CEO's statement may be more effective than an impersonal general statement. Employees are more likely to follow his or her example. Alan Greenberg, the Chairman of Bear Stearns, demonstrates how the former Chairman of this brokerage firm could maintain an on-going contact with the firm's members, emphasize the required business aspects, and at the same time specify behavior which he believed was crucial and admonish against violations of fairness and duties to clients.[961] A theme that the Chairman expressed throughout his memos is a requirement for straightforward honesty in dealing with clients.

He never mentioned these words. He attributed the ideas to a consultant. He wrote of a warning which he received from the consultant: "You will do well in commerce as long as thou

---

959 (Institute of Management Accountants Website).

960 American Marketing Association website.

961 Memos From The Chairman, by Alan C. Greenberg, with a Forward by Warren Buffett, Workman Publishing New York 1996.

do not believe thou odor is perfume." The Chairman added that he assured the consultant "that despite our success, we are still trying to be as careful and as punctilious as always." Then the Chairman ended the message in capital letters: Do not make a liar out of me. [962] So long as he was at the helm the firm was deemed one of the best, and sometimes the best brokerage firm around.

5. The nature of decisions to be made

There are various decisions that involve integrity, yet the decisions that specific individuals make will differ by individual. Therefore, another way to improve the effectiveness of a code is to select and highlight positions applicable to decisions made by individuals subject to the Code.

For example, The Code of the Management Accountants Institute suggests linking honesty to the decision by managerial accountants regarding what information to disclose. The Code provides: "Disclose all relevant information that could reasonably be expected to influence an intended user's understanding of the reports, analyses, or recommendations."[963] Relevance may depend on the types of decisions made by members of a professional organization or as individuals in their role as employees of a company. These decisions are often different from those made by members of the general public, by different professional organizations, or by individuals in different positions and levels within the company. Different professional organizations may face different types of decisions.

6. Risk and its avoidance.

The code of American Marketing Association deals with risks associated with product or service usage, product component substitution, extra cost-added features, advertising, sales promotions, the full price, selling or fundraising under the guise of conducting research, research data, and plagiarism. The Accountants' Code addresses honesty issues in concerning professional limitations, unfavorable information and professional judgments or opinions, and relevant information [964]

---

962 *Id.* September 9, 1983.

963 (Institute of Management Accountants Website).

964 (Institute of Management Accountants website). John C. Lere, St. Cloud State University Bruce R. Gaumnitz, St. Cloud State University.

1. Most Code outlines have a similar pattern.

a. High level company personnel, who exercise effective oversight; b. Written policies and procedures; c. Training and education; d. Lines of communication; e. Standards enforced through well-publicized disciplinary guidelines; f. Internal compliance monitoring and response to detected offenses and corrective action plans; g. Periodic "risk assessments" (added by amendment to the original Guideline elements).

In determining what specific actions are necessary to meet those requirements, factors that shall be considered include: (i) applicable industry practice or the standards called for by any applicable governmental regulation; (ii) the size of the organization; and (iii) similar misconduct. Following applicable industry practice or the standards called for by any applicable governmental regulation weighs against a finding of an effective compliance and ethics program.

b. Element One: High Level Company Personnel Who Exercise Effective Oversight

The Governing Authority. Under the Federal Sentencing Guidelines, an organization's governing authority should be knowledgeable about the program and exercise effective oversight. The Guidelines, define "high-level personnel of the organization" as "individuals who have substantial control over the organization or who have a substantial role in the making of policy within the organization. The term includes: a director; an executive officer; or an individual in charge of a major business or functional unit of the organization, such as sales, administration, or finance. The term "substantial authority personnel" means individuals who within the scope of their authority exercise a substantial measure of discretion in acting on behalf of an organization. [965]

When the Guidelines were amended in 2002, the Advisory Committee noted that almost all of the corporate scandals that motivated the passage of the Sarbanes Oxley Act (SOX) and the amendments to the Guidelines were caused by either high level managers or members of the organizations' governing body. These misdeeds lead to "the public's lack of confidence in public markets." These concerns resulted in Guideline provisions that established clear compliance responsibilities for the organization's "governing authority."

The type of knowledge that the governing authority should have includes: practical management information about compliance risks faced by the organization and others with similar operations and the primary program features aimed at counteracting those risks. The governing body will typically obtain this information through reports from senior organization managers. Governing authorities are expected to be proactive in seeking and evaluating information about their organization's compliance programs, evaluating that information when received,

---

[965] *See* Commentary to §8.A.1.2, Application Notes, 3.

and monitoring the implementation and effectiveness of responses when compliance problems are detected.

High-level personnel and other "substantial authority personnel" of the organization must also be knowledgeable about the compliance program and must promote an organizational culture that encourages ethical conduct and a commitment to compliance with the law.

One or more specific individuals within the "high-level personnel" of an organization should be designated as the organizational official or officials with primary responsibility for the operation of the compliance program. This requirement helps to ensure that the official charged with implementing an organization's compliance program has the formal authority, access to senior management, and the respect needed to manage and oversee the implementation of a program

2. Day-to-Day Responsibility.

Specific individuals, often a compliance and ethics officer (CECO), are assigned overall responsibility for the day-to-day operations of the compliance program.

a. The CECO must periodically report status to high-level personnel and/or the governing body, and must have adequate resources, appropriate authority, and direct access to the governing body. The Guidelines reflect the position that the head of an organization's compliance program will have key information necessary for the governing authority to exercise effective oversight, so periodic reports to the governing authority are expected (at least on an annual basis).

b. Written Policies and Procedures and Training. Under the Guidelines an organization must take reasonable steps to communicate to its employees compliance standards and procedures, and other aspects of the compliance and ethics.

3. Adapting the Code to the Corporation's Reality

Adapting the Code to the corporation's reality involves conducting effective training programs, and disseminating information to employees consistent with their respective responsibilities.[966]

a. Formality. The larger the organization, the more appropriate it may be to have a more formal training program with documentation and the dedicated resources and tools to measure the

---

[966] For [a university] this will typically involve developing policies that explain relevant legal requirements to employees, consistent with their job functions, as well as related training programs and/or materials so that employees understand their obligations. Training need not be formal or expensive to be effective and organizations have great leeway in formulating programs that suit their organizational needs and resources. To be effective though, training must do more than impart information; it should be designed to motivate employees to comply with the law. Also, it should be noted that the *Report of the Ad Hoc Advisory Group on the Organizational Sentencing Guidelines* (October 2003) states:

training program's impact. The burden would thereby remain on the organization to explain what training occurred and why the organization considered it effective...

b. Training and other subjects. Training should be provided to the governing body and high-level executives as well as to employees, and where appropriate, to the organization's agents and vendors. The Code will also cover the organization's key legal and ethical obligations, the employees' obligation to comply with these legal obligations, and possible disciplinary sanctions for non-compliance. The Code should also provide a mechanism for reporting compliance concerns and a clear policy of non-retaliation for good faith reports.

c. Lines of Communication. Information about the compliance program must be widely communicated at all levels of an organization. To enhance the effectiveness of the compliance program, the program must establish lines of communication whereby employees and agents may seek guidance and report concerns, including the opportunity to report anonymously (such as a compliance hot line).

d. Assurances. There should be assurances that there will be no retaliation for good faith reporting. Employees should be encouraged to use internal reporting mechanisms to seek advice if they are not sure whether the conduct of concern would be a violation of the law. Reports regarding contacts and activities related to the hotline should be made periodically to the organization's governing authority.

e. Standards enforced. The organization's compliance and ethics program should be promoted and enforced consistently through well-publicized guidelines that provide a number of incentives available to support the compliance and ethics program, such as disciplinary measures for disobeying the law, the organization's policies, or the requirements of the compliance and ethics program.

f. Internal Compliance Monitoring. The organization shall take reasonable steps, including monitoring and auditing, to ensure that the organization's compliance and ethics program is followed, periodically evaluating the effectiveness of the organization's compliance program.

After monitoring and auditing the compliance program, the organization shall take reasonable steps to respond appropriately to any violations of the law or policies to prevent future misconduct, and modify and improve the organization's compliance and ethics program. The *Report of the Ad Hoc Advisory Group on the Organizational Sentencing Guidelines* (October 2003) described monitoring and auditing as "essential" to effective compliance programs for the following reasons.

[A]n increased emphasis on monitoring, auditing, and evaluation practices is justified on three independently sufficient grounds: (1) the recognition of the importance of compliance monitoring, auditing, and evaluation in recent legal standards; (2) practical evidence of the importance of these practices in revealing recent incidents of major corporate misconduct; and (3) privately developed standards and expert opinions identifying monitoring, auditing, and evaluation efforts as important components of effective compliance programs[967]

g. Periodic Compliance Assessments. Determinations of the sorts of periodic compliance assessments that will compose sufficient monitoring, auditing, and evaluation practices will depend on the characteristics and activities of specific organizations. In small organizations, periodic evaluations of compliance in the course of day-to-day business operating practices will often be adequate monitoring steps so that further auditing or evaluations will not be needed. *In larger organizations, however, separate audits of compliance performance will usually be warranted, with such audits being conducted by internal or external parties who are independent of the managers overseeing the performance under scrutiny. Id.* (Emphasis added).

h. Periodic Risk Assessments. For a compliance and ethics program to be truly effective, an organization must periodically access the risk of non-compliance or misconduct and take appropriate steps to design, implement, or modify the program to reduce the risk of non-compliance or misconduct identified through this process.

An organization's activities and related legal obligations may change over time. Periodic compliance risks assessments help to ensure that compliance efforts are designed to mitigate compliance risks in the context of the organization's present legal and operational environment. Thus, a regular, periodic risk assessment should be used to design and implement a range compliance activity, such as developing appropriate compliance program standards and procedures; determining the specific actions that should be taken to ensure compliance with legal requirements; and helping compliance program evaluators target the frequency and content of program monitoring activities.

i. A Sample Risk Assessment Process. The COSO *Internal Controls Integrated Framework* was established in 1992 by the Committee of Sponsoring Organizations (COSO) of the Treadway Commission, which consisted of all of the major U.S. professional accounting organizations. COSO's mission was to establish a methodology to minimize the opportunity for fraud in

---

967 Under the Guidelines, the term "high-level personnel of the organization" means individuals who have substantial control over the organization or who have a substantial role in the making of policy within the organization. The term includes: a director; an executive officer; or an individual in charge of a major business or functional unit of the organization, such as sales, administration, or finance. The term "substantial authority personnel" means individuals who within the scope of their authority exercise a substantial measure of discretion in acting on behalf of an organization. See Commentary to §8.A.1.2, Application Notes, 3.

companies, and to help assure that companies complied with all applicable laws.[968] The methodology helps identify possible risk events; assess the likelihood or frequency of the risk occurring; estimate the significance or impact of the risk events including operational, regulatory, legal, reputational impacts; determine how the risk should be managed; and assess what actions should be taken.[969]

Discussion topics

* In your opinion, do Codes of the sort described here help reduce violations of the law?

* Please note what is *not* included in the requirements concerning the Code. Many books on Codes of Ethics open and start the discussion with the topic of ethics.[970] This requirement is missing here. The word "Ethics" appears in the title of the Code, but nothing directs ethical behavior. Could this be an error or is it intentional? What could be the reasons for omitting the discussion or the requirement?

* Does the Code assure less insider trading? Can we assume that less insider trading by advisory firms are related to Codes of Ethics? Perhaps the employees in these organizations are well rewarded and therefore do not resort to insider trading. Do you agree with this explanation?

* Does a Code invite circumvention, like any other specific law?

* Having read the materials, please prepare an outline of a compliance program regarding prohibited plagiarism, including the definition of the prohibited act.

IV. DUTIES OF CORPORATE PERSONNEL

1. The Governing Authority.

Under the Federal Sentencing Guidelines, "Governing authority" means "(a) the Board of Directors; or ... if the organization does not have a Board of Directors, the highest-level

---

968 The American Institute of Certified Public Accounts (AICPA) Auditing Standards (SAS 78 – AU 319) made the COSO Framework applicable to all U.S. research universities. *See also* SAS 112 and OMB Circulars A-110 and A-133.

969 (Note: *See* program materials and tools in session on *"Developing And Implementing A Compliance Calendar And Other Tools"* for a COSO-based compliance risk assessment tool.

970 Martin T. Biegelman, Building a World-Class Compliance Program ch. 1 (Why Ethics and Compliance Will Always Matter) (2008).

governing body of the organization."[971] . . . The governing authority is ultimately responsible for the activities of the organization and it can only fulfill this responsibility if its members are knowledgeable about management's ethical and legal compliance performance and exercise reasonable oversight with respect to the effectiveness and implementation of the program. When the Guidelines were amended in 2002, the Advisory Committee noted that almost all of the corporate scandals that motivated the passage of The Sarbanes Oxley Act (SOX) and the amendments to the Guidelines were caused by either high level managers or members of the organizations' governing body. These misdeeds lead to "the public's lack of confidence in public markets." . . . . These concerns resulted in Guideline provisions that established clear compliance responsibilities for the organization's "governing authority."

2. The Governing Authority's Knowledge.

The governing authority's knowledge should include practical management information about compliance risks faced by the organization and others with similar operations, and the primary program features aimed at counteracting those risks. The governing body will typically obtain this information through reports from senior organization managers. Governing authorities are expected to be proactive in seeking and evaluating information about their organization's compliance programs, evaluating that information when received, and monitoring the implementation and effectiveness of responses when compliance problems are detected.

3. Governing authorities and their responsibilities.

An organization's "high level" personnel should have overall responsibility for the compliance program to ensure that it is effective.

4. Primary Responsibility.

Under the Guidelines, one or more specific individuals within the "high-level personnel" of an organization should be designated as the organizational official or officials with primary responsibility for the operation of the compliance program. This requirement helps to ensure that the official charged with implementing an organization's compliance program has the formal authority, access to senior management, and the respect needed to manage and oversee the implementation of a program

---

971 *See* Commentary to §8.B.2.1., Application Notes, 1. Definitions.

5. High-level personnel.

High-level personnel and other "substantial authority personnel" of the organization must also be knowledgeable about the compliance program and must promote an organizational culture that encourages ethical conduct and a commitment to compliance with the law. "High-level personnel of the organization" means those individuals who have substantial control over the organization or who have a substantial role in the making of policy within the organization. The term includes: a director; an executive officer; or an individual in charge of a major business or functional unit of the organization, such as sales, administration, or finance. The term "substantial authority personnel" means individuals who within the scope of their authority exercise a substantial measure of discretion in acting on behalf of an organization. *See* Commentary to §8.A.1.2, Application Notes, 3.

6. Day-to-Day Responsibility.

Specific individuals, often a compliance and ethics officer (CECO), are assigned overall responsibility for the day-to-day operations of the compliance program. The CECO must periodically report status to high level personnel and/or the governing body, and have adequate resources, appropriate authority, and direct access to the governing body. The Guidelines reflect the position that the head of an organization's compliance program will have key information necessary for the governing authority to exercise effective oversight, so periodic reports to the governing authority are expected (at least on an annual basis).

7. Written Policies and Procedures and Training.

Under the Guidelines an organization must take reasonable steps to communicate to its employees compliance standards and procedures, and other aspects of the compliance and ethics program by conducting effective training programs, and disseminating information to employees consistent with their respective responsibilities.

Chapter 21

Conclusion

This text is somewhat different from a usual law text: It did not focus on winning in court or on quantification of economics. It did not deal with deterrence in the criminal law sense, that is, by threats of painful punishment. It seems to belong to ethics, which is arguably not a legal category.

Nonetheless, we dealt with the heart of any law: that is, the enforcement of the law. How could people and organizations of actors be induced to follow the rule of law, whether it serves their interest or not, and whether they like the law or not? The following are three possible answers.

One answer could be to increase the threat of pain with violations. This is an approach similar to criminal law punishment. In fact, as we noted, this is the approach that the compliance system in the United States has been taking and is now reconsidering. Another approach is a type of confession after the fact, including disclosure.[972] @@@ Insert Johns material

In fact, even though the practice of the law focuses on the rules and their interpretation, in reality lawyers should learn about the clients and their activities and match their advice and the legal documents they write to the purpose, behavior, and character of their clients. In this book we aimed at matching the lawyer's advisory services with a client's needs and circumstances. The prototype of this client is a small or large organization that seeks to maximize its profits, yet avoid litigation and especially possible violations of the law. This model leads us to a difficult task. After all, lawyers are not lawmakers; they are law interpreters. Neither are they business advisers.

The following is a view of compliance, based on an opinion of Lord Moulton, a British judge and mathematician. He laid out three "domains of Human Action." One domain covers the laws of the land. The law and its rules are compulsory and must be obeyed. The second domain is the area of unrestricted freedom, where everyone is free to do as they please. The third area is a vast area between the two domains: "the Domain of Obedience to the Unenforceable."[973] In Lord Moulton's opinion, this domain was of paramount importance in the life of a nation.

---

972 Christopher J. Christie & Robert M. Hanna, *A Push Down The Road Of Good Corporate Citizenship: The Deferred Prosecution Agreement Between the U.S. Attorney for the District of New Jersey and Bristol-Myers Squibb,Co.*, 43 Am. Crim. L. Rev. 1043, 1045 (2006). The federal securities law is based on disclosure. See 15 U.S.C. § 77e (2012) (prohibiting sale of securities unless registration and disclosure requirements are met).

973 Right Honorable Lord Moulton, *Law and Manners*, Atlantic Monthly, July 1924, at 1.

"The real greatness of a nation," he wrote, "its true civilization, is measured by the extent of this [L]and Of Obedience to the Unenforceable. It measures the extent to which the nation trusts its citizens, and its existence and its area testify to the way they behave in response to that trust."[974] This Domain is preferable to the "iron rule of law" and the "inadequacy of the formal language of statutes."[975]

America is rich in theories concerning the limiting demarcation lines of these domains, although they may be named differently. However, the driving force in the U.S. seems to be towards widening the area of unrestricted freedom. To be sure, we also watch for the first domain, namely, compliance with the law. But we may tend to justify violations or shadows of violations or moves towards violations of the law. Most importantly, we ignore or restrict or tend to shrink the Domain of Obedience to the Unenforceable.

For an antisocial activity, we argue: "Where is it written that we may not do this?" If it is not written, we are free to act. It is not surprising that we are plagued by an enormous number of rules, by conflicts between those who seek more law and enforcement and those who seek more freedom, and by consequent litigation. In fact, when a regulator such as the Securities and Exchange Commission uses its judicial power, there are questions about its crossing the line.

Sensing a need for the Third Domain, Obedience to the Unenforceable, we call it "compliance." That is because enforcement of the law by the regulators and the courts has become difficult, risky, and very costly. Some institutions and corporations have become very large, complex, and international. Their actions and risk-taking affect America's economic well-being. Freedom and law touch and clash, and the domain of Obedience to the Unenforceable is shrinking.

Compliance, however, is not unenforceable. As the materials in our study demonstrate, there are laws that require corporations to establish compliance programs specifically for the purpose of ensuring compliance with the law. Thus, compliance is derived from, and designed to follow, the dictates of the law. Following the evolution of compliance, we find that the laws, the courts, and the regulators have all expanded compliance. Therefore, compliance programs and settlements with regulators seem to fall into the first category of obedience to the law.

Nonetheless, no specific compliance rules can reflect the enormous variety of organizations that have adopted the rules and the programs they required. Thus, the compliance programs differ depending on the business of the corporations, their size, the their type(s) of business, and the laws which they are required to follow. In addition, some businesses and organizations have become too big to regulate. Specific rules would be impossible to itemize and enforce in their case. Therefore, we have developed outlines of compliance programs, and require the subject organizations to fill in the details into these outlines. When the details of the broad category, domain of the law, are filled, the programs are treated as laws. They are not necessarily the product of a consensus, even within the subject-organizations. Their validity is tested and litigated

---

974 *Id.* at 2.

975 *Id.* at 4.

in the courts. And compliance officers who failed to perform might be punished under the law and litigation.

Furthermore, with no consensus on what is the right thing to do, and in a shrinking Third Domain, two other enforcement mechanisms have appeared. One is the rise and encouragement of the whistleblowers, who disagree with their organizations about the legality of certain organizational activities. The whistleblowers are supported and rewarded by the law and law enforcers, and their activities are often likely to lead to litigation. They add to the area of the domain of the law and resulting litigation.

The domain of freedom—the freedom to compete—has grown as well, shrinking the Domain of Obedience to the Unenforceable. In the U.S., competition is highly valued. The market and its competition may be effective for increasing efficiency and benefits to society, however, competition can also corrupt, if based on hidden, poor products and half-truths. Fraud might be discovered, but discovery can take years. Meanwhile, many honest and trustworthy competitive corporations may sustain losses or fail. Moreover, some enterprises may follow the corrupt ones. After all, if the competitors resort to misleading statements and unfair methods of competition, self-protection justifies acting the same way.

Freedom to compete is an acceptable justification in explaining wrongdoing. The limits on wrongfulness are sought in the law. The Domain of Obedience to the Unenforceable is not deemed a high social value or the source of a behavior model. Rather, the focus is on the risk of violating the law and incurring punishment.

These observations do not mean that this Third Domain does not exist in the United States. It means that this domain covers a relatively small area and may be shrinking. It may not be widely supported, both by the trusted actors and the trusting actors. It may mean that winning is a driving purpose which overcomes prohibitions and limitations that are legally unenforceable.

Compliance does not occupy the precise Third Domain of Obedience to the Unenforceable. This Third Domain is described by Lord Moulton as a social consensus: we do things or refrain from doing things, even if we are not forced by law. We self-limit our freedom guided by certain trustworthy social principles. In fact, however, there is a coercive element even in this vast "unenforceable" area. The source of this enforcement is the social group. The group's judgment must be followed because we cannot live alone. We call this type of enforcement "culture."

Culture is "the way we do things in this group, if you want to belong to this group." In the United States, we do not behead people and display their heads on a stick in the streets. We do not cut a thief's hand off. Presumably there will be no, or few, arguments in the United States and other countries on these ways of punishment. Yet, offering future investors a "free lunch," without acknowledging that the investors will pay dearly for the lunch by being induced to invest in certain investments is not considered a wrongful act within some groups. In fact, it might be considered a smart, effective sales technique. In other societies, however, this type of "free lunch" might be considered fraud and cause exclusion from the group.

Culture exists in the animal world. Very few beings, both animals and humans, can live alone. Living beings live in groups and divide tasks in which they specialize. This form of group culture supports survival. The male lion is the strongest as compared to the female and the newly born. The female is the hunter. She is smaller and more ferocious than the male. Yet, the male gets the "lion's share" because the male needs to be larger and stronger to protect the group. All group participants get something and give something. Each receives more than each gives.

In the society of humans, the guidelines may be far more complex, but they can be divided into efforts, contributions, and benefits. No matter how society determines to divide them, if there is voluntary non-coercive behavior about the division of contributions, or any other ways of behavior, this behavior belongs to the Third Domain. It produces a more civilized society. This is what we mean by self-regulation; and this is how we distinguish it from compliance. Compliance is coerced by law. Self-regulation is induced by group values, to which most participants subscribe.

To be sure, in a very large society, the rules of the lion's family may not be apposite. There will always be people who will not follow the Third Domain, and rebel in words or in actions against restricting the total freedom of the Second Domain. A society, in which the number of such individuals is large, would be coercive, if it does not allow the members to express different opinions and behave in different ways.

The line between the laws in the First Domain and the self-regulation in the Third Domain of the Unenforceable may be differently drawn in different societies. Yet, the Third Domain will prevail, even if society members do not agree to the majority's values all the time and in every form. In the vast area of the Third Domain, members do not resort to coercion or to the law on the one hand or to asserting unlimited freedom on the other hand. They might argue and convince, or argue and be convinced, or be unhappy, but follow nonetheless.

Why should the Third Domain be the largest? One answer can be found in the list of results that Judge Moulton predicted when the Third Domain becomes smaller. He noted the "iron rule of law" and the "inadequacy of the formal language of statutes."[976] Judge Moulton, however, did not envision a Third Domain as a wide-open, wild area where people could do what they wished. He envisioned rules that he called "unenforceable." I assume that what he meant is rules that do not belong to the legal area and are not enforceable as legal rules.

In fact, however, these rules are enforceable, but in different ways. One form of enforcing "unenforceable rules" draws on the society's culture. The other form is more personal, drawing on the benefits of bargains and cooperation. Hence, most parties follow the bargains for self-benefit. The balance between the first two Domains is the balance that would lead to the "iron rule of law." That would widen the Third Domain.

How can we determine where the lines should be drawn and the gray areas spread? One shining star to point the way to self-regulation is to measure the coercion, conflicts, and litigation

---

976 Right Honorable Lord Moulton, *Law and Manners*, Atlantic Monthly, July 1924, at 4.

in either the Domain of Freedom or the Domain of the Law. To be sure, directive signs will be supported by either of two calls: the call for freedom or the call for coercion. But when these calls rise, and when their results show up, we know that we have lost our way to self-regulation. They we should seek to the First and Second Domains and widen the Third Domain. We should recognize where our culture has been leading us, and work to broaden our Land Of Obedience to the Unenforceable.

Professor Thomas C. Schelling's seminal work, *The Strategy of Conflict*, can guide our inquiry. The work of Professor Schelling deals with war. And yet the analysis, system, and ideas of his work can be applied and guide our inquiry in the context of "Obedience to the Unenforceable." This analysis is "concerned not just with enemies who dislike each other but with parties who distrust or disagree with each other."[977]

Professor Schelling includes not only the division of gains and losses, but also the possibility of shared loss or gain. In such a case, the interest is in reaching a "mutually advantageous" result. This is a bargaining process, in which no one wins or loses the entire loaf, and both parties can receive "a fair part of it."

For example, a successful union strike is not a strike that destroys the employer.[978] The context of the strike has a number of elements. The employees depend on the employer for their livelihood. The company depends on the employees for its existence. That interdependence is a driving force for reaching an agreement that benefits both but will not maximize the benefits of either. Deterrence, Professor Schelling writes, is "in fact a theory of the skillful nonuse of nonmilitary forces."[979] A similar analysis applies to the threat by regulators under the law, as well as in family relationships. Deterrence becomes necessary and required both in the context of conflict and in the context of common interest. We can apply the same concept to deterrence of crimes or unsocial activities in everyday affairs.[980] The same rationale can be useful to the managers and controlling persons in a corporation.

Deterrence is concerned with the choices that the other party will make, by influencing its expectations of how we will behave. It involves confronting the party with evidence for believing that our behavior will be determined by this other party's behavior.[981] This idea leads to the question: What is a threat? Can one threaten that he or she will "probably" exercise the punishment? In compliance there are a number of questions to "clarify." The law and law enforcement may not be clear either. Compliance enforcement within the corporation may be even less clear, as well as inconsistent. But some signals may be effective nonetheless. "Possibilities" may be sufficient to deter.

---

977 . Thomas C. Schelling, The Strategy of Conflict 5 (1980).

978 *Id* at 6.

979 *Id.* at 9.

980 *Id.* at 12.

981 *Id.* at 13.

In Professor Schelling's opinion deterrence must be accompanied by mutuality of accommodation and common interest. Antagonism must be incomplete.[982] When trust and good faith exist, there is less need for deterrence. But when they do not exist, other norms of deterrence emerge, as they did in the ancient world. These include, for example, hostage taking, or drinking wine from the same glass as that of the opponent—demonstrating the absence of poison—or meeting in a public place, where neither party has a coercive force behind it.

In describing the binding power of the promise in the bargain Professor Schelling makes an interesting observation. The terms of the obligation of a promise must be observable. So the information should cover what the salesperson is paid when he or she made a sale, not necessarily the extent to which he or she spent more or less efforts on the sale.[983] Each party must be confident that the other will not jeopardize future opportunities by destroying trust at the outset. This is one of the values of a piecemeal bargain Professor Schelling describes: each person's gain at a particular segment of the agreement depends on a particular gain for the other as well.[984]

There are situations in which the parties either win together or lose together: the "win-win" situation. Their interests and rewards are identical. On the other extreme is a situation where if one wins the other must lose: the "zero-sum game." Such are the sports games of today. In contrast, bargaining positions can be a mix of conflict and mutual dependence.[985] "The coordination game probably lies behind the stability of institutions and traditions and perhaps the phenomenon of leadership itself." These become relevant by being "solutions" to the coordination game, writes Professor Schelling. Evasions will be small and accepted in order to avoid "overwhelming the authorities." People may either reciprocate honesty or fear, both justifying their own expectations.[986]

Uncertainty can create and occupy a large free space between total freedom and the law's constraints. It can offer a bargaining and a cooperation space. On the other hand, demand for certainly in the law and claim for total freedom makes their space larger, and may shrink the space between them. To regulate this shrinking area of unenforceability we use traditions or other cultural agreements, which most people can then obey, so long as all interested parties follow the tradition in their bargaining.[987]

It is difficult to communicate intentions unless they take a form of actual action. With action, however, bargaining may have a more restricted impact: you have to believe in the possible intention without actually seeing it manifested in action. Talk can be cheap as compared to action. More importantly, without action, one is less certain about the other party's value

---

982 *Id.* at 15.

983 *Id.* at 44.

984 *Id.* at 45-52.

985 *Id.* at 87.

986 *Id.* at 91-92.

987 *Id.* at 107-08.

system.[988] And even after the other party has made a commitment, it is just a first move in the bargain. A commitment limits one party's options but does not eliminate them completely. There are other conditions that remain undetermined. Similarly, a threat does not necessarily close all doors to bargaining.[989] It also leaves some options open, as do enforceable promises.[990] These constitute "strategic moves."

A strategic move, writes Professor Schelling, is a "move that influences the other person's choice, in a manner favorable to one's self, by affecting the other person's expectations on how one's self will behave."[991] Therefore it is important for the parties to make sure that their expectations will not be uncovered by the other parties.

To be effective, threats must be real. But if they have to be carried out, both parties may be hurt. However, threats may be unenforceable if rendered by a third party. In such a case they are real, but not entirely complete. And if the threat is carried out inadvertently, it can be truly harmful to all parties. Threatening a limited adverse action rather than a full-fledged adverse action may have the advantage of less harm if the other party does not heed the threat and it has to be carried out.[992] Yet, even such a limited adverse action may bring reprisals.

The more important distinction by Professor Schelling is the difference between a threat made to require an action and a threat made to prevent an action.[993] If, as we noted, the bargain would benefit both parties, the absence of a bargain would hurt; yet it would hurt less than if the action of one party would hurt more. Actions might hurt more than threats.

It should be noted that parties, including governments, corporations, and individuals, act under constraints. Depending on whether the constraints are small or large, whether the threats are serious or insignificant, both parties may harm (more or less) one or usually both, parties.[994]

With these strategies in mind Lord Moulton's observation may suggest a route towards self-regulation. First, self-regulation occupies the Domain of Obedience to the Unenforceable. Second, within this domain there are pressures to comply with the rules based on the values of the community. The rules are neither the laws nor the unlimited freedoms, but social mechanisms that Professor Schelling has taught us, and other rules of behavior we might uncover.

In addition, self-regulation could be viewed in a very different way. It is a risk-limiting mechanism. In this view, the law, like financial losses, is an unfair or unnecessary limitation to our well-being and profitability, which we are entitled to. Managers of corporations, of banks, or of any institution should be tasked with "profit maximizing." Those who are protected by the

---

988 *Id.* at 117.

989 *Id.* at 122-23.

990 *Id.* at 134.

991 *Id.* at 160.

992 *Id.* at 187-89.

993 *Id.* at 194-98.

994 *Id.* at 201-03.

law, at the managers' expense, are unworthy of the protection, especially if the law limits the managers' maximization of benefits. Maximizing profits is IT!

In general, we should seek ways to gain the most at the least risk of loss. Among the risks are the risks of being punished if we violate the law. We try to avoid these violations not because we love the law, nor because we believe that the law is just or good, but because we might suffer undesirable losses if we are found to have violated the law. This approach involves the view that maximizing profits is good, and whenever the law prevents us from such gains, the law as bad. Thus, even when we view the law as limiting and hindering our well being unjustly or stupidly, we seek to avoid violating the law in order not to suffer the consequences. In this view, the law is like any danger that we would avoid, be it sickness or a highway collision; be it a hindrance to happiness or a protection.

In February 2016, FINRA, the self-regulator of broker-dealers, required broker-dealers to answer questions concerning their "cultural values." The following is a summary of the requirements:

(1) "A summary of the key policies and processes by which the firm establishes cultural values."

(2) "A description of the processes employed by executive management, business unit leaders, and control functions in establishing, communicating, and implementing your firm's cultural values."

(3) "A description of how your firm assesses and measures the impact of cultural values (to the extent assessments and measures exist) and whether they have made a difference at your firm in achieving desired behaviors."

(4) "A summary of the processes your firm uses to identify policy breaches, including the types of reports or other documents your firm relies on in determining whether a breach of its cultural values has occurred."

(5) "A description of how your firm addresses cultural value policy or process breaches once discovered."

(6) "A description of your firm's policies and processes, if any, to identify and address subcultures within the firm that may depart from or undermine the cultural values articulated by your board and senior management[.]"

(7) "A description of your firm's compensation practices and how they reinforce your firm's cultural values."

(8) "A description of the cultural value criteria used to determine promotions, compensation or other rewards."[995]

Responding to this initiative, Matthew Reynolds commented that culture, without which the rules have weak effect, must be established by the leadership. In his opinion FINRA seeks corporate leaders to "lead by example."[996]

To be sure, cost/benefit calculations and profits maximization are important. But it seems that higher on the list of objectives is a very similar future shared by business leaders. In a letter, Virginia M. Rometty, Chairman, President, and Chief Executive of IBM wrote: "In the end, the most important challenges we face are not about technology, but about values. Whether the question is civil liberties and national security, or privacy and convenience, or some professions rising while others decline, our path to this enormously hopeful future will depend on the creation of mutual value, transparency and above all, trust."[997]

Concluding Assignment

What approach would reduce fraud and violations of the law? Have the securities and banking acts of the 1930s and 1940s reduced fraud? Arguably, they did not. What has reduced fraud was the investors and depositors' memory and caution triggered by the 1929 crash. As the memory of the Great Depression has worn off, so has the investors' and regulators' related caution. To be sure, the restrictive laws of the 1930s and 1940s have been relaxed. Perhaps both reflected the national mood and fading memory. Yet, we experienced the 2008 market crash. Did that event and the laws that followed have the same effect as the laws that followed the 1929 market crash? If not, why not?

Please prepare answers to the following list of questions. You answers may be based on imaginary facts. These facts, however, should be based on a plan, which you would prepare for the corporation's management.

*How, in your opinion, is compliance evolving? How would you prepare yourself and others for a more final, if not the final stage, of self-regulation?

---

995 FINRA, *Establishing, Communicating and Implementing Cultural Values* (Feb. 2016), *available at* http://www.finra.org/industry/establishing-communicating-and-implementing-cultural-values (last visited Sept. 9, 2016).

996 Matthew Reynolds, *FINRA Now Playing Culture Cop*, WEALTHMANAGEMENT.Com, Feb. 25, 2016, *available at* http://wealthmanagement.com/regulation-compliance/finra-now-playing-culture-cop (last visited Sept. 11, 2016). "Matthew Reynolds is the Chief Operating & Compliance Officer at Chicago, Ill.-based financial services firm Noyes and its subsidiaries, David A. Noyes & Company, Member FINRA and Noyes Advisors, LLC, a registered investment advisor with the SEC." *Id.*

997 Virginia M. Rometty, *Chairman's Letter, in* IBM, 2015 ANNUAL REPORT , *available at* http://www.ibm.com/annualreport/2015/chairmans-letter/ (last visited Sept. 11, 2016).@@@

*In the beginning of 2017, large institutions are hard pressed to contract their size and become more manageable. Do you believe that this is the solution to corporate self-regulation?

*What can be done to ensure institutional self-regulation and legal behavior?

————

CPSIA information can be obtained
at www.ICGtesting.com
Printed in the USA
BVHW011917110222
628798BV00016B/220